JANE'S
FIGHTING SHIPS
OF WORLD WAR I

FOREWORD BY CAPTAIN JOHN MOORE RN

JANE'S
FIGHTING SHIPS
OF WORLD WAR I

FOREWORD BY CAPTAIN JOHN MOORE RN

MILITARY PRESS

NEW YORK

PUBLISHER'S NOTE

The editors and publishers of *Jane's Fighting Ships of World War I* wish to state that, in reproducing pictures and typematter from wartime editions of Jane's *All the World's Ships* they have done their best to ensure the retention of as much of the original detail of the material as possible. They are aware, however, that some of the original pictures are of poor quality, but since no others are available these have been included in the interests of completeness.

To provide readers with the most comprehensive record of the ships that fought in World War I the compiler of *Jane's Fighting Ships of World War I*, John Moore, has supplemented the 1919 material by extracting entries on significant ships from the 1914 edition.

Jane's Fighting Ships of World War I
Originally published by Jane's Publishing Company 1919

This 1990 edition published by Military Press
distributed by Crown Publishers, Inc., 225 Park Avenue South,
New York, New York 10003.

By arrangement with the proprietor

Printed and bound in Italy

ISBN 0-517-03375-5

h g f e d c d a

CONTENTS.

ABBREVIATIONS, MAJORITY INTRODUCED
IN THIS EDITION

AA. . . . . Anti-Aircraft
C.M.B. . . . . . Coastal Motor Boat
D.A.M.S. . . Defensively Armed Merchant Ship
D.C. . . . . Depth Charge
Dir. Con. . . Director Controlled
M.L. . . . . Motor Launch
PV. . . . . Paravane
R.F. . . . . Range Finder
R.F.A. . . . . . Royal Fleet Auxiliary
S.D.V. . . . . . . Submarine Decoy Vessel
SL. . . . . Searchlight
S/M . . . . Submarine

* Including Ships salved at Scapa Flow and those named for
  surrender in Peace Treaty.

FOREWORD

ONE hundred and one years separated the Battle of Malaga, an indecisive battering between the French and British fleets in 1704, and the Battle of Trafalgar. A study of the diagrams and paintings of these two encounters shows little difference in the form of the ships and the make-up of the fleets engaged in these two battles. One hundred years after Trafalgar the Japanese and Russian fleets met in the Battle of Tsushima. Any comparison between the pictures of these two actions is impossible for the Industrial Revolution had, by the beginning of the 20th Century, changed the shape of navies beyond recognition. Propulsion was by steam not sails, hulls were of steel not wood, guns were breech-loading rather than muzzle-loading with ranges in miles not hundreds of yards. In all this century of transformation there had been no major fleet action to guide peoples' minds in the search for effective ways of harnessing and directing this astounding increase in naval power – strategy and tactics lagged far behind the advances in material affairs.

By the time of Tsushima there was no excuse for any student of naval warfare being ignorant of the capabilities of the world's navies. In 1898 a British journalist published the first volume of what was to become the world's greatest naval reference book, accepted as a symbol of accuracy and authority from then until the present day. Fred T. Jane produced "All the World's Fighting Ships", a title which soon became "Jane's Fighting Ships" and, subsequently, just plain "Jane's". As is always the case, the more the book was used the more contributors it attracted and the wider became its coverage. Jane travelled widely in his search for information and by 1914, the starting point for this reprint, it had become, without breaching security or confidences, a necessary reference book amongst all concerned with naval affairs.

That 1914 edition is of enormous value in that it shows the diversity of naval thought, design and application which had taken place in Jane's life-time. Born during the American Civil War and dying in the second year of World War One, he had lived through an extraordinary period of upheaval in naval matters. Not only had fundamental changes in construction, propulsion and gunnery taken place but the first elements of what is now known as C3 (command, control and communications) were evident, and two totally new elements in the naval equation, the submarine and the aircraft, had appeared. Jane appreciated the importance of the flying machine and, with only half a dozen flights of more than a mile in the record books, he produced "All the World's Air-Ships (Flying Annual)" in 1909, the first comprehensive guide to the early aircraft.

The submarine had a longer history than the aeroplane but its potential was equally under-estimated by a high proportion of naval officers. During the American Civil War semi-submersibles were employed, some as monitors but, more importantly, some as attack craft. These last were armed with a charge mounted on a spar in the bows and rammed the target, an operation not dissimilar to Japanese suicide operations in World War Two. They had some successes but the true submersible with far greater potential was only a few years ahead. Intrepid inventors in France and Spain preceded the Irishman John Holland who built

his submarines in the USA using a petrol engine for surface propulsion and an electric motor when dived. A series of inventions and developments between 1880 and 1910 transformed the early submersibles into formidable, long-range boats. The diesel engine replaced the petrol and heavy oil engines, storage batteries were improved, a proper periscope was designed, wireless telegraphy was fitted, a gun was mounted on the casing and, most important of all, the torpedo was enabled to run a steady course under the control of its own gyroscope.

The whole concept was so much at variance with the centuries-old doctrine of the battle fleet being the hub of all naval power that it was left to a few enthusiasts, supported by a small group of imaginative senior officers, to devise tactics for submarine operations in war time. This blindness to the potential threat is even more incomprehensible when one sees in this book that there were well over 300 submarines in commission in 1914, a considerable proportion being of modern construction.

This lack of appreciation was evident in many other areas of naval affairs. In part this was due to the failure by most navies to provide a Naval Staff – what Winston Churchill later referred to as "a group of intelligent officers given time to think." What policies were made wer normally generated by senior officers relying on their experience. As this often stretched back to the days of sail and very few had any practical wartime experience, it is hardly surprising that the results were generally unsatisfactory. Arguments raged in public on the merits and demerits of various designs of ships but very rarely was there any informed discussion on such matters as the role of a navy, where it should fit into the country's overall strategy and what influence modern developments should have on the tactics and handling of a fleet.

Had any navy allowed their group of intelligent officers time to think, such matters as the increasing range of guns, the formidable effect of modern explosive shells, the danger from mines, the likelihood of a fleet being directed by wireless rather than signal flags, the necessity to provide means of fire control for the increasingly long ranged artillery, the threat from submarines and lastly, but of cardinal importance, the protection of merchant ships, might have been on their agenda.

This book gives a very clear picture of the manner in which naval affairs had been handled up to 1914, the results of this activity and the measures which had to be put in hand to redress the balance. At the outbreak of war on August 4 1914 there were eight major naval powers – Great Britain, Germany, USA, France, Italy, Austro-Hungary and Russia. Of these only Japan and Russia had any experience of major naval engagements in recent years, the battles of the Spanish-American war being somewhat static by comparison. The Battle of Tsushima in 1905 was the only action in which the opposing fleets had sufficient sea-room in which to manoeuvre.

Comparison of the fleets of the eight navies shows many similarities. The battleships were the centre of all plans and the change in the design of these huge ships which followed the arrival of HMS Dreadnought is 1906 is most marked. In that year both the USA and Germany laid down ships which incorporated certain of the major features of Dreadnought, in

particular the mounting of an increased battery of large calibre guns at the expense of the profusion of smaller weapons in previous designs. The aim was simple – to provide the heaviest broadside possible at the greatest range attainable. By 1909 the Japanese, Italians and Russians had followed suit with the French and Austrians a year behind – with building times of two and a half to three years the first three navies in the race had a clear numerical advantage. By the time the first French battleship to the new design was laid down, the USA had completed four, Germany five and Great Britain twelve. The race was on.

The second improvement which was included in HMS Dreadnought's design was the use of steam turbines in place of reciprocating machinery. This more efficient arrangement provided an increase of speed of some three knots in the battleships and nine knots in the battle-cruisers and both the USA and Germany were quick to follow.

Thus by the start of World War One there were 83 of this new type of ship in commission world-wide – 31 in Great Britain, 18 in Germany, 10 in the USA and France, 5 in Japan, 4 in Italy, 3 in Austria-Hungary and 2 in Russia. To provide the backing considered necessary for such battle-fleets, large squadrons of cruisers and numerous destroyer flotillas had been built. These are all laid out in the back of this book but extraordinary gaps exist in all the navies of 1914 – the war-time building and acquisition programmes of minesweepers point a need which was not appreciated pre-war; the range of destroyers and what few other escorts there were was inadequate for long distance convoy escort and this was a design failure which was to persist well on into World War Two. These are the most evident deficiences at a time when the range and effectiveness of submarines were increasing rapidly. Fortunately for the Allies, the German Naval Staff had been slow to appreciate the potential of their underwater fleet otherwise the crisis of 1917 might not have been surmounted by the Allied navies and the war would have been lost.

The 1919 edition illustrates the first steps towards the great carrier battles of the Pacific war of 1942-45. The three true aircraft carries Argus, Furious and Vindictive of the Royal Navy were adaptations while HMS Hermes, laid down in January 1918, was the first of this type to be designed from the keel up. Learning had been swift, frequently painful but naval warfare would never be the same again.

What followed World War One showed only too clearly how little had been learned by the politicians concerning naval affairs. The Washington Naval Conference of 1921-22 concerned itself chiefly with the limitation of battle-ship building. Where submarines were concerned, there was an unfruitful outcry to have them outlawed – an unlikely approach to those countries which had appreciated their value. As for aircraft-carriers, they were classified as auxiliaries. This conference and its successors were of no value in achieving their objectives because they concentrated on the wrong things. between the wars many naval officers were laggardly in appreciating the lessons of 1914-18 but one had to search diligently to find any politicians who gave the matter more than a passing thought. Had Fred T. Jane survived, his comments would have been of the greatest interest.

John Moore

PREFACE.

Preface.

WORK on the present Edition of "FIGHTING SHIPS" was begun in December, 1918, and was pushed on without intermission during the succeeding months. The results now presented, although a little delayed, will, we feel sure, be satisfactory to our readers.

The labour incurred in preparing this Edition has been exceptionally heavy; we doubt if any issue of our Annual has occasioned so much anxiety. The Editors have had to deal with large masses of information, withheld from publication by the belligerent Naval Powers since 1914. They have also had to investigate the demobilisation of the War Fleets to a peace footing. The indeterminate state of the late Enemy Navies, and the chaotic conditions of the Russian Fleet, have presented very perplexing problems.

Dealing, as is our custom, with the various sections of this book in sequence, we offer the following comments on the present Edition.

Glossary.

The glossary of technical terms was overhauled thoroughly last year, and brought up-to-date. This year, our lists of foreign naval expressions have been completed by the addition of French and Swedish terms.

British Navy.

Various new Maps have been added, and the Gunnery Tables have been renovated by Captain R V. Walling, R.G.A. (retired). Mr. E. L. King has kindly allowed us to make use of his "Silhouettes of Effective British Warships." These drawings depart very largely from the usual scale and form of "FIGHTING SHIPS" Silhouettes. We should be glad to have our readers' opinions, whether Mr. King's form of drawings should be generally adopted for all Navy sections. The British Ship Pages have been entirely renovated this year. Plans and illustrations of British Warship types have been prepared on a lavish scale. Since the signing of the Armistice, the Admiralty have been able to release much information which, undoubtedly, has raised the standard of accuracy in British Warship data. All textual details are founded on the latest and most reliable information that can be secured. One of the most interesting features added is Aircraft recognition views, presenting British Warships from a new angle of vision. We tender our grateful thanks to British Shipbuilders, for the very large amount of information they have kindly placed at our disposal. Exigencies of space have prevented us from using all the excellent photographs furnished to us by British Shipbuilders. The views which we could not use have been presented to the Imperial War Museum, where they will form a permanent record of the magnificent output of British shipyards during the war.

United States.

This section has been revised from the latest official data, placed at our disposal by the U.S. Naval Headquarters in London. We are happy to say that we have, once more, the valuable services of Lieut. Henry Reuterdahl, U.S. N.R.F., the distinguished naval artist and critic. It is largely through his kind assistance that we are able to publish so many new and up-to-date illustrations of U.S. Warships.

Japan.

The Navy Department, Tokyo, has once again verified all the technical details of this section. A considerable number of Japanese Minelayers and Fleet Auxiliaries, hitherto unheard of, have been added. Some very valuable notes, received shortly before publication, are given on an Addenda page.

France.

During his attendance at the Versailles Peace Conference, Capt. R. V. Walling, R.G.A., approached Mons. Leygues (the Minister of Marine) and Admiral le Bon (then Chief of Staff) on our behalf, with a view to the French Navy Section being officially revised. M. Leygues and Admiral le Bon readily assented to the proposals made, and authoritative details of French warships are now given. We may add that very cordial relations have been established between "FIGHTING SHIPS" and Capitane le Marquis de Balincourt, Editor of our esteemed contemporary "Flottes de Combat." We are indebted to Capitane le Marquis de Balincourt for a large series of very useful notes, dealing with the World's Navies.

Italy.

Pressure of work again prevents Mr. Charles de Grave Sells from preparing his Engineering Article, but it was largely through his kind interest that we secured an official revision of our Italian Navy Section. Attention is called to that extraordinary creation, the Monitor *Faa' de Bruno*—a vessel which approaches the future naval "hippopotami," as defined by Admiral of the Fleet, Lord Fisher of Kilverstone.

Minor Navies.

During the war, the edicts of the Allied Censors debarred us from paying too close attention to the Allied Navies. The barriers erected by our late Enemies also made it very difficult—at times—to secure information regarding their Fleets. Attention was therefore concentrated on the field of the Neutral Navies and these were put in a satisfactory condition. This year the Minor Navies have not been neglected, but have been checked from the latest official information. Among the new Navy Sections will be found the Belgian and Esthonian Navies. Details were specially prepared for us by the Naval Staff at Reval at the request of Mr. John Piitka, the Marine Agent of Estonia in London. The Hellenic Naval Section has been revised by command of Admiral Condouriotis, the Minister of Marine. The Chinese and Siamese pages, although they occupy but a small space, given a considerable amount of trouble during the past four years. It was found extremely difficult to secure reliable details of these Navies. Thanks to the kindness of Correspondents, they have both been brought up-to-date.

Late Enemy and Russian Navies.

The treatment of these Sections has been the subject of much anxious thought. No steps have yet been taken to dispose of the German ships salved at Scapa Flow. Although the future establishment of the German Navy is strictly laid down in the Peace Treaty, Germany has (as yet) taken no steps to reduce her Navy to the status required by the Allies. The Austrian Fleet, the Hungarian Danube Flotilla, the Bulgarian and Turkish Fleets are all interned under Allied and U.S. supervision. The disposal of the warships belonging to these Powers is still a matter of pure speculation. The Russian Fleet is rent between contending factions, and various units of the Russian Navy have been temporarily added to the Allied Navies. All these Navies have been relegated to the end of this Edition, on the ground that they cannot be considered as effective fighting forces at the present moment.

Special Article.

Five years have elapsed since Illustrations of British Warships have been allowed to appear in "FIGHTING SHIPS." British Illustrations have been re-instated, but H.M. Ships appear in so altered a guise, compared with their 1914 build, that some lay and foreign readers may be perplexed by the changes carried out between 1914 and 1919. A short and non-technical article has been prepared by the Editors, dealing with the War's influence on British Naval Construction. It consists largely of notes, generally covering all British Warship types, which could not be accommodated in the British Navy section without an undue degree of repetition.

War Loss Section.

Mr. Francis E. McMurtrie has prepared a Final Summary of the naval casualties of the late War, based on official and authoritative information. The lists given afford the most complete compendium of information on this subject ever presented; they are the outcome of the perseverance and care of Mr. McMurtrie in collecting information. The long tables detailing the circumstances and dates of destruction of German Submarines will be scanned with interest.

Conclusion.

It may be finally said that, in this Edition, there is only one page which was transferred in unaltered form from 1918 "FIGHTING SHIPS." Particulars of the world's warships now given are based on highly reliable information. The number of illustrations added or renovated this year runs to nearly eight hundred.

Shortly before his lamented death, the late Mr. Fred T. Jane made arrangements that this annual should be edited in conjunction by Dr. Oscar Parkes and Mr. Maurice Prendergast.

These plans have been held in abeyance. Dr. Oscar Parkes joined H.M. Navy in 1916, as Surgeon-Lieutenant, R.N. Being stationed in the Mediterranean, he was unable to give the degree of assistance planned by the late Mr Jane. Mr. Maurice Prendergast therefore carried on the work of Editorship up to the date of the Armistice. Surgeon-Lieut. Oscar Parkes, O.B.E., R.N. has now joined Mr. Prendergast as Joint Editor, and is largely responsible for the splendid series of British Warship Photographs added to this Edition. To them, our Editors, we offer our cordial thanks for their labours in preparing our present Edition—an Edition which we know has been anxiously awaited by our patrons. Under the control of Surgeon-Lieut. Parkes, R.N. and Mr. Prendergast —and through the assistance of our innumerable correspondents throughout the world — future Editions of "FIGHTING SHIPS" will not fall below the high standard of the Edition we now issue.

The copyright of all Plans, Silhouettes and Sketches appearing in this book is strictly reserved. Photographs may not be reproduced without express permission. We are compelled to lay emphasis on this, on account of the increasing infringements by foreign naval books and periodicals.

THE PUBLISHERS.

"OVERY HOUSE,"
100, SOUTHWARK STREET,
LONDON, S.E. 1.

GLOSSARY OF TECHNICAL TERMS.

ENGLISH.	GERMAN.	FRENCH.	ITALIAN.	RUSSIAN.	SPANISH.	SWEDISH.	DUTCH.
1 Abaft	1 Achtern (adv) hinter (prep); achterlicher als quer ab (abaft the beam)	1 Sur l'arrière	1 A poppa	1 Korma	1 A popa	1 Akterligt	1 Achterlijker dan dwars
2 Abeam	2 dwars ab, quer ab	2 Par le travers	2 Per traverso	2 Poperek	2 Por el través	2 Tvärs ut /direction/	2 Dwars
3 Above water	3 Ober wasser	3 Au dessus de l'eau	3 Sopracqua	3 Nadvodnie	3 Sobre el agua	3 Ofvervattens	3 Boven water
4 Accommodation hulk	4 Wohnschiff	4 Caserne flottant / 4 Ponton	4 Pontone d'accomodamento		4 Ponton de comodidad	4 Logementsfartyg	4 Accomodatie legger
5 Ahead	5 Vorwärts	5 Avant	5 A prora (davanti)	5 Vpered	5 A proa	5 Förut /direction/. Framat /movement/	5 Vooruit
6 Air lock	6 Luftverschluss (?)	6 Ecluse de chauffe/sas	6 Serratura d'aria		6 Cerradura de aire	6 Luftsluss	
7 Amidships	7 Mittschiffs	7 Au milieu	7 Al centro	7 Vseredinu	7 Al centro	7 Midskepps	7 Midscheeps
8 Ammunition ship	8 Munitionsschiff	8 Porte-munitions	8 Nave di munizioni	8 Soodno s ammunicziei; boevimi pripasami	8 Buque de municiónes	8 Ammunitionsfartyg	8 Ammunitie schip
9 Anti-aircraft (gun)	9 Fliegerabwehrgeschütz kanone (abbrev. Flak)	9 Canon contre-aeriens	9 Cannone anti-aeroplani	9 Protivo-aeroplanniya	9 Cañon antiaeroplanos	9 Luftförsvarskanon /generally "Luftkanon"/	9 Anti-luchtschip (kanon)
10 A.P. (projectile)	10 Panzersprenggranate	10 Projectil de rupture	10 Proiettile	10 Probivanshii-bronu	10 Proyectil	10 Halvpansargranat	
11 Armament	11 Armierung	11 Armamento	11 Armamento	11 Vo-oroojenie	11 Armamento	11 Bestyckning	11 Bewapening
12 Armed liner, or Auxiliary cruiser	12 Hilfskreuzer	12 Croiseur auxiliaire	12 Nave armata / incrociatore ausilare	12 Vo-oroojennii passajirskii-parokhod; Vspomogatelnii krieser	12 Buque armado/o crucero auxiliar	12 Hjälpkryssare	12 Gewapende lyner of hulp kruiser
13 Armour	13 Panzer	13 Cuirasse	13 Corazzato	13 Bronia	13 Coraza Blindage	13 Pansar	13 Pantser
14 Armoured cruiser	14 Panzerkreuzer	14 Croiseur cuirassé	14 Incrociatore corazzati	14 Bronenosnii-kreiser	14 Crucero acorazado	14 Pansarkryssare	14 Gepantserde Kruiser
15 Astern	15 Rückwärts	15 Arrière	15 A poppa	15 Nazad	15 A popa	15 Back	15 Achteruit
16 Athwartship	16 dwarsschiffs	16 Par le travers (d'un navire)		16 Soodno-na-traverse	16 Por el través del buque	16 Tvärskepps	
17 Awash	17 im uberflüten Zustand		17 A fior d'acqua	17 Vroven-s-vodoi	17 A flor de agua	17 I övervattensläge	
18 Barbettes	18 Barbetten	18 Barbettes	18 Barbette	18 Barbetten	18 Torres-barbetas	18 Barbettorn	18 Barbette
19 Bases (of barbettes)	19 Trunk (Schacht)	19 Au dessous la tourelle	19 Piattoforme	19 Vnizu	19 Plataformas	19 Fasta torn	19 Torenwal
20 Battery	20 Batterie	20 Batterie	20 Batteria	20 Batareya	20 Bateria	20 Batteri	20 Battery
21 Battle-cruiser	21 Panzerkreuzer	21 Cuirassé rapide. 21 Croiseur de bataille.	21 Incrociatore di battaglia	21 Boevoi kreiser	21 Crucero de batalla	21 Slagkryssare	21 Slag kruiser
22 Battleship	22 Linienschiff	22 Cuirassé d'escadre	22 Nave da battaglia	22 Bronenosets	22 Acorazado	22 Slagskepp	22 Slagschip
23 Beam	23 Breite	23 Largeur	23 Larghezza	23 Shirina	23 Manga	23 Bredd	23 Breedte
24 Before	24 vorn; vor (prep.) vorlicher als quer ab (before the beam)	24 Avant.	24 Avanti	24 Pered; pred	24 A proa	24 Förut	24 Voor
25 Belt	25 Gürtel	25 Ceinture	25 Cintura	25 Poyass	25 Faja	25 Gördelpansar	25 Gordel
26 Bilge k.	26 Schlingerkiel	26 Quille de roulis	26 Chiglia di rollio	26 Bokovoi keel	26 Quilla de pantoque	26 Slingerköl	26 Kimkiel
27 Binnacle	27 Kompassgehäuse	27 Boussole	27 Abitacolo		27 Bitácora	27 Nakterhus	27 Nachthuis

JAPANESE (pronounce as French).

English	Romaji	No.	Japanese
Fighting tops	Sento-Shorou	79	戰鬪檣樓
Ends	Hashi	77	兩端
Draught	Kissui	70	吃水
Displacement	Hai-sui-Tonsu	65	排水噸數
Destroyer	Kuchiku-tei	62	驅逐艦
Deck	Kanpan	51	甲板
Cruiser	Junyo-Kan	50	巡洋艦
C.T. (Conning tower)	Shireto	46	司令塔
Complement	Teiin	45	定員
Coal	Shekitan	41	石炭
c/m (Centi-metre)			センチメーター
Casemates	Kuku-Hodai	38	穹窖砲臺
Capacity	Yorio	36	容量
Bunkers	Shekitanko	34	石炭庫
Bulkheads	Kakuheki	33	隔壁
Bridge	Kenkio	32	艦橋
Boilers	Kikan	29	汽罐
Bow	Kanshu	31	艦首
Belt	Kotai	25	甲帶
Beam	Haba	23	巾
Battleship	Shento-Kan	22	戰鬪艦
Battery	Hodai	20	砲臺
Bases (of barbettes, etc.)	Holo-no-Kibu	19	砲塔の基部
Barbettes	Rotote	18	露砲塔
Astern	Tomo	15	艦後
Armoured Cruiser	Kotetsu Junyo-Kan	14	甲鐵巡洋艦
Armour	Kotetsu	13	甲鐵
Amidships	Chuo	7	中央
Ahead	Omote	5	艦前
Above water		3	水上

ENGLISH.	GERMAN.	FRENCH.	ITALIAN.	RUSSIAN.	SPANISH.	SWEDISH.	DUTCH.
B.L. (gun)	28 Hinterlader	28 Canon culasse	28 Cannone a retrocarica	28 Zaryajansheesyas kazennoi chasti	28 Cañón de retrocarga	28 Bakladdningskanon	
Boilers	29 Kessel	29 Generateurs	29 Caldaie	29 Kotli	29 Calderas	29 Ångpannor	2 Ketels
Boom (port defence)	30 Hafensperre	30 Estacade	30 Asta da bome (per difesa portuale)		30 Cadena de troncos (para defensa de puerto)	30 Bomstängsel	30 Sluitboom
Bow	31 Bug	31 Avant	31 Prora	31 Noss	31 Proa	31 Bog	31 Boeg
Bridge	32 Kommando-Brücke	32 Pont	32 Ponte di comando	32 Most	32 Puente	32 Brygga	32 Brug
Bulkheads	33 Schötten	33 Traverses	33 Paratie	33 Pereborki	33 Manpanos	33 Skott	33 Schot
Bunker (coal)	34 Kohlenbunker	34 Soute à charbon	34 Carbone per carboniere	34 Oogolnaya yama. To bunker, groozitsya ooglem	34 Carbón de lascarboneras	34 Kolboxar	34 Bunker (Kolen)
Camouflage	35 Unsichtbarmalen	35 Camouflage	35 Camuffamento or "Camouflage"	35 Iskoostvennoe prikpitie	35 "Camouflage"	35 Maskering	35 Identiteits verberging
Capacity	36 Capacität	36 Enposant de charge	36 Capacita	36 Poinyestchenie	36 Capacidad	36 Kapacitet	36 Vermogen
Capstan	37 Ankerspill, Ankerwinde	37 Cabestan	37 Argano		37 Cabrestante	37 Ankarspel, Spel	37 Spil
Casemates	38 Casematten	38 Casemates	38 Casamette	38 Kazemat	38 Casamatas	38 Casematter	38 Kazemat
Centre-, (keel-) line	39 Kiellinie	39 Quille centrale/mediane	39 Paramezzale centrale	39 Srednyaya liniya; diametralnaya ploskost	39 Sobrequilla central	39 Midskeppslinje	39 Midden (kiel) lijn
Chart house	40 Kartenhaus		40 Sala nautica	40 Shtoormanskaya roobka	40 Caseta de derrota	40 Styrhytt	40 Kaarthuis
Coal	41 Kohlenvorrat	41 Charbon	41 Carbone	41 Ugol	41 Carbon	41 Kol	41 Steenkolen
Coast defence ship	42 Küstenpanzerschiff	42 Garde-côtes.	42 Nave per difesa della costa	42 Soodno beregovoi oboroni	42 Buque para defensa de costas	42 Kustförsvarsfartyg	42 Kust verdedigings schip
Coastguard vessel	43 Küstenschutzschiff	43 Navire garde-côtes	43 Nave guarda costas	43 Soodno beregovoi okhrani	43 Buque guarda costa	43 Kustbevakningsfartyg	43 Kust bewakings schip
Compass	44 Kompass	44 Boussole	44 Bussola		44 Brújula	44 Kompass	44 Kompass
Complement	45 Besatzung	45 Équipage	45 Equipaggio	45 Kompleki	45 Dotacion	45 Besättning	45 Bemanning
C.T. (conning tower)	46 Kommando Turm	46 Block-haus (C.T.)	46 Torre di comando	46 Roolevaia bashnia	46 Torre de mando	46 Stridstorn	46 Commando-toren
Crane	47 Kran	47 Grue	47 Grua	47 Kran	47 Grua	47 Kran	47 Kraan
"Creep" (anti-submarine)	48 U – drache (?)	48 Gerbe sousmarine	48 "Serpeggiare" (anti-sommergibile)	48 Tral	48 Arrastramiento (anti-submarino)		48 —
Crow's nest	49 Krähennest	49 Nid de pie	49 Gabbia di crocetta		49 Garita para el vijía	49 Utkikskorg	49 Kraaie nest
Cruiser	50 Kreuzer	50 Croiseur	50 Incrociatore	50 Kreiser	50 Crucero	50 Kryssare	50 Kruiser
Deck	51 Deck	51 Pont	51 Ponte	51 Palooba	51 Cubierta	51 Däck	51 Dek
Depôt ship	52 Stammschiff, Mutterschiff	52 Soutien/Convoyeur de	52 Nave di deposito/Nave appoggio	52 Soodno sklad; soodno baza	52 Buque de depósito	52 Depotfartyg	52 Depot schips
,, (torpedo craft) 53	,, (für Torpedofahrzeuge) 53	,, (Torpilleurs). 53	,, Siluranti 53		,, (torpederos) 53	,, för torpedbåtar 53	Depot (torpedo vaartuig) 53
,, (destroyers) 54	,, (,, Zerstörer) 54	,, (Destroyers). 54	,, Cacciatorpediniere 54	54 Soodno-matka dlya kontr-minonosetzev	,, (cazatorpederos) 54	,, ,, jagare 54	,, (torpedo jagers) 54

JAPANESE. (pronounce as French.)

English	Romaji	No.	Japanese
Water line	Suisen	216	氷線
Upper deck	Jokanpan	213	上甲板
Turrets	Yhoto	212	圍砲塔
Trials	Shi Unten (Kokoromi)	206	試運轉
Tons	Unten	194	噸
Torpedo tubes	Suirai Hatsushatusuan	193	水雷發射管
Torpedo boat	Suirai-Tei	192	水雷艇
Torpedo	Suirai	191	水雷
Submerged	Suichu	182	水中
Submarine	Slen-sui	180	潛水
Stern	Kanbi	179	艦尾
Starboard (side)	Ugen	178	右舷
Speed	Sokurioku	176	速力
Shields	Tate	173	楯
Screens	Kakubo	167	スクリール
Ram	Shodo	155	撞頭
Protection to vitals	Yobu-Bogio	150	要部防禦
Port (side)	Sagen	147	左舷
Normal displacement	Kitei	135	規定
m/m (Millimetre)			ミリメーター
M. (Metre)			メーター
Masts	Hobashira	123	檣
Main (-deck)	Chukan-pan	121	中甲板
Machinery		119	機械
Lower (-deck)	Gekan-pan	118	下甲板
Liquid fuel	Yokitai-Nenrio	117	液体燃料
L. (Length)	Nagasa	113	長
Kts. (Knots)		112	節
Hoods	Uogai	101	砲蓋
Guns	Hou	95	砲
Funnels	Yeutotsu or Entotsu	92	烟突

ENGLISH.	GERMAN.	FRENCH.	ITALIAN.	RUSSIAN.	SPANISH.	SWEDISH.	DUTCH.
55 Depôt ship (T.B.)	55 Stammschiff (für Torpedoboote)	55 Soutien de (Torpilleurs)	55 Nave appoggio (torpedine)		55 Buque de déposito (torpederos)	55 Depotfartyg för torpedbåtar	55 Depôt (T.B.)
56 „ (M.L.)	56 „ („ Motorboote)	56 „ (Vedettes).	56 „ (moto-scafo)		56 „ (lancha de motor)	56 „ „ motorbåtar	56 „ (M.L.)
57 „ (submarines)	57 Mutterschiff (für Unterseeboote)	57 „ (Sous-marins).	57 „ (sommergibili)	57 Soodno-matka dlya podvodnikh lodok	57 „ (submarinos)	57 „ förundervattensbåtar	57 „ (onderseeërs)
58 Depression (of guns)	58 Senkung	58 Angle negatif de pointage	58 Depressione (cannone)	58 Oogol snijeniya	58 Puntería baja (de las piezas)	58 Dumpning	
59 Depth charge	59 Wasserbombe	59 Charge de fond	59 Carica di fondo (esplosivo)	59 Bomba dlya vzriva pod vodoi	59 Carga de fondo (explosiva)	59 Vattenbomb	59 Diepte lading
60 Derrick	60 Ladebaum	60 Mât de charge	60 Albero da carico	60 Nod-emnaya strela	60 Pescante de carga	60 Bom	60 Laadboom
61 Despatch vessel	61 Aviso	61 Aviso	61 Nave per dispacci	61 Posilnoe soodno	61 Buque de aviso	61 Avisofartyg	61 Koerier schip
62 Destroyer	62 Zerstörer	62 Contre-torpilleur	62 Caccia-torpediniere	62 Kontr-minonosets	62 Cazatorpederos	62 Jagare	62 Torpedobootjager
63 Diesel engine	63 Dieselmaschine, Ölmaschine, Olmotor	63 Moteur Diesel	63 Macchina "Diesel"	63 Dizel-motor	63 Máquina "Diesel"	63 Dieselmotor	63 Diesel machine
64 Dirigible	64 Lenkbares Luftschiff	64 Dirigeable.	64 Dirigibile	64 Derijabl	64 Dirigible	64 Luftskepp	64 Bestuurbare
65 Displacement	65 Deplacement	65 Déplacement	65 Dislocamento	65 Vodoizmiestchenie	65 Desplazamiento	65 Deplacement	65 Waterverplaatsing
66 Division (of fleet)	66 Division	66 Division	66 Divisione (di una flotta)	66 Deviziya; devizion	66 División (de una flota)	66 Division	66 Eskader
67 Dock (floating)	67 Schwimmdock	67 Dock (flottant).	67 Bacino (galleggianto)	67 Dok (plavoochii)	67 Dique flotante	67 Flytdocka	67 Dok (dryvend)
68 „ (graving)	68 Trockendock	68 Cale sèche	68 Bacino (di carenaggio)	68 Dok (sookhoi)	68 Dique seco	68 Torrdocka	68 „ (droog)
69 Dockyard (D.Y.)	69 Werft	69 Arsenal	69 Arsenale	69 Shipyard, Verv.	69 Arsenal	69 Varv	69 „ werf
70 Draught (mean)	70 mittlerer Tiefgang	70 Tirant d'eau	70 Immersione media		70 Calado medio	70 Djupgående, medel—	70 Diepang (gemiddeld)
71 „ (max.)	71 grösster Tiefgang	71 Tirant d'eau maximum	71 Immersione massima		71 Calado máximo	71 „ maximi—	71 „ (grootste)
72 Dreadnought	72 Dreadnought	72 Dreadnought	72 Dreadnought	72 Drednaoot	72 Dreadnought	72 Dreadnought	
73 Drifter	73 Drifter, Dampflogger	73 Chalutier	73 Nave di pesca ("Drifter")	73 Maloe soodno	73 Vapor de pesca ("Drifter")		73 Smak
74 Echelon	74 Staffellinie	74 Echelon. 74 En quinconce.	74 Linea in "Echelon"	74 Eshelon	74 Linea en escalones	74 Flankformering	
75 "Electric drive"	75 elektrische Antrieb	75 Commande electrique	75 Comando elettrico		75 Impulsión electrica	75 Elektrisk drift	
76 Elevation (of guns)	76 Höhewichtung, Elevation	76 Angle de pointage positif	76 Elevazione (cannone)	76 Oogol vozvosheniya	76 Elevación (tiro de cañón)	76 Elevation	
77 Ends	77 Ends	77 Extrémités	77 Estremita	77 Krai	77 Extremos	77 Stävar	77 Einden
78 Examination Vessel	78 Untersuchungschiff	78 Arraisonneur	78 Nave d'ispezione		78 Buque de inspección	78 Undersökningsfartyg	78 Onderzoekings schip
79 Fighting tops	79 Marsen	79 Hunes	79 Coffe militari	79 Poostchechnii mars	79 Cofas militares	79 Stridsmärsar	79 Gevechtsmars
80 Fire Control	80 Feuerleitung	80 Direction de tir	80 Controllo del tiro	80 Kontrol ognya	80 Regulator de tiro	80 Eldledning	80 Controle by het vuren
81 „ top	81 Artilleriestand im Topp	81 Hune télémètrique.	81 „ (coffa)		81 „ „ (cofa)	81 Eldledningsmärs	
82 Fire director	82 Zentralabfeuerung	82 Direction du feu	82 Direttore de tiro	82 Mekhanizm oopot reblyaemii pri strelbl zalpom	82 Director de tiro	82 Centralavfyrning	
83 Fisheries vessel	83 Fischerieschutzboot	83 Garde-pêche. 84 Navire amiral	83 Nave peschiera	83 Maloe voennoe soodno dlya ohhrani ribnikh promislov	83 Buque de pesquería	83 Fiskeri-inspektionsfartyg	83 Controle schip (visschery
84 Flagship	84 Flaggschiff		84 Nave ammiraglia	84 Flagmanskii korabl	84 Buque almirante	84 Flaggskepp	84 Vlagschip
85 Fleet	85 Flotte	85 Flotte.	85 Flotta		85 Flota	85 Flotta	85 Vloot
86 Flotilla	86 Flotille	86 Flotille.	86 Flottiglia	86 Flotiliya	86 Esquadrilla	86 Flottilj	86 Flotilje
87 „ leader	87 Führerschiff	87 Conducteur de flotille.	87 Nave capofilo	87 Soodno vedooshii flotiliu	87 Buque cabo de fila	87 Flottiljchefsfartyg	87 „ leider
88 Forecastle	88 Back	88 Gaillard d'avant.	88 Castello di prua	88 Bak	88 Castillo	88 Back	88 Logies
89 Foremast	89 Fockmast	89 Mât de nusaine	89 Albero di trinchetto		89 Palo trinquete	89 Fockmast, Förligmast	89 Fokkemast
90 Freeboard	90 Freibord	90 Franc-bord	90 Bordo libero	90 Zapas plavoochesti soodna	90 Obra muerta	90 Fribord	90 Uitwatering
91 Full load displ't	91 Gesamte Wasserverdrängung	91 Deplacement en plein charge	91 Carico completo (dislocamento)	91 Vodvizmeshenie v polnom groozoo	91 Cargamento completo (desplazamiento)	91 Deplacement, fullt rustad	91 Volle lading merk
92 Funnels	92 Schornsteine	92 Cheminées	92 Fumaioli	92 Trubi	92 Chimeneas	92 Skorstenar	92 Schoorsteen
93 Fuze	93 Zünder	93 Amorce	93 Spoletta	93 Vzrivatel	93 Espoleta	93 Tändrör	93 Grut
94 Gunboat	94 Kanonenboot	94 Cannonière	94 Cannoniera	94 Kanonerskaya lodka	94 Lancha cañonera	94 Kanonbåt	94 Kanonneerboot
95 Guns	95 Geschütze	95 Artillerie	95 Cannoni	95 Orudiia	95 Cañones	95 Kanoner	95 Kanonnen
96 Gyroscopic compass	96 Kreiselkompass	96 Compas gyroscopique	96 Busola giroscopica	96 Jiroskop	96 Brújula giroscópica	96 Gyroskopkompass	96 Gyroskoop kompas
97 Hawse	97 Klüse	97 Crussiere	97 "Hawse" (apertura per la catena dell 'ancora)	97 Kluz	97 Escobén	97 Klys	97 Slang
98 H.E. (bursting charge	98 Sprengladung	98 Haut explosif	98 Alto esplosivo	98 Silno-vzrivchatii	98 Fuerte explosivo	98 Sprängladdning	
99 H.E. (shell)	99 Sprenggeschoss, Sprenggranate	99 Obu à grande capacité	99 Granata di alto esplosivo	99 Silno-vzrivchatii snaryud	99 Granada de fuerte explosivo	99 Sprängranat	
100 Hoist (ammunition)	100 Munitionsaufzug	100 Monte-charges.	100 Elevatore di munizioni	100 Podem (in full, podemnaya mashina)	100 Ascensor para municiónes	100 Ammunitionshiss	100 Hysche (ammunitie
101 Hoods	101 Kuppel	101 Carapaces	101 Scudi	101 Pokrishki	101 Carapachos	101 Kåpor	101 Pantserkoepel
102 "Horns" (of mine)	102 Kontakte, Fühlhörner (?)	102 Antennes	102 Corna (di una mina)		102 Conteras (de una mina)	102 Horn	102 "Hoorns" (van mi
103 Hospital ship	103 Hospitalschiff, Lazarettschiff	103 Navire-hôpital	103 Nave ospedale	103 Gospitalnoe soodno	103 Buque-hospital	103 Lasarettsfartyg	103 Hospitaal schip
104 Hull	104 Rumpf	104 Coque	104 Scafo	104 Korpoos; koozov soodna	104 Casco	104 Skrov	104 Hol
105 Hulk	105 Hulk	105 Ponton	105 Pontone	105 Blokshiv	105 Pontón	105 Pråm	105 Legger
106 Hydroplane (boat)	106 Gleitboot	106 Hydroplane (bateau)	106 Idroplano (battello)	106 gidroplane	106 Hidroplane (buque)	106 Hydroplan	
107 „ (in subs.)	107 Tiefenruder					107 Djuproder	
108 Ice-breaker	108 Eisbrecher	108 Brise-glace.	108 Rompighiaccio	108 Ledokol	108 Rompehielos	108 Isbrytare	108 Ysbreeker
109 Jumping wire	109 Minenabweiser, Minendraht	109 Orin.	109 Salto del filo (?)		109 Paso del alambre	109 Avledarewire	
110 Kite-balloon	110 Drache	110 Saucisse /"Captif"	110 Pallone a cervo-volante	110 Zmeikovii aerostat	110 Globo-cometa cautivo	110 Ballong	110 Kabel ballon
111 Kite-balloon ship	111 Drachenschiff	111 Navire porte ballon captif	111 „ id (nave d'appoggio)	111 Soodno-matkadlya zmeikovikh aerostatov	111 „ (buque portador)	111 Ballongfartyg	111 „ „ schip
112 Kts. (Knots)	112 See-meilen (or knotten)	112 Noeuds	112 Nodi	112 Uzell	112 Millas	112 Knop	112 Knoopen (mylen)
113 Length (*p.p.*)	113 Länge zwischen den Perpendikeln	113 Longueur (entre perpendiculaires)	113 Lunghezza tra le perpendicolari		113 Eslora entre perpendiculares	113 Längd mellan perpendiklarne	113 Lengte (p.p.)
114 „ (*w.l.*)	114 Länge auf der Wasserlinie (?)	114 „ (à la flottaison)	114 Lunghezza alla linea di carico		114 Eslora en la linen de ague, máxima	114 „ i vattenlinjen	114 „ (w.l.)
115 „ (*o.a.*)	115 Länge uber alles	115 „ (totale)	115 Lunghezza massima		115 Eslora de fuera a fuera de miembros	115 „ överallt	115 „ (grooste)
116 Light cruiser	116 kleiner Kreuzer	116 Croiseur léger	116 Incrociatore leggiera	116 Legdii kreiser	116 Crucero ligero	116 Lätt kryssare	
117 Liquid Fuel	117 Heizoil	117 Combustible liquide	117 Combustibile liquido	117 Jhidkoe toplivo	117 Combustibele liquido	117 Brännolja	117 Vloeibare brandstof
118 Lower deck	118 Zwischen-deck	118 Faux pont	118 Ponte inferiore	118 Nijhniaia paluba	118 Cubierta baja	118 Mellandäck, Trossdäck	118 Tusschendeks
119 Machinery	119 Maschinen	119 Machines	119 Machinaria	119 Mekhanizm	119 Máquinas	119 Maskineri	119 Werktuigen (machi
120 Magazine	120 Munitionskammer	120 Soute.	120 Magazino-deposito munizioni	120 Sklad; magazin	120 Pañol de municiónes	120 Ammunitionsdurk	120 Magazyn
121 Main-deck	121 Batterie deck	121 Pont de batterie	121 Ponte principale	121 Glavnaia paluba	121 Cubierta principal	121 Huvuddäck	121 Kuildek
122 Mainmast	122 Grossmast		122 Albero di maestra		122 Palo mayor	122 Stormast	122 Groote mast
123 Mast	123 Mast	123 Mât.	123 Albero		123 „ macho	123 Mast	123 Mast
124 „ (tripod)	124 Dreibein, Dreifussmast	124 „ (tripode).	124 „ (treppiedi)	124 Machta trepojnaya	124 „ trípode	124 Tripodmast	
125 „ (lattice)	125 Gittermast	125 „ (en treillis)	125 „ (graticcio)	125 Reshetchataya machta	125 „ de celosía	125 Gallermast	
126 Microphone	126 Geräuschempfänger	126 Microphone	126 Microfono	126 Mikrofon	126 Micrófono	126 Mikrofon	126 Microphone
127 Mine	127 Mine	127 Mine	127 Mina	127 Mina	127 Mina	127 Mina	127 Mijn
128 Mine-layer	128 Minenleger	128 Mouilleurs de mines 128 Pose-mines	128 Posa-mina	128 Minnii zagraditel	128 Colocador de minas	128 Minutläggningsfartyg	128 Mijn legger
129 Mine-sweeper	129 Minensucher	129 Dragueurs de mines	129 Draga-mina	129 Minnii tralshik	129 Rastreador de minas	129 Minsvepningsfartyg	129 Mijn veeger
130 Mizzen-mast	130 Besanmast	130 Mât de artimon.	130 Albero di mezzana		130 Palo mesana	130 Mesanmast	130 Bezaans mast
131 M.L. (motor launch)	131 Motorboot	131 Vedette	131 Lancia a motore	131 Motornoe patrolnoe soodno (literally, motor patrol vessel)	131 Lancha de motor	131 Motorbåt	131 M.L. motor launch
132 M. S. (motor ship)	132 Motorschiff	132 Bateau automobile	132 Nave a motore	132 Motornoe soodna	132 Buque de motor	132 Motorfartyg	132 M.S. motor schip
133 Monitor	133 Monitor	133 Monitor	133 Monitor	133 Monitor	133 Monitor	133 Monitor	133 Monitor
134 Navy yard	134 Marinewerft	134 Arsenal	134 Cantiere dello stato	134 Admiralteistve	134 Arsenal del estado	134 Orlogsvarv	134 Marine werf
135 Normal displ't	135 Normale Wasserdrängung	135 Deplacement normal	135 Dislocamento normale	135 Normalnoe vodoizmeshenie	135 Desplazamiento normal	135 Normal deplacement	135 Normale water verplaats
136 Net Cutter	136 Netzschere	136 Coupe-filets	136 Taglia-rete		136 Cortador de redes	136 Nätsax	136 Net breeker
137 Net layer	137 Netzleger	137 Mouilleur de filets	137 Posa-rete		137 Colocador de redes	137 Nätutläggningsfartyg	137 Net legger
138 Oil tanker	138 Öldampfer, Tankdampfer	138 Pétrolier	138 Nave petroliera a cisterna	138 Nalivnoe soodno	138 Buque de cisterna petrolero	138 Oljetankfartyg	138 Olie tankship.
139 Paddle-wheel	139 Rad	139 Roue	139 Ruote a palette	139 Grebnoe parokhodnoe koleso	139 Rueda de paletas	139 Skovelhjul	139 Wiel (raderboot)
140 „ steamer	140 Raddampfer	140 Navire à roues.	140 Piroscafo a ruote		140 Vapor de ruedas	140 Hjulångare	140 Raderboot

ENGLISH.	GERMAN.	FRENCH.	ITALIAN.	RUSSIAN.	SPANISH.	SWEDISH.	DUTCH.
141 Patrol boat/vessel	141 Vorpostenboot, Fahrzeug	141 Patrouilleur	141 Battelo / nave di pattuglia	141 Patrolnoe soodno	141 Buque de patrulla/ Lancha de patrulla	141 Bevakningsbåt	141 Patrouille boot
142 Periscope	142 Sehrohr	142 Periscope	142 Periscopio	142 Periskop	142 Periscopio	142 Periskop	142 Periskoop
143 Pilot vessel	143 Lotsenboot	143 Bateau pilote	143 Battello pilota		143 Bote de práctico	143 Lotsbåt	143 Loods boot
144 Pinnace (steam)	144 Dampfpinasse	144 Chaloupe à vapeur	144 Canotto a vapore	144 Kater	144 Pinaza de vapor	144 Ångslup	144 Stoom barkes
145 Pole mast	145 Stangenmast	145 Mât gaule.	145 Albero a palo		145 Palo enterizo ó tiple	145 Pålmast	
146 Poop	146 Poop, Hinterschiff	146 Dunette.	146 Cassero di poppa	146 Korma ; oot	146 Toldilla	146 Poop, Hytta	146 Poep
147 Port (side)	147 Backbord	147 Babord	147 Sinistra	147 Lievii	147 Babor	147 Babord	147 Bakboord
148 Powder (propellant)		148 Charge d'explosion	148 Polvere impellente	148 Porokhovoi	148 Pólvora impelente	148 Krut	148 Poeder
149 Propeller	149 Schraube, Propeller	149 Helice	149 Elica	149 Grebnoi vint	149 Hélice	149 Propeller	149 Schroef
150 Protection to vitals	150 Schutz an vitalen stellen	150 Protection des machines	150 Protezione delle parti vitali	150 Zastchita	150 Protection de las partes vitales	150 Skydd för vitala delar	150 Bescherming der vitale deelen
151 Protective deck	151 Schutzdeck	151 Pont cuirassé.	151 Coperta proteggente	151 Bronevaya palooba	151 Cubierta de protección	151 Pansardäck	151 Beschermings dek
152 Q.F.(=R.F. in U.S.)	152 Schnell Feuer Geschutz	152 à tir rapide	152 Tiro rapido	152 Skorostrelnii	152 Tiro rápido	152 Snabbskjutande kanon	152 Snelvuur
153 Radius of action	153 Fahrbereich, Aktionsradius	153 Rayon d'action.	153 Raggio d'azione	153 Radius deistviya	153 Radio de acción	153 Aktionsradie	153 Straal van actie
154 Rake (of masts, &c.)	154 Rak	154 Incliné/e/s sur l'arriere	154 Inclinazione (di nu albero)	154 Ooklon	154 Inclinación (de un palo)	154 Fall /på master. etc./	154 Hang (van masten)
155 Ram	155 Ramsporn	155 Eperon	155 Sperone	155 Tarann	155 Espolon	155 Ramm	155 Ram
156 Range yds./metres)	156 Entfernung, Schlussweite	156 Portée	156 Portate—yarde/metri	156 Dalnost boya	156 Alcance yardas/metros	156 Avstånd	156 Afstand (yds./meters)
157 Range-finder	157 Entfernungsmesse	157 Télémètre.	157 Telemetro	157 Dalnomer	157 Telémetro	157 Avståndsmätare	157 Afstand zoeker
158 Repair ship	158 Reparaturschiff	158 Transport/Navire-atelier.	158 Nave per riparazione	158 Plavoochaya masterskaija	158 Buque de reparaciones	158 Verkstadsfartyg	158 Reparatie schip
159 River gunboat	159 Flusskanonenboot	159 Cannonière de riviere	159 Cannoniera da fiume	159 Rechnaya kanonerskaya lodka	159 Lancha cañónera de río	159 Flodkanonbåt	159 Rivier kanonneerboot
160 River monitor	160 Flussmonitor	160 Monitor de riviere	160 Monitor da fiume		160 Monitor de río	160 Flodmonitor	160 Rivier monitor
161 Royal yacht	161 Königliche Yacht	161 Yacht royal/impérial/ présidentiel	161 Yacht reale	161 Korolevskaya yakhta	161 Yate real	161 Kunglig yacht	161 Koninklijk yacht
162 Rudder	162 Ruder, Steuerruder, Seitenruder, Ventikalruder	162 Gouvernail.	162 Timone	162 Rool	162 Timón	162 Roder	162 Roer
163 Salvage ship	163 Bergungsschiff	163 Navire releveur	163 Nave di salvataggio	163 Spasatelnoe soodno	163 Buque de salvamento	163 Bärgningsfartyg	163 Bergings schip
164 S. S. (steamship)	164 Dampfer	164 Navire à vapeur	164 Vapore		164 Buque de vapor	164 Ångfartyg	164 S.S. (stoomschip)
165 S. V. (sailing vessel)	165 Segler	165 Voilier	165 Bastimento a vela		165 Buque de vela	165 Segelfartyg	165 Z.S. (zeilschip)
166 Scout	166 Aufklärungskreuzer	166 Eclaireur/Estafette	166 Nave esploratrice	166 Raabedchik	166 Buque explorador	166 Spaningsfartyg	166 Verkenaer
167 Screens	167 Splitter-traversen	167 Écrans	167 Schermi	167 Shirmi	167 Pantallas	167 Splintskärmar	167 Splinterschilden Schermen
168 Seaplane	168 Wasserflugzeug	168 Hydravion.	168 Idrovolante	168 Gidroaeroplan	168 Hidrovolante	168 Hydroaeroplan	168 Water vliegtuig
169 Seaplane-carrier	169 Flugzeugmutterschiff	169 Porte-avions.	169 „ (nave appoggio)	169 Soodno-matka dlya gidroaeroplanov	169 „ (buque portador)	169 Flygmaskins— depotfartyg	169 Watervliegtuig drager
170 Searchlight	170 Scheinwerfer	170 Projecteur	170 Proiettore	170 Projektor	170 Proyector	170 Strålkastare	170 Zoeklicht
171 Searchlight-top	171 Scheinwerfertopp	171 Hune à projecteurs	171 „ (coffa)		171 „ (cofa)	171 Strålkastaremast	171 Controle top zoeklicht
172 Sheer (of hull)	172 Sprung		172 Cervatura dello scafo		172 Arrufo del casco	172 Sprang	172 Geer (van hol)
173 Shields	173 Schützschildern	173 Boucliers.	173 Scudi	173 Stehit	173 Mantelete	173 Sköldar	173 Schilden
174 Sloop	174 Sloop, U-bootsabwehrkreuzer	174 Aviso(?)	174 Scialuppa	174 Shlup	174 Balandra		174 Sloep
175 Sounding machine	175 Lotmaschine	175 Sonde/Appareil	175 Macchina da scandaglio		175 Aparato para sondar		175 Diepte peiling machine
176 Speed	176 Geschwindigkeit	176 Vitesse	176 Velocita	176 Skorost khoda	176 Velocidad	176 Fart	176 Vaart, Snelheid
177 Squadron (of fleet)	177 Geschwader	177 Escadre	177 Squadra (di una flotta)	177 Eskadra ; brigada	177 Escuadra de una flota	177 Eskader	177 Eskader (van vloot)
178 Starboard	178 Steuerbord	178 Tribord	178 Dritta	178 Pravaia storona	178 Estribor	178 Styrbord	178 Stuurboord
179 Stern	179 Heck	179 Arrière	179 Poppa	179 Korma	179 Popa	179 Akter	179 Hek
180 Submarine	180 Untersee-Boote	180 Sousmarin	180 Sottomarino	180 Podvodnaia lodka	180 Submarino	180 Undervattensbat	180 Onderzeetorpedoboot
181 Submarine-chaser	181 U-bootsjäger	181 Contre-sousmarins	181 Cacciasommergibili		181 Caza-submarino	181 U-båtsjagare	181 Onderzeeër jager
182 Submerged	182 Unterwasser	182 Submergé	182 Subacqueo	182 Podvodnii	182 Sumergido	182 Under vattnet	182 Onderwater
183 Submersible	183 Tauchboot	183 Submersible	183 Sommergibile	183 Opooskanshiisya pod vodoo ; mogooshii opooskatsya	183 Sumergible	183 Dykbåt	183 Duikboot
184 Super-firing (guns)	184 Übereinandergestellt	184 Superposé/e/s (canons.)		184 Strelba s visshei pozitsii cherez nizshoon		184 Överhöjda kanoner	
185 Supply ship	185 Proviantschiff	185 Ravitailleur/Transport vivres	185 Nave di provviste		185 Buque de abastecimiento	185 Provianfartyg	185 Toever schip
186 Surveying ship	186 Vermessungsschiff	186 Navire pour Service Hydrographique	186 Nave idrografica	186 Opisnoe soodno	186 Buque hidrográfico	186 Sjömätningsfartyg	186 Controle schip
187 Tank vessel (for water)	187 Wasserfahrzeug	187 Citerne	187 Nave-cisterna (acqua)	187 Nalivnoe soodno	187 Buque de cisterna (agua)	187 Vattenbat	187 Tank schip (voor water)
188 Tender	188 Beiboot, Tender	188 Annexe	188 Battello d'avviso	188 Tender	188 Bote-aviso	188 Hjälpfartyg	188 Lichter
189 Topmast	189 Marsstänge	189 Mât de hune	189 Albero di freccia	189 Stenga	189 Mastelero de galope	189 Stäng	189 Steng
190 Top gallant mast	190 Bramstänge	190 Mât de perroquet	190 Albero di velaccio	190 Bram-stenga	190 Mastelero de juanete	190 Bramstäng	190 Bovenbram steng
191 Torpedo	191 Torpedo	191 Torpille	191 Siluro	191 Mina	191 Torpedo	191 Torped	191 Torpedo
192 Torpedo boat	192 Torpedo boot	192 Torpilleur	192 Torpediniera	192 Minonosets	192 Torpedero	192 Torpedbat	192 Torpedoboot
193 Torpedo tubes	193 Torpedo lancier-röhre	193 Tubes lance torpille	193 Tubi lancia siluri	193 Minnie aparati	193 Tubos lanza torpedos	193 Torpedtub	193 Lanceerinridiling (Cuis of Kanon)
194 Tons	194 Tonnen	194 Tonnes	194 Tonnelate	194 Tonni	194 Toneladas	194 Ton	194 Tonnen
195 Training ship	195 Schulschiff	195 Navire-École	195 Nave scuola di marina	195 Oochebnoe soodno	195 Buque escuela de marina	195 Övningsfartyg	195 Opleidings schip
196 „ (boys)	196 Schiffsjungen-schulschiff	196 „ mousses	196 „ (ragazzi)		196 „ (muchachos)	196 Skeppsgossefartyg	196 „ (jongens)
197 „ (engineers)	197 Maschinenschulschiff	197 „ mecaniciens	197 „ (macchinisti)		197 „ (máquinistas)	197 Maskinistskolfartyg	197 „ (machinisten)
198 „ (gunnery)	198 Artillerieschulschiff	198 „ de cannonage	198 „ (artiglieria)		198 „ (artilleria)	198 Artilleriskolfartyg	198 „ (kanonneers)
199 Training ship (midshipmen, &c.)	199 Kadettenschulschiff	199 „ d'application	199 „ (guardie-marine)		199 „ (guardia-marinas)	199 Kadettfartyg	199 „ (adelborsten, etc.)
200 Training ship (navigation)	200 Navigationsschulschiff	200 „ navigation	200 „ (navigazione)		200 „ (navegacion)	200 Skolfartyg	200 „ (navigatie)
201 „ (mine)	201 Minenschulschiff	201 „ de torpilles	201 „ (mina)		201 „ (minas)	201 Minskolfartyg	201 „ (mijn)
202 „ (stokers)	202 Heizerschulschiff	202 „ de chauffe	202 „ (fuochisti)		202 „ (fogoneros)	202 Eldareskolfartyg	202 „ (stokers)
203 „ (torpedo)	203 Torpedoschulschiff	203 „ de torpilles automobils	203 „ (siluri)		203 „ (torpedos)	203 Torpedskolfartyg	203 „ (torpedo)
204 Transport	204 Transporten, Transportdampfer	204 Transport	204 Trasporto	204 Transport ; transportnoe soodno	204 Buque transporte	204 Transport	204 Transport
205 Trawler	205 Fischdampfer	205 Chalutier	205 "Trawler"	205 Tralooer	205 "Trawler" (Buque de pesca)	205 Trawlare, Fiskeangare	205 Stoom visscherman
206 Trials	206 Probefahrten	206 Essais	206 Prove	206 Ispitaniia	206 Pruebas	206 Provturer	206 Proeftocht
207 Trimming tank	207 Trimmtank	207 "Trimming tank" (cisterna di assetamento)	207 "Trimming tank" (cisterna di assettamento)	207 Ooravnitelnaya sisterna	207 "Trimming tank" (cisterna de equilibración)	207 Trimtank	207 Ballast tank
208 Tug	208 Schleppdampfer	208 Remorqueur	208 Rimorchiatore	208 Booksir ; booksirnoe soodno	208 Remolcador	208 Bogserbåt	208 Sleep boot
209 Turbo-generator	209 Turbogenerator	209 Turbo-moteur	209 Turbo generatore		209 Turbo-generador	209 Turbingenerator	
210 Turbine	210 Turbine	210 Turbine	210 Turbina	210 Turbina	210 Turbina	210 Turbin	210 Turbine
211 „ (geared)	211 Turbine mit Reduziervorrichtung, Turbine mit mehrfacher Übersetzung	211 Turbines à engrenages	211 Turbina ad ingranaggio		211 Turbina con engranaje	211 Utväxlad turbin	
212 Turrets	212 Türme	212 Tourelles	212 Torri	212 Bashnia	212 Torres	212 Torn	212 Torens
213 Upper deck	213 Oberdeck	213 Pont de gaillards	213 Ponte superiore	213 Verkhniaia paluba	213 Cubierta alta	213 Övre däck	213 Opperdek
214 Uptake (to funnels)	214 Rauchfang, Exhaustor	214 Base de cheminées	214 Cassa a fumo (nel fumaiolo)	214 Naroojnaya dimovaya trooba	214 Flus de reunión de chimenea	214 Rökupptag	
215 Ventilator	215 Ventilator, Lüfter	215 Ventilateur	215 Ventilatore	215 Ventilyator	215 Ventilador	215 Ventilator	215 Luchtkoker
216 Water line	216 Wasserlinie	216 Flottaison	216 Linea d'acqua	216 Vaterliniia	216 La linea de flotacion	216 Vattenlinje	216 Waterlyn
217 Wireless telegraphy (W/T)	217 Funkentelegraphie (F.T.) ; drachtlose Telegraphie	217 Telegraphie sans fils (T.S.F.)	217 Radiotelegrafia	217 Bezprovolornoe telegrafirovanie	217 Radio-telegrafia	217 Gnisttelegrafi, Radiotelegrafi	217 Telegraphie zonder draad
218 „ aerials	218 Antennen, Luftdrähte	218 Antennes de T.S.F.	218 „ (antenne)	218 Anteni	218 „ (antenas)	218 Antenner, Luftnät	
219 „ spreaders	219 Antennen spr (?)	219 Deflecteurs de T.S.F.	219 „ (Stendadori ærei)		219 (Extendores aéreos)	219 Spröt för gnistnät	
220 Watertight door	220 Wasserdichte Tür	220 Porte de cloison etanche	220 Porta stagna	220 Vodoneproniczaemaya dver	220 Puerta estanca	220 Vattentät dörr	220 Waterdichte deur
221 „ compartment	221 Wasserdichte Abteilung	221 Cloison etanche	221 Compartimento stagno	221 Vodoneproniczaemoe otdelenie	221 Compartimento estanco	221 Vattentät avdelning	221 Waterdichte afdeeling
222 Yacht (steam)	222 Dampfyacht	222 Yacht (à vapeur)	222 Yacht a vapore	222 Yakhta (parovaya)	222 Yate de vapor	222 Ångyacht	222 Yacht (stoom)

BRITISH DOCKYARD—HOME WATERS.

(All maps divided into 2000 yard squares. Soundings in fathoms. Heights in feet).

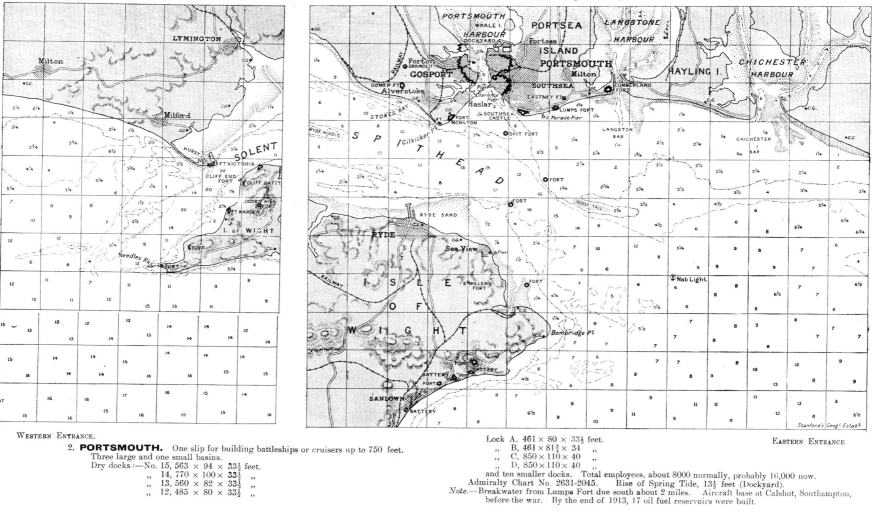

WESTERN ENTRANCE.

EASTERN ENTRANCE.

2. PORTSMOUTH. One slip for building battleships or cruisers up to 750 feet.
Three large and one small basins.
Dry docks:—No. 15, 563 × 94 × 33½ feet.
    ,, 14, 770 × 100 × 33½ ,,
    ,, 13, 560 × 82 × 33½ ,,
    ,, 12, 485 × 80 × 33½ ,,

Lock A. 461 × 80 × 33½ feet.
  ,, B, 461 × 81¾ × 34 ,,
  ,, C, 850 × 110 × 40 ,,
  ,, D, 850 × 110 × 40 ,,
and ten smaller docks. Total employees, about 8000 normally, probably 16,000 now.
Admiralty Chart No. 2631-2045. Rise of Spring Tide, 13½ feet (Dockyard).
Note.—Breakwater from Lumps Fort due south about 2 miles. Aircraft base at Calshot, Southampton, before the war. By the end of 1913, 17 oil fuel reservoirs were built.

BRITISH NAVAL PORTS AND HARBOURS—HOME WATERS.

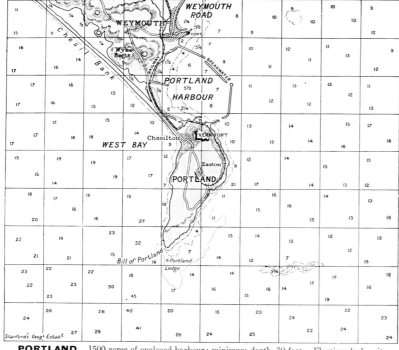

PORTLAND. 1500 acres of enclosed harbour; minimum depth, 30 feet. Floating dock suitable for destroyers. Coaling station. N. and E. entrances 700 feet wide. Strongly fortified.
Admiralty Chart No. 2255. Rise of Spring Tide, 9 feet (Bill of Portland); 6¾ feet (Breakwater).

Other Naval Harbours and Stations in Home Waters.

BEREHAVEN. Good anchorage. **SCILLY.** The anchorage is moderately good. The entrance is very narrow, difficult and dangerous. **LOUGH SWILLY & BUNCRANA.** Very moderately fortified. Good anchorage. **KINGSTOWN** (DUBLIN), **TORBAY, FALMOUTH, CROMARTY FIRTH, MORAY FIRTH,** (SCOTLAND, E. COAST), **SCAPA FLOW, LOCH EWE, LAMLASH,** &c. **CAMPBELTOWN.** Submarine Training Station. **SHANDON, GARELOCH.** Anti-Submarine Station, for Experiments and Training.

DOVER. New harbour, 610 acres; depth of 30 feet at low water over half the area. E. entrance, 1 cable; W. entrance, 800 feet. Coaling station. Well fortified. Floating dock for Destroyers.

Moorings for 16 battleships, 5 large cruisers, 7 *Counties*, 4 small cruisers, and for destroyers.

(The tide at entrance is very strong, making ingress difficult).
Admiralty Chart No. 1698-1828.
Rise of Spring Tide, 18¾ feet.

West Coast (Wales).

PEMBROKE. Building yard. Two large slips. Dry docks:—One, 404 × 75 × 24¾ feet (high water). About 2500 employees.
Admiralty Chart No. 915-2393.
Rise of Spring Tide, 22½ feet (Dockyard).

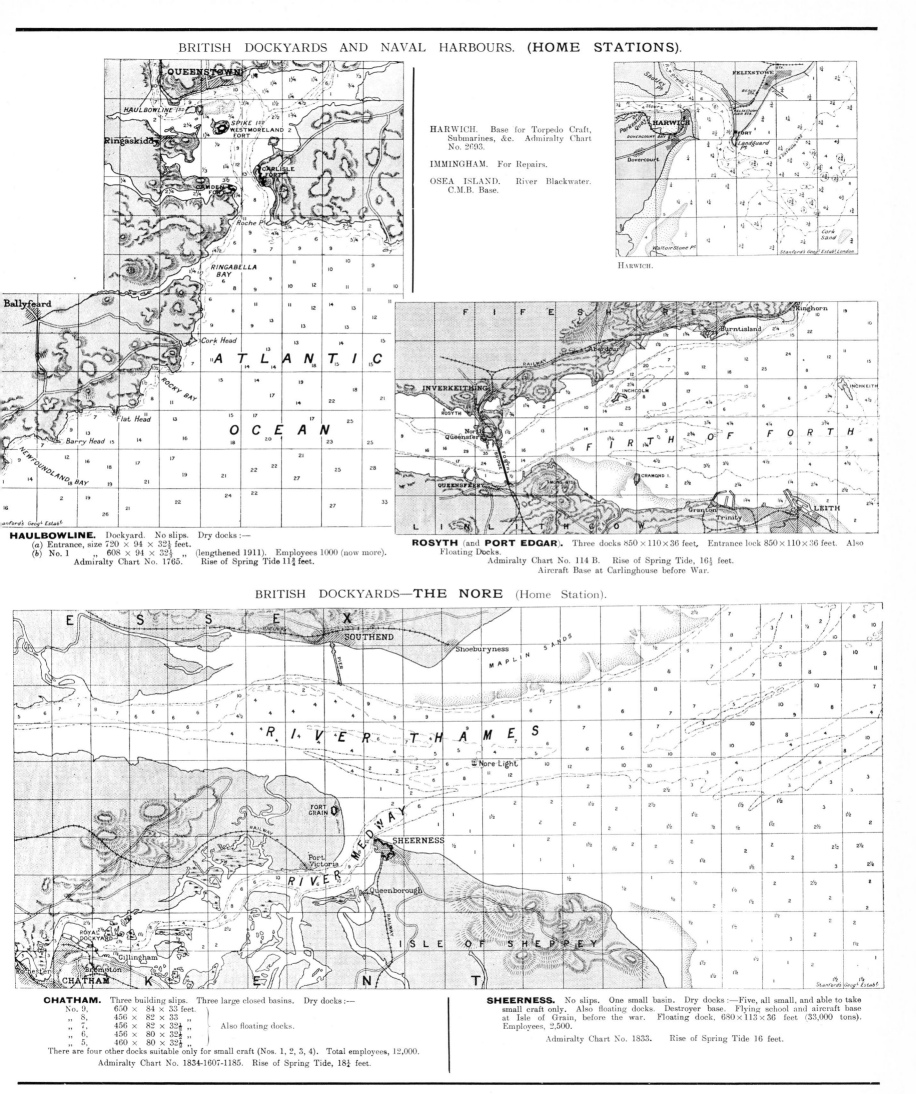

HARWICH. Base for Torpedo Craft, Submarines, &c. Admiralty Chart No. 2693.

IMMINGHAM. For Repairs.

OSEA ISLAND. River Blackwater. C.M.B. Base.

HARWICH.

HAULBOWLINE. Dockyard. No slips. Dry docks :—
(a) Entrance, size 720 × 94 × 32½ feet.
(b) No. 1 ,, 608 × 94 × 32½ ,, (lengthened 1911). Employees 1000 (now more).
Admiralty Chart No. 1765. Rise of Spring Tide 11¾ feet.

ROSYTH (and **PORT EDGAR**). Three docks 850 × 110 × 36 feet. Entrance lock 850 × 110 × 36 feet. Also Floating Docks.
Admiralty Chart No. 114 B. Rise of Spring Tide, 16½ feet.
Aircraft Base at Carlinghouse before War.

BRITISH DOCKYARDS—THE NORE (Home Station).

CHATHAM. Three building slips. Three large closed basins. Dry docks :—

No. 9,	650 × 84 × 33 feet.	
,, 8,	456 × 82 × 33 ,,	
,, 7,	456 × 82 × 32½ ,,	Also floating docks.
,, 6,	456 × 80 × 32½ ,,	
,, 5,	460 × 80 × 32½ ,,	

There are four other docks suitable only for small craft (Nos. 1, 2, 3, 4). Total employees, 12,000.
Admiralty Chart No. 1834-1607-1185. Rise of Spring Tide, 18¼ feet.

SHEERNESS. No slips. One small basin. Dry docks :—Five, all small, and able to take small craft only. Also floating docks. Destroyer base. Flying school and aircraft base at Isle of Grain, before the war. Floating dock, 680 × 113 × 36 feet (33,000 tons). Employees, 2,500.
Admiralty Chart No. 1833. Rise of Spring Tide 16 feet.

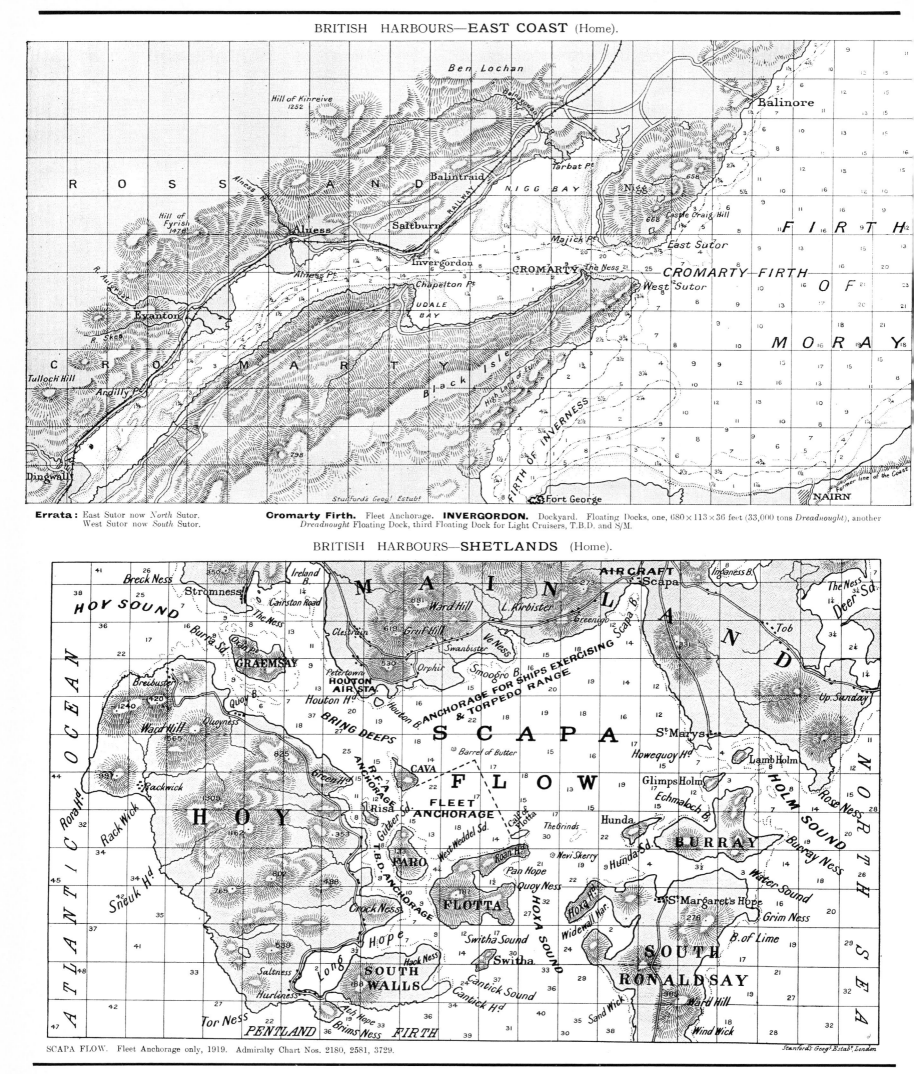

Errata: East Sutor now *North* Sutor.
West Sutor now *South* Sutor.

Cromarty Firth. Fleet Anchorage. **INVERGORDON.** Dockyard. Floating Docks, one, 680 × 113 × 36 feet (33,000 tons *Dreadnought*), another *Dreadnought* Floating Dock, third Floating Dock for Light Cruisers, T.B.D. and S/M.

BRITISH HARBOURS—**SHETLANDS** (Home).

SCAPA FLOW. Fleet Anchorage only, 1919. Admiralty Chart Nos. 2180, 2581, 3729.

(To uniform scale.   Divided into 2000 yard squares.   Soundings in fathoms).

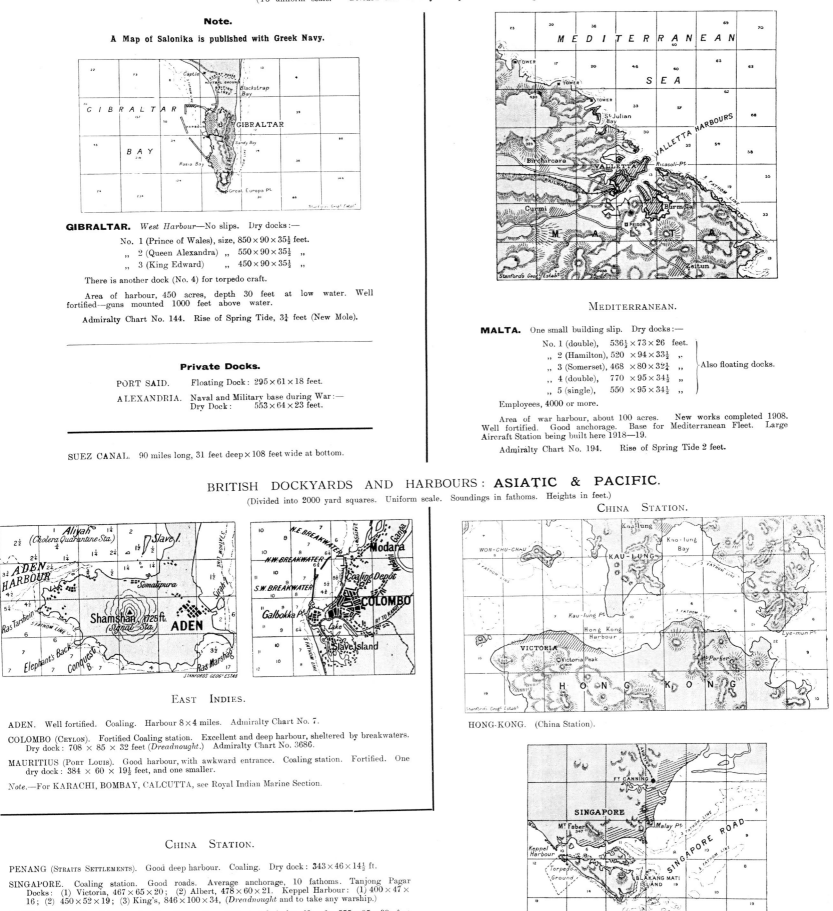

Note.

A Map of Salonika is published with Greek Navy.

GIBRALTAR. *West Harbour*—No slips.   Dry docks:—

No. 1 (Prince of Wales), size, 850 × 90 × 35½ feet.

,,   2 (Queen Alexandra) ,,   550 × 90 × 35½ ,,

,,   3 (King Edward)   ,,   450 × 90 × 35½ ,,

There is another dock (No. 4) for torpedo craft.

Area of harbour, 450 acres, depth 30 feet at low water. Well fortified—guns mounted 1000 feet above water.

Admiralty Chart No. 144.   Rise of Spring Tide, 3¼ feet (New Mole).

Private Docks.

PORT SAID.   Floating Dock: 295 × 61 × 18 feet.

ALEXANDRIA.   Naval and Military base during War:—
Dry Dock: 553 × 64 × 23 feet.

SUEZ CANAL.   90 miles long, 31 feet deep × 108 feet wide at bottom.

MEDITERRANEAN.

MALTA.   One small building slip.   Dry docks:—

No. 1 (double),	536½ × 73 × 26 feet.	
,, 2 (Hamilton),	520 × 94 × 33¼	,,
,, 3 (Somerset),	468 × 80 × 32¼	,,
,, 4 (double),	770 × 95 × 34½	,,
,, 5 (single),	550 × 95 × 34½	,,

Also floating docks.

Employees, 4000 or more.

Area of war harbour, about 100 acres.   New works completed 1908. Well fortified.   Good anchorage.   Base for Mediterranean Fleet.   Large Aircraft Station being built here 1918—19.

Admiralty Chart No. 194.   Rise of Spring Tide 2 feet.

BRITISH DOCKYARDS AND HARBOURS: ASIATIC & PACIFIC.

(Divided into 2000 yard squares. Uniform scale. Soundings in fathoms. Heights in feet.)

CHINA STATION.

EAST INDIES.

ADEN.   Well fortified.   Coaling.   Harbour 8 × 4 miles.   Admiralty Chart No. 7.

COLOMBO (CEYLON).   Fortified Coaling station.   Excellent and deep harbour, sheltered by breakwaters. Dry dock: 708 × 85 × 32 feet (*Dreadnought.*)   Admiralty Chart No. 3686.

MAURITIUS (PORT LOUIS).   Good harbour, with awkward entrance.   Coaling station.   Fortified.   One dry dock: 384 × 60 × 19½ feet, and one smaller.

Note.—For KARACHI, BOMBAY, CALCUTTA, see Royal Indian Marine Section.

HONG-KONG.   (China Station).

CHINA STATION.

PENANG (STRAITS SETTLEMENTS).   Good deep harbour.   Coaling.   Dry dock: 343 × 46 × 14½ ft.

SINGAPORE.   Coaling station.   Good roads.   Average anchorage, 10 fathoms.   Tanjong Pagar Docks: (1) Victoria, 467 × 65 × 20 ; (2) Albert, 478 × 60 × 21.   Keppel Harbour: (1) 400 × 47 × 16 ; (2) 450 × 52 × 19 ; (3) King's, 846 × 100 × 34, (*Dreadnought* and to take any warship).

HONG KONG.   Repairing yard.   No slips.   Dry docks:—Admiralty No. 1, 555 × 95 × 39 feet (*Dreadnought.*)   New dock: Quarry Bay, (Butterfield & Swire) 750 × 88 × 34½ feet (*Dreadnought.*) At Kau-Lung (see map): No. 1, 700 × 86 × 30 feet (*Dreadnought.*)   Hope Dock, 432½ × 84 × 24 feet. Cosmopolitan, 466 × 85½ × 20 feet.   Also three smaller, able to take torpedo craft, etc.

N.B.—All the foregoing, except the two first, are the property of the Hong Kong & Whampoa Dock Co., Ltd.   Area of basin (tidal), 9½ acres.   Average depth of harbour, 40 feet.   Admiralty Charts No. 1180-1459.   Rise of Spring Tide, 8 feet.

WEI-HAI-WEI (CHINA).   Anchorage.   Unfortified base.   Coaling station.

SINGAPORE.   (China Station).

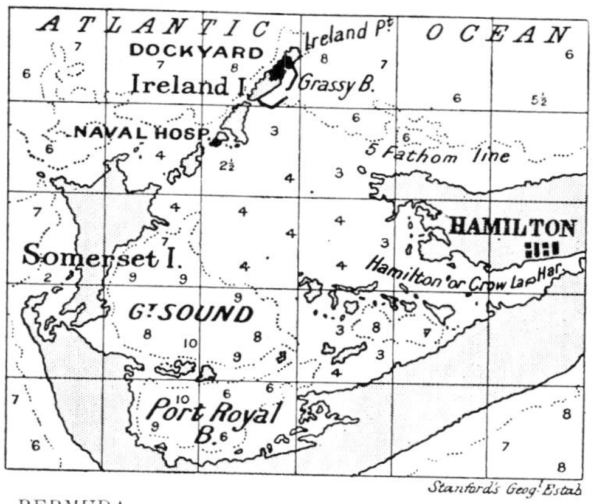

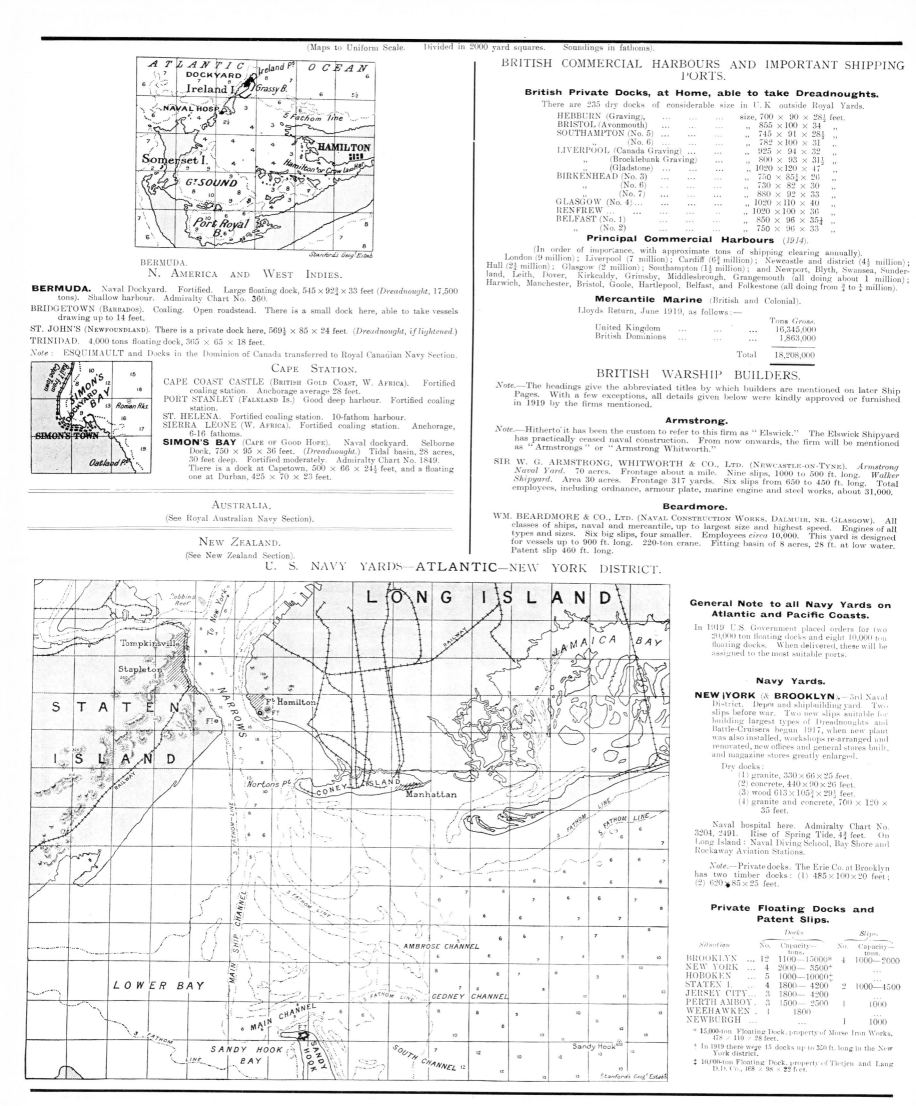

BERMUDA.

N. America and West Indies.

BERMUDA. Naval Dockyard. Fortified. Large floating dock, 545 × 92¾ × 33 feet (*Dreadnought*, 17,500 tons). Shallow harbour. Admiralty Chart No. 360.

BRIDGETOWN (Barbados). Coaling. Open roadstead. There is a small dock here, able to take vessels drawing up to 14 feet.

ST. JOHN'S (Newfoundland). There is a private dock here, 569½ × 85 × 24 feet. (*Dreadnought, if lightened.*)

TRINIDAD. 4,000 tons floating dock, 365 × 65 × 18 feet.

Note: ESQUIMAULT and Docks in the Dominion of Canada transferred to Royal Canadian Navy Section.

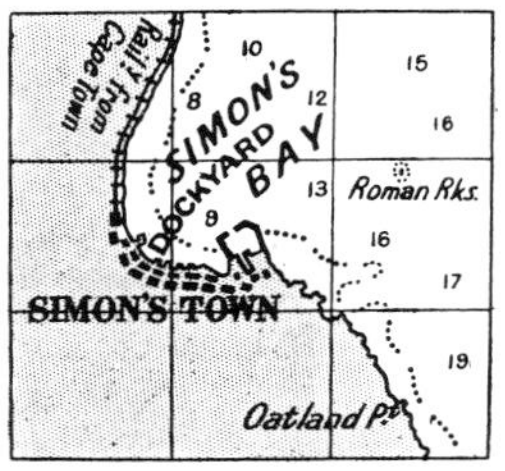

Cape Station.

CAPE COAST CASTLE (British Gold Coast, W. Africa). Fortified coaling station. Anchorage average 28 feet.

PORT STANLEY (Falkland Is.) Good deep harbour. Fortified coaling station.

ST. HELENA. Fortified coaling station. 10-fathom harbour.

SIERRA LEONE (W. Africa). Fortified coaling station. Anchorage, 6-16 fathoms.

SIMON'S BAY (Cape of Good Hope). Naval dockyard. Selborne Dock, 750 × 95 × 36 feet. (*Dreadnought.*) Tidal basin, 28 acres, 30 feet deep. Fortified moderately. Admiralty Chart No. 1849. There is a dock at Capetown, 500 × 66 × 24½ feet, and a floating one at Durban, 425 × 70 × 23 feet.

Australia.

(See Royal Australian Navy Section).

New Zealand.

(See New Zealand Section).

BRITISH COMMERCIAL HARBOURS AND IMPORTANT SHIPPING PORTS.

British Private Docks, at Home, able to take Dreadnoughts.

There are 235 dry docks of considerable size in U.K outside Royal Yards.

HEBBURN (Graving), ...	size, 700 × 90 × 28½ feet.
BRISTOL (Avonmouth)	„ 855 × 100 × 34 „
SOUTHAMPTON (No. 5)	„ 745 × 91 × 28½ „
„ (No. 6)	„ 782 × 100 × 31 „
LIVERPOOL (Canada Graving)	„ 925 × 94 × 32 „
„ (Brocklebank Graving) ...	„ 800 × 93 × 31½ „
„ (Gladstone)	„ 1020 × 120 × 47 „
BIRKENHEAD (No. 3)	„ 750 × 85¼ × 26 „
„ (No. 6)	„ 730 × 82 × 30 „
„ (No. 7)	„ 880 × 92 × 33 „
GLASGOW (No. 4)	„ 1020 × 110 × 40 „
RENFREW	„ 1020 × 100 × 36 „
BELFAST (No. 1)	„ 850 × 96 × 35¼ „
„ (No. 2)	„ 750 × 96 × 33 „

Principal Commercial Harbours (*1914*).

(In order of importance, with approximate tons of shipping clearing annually).

London (9 million); Liverpool (7 million); Cardiff (6¾ million); Newcastle and district (4½ million); Hull (2¼ million); Glasgow (2 million); Southampton (1½ million); and Newport, Blyth, Swansea, Sunderland, Leith, Dover, Kirkcaldy, Grimsby, Middlesbrough, Grangemouth (all doing about 1 million); Harwich, Manchester, Bristol, Goole, Hartlepool, Belfast, and Folkestone (all doing from ¾ to ¼ million).

Mercantile Marine (British and Colonial).

Lloyds Return, June 1919, as follows:—

	Tons *Gross.*
United Kingdom	16,345,000
British Dominions	1,863,000
Total	18,208,000

BRITISH WARSHIP BUILDERS.

Note.—The headings give the abbreviated titles by which builders are mentioned on later Ship Pages. With a few exceptions, all details given below were kindly approved or furnished in 1919 by the firms mentioned.

Armstrong.

Note.—Hitherto it has been the custom to refer to this firm as "Elswick." The Elswick Shipyard has practically ceased naval construction. From now onwards, the firm will be mentioned as "Armstrongs" or "Armstrong Whitworth."

SIR W. G. ARMSTRONG, WHITWORTH & CO., Ltd. (Newcastle-on-Tyne). *Armstrong Naval Yard.* 70 acres. Frontage about a mile. Nine slips, 1000 to 500 ft. long. *Walker Shipyard.* Area 30 acres. Frontage 317 yards. Six slips from 650 to 450 ft. long. Total employees, including ordnance, armour plate, marine engine and steel works, about 31,000.

Beardmore.

WM. BEARDMORE & CO., Ltd. (Naval Construction Works, Dalmuir, nr. Glasgow). All classes of ships, naval and mercantile, up to largest size and highest speed. Engines of all types and sizes. Six big slips, four smaller. Employees *circa* 10,000. This yard is designed for vessels up to 900 ft. long. 220-ton crane. Fitting basin of 8 acres, 28 ft. at low water. Patent slip 460 ft. long.

U. S. NAVY YARDS—ATLANTIC—NEW YORK DISTRICT.

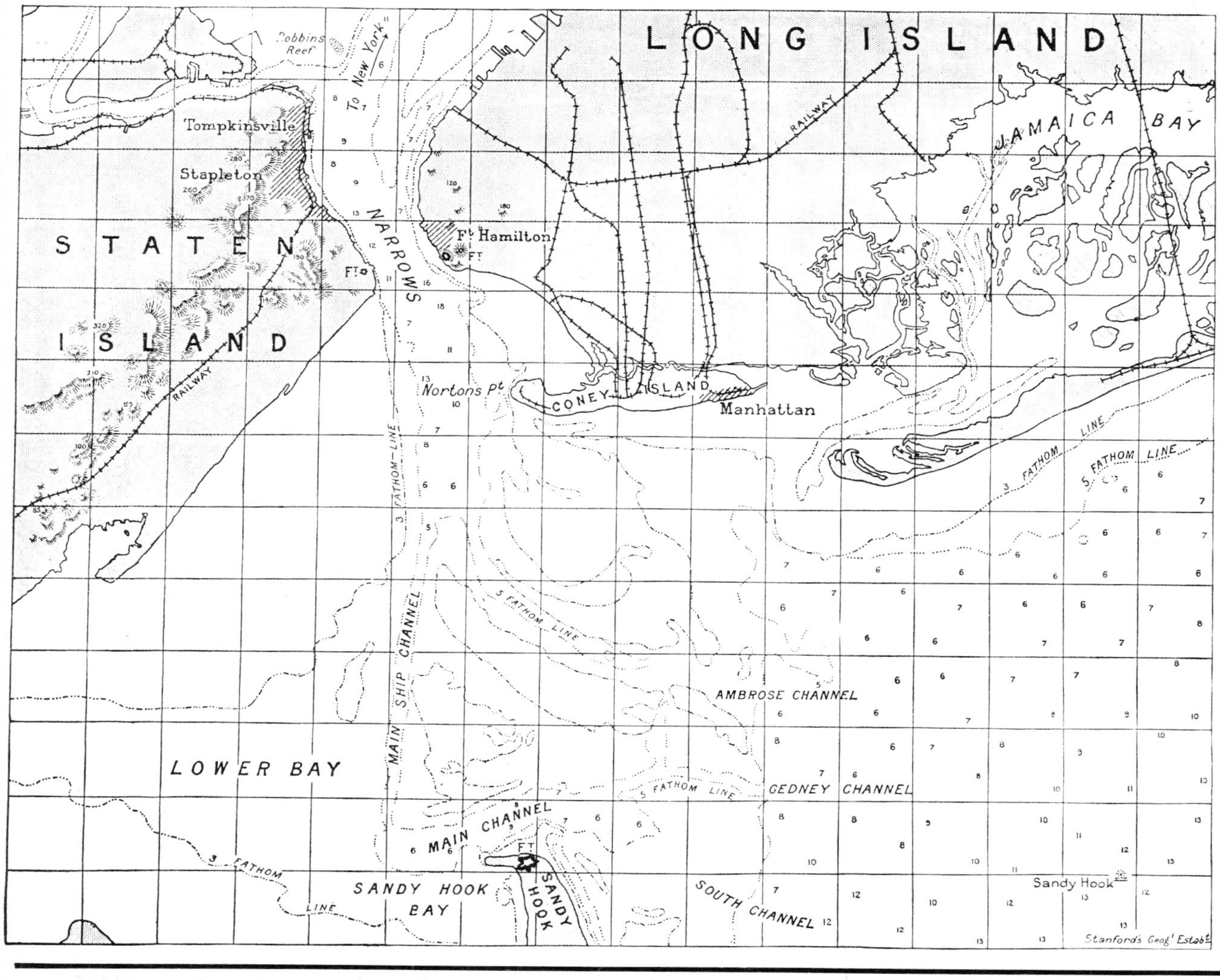

General Note to all Navy Yards on Atlantic and Pacific Coasts.

In 1919 U.S. Government placed orders for two 20,000 ton floating docks and eight 10,000 ton floating docks. When delivered, these will be assigned to the most suitable ports.

Navy Yards.

NEW YORK (& **BROOKLYN**).—3rd Naval District. Depot and shipbuilding yard. Two slips before war. Two new slips suitable for building largest types of Dreadnoughts and Battle-Cruisers begun 1917, when new plant was also installed, workshops re-arranged and renovated, new offices and general stores built, and magazine stores greatly enlarged.

Dry docks:
- (1) granite, 330 × 66 × 25 feet.
- (2) concrete, 440 × 90 × 26 feet.
- (3) wood 613 × 105¾ × 29½ feet.
- (4) granite and concrete, 700 × 120 × 35 feet.

Naval hospital here. Admiralty Chart No. 3204, 2491. Rise of Spring Tide, 4¾ feet. On Long Island: Naval Diving School, Bay Shore and Rockaway Aviation Stations.

Note.—Private docks. The Erie Co. at Brooklyn has two timber docks: (1) 485 × 100 × 20 feet; (2) 620 × 85 × 25 feet.

Private Floating Docks and Patent Slips.

Situation	*Docks* No.	*Docks* Capacity—tons.	*Slips* No.	*Slips* Capacity—tons.
BROOKLYN ...	12	1100—15000*	4	1000—2000
NEW YORK ...	4	2000—3500†		...
HOBOKEN ...	5	1000—10000‡		...
STATEN I. ...	4	1800—4200	2	1000—4500
JERSEY CITY ...	3	1800—4200		...
PERTH AMBOY .	3	1500—2500	1	1000
WEEHAWKEN .	1	1800		...
NEWBURGH ...		...	1	1000

* 15,000-ton Floating Dock, property of Morse Iron Works, 478 × 110 × 28 feet.

† In 1919 there were 15 docks up to 350 ft. long in the New York district.

‡ 10,000-ton Floating Dock, property of Tietjen and Lang D.D. Co., 168 × 98 × 22 feet.

U. S. NAVY YARDS.—ATLANTIC.—HAMPTON ROADS NAVY OPERATING BASE.

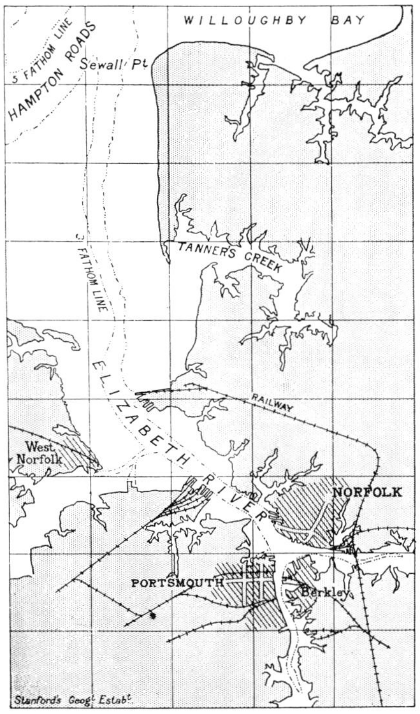

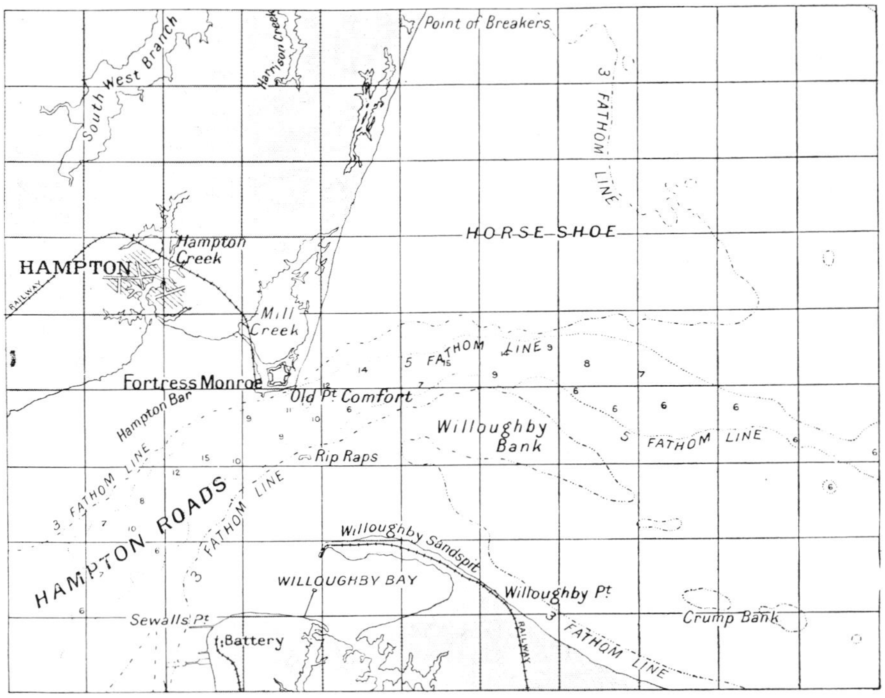

A (Norfolk chart on left joins here.) A

(Hampton Roads as above Map.)

NORFOLK, Va.—5th Naval District. To be the dockyard section of the Hampton Roads Navy Operating Base. Depôt and shipbuilding yard. Naval hospital here. One or more slips for building Dreadnoughts or Battle-Cruisers begun 1917. (1) Wood dock, $460 \times 85 \times 25\frac{1}{2}$ feet; (2) granite, $303 \times 60 \times 25\frac{1}{4}$ feet; (3) granite dock, $550 \times 112 \times 34$ feet. New 1917-18 dock, over 1000 ft. long $\times 110 \times 43\frac{1}{2}$ feet, divisible into 2 sections, about 650 and 350 feet long; to have electric towing gear, 50-ton electric crane, and hydraulic lifts for rapid handling of repair materials, &c. Capable of being emptied in 30 mins.; floating pontoon crane 150 tons, and auxiliary 25 tons on hoist. In 1917 new foundry, workshops, and plant for making mines begun, new plant installed and old renovated. Three patent slips here each 1500 tons. Admiralty Chart No. 2818,2843a.

HAMPTON ROADS NAVY OPERATING BASE (continuation to N. and N.W. of Norfolk Chart).—5th Naval District. Site on ground of Jamestown Exposition was purchased here in 1917, where it is intended that in conjunction with the Norfolk N.Y., a great Naval Base shall be established which will be developed into the principal warship port on the Atlantic coast. Plans as laid down during 1917 by the Navy Department, contemplated the following works: Submarine and Aviation Bases; Training Station for 10,000 men; Fuel Station (for coal and oil); Depots for fleet stores, mines, torpedoes and anti-submarine nets, &c.

U. S. YARDS, HARBOURS, Etc.—ATLANTIC.

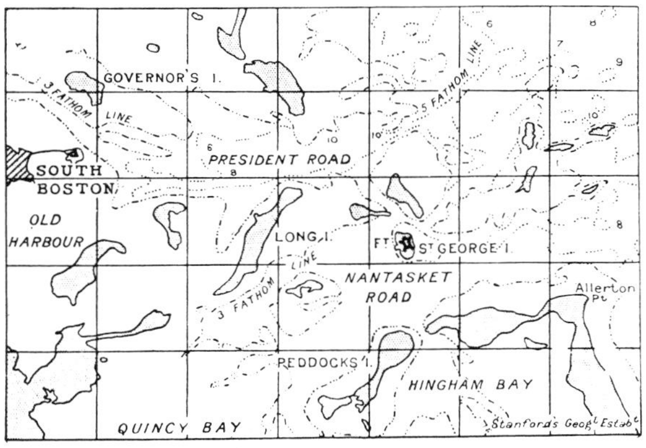

Admiralty Chart No. 1227,2482. Rise of Spring Tide, 5 feet (Charlestown Naval Yard).

Navy Yards (Atlantic Coast).

BOSTON, Mass.—1st Naval District. Depôt. One granite dock, $389 \times 46 \times 26$ feet; one granite and concrete dock, $729 \times 101\frac{1}{2} \times 30\frac{1}{2}$ feet. Naval hospital here. Also two wooden private docks and four patent slips 1000–2300 tons.

LEAGUE ISLAND, PHILADELPHIA Pa.—4th Naval District. Depôt. Two new slips to build Dreadnoughts or Battle-Cruisers. New workshops, foundry and Marine Barracks, 1917-18. One wooden dock, $420 \times 89 \times 25\frac{1}{2}$ feet; second dock, granite and concrete, $707 \times 104 \times 30$ feet. New dock, $1022 \times 144 \times 43\frac{1}{2}$ feet, divisible into two sections, viz., 684 feet outer section and 338 feet inner section. Pier 1000 feet long, with 350-ton crane. Aircraft base and flying ground; also Government seaplane factory. Naval hospital here.

WASHINGTON. No docks. Yard devoted to ordnance construction. Naval hospital here.

PORTSMOUTH, N.H.—1st Naval District. One granite and concrete, $720 \times 101\frac{1}{2} \times 30\frac{2}{3}$ feet. Naval hospital here.

CHARLESTON, S.C.—6th Naval District. 2nd class Navy yard. Dry dock, $503 \times 113 \times 34\frac{1}{4}$ feet.

Naval Stations.

NARRAGANSET BAY, R.I.

NEWPORT, R.I.—2nd Naval District. Chief torpedo station. Manufactory of torpedoes, etc. Naval war college and apprentice-training station. Naval hospital and coal depôt.

CAPE MAY, N.J.—4th Naval District. Base for Submarines and Navy Airships. 349 acres bought 1919 for developing this Station.

NEW LONDON, Conn.—2nd Naval District. Submarine Training Station.

Note.—Charleston, Norfolk, and Bradford, R.I., are stations for petrol and oil fuel. A large number of Naval Stations and Training Camps, Aviation Schools, &c., created during the war have been abolished. 9th, 10th and 11th Naval Districts are on the Great Lakes. Doubtful if any stations are maintained there now.

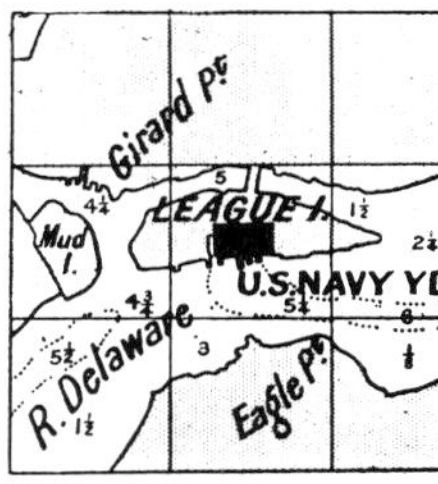

League Island.
Admiralty Chart No. 2564.

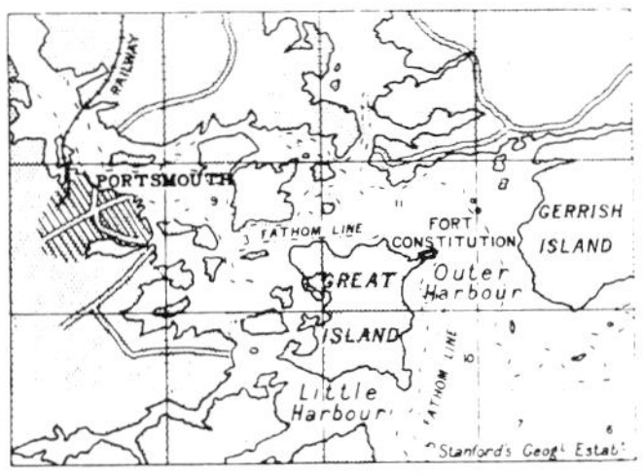

Portsmouth N.H.
Admiralty Chart No. 2482,2487.
Rise of Spring Tide, $8\frac{1}{2}$ feet.

PRIVATE DOCKS, &c.

(exclusive of those in New York and Brooklyn districts, previously listed).

NEW LONDON (Conn.), three patent slips, 1000–2000 tons. PHILADELPHIA, one floating dock (3500 tons) and two patent slips (1000 and 2300 tons). CAMDEN (N.J.), three patent slips, 1200–1500 tons. BALTIMORE (Md.), Wm. Skinner & Sons dry dock, $600 \times 80 \times 22\frac{1}{2}$ feet. Columbian Iron-works Dock (wood), $437 \times 80 \times 21$ feet. Maryland Steel Co., Sparrow Point, wood and steel floating dock, 20,000 tons. Also one 3000 ton floating dock and two patent slips (2000 and 1500 tons). At Portland (Me.), Savannah (Ga.), Jacksonville (Fla.), small patent slips of 1200 tons (Jacksonville, one 4500 ton floating dock).

Mercantile Ports (Atlantic Coast *.

(In order of importance, with approximate tons of shipping cleared per year in brackets).

New York, N.Y. ($13\frac{1}{3}$ million ?); Boston, Mass. ($1\frac{3}{4}$ million); Philadelphia, Pa. ($2\frac{1}{3}$ million); Baltimore, Md. ($1\frac{1}{4}$ million); Hampton Roads, Va. ($\frac{3}{4}$ million); Portland, Me. ($\frac{1}{3}$ million).

* Figures compiled 1913-14. Post-war statistics not available yet.

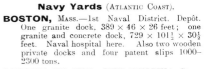

U. S. PRIVATE SHIPYARDS.—ATLANTIC.

(Warship builders *only*. Revised from details furnished by firms named, 1919.)

Bath I.W.

BATH IRONWORKS (Bath, Me.). Build battleships, scout cruisers, destroyers and torpedo vessels, mercantile vessels of fast passenger types and large steam yachts of very fast design. Slips : one 600 ft., one 500 ft., three 350 ft. Cranes : one 100-ton stiff leg derrick (electric), one 35-ton floating sheer-legs (steam), three 15-ton electric locomotive cranes for steel runways. Yard covers 13 acres. Water-front 1000 feet. Plant up-to-date. Yard builds boilers, engines, equipment for ships, &c. Employees : 1300 (peace), 2000 (war).

Bethlehem Fore River.

FORE RIVER PLANT, BETHLEHEM SHIPBUILDING CORPORATION (Quincy, Mass.). 21 launching slips, 41 building slips, 20 building slips for submarines and four for 300 ft. destroyers. One 20-ton lift hammer-head crane, one 75-ton lift gantry crane, 16 overhead cranes over slips, capacity 5 and 10 tons and one 50-ton lift overhead crane. Yard covers 85 acres and water-front 1¼ miles. Yard builds boilers, machinery and equipment. Plant thoroughly modern. Employees, 14,356.

Bethlehem Squantum.

NAVAL DESTROYER PLANT, BETHLEHEM SHIPBUILDING CORPORATION (Squantum, Mass.). 10 building slips with electric bridge cranes and three wet slips. Maximum length of slips 310 ft. (*n.p.*). One 20-ton stiff leg derrick ; one 10-ton guy derrick ; wet slips have one 25-ton and two 10-ton bridge cranes. Yard covers 60 acres approximately. Water-front about 3600 feet. Boilers, engines, &c., supplied by other Bethlehem Plants. Employees, about 9000.

Cramps.

MESSRS. THE WM. CRAMP & SONS SHIP & ENGINE-BUILDING CO. (Philadelphia, Pa.). Build dreadnoughts, battle cruisers, scout cruisers, destroyers and mercantile vessels of all types. 8 slips. Longest ship which can be built, 850 feet. One 100-ton floating derrick with 25-tons auxiliary lift ; one 70-ton lift revolving hammer-head crane ; numerous other cranes to lift 5— 25 tons. Graving dock 433 ft. *over all* ; width at entrance 69 ft. (top), 48 ft. (bottom) ; depth of water 20½ ft. H.W.O.S. and 15½ ft. L.W.O.S. Patent slips : one 3000-ton and one 1000-ton railways. Area of yard 175 acres. Water-front 6300 ft. Yard builds boilers, machinery and naval equipment. Plant is up-to-date. Employees, 7000 (peace), 11,500 (war).

Fore River.

FORE RIVER CO. (Quincy, Mass.). Nine big slips. Area, 40 acres. Yard railway of 4 miles. Depth of water in channel, 33 feet. Employees, about 12,000 now. New Yard, 1917-18.

Note.—This firm has made no return of its shipyard, plant, &c., for several years past. Above details may not be correct now.

Harlan, Wilmington.

(Late Harlan & Hollingsworth Co.)

HARLAN SHIPBUILDING PLANT (Wilmington, Delaware). 35 acres. Water frontage, 1800 feet. Depth at low tide, 22 feet. 5 slips, able to build up to 15,000 tons. Dry dock, 330×90×13½ feet. Equipment thoroughly up-to-date. Employees, 1000.

Note.—Above details are not up-to-date.

Hollands.

ELECTRIC BOAT CO. (Groton, Conn.) Submarines of the "Holland" type, which are chiefly built at the Fore River Co.'s Yard.

Lake C0.

LAKE TORPEDO BOAT CO. (Bridgeport, Con.). Submarines of the "Lake" type.

Newport News.

NEWPORT NEWS SHIPBUILDING & DRY DOCK COMPANY (Newport, Va.). 125 acres. Deep water alongside. Water-front, ¾ mile. One 140-ton revolving derrick, one 100-ton sheer-leg, one 50-ton floating derrick, one 10-ton ditto. Very large modern shops. Total employees 11,500. Eight big slips. Dry docks : (2) 804×80×30 feet ; (3) 537½×79×24½ feet ; (1) 593×50×24½ feet.

New York S.B. Co.

NEW YORK SHIPBUILDING CO. (Camden, N.J.). Can build dreadnoughts, cruisers, destroyers, mine-layers and sweepers, naval tenders and all classes of mercantile vessels, with boilers, machinery, and all equipment. 9 big slips, 4 smaller and 10 for destroyers. Yard can build ships up to 1000 ft. long, and covers 190.6 acres. Water-front about ⅜ths of a mile. Plant up-to-date. All machine tools and cranes electrically driven. Hydraulic and compressed air plant. Employees about 7000 (peace), 19,000 (war).

Todd, Brooklyn.

TODD SHIPYARDS CORPORATION (Tebo Yacht Basin Yard, Brooklyn, N.Y.). Three slips, 250 ft. long. Two 30-ton floating cranes. Two floating docks : (1) 105×23 ft. to lift 600 tons *d.w.* (2) 150×64 ft. to lift 1100 tons *d.w.* Yard covers 25 acres. Plant is modern. Employees, 1000. Associated firms :—Robin D.D. & Repair Co., Brooklyn, N.Y. ; Tietjen & Lang D.D. Co., Hoboken (10,000-ton floating dock) ; Clinton Plant, Brooklyn ; Quintard Iron Works, N.Y. (build engines, &c., for ships built by Todd Co.) ; White Fuel Oil Engineering Co., N.Y. Also see Pacific Coast for Tacoma Yard.

Also a very large number of other shipyards solely engaged on mercantile construction.

U. S. NAVY YARDS, STATIONS, &c.—GULF COAST, CARIBBEAN, &c.

SAN JUAN, PUERTO RICO.

Admiralty Chart No. 478,3408.   Rise of Spring Tide, 1 foot.

NEW ORLEANS, La.—8th Naval District. Floating dock, 525×100×28¼ feet.

PENSACOLA, Fla.—8th Naval District. 2nd class yard. 8th Naval District. Big new Aviation Station for seaplanes, dirigibles, kite-balloons, &c. Floating dock, 450×82×27 feet (12000 tons).

KEY WEST.—7th Naval District. No docks. Submarine and Aircraft Station.

Small Naval Stations may also exist at San Juan (Porto Rico) and St. Thomas (Virgin Islands).

Private Docks.

NEW ORLEANS : Government dock, 525×100×28 feet, and two floating docks, 2000 and 2500 tons.
MOBILE (Ala.) : Pinto Dry Dock, 232×86×17 feet, and two floating docks, 1000 and 1100 tons.

Private Shipyards.

Various New Yards established 1917-18. Do not undertake Naval construction, all being devoted to mercantile contracts.

Mercantile Ports.*

(In order of importance and approximate tons of shipping cleared annually).

New Orleans (2½ million) ; Galveston, Texas (½ million) ; Mobile, Ala. (¼ million) ; Pensacola, Fla. (½ million) ; Savannah, Ga. (⅓ million) ; Key West (½ million).

* 1914 figures : post-war statistics not available.

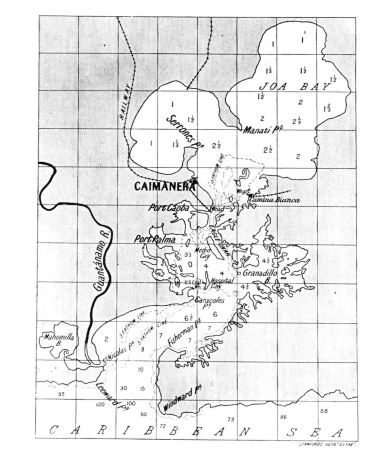

GUANTANAMO BAY (Cuba). Fleet Anchorage and Exercising Grounds. Small repairs undertaken here. Fuel Depôt. Admiralty Chart No. 904.

U. S. A.—PANAMA CANAL ZONE.

Canal about 50 miles long. Channel 300–1000 feet wide at bottom; depth 41–85 feet. Time of passage about 10 hours.

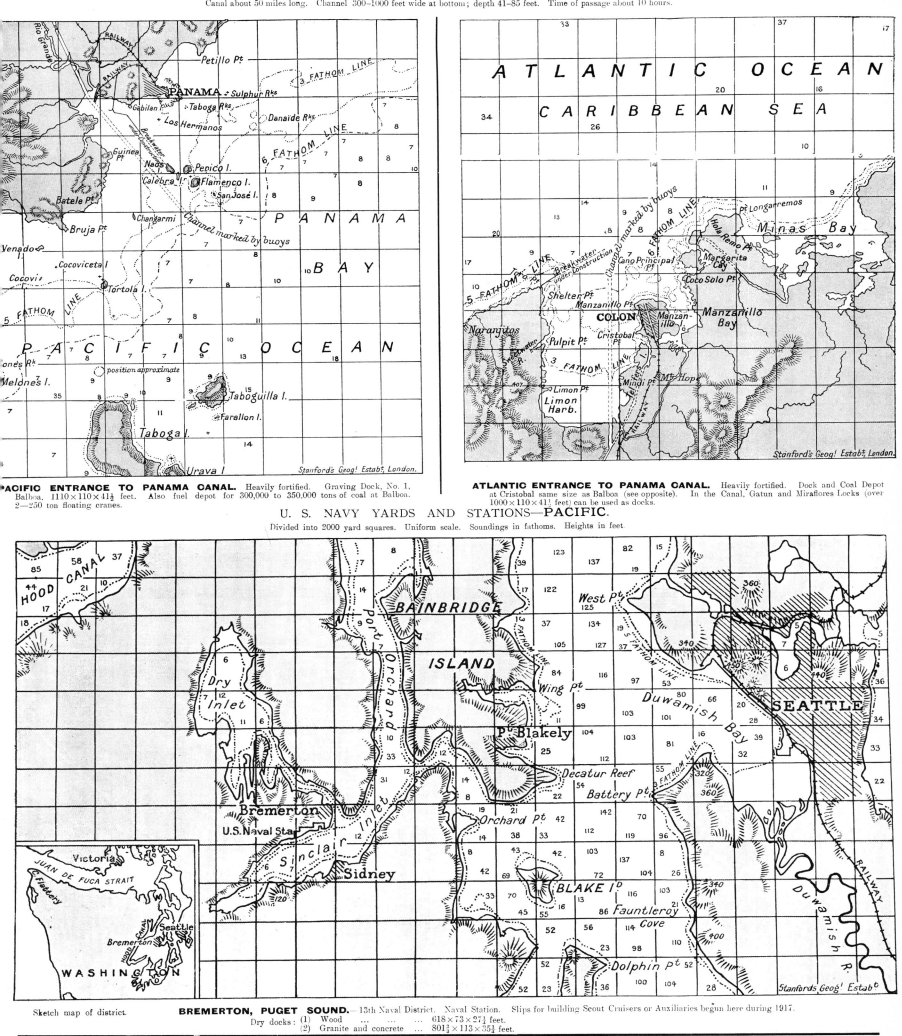

PACIFIC ENTRANCE TO PANAMA CANAL. Heavily fortified. Graving Dock, No. 1, Balboa. 1110×110×41½ feet. Also fuel depot for 300,000 to 350.000 tons of coal at Balboa. 2—250 ton floating cranes.

ATLANTIC ENTRANCE TO PANAMA CANAL. Heavily fortified. Dock and Coal Depot at Cristobal same size as Balboa (see opposite). In the Canal, Gatun and Miraflores Locks (over 1000×110×41½ feet) can be used as docks.

U. S. NAVY YARDS AND STATIONS—PACIFIC.

Divided into 2000 yard squares. Uniform scale. Soundings in fathoms. Heights in feet.

Sketch map of district.

BREMERTON, PUGET SOUND. 13th Naval District. Naval Station. Slips for building Scout Cruisers or Auxiliaries begun here during 1917.

Dry docks: (1) Wood ... ... 618×73×27½ feet.
(2) Granite and concrete ... 801⅓×113×35¼ feet.

U. S. HARBOURS.—PACIFIC.

Divided into 2000 yard squares. Uniform scale. Soundings in fathoms. Heights in feet.

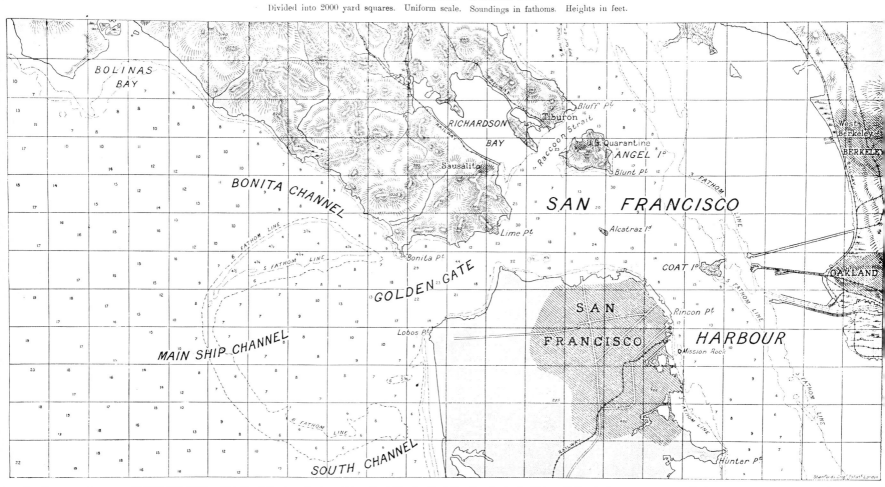

San Francisco Harbour. **MARE ISLAND.**—12th Naval District. Depôt and Navy Yard (22 miles N. of San Francisco), of which small Map is given on next page. Slip to build Dreadnoughts of 600 feet length, or above, begun at Mare Island in 1916 or 1917. Destroyers also built. Dry Docks: (1) Granite ... 418 × 88 × 27½ feet.
(2) Concrete ... 883 × 102 × 31½ „

U. S. HARBOURS, Etc.—PACIFIC & ASIATIC.

Principal Private Yards.—Pacific Coast.

Note : No Pacific Coast Shipyards have made returns for several years past.

BETHLEHEM SHIPBUILDING CORPORATION (San Francisco). Large new yard and engine shops at Alameda, new yard projected at Risdon. Builds Destroyers.

CALIFORNIA SHIPBUILDING CO. (Long Beach, Cal.), Submarine builders.

MORAN & CO. (Seattle, Puget Sound). One big slip. Floating dock 468 × 85 × 27½ feet (12,000 tons) and another *smaller.*

SEATTLE DRY DOCK AND CONSTRUCTION CO. (Seattle, Washington). Now controlled by Skinner & Eddy, Seattle. Floating dock, 325 × 100 (extreme) × 25 feet, for 6000 tons; one floating dock for 2500 tons; one patent slip, 3000 tons.

TODD DRY DOCKS & CONSTRUCTION CO. (Tacoma, Washington). No details available. Is building Cruisers. 12,000 ton floating dock completing at end of 1918.

⊙ UNION IRON WORKS CO. (San Francisco). (Affiliated to the Bethlehem Shipbuilding Co.) 38 acres. Three dry docks (Hunters Point): (1) 750 × 103 × 30 feet (28,000 tons), (2) 485 × 97 × 24 feet (10,000 tons), (3) 1110 × 110 × 41½ feet. Three small floating docks of 2500 and 1800 tons and a third of unknown capacity. Six slips of 600 feet long, fully equipped with electric cranes, etc., and 4 smaller. Five wharves 585 × 50 feet, berthing for 15 average sized vessels. One sheer leg 100 tons, one 40 tons. 2 marine railways. All plant dates from 1910 or later. *Employees :* Average 2300. Enlarged 1917.

* Details not revised since 1914. Title may have been altered to BETHLEHEM UNION PLANT.

Also 30–40 new shipyards on Pacific coast, but these are engaged in mercantile construction only.

Mare Island. Admiralty Chart No. 2887.

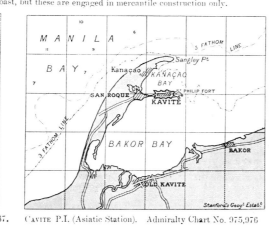

Cavite P.I. (Asiatic Station). Admiralty Chart No. 975,976

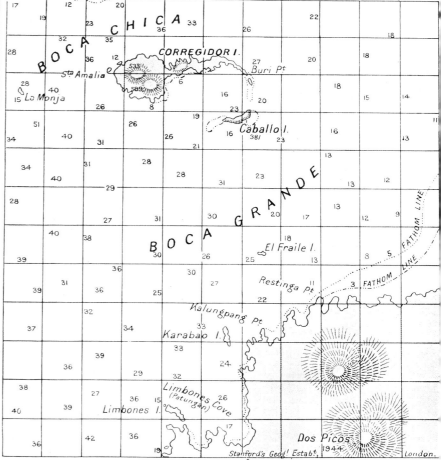

Entrance to Manila Bay. (Asiatic Station).

U. S. HARBOURS, Etc.—PACIFIC & ASIATIC.

Divided into 2000 yard squares.   Uniform scale.   Soundings in fathoms.   Heights in feet.

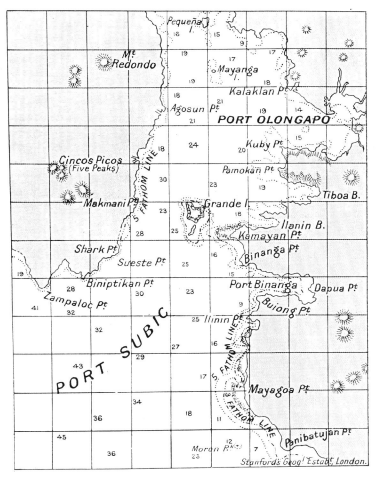

OLONGAPO & PORT SUBIC.

Naval Hospital.

LAS ANIMAS, Cal.

Naval Stations.—2ND CLASS, PACIFIC.

PEARL HARBOUR (1) Honolulu. (2) Pearl Harbour, on S. side of Island of Oahu, about 10–15 miles west of Honolulu. Large dock here, 1001 × 114 × 34¾ feet.
TUTUILA (SAMOA).

Asiatic Naval Stations.

CAVITE (P.I.) Small dry dock at Manila. Maps on preceding page.
OLONGAPO (P.I.) Dewey Floating dock, 18,500 tons, 501′ 0¾″ × 100′ ×37′ 0″ ?

Chief Mercantile Ports.—PACIFIC COAST.

Seattle (2¼ million) ; San Francisco (1¼ million).

* These figures were compiled before 1914, and can no longer be regarded as really trustworthy.

TUTUILA (SAMOA).
Admiralty Chart No. 1730.

JAPANESE DOCKYARDS.

Divided into 2000 yard squares.   Uniform scale.   Soundings in fathoms.   Heights in feet.

YOKOSUKA

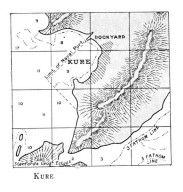

KURE

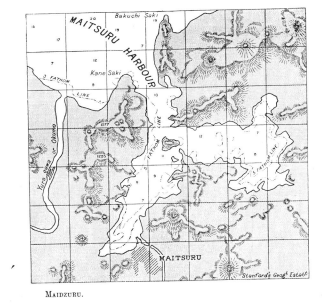

MAIDZURU.

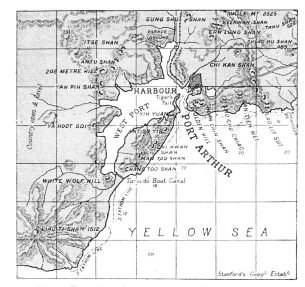

RYOJUN (PORT ARTHUR).

Imperial Dockyards.   Principal Naval Harbours (*Ching-ju-fu*).

YOKOSUKA (in Sagami).   Fleet Base, Dockyard, T.B.D., Submarine and Aircraft Stations. Fortified. Six slips, one for battle-cruisers, two for Dreadnoughts, three smaller. Docks No. 5, 747×115×41 feet, able to take any ship, and No. 4, 538×98½×32. Also one dock (No. 2) 447×94½×29 feet ; two others : No. 1, 298×82×21 feet ; No. 3, 265×45×18 feet. Employees (in 1914) 8000. Naval Engineering Academy here. Naval Aviation Station at Oihama. Admiralty Chart No. 997.

KURE (in Aki).   Fleet Base, Dockyard, T.B.D., and Aircraft Base.   Three slips. Docks No. 1, 413×58½×28 feet ; No. 2, 485½ × 81 × 35½ feet. No. 3, 666×100×34 feet. Perhaps a fourth big dock. Ordnance and Armour Plate built here. Cadets Academy at Etajima. Admiralty Chart No. 3469.

* **SASEBO** (in Hizen).   Fleet Base, Dockyard, T.B.D. and Aircraft Base. One slip. There are four docks here : (1) 435×94× 29 ; (2) 475×85×32 ; (3) 538×93½×33 feet. (4) 777×111 ×38 feet. Perhaps a fifth big dock. There is also a floating dock for torpedo craft here (1500 tons). Admiralty Chart No. 359.

* *See next page for Map.*

MAIDZURU (or MAIZURU) (in Tango). Admiralty Chart No. 2174. One dock 450 feet long, one small for t.b. (completed 1908), a third dock 540 feet long completed 1913. Perhaps a fourth dock.
RYOJUN (PORT ARTHUR). Dry docks : No. 1, 370×72×30 feet ; No. 2, 500×92½×32 feet. Admiralty Chart No. 1236-1798.
DAIREN (Dalny).   Naval dock, 381×43×19¾ feet.
CHINKAI (Korea), previously known as Masampo.

JAPANESE DOCKYARDS.

Divided into 2000 yard squares.　　Uniform scale.　　Soundings in fathoms.　　Heights in feet.

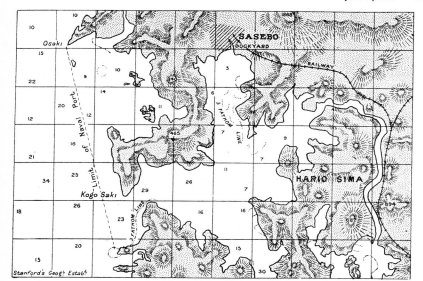

SASEBO.

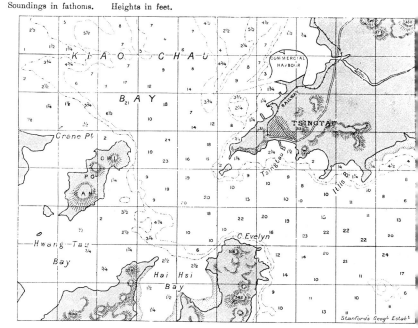

Lesser Naval Harbours (Yoko).

OMINATO. Torpedo base. } Repair Stations for T.B.D., &c. Small 1500 ton Floating
BAKO (Pescadores). } Dock at each.

Mercantile Marine.

June, 1919, 2,325,000 tons *gross*. A considerable amount of new mercantile tonnage is being built.

Coinage.

Yen (100 sen) = 2s. 0¼d. British, $0.50 U.S.A., *about*.

Principal Mercantile Ports.

Yokohama, Hakodate, Nagasaki, Moji, Kobé, Dairen (Dalny).

Overseas Possessions.

Formosa, Karafuto (Saghalien), Pescadores. Protectorate in Chosen (Korea). Kiaochau Peninsula and Tsingtao leased from China.

KIAO-CHAU and TSINGTAO (China). German naval base in the Far East, occupied by the Anglo-Japanese Expeditionary Army, 1914. There used to be a floating dock here, 410 × 100 × 30 feet (12,000 tons), but it was probably destroyed by the Germans before surrender. Tsingtao is only being used as a commercial harbour, but the naval base facilities, created during German occupation, are at the disposal of Japanese warships in any emergency.

Private Docks.

Details of Private Docks will be found on a later page (after the Silhouettes), with a full description of the Private Japanese Shipbuilding Yards.

FRENCH NAVAL BASES.

CHANNEL.

For Charts, see preceding page.

DUNKIRK. Fine harbour. Breakwater. Torpedo, Submarine and Aircraft base. There are five docks here—one 622 × 69 × 26¼, two 357¼ × 46 × 26 or 21 feet, and one smaller.

CALAIS. Torpedo and submarine base. Dock, 426¼ × 69 × 28½.

Private Docks.

BOULOGNE. Floating Dock, 236¼ × 62¼ feet (1000 tons).
DIEPPE. Dry Dock, 361 × 59 × 27 feet.
HAVRE. (No. 4). 674¼ × 98⅔ × 28½ feet; also 2 large and 3 small docks.
GRANVILLE. Dry Dock, 223 × 46½ × 23 feet.
PAIMPOL. Dry Dock, 229½ × 36 × feet.

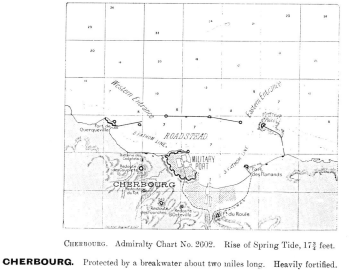

CHERBOURG. Admiralty Chart No. 2602.　Rise of Spring Tide, 17¾ feet.

CHERBOURG. Protected by a breakwater about two miles long. Heavily fortified.

Dry Docks.

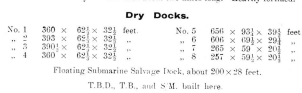

No. 1	360 × 62¼ × 32¼ feet	No. 5	656 × 93¼ × 39½ feet
„ 2	393 × 62¼ × 32¼ „	„ 6	606 × 69¼ × 29¼ „
„ 3	390½ × 62¼ × 32¼ „	„ 7	265 × 59 × 20½ „
„ 4	360 × 62¼ × 32¼ „	„ 8	257 × 59½ × 20½ „

Floating Submarine Salvage Dock, about 200 × 28 feet.

T.B.D., T.B., and S.M. built here.

ATLANTIC COAST.

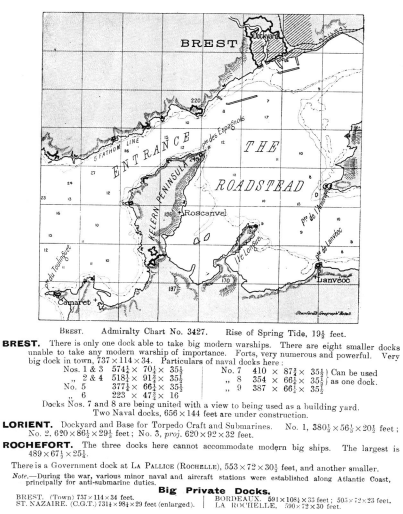

BREST.　Admiralty Chart No. 3427.　Rise of Spring Tide, 19½ feet.

BREST. There is only one dock able to take big modern warships. There are eight smaller docks unable to take any modern warship of importance. Forts, very numerous and powerful. Very big dock in town, 737 × 114 × 34. Particulars of naval docks here:—

Nos. 1 & 3	574½ × 70¼ × 35½	No. 7	410 × 87¾ × 35½	} Can be used
„ 2 & 4	518½ × 91¾ × 35½	„ 8	354 × 66¼ × 35½	} as one dock.
No. 5	377¼ × 66¼ × 35½	„ 9	387 × 66¼ × 35½	
„ 6	223 × 47¾ × 16			

Docks Nos. 7 and 8 are being united with a view to being used as a building yard.
Two Naval docks, 656 × 144 feet are under construction.

LORIENT. Dockyard and Base for Torpedo Craft and Submarines. No. 1, 380½ × 56½ × 20½ feet; No. 2, 620 × 86½ × 29½ feet; No. 3, *proj.* 620 × 92 × 32 feet.

ROCHEFORT. The three docks here cannot accommodate modern big ships. The largest is 489 × 67½ × 25¼.

There is a Government dock at LA PALLICE (ROCHELLE), 553 × 72 × 30½ feet, and another smaller.

Note.—During the war, various minor naval and aircraft stations were established along Atlantic Coast, principally for anti-submarine duties.

Big Private Docks.

BREST. (Town) 737 × 114 × 34 feet.
ST. NAZAIRE. (C.G.T.) 731¼ × 98¼ × 29 feet (enlarged).
BORDEAUX. 591 × 108½ × 33 feet; 505 × 72 × 23 feet.
LA ROCHELLE. 590 × 72 × 30 feet.

FRENCH NAVAL BASES—MEDITERRANEAN.

(To uniform scale. Divided into 2000 yard squares. Soundings in fathoms. Heights in feet.) **Dockyards named in heavy type.**

TOULON. Very strongly fortified. Aircraft and Submarine base. Destroyers, T.B. and Submarines built here in Dockyard.

Dry Docks.

MISSIESSY.	No. 1	$427 \times 93\frac{1}{4} \times 30\frac{1}{2}$	CASTIGNEAU. No. 1 $325 \times 70\frac{1}{2} \times 25\frac{1}{2}$
,,	,, 2	$427 \times 93\frac{1}{4} \times 30\frac{1}{2}$	,, ,, 2 $385\frac{1}{2} \times 70\frac{1}{4} \times 27\frac{1}{2}$
,,	,, 3	$585 \times 93\frac{1}{4} \times 30\frac{1}{2}$	,, ,, 3 $535 \times 75\frac{1}{2} \times 27\frac{1}{2}$
,,	,, 4	$600 \times 92 \times 32\frac{1}{2}$	

Floating dock for torpedo craft. Submarine Floating Salvage Dock, "Atlas" $300 \times 42\frac{2}{3}$ feet, 1000 tons lift. Also 3 small docks in the Arsenal Principal.

Naval Aviation Centres.

Very large establishment at Fréjus, St. Raphael, near Toulon. Also Training School at Berre, near Marseilles.

Naval Bases.—(Continued).

AJACCIO. } Fortified harbours used by the French fleet. No docks.
BONIFACIO. }

ALGIERS. Coaling Station. Two dry docks (No. 1) $455 \times 74 \times 28$ feet; (No. 2) $268 \times 54 \times 19$ feet. Average depth of harbour, 8 fathoms.

ORAN. Torpedo base. Excellent harbour, with an average depth of five fathoms. Two breakwaters. Fortified. Floating Submarine Salvage Dock 210×64 feet.

BIZERTA. Submarine and Aircraft base. Lies inside a narrow channel. One large dock suitable for any warship, one small one. Floating dock for torpedo craft. (No. 1) $656 \times 90\frac{1}{2} \times 33\frac{1}{2}$; (No. 3) $295 \times 46\frac{1}{2} \times 17\frac{1}{4}$; (No. 4) $656\frac{1}{4} \times 90\frac{1}{2} \times 33\frac{1}{2}$. Submarine Salvage Ship *Vulcain* stationed here.

Note.—Temporary Naval Base established at Beyrout. During the War the French Fleet was first based at Malta, but was transferred to Corfu. Milo, Mudros, Salonika, Salamina, Gulf of Patras, were netted for use as anchorages for French Warships.

ORAN. Admiralty Chart No. 812.

BIZERTA. Admiralty Chart No 1569.

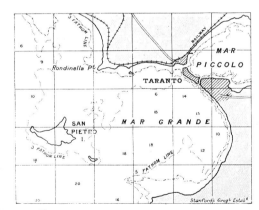

TOULON. Admiralty Chart No. 151-2608

AJACCIO. Admiralty Chart No. 429.

Large Private Docks (*Mediterranean*).

MARSEILLES.—(No. 1) $595\frac{1}{2} \times 61 \times 22\frac{1}{2}$ feet, and No. 7, $669\frac{1}{4} \times 82 \times 29\frac{1}{2}$ feet.

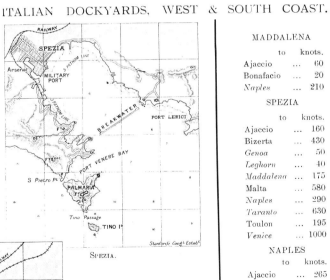

FRENCH **COLONIAL** NAVAL BASES.

African W. Coast.

DAKAR (Senegal). Naval dry dock here, $629\frac{3}{4} \times 92\frac{2}{3} \times 30\frac{1}{2}$ feet.

African E. Coast.

Also one or two small Naval Stations in Madagascar; location not known.

DAKAR (Senegal). Admiralty Chart No. 1001.

In the Far East.

SAIGON. Situated 42 miles up the Donnoi River, Anchorage average, 9 fathoms. One large dry dock $518 \times 72 \times 30$ feet, and two small ones. Floating Dock 400×66 feet, 10,000 tons lift. Slip for building ships up to 300 feet long.

ITALIAN DOCKYARDS, WEST & SOUTH COAST.

TARANTO.

SPEZIA.

TABLE OF DISTANCES.

MADDALENA	to knots.
Ajaccio	60
Bonafacio	20
Naples	210

SPEZIA	to knots.
Ajaccio	160
Bizerta	430
Genoa	50
Leghorn	40
Maddalena	175
Malta	580
Naples	290
Taranto	630
Toulon	195
Venice	1000

NAPLES	to knots.
Ajaccio	265
Bizerta	315
Bonafacio	225
Maddalena	210

TARANTO	to knots.	VENICE	to knots.
Bizerta	550	Pola	75
Malta	310	*Taranto*	575
Messina	220	Toulon	1197
Naples	380		
Venice	575		

TRIESTE to

	MILES.		MILES.
Brindisi	372	*Pola*	61
Cattaro	337	Smyrna[⊛]	902
Constantinople[⊛]	1050	,, [†]	1000
,, [†]	1152	Salonika[⊛]	950
Corfu	480	,, [†]	1049
Fiume	110	Toulon	1169
Gibraltar	1648	Wilhelmshaven[§]	3207
Malta	730	,, [‡]	3744
Piraeus[⊛]	708	Zeebrugge[§]	3050
,, [†]	839	,, [‡]	3756

⊛ By Canal of Corinth.
† By Cape Matapan.
§ By English Channel.
‡ By North of Scotland and West of Ireland.

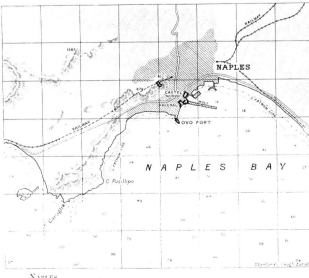

NAPLES.

Royal Dockyards.

SPEZIA. Docks: No. 5, $702 \times 105\frac{1}{2} \times 33$ feet; No. 6, $508 \times 90 \times 33$ feet; No. 4, $354\frac{1}{2} \times 71\frac{1}{2} \times 29$ feet; Nos. 3 and 2, $430 \times 77 \times 30$ feet; No. 1, $358 \times 71 \times 30$ feet. Two large slips. (At Muggiano, there is a special testing dock for submarines belonging to Fiat-San-Giorgio Co.) Total employees about 5300. Admiralty Chart No. 155.

NAPLES (NAPOLI). One small Government dock, $247 \times 62 \times 19\frac{1}{2}$ feet. New large dock, *projected*, 1918. One small slip. Total employees 3029. Good anchorage. Commercial harbour and various new harbour works *projected*. There are two municipal docks (*c.* preceding page). Admiralty Chart No. 1728.

CASTELLAMARE. No docks. Building yard. Two large slips, two small. Total employees 1920.

TARANTO. One dock, "Principe do Napoli," $709 \times 108 \times 32\frac{1}{2}$ feet (2 sections). Floating dock, $365 \times 61 \times 25$ feet (4800 tons), and another smaller (2900 tons). One large slip. Total employees 1561. Admiralty Chart No. 1643. Two 130 ton old Krupps are mounted in a turret on San Pietro.

MADDALENA (Sardinia). No docks. Total employees 113. **MESSINA** (Sicily): Government Dock $343 \times 71\frac{1}{2} \times 26$ feet.

Torpedo Craft, Submarine and Naval Aircraft Stations: Spezia, Naples, Taranto. Also minor Naval Stations at Genoa, Maddalena, Gaeta, Messina.

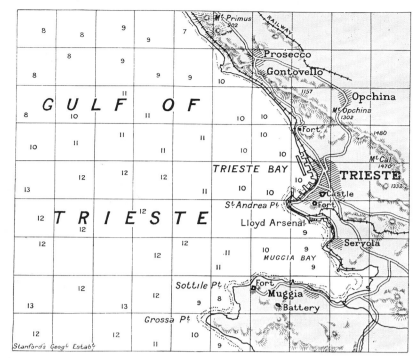

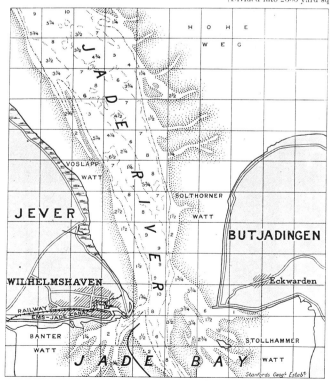

Arsenals.

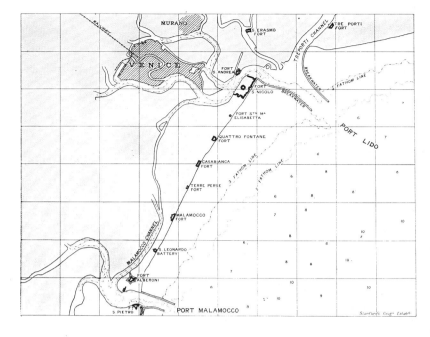

Royal Dockyards.

VENICE (VENEZIA). One dock, No. 4, $656 \times 106 \times 38\frac{1}{2}$ feet; one dock for long cruisers, No. 1, $525 \times 78 \times 25\frac{1}{2}$ feet; one small dock No. 2, for third-class cruisers, $295 \times 59 \times 19\frac{1}{2}$ feet. Two large slips, one small slip. Submarines built in this yard. Employees 2797. Depth of Port Lido, 29 feet. Malamocco, 28 feet at low water. Commercial harbours at both. Admiralty Chart No. 1483.

TRIESTE. No Government docks. One slip. Two Private docks here, $456 \times 73 \times 19$ feet and $360 \times 54 \times 18\frac{3}{4}$ feet; there is a dock at San Rocco, across the bay, $414 \times 66 \times 21$ feet. Two floating of 2,000 and 1,500 tons. Admiralty Chart No. 1434. Rise of Spring Tide, 2 feet.

POLA (Late Austro-Hungarian Naval Base). Heavily fortified. Slips: One 690 feet long and two smaller. Two dry docks: (a) $467 \times 85 \times 27\frac{3}{4}$ feet and (b) $397 \times 86 \times 31\frac{1}{4}$ feet. Floating docks: (c) $585 \times 111 \times 37$ feet (22,500 tons); (d) $459\frac{1}{2} \times 90 \times 32\frac{1}{4}$ feet (15,000 tons); (e) $300 \times 82\frac{1}{2} \times 20$ feet; (f) small, only used for torpedo craft, 1,000 tons lift, completed June, 1914. Employés 4500. 3 slips. Naval hospital. Admiralty Chart No. 202. Rise of Spring Tide, $3\frac{1}{2}$ feet.

Torpedo Craft, Submarine & Naval Aircraft Stations: Venice, Brindisi. Also minor Naval Station at Ancona.

(For BRINDISI, see next page).

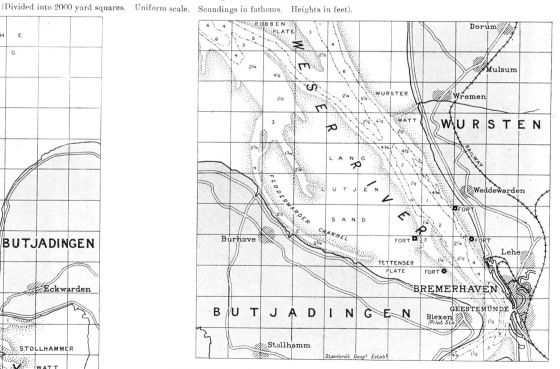

WILHELMSHAVEN. Fleet base; also base for torpedo craft, and seaplanes. Two large basins. Harbour for torpedo craft inside yard.

Docks (Graving): Nos. (1), (2) and (3), $625 \times 99\frac{1}{2} \times 36$ feet; No. (4), $584 \times 101 \times 35$ feet; No. (5), $584 \times 101 \times 35$ feet; No. (6), $584 \times 94 \times 35$ feet; No. (7), $822 \times 131 \times 34$ feet; No. (8), $822 \times 114\frac{3}{4} \times 34$ feet. Five building slips, (1) 600 feet, (2) 345 feet, (3) 300 feet, (4) about 600 feet. Men employed, about 11,500. Machinery: 38 of 9300 H.P. Admiralty Chart No. 3346. Rise of Spring Tide, $11\frac{1}{2}$ feet. Harbour has to be dredged continually on account of the sand which silts up very badly. Wangeroog (at mouth of Jade) is a minor Naval Station.

BREMERHAVEN. Port for Bremen, which is 50 miles inland of river mouth, and about 28 miles from Bremerhaven. At Bremen are the headquarters of the N. Deutscher Lloyd, and the big shipbuilding firm, Weser Act-Gesellschaft. Trade of the district (Bremerhaven, Vegesack, etc. included) was 2,750,000 tons of shipping cleared annually before the war. Kaiser Dry Dock No. 1, $741 \times 98 \times 35$ feet, can take ships up to 50,000 tons. Another (N.D.L. floating) $450 \times 58 \times 19\frac{1}{2}$ feet. At Bremerhaven, Seebeck Co. has one dock (No. 1) $550 \times 65 \times 21$ feet, and three smaller. At Geestemünde, the same firm has two docks, each $547 \times 80 \times 18$ feet. Also at Geestemünde, two smaller dry docks; and at Hammelwarden, one small dry dock. At Bremen, one floating dock, $490 \times 90 \times 23$ feet (12,000 tons), and another smaller (3000 tons). Geestemünde, Bremen, and Bremerhaven are minor Naval Stations. Naval Hospital, Barracks, &c., at Lehe, near Bremerhaven.

Admiralty Chart No. 3346. Rise of Spring Tide, $10\frac{3}{4}$ feet.

GERMAN HARBOURS:—NORTH SEA (*Continued.*)

(Divided into 2000 yard squares. Uniform scale. Soundings in fathoms.)

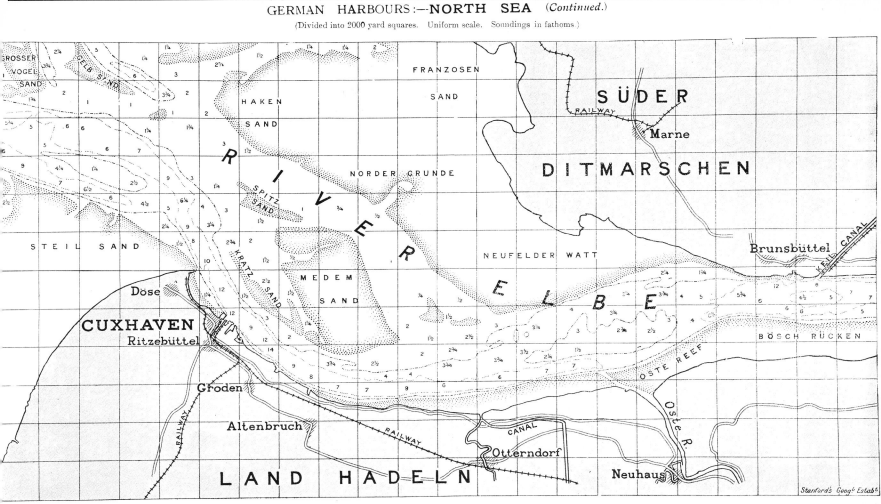

CUXHAVEN (and North Sea entrance to Kiel Canal).

CUXHAVEN. Port for Hamburg, which is 65 miles from the sea, and headquarters of the H.A.P.A.G. (Hamburg-American Line). Mine and Torpedo Station at Groden. Ammunition Stores; Naval Airship and Seaplane Base; Naval Hospital and Barracks; W/T. Station. Before the war, trade of Hamburg and Cuxhaven amounted to about 9,500,000 tons of shipping cleared per. annum. Very strongly fortified. A dredged channel for Destroyers is believed to exist north of Medem Sand. Brunsbüttel coaling basin 1700×680 feet area. Naval Airship Station at Fuhlsbüttel, near Hamburg. Admiralty Chart No. 3261. Rise of Spring Tide, 10¼ feet.

505

GERMAN HARBOURS:—NORTH SEA (*Continued.*)

(To Special Scale. Divided into 4000 yard squares. Soundings in fathoms.)

Map is to Special Scale: see Note inset.

EMDEN. New and large W/T. Station. One floating dock (Inner Harbour) 284½ × 59½ × 17¾ feet (3500 tons). 1 smaller (2500 tons). Lock between Inner Harbour and Ems River 853 × 131 × 43 feet. Inner and Outer Harbours 37 feet deep connected by dredged channel 40 feet deep. There is a small canal (Ems-Jade) between this port and Wilhelmshaven, which was only suitable for small vessels of shallow draught in 1914. The Borkum is fortified. Big Naval W/T. Station at Norddeich. Admiralty Chart No. 3761.

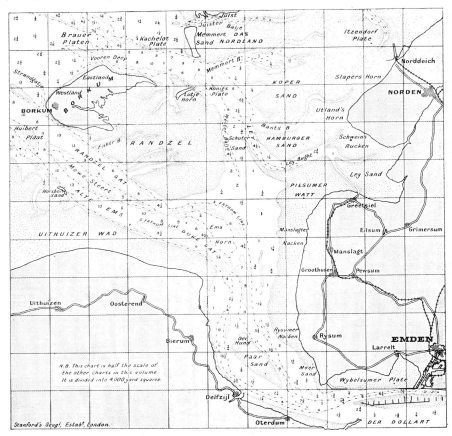

Note.—Channel along Wybelsumer Plate from Ems River into Port said to be dredged now to 5 fathoms. Channel out to Borkum may also be dredged.

KIEL CANAL.

Length : 61½ miles. Width at surface : 394 feet and 144 feet at bottom. New double locks : 1082 × 147 × 36 feet. Old locks (at Holtenau and Brunsbüttel) : 482 × 82 × 29½ feet. Sidings : 4 of 3600 × 540 feet, 11 other bays of 984 feet for turning. Speed of ships : 10 kts. for large, 15 kts. for small. Time of passage : 7 to 10 hours, according to size of ships ; but 16 battleships can, in emergency, pass in 6 hours.

Naval Airship Stations.

AHLHORN
FRIEDRICHSHAVEN
KONIGSBERG (Seerappen)
NIEDERGORSDORF

NORDHOLZ
STOLP (in Pommern)
WITTMUNDHAFEN

NORTH SEA Seaplane Bases.

BORKUM
HELIGOLAND
LIST

NORDENEY
WILHELMSHAVEN

BALTIC Seaplane Bases.

APENRADE
BUG (Rügen Island)
DANZIG
FLENSBURG
HOLTENAU
NEST

KIEL
PUTZIG
SEERAPPEN
SEDDIN
WIEK (Rügen Island)
WARNEMÜNDE

Note.

The following details of Principal Private Yards in North Sea and Baltic relate to conditions up to August, 1914.

NORTH SEA (Nordsee).

Principal Private Yards :

BLOHM & VOSS (HAMBURG). Ten *Slips* (four 600 feet long, five each about 500 feet long, and one slip 328 feet). Five *Docks* (floating). (1) 320 × 52 × 18. (2) 355 × 52 × 18. (3) 558 × 88 × 25. (4) 595 × 88 × 25. (5) 728 × 123 × 36 feet (46,000 tons). Possibly a sixth (40,000 tons) intended originally for Pola D.Y. (Austria-Hungary). Probably build submarines and destroyers now. *Employees,* 10,000. *Machinery.* 10,000 H.P. Bought Janssen & Schmilinsky Yard for extensions, 1917, with dock 400 × 50 × 16 feet.

A. G. WESER (BREMEN). Five *Slips* (one of 650 feet. one of 328 feet, one small). Three *Docks* (floating) of small size. Build submarines. *Employees,* 6000. *Machinery,* 4220 H.P.

BREMER-VULKAN (VEGESACK). Six *Slips* (one of 650 feet, two about 500 feet, three smaller). *Docks,* one floating. Probably build submarines and destroyers now. *Employees,* about 3100. *Machinery,* 2800 H.P.

VULCAN (HAMBURG). Two *Slips,* 650 feet or so. Four floating docks : No. 4, 605 × 85 × 28 feet (17,500 tons) ; No. 3, 610 × 106 × 28 feet (27,000 tons). Another dock, 723¾ × 108½ × 32¾ feet (32,000 tons) may exist. Two smaller floating docks, 433 × 70 × feet (6000 tons) and 510 × 82 × feet (11,000 tons). *Employees,* about 9000. H.P. 6500.

JOHANN C. TECKLENBORG (GEESTEMÜNDE). Six *Slips* (two of 600 feet, two about 500 feet, two smaller). 2600 men. H.P. 2600. Two dry docks.

REIHERSTIEG SCHIFFSWERFTE (HAMBURG). One *Slip* about 550 feet, one about 400, five small. *Docks :* one (floating) 511½ × 97 × 26 feet (20,000 tons), three smaller. *Employees,* about 2000. H.P. about 4000. Bought J. & N. Wichorst Yard, 1917, for extensions.

BALTIC (Ostsee).

(A)—Principal Private Yards.

HOWALDT (KIEL). Nine *Slips* (two over 700 feet, one about 500 feet, six smaller). *Docs :* one floating (11,000 tons). *Employees,* about 3500. *Machinery :*

KRUPP'S GERMANIA (KIEL). Nine *Slips* (five of 700 to 520 feet, the rest smaller). Submarines built here for which 10-12 slips were available in 1914. *Employees,* 6400. *Machinery,* 4000 H.P. *Docks :* None.

SCHICHAU (ELBING). Twenty-seven *Slips* (six over 650 feet long, the others all small). Two (six ?) *Docks* (floating) for torpedo craft. *Employees,* about 10,000. *Machinery,* 5000 H.P.

VULCAN (BREDOW-STETTIN). Seven *Slips* (two over 650 feet, two about 500 feet, three about 350 feet or so). Two *Docks* (floating). (1) 416 × 58 × 17 feet. (2) 300 × 37 × 14½ feet. *Employees,* 7000.

GERMAN HARBOURS—BALTIC.

(Uniform Scale. Divided into 2000 yard squares. Soundings in fathoms).

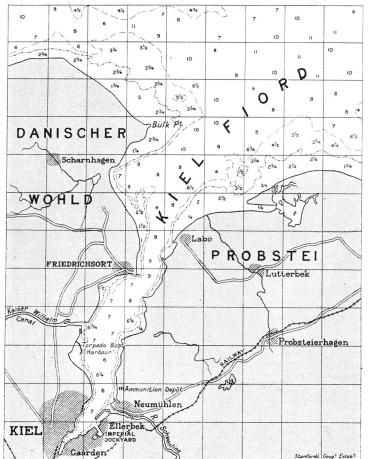

KIEL (and Baltic entrance to Kiel Canal). Fleet, torpedo craft, and seaplane bases and training stations. Two large basins. Docks : (1) 423 × 71 × 28. (2) 382 × 70 × 25½ (3) 362 × 64½ × 22½ (4) 344 × 67 × 16 (5) 570 × 94 × 30 (6) 570 × 94 × 30. Also one floating dock (40,000 tons), 660 × 96 × 32 feet, and five small floating. Another 36,000 ton floating, and 1 small private floating dock (Swentine). Two building slips. (1) 427 feet. (2) 427 feet. Men employed, *about* 10,500. Machinery : 109 of 23,240 H.P. Admiralty Chart, No. 33.

GERMAN DOCKYARDS.—BALTIC—(Continued).

(Divided into 2000 yard squares. Uniform Scale. Soundings in fathoms).

Other smaller Naval Stations in 1914 in Baltic, were:—

FRIEDRICHSORT (see Kiel Map). Torpedo manufactory and range; munitions and mine depots; naval hospital and barracks.
DIETRICHSDORF: Ammunition depot.
WARNEMÜNDE: Seaplane base 1914—19.
NEUMÜNSTER 1 H: Big naval W/T. station.
SONDERBURG: Naval hospital and barracks.

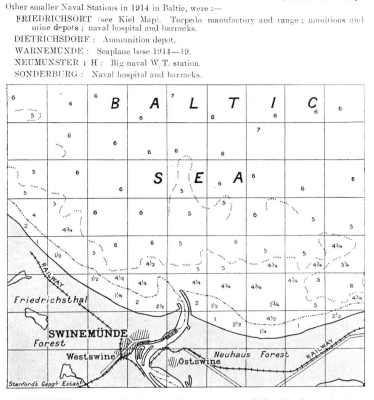

SWINEMÜNDE. Port for Stettin, a smaller naval station, which is 36 miles up the river. Trade of Stettin and Swinemünde is about 1,300,000 tons of shipping cleared annually, but is much greater at present. No docks here suitable for large warships.

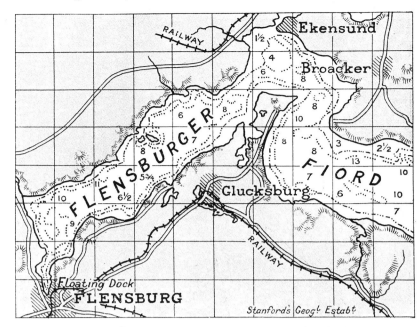

FLENSBURG - MURWICK. Seaplane Station. Smaller Naval Station in 1914, with Gunnery and Torpedo Schools, Naval Hospital and Barracks. Floating Pontoon Dock, 280×49×19 feet. 2,800 tons.

Note.

By plebiscite of the population of Slesvig, Flensburg may become a Danish Port in the near future.

ROYAL DOCKYARDS—HOME WATERS.

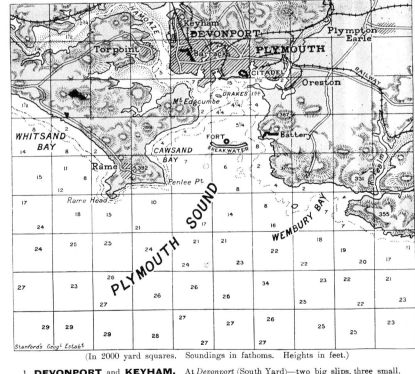

(In 2000 yard squares. Soundings in fathoms. Heights in feet.)

ROSYTH		Portland 55	Constantinople...702	Singapore... ...1600	Madagascar ...1800
	to knots.	Wilhelmshaven 620	Port Said... ...920	Sydney(N.S.W.) 5450	Port Elizabeth 428
Aberdeen 95			Sevastopol ...1000		Portsmouth ...5960
Dover 473		DEVONPORT	Spezia 580	SINGAPORE	St. Helena ...1710
Helder 360		to knots.	Suda Bay ... 575	to knots.	Teneriffe 4470
Hull 260		Berehaven ...375	Suez 1010	Bangkok 820	
Kronstadt ...1345		Brest 140	Toulon 612	Batavia 500	ESQUIMAULT
Newcastle ...130		Cape of Good		Devonport...8020	to knots.
Portsmouth ...570		Hope 5890	ADEN	Hong Kong ...1430	Honolulu 2410
Sheerness... ...458		Cherbourg ...110	to knots.	Manila 1320	San Francisco... 750
Wilhelmshaven 445		Gibraltar 1050	Batavia 3950	Saigon 648	Seattle 76
		Lorient 233	Beira 2824		Yokosuka... ...4300
SHEERNESS		New York ...2905	Bombay 1652	HONG-KONG	
	to knots.	Portland 100	Cape Town ... 4450	to knots.	SYDNEY (N.S.W.)
Dover 45		Queenstown ...292	Colombo 2100	Devonport ...9450	to knots.
Dunkirk 70		Rochefort 370	Delagoa Bay ...3340	Kiao-chau ...1270	Adelaide 1076
Helder 190		Toulon 1764	Devonport... ...4350	Manila 650	Auckland... ...1280
Hull 200			Durban 3650	Nagasaki ...1067	Batavia 4476
Kronstadt ...1200		GIBRALTAR	Karachi 1470	Port Arthur ...1415	Brisbane 510
Newcastle ...328		to knots.	Mauritius... ...2600	Saigon 930	Cape of Good
Portsmouth ...150		Ajaccio 1000	Suez 1310	Shanghai ... 870	Hope 6157
Wilhelmshaven 270		Algiers 420	Tamatave ...2290	Ta-kau(Formosa) 340	Colombo 5450
		Berehaven ...1170	Zanzibar 1770	Vladivostock ...1927	Devonport
PORTSMOUTH		Bizerta 875		Wei-hai-wei ...1470	(via Cape)...12,047
	to knots.	Brest 953	COLOMBO	Yokosuka... ...1620	Hobart 630
Barbados ...3600		Devonport ...1050	to knots.		Melbourne ... 570
Berehaven ...375		Malta 980	Bombay 900	CAPE OF GOOD	Singapore ...4980
Brest 226		Oran 225	Calcutta ...1240	HOPE	Wellington,
Cherbourg ...72		Toulon 713	Devonport... ...6450	to knots.	(N.Z.) 1234
Devonport ...155			Fremantle	Ascension... ...2395	
Gibraltar 1200		MALTA	(W.A.) 3105	Durban 812	
Lorient 331		to knots.	Karachi 1400	Falkland Isles 4800	
New York... ...3080		Aden 2320	Penang 1280	Fremantle	
Pernambuco ...3900		Ajaccio 450	Rangoon 1207	(W.A.) 4850	
		Bizerta 240		Hobart 5527	

1. DEVONPORT and KEYHAM. At *Devonport* (South Yard)—two big slips, three small.
Dry docks:—No. 3, could just take *Duncan* class, size 430 × 93 × 34¾ feet, and three others, of which one (No. 2 Dock) can take a second class cruiser; other two suitable for small craft only. At *Keyham* (North Yard)—No slips. New basin, 35½ acres, depth, 32½ft. Tidal basin, 10 acres, depth, 32ft.

Dry Docks in New Extension:—
Entrance lock, 730* × 95 × 44 feet.
No. 9 (double) 745 × 95 × 32 „
Keyham (North Yard) No. 10 (double) 741 × 95 × 44 feet.
„ 8 659 × 95 × 32 „
* Can be lengthened 86 feet.

In the old part of the yard there are three docks, of which one (No. 7) can take a second class cruiser; the others small craft only. Total employees for the two yards, 14,000—15,000.

Admiralty Chart No. 1267. Rise of Spring Tide 15½ feet (Dockyard).

(ROYAL) BRITISH NAVY.

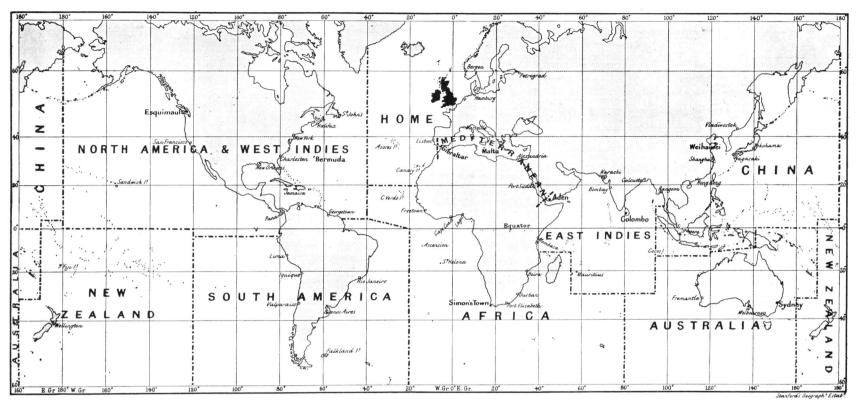

LIMITS OF BRITISH NAVAL STATIONS, 1919.

From Chart furnished by courtesy of the Hydrographic Department, Admiralty.

BRITISH NAVY.

Diesel Engine Builders.

(From " The Motorship," New York.)

	Type of Engine.
Cammell Laird & Co., Birkenhead	Fullagar (2-cycle)
North British Diesel Engine Co., Glasgow ..	————?———— (4-cycle)
Clyde Shipbuilding & Engineering Co., Govan, Glasgow ..	Carels (2-cycle)
Harland & Wolff Diesel Dept., Glasgow ..	Burmeister & Wain (4-cycle)
Wm. Doxford & Sons (Northumberland Shipbuilding Co., Ltd.), Sunderland	Junkers (2-cycle, Solid-injection)
Wallsend Slipway, Wallsend-on-Tyne	Werkspoor (4-cycle)
North Eastern Marine Engineering Co., Wallsend-on-Tyne	Carels (2-cycle)
John I. Thornycroft & Co., London	Sulzer (2-cycle)
Wm. Denny Bros. & Co., Ltd., Dumbarton	White M.A.N. (2-cycle)
J. Samuel White & Co., East Cowes	Vickers (4-cycle)
Vickers Limited, Barrow-in-Furness ..	Mirrlees (4-cycle)
Mirrlees, Bickerton & Day, Stockton-on-Tees ..	Willans (4-cycle)
Willans, Robinson & Co., Rugby ..	M.A.N. (2-cycle)
Yarrows Limited, Scotstoun	M.A.N. (2-cycle)
Fairfield Shipbuilding & Engineering Co., Port Glasgow ..	Ansaldo-Fiat (2-cycle)
Scotts Shipbuilding & Engineering Co., Greenock ..	————?————
Alex. Stephen & Sons, Linthouse (Glasgow) ..	
Sir W. G. Armstrong, Whitworth & Co., Newcastle-on-Tyne	Armstrong-Whitworth (2 & 4-cycle)
Richardsons Westgarth, Middlesborough	Carels (2-cycle)
Wm. Beardmore & Co., Ltd., Dalmuir ..	Beardmore & Tosi (4-cycle)
Swan, Hunter & Wigham Richardsons Ltd., Newcastle-on-Tyne	Neptune & Polar (2-cycle)
Palmers Shipbuilding & Engineering Co., Jarrow-on-Tyne	————?————
Barclay, Curle & Co., Glasgow	Burmeister & Wain (4-cycle)
Norris, Henty & Gardners Ltd., Patricroft ..	Gardner (4-cycle)
Union Ship Engineering Co. Ltd., Montrose	————?———— (4-cycle)
Ruston & Hornsby, Lincoln	Nelseco† (4-cycle)

* Also building engines in association with Messrs. Petters, Yeovil.

† Several other British engineering companies also built the Nelseco (American) marine Diesel engine during the war.

Uniforms.

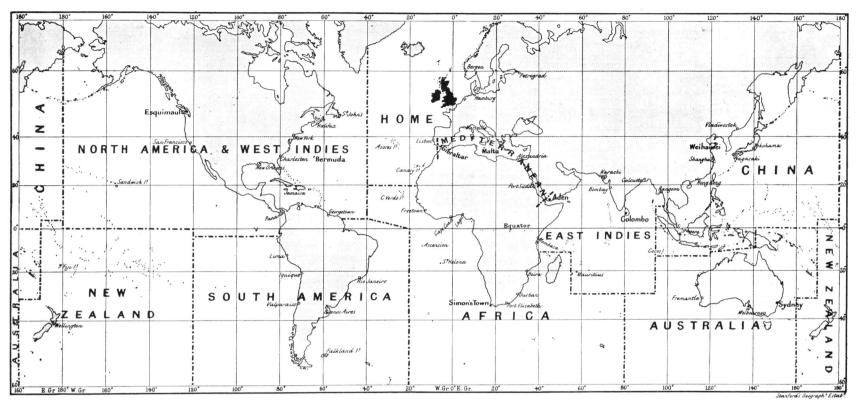

Admiral — Vice-Admiral — Rear-Admiral — Commodore — Captain — Commander — Lieutenant-Commander — Lieutenant (under 8 years) — Sub-Lieut.

Admiral of the fleet one stripe more than a full Admiral.

In relative ranks, Engineers have the same *with the curl*, and with purple between the stripes (1915 change).
" " Surgeons " " " " red " " (1918 change).
" " Paymasters " " " " white " " (" ").
" " Naval Instructors " " " " blue " " (" ").

Note.—On the right sleeve only, inverted chevrons are worn for every year of War Service since August 5th, 1914. The first and lowest chevron in silver is for War Service up to Dec. 31st, 1914. The upper gold chevrons are for each year's service from Jan. 1st, 1915. Also worn by the Royal Marines, R.A.N., R.C.N., R.N.R., R.F.R., R.N.V.R., R.N. Sick Berth Reserve and officers of the Mercantile Marine serving in H.M. Ships and Auxiliaries.

Personnel and Navy Estimates. 1919-20.

Provisional Estimates have only been presented to Parliament, for the sum of £149,200,000, but it is noted that revised and detailed Estimates will be presented at a later date in the Financial Year. Personnel is estimated at 280,000 officers, seamen, boys, coastguards and Royal Marines, but this total is being rapidly decreased by demobilisation and discharges. It was 180,000 in August, 1919. and will be about 147,000 in Jan., 1920.

Admiralty (October, 1919).

First Lord	..	The Right Hon. Walter Long, M.P.
First Lord and Chief of Staff	..	Admiral Earl Beatty, G.C.B., D.S.O., &c.
Deputy First Sea Lord	..	..
Deputy Chief of Staff	..	..
Assistant Chief of Staff	..	..
Second Sea Lord ..	..	..
Third Sea Lord and Controller	..	..
Fourth Sea Lord ..	..	..
Civil Lord	..	..
Chief Constructor ..	..	Sir Eustace H. Tennyson D'Eyncourt, K.C.B.

(Maintenance Operations.)

BRITISH NAVAL ORDNANCE, HEAVY, B.L. (Capt. R. V. WALLING, R.G.A., retired).

NOTE.—All details are unofficial, but believed to be approximately correct. Particulars given, for reference purposes, of some older marks of guns, now dismounted from H.M. Ships.

Designation, Calibre, ins.	Mark.	Length. (cals.)	Weight of piece without B.M. (tons cwts. qrs.)	Weight of Projectile (lbs.)	M.V. (f.s.)	M.E. (f.t.)	Weight of Charge (lbs.)	Max. R.P.M.	REMARKS.
18	I	35 ?	150 0 0 ?	3,600 ?	?	?	?	?	Monitors and "Furious" originally mounted these pieces, but they have been removed.
15	"B"	45	96 0 0	1950	2500	84,500	450	1.2	Particulars doubtful. Mk. I also reported to be 42 cals. long.
15	I	45	96 0 0	1920	2655	84,070	428	1.2	
13.5	V	45	74 18 1	1250	2700	63,190	296	1.5	With tapered inner "A" tube, without forward step, weighs 1 cwt. more. Obsolete Marks : I ; II ; III ; IIIa, b, c, d, e, and f ; IV.
12	XII	50	65 13 1	850	3010	53,400	307	2	Dreadnoughts and Battle Cruisers.
12	XI } XI*	50	65 13 1	850	3010	53,046	307	2	
12	X	45	56 16 1	850	2800	47,800	258	2	Mk. IX guns in "King Edward" class only :—Wt. of Charge, 254 lbs. Marks : VI, IV, V, Vw, VIII. VIIIe, VIIIv, IX, IXe, IXv, IXw, X, X*, XI, XI* and XII have been introduced into the Naval Service.
12	X*	45	56 12 1	850	2650	39,200	246	2	
12	IX	40	50 0 0	850	2650	39,200	246	2	
10	VII	45	30 4 2	500	2850	26,945	$146\frac{3}{4}$	3	Only mounted in "Triumph," now sunk.
10	VI } VI*	45	36 10 0	500	2800	27,181	$146\frac{3}{4}$	3	Only mounted in "Swiftsure." Mk. VI*, land guns. Wt. given is that without "Ring, connecting hydraulic buffer." A Mk. V pattern was sealed, but the gun was never made.
9.2	XI	50	28 0 0	380	3000	23,700	$128\frac{1}{2}$	4	
9.2	XI*	50	27 15 2	380	3000	22,930	$128\frac{1}{2}$	4	Only two Mk. Xv guns in the Service. There is one Mk. X/IX gun for Naval Service.
9.2	Xv	46	27 19 0	380	2800	20,685	120	4	"Terrible" only ; two guns from "Powerful" mounted in R.G.A. Battery at Scapa Flow.
9.2	X	46	27 19 0	380	2800	20,685	120	4	Twenty different Marks have been made and fourteen introduced in Naval Service.
9.2	VIII	40	24 6 3	380	2347	14,520	66	4	
14	I	45	85 0 0	1400	2700	70,770	324	2	Elswick Ordnance Co., "Armstrong" design. H.M.S. "Canada" only.
14	?	45	70 6 0	1400	2600	65,700	?	?	Bethlehem guns, mounted in monitors only ("Abercrombie" class).

MEDIUM, B.L.

Designation, Calibre, ins.	Mark.	Length. (cals.)	Weight of piece without B.M. (tons cwts. qrs.)	Weight of Projectile (lbs.)	M.V. (f.s.)	M.E. (f.t.)	Weight of Charge (lbs.)	Max. R.P.M.	REMARKS.
7.5	III } III*	50	15 9 3	200	3000	12,481	$54\frac{1}{4}$	5	Monitors, removed from "Swiftsure," Mks. IV and IV* were for "Triumph," sunk. New Mark in "Hawkins" and "Raleigh," of which no details available.
7.5	II** } V	50	14 16 2	200	2800	12,500	61	5	
7.5	I	45	13 9 2	200	2600	9340	61	5	"Devonshire" class only. Other Marks in Naval Service : I* and I** of 45 cal./L ; II and II* of 50 cal./L.
6	XVIII	50	?	100	?	?	?	7	New ships.
6	XIV	50	?	100	3100	6665	?	7	"Cleopatra" class.
6	XI* } XI	50	8 8 2	100	3000	6240	$32\frac{1}{12}$	7	Mk. VIII left hand guns for "T" mounting in "County" class.
6	VIII } VII	45	7 7 2	100	2750	5250	23	7	Many new Marks of 6 in. introduced during the War, including a short Mk. XIX for L.S. (Travelling Carriage.)
5.5	I	50	6 10 0	115	2870	6000 (?)	?	8	Woolwich Arsenal. Details doubtful. Mounted in "Furious" and "Hood," "Birkenhead" and "Chester." 5.5 guns and mountings by Coventry Ordnance Co.
4.7	I	50	3 14 0	45	3000	2800	14	12	Woolwich Arsenal. Modified 4.7 inch Q.F. V (L.S.). New T.B.D.'s.

Also :—
Q.F. 6 in., many marks } quite obsolete, but were mounted in D.A.M.S. and S.D.V.
Q.F.C. 6 in., ,, ,, } during the War.
Q.F. 4.7 in. Mk. V, Land Service only.

Mk. IV, three-motion B.M., Mk. IV "B," same, converted to single-motion.
Mk. III, ,, Mk. III "B" ,, ,,
Mk. II, ,, Mk. II "B" ,, ,,
Mk. I, ,, Mk. I "B" ,, ,,

BRITISH NAVAL ORDNANCE, TORPEDOES, MINES, &c.

Torpedoes.
No official details available. Various Marks of 21 inch, 18 inch and 14 inch torpedoes said to be in service ; the first two with heaters, the third without. Also a specially light 14 inch mark for use by "Cuckoo" type Torpedo-dropping Seaplanes and C.M.B.

Mines.
No official figures available. Among the various Marks of mines produced during the War, the following are said to exist : (a) Spherical types with swinging-bar contact, either above or below mine ; (b) "British Elia" type—may be the same as (a) just described ; (c) Pear-shaped and spherical types with horn contacts ; reported to be very like German mines ; (d) Special types for laying by Destroyers, Submarines and C.M.B.

Aircraft Bombs.
There are only vague and unofficial references to these types : Experimental 3300 lb. type ; 1650 lb. type (with bursting charge of 1100 lbs. T.N.T.), 530 lb., 230 lb. (with A.P. nose ?), 112 lb. and 100 lb. Fuzes said to be impact, delay action and special types for use against submarines.

Depth Charges.
Only mark reported is 300 lb. type.

Searchlights.
36 inch, 24 inch, 20 inch (all controlled in latest ships). About 8—36 inch and 2—24 inch (Signalling) in Dreadnoughts and Battle Cruisers ; 4—36 inch in Light Cruisers ; 1—24 inch or 20 inch in T.B.D. Twin 24 inch mountings were used in *Iron Duke, King George, Orion, Colossus, Neptune, Lion* and *New Zealand* Classes, but these are said to have been replaced by single 36 inch controlled S.L.

Paravanes (PVs.)
No official details available. Reported that there are about twenty marks, roughly divided into "M," "B" and "C" patterns. "M" type said to be "otter gear" of simple design for use by mercantile craft up to 18 kts. speed, keeping depth by ordinary form of hydrostatic valve. "B" type said to be for Battleships and older Cruisers up to 22 kts. speed ; "C" pattern for Light Cruisers, &c., up to 28 kts. speed. Depth kept in these by hydrostatic valves, plus "mercury oscillators," the hydrostatic valve by itself being too sluggish to prevent the PVs. "porpoising." Length about 12 feet, breadth about 7 feet across spread of 'planes. Destroyers reported to use special types of PVs., viz., H.S.S.S. and H.S.M.S. PVs. towed in large ships by chains from skeg (or PV. plate) attached to forefoot, under stem ; also by sliding bar shoes at stem. Destroyers and vessels of light draught can tow their PVs. from stern.

Naval Ordnance.—*continued.*

Also (for Anti-Submarine purposes) :—
11 inch howitzer mounted in some ships of "Devonshire" and "County Classes."
200 lb. stick bomb howitzer in some Special Service Vessels.
Thornycroft Depth Charge Thrower in Destroyers, P-boats, some Sloops and Special Service Vessels.

Also :—
Q.F., 12 pr. 12 cwt. Mk. I.
,, 12 pr. Mk. II (war model) : mostly for merchantmen.
,, 12 pr. 18 cwt. Mk. I. for "G," "H" and "I" classes of T.B.D.
,, 12 pr. 8 cwt. Mk. I (boat gun).
,, 14 pr. Mk. I (H.M.S. "Swiftsure"—now removed).
,, 6 pr.
,, 3 pr. } have been used as A.A. guns.
,, 3 pr. (semi-automatic, Vickers design) } Saluting guns in big ships.
,, 2¼ pdr. (automatic) modified "pom-pom" for A.A. work.
,, 77 mm.—captured German field guns, adapted for use in some submarines.

Machine Guns :—
.303 inch Vickers.
.303 inch Maxim.
.303 inch Lewis.

Rifles :—
.303 inch Lee-Enfield (Long).

Pistols :—
.45 inch Webley automatic (H.V.).

BRITISH WARSHIPS: RECOGNITION SILHOUETTES.
By E. L. KING.

ONE FUNNEL.

O & ONE FUNNEL.

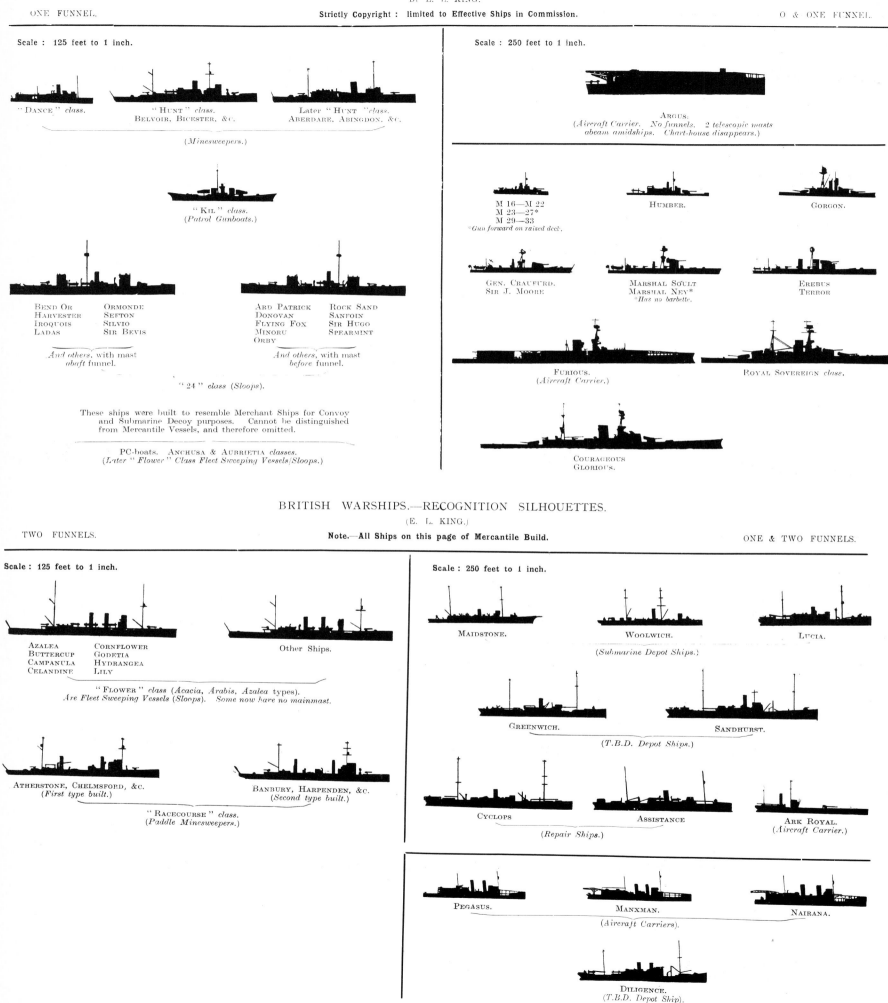

Scale : 125 feet to 1 inch.

"DANCE" *class.*

"HUNT" *class.*
BELVOIR, BICESTER, &c.

Later "HUNT" *class.*
ABERDARE, ABINGDON, &c.

(Minesweepers.)

"KIL" *class.*
(Patrol Gunboats.)

BEND OR	ORMONDE
HARVESTER	SEFTON
IROQUOIS	SILVIO
LADAS	SIR BEVIS

And others, with mast
abaft funnel.

ARD PATRICK	ROCK SAND
DONOVAN	SANFOIN
FLYING FOX	SIR HUGO
MINORU	SPEARMINT
ORBY	

And others, with mast
before funnel.

"24" *class (Sloops).*

These ships were built to resemble Merchant Ships for Convoy
and Submarine Decoy purposes. Cannot be distinguished
from Mercantile Vessels, and therefore omitted.

PC-boats. ANCHUSA & AUBRIETIA *classes.*
(Later "Flower" Class Fleet Sweeping Vessels/Sloops.)

Scale : 250 feet to 1 inch.

ARGUS.
*(Aircraft Carrier. No funnels. 2 telescopic masts
abeam amidships. Chart-house disappears.)*

M 16—M 22
M 23—27*
M 29—33
*Gun forward on raised deck.

HUMBER.

GORGON.

GEN. CRAUFURD.
SIR J. MOORE.

MARSHAL SOULT
MARSHAL NEY*
*Has no barbette.

EREBUS
TERROR

FURIOUS.
(Aircraft Carrier.)

ROYAL SOVEREIGN *class.*

COURAGEOUS
GLORIOUS.

BRITISH WARSHIPS.—RECOGNITION SILHOUETTES.
(E. L. KING.)

TWO FUNNELS.

Note.—All Ships on this page of Mercantile Build.

ONE & TWO FUNNELS.

Scale : 125 feet to 1 inch.

AZALEA	CORNFLOWER
BUTTERCUP	GODETIA
CAMPANULA	HYDRANGEA
CELANDINE	LILY

Other Ships.

"FLOWER" *class (Acacia, Arabis, Azalea types).*
Are Fleet Sweeping Vessels (Sloops). Some now have no mainmast.

ATHERSTONE, CHELMSFORD, &c.
(First type built.)

BANBURY, HARPENDEN, &c.
(Second type built.)

"RACECOURSE" *class.*
(Paddle Minesweepers.)

Scale : 250 feet to 1 inch.

MAIDSTONE.

WOOLWICH.

LUCIA.

(Submarine Depot Ships.)

GREENWICH.

SANDHURST.

(T.B.D. Depot Ships.)

CYCLOPS

ASSISTANCE

ARK ROYAL.
(Aircraft Carrier.)

(Repair Ships.)

PEGASUS.

MANXMAN.

NAIRANA.

(Aircraft Carriers).

DILIGENCE.
(T.B.D. Depot Ship).

BRITISH WARSHIPS.—RECOGNITION SILHOUETTES.
(E. L. KING).

TWO FUNNELS.   TWO FUNNELS.

Scale of all : 250 feet to 1 inch.

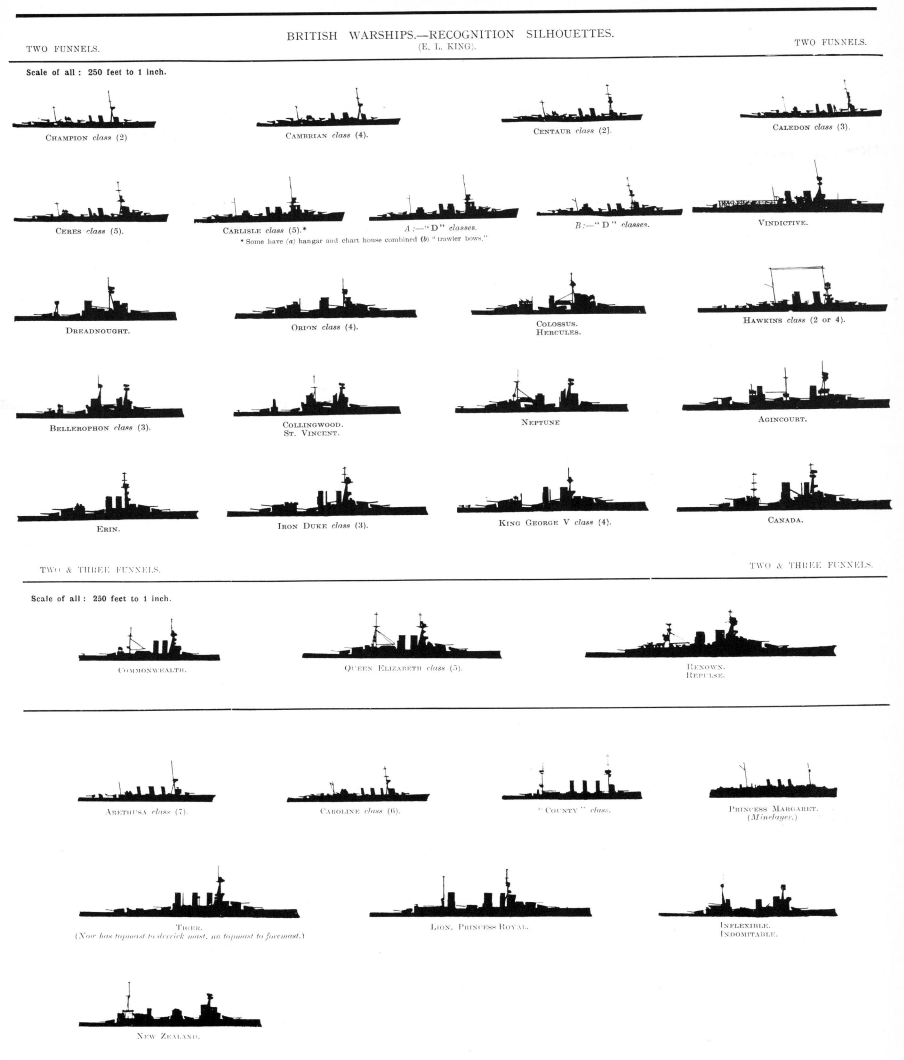

CHAMPION *class* (2).

CAMBRIAN *class* (4).

CENTAUR *class* (2).

CALEDON *class* (3).

CERES *class* (5).

CARLISLE *class* (5).*

A:—"D" *classes.*

B:—"D" *classes.*

VINDICTIVE.

* Some have (*a*) hangar and chart house combined (*b*) "trawler bows."

DREADNOUGHT.

ORION *class* (4).

COLOSSUS.
HERCULES.

HAWKINS *class* (2 or 4).

BELLEROPHON *class* (3).

COLLINGWOOD.
ST. VINCENT.

NEPTUNE

AGINCOURT.

ERIN.

IRON DUKE *class* (3).

KING GEORGE V *class* (4).

CANADA.

TWO & THREE FUNNELS.   TWO & THREE FUNNELS.

Scale of all : 250 feet to 1 inch.

COMMONWEALTH.

QUEEN ELIZABETH *class* (5).

RENOWN.
REPULSE.

ARETHUSA *class* (7).

CAROLINE *class* (6).

"COUNTY" *class.*

PRINCESS MARGARET.
(*Minelayer.*)

TIGER.
(*Now has topmast to derrick mast, no topmast to foremast.*)

LION. PRINCESS ROYAL.

INFLEXIBLE.
INDOMITABLE.

NEW ZEALAND.

BRITISH WARSHIPS.—RECOGNITION SILHOUETTES.

(E. L. KING).

FOUR FUNNELS.   FOUR FUNNELS.

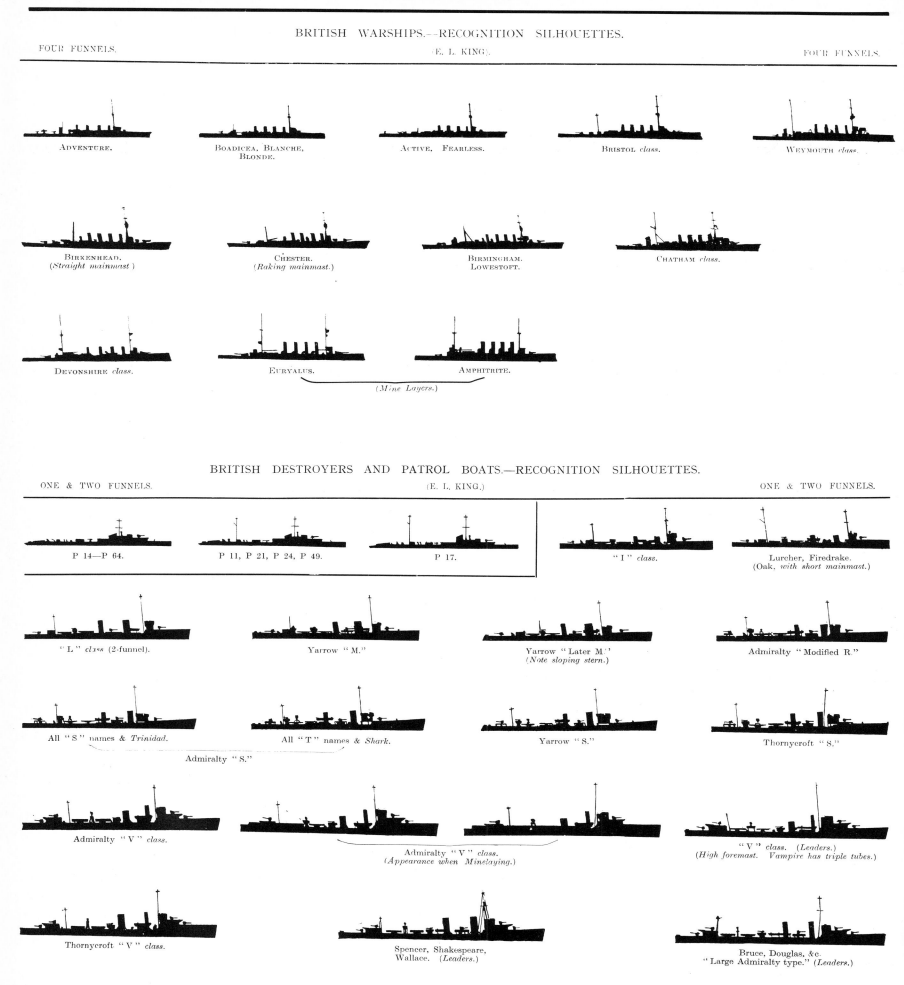

ADVENTURE.

BOADICEA, BLANCHE,
BLONDE.

ACTIVE, FEARLESS.

BRISTOL *class.*

WEYMOUTH *class.*

BIRKENHEAD.
(Straight mainmast.)

CHESTER.
(Raking mainmast.)

BIRMINGHAM.
LOWESTOFT.

CHATHAM *class.*

DEVONSHIRE *class.*

EURYALUS.

AMPHITRITE.

(Mine Layers.)

BRITISH DESTROYERS AND PATROL BOATS.—RECOGNITION SILHOUETTES.

(E. L. KING.)

ONE & TWO FUNNELS.   ONE & TWO FUNNELS.

P 14—P 64.

P 11, P 21, P 24, P 49.

P 17.

"I" *class.*

Lurcher, Firedrake.
(Oak, *with short mainmast.*)

"L" *class* (2-funnel).

Yarrow "M."

Yarrow "Later M."
(Note sloping stern.)

Admiralty "Modified R."

All "S" names & *Trinidad.*

All "T" names & *Shark.*

Yarrow "S."

Thornycroft "S."

Admiralty "S."

Admiralty "V" *class.*

Admiralty "V" *class.*
(Appearance when Minelaying.)

"V" *class.* (Leaders.)
(High foremast. Vampire has triple tubes.)

Thornycroft "V" *class.*

Spencer, Shakespeare,
Wallace. *(Leaders.)*

Bruce, Douglas, &c.
"Large Admiralty type." *(Leaders.)*

BRITISH DESTROYERS.—RECOGNITION SILHOUETTES.

(E. L. KING.)

THREE & FOUR FUNNELS.   THREE & FOUR FUNNELS.

Scale of all : 125 feet to 1 inch.

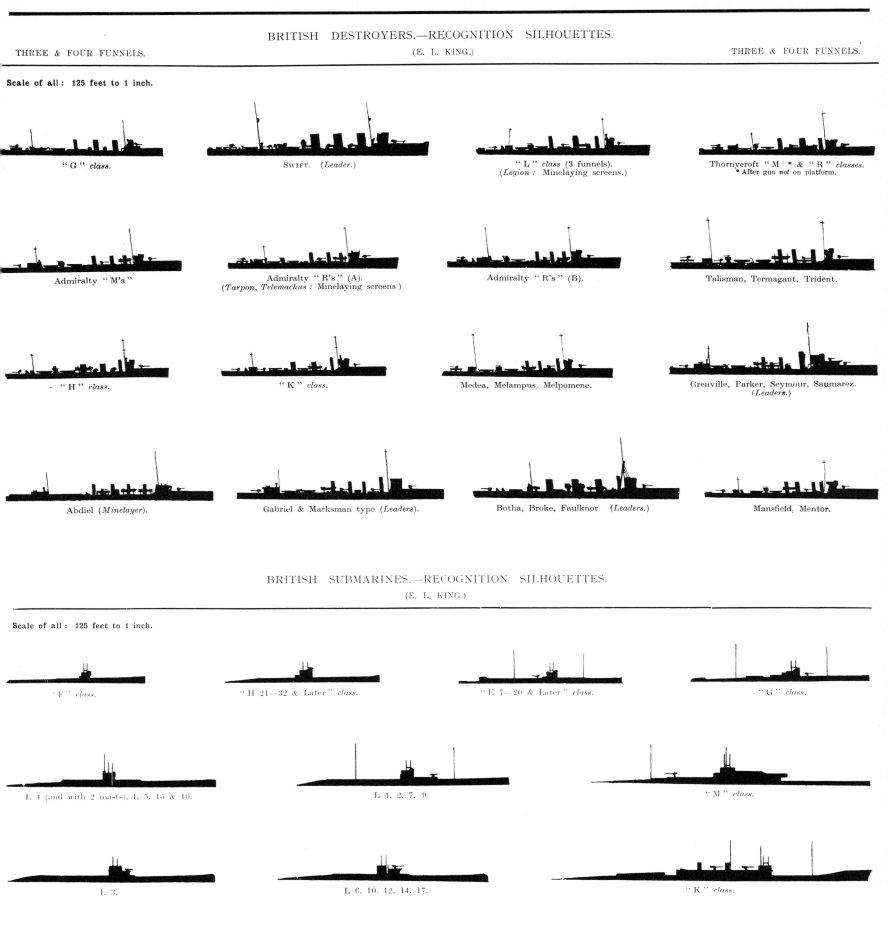

"G" class.

SWIFT. (Leader.)

"L" class (3 funnels).
(Legion : Minelaying screens.)

Thornycroft "M"* & "R" classes.
* After gun not on platform.

Admiralty "M's"

Admiralty "R's" (A).
(Tarpon, Telemachus : Minelaying screens)

Admiralty "R's" (B).

Talisman, Termagant, Trident.

"H" class.

"K" class.

Medea, Melampus, Melpomene.

Grenville, Parker, Seymour, Saumarez.
(Leaders.)

Abdiel (Minelayer).

Gabriel & Marksman type (Leaders).

Botha, Broke, Faulknor. (Leaders.)

Mansfield, Mentor.

BRITISH SUBMARINES.—RECOGNITION SILHOUETTES.

(E. L. KING.)

Scale of all : 125 feet to 1 inch.

"F" class.

"H 21—32 & Later" class.

"E 7—20 & Later" class.

"G" class.

L 4 (and with 2 masts), L 5, 15 & 16.

L 1, 2, 7, 9.

"M" class.

L 3.

L 6, 10, 12, 14, 17.

"K" class.

"R" class.

BRITISH NAVY.

ADDENDA AND CORRECTIONS :—1.

NAVAL ORDNANCE : MEDIUM B.L. Following are correct details of 5.5 inch. Length, 59 cals. Weight of gun, 6 tons 4 cwt. Weight of projectile, 82 lbs. M. V., 2950 ft.-secs. M. E., 4520 ft.-tons. Weight of charge, 23½ lbs. Rounds per minute : 12. *Remarks.*— Mounted in *Hood*. Range, at 30° elevation : 12,000 yards.

The Russian (Black Sea) Dreadnought, **VOLYA** was temporarily taken over by the British Navy during 1919 ; reported to have joined Gen. Denikin's Naval Forces in the Black Sea and to have been re-named **GENERAL ALEXEIEFF.**

INDOMITABLE to be sold.

CAPETOWN to be towed to Pembroke D.Y. for completion.

Unofficially reported that *EFFINGHAM* will be built as an Aircraft carrier.

CALLIOPE (and other Light Cruisers) no longer have searchlight and control tower amidships.

FOX for disposal.

Monitors.

Marshal Soult.

Monitors—*continued.*

Roberts. *Official R.A.F. Photo.*

Note.—*Roberts* is not included in the Post-War Fleet Organization. The above photograph has, however, been selected as an illustration, because it gives, by far, the best impression of the box-like hull and huge beam of the big Monitors. The projection of the " bulges " is also very clear in the above view. The formation and throwing-off of the coarse bow-wave are also worth noting.

BRITISH NAVY.

ADDENDA & CORRECTIONS :—2.

Monitors—*Continued.*

HUMBER, M 33 for sale. **M 31** to be converted for Minelaying.

M 19 (of M 19—27 class). **M 23** for sale.

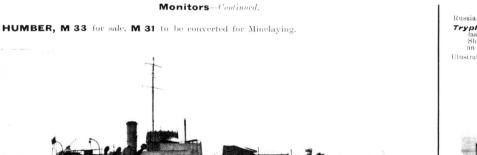

M 16 (of M 16—18 class).

Destroyers.

Russian (Black Sea) Destroyer **Derski** has been temporarily taken over by British Navy.
Tryphon (Yarrow " S " Type) did not go aground on Danish Coast, as stated. She went aground at Tenedos about last June and lay there on her beam-ends for three weeks. She was salved and brought to Pera for temporary repairs. She was then towed to Malta but nearly sank on passage. She is said to be too badly damaged for any further use, but an H.M.S. *Triton*—perhaps *Tryphon*—was recently reported as repairing by Yarrows.
Illustration of **Taurus** (Thornycroft " R ") is really **Patriot** (Thornycroft " M ").

Trident. *Photo. Cribb, Southsea.*

Nizam to be sold.

D.C.B. (*Depth Charge Boats*).

These are a modified type of C.M.B. without torpedoes in troughs but carrying Thornycroft Depth Charge Throwers or U. S. type Y-guns and special load of Depth Charges.
About 100 M.L. (Motor Launches) have been sold.

Submarines.

Delete: **F** Class Submarines and **E 54**; all are for sale. *Delete*: **L 55,** lost 1919.

Aircraft Carriers.

VINDICTIVE reported very badly damaged by grounding in the Baltic. **NAIRANA** re-conditioned for mercantile service. **EAGLE** to be towed to Portsmouth D.Y. for completion.

Minesweepers.

Delete: **KINROSS** (of later " Hunt " Class), lost in .Egean, 1919. **FANDANGO** (not listed) of " Dance " Class, armed with 1—6 pdr. A.A. gun, lost 1919.

Salvage Vessel.

MELITA for sale.

1913-14 BRITISH DREADNOUGHTS.

(Royal Sovereign Class.)

SOVEREIGN (29th April, 1915), **ROYAL OAK** (17th Nov., 1914), **RESOLUTION** (14th Jan., 1916), **RAMILLIES** (12th Sept., 1916), **REVENGE** (29th May, 1915).

Normal displacement, 25,750 tons (about 31,250-33,500 tons *full load*). Complement, 937-997.. Length (*over all*), 624¼ feet. Beam, 88½ feet.* *Mean* draught, 27 feet. Length (*p.p.*), 580 feet.

*For *R.S.* and *R.O.* With bulge protection, *Revenge* and *Resolution* 101′ 5″, *Ramillies* 102½ feet.

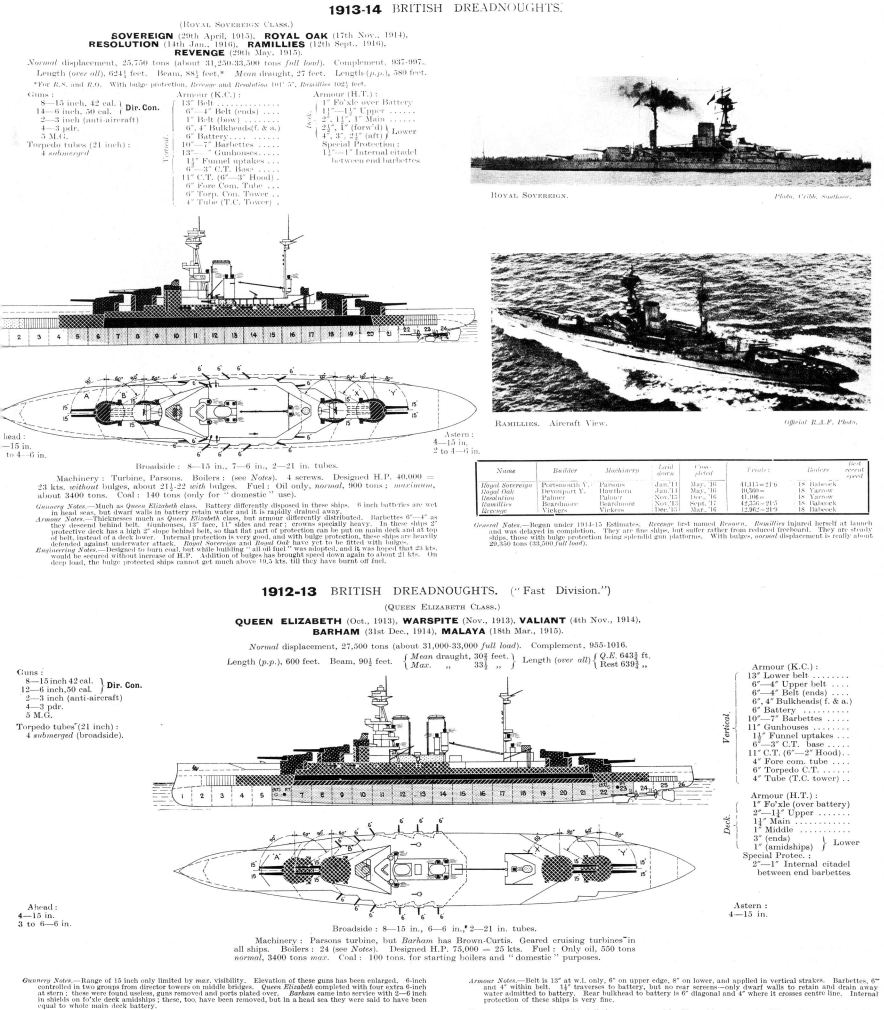

Guns:
- 8—15 inch, 42 cal. } **Dir. Con.**
- 14—6 inch, 50 cal. }
- 2—3 inch (anti-aircraft)
- 4—3 pdr.
- 5 M.G.

Torpedo tubes (21 inch):
- 4 *submerged*

Armour (K.C.):

Vertical.
- 13″ Belt ....
- 6″—4″ Belt (ends) ....
- 1″ Belt (bow) ....
- 6″, 4″ Bulkheads(f. & a.)
- 6″ Battery.... ......
- 10″—7″ Barbettes .....
- 13″— ″ Gunhouses.....
- 1½″ Funnel uptakes ...
- 6″—3″ C.T. Base .....
- 11″ C.T. (6″—3″ Hood) .
- 6″ Fore Com. Tube ...
- 6″ Torp. Con. Tower ..
- 4″ Tube (T.C. Tower) .

Armour (H.T.):

Deck.
- 1″ Fo'xle over Battery
- 1¼″—1½″ Upper ......
- 2″, 1½″, 1″ Main ......
- 2½″, 1″ (forw'd) } Lower
- 4″, 3″, 2½″ (aft) }

Special Protection:
- 1½″—1″ Internal citadel between end barbettes

Royal Sovereign. *Photo, Cribb, Southsea.*

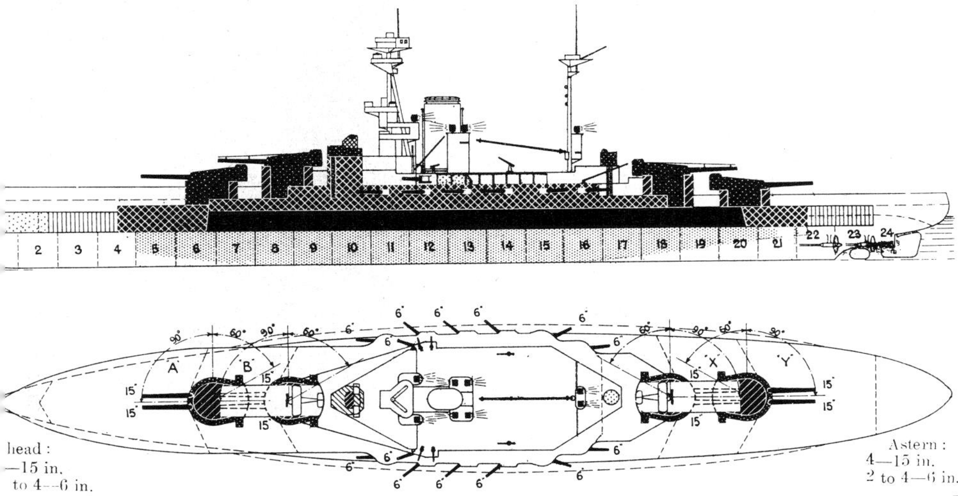

Ahead: 4—15 in. 2 to 4—6 in.

Astern: 4—15 in. 2 to 4—6 in.

Ramillies. Aircraft View. *Official R.A.F. Photo.*

Broadside: 8—15 in., 7—6 in., 2—21 in. tubes.

Machinery: Turbine, Parsons. Boilers: (see *Notes*). 4 screws. Designed H.P. 40,000 = 23 kts. *without* bulges, about 21½-22 *with* bulges. Fuel: Oil only, *normal*, 900 tons; *maximum*, about 3400 tons. Coal: 140 tons (only for "domestic" use).

Name	*Builder*	*Machinery*	*Laid down*	*Completed*	*Trials:*	*Boilers*	*Best recent speed*
Royal Sovereign	Portsmouth Y.	Parsons	Jan.'14	May, '16	41,115 = 21·6	18 Babcock	
Royal Oak	Devonport Y.	Hawthorn	Jan.'14	May, '16	40,360 =	18 Yarrow	
Resolution	Palmer	Palmer	Nov.'13	Dec., '16	41,406 =	18 Yarrow	
Ramillies	Beardmore	Beardmore	Nov.'13	Sept. '17	42,356 = 21·5	18 Babcock	
Revenge	Vickers	Vickers	Dec.'13	Mar., '16	42,962 = 21·9	18 Babcock	

Gunnery Notes.—Much as *Queen Elizabeth* class. Battery differently disposed in these ships. 6 inch batteries are wet in head seas, but dwarf walls in battery retain water and it is rapidly drained away.

Armour Notes.—Thicknesses much as *Queen Elizabeth* class, but armour differently distributed. Barbettes 6″—4″ as they descend behind belt. Gunhouses, 13″ face, 11″ sides and rear; crowns specially heavy. In these ships 2″ protective deck has a high 2″ slope behind belt, so that flat part of protection can be put on main deck and at top of belt, instead of a deck lower. Internal protection is very good, and with bulge protection, these ships are heavily defended against underwater attack. *Royal Sovereign* and *Royal Oak* have yet to be fitted with bulges.

Engineering Notes.—Designed to burn coal, but while building "all oil fuel" was adopted, and it was hoped that 23 kts. would be secured without increase of H.P. Addition of bulges has brought speed down again to about 21 kts. On deep load, the bulge protected ships cannot get much above 19.5 kts. till they have burnt off fuel.

General Notes.—Begun under 1914-15 Estimates. *Revenge* first named *Renown*. *Ramillies* injured herself at launch and was delayed in completion. They are fine ships, but suffer rather from reduced freeboard. They are steady ships, those with bulge protection being splendid gun platforms. With bulges, *normal* displacement is really about 29,350 tons (33,500 *full load*).

1912-13 BRITISH DREADNOUGHTS. ("Fast Division.")

(Queen Elizabeth Class.)

QUEEN ELIZABETH (Oct., 1913), **WARSPITE** (Nov., 1913), **VALIANT** (4th Nov., 1914), **BARHAM** (31st Dec., 1914), **MALAYA** (18th Mar., 1915).

Normal displacement, 27,500 tons (about 31,000-33,000 *full load*). Complement, 955-1016.

Length (*p.p.*), 600 feet. Beam, 90½ feet. { *Mean* draught, 30⅔ feet. *Max.* ,, 33½ ,, } Length (*over all*) { *Q.E.* 643¾ ft. Rest 639¾ ,, }

Guns:
- 8—15 inch 42 cal. } **Dir. Con.**
- 12—6 inch, 50 cal. }
- 2—3 inch (anti-aircraft)
- 4—3 pdr.
- 5 M.G.

Torpedo tubes (21 inch):
- 4 *submerged* (broadside).

Armour (K.C.):

Vertical.
- 13″ Lower belt ....
- 6″—4″ Upper belt ....
- 6″—4″ Belt (ends) ....
- 6″, 4″ Bulkheads(f. & a.)
- 6″ Battery ....
- 10″—7″ Barbettes .....
- 11″ Gunhouses ....
- 1½″ Funnel uptakes ...
- 6″—3″ C.T. base .....
- 11″ C.T. (6″—2″ Hood)..
- 4″ Fore com. tube ....
- 6″ Torpedo C.T. ......
- 4″ Tube (T.C. tower) ..

Armour (H.T.):

Deck.
- 1″ Fo'xle (over battery)
- 2″—1¼″ Upper ....
- 1¼″ Main ....
- 1″ Middle ....
- 3″ (ends) } Lower
- 1″ (amidships) }

Special Protec.:
- 2″—1″ Internal citadel between end barbettes

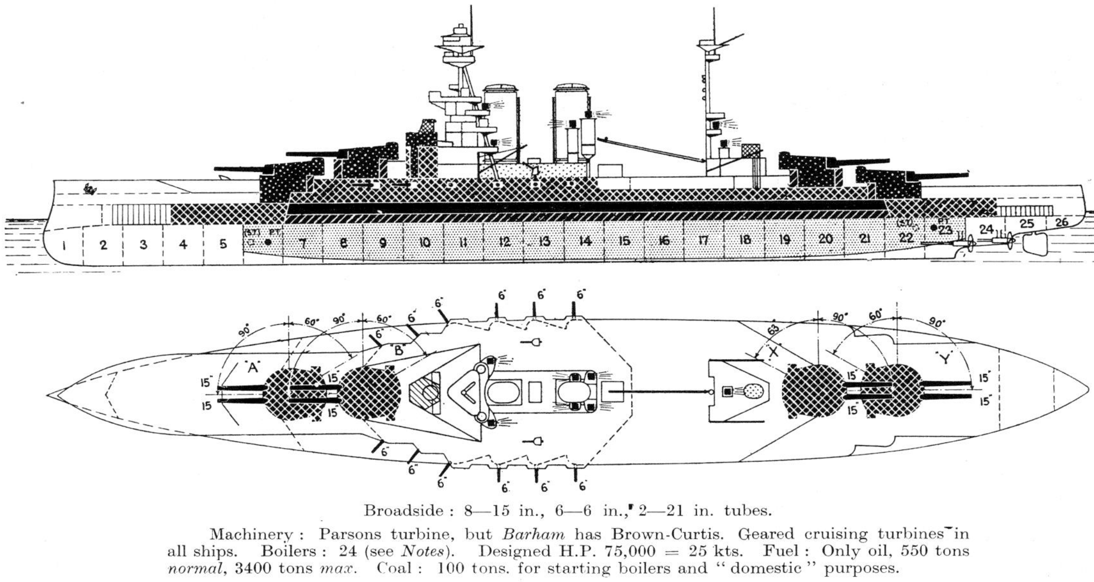

Ahead: 4—15 in. 3 to 6—6 in.

Astern: 4—15 in.

Broadside: 8—15 in., 6—6 in., 2—21 in. tubes.

Machinery: Parsons turbine, but *Barham* has Brown-Curtis. Geared cruising turbines in all ships. Boilers: 24 (see *Notes*). Designed H.P. 75,000 = 25 kts. Fuel: Only oil, 550 tons *normal*, 3400 tons *max*. Coal: 100 tons. for starting boilers and "domestic" purposes.

Gunnery Notes.—Range of 15 inch only limited by *max.* visibility. Elevation of these guns has been enlarged. 6-inch controlled in two groups from director towers on middle bridges. *Queen Elizabeth* completed with four extra 6-inch at stern; these were found useless, guns removed and ports plated over. *Barham* came into service with 2—6 inch in shields on fo'xle deck amidships; these, too, have been removed, but in a head sea they were said to have been equal to whole main deck battery.

Armour Notes.—Belt is 13″ at w.l. only, 6″ on upper edge, 8″ on lower, and applied in vertical strakes. Barbettes, 6″ and 4″ within belt. 1½″ traverses to battery, but no rear screens—only dwarf walls to retain and drain away water admitted to battery. Rear bulkhead to battery is 6″ diagonal and 4″ where it crosses centre line. Internal protection of these ships is very fine.

Engineering Notes.—"All oil" installation very successful. These ships steam splendidly, and can maintain a high average speed for long periods. H.P. turbines on wing shafts, with cruising turbines geared at forward end; L.P. turbines on inner shafts.

1912-13 BRITISH DREADNOUGHTS. ("Fast Division.")

QUEEN ELIZABETH.*
*Other ships without fore topmast, as *Warspite* view.

Photo, Graphic Union.

WARSPITE.

Photo, Cribb, Southsea.

Name.	Builder.	Machinery.	Laid down.	Completed.	Trials.	Boilers.	Best recent speed.
Queen Elizabeth	Portsmouth	Wallsend	Oct. '12	Jan., '15	57,130 =	24 Babcock	
Warspite	Devonport	Hawthorn	Oct. '12	Mar., '15	77,510 =	24 Yarrow	
Valiant	Fairfield	Fairfield	Jan.'13	Feb., '16	71,112 =	24 Babcock	
Barham	Clydebank	Clydebank	Feb.'13	Oct., '15	76,575 =	24 Yarrow	
Malaya	Elswick	Wallsend	Oct.'13	Feb.'16	76,074 =	24 Babcock	

Note.—First four begun under 1912 Estimates. *Malaya*, extra ship, gift of Federated Malay States. Estimated cost (average), £2,500,000 per ship = £90 per ton. At the Battle of Jutland, *Warspite, Valiant, Barham* and *Malaya* supported the First Battle-Cruiser Squadron. *Queen Elizabeth*, Flagship, C.-in-C., Grand Fleet, 1917-18. *Barham* grounded on May Island during War and badly injured herself, but was salved and repaired. In appearance and general design, these five ships are the finest in the British Navy. Their decks are remarkably clear, and internal arrangements are very spacious. Taken all round, they present the most successful type of capital ship yet designed.

MALAYA (Aircraft view).

Official R.A.F. Photo.

1912 BRITISH DREADNOUGHTS.

(IRON DUKE CLASS.)

BENBOW (Nov., 1913), **EMPEROR OF INDIA** (ex-*Delhi*, Nov., 1913),
IRON DUKE (Oct., 1912), **MARLBOROUGH** (Nov., 1912).

Normal displacement, 25,000 tons. *Full load*, 28,800 tons. Complement, 995 to 1022.

Length (o.a.), 622¾ feet. Beam, 89½ feet. { *Mean* draught, 28½ feet. } Length (p.p.), 580 feet
{ *Max.* " 32¾ " }

Guns :
  10—13·5 inch (M.V.) |
  12—6 inch, 50 cal. | **Dir. Con.**
  2—3 inch (anti-aircraft)
  4—3 pdr.
  5 M.G.
  (1 landing)
Torpedo tubes (21 inch) :
  4 submerged (broadside)

Armour (K.C.) :
Vertical.
  12"-8" Lower belt ......
  9" Middle belt ......
  8" Upper belt ....
  6"—4" Belt (ends) ...
  8", 6", 4" Bulkheads (f. & a.) ....
  6" Battery* ....
  10"—7" Barbettes .....
  11"— " Gunhouses...
  1½" Funnel uptakes ...
  6"—3" C.T. base .....
  11" C.T. (4"—3" hood)..
  6" Fore com. tube ....
  6" Torpedo C.T. .....
  4" After com. tube ...

Armour (H.T.) :
Deck.
  1" Fo'xle (over battery)
  2"—1½" Upper ....
  1" (amidships) }
  2½"—1½" (aft) } middle
  2½"—1" Lower ....
Special Protection :
  1½"—1" Screens to Mags., shell and engine rooms

* *See Notes.*

IRON DUKE.

Gunnery Notes.—Originally had 2—6 inch in casemates at stern, but these were found utterly useless. Ports were sealed up and guns re-mounted on forecastle deck. Forward 6-inch battery used to be swamped out in head seas. Rubber sealing joints for gun-ports were designed and added at Scapa Flow.

Armour Notes.—Belt is 12" at w.l. only and 8" on lower edge. Barbettes, 6" and 3" as they descend through decks behind belt. Battery has 1" traverses and 4" bulkhead completely athwartships, just before fore funnel. Internal protection more complete than in *King George V* class, but, all the same, screens do not completely extend between end barbettes. At Jutland, *Marlborough* was torpedoed over boiler rooms, where there is *no* internal protection. Lord Jellicoe is therefore in error when he says that the torpedo struck " at about one of the most favourable spots for the ship."

Name.	Builder.	Machinery.	Laid down.	Completed.	50 hrs.	Full power.	Boilers.	Best recent speed.
Benbow	Beardmore	Beardmore	May '12	Oct. '14		32530 = 21·5	18 Babcock	
E. of India	Vickers	Vickers	May '12	Nov. '14		29654 =	Yarrow	
Iron Duke	Portsmouth Y	Laird	Jan. '12	Mar. '14	20,875 = 19	30010 = 21·6	18 Babcock	
Marlborough	Devonport Y	Hawthorn	Jan. '12	June '14		32013 = 21·6	Yarrow	

Note.—Begun under the 1911 Estimates. Derived from *Orion* class through *King George* type. Average cost about £1,891,600. *Emperor of India* was originally named *Delhi*. *Iron Duke*, Flagship, C.-in-C., Grand Fleet, 1914-16.

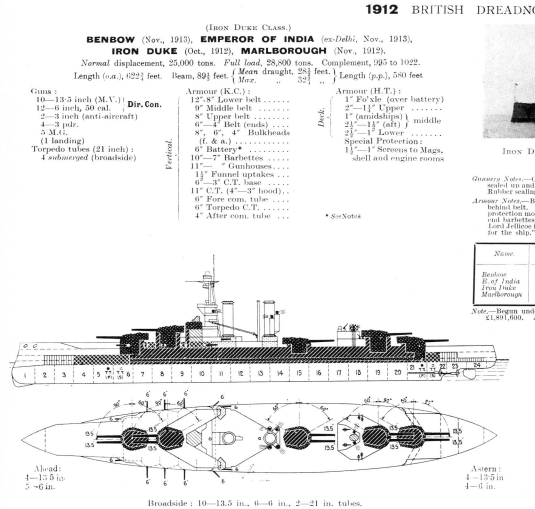

Ahead :
4—13·5 in.
5—6 in.

Astern :
4—13·5 in.
4—6 in.

Broadside : 10—13·5 in., 6—6 in., 2—21 in. tubes.

Machinery : Turbine (Parsons). Boilers : (see *Notes*). Designed H.P. 29,000 = 21 kts.
Coal : *normal*, 1000 tons ; *maximum*, 3250 tons. Oil : *normal*, 1050 tons ; *max.*, 1600 tons.

1911 BRITISH DREADNOUGHT (*purchased 1914*).

CANADA (ex *Almirante Latorre*), (Nov., 1913.)
Displacement, 28,000 tons (about 32,000 *full load*). Complement (1176).

Length (*p.p.*), 625 feet. Beam, 92½ feet. { Mean draught, 29 feet. } Length (*over all*), 661 feet.
                                          { Max.   „   32   „ }

Guns (Elswick) :
10—14 inch, 45 cal. ⎫ **Dir. Con.**
12—6 inch 50 cal. ⎭
2—3 inch (anti-aircraft)
4—3 pdr.
 (2 landing)
4 M.G.
Torpedo tubes (21 inch) :
 4 *submerged*

Armour :
Vertical.
9″ Lower belt . . . . . .
7″ Middle belt . . . . . .
4½″ Upper belt . . . . . .
6″—4″ Belt (ends) . . . .
4½″, 4″ B'lkh'ds (f. & a.)
6″ Batteries . . . .
10″ Barbettes . . . .
10″— „ Gunhouses . . . . .
3″ C.T. base* . . . .
11″ C.T. (6″—3″ hood) . .
6″ Fore com. tube . . . .
6″ Torpedo C.T. . . . . .
6″ Aft com. tube . . . . .
*Not shown on plans.

Armour :
Decks.
1″ Shelter (over case-mates) . . . .
1″ Fo'xle (over battery)
1½″ Upper (outside battery) . . . .
1½″ Main (aft) . . . . . .
1″ Protective . . . .
2″ (forward) ⎫ lower . . .
4″ (aft)   ⎭
Special Protec. :
2″—1½″ Internal screens
 (mags.. &c.) . . . . . .

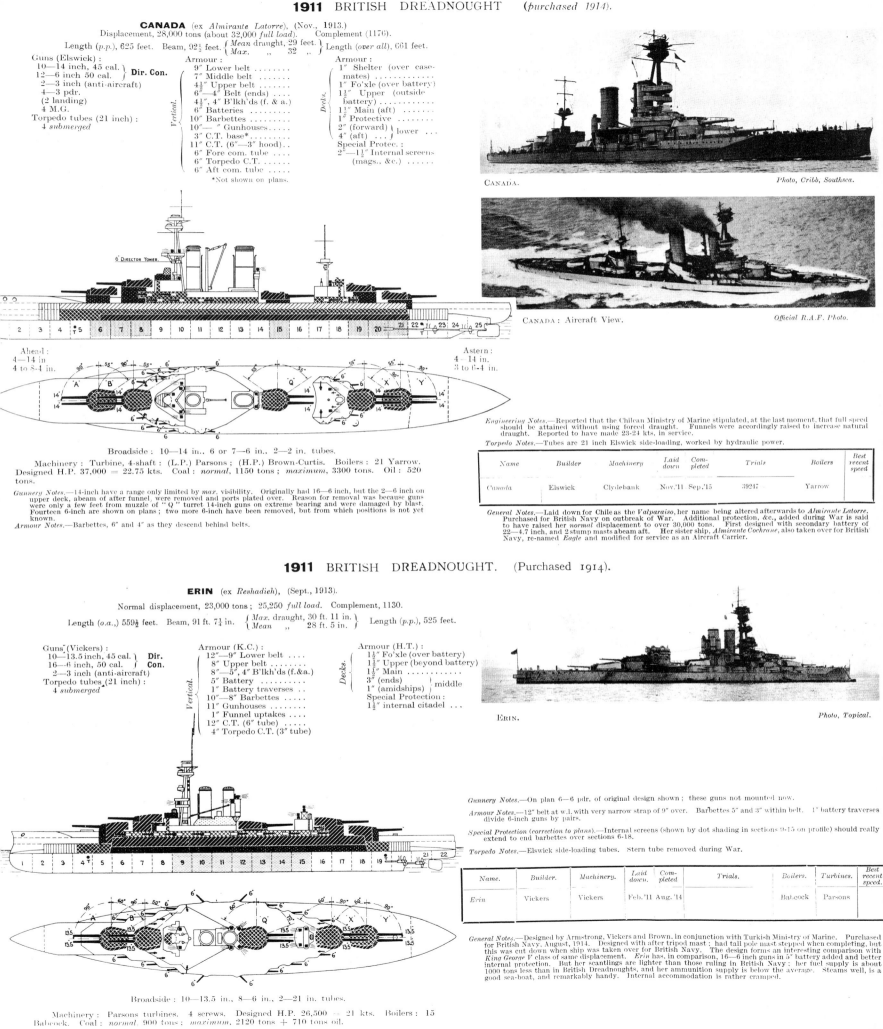

CANADA. *Photo, Cribb, Southsea.*

CANADA : Aircraft View. *Official R.A.F. Photo.*

Ahead :
4—14 in.
4 to 8-4 in.

Astern :
4—14 in.
3 to 6-4 in.

Broadside : 10—14 in.. 6 or 7—6 in.. 2—2 in. tubes.

Machinery : Turbine, 4-shaft : (L.P.) Parsons ; (H.P.) Brown-Curtis. Boilers : 21 Yarrow.
Designed H.P. 37,000 = 22.75 kts. Coal : *normal*, 1150 tons ; *maximum*, 3300 tons. Oil : 520 tons.

Gunnery Notes.—14-inch have a range only limited by *max.* visibility. Originally had 16—6 inch, but the 2—6 inch on upper deck, abeam of after funnel, were removed and ports plated over. Reason for removal was because guns were only a few feet from muzzle of " Q " turret 14-inch guns on extreme bearing and were damaged by blast. Fourteen 6-inch are shown on plans ; two more 6-inch have been removed, but from which positions is not yet known.
Armour Notes.—Barbettes, 6″ and 4″ as they descend behind belts.

Engineering Notes.—Reported that the Chilean Ministry of Marine stipulated, at the last moment, that full speed should be attained without using forced draught. Funnels were accordingly raised to increase natural draught. Reported to have made 23-24 kts. in service.
Torpedo Notes.—Tubes are 21 inch Elswick side-loading, worked by hydraulic power.

Name	Builder	Machinery	Laid down	Com-pleted	Trials	Boilers	Best recent speed
Canada	Elswick	Clydebank	Nov.'11	Sep.'15	39247	Yarrow	

General Notes.—Laid down for Chile as the *Valparaiso*, her name being altered afterwards to *Almirante Latorre*. Purchased for British Navy on outbreak of War. Additional protection, &c., added during War is said to have raised her *normal* displacement to over 30,000 tons. First designed with secondary battery of 22—4.7 inch, and 2 stump masts abeam aft. Her sister ship, *Almirante Cochrane*, also taken over for British Navy, re-named *Eagle* and modified for service as an Aircraft Carrier.

1911 BRITISH DREADNOUGHT. (Purchased 1914).

ERIN (ex *Reshadieh*), (Sept., 1913).

Normal displacement, 23,000 tons ; 25,250 *full load*. Complement, 1130.

Length (*o.a.*) 559½ feet. Beam, 91 ft. 7¼ in. { Max. draught, 30 ft. 11 in. } Length (*p.p.*), 525 feet.
                                               { Mean   „   28 ft. 5 in. }

Guns (Vickers) :
10—13.5 inch, 45 cal. ⎫ **Dir. Con.**
16—6 inch, 50 cal.   ⎭
2—3 inch (anti-aircraft)
Torpedo tubes (21 inch) :
 4 *submerged*

Armour (K.C.) :
Vertical.
12″—9″ Lower belt . . . .
8″ Upper belt . . . . . .
8″—5″, 4″ B'lkh'ds (f.&a.)
5″ Battery . . . .
1″ Battery traverses . . .
10″—8″ Barbettes . . . . .
11″ Gunhouses . . . . . .
1″ Funnel uptakes . . . .
12″ C.T. (6″ tube) . . . .
4″ Torpedo C.T. (3″ tube)

Armour (H.T.) :
Decks.
1½″ Fo'xle (over battery)
1½″ Upper (beyond battery)
1½″ Main . . . .
3″ (ends) ⎫ middle
1″ (amidships) ⎭
Special Protection :
1½″ internal citadel . . .

ERIN. *Photo, Topical.*

Gunnery Notes.—On plan 6—6 pdr. of original design shown ; these guns not mounted now.

Armour Notes.—12″ belt at w.l. with very narrow strap of 9″ over. Barbettes 5″ and 3″ within belt. 1″ battery traverses divide 6-inch guns by pairs.

Special Protection (correction to plans).—Internal screens (shown by dot shading in sections 9-15 on profile) should really extend to end barbettes over sections 6-18.

Torpedo Notes.—Elswick side-loading tubes. Stern tube removed during War.

Name.	Builder.	Machinery.	Laid down.	Com-pleted.	Trials.	Boilers.	Turbines.	Best recent speed.
Erin	Vickers	Vickers	Feb.'11	Aug.'14		Babcock	Parsons	

General Notes.—Designed by Armstrong, Vickers and Brown, in conjunction with Turkish Ministry of Marine. Purchased for British Navy, August, 1914. Designed with after tripod mast ; had tall pole mast stepped when completing, but this was cut down when ship was taken over for British Navy. The design forms an interesting comparison with *King George V* class of same displacement. *Erin* has, in comparison, 16—6 inch guns in 5″ battery added and better internal protection. But her scantlings are lighter than those ruling in British Navy ; her fuel supply is about 1000 tons less than in British Dreadnoughts, and her ammunition supply is below the average. Steams well, a good sea-boat, and remarkably handy. Internal accommodation is rather cramped.

Broadside : 10—13.5 in.. 8—6 in.. 2—21 in. tubes.

Machinery : Parsons turbines. 4 screws. Designed H.P. 26,500 = 21 kts. Boilers : 15 Babcock. Coal : *normal* 900 tons ; *maximum*, 2120 tons + 710 tons oil.

1911 BRITISH DREADNOUGHT. (*Purchased 1914.*)

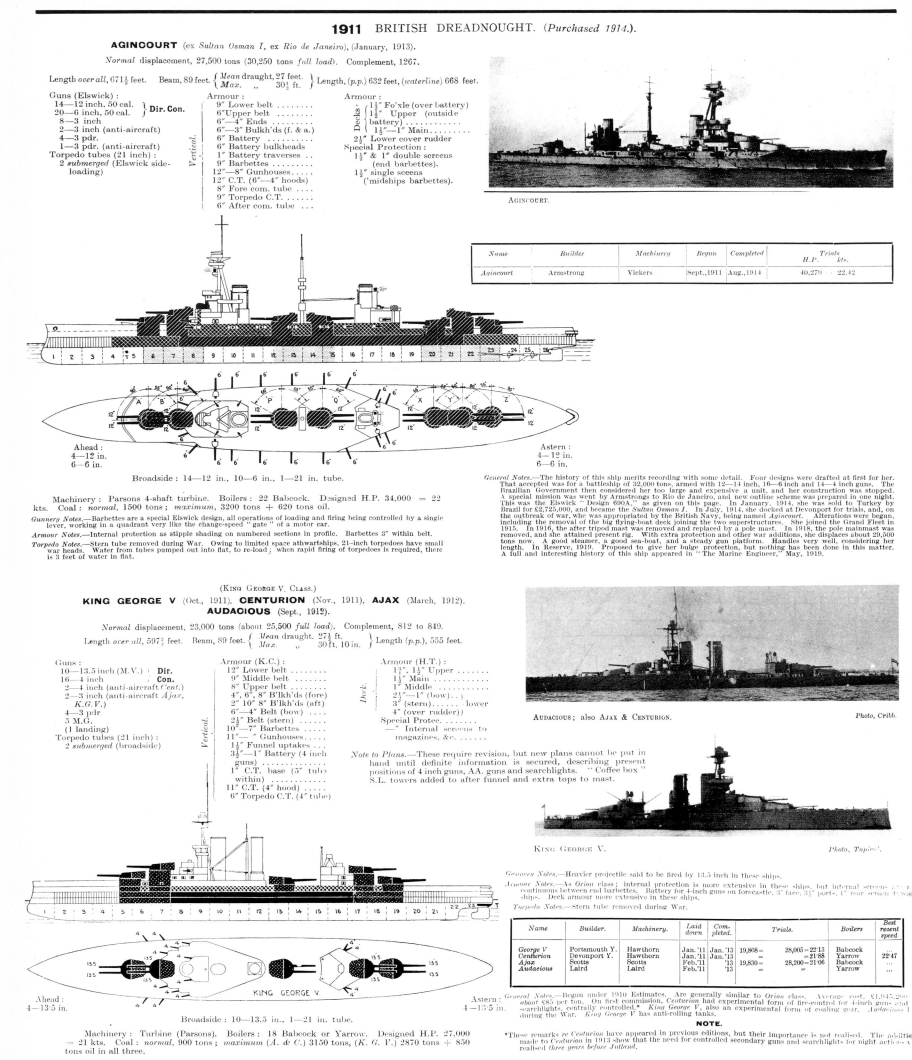

AGINCOURT (ex *Sultan Osman I*, ex *Rio de Janeiro*), (January, 1913).

Normal displacement, 27,500 tons (30,250 tons *full load*). Complement, 1267.

Length *over all*, 671½ feet. Beam, 89 feet. { *Mean* draught, 27 feet. *Max.* „ 30½ ft. } Length, (*p.p.*) 632 feet, (*waterline*) 668 feet.

Guns (Elswick) :
14—12 inch, 50 cal. } **Dir. Con.**
20—6 inch, 50 cal.
8—3 inch
2—3 inch (anti-aircraft)
4—3 pdr. (anti-aircraft)
1—3 pdr.
Torpedo tubes (21 inch) :
2 *submerged* (Elswick side-loading)

Armour : (Vertical)
9″ Lower belt . . . .
6″ Upper belt . . . .
6″—4″ Ends . . . .
6″—3″ Bulkh'ds (f. & a.)
6″ Battery . . . .
6″ Battery bulkheads
1″ Battery traverses . .
9″ Barbettes . . . .
12″—8″ Gunhouses . . . . .
12″ C.T. (6″—4″ hoods)
8″ Fore com. tube . . . . .
9″ Torpedo C.T. . . . . . .
6″ After com. tube . . . .

Armour : (Decks)
1½″ Fo'xle (over battery)
1½″ Upper (outside battery) . . . .
1½″—1″ Main . . . . . .
2½″ Lower cover rudder
Special Protection :
1½″ & 1″ double screens (end barbettes).
1½″ single sceens ('midships barbettes).

Name	Builder	Machinery	Begun	Completed	Trials	
					H.P.	kts.
Agincourt	Armstrong	Vickers	Sept.,1911	Aug.,1914	40,279	22.42

AGINCOURT.

Broadside : 14—12 in., 10—6 in., 1—21 in. tube.

Ahead :
4—12 in.
6—6 in.

Astern :
4—12 in.
6—6 in.

Machinery : Parsons 4-shaft turbine. Boilers : 22 Babcock. Designed H.P. 34,000 = 22 kts. Coal : *normal*, 1500 tons ; *maximum*, 3200 tons + 620 tons oil.

Gunnery Notes.—Barbettes are a special Elswick design, all operations of loading and firing being controlled by a single lever, working in a quadrant very like the change-speed "gate" of a motor car.

Armour Notes.—Internal protection as stipple shading on numbered sections in profile. Barbettes 3″ within belt.

Torpedo Notes.—Stern tube removed during War. Owing to limited space athwartships, 21-inch torpedoes have small war heads. Water from tubes pumped out into flat, to re-load ; when rapid firing of torpedoes is required, there is 3 feet of water in flat.

General Notes.—The history of this ship merits recording with some detail. Four designs were drafted at first for her. That accepted was for a battleship of 32,000 tons, armed with 12—14 inch, 16—6 inch and 14—4 inch guns. The Brazilian Government then considered her too large and expensive a unit, and her construction was stopped. A special mission was went by Armstrongs to Rio de Janeiro, and new outline scheme was prepared in one night. This was the Elswick "Design 690A," as given on this page. In January, 1914, she was sold to Turkey by Brazil for £2,725,000, and became the *Sultan Osman I*. In July, 1914, she docked at Devonport for trials, and, on the outbreak of war, whe was appropriated by the British Navy, being named *Agincourt*. Alterations begun, including the removal of the big flying-boat deck joining the two superstructures. She joined the Grand Fleet in 1915. In 1916, the after tripod mast was removed and replaced by a pole mast. With extra protection and other war additions, she displaces about 29,500 tons now. A good steamer, a good sea-boat, and a steady gun platform. Handles very well, considering her length. In Reserve, 1919. Proposed to give her bulge protection, but nothing has been done in this matter. A full and interesting history of this ship appeared in "The Marine Engineer," May, 1919.

(KING GEORGE V. CLASS.)

KING GEORGE V (Oct., 1911), **CENTURION** (Nov., 1911), **AJAX** (March, 1912). **AUDACIOUS** (Sept., 1912).

Normal displacement, 23,000 tons (about 25,500 *full load*). Complement, 812 to 849.

Length *over all*, 597⅔ feet. Beam, 89 feet. { *Mean* draught. 27½ ft. *Max.* „ 30 ft. 10 in. } Length (*p.p.*), 555 feet.

Guns :
10—13.5 inch (M.V.) **Dir.**
16—4 inch **Con.**
2—4 inch (anti-aircraft *Cent.*)
2—3 inch (anti-aircraft *Ajax, K.G.V.*)
4—3 pdr
5 M.G.
(1 landing)
Torpedo tubes (21 inch) :
2 *submerged* (broadside)

Armour (K.C.) : (Vertical)
12″ Lower belt . . . .
9″ Middle belt . . . .
8″ Upper belt . . . .
4″, 6″, 8″ B'lkh'ds (fore)
2″ 10″ 8″ B'lkh'ds (aft)
6″—4″ Belt (bow)
2½″ Belt (stern)
10″—7″ Barbettes . . . . .
11″—″ Gunhouses . . . .
1½″ Funnel uptakes . . .
3½″—1″ Battery (4 inch guns) . . . .
1″ C.T. base (5″ tube within)
11″ C.T. (4″ hood) . . . . .
6″ Torpedo C.T. (4″ tube)

Armour (H.T.) : (Deck)
1¾″, 1½″ Upper . . . . . .
1½″ Main . . . .
1″ Middle . . . .
2½″—1″ (bow) . . . . . .
3″ (stern) . . . . . lower
4″ (over rudder))
Special Protec.
—″ Internal screens to magazines, &c. . . . . . .

Note to Plans.—These require revision, but new plans cannot be put in hand until definite information is secured, describing present positions of 4 inch guns, AA. guns and searchlights. "Coffee box" S.L. towers added to after funnel and extra tops to mast.

AUDACIOUS ; also AJAX & CENTURION.   *Photo, Cribb.*

KING GEORGE V.   *Photo, Topical.*

Gunnery Notes.—Heavier projectile said to be fired by 13.5 inch in these ships.

Armour Notes.—As *Orion* class ; internal protection is more extensive in these ships, but internal screens are continuous between end barbettes. Battery for 4-inch guns on forecastle, 3″ face, 3½″ ports, 1″ rear screen to these ships. Deck armour more extensive these ships.

Torpedo Notes.—Stern tube removed during War.

Name	Builder.	Machinery.	Laid down	Completed	Trials.		Boilers	Best recent speed
George V	Portsmouth Y.	Hawthorn	Jan. '11	Jan. '13	19,808 =	22·13	Babcock	
Centurion	Devonport Y.	Hawthorn	Jan. '11	Jan. '13	=	21·88	Yarrow	22·47
Ajax	Scotts	Scotts	Feb.'11	'13	19,830 =		Babcock	...
Audacious	Laird	Laird	Feb.'11	'13	28,200 =	21·06	Yarrow	...

Broadside : 10—13.5 in., 1—21 in. tube.

Ahead :
4—13.5 in.

Astern :
4—13.5 in.

KING GEORGE V

Machinery : Turbine (Parsons). Boilers : 18 Babcock or Yarrow. Designed H.P. 27,000 = 21 kts. Coal : *normal*, 900 tons ; *maximum* (*A. & C.*) 3150 tons, (*K. G. V.*) 2870 tons + 850 tons oil in all three.

General Notes.—Begun under 1910 Estimates. Are generally similar to *Orion* class. Average cost, £1,945,200 about £85 per ton. On first commission, *Centurion* had experimental form of fire-control for 4-inch guns and searchlights, centrally controlled.* *King George V,* also experimental form of coaling gear. *Audacious* during the War. *King George V* has anti-rolling tanks.

NOTE.

These remarks re Centurion have appeared in previous editions, but their importance is not realised. The additions made to Centurion in 1913 show that the need for controlled secondary guns and searchlights for night actions was realised three years before Jutland.

1909 BRITISH DREADNOUGHTS.

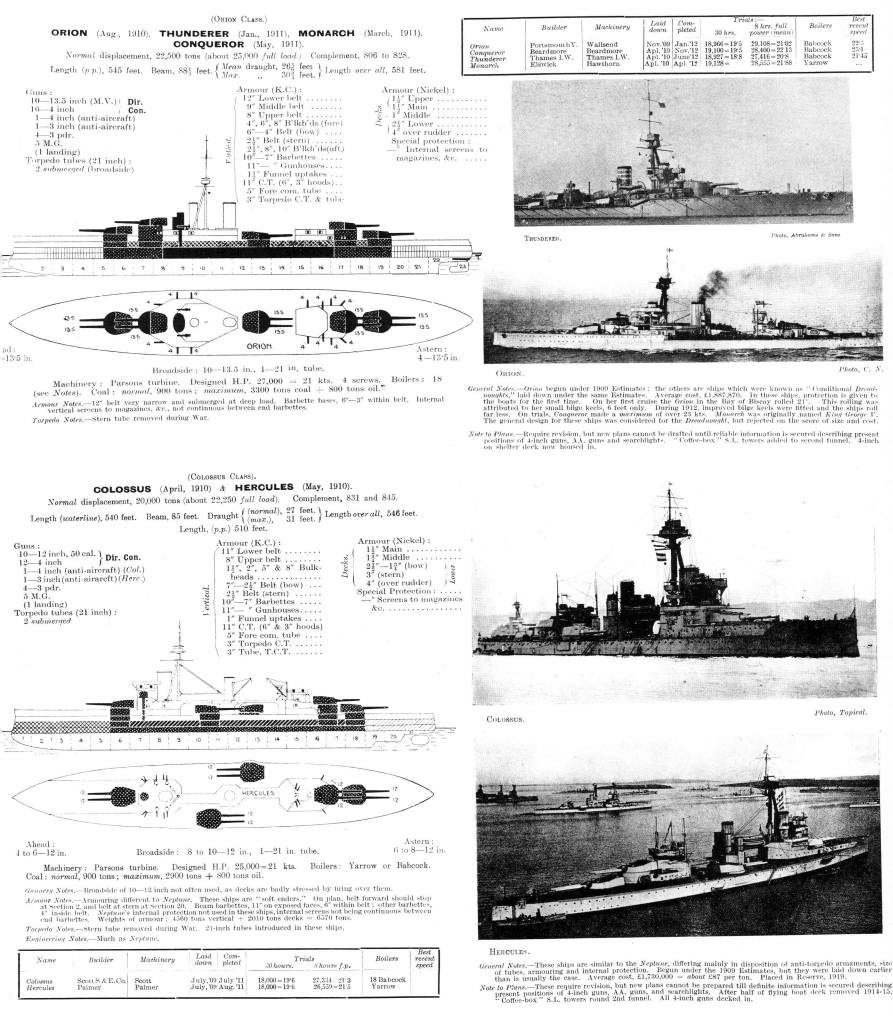

(ORION CLASS.)

ORION (Aug., 1910). **THUNDERER** (Jan., 1911), **MONARCH** (March, 1911), **CONQUEROR** (May, 1911).

Normal displacement, 22,500 tons (about 25,000 *full load*.)   Complement, 806 to 828.

Length (p p.), 545 feet.   Beam, 88½ feet. { *Mean* draught, 26⅝ feet. } Length *over all*, 581 feet.
{ *Max.,*   30¾ feet. }

Guns :
10—13.5 inch (M.V.) **Dir.**
16—4 inch **Con.**
1—4 inch (anti-aircraft)
1—3 inch (anti-aircraft)
4—3 pdr.
5 M.G.
(1 landing)
Torpedo tubes (21 inch) :
2 *submerged* (broadside)

Armour (K.C.) :
12″ Lower belt ....
9″ Middle belt ......
8″ Upper belt ......
4″, 6″, 8″ B'lkh'ds (fore)
6″—4″ Belt (bow) ....
2½″ Belt (stern) ....
2½″, 8″, 10″ B'lkh'ds (aft.)
10″—7″ Barbettes ....
11″— ″ Gunhouses ....
1½″ Funnel uptakes ...
11″ C.T. (6″, 3″ hoods)..
5″ Fore com. tube ....
3″ Torpedo C.T. & tube

Armour (Nickel) :
1½″ Upper ....
1¾″ Main ....
1″ Middle ....
2½″ Lower ....
4″ over rudder ......
Special protection :
— Internal screens to magazines, &c. .....

Broadside : 10—13.5 in., 1—21 in. tube.

ad : —13.5 in.   Astern : 4—13.5 in.

Machinery : Parsons turbine. Designed H.P. 27,000 = 21 kts.   4 screws.   Boilers : 18 (see *Notes*).   Coal : *normal*, 900 tons ; *maximum*, 3300 tons coal + 800 tons oil.

Armour Notes.—12″ belt very narrow and submerged at deep load. Barbette bases, 6″—3″ within belt. Internal vertical screens to magazines, &c., not continuous between end barbettes.

Torpedo Notes.—Stern tube removed during War.

Name	Builder	Machinery	Laid down	Completed	Trials :—		Boilers	Best recent speed
					30 hrs.	8 hrs. full power (mean)		
Orion	Portsmouth Y.	Wallsend	Nov.'09	Nov.'12	18,966=19·5	29,108=21·02	Babcock	22·5
Conqueror	Beardmore	Beardmore	Apl.'10	Nov.'12	19,100=19·5	28,400=22·13	Babcock	23·1
Thunderer	Thames I.W.	Thames I.W.	Apl.'10	June'12	18,927=18·8	27,416=20·8	Babcock	21·45
Monarch	Elswick	Hawthorn	Apl.'10	Apl.'12	19,128=	28,555=21·88	Yarrow	...

THUNDERER.   *Photo, Abrahams & Sons*

ORION.   *Photo, C. N.*

General Notes.—Orion begun under 1909 Estimates : the others are ships which were known as "Conditional *Dreadnoughts*," laid down under the same Estimates. Average cost, £1,887,870. In these ships, protection is given to the boats for the first time. On her first cruise the *Orion* in the Bay of Biscay rolled 21°. This rolling was attributed to her small bilge keels, 6 feet only. During 1912, improved bilge keels were fitted and the ships roll far less. On trials, *Conqueror* made a *maximum* of over 23 kts. *Monarch* was originally named *King George V*. The general design for these ships was considered for the *Dreadnought*, but rejected on the score of size and cost.

Note to Plans.—Require revision, but new plans cannot be drafted until reliable information is secured describing present positions of 4-inch guns, AA. guns and searchlights. "Coffee-box" S.L. towers added to second funnel. 4-inch on shelter deck now housed in.

(COLOSSUS CLASS).

COLOSSUS (April, 1910) & **HERCULES** (May, 1910).

Normal displacement, 20,000 tons (about 22,250 *full load*).   Complement, 831 and 845.

Length (*waterline*), 540 feet.   Beam, 85 feet.   Draught { (*normal*), 27 feet. } Length *over all*, 546 feet.
{ (*max.*), 31 feet. }
Length, (p.p.) 510 feet.

Guns :
10—12 inch, 50 cal. **Dir. Con.**
12—4 inch
1—4 inch (anti-aircraft) (*Col.*)
1—3 inch (anti-aircraft) (*Herc.*)
4—3 pdr.
5 M.G.
(1 landing)
Torpedo tubes (21 inch) :
2 *submerged*

Armour (K.C.) :
11″ Lower belt ....
8″ Upper belt ......
1½″, 2″, 5″ & 8″ Bulkheads ....
7″—2½″ Belt (bow) ...
2½″ Belt (stern) ....
10″—7″ Barbettes ....
11″— ″ Gunhouses .....
1″ Funnel uptakes ...
11″ C.T. (6″ & 3″ hoods)
5″ Fore com. tube ....
3″ Torpedo C.T. .....
3″ Tube, T.C.T. ......

Armour (Nickel) :
1½″ Main ....
1¾″ Middle ....
2¼″—1¾″ (bow) ..
3″ (stern) ....
4″ (over rudder) ...
Special Protection : .....
— ″ Screens to magazines &c. .....

Ahead : 4 to 6—12 in.   Broadside : 8 to 10—12 in., 1—21 in. tube.   Astern : 6 to 8—12 in.

Machinery : Parsons turbine. Designed H.P. 25,000 = 21 kts.   Boilers : Yarrow or Babcock. Coal : *normal*, 900 tons ; *maximum*, 2900 tons + 800 tons oil.

Gunnery Notes.—Broadside of 10—12 inch not often used, as decks are badly stressed by firing over them.

Armour Notes.—Armouring different to *Neptune*. These ships are "soft enders." On plan, belt forward should stop at Section 2, and belt at stern at Section 20. Beam barbettes, 11″ on exposed faces, 6″ within belt ; other barbettes, 4″ inside belt. *Neptune's* internal protection not used in these ships, internal screens not being continuous between end barbettes. Weights of armour : 4560 tons vertical + 2010 tons decks = 6570 tons.

Torpedo Notes.—Stern tube removed during War. 21-inch tubes introduced in these ships.

Engineering Notes.—Much as *Neptune*.

Name	Builder	Machinery	Laid down	Completed	Trials		Boilers	Best recent speed
					30 hours.	8 hours f.p.		
Colossus	Scott S.& E. Co.	Scott	July, '09	July '11	18,000=19·6	27,334=21·3	18 Babcock	
Hercules	Palmer	Palmer	July, '09	Aug.'11	18,000=19·6	26,559=21·5	Yarrow	

COLOSSUS.   *Photo, Topical.*

HERCULES.

General Notes.—These ships are similar to the *Neptune*, differing mainly in disposition of anti-torpedo armaments, size of tubes, armouring and internal protection. Begun under the 1909 Estimates, but they were laid down earlier than is usually the case. Average cost, £1,730,000 = *about* £87 per ton. Placed in Reserve, 1919.

Note to Plans.—These require revision, but new plans cannot be prepared till definite information is secured describing present positions of 4-inch guns, AA. guns, and searchlights. After half of flying boat deck removed 1914-15. "Coffee-box" S.L. towers round 2nd funnel. All 4-inch guns decked in.

1909 BRITISH DREADNOUGHTS.

NEPTUNE (Sept., 1909).

Normal displacement, 19,900 tons (about 22,000 *full load*). Complement, 813.

Length (*waterline*), 540 feet. Beam, 85 feet. { Draught (*normal*), 27 feet. } Length *over all*, 546 feet (p.p. 510 feet).
{ „ (*max.*), 30 „ }

Guns :
10—12 inch, 50 cal. } Dir.
12—4 inch } Con.
2—3 inch (anti-aircraft)
4—3 pdr.
5 M.G.
(1 landing)
Torpedo tubes (18 inch) :
2 submerged

Armour (K.C.) :
Vertical
10" Lower belt . . . .
8" Upper belt . . . .
5" & 8" Bulkheads . . . .
7"—2½" Belt (bow) . . .
2½" Belt (stern) . . . .
9" Barbettes . . . .
11"—" Gunhouses . . . .
11" C.T. (5" tube) . . . . .
1½" Torpedo C.T. . . . . .
1" Funnel uptakes . . . .

Armour (Nickel) :
Decks
1½" Main . . . .
1¾" Middle . . . .
1½" (bow) } lower
3" (stern) }
Special protection :
"—" Internal screens over magazines and machinery spaces
" Bulkheads to keel. . . .

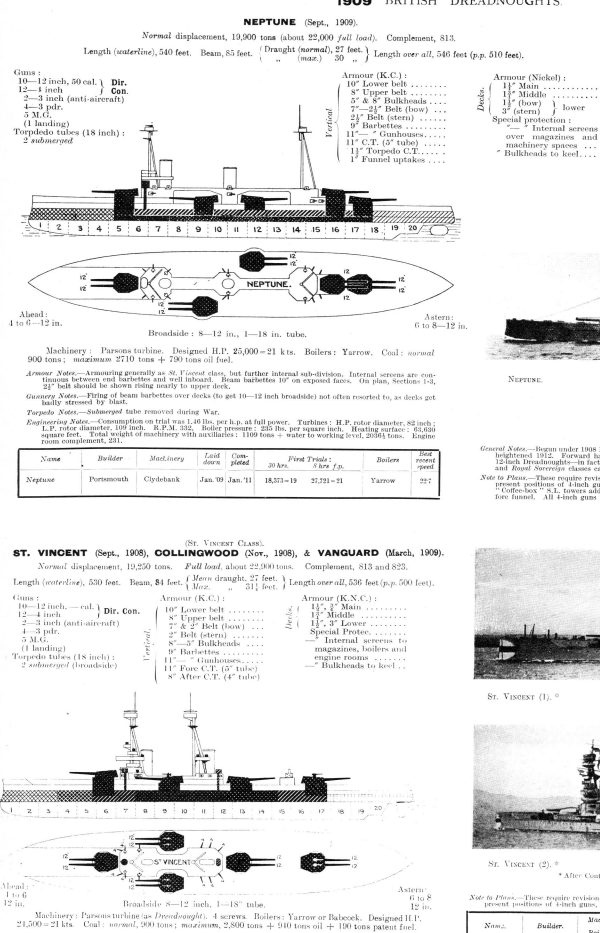

Ahead :
4 to 6—12 in.

NEPTUNE.

Astern :
6 to 8—12 in.

Broadside : 8—12 in., 1—18 in. tube.

Machinery : Parsons turbine. Designed H.P. 25,000 = 21 k ts. Boilers : Yarrow. Coal : *normal* 900 tons ; *maximum* 2710 tons + 790 tons oil fuel.

Armour Notes.—Armouring generally as *St. Vincent* class, but further internal sub-division. Internal screens are continuous between end barbettes and well inboard. Beam barbettes 10" on exposed faces. On plan, Sections 1-3, 2½" belt should be shown rising nearly to upper deck.

Gunnery Notes.—Firing of beam barbettes over decks (to get 10—12 inch broadside) not often resorted to, as decks get badly stressed by blast.

Torpedo Notes.—Submerged tube removed during War.

Engineering Notes.—Consumption on trial was 1.46 lbs. per h.p. at full power. Turbines : H.P. rotor diameter, 82 inch ; L.P. rotor diameter, 109 inch. R.P.M. 332. Boiler pressure : 235 lbs. per square inch. Heating surface : 63,630 square feet. Total weight of machinery with auxiliaries : 1109 tons + water to working level, 2036¼ tons. Engine room complement, 231.

NEPTUNE. *Photo, Sadler & Renouf.*

| Name | Builder | Machinery | Laid down | Completed | First Trials : | | Boilers | Best recent speed |
					30 hrs.	8 hrs f.p.		
Neptune	Portsmouth	Clydebank	Jan. '09	Jan. '11	18,373 = 19	27,721 = 21	Yarrow	22·7

General Notes.—Begun under 1908 Estimates. Cost to build, £86.8 per ton. Cost of machinery, £258,000. Fore funnel heightened 1912. Forward half of flying decks removed, 1914-15. Has the best internal protection of all the 12-inch Dreadnoughts—in fact her internal protection was not equalled in later Battleships till the *Queen Elizabeth* and *Royal Sovereign* classes came into service. Placed in Reserve, 1919.

Note to Plans.—These require revision, but new plans cannot be prepared till definite information is secured regarding present positions of 4-inch guns, AA. guns and searchlights. Fore half of flying boat deck removed, 1914-15. "Coffee-box" S.L. towers added to 2nd funnel and mainmast, director top to foremast and "clinker screen" to fore funnel. All 4-inch guns decked in.

(St. Vincent Class).

ST. VINCENT (Sept., 1908), COLLINGWOOD (Nov., 1908), & VANGUARD (March, 1909).

Normal displacement, 19,250 tons. *Full load*, about 22,900 tons. Complement, 813 and 823.

Length (*waterline*), 530 feet. Beam, 84 feet. { Mean draught, 27 feet. } Length *over all*, 536 feet (p.p. 500 feet).
{ Max. „ , 31¼ feet. }

Guns :
10—12 inch. — cal. } Dir. Con.
12—4 inch
2—3 inch (anti-aircraft)
4—3 pdr.
5 M.G.
(1 landing)
Torpedo tubes (18 inch) :
2 submerged (broadside)

Armour (K.C.) :
Vertical
10" Lower belt . . . .
8" Upper belt . . . .
7" & 2" Belt (bow) . . . . .
2" Belt (stern) . . . .
8"—5" Bulkheads . . . .
8" Barbettes . . . .
11"—" Gunhouses. . . . .
11" Fore C.T. (5" tube) . .
8" After C.T. (4" tube) . .

Armour (K.N.C.) :
Decks
1½", ¾" Main . . . .
1¾" Middle . . . .
1½", 3" Lower . . . .
Special Protec. . . . . . .
—" Internal screens to magazines, boilers and engine rooms . . . .
—" Bulkheads to keel . .

Ahead :
4 to 6—12 in.

Broadside 8—12 inch, 1—18" tube.

ST VINCENT

Astern :
6 to 8—12 in.

Machinery : Parsons turbine (as *Dreadnought*). 4 screws. Boilers : Yarrow or Babcock. Designed H.P. 21,500 = 21 kts. Coal : *normal*, 900 tons ; *maximum*, 2,800 tons + 940 tons oil + 190 tons patent fuel.

Torpedo Notes.—Stern tube removed during War.

Armour Notes.—Armour generally as *Bellerophon* class, but thinner belt at bow and stern. On plans, bow belt in Sections 1-3 should be shown rising almost to upper deck. Internal screens are continuous between end barbettes and well inboard. Barbette bases, 10".

Engineering Notes.—In this class (and all later Dreadnoughts up to *Iron Duke* class), no cruising turbines. An extra stage at forward end of H.P. turbine is used when running at cruising speed. For full speed, bye-pass valves used. H.P. rotor diameter, 68 inch. L.P. rotor diameter, 92 inch. 324 R.P.M. Pressure, 235 lbs. Heating surface : 63,414 square feet. Weight of main and auxiliary engines : 1072½ tons + water to working level = 1983½ tons. Average consumption on trials : 1.8 lbs. per H.P.

ST. VINCENT (1). *

ST. VINCENT (2). *

* After Control Top removed since above photographs were taken.

Note to Plans.—These require revision, but new plans cannot be prepared till definite information is secured describing present positions of 4-inch guns, AA. guns and searchlights.

Name.	Builder.	Machinery and Boilers by.	Laid down.	Completed.	Last refit.	Trials.	Boilers.	Best recent speed.
St. Vincent	Portsmouth	Scott Eng. & S. Co.	Dec. '07	Jan., '10		= 21·9	Babcock	22·5
Collingwood	Devonport	Hawthorn L.	Feb.'08	Jan., '10		26,319 = 21·5	Yarrow	22
Vanguard	Vickers	Vickers	April '08	Feb., '10		= 22·1	Babcock	22·4

General Notes.—Begun under 1907 Estimates. These ships are simply enlarged *Bellerophons* and second improvements on original *Dreadnought* design. *Collingwood* did not reach designed speed on first trials. Internal protection is very complete. Underwent large refit in 1912-13. *Vanguard* lost by explosion during the War. *St. Vincent* and *Collingwood* in Reserve or employed as Gunnery Training Ships in 1919.

1907 BRITISH DREADNOUGHTS.

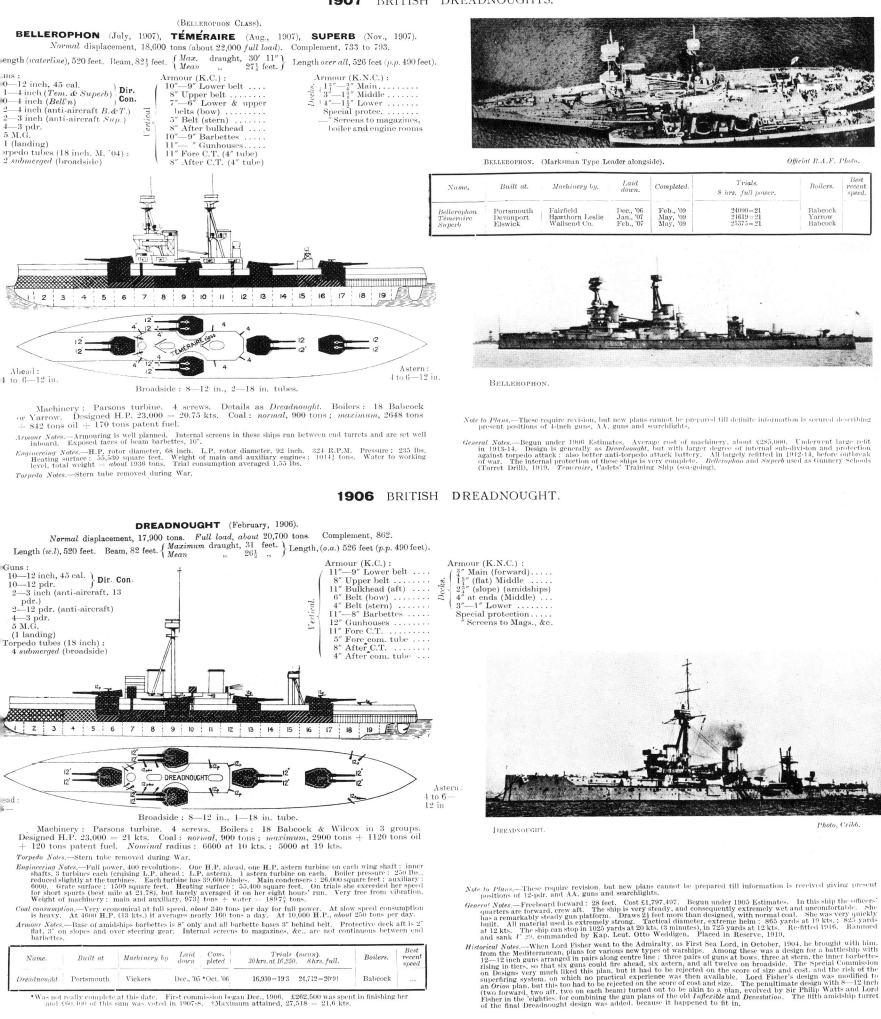

(Bellerophon Class).

BELLEROPHON (July, 1907), **TÉMÉRAIRE** (Aug., 1907), **SUPERB** (Nov., 1907).

Normal displacement, 18,600 tons (about 22,000 *full load*). Complement, 733 to 793.

ength (*waterline*), 520 feet. Beam, 82½ feet. { *Max.* draught, 30′ 11″ / *Mean* „ 27¼ feet. } Length *over all*, 526 feet (*p.p.* 490 feet).

ıns :
0—12 inch, 45 cal. } Dir.
1—4 inch (*Tem. & Superb*) } Con.
0—4 inch (*Bell'n*)
2—4 inch (anti-aircraft *B.&T.*)
2—3 inch (anti-aircraft *Sup.*)
4—3 pdr.
5 M.G.
1 (landing)
rpedo tubes (18 inch, M. '04) :
2 *submerged* (broadside)

Armour (K.C.) :
Vertical
10″—9″ Lower belt ....
8″ Upper belt ....
7″—6″ Lower & upper belts (bow) ....
5″ Belt (stern) ....
8″ After bulkhead ....
10″—9″ Barbettes .....
11″— ″ Gunhouses.....
11″ Fore C.T. (4″ tube)
8″ After C.T. (4″ tube)

Armour (K.N.C.) :
Decks
1¾″—¾″ Main.........
3″—1¾″ Middle ....
4″—1½″ Lower ....
Special protec. ....
—″ Screens to magazines, boiler and engine rooms

Bellerophon. (Marksman Type Leader alongside). *Official R.A.F. Photo.*

Name.	*Built at.*	*Machinery by.*	*Laid down.*	*Completed.*	*Trials. 8 hrs. full power.*	*Boilers.*	*Best recent speed.*
Bellerophon	Portsmouth	Fairfield	Dec., '06	Feb., '09	24030=21	Babcock	
Téméraire	Devonport	Hawthorn Leslie	Jan., '07	May, '09	21619=21	Yarrow	
Superb	Elswick	Wallsend Co.	Feb., '07	May, '09	25375=21	Babcock	

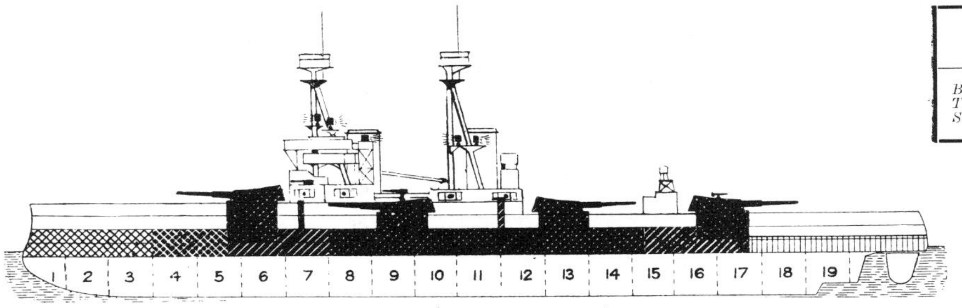

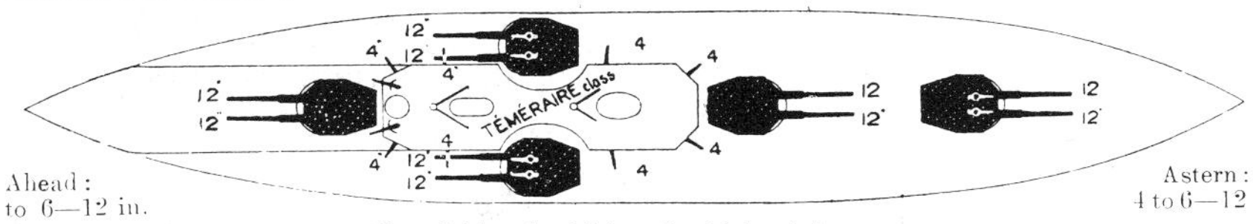

Ahead :
4 to 6—12 in.

Astern :
4 to 6—12 in.

Broadside : 8—12 in., 2—18 in. tubes.

Bellerophon.

Machinery : Parsons turbine. 4 screws. Details as *Dreadnought*. Boilers : 18 Babcock or Yarrow. Designed H.P. 23,000 = 20.75 kts. Coal : *normal*, 900 tons ; *maximum*, 2648 tons + 842 tons oil + 170 tons patent fuel.

Armour Notes.—Armouring is well planned. Internal screens in these ships run between end turrets and are set well inboard. Exposed faces of beam barbettes, 10″.

Engineering Notes.—H.P. rotor diameter, 68 inch. L.P. rotor diameter, 92 inch. 324 R.P.M. Pressure : 235 lbs. Heating surface : 55,530 square feet. Weight of main and auxiliary engines : 1014½ tons. Water to working level, total weight = *about* 1936 tons. Trial consumption averaged 1.55 lbs.

Torpedo Notes.—Stern tube removed during War.

Note to Plans.—These require revision, but new plans cannot be prepared till definite information is secured describing present positions of 4-inch guns, AA. guns and searchlights.

General Notes.—Begun under 1906 Estimates. Average cost of machinery, about £285,000. Underwent large refit in 1913-14. Design is generally as *Dreadnought*, but with larger degree of internal sub-division and protection against torpedo attack : also better anti-torpedo attack battery. All largely refitted in 1912-14, before outbreak of war. The internal protection of these ships is very complete. *Bellerophon* and *Superb* used as Gunnery Schools (Turret Drill), 1919. *Téméraire*, Cadets' Training Ship (sea-going).

1906 BRITISH DREADNOUGHT.

DREADNOUGHT (February, 1906).

Normal displacement, 17,900 tons. *Full load, about* 20,700 tons. Complement, 862.

Length (*w.l.*), 520 feet. Beam, 82 feet. { *Maximum* draught, 31 feet. / *Mean* „ 26½ „ } Length, (*o.a.*) 526 feet (*p.p.* 490 feet).

Guns :
10—12 inch, 45 cal. } Dir. Con.
10—12 pdr. }
2—3 inch (anti-aircraft, 13 pdr.)
2—12 pdr. (anti-aircraft)
4—3 pdr.
5 M.G.
(1 landing)
Torpedo tubes (18 inch) :
4 *submerged* (broadside)

Armour (K.C.) :
Vertical
11″—9″ Lower belt ....
8″ Upper belt ....
11″ Bulkhead (aft) ....
6″ Belt (bow) ....
4″ Belt (stern) ....
11″—8″ Barbettes .....
12″ Gunhouses ....
11″ Fore C.T. ....
5″ Fore com. tube ....
8″ After C.T. ....
4″ After com. tube ...

Armour (K.N.C.) :
Decks
¾″ Main (forward).....
1¾″ (flat) Middle .....
2¾″ (slope) (amidships)
4″ at ends (Middle) ...
3″—1″ Lower ....
Special protection.....
″ Screens to Mags., &c.

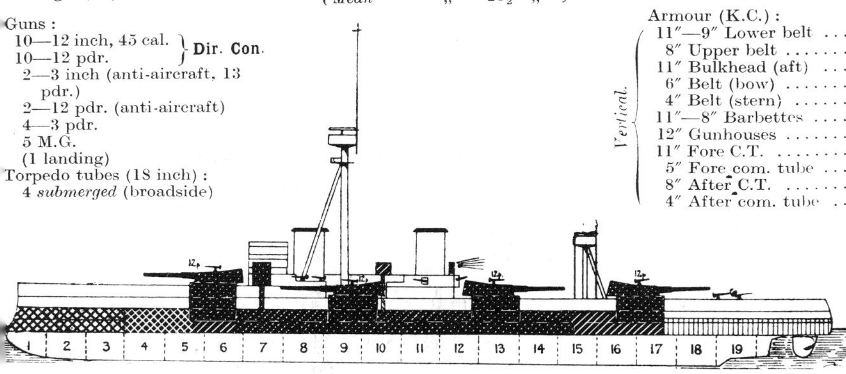

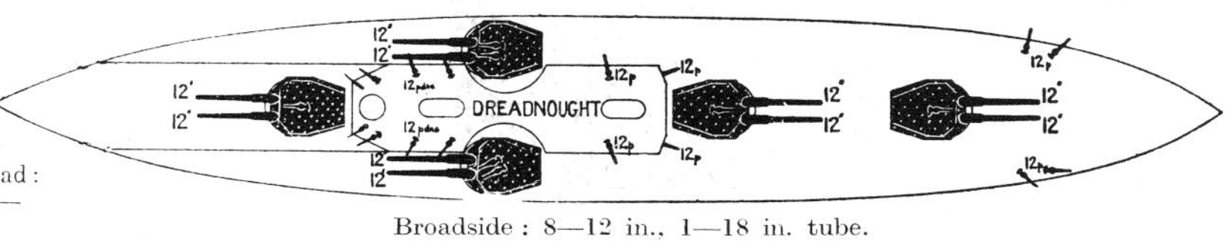

ead :
—

Astern :
4 to 6—
12 in.

Broadside : 8—12 in., 1—18 in. tube.

Dreadnought. *Photo, Cribb.*

Machinery : Parsons turbine. 4 screws. Boilers : 18 Babcock & Wilcox in 3 groups. Designed H.P. 23,000 = 21 kts. Coal : *normal*, 900 tons ; *maximum*, 2900 tons + 1120 tons oil + 120 tons patent fuel. *Nominal* radius : 6600 at 10 kts. ; 5000 at 19 kts.

Torpedo Notes.—Stern tube removed during War.

Engineering Notes.—Full power, 400 revolutions. One H.P. ahead, one H.P. astern turbine on each wing shaft ; inner shafts, 3 turbines each (cruising L.P. ahead ; L.P. astern). 1 astern turbine on each. Boiler pressure : 250 lbs., reduced slightly at the turbines. Each turbine has 39,600 blades. Main condensers : 26,000 square feet ; auxiliary : 6000. Grate surface : 1599 square feet. Heating surface : 55,400 square feet. On trials she exceeded her speed for short spurts (best mile at 21.78), but barely averaged it on her eight hours' run. Very free from vibration. Weight of machinery : main and auxiliary, 973½ tons + water = 1897¾ tons.

Coal consumption.—Very economical at full speed, *about* 340 tons per day for full power. At slow speed consumption is heavy. At 4600 H.P. (13 kts.) it averages nearly 160 tons a day. At 10,000 H.P., *about* 250 tons per day.

Armour Notes.—Base of amidships barbettes is 8″ only and all barbette bases 3″ behind belt. Protective deck aft is 2″ flat, 3″ on slopes and over steering gear. Internal screens to magazines, &c., are not continuous between end barbettes.

Name.	*Built at*	*Machinery by*	*Laid down*	*Com-pleted*	*Trials (mean). 30 hrs. at 16,250.*	*8 hrs. full.*	*Boilers.*	*Best recent speed*
Dreadnought	Portsmouth	Vickers	Dec., '05	*Oct. '06	16,930=19·3	24,712=20·9†	Babcock	...

*Was not really complete at this date. First commission began Dec., 1906. £262,500 was spent in finishing her and £60,400 of this sum was voted in 1907-8. †Maximum attained, 27,518 = 21.6 kts.

Note to Plans.—These require revision, but new plans cannot be prepared till information is received giving present positions of 12-pdr. and AA. guns and searchlights.

General Notes.—Freeboard forward : 28 feet. Cost £1,797,497. Begun under 1905 Estimates. In this ship the officers' quarters are forward, crew aft. The ship is very steady, and consequently extremely wet and uncomfortable. She has a remarkably steady gun platform. Draws 2½ feet more than designed, with normal coal. She was very quickly built. All material used is extremely strong. Tactical diameter, extreme helm : 865 yards at 19 kts. ; 825 yards at 12 kts. The ship can stop in 1025 yards at 20 kts. (3 minutes), in 725 yards at 12 kts. Re-fitted 1916. Rammed and sank *U 29*, commanded by Kap. Leut. Otto Weddigen. Placed in Reserve, 1919.

Historical Notes.—When Lord Fisher went to the Admiralty, as First Sea Lord, in October, 1904, he brought with him, from the Mediterranean, plans for various new types of warships. Among these was a design for a battleship with 12—12 inch guns arranged in pairs along centre line ; three pairs of guns at bows, three at stern, the inner barbettes rising in tiers, so that six guns could fire ahead, six astern, and all twelve on broadside. The Special Commission on Designs very much liked this plan, but it had to be rejected on the score of size and cost, and the risk of the superfiring system, on which no practical experience was then available. Lord Fisher's design was modified to an *Orion* plan, but this too had to be rejected on the score of cost and size. The penultimate design with 8—12 inch (two forward, two aft, two on each beam) turned out to be akin to a plan, evolved by Sir Philip Watts and Lord Fisher in the 'eighties, for combining the gun plans of the old *Inflexible* and *Devastation*. The fifth amidship turret of the final Dreadnought design was added, because it happened to fit in.

1915 BRITISH BATTLE CRUISERS

(RENOWN CLASS.)

REPULSE (8th January, 1916). **RENOWN** (4th March, 1916).

Normal displacement, 26,500 tons (about 32,000-32,700 *full load*).   Complement, Renown, 999 ; Repulse 1016.

Length (p.p.), 750 feet. { o.a. 794 feet *Repulse* / o.a. 794 feet 1½in. *Renown* }   Beam { Repulse 90 feet* / Renown 90 feet 2 in.* }   Draught { Repulse 26¼ feet (*mean*), 30½ feet (*max.*) / Renown 26⅔ feet (*mean*), 30 feet (*max.*) }

*Outside bulges:

Guns :
6—15 inch, 42 cal. **} Dir.**
17—4 inch, 50 cal. **} Con.**
2—3 inch (anti-aircraft)
4—3 pdr.
5 M.G.
(1 landing)
Torpedo tubes (21 inch) :
2 *submerged**
*See Torpedo Notes.

Armour (K.C.) :
(Vertical.)
6" (amidships) ....
4" (within bow) } Lower
3" (stern) } belt
4" Fore b'lkhead
3" After b'lkh'd
1½" Upper belt ......
7"—4" Barbettes .....
11"—7" Gunhouses ...
1½" Funnel uptakes ...
2" C.T. base (3" tube within) ....
10" C.T. ....
6" Sighting hood over C.T. ....
3" Torpedo C.T. .....

Armour (H.T.) :
(Decks)
1½"—½" Fo'xle ......
1"—1½" Upper ....
3"—¾" Main (2" slopes)
2½" Bow } Lower
3½"—3" Stern }
—" Barbettes ....
3" C.T. and hood ...
1½" Torpedo C.T. ....
Special protection :
Modified bulges about 20 ft. deep, filled with oil ....

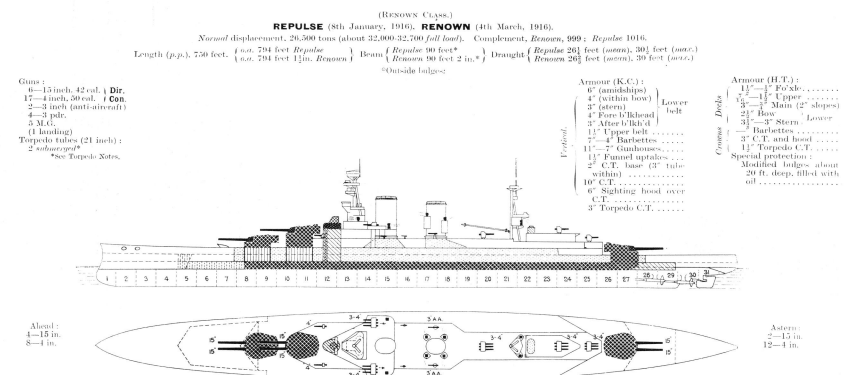

Ahead :
4—15 in.
8—4 in.

Astern :
2—15 in.
12—4 in.

Broadside : 6—15 in., 13—4 in., 1—21 in. tube.

Machinery : Brown-Curtis (direct drive) turbines. 4 screws. Boilers : 42 Babcock & Wilcox. Designed H.P. not exactly specified, but expected to be 110,000 to 120,000 S.H.P. for 30 kts. In service, S.H.P. 112,000 = about 31.5 kts. Fuel (oil only) : 1000 tons *normal* ; *Repulse* 4243 tons *maximum* ; *Renown* 4289 tons *maximum*.

Gunnery Notes.—15-inch have range only limited by maximum visibility. Director tower under control tower on foremast. 4-inch triples have 2 director towers, and all guns can be worked from either tower or half the 4-inch from one tower. If towers are destroyed, 4-inch can work independently. 4-inch triples are clumsy and not liked. They are not mounted in one sleeve ; have separate breech mechanism ; gun crew of 23 to each triple. First salvo fired by forward 15-inch of *Renown* did considerable damage forward, and she had to be docked for repairs.
Torpedo Notes.—*Submerged* tubes a failure. *Renown*, on 1919 re-fit, reported to have had *submerged* tubes removed and replaced by 8 *above water* tubes in 4 twin mountings on main deck.
Armour Notes.—Armouring adapted from *Invincible* and *Indefatigable* classes. Belt *about* 9¼ ft. deep. *Special Protection.*—Projected that bulges be deepened. *Renown* may have had bulges enlarged on her 1919 re-fit, and her beam may be larger now.
Engineering Notes.—Turbines similar to *Tiger*. For full description, v. "Engineering," April 11th, 1919. Boilers : 250 lbs. per sq. in. Heating surface : 157,206 sq. ft. Consumption at full speed : *about* 1400 tons oil fuel per day.
Aircraft Notes.—Two aeroplanes carried on flying-off platforms on crowns of " B " and " Y " turrets.

Name	Builder	Machinery	Begun*	Completed	Trials : H.P.	kts.	Where run
Repulse	Clydebank	Clydebank	Jan.25,'15	Aug.,1916	119,025	31.7	Skelmorlie (deep load)
Renown	Fairfield	Fairfield	Jan.25,'15	Sept.,1916	126,300	32.68	Arran (normal load)

*To Battle Cruiser design.

General Notes.—Provided for by 1914-15 Navy Estimates : first designed as slightly modified *Royal Sovereigns*, contracted for on that basis, and begun 1914, but building was not pushed on actively after the outbreak of War. After the Falklands Battle it was decided that these two ships should be re-designed as Battle Cruisers. Outline design was prepared in ten days, and builders received sufficient details by January 21st, 1915, to begin building, but full designs were not finished and approved till April, 1915. Intended that they should be completely built in fifteen months, but this time was somewhat exceeded. Both ships have turned out remarkably well and reflect great credit on their designers and builders. Internally, they are most spacious, but they are lightly built, and their guns " shake them up " considerably. Remarkable speeds have been claimed for these ships. When attempting to intercept enemy warships in November, 1917, *Renown* is said to have touched 41 kts. Be this as it may, they have certainly done 33-34 kts. in service. Reported to have cost about three to four millions each.

1915 BRITISH BATTLE CRUISERS. (Illustrations.)

(For Plan and Description, v. opposite page.)

RENOWN.

RENOWN.   REPULSE.

Photo, Sub-Lieut Vickers, R.N.

1911 BRITISH BATTLE-CRUISERS. No. **22 & 27** (Dreadnoughts).

QUEEN MARY (March, 1912), & **TIGER** (1913).

Normal displacement, 27,000 tons. *Full load,* tons. Complement

Length (*waterline*), 720 feet. Beam, 87 feet. *Maximum* draught, 30 feet. Length *over all*, 725 feet.

Guns : *(see note)*.
  8—13·5 inch (A⁷)
  16—4 inch
Torpedo tubes (21 inch) :
  2 *submerged* (broadside)
  1 *submerged* (stern)

Armour (Krupp) :
  9″ Belt (amidships) .. *aa*
  4″ Belt (ends) ....

QUEEN MARY.   *Photo, Abrahams & Sons.*

TIGER (present appearance).   *Photo, Renouf.*

Note.—*Tiger* tripod forward. Rumoured that her secondary battery may possibly consist of 12—6 inch guns instead of 16—4 inch as *Queen Mary.*

Machinery : Turbine (Brown-Curtis). Boilers : Babcock. Designed H.P. 75,000 = 27 kts. Coal: *normal*, 1000 tons; *maximum* 3500 tons + oil, 1000 tons.

TIGER approximate sketch.

Name	Builder	Machinery	Laid down	Completed	Trials	Boilers	Best recent speed
Queen Mary	Palmer	Clydebank	Mar. '11	1913		Yarrow	33
Tiger	Clydebank	Clydebank	June '12	May '14		Babcock	

Tiger, 1911-12 estimates. *Queen Mary,* 1910-11 estimates.

1912 BRITISH BATTLE CRUISER.

TIGER (Dec., 1913).

Normal displacement, 28,500 tons. *Full load, about* 35,000 tons. Complement 1185.

Length (*waterline*), 675 feet. Beam, 90½ feet. { *Mean* draught, 28⅓ feet. { Length (*o.a.*) 704 feet. { *Max.* „ 34 „ { Length (*p.p.*) 660 feet.

Guns :
  8—13·5 inch (M.V.) } **Dir.**
  12—6 inch (M. XII) } **Con.**
  2—3 inch (anti-aircraft)
  4—3 pdr.
  5 M.G.
  (1 landing)
Torpedo tubes (21 inch) :
  4 *submerged* (broadside)

Armour (K.C.) :
  Vertical.
  9″ Lower belt ....
  6″ Upper belt ....
  3″ Under lower belt ..
  4″ Bulkheads..........
  6″ Battery (1″ traverses)
  5″, 4″ Battery Bulk'ds)
  6″ Casemates (2″ rear)
  9″—8″ Barbettes ......
  9″ Gunhouses ....
  2″ C.T. base..........
  4″ Com tube ....
  10″ C.T. ....
  6″—3″ hood over C.T.
  6″ Torpedo C.T. (4″ tube)..............

Armour (H.T.) :
  Deck.
  1½″—1″ Fo'xle........
  1½″—1″ Upper ......
  1″ Amidships } Lower
  3″ Bow }
  Special protection :
  2½″—1″ H.T. magazine screens ....

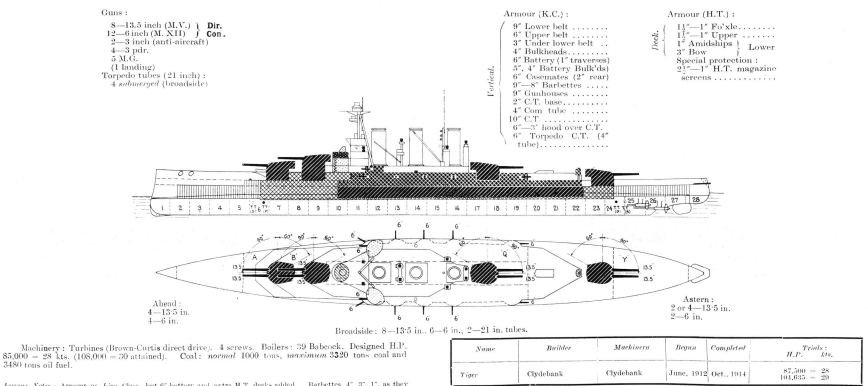

Ahead :
  4—13·5 in.
  4—6 in.

Astern :
  2 or 4—13·5 in.
  2—6 in.

Broadside: 8—13·5 in., 6—6 in., 2—21 in. tubes.

Machinery : Turbines (Brown-Curtis direct drive). 4 screws. Boilers : 39 Babcock. Designed H.P. 85,000 = 28 kts. (108,000 = 30 attained). Coal : *normal* 1000 tons, *maximum* 3320 tons coal and 3480 tons oil fuel.

Armour Notes.—Armour as *Lion* Class, but 6″ battery and extra H.T. decks added. Barbettes, 4″, 3″, 1″, as they descend through decks behind belts. ¾″ rear screen to 6″ battery. Internal magazine protection is not continuous between barbettes.

Engineering Notes.—4-shaft turbines in 2 sets, each set has H.P. ahead and H.P. astern turbine on wing shaft, one L.P. ahead and one L.P. astern, in same casing on inner shaft. Boilers in 5 rooms. The enormous fuel capacity (6800 tons coal and oil) does not give this ship any exceptional radius of action, for she burns about 1200 tons of fuel per day at 60,000 S.H.P.

Name	Builder	Machinery	Begun	Completed	Trials :	
					H.P.	kts.
Tiger	Clydebank	Clydebank	June, 1912	Oct., 1914	87,500 = 28	
					104,635 = 29	

General Notes.—Begun under 1911 Estimates by J. Brown & Co., Clydebank : machinery by builders. Completed October, 1914. Estimated cost was £2,593,095, but this was exceeded. As first designed, this ship was to have been very much like the *Lion* class. A year after the *Tiger* was laid down the Japanese battle-cruiser *Kongo* was completed and passed her trials. Comparison between the *Lion* and *Kongo* designs showed the Japanese ship to be superior in armament and protection. Work was suspended on the *Tiger*, and her design was altered to embody certain improvements displayed by the *Kongo*. These alterations resulted in the *Tiger* being one and a half years on the stocks before launching. Until *Hood* was launched in 1918, *Tiger* was the largest ship in H.M. Navy. She was also a remarkably handsome ship until the present hideous rig was adopted in 1918.

1909 BRITISH BATTLECRUISERS.

(LION CLASS.)

LION (August, 1910), **PRINCESS ROYAL** (April, 1911).

Normal displacement, 26,350 tons. *Full load*, 29,700 tons. Complement, 1085 & 1061.

Length (w.l.), 675 feet. Beam, 88½ feet. {*Mean* draught, 27⅜ feet.} {*Length over all*, 700 feet.
{*Max.* draught, 31⅜ feet.} {*Length p.p.*, 660 feet.

Guns :
8—13.5 inch (M.V.) } **Dir. Con.**
16—4 inch, 50 cal. }
2—3 inch (anti-aircraft)
4—3 pdr.
(P.R. 2—2 pdr. pom-pom)
5 M.G.
(1 landing)
Torpedo tubes (21 inch) :
2 *submerged* (broadside)

Armour :
Decks : { 1″ Upper . . . .
{ 1½″—1″ Amidships } Lower
{ 2½″ Ends }

Special protection :
—″ Magazine screens

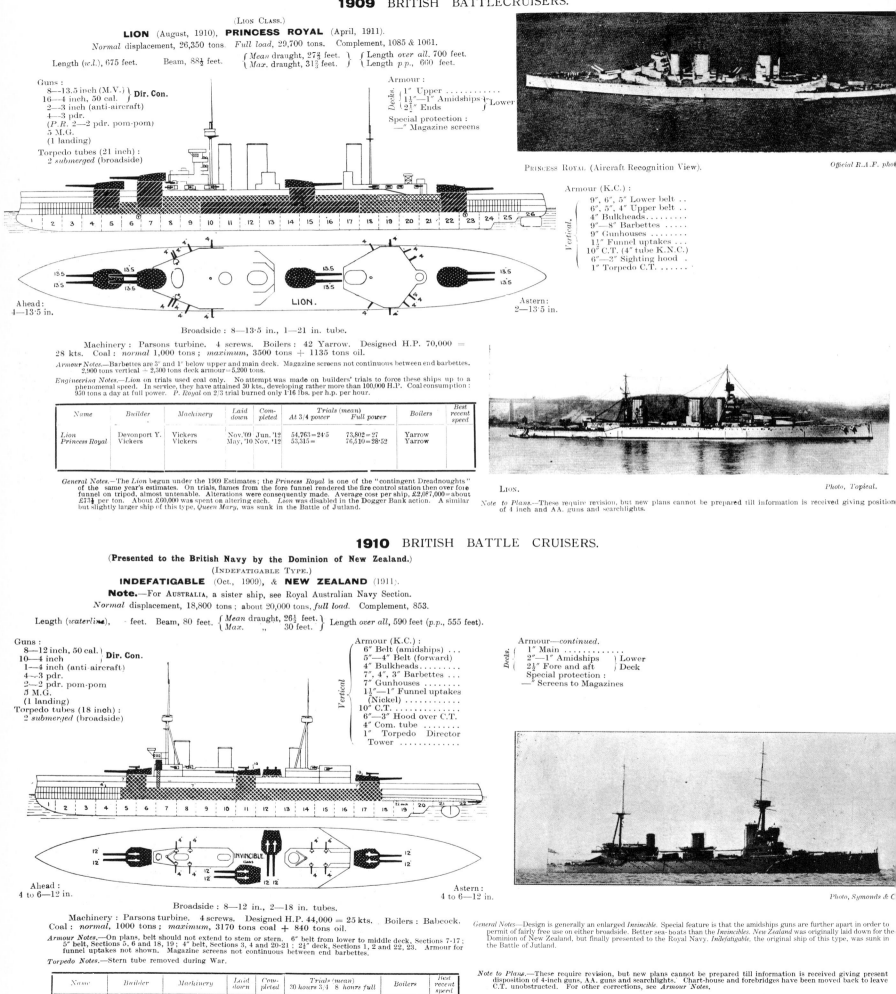

PRINCESS ROYAL (Aircraft Recognition View).

Official R.A.F. photo

Armour (K.C.) :
Vertical { 9″, 6″, 5″ Lower belt . .
{ 6″, 5″, 4″ Upper belt . .
{ 4″ Bulkheads. . . . .
{ 9″—8″ Barbettes . . . . .
{ 9″ Gunhouses . . . . . .
{ 1½″ Funnel uptakes . . .
{ 10″ C.T. (4″ tube K.N.C.)
{ 6″—3″ Sighting hood . .
{ 1″ Torpedo C.T. . . . . . .

Ahead :
4—13·5 in.

Astern :
2—13·5 in.

LION.

Broadside : 8—13·5 in., 1—21 in. tube.

Machinery : Parsons turbine. 4 screws. Boilers : 42 Yarrow. Designed H.P. 70,000 = 28 kts. Coal : *normal* 1,000 tons ; *maximum*, 3500 tons + 1135 tons oil.

Armour Notes.—Barbettes are 3″ and 1″ below upper and main deck. Magazine screens not continuous between end barbettes. 2,900 tons vertical + 2,300 tons deck armour=5,200 tons.

Engineering Notes.—Lion on trials used coal only. No attempt was made on builders' trials to force these ships up to a phenomenal speed. In service, they have attained 30 kts., developing rather more than 100,000 H.P. Coal consumption : 950 tons a day at full power. P. Royal on 2/3 trial burned only 1·16 lbs. per h.p. per hour.

| Name | Builder | Machinery | Laid down | Com-pleted | Trials (mean) | | Boilers | Best recent speed |
					At 3/4 power	Full power		
Lion	Devonport Y.	Vickers	Nov.'09	Jun. '12	54,763=24·5	73,802=27	Yarrow	
Princess Royal	Vickers	Vickers	May, '10	Nov. '12	53,315=	76,510=28·52	Yarrow	

General Notes.—The *Lion* begun under the 1909 Estimates ; the *Princess Royal* is one of the "contingent Dreadnoughts" of the same year's estimates. On trials, flames from the fore funnel rendered the fire control station then over fore funnel on tripod, almost untenable. Alterations were consequently made. Average cost per ship, £2,087,000 = about £73½ per ton. About £60,000 was spent on altering each. *Lion* was disabled in the Dogger Bank action. A similar but slightly larger ship of this type, *Queen Mary*, was sunk in the Battle of Jutland.

LION.

Photo, Topical.

Note to Plans.—These require revision, but new plans cannot be prepared till information is received giving positions of 4 inch and AA. guns and searchlights.

1910 BRITISH BATTLE CRUISERS.

(Presented to the British Navy by the Dominion of New Zealand.)

(INDEFATIGABLE TYPE.)

INDEFATIGABLE (Oct., 1909), & **NEW ZEALAND** (1911).

Note.—For AUSTRALIA, a sister ship, see Royal Australian Navy Section.

Normal displacement, 18,800 tons ; about 20,000 tons, *full load*. Complement, 853.

Length (waterline), - feet. Beam, 80 feet. {*Mean* draught, 26½ feet.} Length *over all*, 590 feet (p.p. 555 feet).
{*Max.* „ 30 feet.}

Guns :
8—12 inch, 50 cal. } **Dir. Con.**
10—4 inch }
1—4 inch (anti-aircraft)
4—3 pdr.
2—2 pdr. pom-pom
5 M.G.
(1 landing)
Torpedo tubes (18 inch) :
2 *submerged* (broadside)

Armour (K.C.) :
Vertical { 6″ Belt (amidships) . . .
{ 5″—4″ Belt (forward)
{ 4″ Bulkheads. . . . .
{ 7″, 4″, 3″ Barbettes . . .
{ 7″ Gunhouses . . . .
{ 1½″—1″ Funnel uptakes
{ (Nickel) . . . .
{ 10″ C.T. . . . .
{ 6″—3″ Hood over C.T.
{ 4″ Com. tube . . . .
{ 1″ Torpedo Director
{ Tower . . . .

Armour—*continued*.
Decks. { 1″ Main . . . .
{ 2″—1″ Amidships } Lower
{ 2½″ Fore and aft } Deck
Special protection :
— Screens to Magazines

Ahead :
4 to 6—12 in.

Astern :
4 to 6—12 in.

Broadside : 8—12 in., 2—18 in. tubes.

Machinery : Parsons turbine. 4 screws. Designed H.P. 44,000 = 25 kts. Boilers : Babcock. Coal : *normal*, 1000 tons ; *maximum*, 3170 tons coal + 840 tons oil.

Armour Notes.—On plans, belt should not extend to stem or stern. 6″ belt from lower to middle deck, Sections 7-17 ; 5″ belt, Sections 5, 6 and 18, 19 ; 4″ belt, Sections 3, 4 and 20-21 ; 2½″ deck, Sections 1, 2 and 22, 23. Armour for funnel uptakes not shown. Magazine screens not continuous between end barbettes.

Torpedo Notes.—Stern tube removed during War.

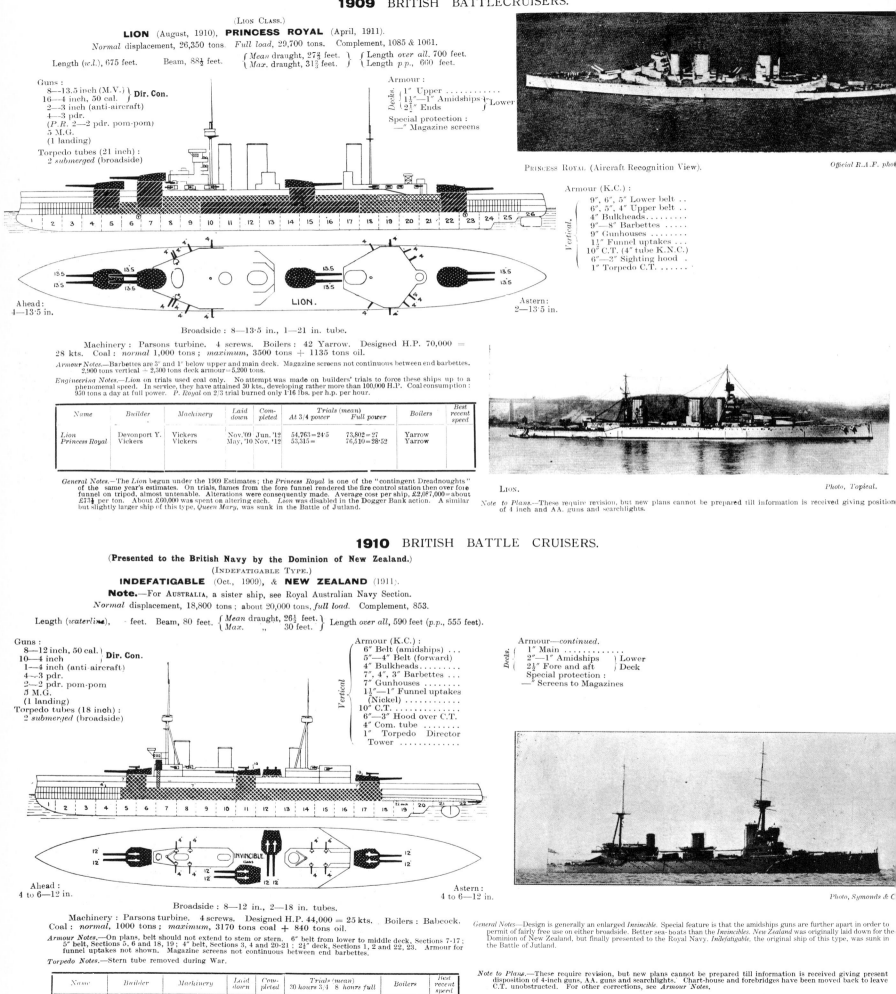

Photo, Symonds & Co.

General Notes.—Design is generally an enlarged *Invincible*. Special feature is that the amidships guns are further apart in order to permit of fairly free use on either broadside. Better sea-boats than the *Invincibles*. *New Zealand* was originally laid down for the Dominion of New Zealand, but finally presented to the Royal Navy. *Indefatigable*, the original ship of this type, was sunk in the Battle of Jutland.

Note to Plans.—These require revision, but new plans cannot be prepared till information is received giving present disposition of 4-inch guns, AA. guns and searchlights. Chart-house and forebridges have been moved back to leave C.T. unobstructed. For other corrections, see *Armour Notes*.

| Name | Builder | Machinery | Laid down | Com-pleted | Trials (mean) | | Boilers | Best recent speed |
					30 hours 3/4	8 hours full		
Indefatigable	Devonport	Clydebank	Feb.'09	Feb '11	32,000=24·6	=26·7	Babcock	
New Zealand	Fairfield	Fairfield	1910	Jan.'12	=24·8	29,000=27	Babcock	29·13

1906 BRITISH BATTLE CRUISERS.

(INVINCIBLE CLASS).

INVINCIBLE (April, 1907), **INFLEXIBLE** (June, 1907), & **INDOMITABLE** (March, 1907).

Normal Displacement, 17,250 tons (about 20,000 *full load*. Complement, 837.

Length (*waterline*), 560 feet. Beam, 78ft. 10 in. { Mean draught, 26 feet. / Max. ,, 29¾ feet. } Length *over all*, 567 feet (*p.p.* 530).

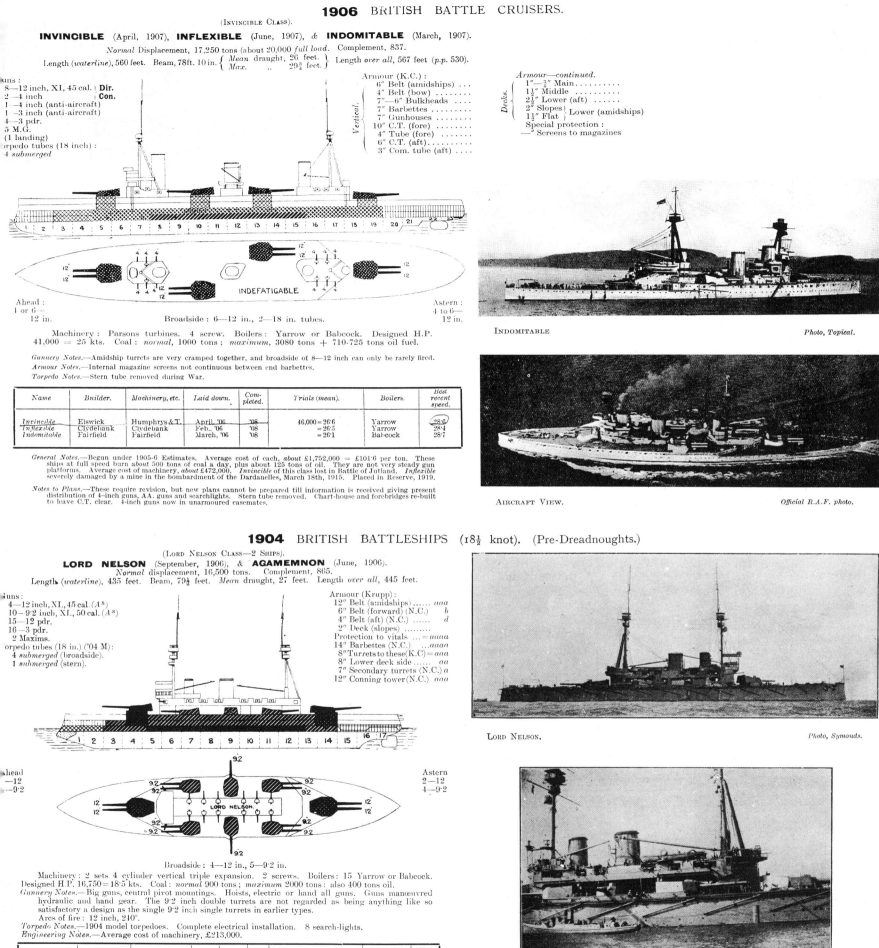

Guns :
8—12 inch, XI, 45 cal. } **Dir.**
2—4 inch } **Con.**
1—4 inch (anti-aircraft)
1—3 inch (anti-aircraft)
4—3 pdr.
5 M.G.
(1 landing)
Torpedo tubes (18 inch) :
4 submerged

Armour (K.C.) :
Vertical. {
6″ Belt (amidships) ...
4″ Belt (bow) ....
7″—6″ Bulkheads ......
7″ Barbettes ....
7″ Gunhouses ....
10″ C.T. (fore) ......
4″ Tube (fore) ......
6″ C.T. (aft) ......
3″ Com. tube (aft) ....
}

Armour—continued.
Decks. {
1″—¾″ Main ....
1½″ Middle ....
2½″ Lower (aft) .....
2″ Slopes } Lower (amidships)
1½″ Flat }
}
Special protection :
—″ Screens to magazines

Ahead :
4 or 6—
12 in.

Broadside : 6—12 in., 2—18 in. tubes.

Astern :
4 to 6—
12 in.

INDEFATIGABLE

INDOMITABLE   *Photo, Topical.*

AIRCRAFT VIEW.   *Official R.A.F. photo.*

Machinery : Parsons turbines. 4 screw. Boilers : Yarrow or Babcock. Designed H.P. 41,000 = 25 kts. Coal : *normal*, 1000 tons ; *maximum*, 3080 tons + 710-725 tons oil fuel.

Gunnery Notes.—Amidship turrets are very cramped together, and broadside of 8—12 inch can only be rarely fired.
Armour Notes.—Internal magazine screens not continuous between end barbettes.
Torpedo Notes.—Stern tube removed during War.

Name	Builder.	Machinery, etc.	Laid down.	Com-pleted.	Trials (mean).	Boilers.	Best recent speed.
Invincible	Elswick	Humphrys & T.	April, '06	'08	46,000 = 26·6	Yarrow	28·6
Inflexible	Clydebank	Clydebank	Feb., '06	'08	= 26·5	Yarrow	28·4
Indomitable	Fairfield	Fairfield	March, '06	'08	= 26·1	Babcock	28·7

General Notes.—Begun under 1905-6 Estimates. Average cost of each, *about* £1,752,000 = £101·6 per ton. These ships at full speed burn *about* 500 tons of coal a day, plus about 125 tons of oil. They are not very steady gun platforms. Average cost of machinery, *about* £472,000. *Invincible* of this class lost in Battle of Jutland. *Inflexible* severely damaged by a mine in the bombardment of the Dardanelles, March 18th, 1915. Placed in Reserve, 1919.

Notes to Plans.—These require revision, but new plans cannot be prepared till information is received giving present distribution of 4-inch guns, AA. guns and searchlights. Stern tube removed. Chart-house and forebridges re-built to leave C.T. clear. 4-inch guns now in unarmoured casemates.

1904 BRITISH BATTLESHIPS (18½ knot). (Pre-Dreadnoughts.)

(LORD NELSON CLASS—2 SHIPS).

LORD NELSON (September, 1906), & **AGAMEMNON** (June, 1906).

Normal displacement, 16,500 tons. Complement, 865.

Length (*waterline*), 435 feet. Beam, 79½ feet. *Mean* draught, 27 feet. Length *over all*, 445 feet.

Guns :
4—12 inch, XI, 45 cal. (A⁵)
10—9·2 inch, XI, 50 cal. (A³)
15—12 pdr.
16—3 pdr.
2 Maxims.
Torpedo tubes (18 in.) ('04 M)
4 submerged (broadside).
1 submerged (stern).

Armour (Krupp) :
12″ Belt (amidships) ...... *aaa*
6″ Belt (forward) (N.C.) *b*
4″ Belt (aft) (N.C.) ...... *d*
2″ Deck (slopes) ....
Protection to vitals ... = *aaaa*
14″ Barbettes (N.C.) ...... *aaaa*
8″Turrets to these(K.C) = *aaa*
8″ Lower deck side ...... *aa*
7″ Secondary turrets (N.C.) *a*
12″ Conning tower(N.C.) *aaa*

LORD NELSON.   *Photo, Symonds.*

Ahead
2—12
4—9·2

LORD NELSON.

Astern
2—12
4—9·2

Broadside : 4—12 in., 5—9·2 in.

Machinery : 2 sets 4 cylinder vertical triple expansion. 2 screws. Boilers : 15 Yarrow or Babcock. Designed H.P. 16,750 = 18·5 kts. Coal : *normal* 900 tons ; *maximum* 2000 tons : also 400 tons oil.

Gunnery Notes.—Big guns, central pivot mountings. Hoists, electric or hand all guns. Guns manœuvred hydraulic and hand gear. The 9·2 inch double turrets are not regarded as being anything like so satisfactory a design as the single 9·2 inch single turrets in earlier types.
Arcs of fire : 12 inch, 240°.
Torpedo Notes.—1904 model torpedoes. Complete electrical installation. 8 search-lights.
Engineering Notes.—Average cost of machinery, £213,000.

Name.	Builder	Machinery	Laid down	Com-pleted	Last refit	Trials		Boilers	Best recent speed
Lord Nelson	Palmer	Palmer	Nov., '04	1908	...	...	17,415 = 18·9	Babcock	19
Agamemnon	Beardmore	Hawthorn Leslie	Oct., '04	1907	...	...	17,285 = 18·8	Yarrow	18·9

General Notes.—Estimates 1904-05. Estimated cost about £1,500,000 per ship. Designed by Sir P. Watts. These ships have an abnormally small tactical diameter and can practically spin round on their sterns. They heel considerably in doing so. In appearance they are quite unlike other British ships and have a distinctly French look.

LORD NELSON   AGAMEMNON

Photo, Oscar Parkes, Esq.

1902 BRITISH BATTLESHIPS (18-19 knot).

(KING EDWARD CLASS—8 SHIPS).

COMMONWEALTH (May, 1903), **KING EDWARD** (July, 1903), **DOMINION** (August, 1903), **HINDUSTAN** (December, 1903), **ZEALANDIA** (*ex New Zealand*), (February, 1904), **HIBERNIA** (June, 1905), **AFRICA** (May, 1905) and **BRITANNIA** (December, 1904).

Normal displacement, 16350 tons. *Full load*, 17,500 tons. Complement, 777.
Length (*waterline*), 439 feet. *Beam*, 78 feet. *Mean draught*, 26¾ feet. *Length over all*, 453¾ feet.

Guns:
4—12in. IX, 40 cal. (*AAAA*)
4—9·2 in., IX, 45 cal. (*AA*)
10—6 in., VII.
12—12 pdr.
14—3 pdr.
2 Maxims.
Torpedo tubes
(18 inch):
4 *submerged*
(broadside).
1 *submerged* (stern)

Armour (Krupp):
9″ Belt (amidships) .... *aa*
6—2″ Belt (forward) .... *a-f*
2″ Deck (slopes) ....
Protection to vitals ....= *aaa*
12″ Barbettes (N.C.) .... *aaa*
8″ Turrets to these (K.C.) = *aaa*
8″ Lower deck side .... *aa*
7″ Battery .... *a*
7″ Secondary turrets .... *a*
12″ Conning tower .... *aaa*

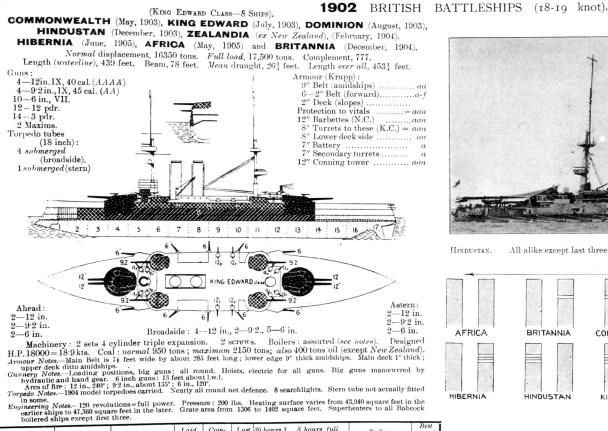

HINDUSTAN. All alike except last three, which have a double top on foremast and top mast abaft. *Photo, Cr*

Ahead:
2—12 in.
2—9·2 in.
2—6 in.

Astern:
2—12 in.
2—9·2 in.
2—6 in.

Broadside: 4—12 in., 2—9·2 in., 5—6 in.

Machinery: 2 sets 4 cylinder triple expansion. 2 screws. Boilers: assorted (*see notes*). Designed H.P. 18000 = 18·9 kts. Coal: *normal* 950 tons; *maximum* 2150 tons; *also* 400 tons oil (except *New Zealand*).
Armour Notes.—Main Belt is 7½ feet wide by about 285 feet long; lower edge 9″ thick amidships. Main deck 1″ thick; upper deck ditto amidships.
Gunnery Notes.—Loading positions, big guns: all round. Hoists, electric for all guns. Big guns manœuvred by hydraulic and hand gear. 6 inch guns: 13 feet about l.w.l.
Arcs of fire: 12 in., 240°; 9·2 in., about 135°; 6 in., 120°.
Torpedo Notes.—1904 model torpedoes carried. Nearly all round net defence. 8 searchlights. Stern tube not actually fitted in some.
Engineering Notes.—120 revolutions = full power. Pressure: 200 lbs. Heating surface varies from 43,940 square feet in the earlier ships to 47,360 square feet in the later. Grate area from 1306 to 1402 square feet. Superheaters to all Babcock boilered ships except first three.

AFRICA | BRITANNIA | COMMONWEALTH | DOMINION

HIBERNIA | HINDUSTAN | KING EDWARD

LAST THREE | FIRST F

HIBERNIA, AFRICA and BRITAN
All alike except that *Africa* has
standard compass.

Name.	Builder.	Machinery.	Laid down.	Com-pleted.	Last refit	30 hours ½ power.	8 hours full power.	Boilers.	Best recent speed.
Commonwealth	Fairfield	Fairfield	June '02	1905	1907	12,769 = 17·9	18,538 = 19·01	16 Babcock	18·7
King Edward	Devonport	Harland & W.	Mar. '02	1905	1907	12,884 = 17·5	18,138 = 19·04	10 Babcock, 6 Cyl.	19·1
Dominion	Vickers	Vickers	May '02	1905	1907	12,843 = 18·3	18,439 = 19·35	16 Babcock	18·2
Hindustan	Clydebank	Clydebank	Oct. '02	1905	1907	12,926 = 17·7	18,521 = 19·08	18 Babcock, 3 Cyl.	18·7
Zealandia	Portsmouth	Humphrys & T.	Feb. '03	1905	1907	12,981 = 16·9	18,440 = 18·6	12 Niclausse, 3 Cyl.	18·9
Africa	Clydebank	Clydebank	Jan. '04	1906	1907	12,860 = 17·5°	18,624 = 18·95°	Babcock	18·2
Britannia	Portsmouth	Humphrys & T.	Feb. '04	1906	1907	13,087 = 16·8	18,725 = 18·74	Babcock & Cyl.	17·5
Hibernia	Devonport	Harland & W.	Jan. '04	1906	1907	12,700 = 15·5	18,112 = 18·12°	Babcock	18·8

All were light on first trials

Class distinction.—To be recognised at once by rig and by the enormous funnels. No after-bridge.

General Notes.—Tactical diameter very small, about 310 yards at 15 knots. Extremely handy. Cost per ship about £1,. The last British battleships designed by Sir William White. Estimates '01-'02, (3 ships), '02-'03, (2 ships), and '03-'04, (3 ships).

Coal consumption: Averages 11 tons an hour at 12,000 H.P., and from 15½-18 tons at full power. The Babcock boilered fitted with superheaters are considerably more economical than those not to be fitted. Economical speed: about 16 kts.

The ships cost about £120,000 per annum each to maintain with full crews; and £60,000 with two-thirds crews.
General Notes—King Edward VII mined off N. Scotland coast Jan. 1916 and Britannia torpedoed by U-boat off Cape Trafalgar 9 Nov. 1918.

1902 BRITISH BATTLESHIPS (20 knot).

SWIFTSURE & TRIUMPH (January, 1903).
(Purchased from Chili, 1903).
Normal displacement, 11,800 tons. Complement, 700.
Length (*waterline*), 458 feet; *Beam*, 71 feet; *Maximum draught*, 24¾ feet; *Length (over all)* 470 feet.

Guns:
4—10 inch, 45 cal. (*AAA*).
14—7·5 inch, II, 50 cal. (*A*).
14—14 pdr.
1—12 pdr., 8 cwt.
4—6 pdr.
4 Maxims.
Torpedo tubes (Elswick, 18 in.):
2 *submerged*.

Armour (Krupp):
7″ Belt (amidships) ... *a*
3″ Belt (ends) ... *e*
10″ Bulkheads .... *aaa*
1½″ Deck (amidships) ...
Protection to vitals ...= *aa*
3″ Deck (outside citadel)
10″ Barbettes .... *aa*
8″—6″ Turrets (K.C.) = *aaa-aa*
6″ Lower deck............ *a*
7″ Battery................. *a*
7″ Casemates (4) (N.C.) *a*
10″ Conning tower ...... *aa*
(*Total weight:* about 3200 tons).

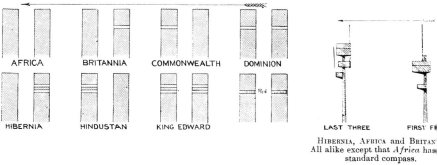

SWIFTSURE. *Photo, Symonds.*

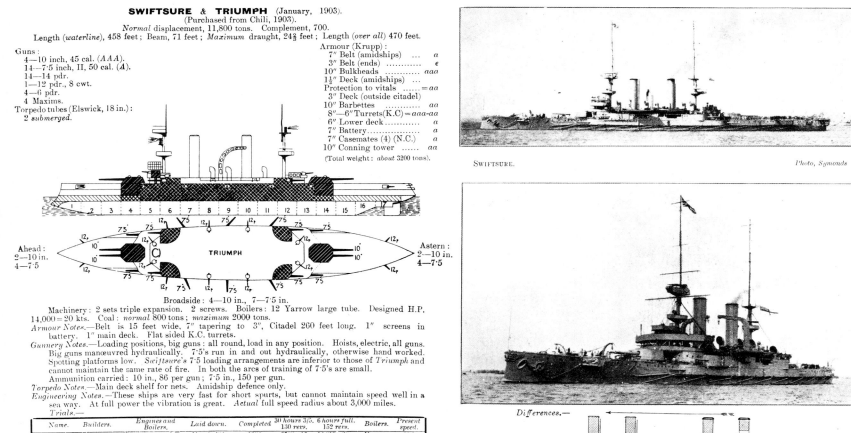

Ahead:
2—10 in.
4—7·5

Astern:
2—10 in.
4—7·5

TRIUMPH

Broadside: 4—10 in., 7—7·5 in.

Machinery: 2 sets triple expansion. 2 screws. Boilers: 12 Yarrow large tube. Designed H.P. 14,000 = 20 kts. Coal: *normal* 800 tons; *maximum* 2000 tons.
Armour Notes.—Belt is 15 feet wide, 7″ tapering to 3″, Citadel 260 feet long. 1″ screens in battery. 1″ main deck. Flat sided K.C. turrets.
Gunnery Notes.—Loading positions, big guns: all round, load in any position. Hoists, electric, all guns. Big guns manœuvred hydraulically. 7·5's run in and out hydraulically, otherwise hand worked. Spotting platforms low. *Swiftsure's* 7·5 loading arrangements are inferior to those of *Triumph* and cannot maintain the same rate of fire. In both the arcs of training of 7·5's are small.
Ammunition carried: 10 in., 86 per gun; 7·5 in., 150 per gun.
Torpedo Notes.—Main deck shelf for nets. Amidship defence only.
Engineering Notes.—These ships are very fast for short spurts, but cannot maintain speed well in a sea way. At full power the vibration is great. *Actual* full speed radius about 3,000 miles.
Trials.—

Name.	Builders.	Engines and Boilers.	Laid down.	Completed.	30 hours 3/5. 130 revs.	6 hours full. 152 revs.	Boilers.	Present speed.
Swiftsure	Elswick	Humphrys and T.	March, '02	1904	8700 = 17	14,018 = 20	Yarrow	19·1
Triumph	Vickers	Vickers	March, '02	1904		14,090 = 20·17	Yarrow	19·3

Coal consumption averages at 10,000 H.P. 9 tons per hour; at 14,000 H.P. (20 kts.) 12—13 tons per hour. Both ships tended to be "coal eaters" originally, but in service have proved very fairly economical as a rule. In 1907 manœuvres both ships averaged about 18 kts.
General Notes.—Purchased from Chili for £949,900 each. Scantlings much lighter than in normal British ships. Designed by Sir E. J. Reed.

"Triumph torpedoed off Gallipoli, May 1915."

Differences.—

SWIFTSURE
Higher cowls.
Bow scroll.
Very conspicuous fire controls.

TRIUMPH
Low cowls.
No bow scroll.

1901 BRITISH BATTLESHIPS

(QUEEN CLASS—2 SHIPS).

QUEEN (March, 1902) & **PRINCE OF WALES** (March, 1902).

Displacement, 15,000 tons. Complement, 750 (flagship, 789).

Length (waterline), 411 feet. Beam, 75 feet. Maximum draught, 29 feet. Length over all, 430 feet.

Guns :
4—12 inch, IX, 40 cal. (AAAA)
12—6 inch, VII, 45 cal.
16—12 pdr., 12 cwt.
2—12 pdr., 8 cwt.
6—3 pdr.
2 Maxims.
Torpedo tubes (18 inch) :
4 submerged.
(Total weight with ammunition 1200 tons.)

Armour (Krupp) :
9″ Belt (amidships) ....aa
6″—2″ Belt (bow)..............a-f
12″ After bulkhead ....aaa
3″ Armour deck...................
Protection to vitals ....=aaa
12″ Barbettes ....aaa
10″—8″ Turrets (K.C) = aaa-aa
6″ Casemates (12) (N.C.) ...... b
12″ Conning tower (N.C.) ...aaa
(Total weight 4295 tons).

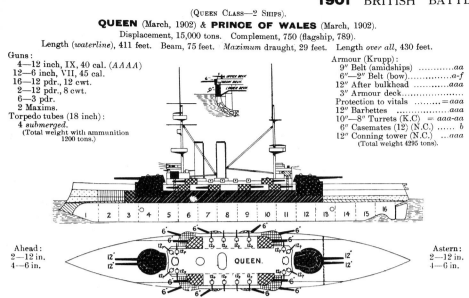

QUEEN.   Photo, Symonds.

Broadside : 4—12 in., 6—6 in.

Ahead :
2—12 in.
4—6 in.

Astern :
2—12 in.
4—6 in.

QUEEN   PRINCE OF WALES

Machinery : 2 sets 3 cylinder vertical inverted triple expansion. 2 screws. Boilers : Queen, 15 Babcock, Prince of Wales, 20 Belleville. Designed H.P. 15,000=18 kts. Coal : normal 900 tons ; maximum 2100 tons.

Armour Notes.—Belt is 15 feet wide by 300 feet long, from bow. Flat-sided turrets, K.C.

Gunnery Notes.—Loading positions, big guns : all round. Hoist, for 6 inch, electric. Big guns manœuvred by hydraulic gear. Arcs of fire : Big guns, 260° ; secondary guns, 120°. Fire control fitted or fitting as plan. Ammunition carried : 12 in., 80 rounds per gun ; 6 in., 200 per gun.

Torpedo Notes.—Main deck shelf for nets. Defence almost all round. 2 torpedo launches carried. 8 searchlights.

Engineering Notes.—Pressure 300 lbs. at boilers, reduced to 250 at engines. Heating surface, Queen 38,400 sq. feet ; Prince of Wales 37,000 sq. feet.

Name.	Built at	Engines & Boilers by	Laid down	Completed	30 hours 4/5 power. 101 revs.	8 hours full power. 110 revs.	Boilers.	Speed last sea trial.
Queen	Devonport	Harland & Wolff	March, '01	1904	11,670=16·97	15,556=18·39	Babcock	18
Prince of Wales	Chatham	Greenock Foundry	March, '01	1904	11,669=17·04	15,364=18·45	Belleville	18

Coal consumption in service : Averages 9 tons an hour at 10,000 H.P. (15 kts.), 12—14 at 15,000 H.P. (18 kts.). On first trials the Queen was the more economical of the two especially at mean powers

General Notes.—Very handy ships. Slightly improved Londons. Open 12 pdr. batteries and kidney-shaped fighting tops. Cost per ship averaged just over £1,000,000.

Class distinctions.—Kidney-shape lower tops. Open 12 pdr. battery. Flat-sided turrets. No scuttles to lower deck forward.

1898 BRITISH BATTLESHIPS (19 knot).

(DUNCAN CLASS—5 SHIPS.)

RUSSELL (February, 1901), **ALBEMARLE** (March, 1901), **DUNCAN** (March, 1901), **CORNWALLIS** (July, 1901), **EXMOUTH** (August, 1901).

Normal displacement, 14,000 tons. Complement, 750 (flagships 778).

Length (waterline), 418 feet. Beam, 75½ feet. Maximum draught, 27¼ feet. Length over all, 429 feet.

Guns :
4—12 inch, IX. (AAAA).
12—6 inch, VII.
12—12 pdr.
6—3 pdr.
2 Maxims.
Torpedo tubes (18 inch) :
4 submerged.

Armour (Krupp) :
7″ Belt (amidships) ...... a
5″—3″ Belt (bow)........ b-c
1½″ Belt (aft) ....
2½″ Deck (on slopes) ...
Protection to vitals ......=aa
11″ Barbettes (N.C.) ...... aa
6″ Turrets (K.C.).........=aa
6″ Casemates (12) ...... b
12″ Conning tower ......aaa
(Total weight about 3500 tons.)

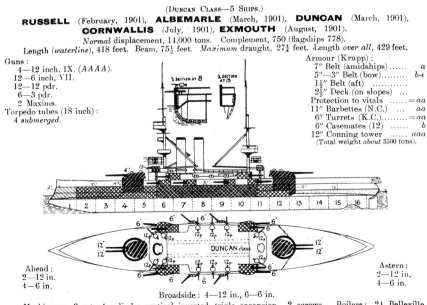

Broadside : 4—12 in., 6—6 in.

Ahead :
2—12 in.
4—6 in.

Astern :
2—12 in.
4—6 in.

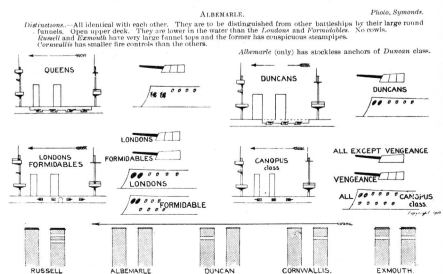

ALBEMARLE.   Photo, Symonds.

Distinctions.—All identical with each other. They are to be distinguished from other battleships by their large round funnels. Open upper deck. They are lower in the water than the Londons and Formidables. No cowls. Russell and Exmouth have very large funnel tops and the former has conspicuous steampipes. Cornwallis has smaller fire controls than the others.

Albemarle (only) has stockless anchors of Duncan class.

QUEENS   DUNCANS   DUNCANS

LONDONS

LONDONS FORMIDABLES   FORMIDABLES   CANOPUS class   ALL EXCEPT VENGEANCE

LONDONS   VENGEANCE

FORMIDABLE   ALL CANOPUS class

Machinery : 2 sets 4 cylinder vertical inverted triple expansion. 2 screws. Boilers : 24 Belleville.

Coal : normal 900 tons ; maximum 2000 tons. Designed H.P. 18,000=19 kts. Nominal radius 7,200 at 10 kts.

Armour Notes.—Main belt is 14 feet wide by 285 feet long ; lower edge is full thickness. Flat-sided turrets (K.C.)

Gunnery Notes.—Loading positions, big guns : all round. Hoists, for 6 inch, electric and hand. Big guns manœuvred by hydraulic gear. Fire control stations fitted 1905-6.

Arcs of fire : 12 in., 240° ; 6 in., 120°.

Engineering Notes.—Machinery, etc., weighs 1580 tons.

Name.	Builder.	Engines by	Laid down	Completed	Last big Refit.	30 hours at 4/5.	8 hours full.	Boilers.	Last recorded best speed.
Russell	Palmer	Palmer	March, '99	1903	—	13,695=17·95	18,222=19·3	Belleville	19·8
Duncan	Thames I.W.	Thames I.W.	July, '99	1903	—	13,717=18·1	18,232=19·11	Belleville	20·1
Cornwallis	Thames I.W.	Thames I.W.	July, '99	1904	—	13,691=17·91	18,238=18·98°	Belleville	19·56
Exmouth	Laird	Laird	Aug. '99	1903	—	13,774=18	18,346=19·03	Belleville	20·0
Albemarle	Chatham	Thames I.W.	Jan., '00	1903	'09	13,587=17·2°	*18,296=18·6	Belleville	19·8

°Run in bad weather.

Coal consumption averages 2¾ tons an hour at 10 kts.; at 13,000 H.P. (17 kts.) about 10¾ tons an hour ; at 18,000 H.P. (19 kts.) about 15 tons an hour or less. All these ships are excellent steamers, and make or exceed their speeds in almost any weather. Boilers are of 1900 pattern.

General Notes.—The ships are proving very passable sea boats. Hull without armour weighs 9055 tons. Cost per ship, complete, just over £1,000,000. Very handy. Montagu, of this class, wrecked on Lundy, 1906.

Russell mined off Malta May 1916.
Cornwallis sunk by U-boat off Malta Jan. 1917.

1898 BRITISH BATTLESHIPS.—(18 knot)

(LONDON CLASS—3 SHIPS).

LONDON (Sept., 1899), **BULWARK** (Oct., 1899), **VENERABLE** (Nov., 1899).

Displacement, 15,000 tons. Complement, 750 (flagship, 789).

Length (waterline), 411 feet. Beam, 75 feet. Maximum draught, 29 feet. Length over all, 430 feet.

Guns :
1—12 inch, IX., 40 cal. (AAAA).
12—6 inch, VII., 45 cal.
16—12 pdr., 12 cwt.
2—12 pdr., 8 cwt.
6—3 pdr.
2 Maxims.
Torpedo tubes (18 inch) :
4 submerged.
(Total weight with ammunition, 1200 tons).

Armour (Krupp) :
9″ Belt (amidships) .... aa
6″—2″ Belt (bow) .... a-f
12″ After bulkhead .... aaa
3″ Armour deck...............
Protection to vitals ....=aaa
12″ Barbettes .... aaa
10″—8″ Turrets (K.C.) ...aaa-aa
6″ Casemates (12) (N.C.) ... b
12″ Conning tower (N.C.) ... aaa
(Total weight 4295 tons).

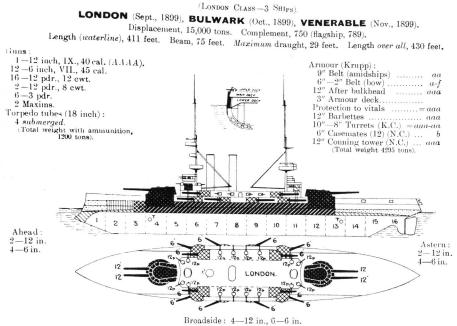

Ahead :
2—12 in.
4—6 in.

LONDON

Astern :
2—12 in.
4—6 in.

Broadside : 4—12 in., 6—6 in.

LONDON.   Photo, Symonds.

Machinery : 2 sets 3 cylinder vertical inverted triple expansion. 2 screws. Boilers : 20 Belleville. Designed H.P. 15,000 = 18 kts. Coal : normal 900 tons ; maximum 2100 tons.

Armour Notes.—Belt is 15 feet wide by 300 feet long, from bow. Flat sided K.C. turrets.

Gunnery Notes.—Loading positions, big guns : all round. Hoist, for 6 inch, electric. Big guns manœuvred, hydraulic gear. Arcs of fire : Big guns, 260° ; secondary guns, 120°.
Ammunition carried : 12 in., 80 rounds per gun ; 6 in. 200 per gun.

Torpedo Notes.—Main deck shelf for nets. Defence almost all round. 2 torpedo launches carried. 6 searchlights.

Engineering Notes.—Pressure, 300 lbs. at boilers, reduced to 250 at engines. Heating surface, 37,000 square feet.

Differences.—

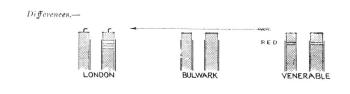

LONDON   BULWARK   VENERABLE

Name.	Built at	Engines by	Laid down	Completed	Last Refit.	30 hours 4/5 power. 161 revs.	8 hours full power. 116 revs.	Boilers.	Speed last sea trial.
London	Portsmouth	Earle	Dec. '98	1902	'08-'09	11,718=16·4	15,261=18·10	Belleville	17·75
Bulwark	Devonport	Hawthorn Leslie	March, '99	1902	nil	11,755=16·8	15,353=18·15	Belleville	18·5
Venerable	Chatham	Maudslay	Nov. '99	1902	'08-'09	11,364=16·8	15,345=18·40	Belleville	18·3

Coal consumption in service : Averages 8¼ tons an hour at 10,000 H.P. (15 kts.), 11¾ at 15,000 H.P. (18 kts.).

General Notes.—Very handy ships   Cost per ship averaged just over £1,000,000.

"Bulwark sunk by internal explosion Nov. 1914."

1898 BRITISH BATTLESHIPS (18 knot).

(FORMIDABLE CLASS—3 SHIPS).

FORMIDABLE (Nov. 1898), **IRRESISTIBLE** (Dec. 1898), & **IMPLACABLE** (March, 1899).

Displacement, 15,000 tons. Complement, 780 (flagship 810).

Length (waterline), 411 feet. Beam, 75 feet. Maximum draught, 29 feet. Length over all, 430 feet.

Guns :
4—12 in., IX, 40 cal. (AAAA)
12—6 in., VII, 45 cal.
16—12 pdr., 12 cwt.
2—12 pdr., 8 cwt.
6—3 pdr.
2 Maxims.
Torpedo tubes (18 inch) :
4 submerged.
(Total weight with ammunition, 1200 tons).

Armour (Krupp) :
9″ Belt (amidships) .... aa
2″ Belt (bow) .... f
1½″ Belt (aft) .... f
12″ Bulkheads .... aaa
3″ Deck (on slopes) ....
Protection to vitals ....=aaa
12″ Barbettes (N.C.) .... aaa
10″—8″ Turrets (N.C.) =aaa-aa
6″ Casemates (12) (N.C.) ... b
12″ Conning tower (N.C.) ... aaa
(Total weight about 4300 tons).

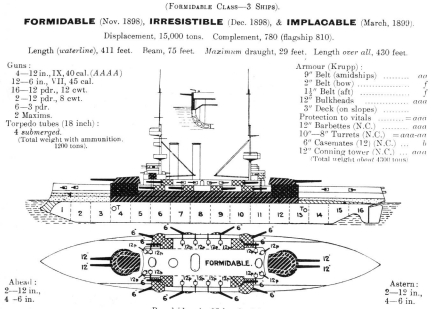

Ahead :
2—12 in.,
4—6 in.

FORMIDABLE.

Astern :
2—12 in.,
4—6 in.

Broadside : 4—12 in., 6—6 in.

IMPLACABLE.   Photo, Symonds.

Machinery : 2 sets 3 cylinder vertical inverted triple expansion. 2 screws. Boilers : 20 Belleville. Designed H.P. 15,000 = 18 kts. Coal : normal 900 tons ; maximum 2200 tons.

Armour Notes.—Belt is 15 feet wide by 216 feet long ; 2″ continuation to bow ; lower edge is normal thickness. Curved turrets of K.N.C.

Gunnery Notes. and Torpedo Notes.—As for later Formidables, previous page.

Engineering Notes.—(See also later Formidables).

Differences—

FORMIDABLE   IMPLACABLE   IRRESISTABLE

Name.	Built at	Engines & Boilers by	Laid down.	Completed	Refit	30 hours 4/5 power.	8 hours full power.	Boilers.	Speed last sea trial.
Formidable	Portsmouth	Earle	March, '98	1901	'08-'09	11,618=17·15	15,511=18·13	Belleville	18·4
Irresistible	Chatham	Maudslay	April, '98	1902	nil	11,626=17·5	15,603=18·20	Belleville	18·5
Implacable	Devonport	Laird	July, '98	1902	'08-'09	11,618=16·81	15,244=18·22	Belleville	18·7

Coal consumption in service averages 8 tons an hour, at 10,000 H.P. (15 kts.), 11½ tons at 15,000 H.P. (18 kts.)

General Notes.—Very handy ships, answer the least touch of helm. Average cost just over £1,000,000 per ship.

Formidable sunk by U-boat off Portland Jan. 1915.
Irristible sunk by U-boat off Gallipoli Mar. 1915.

Class distinctions :—

Formidable London Queen	Fore funnel close to foremast and smaller than after.	Oval turrets. No scuttles lower deck forward. Flat-sided turrets. Open upper deck. Flat-sided turrets.
Duncan	Funnels as in Formidable, but equal sized and big.	Slightly smaller ship. Open upper deck. Flat-sided turrets.
Canopus	Funnels close together, and more amidships.	Shorter masts, closer together, ship lower in water, and generally smaller. Oval turrets.

1896 BRITISH BATTLESHIPS (18¼ knot).

(CANOPUS CLASS—6 SHIPS).

CANOPUS (October, 1897), **GOLIATH** (March, 1898), **ALBION** (June, 1898), **OCEAN** (July, 1898), **GLORY** (March, 1899), *also* **VENGEANCE** (July, 1899).

Displacement, 12,950 tons. Complement, 750 (flagship 780).

Length (*waterline*), 400 feet. Beam, 74 feet. *Maximum* draught, 26½ feet. Length *over all*, 418 feet.

Guns:
- 4—12 inch, VIII, 35 cal. (*AAA*)
- 12—6 inch, *wire*, 40 cal.
- 10—12 pdr., 12 cwt.
- 2—12 pdr., 8 cwt. boat.
- 6—3 pdr.
- 2 Maxims.

Torpedo tubes (18 inch):
- 4 *submerged*.

(Total weight, with ammunition, 1000 tons).

Armour (Harvey-nickel):
- 6″ Belt (amidships) ... b
- 2″ Belt (bow) .... f
- 1½″ Belt (aft) .... f
- 12″ Bulkheads ...... aaa
- 2½″ Deck (on slopes)
- Protection to vitals ... = a
- 12″ Barbettes...... aaa-aa
- 8″ Turrets to these...
- 5″ Casemates (12) ... c
- 12″ Conning tower ... aaa

(Total weight, *about* 3600 tons).

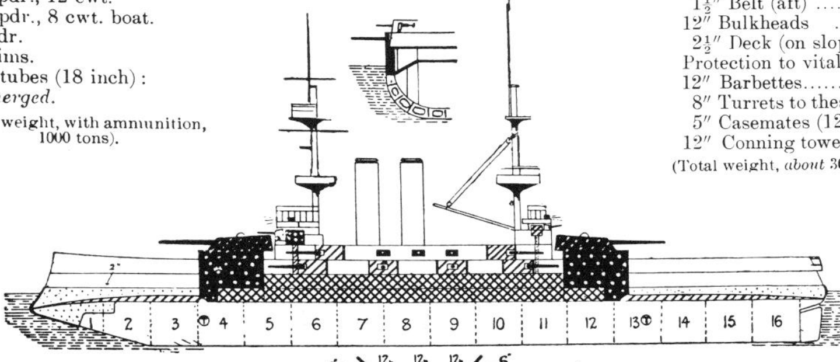

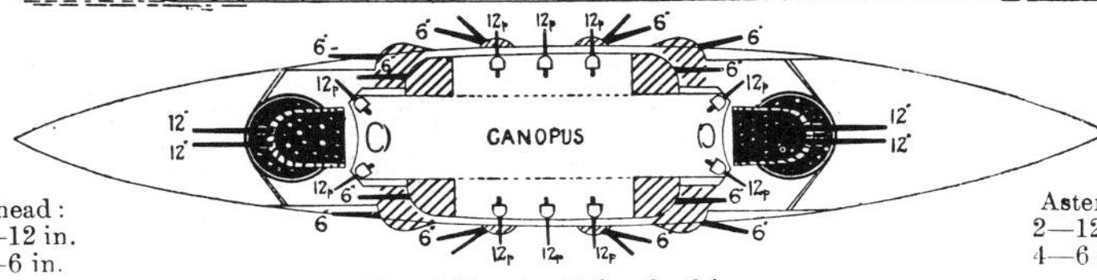

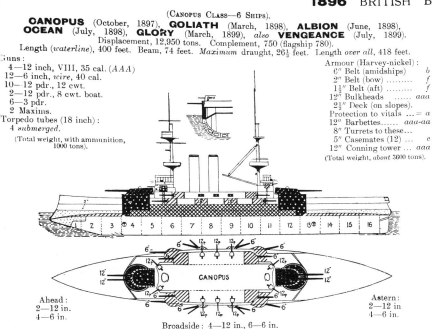

Ahead:
2—12 in.
4—6 in.

Astern:
2—12 in
4—6 in.

Broadside: 4—12 in., 6—6 in.

Machinery: 2 sets 3 cylinder vertical inverted triple expansion. 2 screws. Boilers: 20 Belleville. Designed H.P. 13,500 = 18·25 kts. Coal: *normal* 1000 tons; *maximum* 2300 tons.

Armour Notes.—Belt is 14 feet wide by 210 feet long. Barbettes circular, the thickness given being the maximum. Belt is normal thickness at lower edge. Weight of side armour only, 1740 tons. Main deck 1″ steel. Barbettes 37 feet in diameter. Circular turrets (H.N.)

Gunnery Notes.—Loading positions, big guns: all round. *Vengeance's* load in any position also. Big guns manœuvred: hydraulic and hand gear, Hoists, for 6 inch, electric and hand. Fitting with fire control stations as plan.

Arcs of fire: Big guns, 260°; casemates, 120°.

Torpedo Notes.—Net defence amidships; stowage on shelf at main deck level. Electric machinery: 3 dynamos, 8 electric fans for ventilation.

Name	Built at	Engines and boilers by	Laid down	Completed	Last Refit	30 hours 4/5. 99-102 revs.	8 hours full power. 107-110 revs.	Boilers.	Best recent speed.
Canopus	Portsmouth	Greenock Fdy.	Jan., '97	1900	'07	10,454 = 17·2	13,763 = 18·5	Belleville	16·5
Goliath	Chatham	Penn	Jan., '97	1900	'07	10,413 = 17·3	13,918 = 18·4	Belleville	
Albion	Thames I.W.	Maudslay	Dec., '96	1902	'06	10,809 = 16·8*	13,885 = 17·8*	Belleville	18·2
Ocean	Devonport	Hawthorn Leslie	Feb., '97	1900	'10	10,314 = 16·2	13,728 = 18·5	Belleville	17·8
Glory	Laird	Laird	Dec., '96	1901	'07	10,587 = 16·8	13,745 = 18·1	Belleville	17·6
Vengeance	Vickers	Vickers	Aug., '97	1901	'05	10,387 = 17·2	13,852 = 18·5	Belleville	18

* Run in a gale.

Coal consumption averages: 9 tons an hour at 10,000 H.P. (16·5 kts.), 12½ tons at 13,500 H.P. (18·25 kts.)

In 1907 manœuvres *Vengeance* and *Ocean*, in the chase, beat all the *King Edward* class except *King Edward*; but the ships are getting worn out, and few can now steam well except for short spurts.

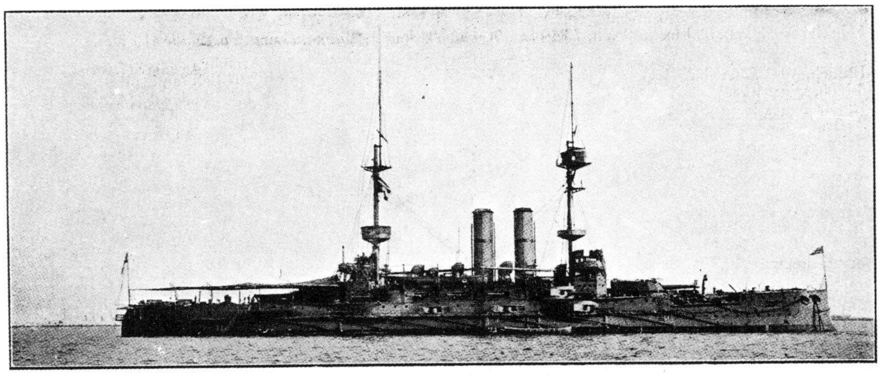

VENGEANCE.

Differences.—

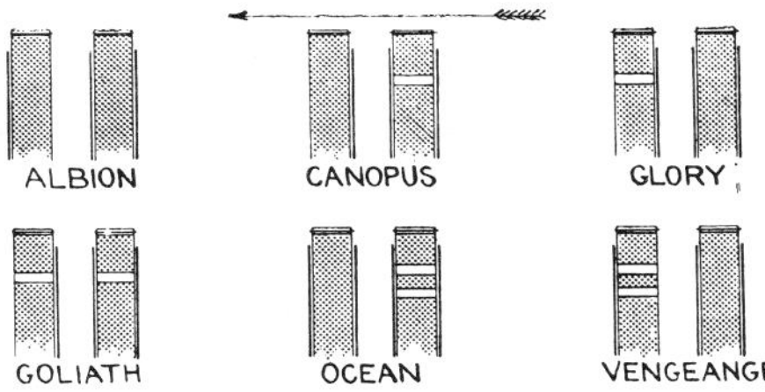

For identifications of class from *Formidables* and *Duncans* see *Formidable* class.

Albion has specially large fire control on fore.

Engineering Notes.—70 revolutions = 12½ kts. Boilers: 15—9 element generators, and 5—8 element generators. Total heating surface (including economisers), 33,700 square feet. Grate area 1055 feet. Pressure, 300 lbs., reduced to 250 lbs. at engines. Distilling machinery: 2 evaporators, capacity 68 tons per 24 hours. Distillers produce 40 tons per day. Auxiliary engines: 4 air compressing, 2 boat hoists, 2 refrigerating, 2 coal hoists, 5 blowing, 2 steam fans. Funnels 11 feet in diameter. Height above furnace bars, 90 feet. Screws: 4 bladed. Diameter of cylinders 30 in., 49 in., and 80 in. Stroke 51 in.

General Notes.—Tactical diameter, extreme helm at 15 kts. 450 yards; with the engines, 350 yards. Cost, *complete*, about £900,000 per ship. Maintenance cost, in full commission, about £94,000 per annum per ship.

1894 BRITISH BATTLESHIPS (16½ knot).

(MAJESTIC CLASS—9 SHIPS).

MAGNIFICENT (December, 1894), **MAJESTIC** (January, 1895), **HANNIBAL** (April, 1895), **PRINCE GEORGE** (August, 1895), **VICTORIOUS** (October, 1895), **JUPITER** (November, 1895), **MARS** (March, 1896), *also* **CÆSAR** (September, 1896), & **ILLUSTRIOUS** (September, 1896).

Displacement, 14,900 tons. Complement, 757.

Length (*waterline*), 399 feet. Beam, 75 feet. *Maximum* draught, 30 feet. Length *over all*, 413 feet.

Guns:
- 4—12 inch, VIII., 35 cal. (*AAA*)
- 12—6 inch, *wire*, 40 cal.
- 16—12 pdr.
- 12—3 pdr.
- 2 Maxims.
- 2—12 pdr. boat guns.

Torpedo tubes (18 inch):
- 4 *submerged*.
- 1 *above water* (stern).

(Total weight with ammunition, 1500 tons).

(Ammunition only, 355 tons).

Armour (Harvey):
- 9″ Belt (amidships) ... a
- 14″ Bulkheads ...... aa
- 4″ Deck (on slopes)
- Protection to vitals = aaa
- 14″ Barbettes .... aa
- 10″ Turrets to these = aa
- 6″ Casemates (12) ... c
- 14″ Conning tower ... aa

(Total weight 4260 tons).

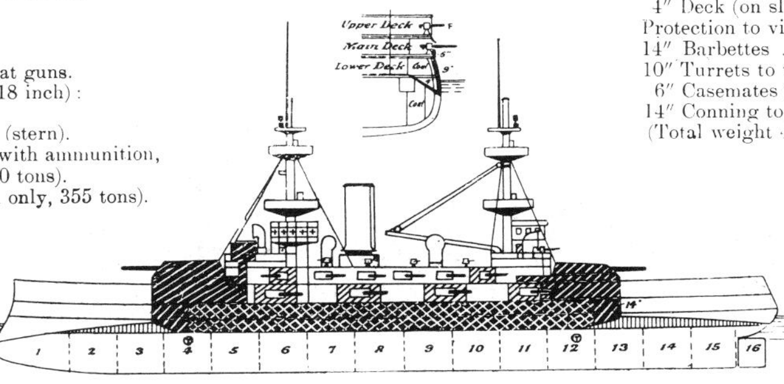

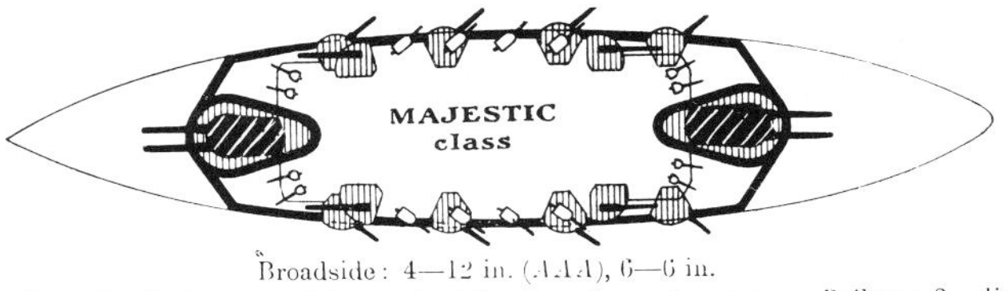

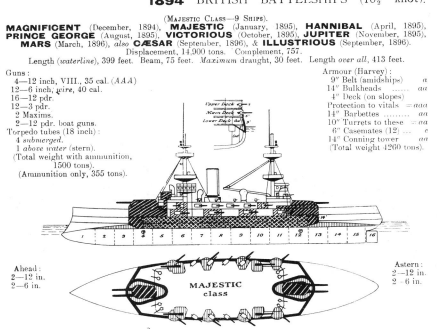

Ahead:
2—12 in.
2—6 in.

Astern:
2—12 in.
2—6 in.

Broadside: 4—12 in. (AAA), 6—6 in.

Machinery: 2 sets 3 cylinder vertical inverted triple expansion. 2 screws. Boilers: 8 cylindrical, with 4 furnaces each. Designed H.P. *natural* 10,000 = 16·5 kts.; *forced* 12,000 = 17·5 kts. Coal: *normal* 1200 tons; *maximum* 2,000 tons (always carried). Oil, 400 tons.

Armour Notes.—Belt is 16 feet wide by 220 feet long. *Cæsar* and *Illustrious* have circular barbettes.

Gunnery Notes.—Loading positions, big guns: all round (end on in first two and all round for a few rounds). Hoists, electric and hand. Big guns manœuvred, hydraulic and hand.

Arcs of fire: Big guns, 260°; Casemates, 120°.

Torpedo Notes.—Midship net defence. Nets stow on main deck shelf in most of the class (all are being so fitted). Two torpedo launches. 6 searchlights.

Engineering Notes.—Machinery and boilers weigh 1,600 tons. 32 furnaces. Heating surface, 24,400 square feet. All fitting or fitted for oil fuel. Screws: 17 feet in diameter, 19¾ feet pitch, 4 bladed. Cylinders: 40, 59 and 88 ins. diameter. Stroke: 51 ins. Pressure: 155 lbs.

Name.	Builder.	Engines by	Laid down	Completed	First trials:— 8 hours nat.	First trials:— 8 hours f. d.	Best recent speed
Magnificent	Chatham	Penn	Dec., '93	1895	10,301 = 16·50	12,157 = 18·4	15·9
Majestic	Portsmouth	Vickers	Feb., '94	1895	10,418 = 16·99	12,097 = 17·9	16·8
Hannibal	Pembroke	Harland & Wolff	April, '94	1897	10,357 = 16·30	12,138 = 18·0	16·2
Prince George	Portsmouth	Humphrys & T.	Sept., '94	1896	10,464 = 16·52	12,253 = 18·3	—
Victorious	Chatham	Hawthorn, L.	May, '94	1897	10,319 = 16·92	12,201 = 18·7	16·4
Jupiter	Clydebank	Clydebank	Oct., '94	1897	10,258 = 15·80	12,475 = 18·4	—
Mars	Laird	Laird	June, '94	1897	10,159 = 15·96	12,434 = 17·7	16·6
Cæsar	Portsmouth	Maudslay	March, '95	1897	10,630 = 16·70	12,652 = 18·7	17
Illustrious	Chatham	Penn	March, '95	1898	10,241 = 15·96	12,112 = 16·5*	16·1

*Bad weather.

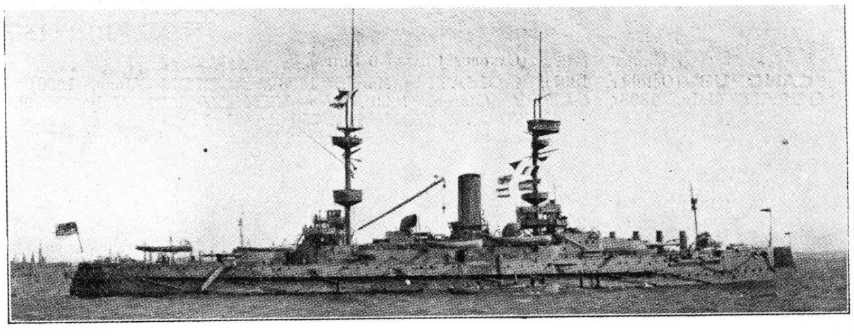

MAGNIFICENT *only*. (Note different rig.) *Photo, Cousens.*

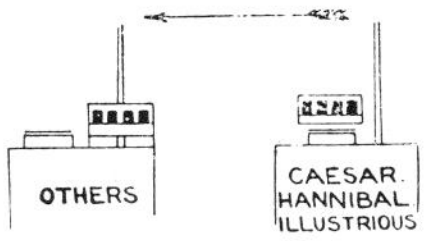

Mars has smaller fire controls than the others.

Cæsar, *Hannibal* and *Illustrious* have the fore-bridge before foremast—the others round about it (*see plan*).

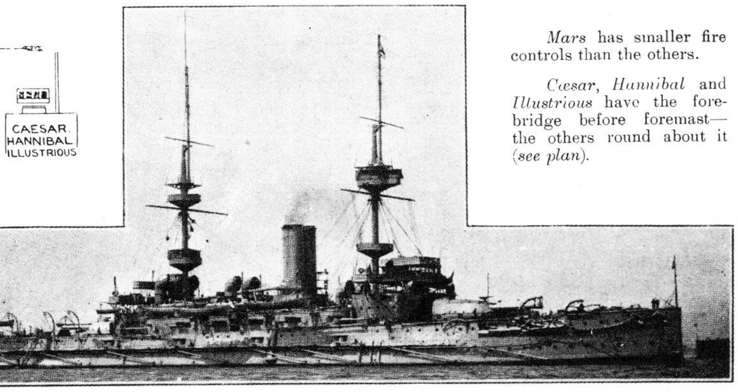

ILLUSTRIOUS. *Photo, Symonds.*

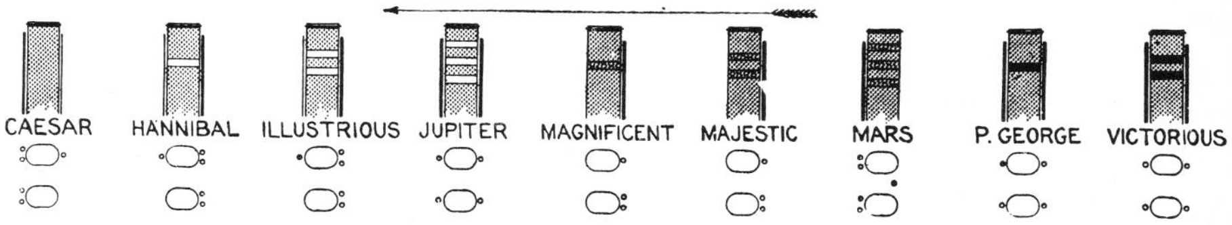

All the ships were *light* on trials and drawing about 2 feet less than the normal. Sea trials run with full coal and stores aboard.

Coal consumption for the class averages: at 8 kts., 1¼ ton an hour; at 8,000 H.P. (15 kts.), 8½ tons; at 10,000 H.P. (16·5 kts.), 10¼ tons. The *Hannibal*, which is the most economical ship, burns somewhat less.

General Notes.—150 w. t. compartments. 208 w. t. doors. Tactical diameter: at 15 kts., 450 yards; with one engine, 350 yards. Ships answer helm very well. Cost nearly £1,000,000 per ship *complete*.

Majestic sunk by U-boat off Gallipoli May 1915

1916 BRITISH CRUISERS.

(COURAGEOUS CLASS—2 Ships).

COURAGEOUS (5th February, 1916), **GLORIOUS** (20th April, 1916).

Normal displacement, *about* 18,600 tons (*about* 22,700 tons *full load*). Complements C. 842. G. 829.

Length $\begin{cases} p.p. & 735 \text{ ft.} \\ o.a. & 786\frac{1}{2} \text{ ft.} \end{cases}$ Beam (outside bulges), 81 ft.   Draughts $\begin{cases} mean & 22\frac{1}{4} \text{ ft.} \\ max. & 26 \text{ ft.} \end{cases}$

Guns :
4—15 inch, 42 cal.
18—4 inch
2—3 inch (anti-aircraft)   } **Dir. Con.**
4—3 pdr.
5 M.G.
(1 landing)
Torpedo tubes (21 in.) :
2 *submerged*
12 *above water* (4 triple deck)

Armour :

Vertical.
3″ Belt (amidships) ...
2″ Belt (within bow) ...
2″ (H.T.) Fore bulkhead
3″—1″ (H.T.) After Bulkhead
1½″ Side over belt ....
7⅞″—3″ Barbettes ....
9″—7″ Gunhouses ....
1″—1½″ Funnel uptakes
2″ C.T. base ....
3″ Tube ....
10″ C.T.
6″ Sighting hood......
3″ Torpedo C.T. (2″ tube)

Armour—continued.

Decks (H.T.)
1″ Forecastle ....
1″ Upper ....
1¾″—¾″ Main (between barbettes) ....
1½″ Lower (stern, flat)
3″ Lower (stern, over rudder) ....
2″ Lower (on slopes) ..
4¼″ Barbettes (since increased) ....
3″ C.T. and sighting hd.
1¾″—¾″ Torpedo C.T.
Torpedo protection (H.T.) :
Modified bulges 25 ft. deep filled with oil fuel ....
1½″—1″ Outer internal screens between barbettes ....
¾″ Inner screen to boiler and engine room vents

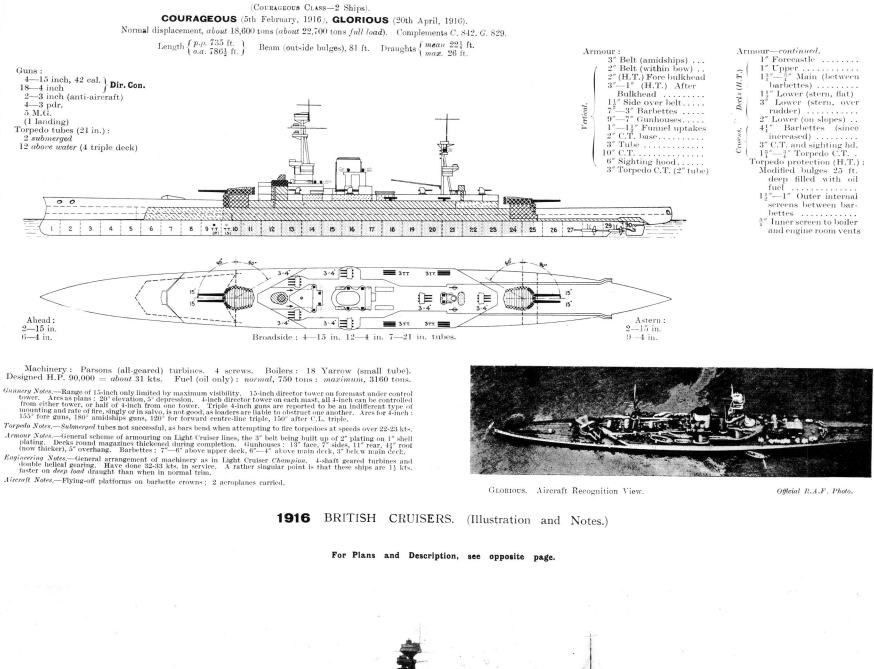

Ahead :
2—15 in.
6—4 in.

Broadside : 4—15 in. 12—4 in. 7—21 in. tubes.

Astern :
2—15 in.
9—4 in.

Machinery : Parsons (all-geared) turbines. 4 screws. Boilers : 18 Yarrow (small tube). Designed H.P. 90,000 = *about* 31 kts. Fuel (oil only) : *normal*, 750 tons : *maximum*, 3160 tons.

Gunnery Notes.—Range of 15-inch only limited by maximum visibility. 15-inch director tower on foremast under control tower. Arcs as plans : 20° elevation, 5° depression. 4-inch director tower on each mast, all 4-inch can be controlled from either tower, or half of 4-inch from one tower. Triple 4-inch guns are reported to be an indifferent type of mounting and rate of fire, singly or in salvo, is not good, as loaders are liable to obstruct one another. Arcs for 4-inch : 155° fore guns, 180° amidships guns, 120° for forward centre-line triple, 150° after C.L. triple.

Torpedo Notes.—*Submerged* tubes not successful, as bars bend when attempting to fire torpedoes at speeds over 22-23 kts.

Armour Notes.—General scheme of armouring on Light Cruiser lines, the 3″ belt being built up of 2″ plating on 1″ shell plating. Decks round magazines thickened during completion. Gunhouses : 13″ face, 7″ sides, 11″ rear, 4¼″ roof (now thicker), 5″ overhang. Barbettes : 7″—6″ above upper deck, 6″—4″ above main deck, 3″ below main deck.

Engineering Notes.—General arrangement of machinery as in Light Cruiser *Champion*. 4-shaft geared turbines and double helical gearing. Have done 32-33 kts. in service. A rather singular point is that these ships are 1½ kts. faster on *deep load* draught than when in normal trim.

Aircraft Notes.—Flying-off platforms on barbette crowns ; 2 aeroplanes carried.

GLORIOUS. Aircraft Recognition View. *Official R.A.F. Photo.*

1916 BRITISH CRUISERS. (Illustration and Notes.)

For Plans and Description, see opposite page.

GLORIOUS.

Photo, Cribb, Southsea.

Name	Builder	Machinery	Begun	Completed	Trials
Courageous	Armstrong	Parsons	May, 1915	Dec., 1916	93,780 = 31·58
Glorious	Harland & Wolff, Belfast	Harland & Wolff	Mar., 1915	Nov., 1916	91,165 = 31·6

General Notes.—Emergency War Programme ships. Design of these ships is said to have been formulated by Admiral of the Fleet Lord Fisher, when First Sea Lord, 1914-15. Their shallow draught is said to have been planned with a view to future operations in the Baltic. In 1915, credits could not be secured for commencing extra Battle Cruisers, taking two years to build. But additional Light Cruisers had been approved, and the opportunity was taken to design these two ships as "Large Light Cruisers." They were designed about January, 1915, and it was intended that they should be finished in a year. Accordingly, the number of big guns and mountings available had to be taken into consideration in planning armament. The twelve months' projected building time was exceeded by six months, as these ships were not commissioned till October, 1916.

The intended Baltic operations having been negatived, a tactical role as "Light Cruiser Destroyers" was assigned to these vessels. The objection is, their end-on fire of two 15-inch guns (when in chase), is too heavy and slow-firing. Against a small and rapidly-moving target, like an enemy Light Cruiser (continually altering her course), two 15-inch guns have only a fair chance of securing hits—but one salvo on the target would probably be decisive.

The lines of these vessels are remarkably fine, the beam at fore barbette being only 71 feet. On her acceptance trials, *Courageous* met heavy weather and was driven hard into a head sea. Her hull became badly strained just before the fore barbette. She was docked and doubling plates added here ; subsequent trials showing that the defect had been overcome. *Glorious* did not develop this weakness, but after twelve months' service she was strengthened in the same way, as a precautionary measure. When running into a head sea, these two ships can easily outstrip destroyers. They are said to have done 35 kts. in service.

These vessels are abnormal in type—so abnormal, they have been dubbed the "Outrageous Class." In 1919, they were laid up in reserve, as their cost of maintenance is very high. It does not appear that they will have a very long life. No figures are available for cost, but they are said to have run to three millions each. A third unit, *Furious*, of slightly modified *Courageous* design, was converted for service as an Aircraft Carrier.

1905 BRITISH CRUISERS (23 knot).

(MINOTAUR CLASS—3 SHIPS.)

MINOTAUR (June, 1906), **DEFENCE** (April, 1907), **SHANNON** (—1906).
Normal displacement, 14,600 tons. Complement, 755.
Length (*waterline*), 520 feet. Beam, 74½ feet. *Maximum* draught, 28 feet. Length *over all*, 525 feet (*p.p.* 490).
(But *Shannon* has 75½ feet beam and a foot less draught.)

Guns :
4—9·2 inch, XI., 50 cal. (A³)
10—7·5 inch, II., 50 cal. (A)
14—12 pdr.
2—12 pdr. Field.
Torpedo tubes (18 inch) :
5 submerged.

Armour (Krupp) :
6" Belt (amidships) .... a
4" Belt (bow) .... d
3" Belt (stern) .... ε
1½"—¾" Deck ....
Protection to vitals .... = aa
7" Barbettes .... a
8"—6" Turrets to these (K.C.) = aa-a
8"—6" Secondary turrets ......aa-a

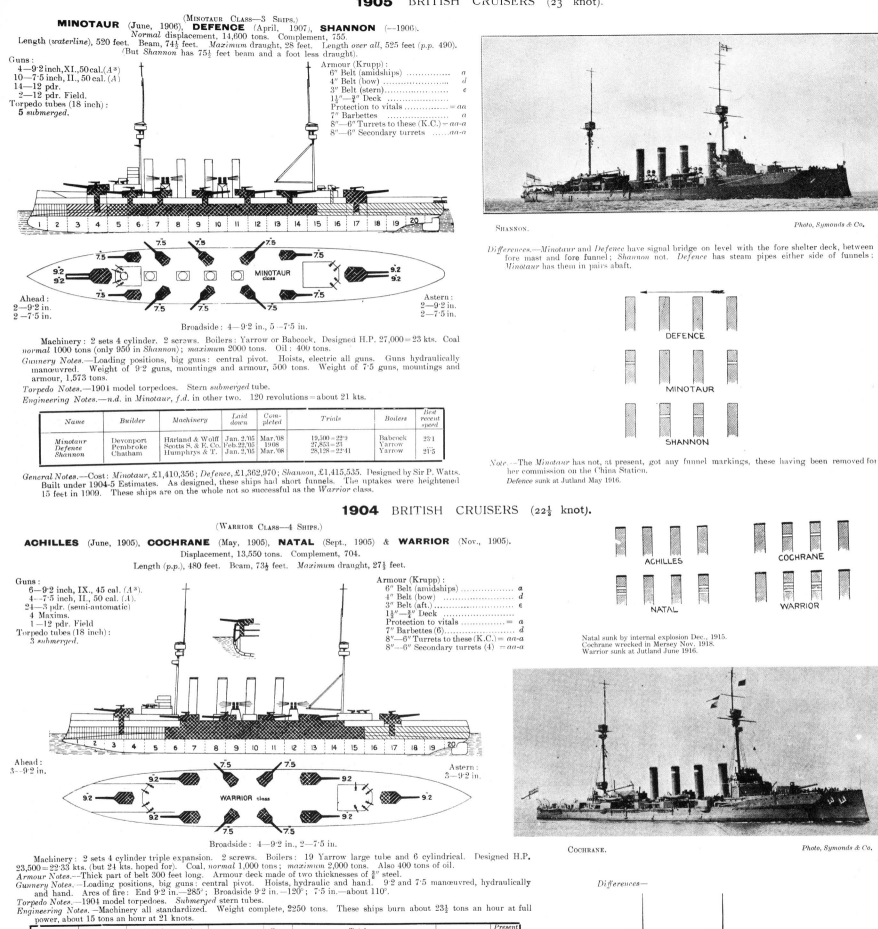

SHANNON.   *Photo, Symonds & Co.*

Differences.—*Minotaur* and *Defence* have signal bridge on level with the fore shelter deck, between fore mast and fore funnel; *Shannon* not. *Defence* has steam pipes either side of funnels: *Minotaur* has them in pairs abaft.

DEFENCE

MINOTAUR

SHANNON

Note.—The *Minotaur* has not, at present, got any funnel markings, these having been removed for her commission on the China Station.

Defence sunk at Jutland May 1916.

Ahead:
2—9·2 in.
2—7·5 in.

Astern:
2—9·2 in.
2—7·5 in.

Broadside: 4—9·2 in., 5—7·5 in.

Machinery : 2 sets 4 cylinder. 2 screws. Boilers: Yarrow or Babcock. Designed H.P. 27,000 = 23 kts. Coal *normal* 1000 tons (only 950 in *Shannon*); *maximum* 2000 tons. Oil : 400 tons.
Gunnery Notes.—Loading positions, big guns: central pivot. Hoists, electric all guns. Guns hydraulically manœuvred. Weight of 9·2 guns, mountings and armour, 500 tons. Weight of 7·5 guns, mountings and armour, 1,573 tons.
Torpedo Notes.—1904 model torpedoes. Stern *submerged* tube.
Engineering Notes.—*n.d.* in *Minotaur*, *f.d.* in other two. 120 revolutions = about 21 kts.

Name	Builder	Machinery	Laid down	Completed	Trials	Boilers	Best recent speed
Minotaur	Devonport	Harland & Wolff	Jan. 2, '05	Mar. '08	19,500 = 22·9	Babcock	23·1
Defence	Pembroke	Scotts S. & E. Co.	Feb. 22, '05	1908	27,853 = 23	Yarrow	
Shannon	Chatham	Humphrys & T.	Jan. 2, '05	Mar. '08	28,128 = 22·41	Yarrow	21·5

General Notes.—Cost: *Minotaur*, £1,410,356; *Defence*, £1,362,970; *Shannon*, £1,415,535. Designed by Sir P. Watts. Built under 1904-5 Estimates. As designed, these ships had short funnels. The uptakes were heightened 15 feet in 1909. These ships are on the whole not so successful as the *Warrior* class.

1904 BRITISH CRUISERS (22⅓ knot).

(WARRIOR CLASS—4 SHIPS.)

ACHILLES (June, 1905), **COCHRANE** (May, 1905), **NATAL** (Sept., 1905) & **WARRIOR** (Nov., 1905).
Displacement, 13,550 tons. Complement, 704.
Length (*p.p.*), 480 feet. Beam, 73½ feet. *Maximum* draught, 27½ feet.

Guns :
6—9·2 inch, IX., 45 cal. (A³).
4—7·5 inch, II., 50 cal. (A).
24—3 pdr. (semi-automatic)
4 Maxims.
1—12 pdr. Field
Torpedo tubes (18 inch) :
3 submerged.

Armour (Krupp) :
6" Belt (amidships) .... a
4" Belt (bow) .... d
3" Belt (aft.) .... ε
1½"—¾" Deck ....
Protection to vitals .... = a
7" Barbettes (6)................... d
8"—6" Turrets to these (K.C.) = aa-a
8"—6" Secondary turrets (4) = aa-a

ACHILLES   COCHRANE

NATAL   WARRIOR

Natal sunk by internal explosion Dec., 1915.
Cochrane wrecked in Mersey Nov. 1918.
Warrior sunk at Jutland June 1916.

Ahead :
3—9·2 in.

Astern :
3—9·2 in.

Broadside: 4—9·2 in., 2—7·5 in.

COCHRANE.   *Photo, Symonds & Co.*

Machinery : 2 sets 4 cylinder triple expansion. 2 screws. Boilers : 19 Yarrow large tube and 6 cylindrical. Designed H.P. 23,500 = 22·33 kts. (but 24 kts. hoped for). Coal, *normal* 1,000 tons; *maximum* 2,000 tons. Also 400 tons of oil.
Armour Notes.—Thick part of belt 300 feet long. Armour deck made of two thicknesses of ⅜" steel.
Gunnery Notes.—Loading positions, big guns: central pivot. Hoists, hydraulic and hand. 9·2 and 7·5 manœuvred, hydraulically and hand. Arcs of fire: End 9·2 in.—285°; Broadside 9·2 in.—120°; 7·5 in.—about 110°.
Torpedo Notes.—1904 model torpedoes. *Submerged* stern tubes.
Engineering Notes.—Machinery all standardized. Weight complete, 2250 tons. These ships burn about 23½ tons an hour at full power, about 15 tons an hour at 21 knots.

Differences—

Copyright

ACHILLES.   WARRIOR.
COCHRANE.   NATAL.

Name.	Builders	Machinery and Boilers made by	Laid down.	Completed	Trials :—		Boilers.	Present best speed.
					4/5 P. (126 R.)	Full p. (139 R.)		
Achilles	Elswick	Hawthorn Leslie	22 Feb., '04	1907	16,009 = 21·5 (max.)	23,968 = 23·27 (max.)	Yarrow & Cyl.	23
Cochrane	Fairfield	Fairfield	24 Mar., '04	1907			,,	22·8
Natal	Vickers	Vickers	6 Jan., '04	1907	15,937 = 21·35	23,344 = 22·4	,,	23·1
Warrior	Pembroke	Wallsend Co.	5 Nov., '03	1907-08		= 22·9	,,	22·9

General Notes.—Design altered since first conception. These were originally to have been sisters to the *Duke of Edinburgh*. Average cost per ship about £1,180,000. Designer: Sir P. Watts. Built under 1903-4 estimates. These ships are singularly successful sea boats, and are held by all who have served in them to be the best cruisers ever turned out.

1903 BRITISH CRUISERS

(DUKE OF EDINBURGH CLASS—2 SHIPS).

DUKE OF EDINBURGH (June 1904), & **BLACK PRINCE** (November, 1904).

Normal displacement, 13,550 tons. Complement, 704.

Length (p.p.), 480 feet. Beam, 73½ feet. *Maximum* draught, 27½ feet.

Guns:
6—9·2 inch, IX., 45 cal. (A³).
10—6 inch, XI., 50 cal.
20—3 pdr. (semi-automatic)
Torpedo tubes (18 inch):
3 submerged.

Armour (Krupp):
6″ Belt (amidships) .... a
4″ Belt (bow) .... d
3″ Belt (aft) .... d
1½″—¾″ Armour deck ....
Protection to vitals .... = a
7″ Barbettes (6) (N.C.) .... a
8″—4″ Turrets to them (K.C.) =aaa-a
6″ Battery (N.C.) .... b

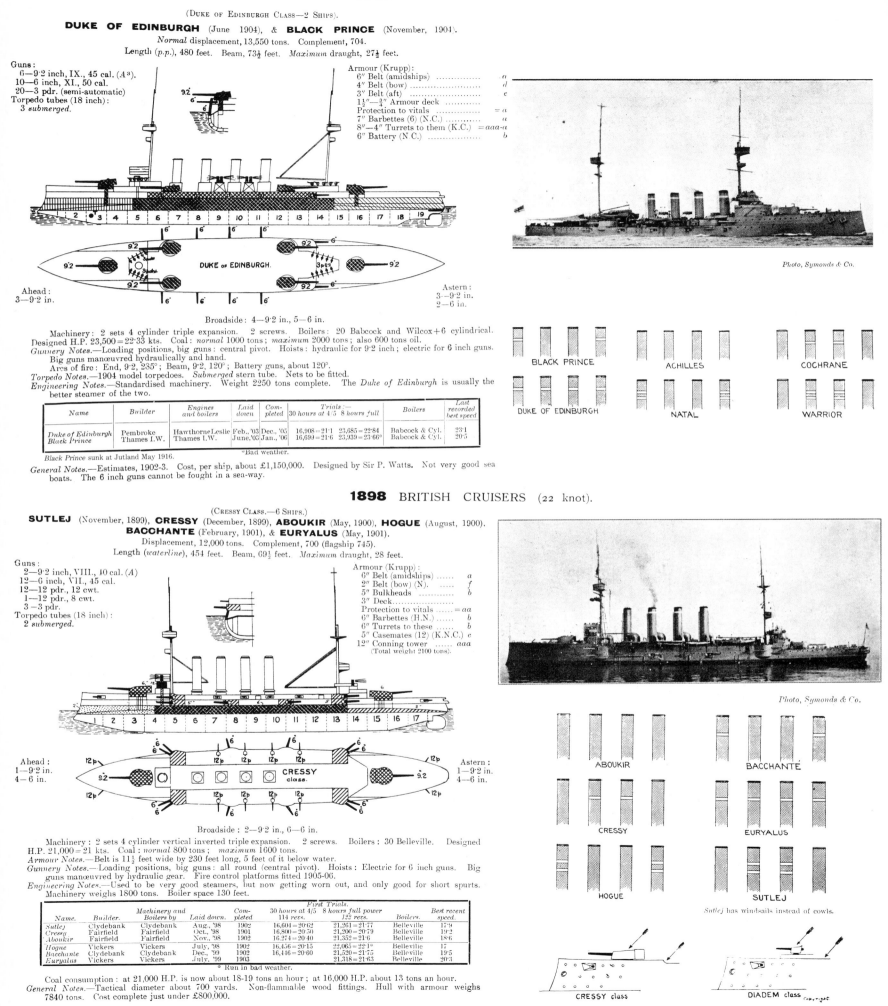

Photo, Symonds & Co.

Ahead:
3—9·2 in.

Astern:
3—9·2 in.
2—6 in.

Broadside: 4—9·2 in., 5—6 in.

BLACK PRINCE   ACHILLES   COCHRANE

DUKE OF EDINBURGH   NATAL   WARRIOR

Machinery: 2 sets 4 cylinder triple expansion. 2 screws. Boilers: 20 Babcock and Wilcox+6 cylindrical.
Designed H.P. 23,500 =22·33 kts. Coal: *normal* 1000 tons; *maximum* 2000 tons; also 600 tons oil.
Gunnery Notes.—Loading positions, big guns: central pivot. Hoists: hydraulic for 9·2 inch; electric for 6 inch guns. Big guns manœuvred hydraulically and hand.
Arcs of fire: End, 9·2, 235°; Beam, 9·2, 120°. Battery guns, about 120°.
Torpedo Notes.—1904 model torpedoes. Submerged stern tube. Nets to be fitted.
Engineering Notes.—Standardised machinery. Weight 2250 tons complete. The *Duke of Edinburgh* is usually the better steamer of the two.

Name	Builder	Engines and boilers	Laid down	Completed	Trials:— 30 hours at 4/5	8 hours full	Boilers	Last recorded best speed
Duke of Edinburgh	Pembroke	Hawthorne Leslie	Feb., '03	Dec., '05	16,908 =21·1	23,685 =22·84	Babcock & Cyl.	23·1
Black Prince	Thames I.W.	Thames I.W.	June,'03	Jan., '06	16,699 =21·6	23,939 =23·66*	Babcock & Cyl.	20·5

*Bad weather.

Black Prince sunk at Jutland May 1916.

General Notes.—Estimates, 1902-3. Cost, per ship, about £1,150,000. Designed by Sir P. Watts. Not very good sea boats. The 6 inch guns cannot be fought in a sea-way.

1898 BRITISH CRUISERS (22 knot).

(CRESSY CLASS.—6 SHIPS.)

SUTLEJ (November, 1899), **CRESSY** (December, 1899), **ABOUKIR** (May, 1900), **HOGUE** (August, 1900).
BACCHANTE (February, 1901), & **EURYALUS** (May, 1901).

Displacement, 12,000 tons. Complement, 700 (flagship 745).

Length (*waterline*), 454 feet. Beam, 69½ feet. *Maximum* draught, 28 feet.

Guns:
2—9·2 inch, VIII., 40 cal. (A)
12—6 inch, VII., 45 cal.
12—12 pdr., 12 cwt.
1—12 pdr., 8 cwt.
3—3 pdr.
Torpedo tubes (18 inch):
2 submerged.

Armour (Krupp):
6″ Belt (amidships) ...... a
2″ Belt (bow) (N). ...... f
5″ Bulkheads .... b
3″ Deck.....................
Protection to vitals ......= aa
6″ Barbettes (H.N.) ...... b
6″ Turrets to these ...... b
5″ Casemates (12) (K.N.C.) c
12″ Conning tower ...... aaa
(Total weight 2100 tons).

Ahead:
1—9·2 in.
4—6 in.

Astern:
1—9·2 in.
4—6 in.

Broadside: 2—9·2 in., 6—6 in.

ABOUKIR   BACCHANTE

CRESSY   EURYALUS

HOGUE   SUTLEJ

Sutlej has windsails instead of cowls.

CRESSY class   DIADEM class

Machinery: 2 sets 4 cylinder vertical inverted triple expansion. 2 screws. Boilers: 30 Belleville. Designed H.P. 21,000 =21 kts. Coal: *normal* 800 tons; *maximum* 1600 tons.
Armour Notes.—Belt is 11½ feet wide by 230 feet long, 5 feet of it below water. Hoists: Electric for 6 inch guns. Big
Gunnery Notes.—Loading positions, big guns: all round (central pivot). Fire control platforms fitted 1905-06.
Engineering Notes.—Used to be very good steamers, but now getting worn out, and only good for short spurts. Machinery weighs 1800 tons. Boiler space 130 feet.

Name	Builder	Machinery and Boilers by	Laid down	Completed	First Trials. 30 hours at 4/5 114 revs.	8 hours full power 122 revs.	Boilers	Best recent speed.
Sutlej	Clydebank	Clydebank	Aug., '98	1902	16,604 =20·62	21,261 =21·77	Belleville	17·9
Cressy	Fairfield	Fairfield	Oct., '98	1901	16,800 =20·50	21,200 =20·79	Belleville	19·2
Aboukir	Fairfield	Fairfield	Nov., '98	1902	16,274 =20·40	21,352 =21·6	Belleville	18·6
Hogue	Vickers	Vickers	July, '98	1902	16,456 =20·15	22,065 =22·1*	Belleville	17
Bacchante	Clydebank	Clydebank	Dec., '99	1902	16,416 =20·60	21,520 =21·75	Belleville	19·5
Euryalus	Vickers	Vickers	July, '99	1903		21,318 =21·63	Belleville	20·3

* Run in bad weather.

Coal consumption: at 21,000 H.P. is now about 18-19 tons an hour; at 16,000 H.P. about 13 tons an hour.
General Notes.—Tactical diameter about 700 yards. Non-flammable wood fittings. Hull with armour weighs 7840 tons. Cost complete just under £800,000.

Hogue, Aboukir and *Cressy* sunk on 22 Sept., 1914 off Holland.

OLD BRITISH CRUISERS.

CARNARVON.

HAMPSHIRE (Sept., 1903) **ROXBURGH** (Jan., 1904) **ARGYLL** (Mar., 1904)
CARNARVON (Oct., 1903), **ANTRIM** (Oct., 1903), **DEVONSHIRE** (April, 1904).

Displacement, 10,850 tons. Complement, 653.

Length (over all), 473½ feet. Beam, 68½ feet. Maximum draught, 25½ feet.

Guns (2—11 inch anti-submarine howitzers may still be mounted in some ships): 4—7·5 inch I, 6—6 inch VII, 8—3 pdr., 5 machine, (1 landing). Torpedo tubes (18 inch): 2 submerged. Armour (Krupp): 6″—4½″ Belt (amidships), 2⅜″ Belt (forward), 2″ Deck (aft), 4½″ Bulkheads (aft), 6″ Barbettes, 7½″—4½″ Hoods to these, 6″ Casemates, 10″ Conning tower (fore). Machinery: 2 sets vertical triple expansion. 2 screws. Boilers, various: 17-15 water-tube and 6 cylindrical. Designed H.P. 20,500 (n.d.), 21,000 (f.d.)=22·25 kts. Coal: normal 800 tons; maximum 1,750 tons (Carnarvon + 250 tons oil).

| Name. | Built at | Laid down. | Completed. | Trials:— | | Boilers 4/5. | Last best speed. |
				30 hours at 4/5.	8 hrs. full power.		
Devonshire	Chatham	March. '02	Aug. '05	14,830=21·0	21,475=23·17	15 Niclausse	23·1
Antrim	Clydebank	Aug., '02	July, '05	14,628=21·21	21,604=23·20	17 Yarrow	22·4
Carnarvon	Beardmore.	Oct., '02	May, '05.	15,212=21·43	21,460=23·1	17 Niclausse	22·1

(Engines by builders, except for Devonshire, which are by Thames Ironworks.)

General Notes.—Cost, per ship, about £850,000. Built under 1901 Estimates. Argyll and Hampshire of this class lost during the war. 1919: Devonshire in Reserve; Antrim for Signals and W/T. experiments. Some of these three ships partially dismantled. Carnarvon, sea-going Training Ship for Cadets. Roxburgh for sale.

Argyll wrecked off Scotland October 1915. Hampshire mined off Orkneys June 1916.

SUFFOLK. **KENT** (Mar 1901), **ESSEX** (Aug., 1901), **MONMOUTH** (Nov., 1901)
LANCASTER (Mar., 1902), **BERWICK** (Sept., 1902), **DONEGAL** (Sept., 1902), **CORNWALL** (Oct., 1902), **CUMBERLAND** (Dec., 1902), and **SUFFOLK** (Jan., 1903). Normal displacement, 9,800 tons. Complement, 690. Length over all, 463½ feet. Beam, 66 feet. Max. draught, 25½ feet. Guns (2—11 inch howitzers may still be in some ships): 6 in., 45 cal., as follows : 4 in Cornwall and Cumberland, 8 in Donegal and Berwick, 10 in Lancaster, 14 in Suffolk, and (in all ships) 4—12 pdr., 2—3 pdr. (anti-aircraft), 2 or 1 machine, (1 landing). Torpedo tubes (18 inch): 2 submerged. Armour (Krupp): 4″ Belt (amidships), 2″ Belt (bow), 5″ Bulkhead (aft), 2″ Deck (aft), 4″ Barbettes (H.N.), 5″ Turrets to these (H.N.), 4″ Casemates (10), 10″ Conning tower. Machinery: 2 sets 4 cylinder vertical triple expansion. 2 screws. Boilers: Various—see Notes. Designed H.P. 22,000=23 kts. Coal: normal 800 tons; maximum 1,730 tons.

Name.	Built at	Machinery	Laid down.	Completed	30 hrs. 4/5.	8 hours full power.	Boilers.	Last recorded best speed.
Essex	Pembroke	Clydebank	Jan., '00	1904	16,132=19·6	22,219=22·8	Belleville	22
Lancaster	Elswick	Hawthorn L.	Mar., '01	1904	16,004=22·0	22,881=24	Niclausse	24·1
Berwick	Beardmore	Humphrys	Apl., '01	1903	16,554=21·7	22,680=23·7	Belleville	24·4
Donegal	Fairfield	Fairfield	Feb., '01	1903	16,333=22·3	22,154=23·7	Belleville	24·3
Cornwall	Pembroke	Hawthorn	Mar., '01	1904	16,487=21·8	22,694=23·6	Babcock	24·0
Cumberland	L. & Glasgow	L. & Glasgow	Feb., '01	1904	16,472=22·1	22,784=23·7	Belleville	24·4
Suffolk	Portsmouth	Humphrys & T.	Mar., '02	1904	16,350=21·2	22,645=23·7	Belleville	23·7

General Notes.—1900 Estimates. Cost about £775,000 each. Bedford, of this class, was wrecked 1910 on the China Station, Monmouth sunk in battle, off Chile, Essex, in 1919, only Harbour Depot and Accommodation Ship for Destroyers in Reserve.

Note.

Following old Cruisers for disposal (will not be required for War Fleet): Leviathan, Edgar.* Following assigned to Special Service (Harbour Duties only): Sutlej, Diadem, Europa, Terrible, Theseus*, Grafton,* Crescent. For sale: King Alfred, Kent, Argonaut, Bacchante, Endymion.* Both Amphitrite and Euryalus converted to Minelayers.

* Fitted with bulge protection.

1898 BRITISH CRUISERS (24 knot).

(DRAKE CLASS—4 SHIPS.)

GOOD HOPE (February, 1901), **DRAKE** (March, 1901), **LEVIATHAN** (July, 1901) and
KING ALFRED (Oct., 1901).

Displacement, 14,100 tons. Complement, 900.

Length (waterline), 515 feet. Beam, 71 feet. Maximum draught, 28 feet. Length over all, 529½ feet.

Guns :
2—9·2 inch IX, 45 cal. (A²)
16—6 inch, VII, 45 cal.
12—12 pdr.
3—3 pdr.
Torpedo tubes (18 inch) :
2 submerged

Armour (Krupp) :
6″ Belt (amidships) ...... a
3″ Belt (bow) c
8″ Bulkheads (aft) (H.N.) a
3″—2″ Deck slopes
Protection to vitals ......= aa
6″ Barbettes (N.C.) ...... b
5″ Turrets to these........ c
6″ Casemates (16) (N.C.) b
12″ Conning tower (H.N.) aaa
(Total weight about 2700 tons).

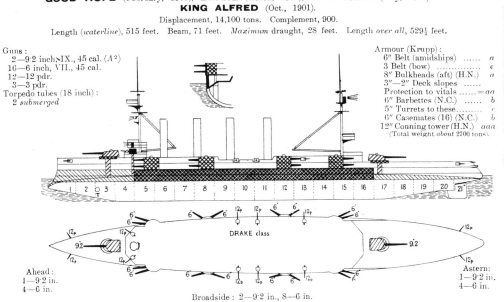

DRAKE class

Ahead :
1—9·2 in.
4—6 in.

Astern :
1—9·2 in.
4—6 in.

Broadside: 2—9·2 in., 8—6 in.

Machinery: 2 sets 4 cylinder vertical inverted triple expansion. 2 screws. Boilers: 43 Belleville. Designed H.P. 30,000=23 kts. Coal: normal 1250 tons : maximum 2500 tons.
Armour Notes—Belt is 11½ feet wide by 400 feet long.
Gunnery Notes—Loading positions, big guns: all round. Hoists, electric for 6 inch guns. Big guns manœuvred by hydraulic gear. Fire controls fitted 1905-06.
Engineering Notes—Machinery, boilers with water, &c., weigh 2,500 tons. Boiler rooms 185 feet long. All the class are excellent steamers. Heating surface, 72,000 square feet. Grate area, 2313 square feet.

| Name | Builder | Machinery | Laid down | Completed | First Trials :— | | Boilers | Last recorded best speed. |
					30 hrs. at 4/5	Full power		
Good Hope	Fairfield	Fairfield	Sept. '99	1902	22,703=22·7	31,071=23·05	Belleville	23·54
Drake	Pembroke	Humphrys & T.	Apl., '99	1902	23,103=22·08	30,849=23·05	Belleville	24·6
King Alfred	Clydebank	Clydebank	Nov., '99	1903	22,540=21·98	30,893=23·46	Belleville	25·1*
Leviathan	Vickers	Vickers	Aug. '99	1903	22,990=21·96	31,203=23·23	Belleville	23·7

* 1907. Mean for best hour. Mean of 8 hours was 24·8.

Coal consumption averages 11 tons an hour at 19 kts. ; and 19-24 tons an hour at 30,000 H.P. (24 kts).
General Notes—Tactical diameter about 750 yards, extreme helm. Cost complete per ship averaged just over £1,000,000.

DRAKE.

Good Hope sunk at Battle of Coronel 1 Nov. 1914.
Drake torpedoed by U-boat 2 Oct. 1917.

Differences :—

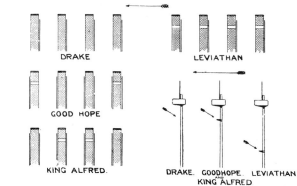

DRAKE   LEVIATHAN

GOOD HOPE

KING ALFRED.

DRAKE. GOODHOPE LEVIATHAN
and
KING ALFRED

Drake has Admiral's bridge forward. No after-bridge. All have now no yards on main mast.

1895 BRITISH CRUISERS (21 knot.)

(DIADEM CLASS).

DIADEM (October, 1896), **EUROPA** (March, 1897), **ARGONAUT** (January, 1898), **ARIADNE** (April, 1898), **AMPHITRITE** (July, 1898), **SPARTIATE** (October, 1898).

(*Niobe* of this class, *see* CANADA).

Displacement, 11,000 tons. Complement, 677.

Length (*waterline*), 450 feet. Beam, 69 feet. *Maximum* draught, 27½ feet. Length *over all*, 462½ feet.

Guns:
16—6 in. wire, 40 cal.
12—12 pdr., 12 cwt.
1—12 pdr., 8 cwt.
3—3 pdr.
Torpedo tubes (18 inch):
2 *submerged*.
Total weight, with ammunition,
652 tons.

Armour:
4″ Armour deck ......= b
Protection to vitals ... = b
6″ Casemates (12)...... b
12″ Conning tower ...aaa
Total weight, 1,900 tons, of
which 1500 is for deck.

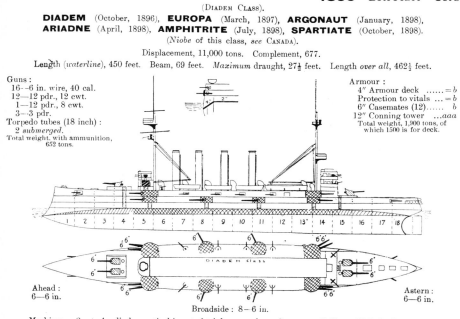

Ahead:
6—6 in.

Astern:
6—6 in.

Broadside: 8—6 in.

Photo, Symonds.

Machinery: 2 sets 4 cylinder vertical inverted triple expansion. 2 screws. Boilers: 30 Bellevilles. Designed H.P. 16,500 = 20·25 in earlier three; 18,000 = 20·75 in later four. Coal: *normal* 1000 tons; *maximum* 2000 tons; 400 tons oil also to be carried.

Gunnery Notes.—Each gun has its own hoist. Electric hoists. Ammunition carried: 200 rounds per gun.

Engineering Notes.—Machinery weighs 1525 tons. Boiler space 132 feet. Heating surface 47,282 square feet. Grate area 1390 feet. Boilers of last four ships are of an improved pattern to those in the three earlier.

Name	Builder	Machinery and Boilers by	Laid down	Com-pleted	Trials:— 30 hours at 4/5.	8 hours full.	Boilers	Best recent speed
								kts.
Argonaut	Fairfield	Fairfield	Nov.'96	1900	13,815 = 19·86	18,894 = 21·17	Belleville	
Ariadne	Clydebank	Clydebank	Oct.'96	1900	14,046 = 20·1	19,156 = 21·50	Belleville	about
Amphitrite	Vickers	Vickers	Dec.'96	1900	13,695 = 19·5	18,229 = 20·78	Belleville	18-19
Spartiate	Pembroke	Maudslay	May'97	1902		18,658 = 21	Belleville	
Diadem	Fairfield	Fairfield	Jan.'96	1899	12,791 = 19·8	17,262 = 20·65	Belleville	about
Europa	Clydebank	Clydebank	Jan.'96	1899	12,739 = 19·3	17,137 = 20·4	Belleville	18-17

Coal consumption is now heavy in all this class. All are getting worn out.

General Notes.—Hull with armour weighs 6975 tons. Tactical diameter about 1000 yards. Average cost per ship, about £600,000. *Niobe* of this class sold to Canada. *Andromeda* struck off effective list. *Argonaut* is used for training stokers.

Differences.—

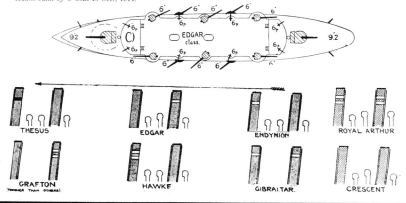

LATER DIADEMS.   EARLY DIADEMS.

Distinction.—From *Cressy* class by being generally "lighter" in appearance, and the absence of large fore and aft turrets.

Ariadne sunk by U-boat off Beachy Head 26 July 1917 when in service as a minelayer.

1893-91 OLD BRITISH CRUISERS.

ROYAL ARTHUR (1891) and **CRESCENT** (1892). 7700 tons. Armament: 1—9·2 inch, 30 cal., 12—6 inch, VII (of which four are in 6″ casemates on main deck, others shields), 12—6 pdr., 5—3 pdr., 2 boat, 2—18 inch *submerged* tubes. Designed H.P. 12,000 = 19·5 kts. Coal: *maximum* 1250 tons. Still steam very well.

EDGAR (1890), **HAWKE** (1891), **ENDYMION** (1891), **THESEUS** (1892), **GRAFTON** (1892) and **GIBRALTAR** (1892). 7350 tons (except *Gibraltar*, which is sheathed and coppered, 7700 tons). Armament: 2—9·2 inch, 30 cal., 10—6 inch VII (four in 6″ main deck casemates, others shields), 12—6 pdr., 5—3 pdr., 2—18 inch *submerged* tubes. Armour: 5″—3″ deck. Designed H.P. 12,000 = 19·5 kts. Coal: *maximum* 1250 tons. Excellent steamers.

St. George, of this class, is a torpedo depôt ship. The *Hawke* lost her ram in collision with the S.S. *Olympic* in 1911 and has now a straight stem.

Hawke sunk by U-boat 15 Oct., 1914.

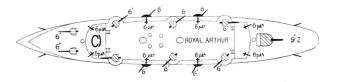

THESUS   EDGAR   ENDYMION   ROYAL ARTHUR

GRAFTON   HAWKE   GIBRALTAR.   CRESCENT

1917-18 BRITISH LIGHT CRUISERS.

(CARLISLE CLASS—5 SHIPS.)

CAIRO (19th Nov., 1918), **CALCUTTA** (——, 1919), **CARLISLE** (9th July, 1918),
CAPETOWN (28th June, 1919) **COLOMBO** (18th Dec., 1918).

Displacement, 4190 tons. Complement, *about* 330-350.

Length $\begin{cases} p.p. \text{ 425 feet} \\ o.a. \text{ 451}\frac{1}{2} \text{ ,,} \end{cases}$ Beam, 43½ feet. Draught $\begin{cases} mean \text{ 14 feet} \\ max. \text{ 16}\frac{1}{2} \text{ ,,} \end{cases}$

Guns :
5—6 inch, 50 cal. (**Dir. Con.**)
2—3 inch AA.
4—3 pdr.
2—2 pdr. pom-pom
1 M.G.
Torpedo tubes (21 inch) :
   8 *above water*, in 4 double
   mountings

Armour (H.T.) :
3″ Side (amidships) ...
2¼″—1½″ Side (bow) ...
2″ Side (stern) ....
1″ Upper deck (amids.)
1″ Deck over rudder ..
(No C.T. or tube)

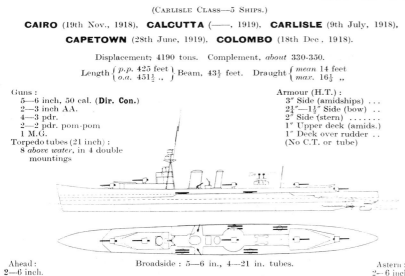

CARLISLE. (*Capetown same.*)

Ahead :
2—6 inch.

Broadside : 5—6 in., 4—21 in. tubes.

Astern :
2—6 inch.

Machinery : Turbines (all-geared), Brown-Curtis or Parsons types. Designed S.H.P. 40,000 = 29 kts. 2 screws. Boilers : — Yarrow. Fuel (oil only) : *normal*, 300 tons ; *maximum*, 950 tons.

Name	Builder	Machinery	Begun	Completed	Trials: H.P. kts.	Turbines
Cairo	Cammell Laird	Cammell Laird	Nov.28,'17	Sep.23,'19		
Calcutta	Vickers	Vickers	1917 ?			
Carlisle	Fairfield	Fairfield	1917	Nov.11,'18	40,930 = 28·45	
Capetown	Cammell Laird	Cammell Laird	Feb.23,'18	1919		
Colombo	Fairfield	Fairfield	1917 ?	June, '19		

General Notes.—Emergency War Programme ships, ordered June-July, 1917, that is, *after* the first three units of " D Class " (*Danae, Dragon, Dauntless*) were ordered. In these ships, " trawler bows " were added, to remedy defects shown by *Ceres* and *Calypso* classes. Conning tower also abolished, and hangar for aeroplanes combined with chart-house. Unofficially referred to as "Repeat C Class."

To distinguish.—From *Danae* and other D Cruisers—*no* 6-inch gun between foremast and first funnel. From *Ceres* class, by " trawler bows " and aeroplane hangar before tripod mast.

" Trawler bow," large forebridges, but *no* hangar.

CAIRO.

1916-18. BRITISH LIGHT CRUISERS.

(" D CLASS," THIRD GROUP— SHIPS.)

DESPATCH (24th Sept., 1919), **DIOMEDE** (29th April, 1919).—For others see *Cancelled Ships*.

Length $\begin{cases} p.p. \text{ feet} \\ o.a. \text{ ,,} \end{cases}$ Beam, feet. Draught $\begin{cases} mean \text{ feet.} \\ max. \text{ ,,} \end{cases}$

(" D CLASS," SECOND GROUP—3 SHIPS.)

DELHI (23rd Aug., 1918), **DUNEDIN** (1919), **DURBAN** (29th May, 1919).

Length $\begin{cases} p.p. \text{ 445 feet} \\ o.a. \text{ 472}\frac{1}{2} \text{ ,,} \end{cases}$ Beam, 46½ feet. Draught $\begin{cases} mean \text{ 14 feet.} \\ max. \text{ 16}\frac{1}{4} \text{ ,,} \end{cases}$

(" D CLASS," FIRST GROUP—3 SHIPS.)

DANAE (26th Jan., 1918), **DAUNTLESS** (10th April, 1918), **DRAGON** (29th Dec., 1917).

Length $\begin{cases} p.p. \text{ 445 feet} \\ o.a. \text{ 471 ,,} \end{cases}$ Beam, 46 feet. Draught $\begin{cases} mean \text{ 14}\frac{1}{2} \text{ feet.} \\ max. \text{ 16}\frac{1}{2} \text{ ,,} \end{cases}$

Displacement (of all above), 4,650 tons. Complement, *about* 350.

Guns :
6—6 inch, 50 cal. (**Dir. Con.**)
2—3 inch AA.
4—3 pdr.
2—2 pom-pom.
1 M.G.
Torpedo tubes (21 inch) :
   12 in 4 triple deck mountings.

Armour (H.T.) :
3″ Side (amidships) ...
2″, 1¾″, 1½″ Side (bow and stern) ....
1″ Upper deck (amids.)
1″ Deck over rudder ..

DANAE.   *Photo, Seward, Weymouth.*

Hangar forward, as *Carlisle*. Bows as *Danae* above.

DRAGON, DAUNTLESS.

Ahead :
2—6 in.

Broadside : 6—6 in., 6—21 in. tubes.

Astern : 2—6 in.

Machinery : Turbines (all-geared), Brown-Curtis or Parsons types. Designed S.H.P. 40,000 = 29 kts. 2 screws. Boilers : Yarrow (small tube). Oil fuel only : *normal*, 300 tons ; *maximum*, 1050 tons.

No hangar, " trawler " bows, high bridges, revolving launching platform for aeroplane abaft fourth 6-inch gun.

Name	Builder	Machinery	Ordered	Begun	Completed	Trials H.P. kts.	Turbines
Despatch	Fairfield*	Fairfield	Mar., 1918	1918			
Diomede	Vickers*	Vickers	Mar., 1918	1918			
Delhi	Armstrong		Sept., 1917	29 Oct., '17	June, 1919	41,000 = 28·5†	
Dunedin	Armstrong		Sept., 1917				
Durban	Scotts*	Scotts	Sept., 1917				Brown-Curtis
Danae	Armstrong	Wallsend	Sept., 1916	Dec., 1916	July, 1918	40,463 =	
Dauntless	Palmer		Sept., 1916		Dec., 1918		
Dragon	Scott	Scott	Sept., 1916	Jan., 1917	Aug., 1918	40,035 =	Brown-Curtis

DELHI.

*Towed to following Dockyards for completion : *Diomede* to Portsmouth, *Despatch* to Chatham, *Durban* to Devonport.
† With PV's. out, and on deep draught.

General Notes.—Emergency War Programme ships. Note that first three were ordered *before* Carlisle class. Design generally as *Ceres* class, but lengthened *about* 20 feet, to add a sixth 6-inch between foremast and first funnel ; also triple tubes. Completion of *Despatch* and *Diomede* may be indefinitely postponed.

Cancelled Ships (Third Group).—*Daedalus* (Armstrong), *Daring* (Beardmore), *Desperate* (——), *Dryad* (Vickers). All ordered March, 1918, with *Diomede* and *Despatch*. Cancelled 1918. Possible that *Desperate* may proceed, so as to complete three ships in third group, as in other two groups. Contractor for *Desperate* not known ; may be Palmer.

1916 BRITISH LIGHT CRUISERS.

(CERES CLASS—5 SHIPS.)

CARDIFF (ex *Caprice*, 12th May, 1917), **CERES** (24th March, 1917), **COVENTRY** (ex *Corsair*, 6th July, 1917), **CURACOA** (5th May, 1917), **CURLEW** (5th July, 1917).

Displacement, 4190 tons. Complement, 327.

Length $\begin{cases} p.p. \ 425 \text{ feet} \\ o.a. \ 450 \ ,, \end{cases}$ Beam, 43½ feet. Draught $\begin{cases} \textit{mean} \ 14 \text{ feet.} \\ \textit{max.} \ 16\frac{1}{4} \ ,, \end{cases}$

Guns :
5—6 inch, 50 cal. (**Dir. Con.**)
2—3 inch AA.
4—3 pdr.
1 M.G.
Torpedo tubes (21 inch) :
8 *above water*, in 4 *double* mountings

Armour (H.T.) :
3″ Side (amidships) . . .
2¼″—1½″ Side (bow) . .
2″ Side (stern) . . . . . .
1″ Upper deck (amids.)
1″ Deck over rudder . .
(Harvey or Hadfield)
3″ C.T. . . . .
— Tube . . . .

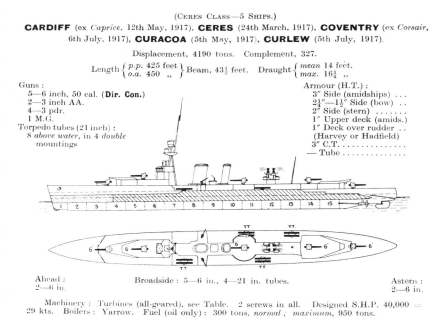

Ahead :
2—6 in.

Broadside : 5—6 in., 4—21 in. tubes.

Astern :
2—6 in.

Machinery : Turbines (all-geared), see Table. 2 screws in all. Designed S.H.P. 40,000 = 29 kts. Boilers : Yarrow. Fuel (oil only) : 300 tons, *normal* ; *maximum*, 950 tons.

Name	Builder	Machinery	Begun	Completed	Trials H.P.	kts.	Turbines
Cardiff	Fairfield	Fairfield	July, 1916	July, 1917	41,450	28·96	B.-Curtis A.G.
Ceres	Clydebank	Clydebank	Apl.26,'16	June, 1917	39,425	29·1	B.-Curtis A.G.
Coventry	Swan Hunter	Wallsend	Aug., 1916	Feb., 1918	39,907		B.-Curtis A.G.
Curacoa	Pembroke D.Y.	Harland & Wolff	July, 1916	Feb., 1918	40,428		B.-Curtis A.G.
Curlew	Vickers	Vickers	Aug., 1916	Dec., 1917	40,240	28·07	Parsons A.G.

CURLEW.

Photo, Seward, Weymouth.

COVENTRY

Photo, Messrs. Swan Hunter & Wigham Richardson, Builders.

General Notes.—All Emergency War Programme ships, ordered April, 1916. Very wet forward, to remedy which defect the later *Carlisle* and *Dragon* classes were given "trawler" bows.

To distinguish : From *Dragon* and "D" Cruisers.—No 6 inch between foremast and first funnel. The same point separates this class from the *Caledon* class.

(IMPROVED BIRMINGHAM CLASS—2 or 4 SHIPS.)

EFFINGHAM (building), *FROBISHER* **HAWKINS** (Oct., 1917), **RALEIGH** (29th Aug., 1919).

Displacement, 9750 tons. Complement, —

Length $\begin{cases} p.p. \ 565 \text{ feet} \\ o.a. \ 605 \ ,, \end{cases}$ Beam $\begin{cases} w.l. \qquad \quad 58^* \text{ feet.} \\ \textit{outside bulges} \ 65 \ ,, \end{cases}$ Draught $\begin{cases} \textit{mean} \ 17\frac{1}{2} \text{ feet.} \\ \textit{max.} \ 20\frac{1}{2} \ ,, \end{cases}$

*Approximate.

Guns :
7—7·5 inch, 50 cal. (**Dir. Con.**)
8—12 pdr.
4—3 inch AA.
4—3 pdr.
2—2 pdr. pom-pom
— M.G.
Torpedo tubes (21 inch) :
4 *above water*
2 *submerged*

Armour (H.T. or Nickel) :
3″—2″ Side (amidships)
2½″—1½″ Side (bow) . .
2½″—2¼″ Side (stern)
1″ Upper deck (amids.)
1½″—1″ Deck over rudder (Hadfield) . .
3″ C.T. . . . .
Anti-Torpedo Protection :
Bulges, 10 ft. deep . .
Unpierced Bulkheads, below lower deck . . .

Ahead :
2 to 4—7·5 in.

Broadside : 6—7·5 in., 3—21 in. tubes.

Astern :
2 to 4—7·5 in.

Machinery : Turbines, Brown-Curtis or Parsons (geared cruising). Designed S.H.P. in *Hawkins*, 60,000 = 30 kts. (other 3 ships, with oil fuel only, expected to develop 70,000 S.H.P. and about 31 kts.). 4 screws. Boilers : 12 Yarrow (small tube). Fuel : *As originally designed.* Coal : *normal*, 800 tons ; *maximum*, 1000 tons + 1600 tons oil. *Hawkins* reported to have these proportions of fuel, but other three ships may be modified to take about 3000 tons oil only, *max.* capacity.

Gunnery Notes.—7·5's are a new semi-auto. B.L. mark on centre-pivot mountings and with H.A. elevation. Unofficially stated that projectile is light and muzzle velocity high, so that guns have practically a range only limited by *maximum* visibility. Armaments originally projected for this class were (*a*) mixed battery of 9·2 inch and 6 inch, (*b*) 14—6 inch.

Torpedo Notes.—Above water tubes are single (side-loading ?), mounted athwartships on upper deck below mainmast. In *Repulse* class, *Glorious* class and *Centaur* class, *submerged* tubes have proved very satisfactory, as bars bend when attempting to fire torpedoes over 20 kts. Possible that *submerged* tubes have not been mounted in *Hawkins*.

Armour and Protection Notes.—Armour on Light Cruiser lines. Estimated that bulges and sub-division will keep ship afloat, even if all three boiler-rooms and both engine-rooms are flooded.

Name	Builder	Machinery	Begun	Completed	Trials H.P.	kts.	Turbines
Effingham	Portsmouth D.Y.		1916 ?	No.			
Frobisher	Devonport D.Y.		1916 ?	No.			
Hawkins	Chatham D.Y.		1916 ?	July25,'19			
Raleigh	Beardmore	Beardmore	Dec.9,'15	No.			Brown-Curtis

Cancelled Ships.—Building of *Effingham* and *Frobisher* has been proceeding intermittently for the past three years, and, in the spring of 1919, *Effingham* was only in frame, and *Frobisher* little advanced. Possible that these two ships may be stopped. *Raleigh* is launched, but her completion is being delayed indefinitely.

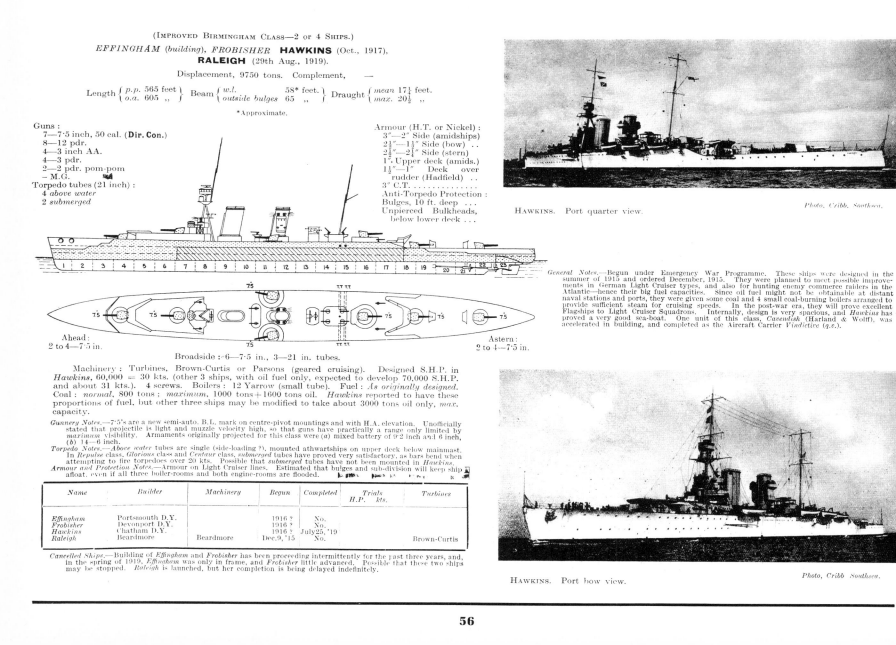

HAWKINS. Port quarter view.

Photo, Cribb, Southsea.

General Notes.—Begun under Emergency War Programme. These ships were designed in the summer of 1915 and ordered December, 1915. They were planned to meet possible improvements in German Light Cruiser types, and also for hunting enemy commerce raiders in the Atlantic—hence their big fuel capacities. Since oil fuel might not be obtainable at distant naval stations and ports, they were given some coal and 4 small coal-burning boilers arranged to provide sufficient steam for cruising speeds. In the post-war era, they will prove excellent Flagships to Light Cruiser Squadrons. Internally, design is very spacious, and *Hawkins* has proved a very good sea-boat. One unit of this class, *Cavendish* (Harland & Wolff), was accelerated in building, and completed as the Aircraft Carrier *Vindictive* (q.v.).

HAWKINS. Port bow view.

Photo, Cribb, Southsea.

1916 BRITISH LIGHT CRUISERS.

(CALEDON CLASS—3 SHIPS.)

CALEDON (25th Nov., 1916), **CALYPSO** (24th Jan., 1917), **CARADOC** (23rd Dec., 1916).

Displacement, 4120 tons. Complement, 344.

Length $\begin{cases} p.p.\ 425\ \text{feet} \\ o.a.\ 450\ ,, \end{cases}$ Beam, $42\frac{3}{4}$ feet. Draught $\begin{cases} mean\ 14\frac{1}{2}\ \text{feet.} \\ max.\ 16\frac{1}{4}\ ,, \end{cases}$

Guns :
5—6 inch, 50 cal. (**Dir. Con.**)
2—3 inch AA.
4—3 pdr.
1 M.G.
Torpedo tube (21 inch) :
8 *above water*, in 4 double mountings

Armour (H.T.) :
3″ Side (amidships) ...
$2\frac{1}{4}$″—$1\frac{1}{4}$″ Side (bow)
$2\frac{1}{2}$″—2″ Side (stern) ..
1″ Upper deck (amids.)
1″ Deck over rudder ..
(Harvey or Hadfield)
6″ C.T. } probably
4″ Tube } removed

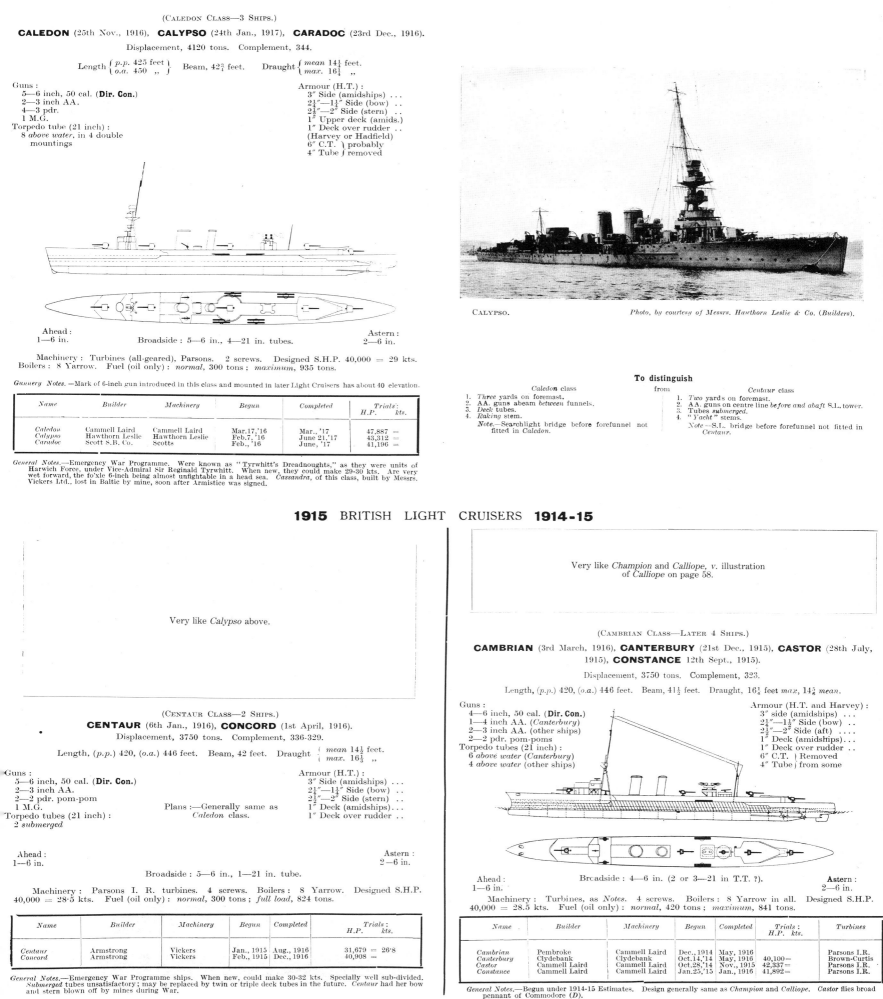

CALYPSO.

Photo, by courtesy of Messrs. Hawthorn Leslie & Co. (Builders).

Ahead :
1—6 in.

Broadside : 5—6 in., 4—21 in. tubes.

Astern :
2—6 in.

Machinery : Turbines (all-geared), Parsons. 2 screws. Designed S.H.P. 40,000 = 29 kts.
Boilers : 8 Yarrow. Fuel (oil only) : *normal*, 300 tons ; *maximum*, 935 tons.

Gunnery Notes.—Mark of 6-inch gun introduced in this class and mounted in later Light Cruisers has about 40 elevation.

To distinguish

	Caledon class	from		*Centaur* class
1.	*Three* yards on foremast.		1.	*Two* yards on foremast.
2.	AA. guns abeam *between* funnels.		2.	AA. guns on centre line *before* and *abaft* S.L. tower.
3.	*Deck* tubes.		3.	Tubes *submerged.*
4.	*Raking* stem.		4.	"*Yacht*" stems.

Note.—Searchlight bridge before forefunnel not fitted in *Caledon*.

Note.—S.L. bridge before forefunnel not fitted in *Centaur.*

Name	Builder	Machinery	Begun	Completed	Trials :	
					H.P.	kts.
Caledon	Cammell Laird	Cammell Laird	Mar.17,'16	Mar., '17	47,887	=
Calypso	Hawthorn Leslie	Hawthorn Leslie	Feb.7, '16	June 21,'17	43,312	=
Caradoc	Scott S.B. Co.	Scotts	Feb., '16	June, '17	41,196	=

General Notes.—Emergency War Programme. Were known as "Tyrwhitt's Dreadnoughts," as they were units of Harwich Force, under Vice-Admiral Sir Reginald Tyrwhitt. When new, they could make 29-30 kts. Are very wet forward, the fo'xle 6-inch being almost unfightable in a head sea. *Cassandra*, of this class, built by Messrs. Vickers Ltd., lost in Baltic by mine, soon after Armistice was signed.

1915 BRITISH LIGHT CRUISERS 1914-15

Very like *Calypso* above.

Very like *Champion* and *Calliope, v.* illustration of *Calliope* on page 58.

(CENTAUR CLASS—2 SHIPS.)

CENTAUR (6th Jan., 1916), **CONCORD** (1st April, 1916).

Displacement, 3750 tons. Complement, 336-329.

Length, (p.p.) 420, (o.a.) 446 feet. Beam, 42 feet. Draught $\begin{cases} mean\ 14\frac{1}{2}\ \text{feet.} \\ max.\ 16\frac{1}{4}\ ,, \end{cases}$

Guns :
5—6 inch, 50 cal. (**Dir. Con.**)
2—3 inch AA.
2—2 pdr. pom-pom
1 M.G.
Torpedo tubes (21 inch) :
2 *submerged*

Plans :—Generally same as *Caledon* class.

Armour (H.T.) :
3″ Side (amidships) ...
$2\frac{1}{4}$″—$1\frac{1}{4}$″ Side (bow) ..
$2\frac{1}{2}$″ Side (stern) ..
1″ Deck (amidships)...
1″ Deck over rudder ..

Ahead :
1—6 in.

Astern :
2—6 in.

Broadside : 5—6 in., 1—21 in. tube.

Machinery : Parsons I. R. turbines. 4 screws. Boilers : 8 Yarrow. Designed S.H.P. 40,000 = 28.5 kts. Fuel (oil only) : *normal*, 300 tons ; *full load*, 824 tons.

Name	Builder	Machinery	Begun	Completed	Trials :	
					H.P.	kts.
Centaur	Armstrong	Vickers	Jan., 1915	Aug., 1916	31,679	= 26·8
Concord	Armstrong	Vickers	Feb., 1915	Jan., 1916	40,908	=

General Notes.—Emergency War Programme ships. When new, could make 30-32 kts. Specially well sub-divided. *Submerged* tubes unsatisfactory ; may be replaced by twin or triple deck tubes in the future. *Centaur* had her bow and stern blown off by mines during War.

(CAMBRIAN CLASS—LATER 4 SHIPS.)

CAMBRIAN (3rd March, 1916), **CANTERBURY** (21st Dec., 1915), **CASTOR** (28th July, 1915), **CONSTANCE** 12th Sept., 1915).

Displacement, 3750 tons. Complement, 323.

Length, (p.p.) 420, (o.a.) 446 feet. Beam, $41\frac{1}{2}$ feet. Draught, $16\frac{1}{4}$ feet *max*, $14\frac{1}{2}$ *mean*.

Guns :
4—6 inch, 50 cal. (**Dir. Con.**)
1—4 inch AA. (*Canterbury*)
2—3 inch AA. (other ships)
2—2 pdr. pom-poms
Torpedo tubes (21 inch) :
6 *above water* (*Canterbury*)
4 *above water* (other ships)

Armour (H.T. and Harvey) :
3″ side (amidships) ...
$2\frac{1}{4}$″—$1\frac{1}{4}$″ Side (bow) ..
$2\frac{1}{2}$″—2″ Side (aft) ....
1″ Deck (amidships)...
1″ Deck over rudder ..
6″ C.T. } Removed
4″ Tube } from some

Ahead :
1—6 in.

Broadside : 4—6 in. (2 or 3—21 in T.T. ?).

Astern :
2—6 in.

Machinery : Turbines, as *Notes*. 4 screws. Boilers : 8 Yarrow in all. Designed S.H.P. 40,000 = 28.5 kts. Fuel (oil only) : *normal*, 420 tons ; *maximum*, 841 tons.

Name	Builder	Machinery	Begun	Completed	Trials :		Turbines
					H.P.	kts.	
Cambrian	Pembroke	Cammell Laird	Dec.,1914	May, 1916	40,100	=	Parsons I.R.
Canterbury	Clydebank	Clydebank	Oct.14,'14	May, 1916			Brown-Curtis
Castor	Cammell Laird	Cammell Laird	Oct.28,'14	Nov., 1915	42,337	=	Parsons I.R.
Constance	Cammell Laird	Cammell Laird	Jan.25,'15	Jan., 1916	41,892	=	Parsons I.R.

General Notes.—Begun under 1914-15 Estimates. Design generally same as *Champion* and *Calliope. Castor* flies broad pennant of Commodore (D).

1914 BRITISH LIGHT CRUISERS (Purchased 1915).

BIRKENHEAD (ex *Antinauarkos Condouriotis*, 18th Jan., 1915). **CHESTER** (8th Dec., 1915).

| | Length (feet). | | Beam. | Draught (feet). | | Displace- | Comple- |
	(p.p.)	(o.a.)	(ft.)	mean	max.	ment (tons)	ment.
Birkenhead	430	446	49⅝	15½	17	5235	452
Chester	430	456½	49⅝	15¼	17¼	5185	402

Guns :
10—5·5 inch (**Dir. Con.**)
1—3 inch AA.
2 or 1—3 pdr. AA.
1 M.G.
Torpedo tubes (21 inch) :
  2 *submerged*

Armour :
  ″ Belt ....
  ″ Ends ....
  ″ Deck ....
  ″ Shields ....
  ″ C.T. ....

No plans available.

BIRKENHEAD.

Ahead :
3—5·5 inch.

Astern :
5—5·5 inch.

Broadside : 6—5·5 in., 1—21 in. tube.

Machinery : Turbines : Parsons (compound re-action). 4 screws. Boilers : 12 Yarrow. Designed S.H.P. : *Birkenhead*, 25,000 = 25 kts. ; *Chester*, 31,000 = 26·5 kts. Fuel : *Birkenhead*, 1070 tons coal + 352 tons oil, both *max.* ; *Chester*, 1172 tons *max.* oil only.

Gunnery Notes.—5·5 inch guns and mountings by Coventry Ordnance Co. They are said to have proved so successful that it was decided to introduce this calibre into the Navy as an official mark of gun.

To distinguish.—*Birkenhead* has *straight* pole mainmast, as above view ; *Chester's* pole mainmast is *raked aft.*

| Name | Builder | Machinery | Begun | Completed | Trials* | |
					H.P.	kts.
Birkenhead	Cammell Laird	Cammell Laird	Mar.21,'14	May, 1915	26,767	=
Chester	Cammell Laird	Cammell Laird	Oct. ,7,'14	May, 1916	31,422	=

*S.H.P. only ; no speeds taken.

General Notes.—Begun for Greek Navy : purchased for British Navy under the War Emergency Programme. These ships have been very well reported on. They are good sea-boats, and the majority of their guns are mounted well above waterline. Steam well and are good for 23 kts. continuous, except in bad head seas. Designed by Messrs. Cammell Laird & Co. as an improvement on the British *Chatham* and Australian *Melbourne* classes.

1914 BRITISH LIGHT CRUISERS.

(CAMBRIAN CLASS—FIRST TWO SHIPS.)

CALLIOPE (Dec. 17th, 1914), **CHAMPION** (May 29th, 1915).

Displacement, 3750 tons. Complement, 324.

Length, 420 (p.p.), 446 (o.a.) feet. Beam, 41½ feet. Draught $\begin{cases} mean\ 14\frac{1}{2}\ feet. \\ max.\ 16\ ,, \end{cases}$

Calliope
Guns :
  4—6 inch (**Dir Con.**)
  2—3 inch AA.
  1 M.G.
Torpedo tubes (2—21 inch*):
  submerged
  4—21 inch above water reported added 1919.

Champion
  4—6 inch (**Dir Con.**)
  1—4 inch AA.
  1—3 pdr. AA.
Torpedo tubes (6—21 inch):
  above water

Armour (H.T.) :
  4″ Side (amidships) ...
  2¼″—1½″ Forward ....
  2½″—2″ Aft ....
  1″ Deck (amidships)...
  1″ Deck over rudder hd.
    (Hadfield)
  6″ C.T. } removed ? ..
  2″ Tube }

CALLIOPE.

Photo, Topical.

Plans generally same as *Cambrian* class on page 57.

Note.

Calliope very badly damaged by oil fuel fire at sea, November, 1919. If not scrapped, she will require extensive re-construction before she can return to service.

Ahead :
1—6 inch.

Astern :
2—6 inch.

Broadside : 4—6 in., —21 in. tubes.

Machinery : Turbines (all-geared), Parsons. Screws : 4 in *Calliope*, 2 in *Champion*. Designed S.H.P. in *Calliope*, 37,500 ; in *Champion*, 40,000 = 28·5 kts. in both ships. Boilers : 8 Yarrow. Fuel (oil only) : 405 tons, *normal* ; *maximum*, 772 tons.

Name	Builder	Machinery	Laid down	Com-pleted	First trials :	Turbines	Boilers	Best recent speed
Calliope	Chatham	Parsons	Jan.'14	June '15	30,917 = 28	Parsons A.G.	Yarrow	
Champion	Hawthorn	Hawthorn	Mar., 9 '14	Dec. 20, '15	{ 30,290 = { 41,000 = 29			

General Notes.—Begun under 1913-14 Estimates, with 6 *Caroline* class, on next page. Same hull, &c., but all-geared turbines adopted. Also carry less oil fuel, have thicker side plating, and—of course—one funnel less.

1913-14 BRITISH LIGHT CRUISERS.

(CAROLINE CLASS—6 SHIPS.)

CAROLINE (Sept. 29th, 1914), **CARYSFORT** (Nov. 14th, 1914), **CLEOPATRA** (Jan. 14th, 1915),
COMUS (16th Dec., 1914), *also* **CONQUEST** (20th Jan., 1915), **CORDELIA** (Feb. 23rd, 1914).

Displacement, 3750 tons. Complement, 325.

Length (*p.p.*), 420 feet. Beam, 41½ feet. Draught, (*max.*) 16, (*mean*) 14½ feet. Length *over all*, 446 feet.

Caroline, Carysfort, Comus
Guns :
4—6 inch (**Dir. Con.**)
2—3 inch AA.
1 M.G.
Tubes :
4—21 inch *above water*
in 2 pairs

Cleopatra
4—6 inch (**Dir. Con.**)
2—4 inch AA.
2—2 pdr. pom-poms
1 M.G.
Tubes :
8—21 inch *above water*
in 4 pairs

Armour (H.T.) :
3″ Side (amidships). 2¼″—1½″ forward, 2¼″—2″ aft. 1″ Deck (amidships), 1″ Deck over rudder head. (Hadfield), 6″ C.T. and 4″ tube, but removed from some.

Conquest
Guns :
4—6 inch (**Dir. Con.**)
1—4 inch AA.
2—2 pdr. pom-poms
1 M.G.
Tubes :
As *Cleopatra*

Cordelia
4—6 inch (**Dir. Con.**)
1—4 inch AA.
1 M.G.
Tubes :
As *Cleopatra*

CAROLINE (and *Carysfort, Comus*).   *Photo, Topical.*

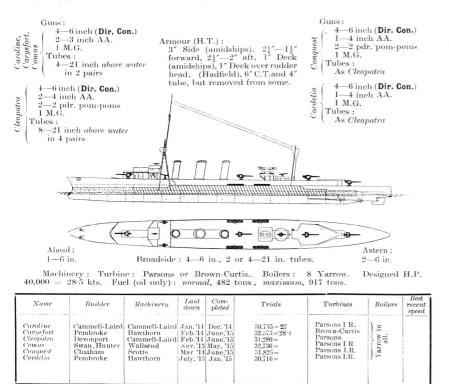

Ahead :
1—6 in.
Broadside : 4—6 in., 2 or 4—21 in. tubes.
Astern :
2—6 in.

Machinery : Turbine : Parsons or Brown-Curtis. Boilers : 8 Yarrow. Designed H.P. 40,000 = 28·5 kts. Fuel (oil only) : *normal*, 482 tons, *maximum*, 917 tons.

Name	Builder	Machinery	Laid down	Completed	Trials	Turbines	Boilers	Best recent speed
Caroline	Cammell-Laird	Cammell-Laird	Jan. '14	Dec. '14	30,735 = 27	Parsons I.R.		
Carysfort	Pembroke	Hawthorn	Feb. '14	June '15	32,573 = 28·4	Brown-Curtis		
Cleopatra	Devonport	Cammell-Laird	Feb. '14	June '15	31,280 =	Parsons	Yarrow in all.	
Comus	Swan, Hunter	Wallsend	Nov. '13	May '15	32,736 =	Parsons I.R.		
Conquest	Chatham	Scotts	Mar. '14	June '15	31,825 =	Parsons I.R.		
Cordelia	Pembroke	Hawthorn	July '13	Jan. '15	30,716 =	Parsons I.R.		

General Notes.—*Caroline* of this class was built within twelve months. Belong to the 1913-14 Estimates. Originally had 2—6 inch and 8—4 inch : re-armed during War.

CLEOPATRA.

CONQUEST.

CORDELIA.

1912-13 BRITISH LIGHT CRUISERS.

(ARETHUSA CLASS—7 SHIPS.)

AURORA (30th Sept., 1913), **GALATEA** (May 14th, 1914), **INCONSTANT** (July 6th, 1914),
ROYALIST (Jan. 14th, 1915), **PENELOPE** (Aug. 25th, 1915), **PHAETON** (Oct. 21st, 1914),
ARETHUSA (Oct. 1913) **UNDAUNTED** (April 28th, 1914).

Displacement, 3500 tons. Complement, 318.

Length (*p.p.*), 410 feet. Beam, 39 feet. {Mean Draught, 13½ feet. Max. ,, 15½ ,, } Length *over all*, 436 feet.

Guns :
Galatea, Inconstant, Phaeton, Royalist :—
3—6 inch } **Dir.**
4—4 inch } **Con.**
2—3 inch AA.
Penelope as above, but 1—4 inch AA. in place of 2—3 inch AA.

Guns :
Undaunted, Aurora :—
2—6 inch } **Dir.**
6—4 inch } **Con.**
1—4 inch AA. } *Undaunted*
2—2 pdr. AA. }
2—3 inch AA.—*Aurora*

Armour (H.T.) :
3″ Amidships.........
2¼—1½″ Forward .....
2¼—2″ Aft ....
1″ Deck (amidships)...
1″ Deck over rudder hd. (Hadfield)
6″ C.T. } Removed from
4″ Tube } some ships

and—in all—
Torpedo tubes : 8—21 inch *above water*

UNDAUNTED (and *Aurora*).   *Photo, Topical.*

Note :—Ships fitted to tow Kite Balloons have aftermast *before* S.L. tower.

Arethusa sunk 11 Feb 1916 off Felixstowe by mine.

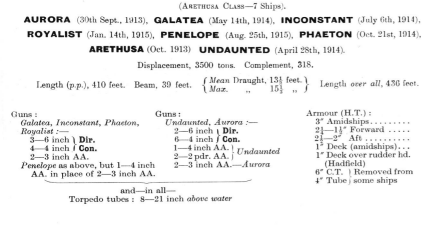

Ahead :
1—6 inch.
Broadside : 2 or 3—6 in., 3 or 2—4 in., 4—21 in. tubes.
Astern :
1—6 inch.
2—4 inch.

Machinery : Turbine (see *Notes*). Boilers : 8 Yarrow in all. Designed H.P. 40,000 = 28.5 kts. Fuel : Oil only, 482 tons *normal* ; 810 tons *maximum*.

Armour Notes.—C.T. removed and replaced by revolving launching platform for a seaplane or aeroplane. Side armour serves dual purpose of providing protection and giving skin plating.

Gunnery Notes.—Beam 4-inch forward very wet and cannot be fought in a head sea. Accordingly, 2—4 inch right forward have been taken out of five ships and a third 6-inch mounted on centre-line between 3rd funnel and S.L. tower.

Name	Builder	Machinery	Laid down	Completed	Trials	Turbines	Boilers	Best recent speed
Aurora	Devonport	Parsons	Oct. '12	Oct. '14	30,417 = 27·1	Parsons I.R.		
Galatea	Beardmore	Beardmore	Jan. '13	Dec. '14	30,796 =	Parsons I.R.		
Inconstant	Beardmore	Beardmore	April '13	Jan. '15	30,357 =	Parsons I.R.	Yarrow small tube in all	
Royalist	Beardmore	Beardmore	June '13	Mar. '15	31,034 =	Parsons I.R.		
Penelope	Vickers	Vickers	Feb. '13	Dec. '14	32,052 =	Parsons I.R.		
Phaeton	Vickers	Vickers	Mar. '13	Feb. '15	34,595 =	Parsons I.R.		
Undaunted	Fairfield	Fairfield	Dec. '12	Sep. '14	32,161 = 27·5	Brown-Curtis		

General Notes.—Built under 1912 Estimates. *Arethusa* of this class lost in the War. All have tripod masts. Very cramped internally.

1912. BRITISH LIGHT CRUISERS

(CHATHAM CLASS—LATER SHIPS.)

NOTTINGHAM (April, 1913), **BIRMINGHAM** (May, 1913), **LOWESTOFT** (April, 1913).

Displacement, 5440 tons. Complement, 433.

Length (p.p.), 430 feet. Beam, 49⅚ feet. { Mean draught, 15¾ feet. Max. „ 17½ „ } Length over all, 457 feet.

Guns:
9—6 inch (**Dir. Con.**)
1—3 inch anti-aircraft
4—3 pdr.
2 machine
Torpedo tubes (21 inch):
2 submerged

Armour (Nickel and H.T.):
3″ Side (amidships) ....
1½″ Side (forward) ....
1¾″ Side (aft) ....

(C.T. removed).

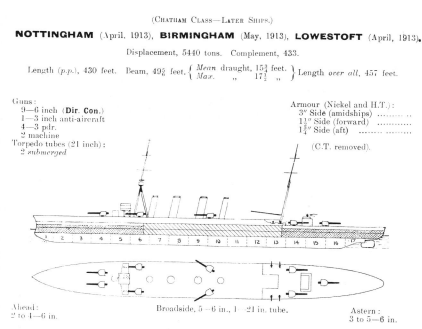

Ahead:
2 to 4—6 in.

Broadside, 5—6 in., 1—21 in. tube.

Astern:
3 to 5—6 in.

Machinery: Parsons turbine. Boilers: 12 Yarrow. Designed H.P. 25,000 = 25·5 kts.
Coal: normal. tons; maximum, 1165 tons + 235 tons oil = 4680 miles at 10 kts.

Name	Builder	Machinery	Laid down	Completed	Trials	Boilers	Best recent speed
Nottingham	Pembroke Y.	Hawthorn	June '12	'14	—	Yarrow	...
Birmingham	Elswick		'12	'11	—	Yarrow	...
Lowestoft	Chatham Y.	...	July, '12	'11	—	Yarrow	...

Belong to 1911 Estimates. Average cost of above two ships £356,768. Nottingham sunk by U-boat 19 Aug. 1916.

BIRMINGHAM.　　　　　Photo, Dr. B. H. Pidcock.

LOWESTOFT.

Following Notes also for Southampton, Dublin and Chatham (next page):—
Armour Notes.—Vertical side plating from 2 ft. 7 in. below w.l. to (a) upper deck amidships, (b) 3 ft. below upper deck fore and aft. Armour is really 2″ nickel amidships, 1″ forward and aft, but side plating is added for total thicknesses given.
Machinery Notes.—Impulse reaction turbines, viz., on each shaft, one ahead impulse turbine plus an ahead reaction turbine, an impulse astern turbine and an astern reaction turbine.

1911 BRITISH LIGHT CRUISERS. 1909

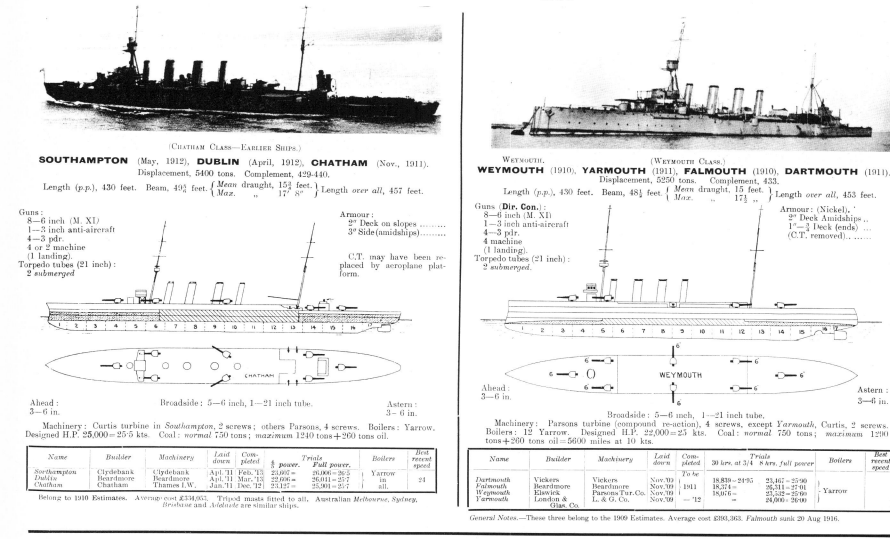

(CHATHAM CLASS—EARLIER SHIPS.)

SOUTHAMPTON (May, 1912), **DUBLIN** (April, 1912), **CHATHAM** (Nov., 1911).

Displacement, 5400 tons. Complement, 429-440.

Length (p.p.), 430 feet. Beam, 49⅚ feet. { Mean draught, 15¾ feet. Max. „ 17′ 8″ } Length over all, 457 feet.

Guns:
8—6 inch (M. XI)
1—3 inch anti-aircraft
4—3 pdr.
4 or 2 machine
(1 landing).
Torpedo tubes (21 inch):
2 submerged

Armour:
2″ Deck on slopes ....
3″ Side (amidships)........

C.T. may have been replaced by aeroplane platform.

CHATHAM

Ahead:
3—6 in.

Broadside: 5—6 inch, 1—21 inch tube.

Astern:
3—6 in.

Machinery: Curtis turbine in Southampton, 2 screws; others Parsons, 4 screws. Boilers: Yarrow.
Designed H.P. 25,000 = 25·5 kts. Coal: normal 750 tons; maximum 1240 tons + 260 tons oil.

Name	Builder	Machinery	Laid down	Completed	½ power Trials Full power		Boilers	Best recent speed
Southampton	Clydebank	Clydebank	Apl. '11	Feb. '13	23,697	26,006=26·5	Yarrow in all.	24
Dublin	Beardmore	Beardmore	Apl. '11	Mar. '13	22,606	26,041=25·7		
Chatham	Chatham	Chatham	Jan. '11	Dec. '12	23,127	25,901=25·7		

Belong to 1910 Estimates. Average cost £334,053. Tripod masts fitted to all. Australian Melbourne, Sydney, Brisbane and Adelaide are similar ships.

WEYMOUTH.　　　　　(WEYMOUTH CLASS.)

WEYMOUTH (1910), **YARMOUTH** (1911), **FALMOUTH** (1910), **DARTMOUTH** (1911).

Displacement, 5250 tons. Complement, 433.

Length (p.p.), 430 feet. Beam, 48½ feet. { Mean draught, 15 feet. Max. „ 17½ „ } Length over all, 453 feet.

Guns (**Dir. Con.**):
8—6 inch (M. XI)
1—3 inch anti-aircraft
4—3 pdr.
4 machine
(1 landing).
Torpedo tubes (21 inch):
2 submerged.

Armour: (Nickel).
2″ Deck Amidships ..
1″—¾″ Deck (ends)..
(C.T. removed).. ......

WEYMOUTH

Ahead:
3—6 in.

Broadside: 5—6 inch, 1—21 inch tube.

Astern:
3—6 in.

Machinery: Parsons turbine (compound re-action), 4 screws, except Yarmouth, Curtis, 2 screws.
Boilers: 12 Yarrow. Designed H.P. 22,000 = 25 kts. Coal: normal 750 tons; maximum 1290 tons + 260 tons oil = 5600 miles at 10 kts.

Name	Builder	Machinery	Laid down	Completed	30 hrs. at 3/4 Trials 8 hrs. full power		Boilers	Best recent speed
Dartmouth	Vickers	Vickers	Nov.'09	To be 1911	18,839 = 24·95	23,467=25·90		
Falmouth	Beardmore	Beardmore	Nov.'09		18,374	26,311=27·01	Yarrow	
Weymouth	Elswick	Parsons Tur. Co.	Nov.'09		18,076	23,532=25·60		
Yarmouth	London & Glas. Co.	L. & G. Co.	Nov.'09	'12		24,000=26·00		

General Notes.—These three belong to the 1909 Estimates. Average cost £393,363. Falmouth sunk 20 Aug 1916.

1908 BRITISH LIGHT CRUISERS.

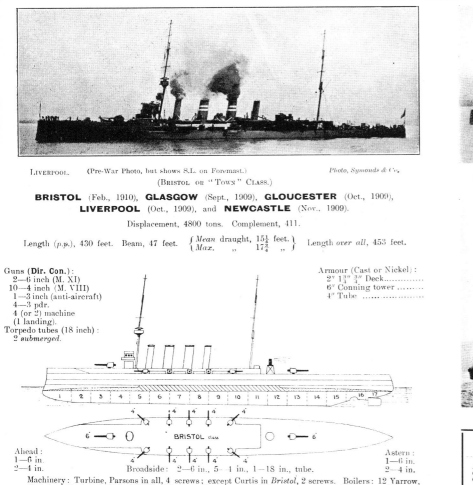

LIVERPOOL. (Pre-War Photo, but shows S.L. on Foremast.) *Photo, Symonds & Co.*

(BRISTOL OR "TOWN" CLASS.)

BRISTOL (Feb., 1910), **GLASGOW** (Sept., 1909), **GLOUCESTER** (Oct., 1909), **LIVERPOOL** (Oct., 1909), and **NEWCASTLE** (Nov., 1909).

Displacement, 4800 tons. Complement, 411.

Length (*p.p.*), 430 feet. Beam, 47 feet. { Mean draught, 15¼ feet. } Length *over all*, 453 feet.
{ Max. „ 17¾ „ }

Guns (**Dir. Con.**):
2—6 inch (M. XI)
10—4 inch (M. VIII)
1—3 inch (anti-aircraft)
4—3 pdr.
4 (or 2) machine
(1 landing).
Torpedo tubes (18 inch):
2 submerged.

Armour (Cast or Nickel):
2" 1¾" ¾" Deck.............
6" Conning tower ....
4" Tube ....

Ahead:
1—6 in.
2—4 in.

Broadside: 2—6 in., 5—4 in., 1—18 in., tube.

Astern:
1—6 in.
2—4 in.

Machinery: Turbine, Parsons in all, 4 screws; except Curtis in *Bristol*, 2 screws. Boilers: 12 Yarrow, small tube. Designed H.P. 22,000 = 25 kts. Coal: *normal* 600 tons; *maximum* 1353 tons + 260 tons oil. Built under 1908 Estimates.

NEWCASTLE. (No topmast to mainmast.)

BRISTOL. (Big top to foremast.)

Name	Builder	Machinery	Laid down	Completed	Trials: ⅘ power.	Full power.	Boilers
Bristol	Brown	Brown	Mar.'09	Feb.'11	11,300 = 24·06	21,927 = 26·84	Yarrow in all.
Glasgow	Fairfield	Fairfield	Mar.'09	Jan.'11	11,055 = 23·7	22,172 = 25·8	
Gloucester	Beardmore	Beardmore	Apl.'09	Jan.'11	13,968 = 23·447	24,335 = 26·296	
Liverpool	Vickers	Vickers	Feb.'09	Oct.'10	13,970 = 23·883	24,178 = 26·171	
Newcastle	Elswick	Wallsend Co.	Mar.'09	Oct.'10	14,038 = 23·312	24,669 = 26·266	

1910-11 BRITISH LIGHT CRUISERS. 1909

FEARLESS.

(BOADICEA TYPE—LAST TWO.)

ACTIVE (Feb., 1911), **AMPHION** (Dec., 1911), **FEARLESS** (June, 1912).

Displacement, 3440 tons. Complement, 325-321.

Length, (*p.p.*) 385, (*o.a.*) 406 feet. Beam, 41½ feet. *Max.* draught, 15 feet 7 ins.

Guns:
Fearless 8— } 4 inch M. VII.
Active 10— }
1—3 inch anti-aircraft
4—3 pdr.
1 machine gun
Torpedo tubes (21 inch):
2 above water

Armour (Hadfield):
1" Deck ....
4" Conning tower.....
2½" Tube ....

"Fearless" attached to Submarines.

(Plan as *Blanche* and *Blonde*).

Machinery: Parsons turbine. Boilers: 12 Yarrow (small tube). Designed H.P. 18,000 = 25 kts. Coal: *normal* 350 tons; *maximum* 780 tons. Also 190 tons oil. Built under 1911 Estimates. *Amphion* of this class sunk, August, 1914.

Name	Builder	Machinery	Laid down	Completed	Trials	Boilers	Best recent speed
Active	Pembroke	Hawthorn	July.'10	1912	= 25·1	Yarrow in all	27
Amphion	Pembroke	Hawthorn	Mar.'11	1912			—
Fearless	Pembroke	Hawthorn	Nov.'11	1913			—

BLANCHE.

(BOADICEA TYPE).

BLANCHE (November, 1909), **BLONDE** (July, 1910).

Normal displacement, 3350 tons. Complement, 314.

Length, (*p.p.*) 385, (*o.a.*) 405 feet. Beam, 41½ feet. *Max.* draught, 15½ feet.

Guns:
8—4 inch (M. VII)
1—4 inch anti-aircraft
4—3 pdr.
1 machine.
Torpedo tubes (18 inch):
2 above water

Armour (Hadfield):
1½" Deck ....
4" Conning tower
2½" Tube.....

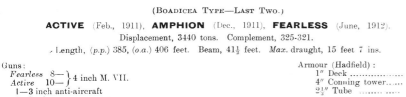

Machinery: Parsons turbine. Boilers: 12 Yarrow. Designed H.P. 18,000 = 24-25 kts. Coal: *normal*, 450 tons; *maximum*, 780 tons coal + 190 tons oil. Both built under 1909 Estimates.

Name	Builder	Machinery	Laid down	Completed	Trials 30 hrs.	8 hrs.	Boilers	Best recent speed
Blanche	Pembroke, Y.	Hawthorn	Ap.'09	1910	15,000 = 22·3	18,542 = 25·67	Yarrow small tube	26·1
Blonde	Pembroke, Y.	Laird	Dec.'09	1911		18,772 = 25·3		

Note to Plans.—2—4 inch removed, but from which positions is not yet known.

1907-9 BRITISH LIGHT CRUISERS. 1903.

(BOADICEA TYPE.)

BOADICEA (May, 1908). **BELLONA** (March, 1909).

Normal displacement, 3300 tons. Complement, 317.

Length (*p.p.*), 385 feet. (*o.a.* 405). Beam, 41 feet. *Mean* draught, $13\frac{1}{2}$ feet ($14\frac{5}{6}$ *max.*).

Guns:
10—4 inch (M. VII.)
1—4 inch anti-aircraft
4—3 pdr.
1 machine.
Torpedo tubes (18 inch):
2 *above water*

Armour: (Hadfield).
1" Deck ....
4" C.T. ....
$2\frac{1}{2}$" Tube ......

Machinery: Parsons turbine Boilers: 12 Yarrow. Designed H.P. 18,000=25 kts. Coal: *normal*, 450 tons; *maximum*, 855 tons coal+200 tons oil.

Name	*Builder*	*Machinery*	*Laid down*	*Completed*	*Trials (mean) Full power.*	*Boilers*	*Best recent speed*
Boadicea	Pembroke Y	Clydebank	July'07	1909	18,536=25·5	Yarrow	27·9

1907 Estimates; *Bellona*, (1908 Estimates.) for sale 1919.

HERMES (April 1898), **HYACINTH** (October, 1898).
HIGHFLYER (June, 1898). Large re-fit, 1919. 5600 tons. Complement, 450. Dimensions: 350 (*p.p.*) × 54 × 22 feet (*max.* draught). Guns: 11—6 inch wire (M. VII, VIII), 6—12 pdr., 4—3 pdr., 4 Maxims, 1 landing. Torpedo tubes (18 inch): 2 *submerged*. Armour: 3" Armour deck, Protection to vitals, 5" Engine hatches, 6" Conning tower. Machinery: 2 sets 4 cylinder triple expansion. 2 screws. Boilers: Belleville. Designed H.P. 10,000 = 19·5 kts. Coal: *normal*, 500 tons; *maximum*, 1120 tons. Complement, 481.
Hermes sunk by U-boat 31 Oct 1914 in Straits of Dover while acting as seaplane carrier.

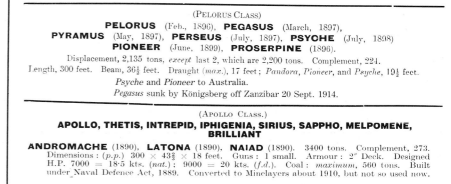

(ASTRÆA CLASS.)

Photo, N. O'Toole, Esq.

ASTRÆA, CHARYBDIS, FORTE, FOX, HERMIONE (—1893).
4360 tons (sheathed and coppered). Complement, 318. Dimensions: (*p.p.*) 320 × $49\frac{1}{2}$ × $21\frac{1}{2}$ feet (*max.* draught). Armament: 2—6 inch, 8—4·7 inch, 1—12 pdr., 2—6 pdr., 1—3 pdr., 4 M.G., 1 landing. Torpedo tubes (18 inch): 3 *above water (may be removed)*. Armour: 2" Deck, 5" Engine hatches, 3" Conning tower. Designed H.P. (*f.d.*) 9000 = 19·5 kts. Coal: *maximum*, 1000 tons. Built under Naval Defence Act, 1889. *Hermione*, Depot Ship at Southampton.

NOTE.—All the old Light Cruisers of "Sentinel" type given below will not be used again for Fleet Service except in emergency.

ATTENTIVE (24th November, 1904).

ADVENTURE (Sept., 1904). By Elswick. Displacement, 2670 tons. Dimensions: 374 × $38\frac{1}{4}$ × $13\frac{1}{2}$ feet (*maximum* draught). Complement, 301. Guns: 2—6 inch, 6—4 inch, 1—3 inch AA., 1—6 pdr., 2—2 pdr. AA. Torpedo tubes (14 inch): 2 *above water*. Armour: 2" Deck. Machinery: 2 sets 6 cylinder. 2 screws. Boilers: $\frac{4}{5}$ Yarrow curved, $\frac{1}{5}$ cylindrical. *About* H.P. 16,000 = 25·5 kts. Coal: *normal*, 150 tons; *maximum*, 455 tons. *Attentive* for Sale.

FORWARD (29th August, 1904),

FORESIGHT (Oct., 1904). By Fairfield. Displacement, 2850 tons. Dimensions: 360 × $39\frac{1}{4}$ × $15\frac{1}{3}$ feet (*maximum* draught). Complement, 298. Guns: 9—4 inch (M. VII), 1—3 inch AA. Torpedo tubes (14 inch): 2 *above water*. Armour: 2" Belt amidships, $1\frac{1}{2}$"—$\frac{5}{8}$" Deck. Machinery: 2 sets 6 cylinder. 2 screws. *About* H.P. 15,000 = $25\frac{1}{4}$ kts. Coal: *normal*, 150 tons; *maximum*, 500 tons. *Forward* for Sale.

PATHFINDER (16th July, 1904), & **PATROL** (13th October, 1904).
Pathfinder sunk by U-boat 5 Sept., 1914.

SENTINEL (April, 1904) and **SKIRMISHER** (Feb., 1905). Both by Vickers, Ltd. Displacement, 2895 tons. Dimensions: 360 × 40 × $14\frac{3}{4}$ feet (*maximum* draught). Complement, 298. Guns (M. VII): 9—4 inch and (in *Sentinel*) 1—3 inch AA., 1—6 pdr. AA., 1—3 pdr. AA., (in *Skirmisher*) 1—3 inch AA., 1—6 pdr. Torpedo tubes (14 inch): 2 *above water*. Armour: $1\frac{1}{2}$"—$\frac{5}{8}$" Deck. Machinery: 2 sets 4 cylinder. 2 screws. H.P. *about* 17,000 = 25 kts. Coal: *normal*, 160 tons; *maximum*, 410 tons.

VINDICTIVE (December, 1897).
Displacement, 5750 tons. Complement, 480.
Length, 320 feet. Beam, $57\frac{1}{2}$ feet. *Maximum* draught, 24 feet
Sunk as blockship at Ostend May 10 1918.

(TOPAZE CLASS.)

DIAMOND (Jan., 1904), **SAPPHIRE** (March, 1904).
TOPAZE (July, 1903), **AMETHYST** (Nov., 1903). Displacement, 3000 tons. Complement, 290-300. Dimensions: 360 × 40 × $14\frac{1}{2}$ feet (*mean* draught). Guns: *Topaze*, 12—4 inch, 1—6 pdr. AA., 2—3 pdr. AA., 1—6 pdr., 3 M.G.; *Amethyst*, 2—6 inch, 8—4 inch, 2—3 pdr., 3 M.G. Torpedo tubes (18 inch): 2 *above water*. Armour (steel): 2" Deck. Machinery: 2 sets triple expansion, except *Amethyst*, Parsons turbine. 2 screws. Boilers: Normand-Laird in *Topaze*, Yarrow in *Amethyst*. *Max.* H.P. *Topaze*, 9800 = 22·2 kts.; *Amethyst*, 12,000 = 23·4 kts. *nominal*. Coal: *normal*, 300 tons; *maximum*, 750 tons. Built under 1902-3 Estimates.

(ECLIPSE CLASS.)

ECLIPSE (July, 1894), **TALBOT** (April, 1895), **MINERVA** (Sept., 1895), **VENUS** (Sept., 1895)
JUNO (Nov., 1895), **DIANA** (Dec., 1895), **DIDO** (March, 1896),
DORIS (March, 1896), & **ISIS** (June, 1896) Displacement, 5600 tons. Complement, 393. Dimensions: 364 (*w.l.*) × 54 × 23 feet (*max.* draught). Length *over all*, $370\frac{1}{2}$ feet. Guns: 9—6 inch, 45 cal. M. VII, 4—12 pdr., 12 cwt., 1—3 pdr., 2 M.G. Torpedo tubes (18 inch): 2 *submerged*, 1 *above water* (stern). Armour: $2\frac{1}{2}$" Armour deck, Protection to vitals, 6" Engine hatches, 6" Conning tower (Harvey). Machinery: 2 sets inverted triple expansion. 2 screws. Boilers: 8 single-ended cylindrical. Designed H.P. *natural* 8000 = 18·5 kts.; *forced* 9600 = 19·5 kts. Coal: *normal*, 550 tons; *maximum*, 1065 tons.

(PELORUS CLASS)

PELORUS (Feb., 1896), **PEGASUS** (March, 1897),
PYRAMUS (May, 1897), **PERSEUS** (July, 1897), **PSYCHE** (July, 1898)
PIONEER (June, 1899), **PROSERPINE** (1896).
Displacement, 2,135 tons, *except* last 2, which are 2,200 tons. Complement, 224.
Length, 300 feet. Beam, $36\frac{1}{2}$ feet. Draught (*max.*), 17 feet; *Pandora*, *Pioneer*, and *Psyche*, $19\frac{1}{2}$ feet.
Psyche and *Pioneer* to Australia.
Pegasus sunk by Königsberg off Zanzibar 20 Sept. 1914.

(APOLLO CLASS.)

APOLLO, THETIS, INTREPID, IPHIGENIA, SIRIUS, SAPPHO, MELPOMENE, BRILLIANT
ANDROMACHE (1890), **LATONA** (1890), **NAIAD** (1890). 3400 tons. Complement, 273. Dimensions: (*p.p.*) 300 × $43\frac{3}{4}$ × 18 feet. Guns: 1 small. Armour: 2" Deck. Designed H.P. 7000 = 18·5 kts. (*nat.*); 9000 = 20 kts. (*f.d.*). Coal: *maximum*, 560 tons. Built under Naval Defence Act, 1889. Converted to Minelayers about 1910, but not so used now.

Thetis, *Intrepid*, *Iphigenia*, *Brilliant* and *Sirius* sunk as blockships at Zeebrugge 23 April 1918.

BRITISH NAVY.

Coast Defence Vessel.

Photo, Cribb, Southsea.

GORGON (ex *Nidaros*, 9th June, 1914).

Displacement, 5700 tons. Complement, 303.

Length (*o.a.*), 310 feet. Beam, 73⅜ feet. *Max.* Draught, 16½ feet.

Guns (Elswick):
2—9·2 inch
6—6 inch
2—3 inch anti-aircraft.
4—2 pdr. pom-poms.

Armour:
*7″ Belt ....
*4″ Ends ....
2″ Deck ....
4″ Citadel ....
8″ Turrets ....
6″ Secondary guns ....
8″ Fore C.T. ....
6″ Aft C.T. ....
* Not fitted ?

Machinery: Triple expansion. 2 screws. Boilers: Yarrow. Designed H.P. 4000 = 13 kts. Coal: *maximum* 364 tons + 170 tons oil.

Name	*Builder*	*Machinery*	*Begun*	*Completed*	*Trials.*
Gorgon	Armstrong	H. Leslie	June, 1913	June, 1918	

Notes.—There were originally two ships in this class, begun at Elswick in May-June, 1913, for the Norwegian Navy, as the Coast Service Battleships *Bjoergvin* and *Nidaros*. Construction was stopped when war began, and they lay in the Tyne in an incomplete condition until 1915, when they were taken over for the British Navy and named *Glatton* (ex *Bjoergvin*) and *Gorgon* (ex *Nidaros*). *Glatton* blew up at Dover during September, 1918. As originally designed, this ship had a beam of 55¾ feet and a speed of 15 kts. Beam has been increased and speed reduced by the addition of "blisters" to the hull. The belt may never have been fitted.

Monitors

EREBUS.

EREBUS (19th June, 1916), **TERROR** (18th May, 1916).

Displacement, 8000 tons. Complements, 226 and 223.

Length, (*p.p.*) 380, (*o.a.*) 405 feet. Beam, 88 feet. *Mean* Draught, 11 feet.

Guns:
2—15 inch, 42 cal. (**Dir. Con.**)
8—4 inch
2—12 pdr.
2—3 inch (anti-aircraft)
2—2 pdr. (anti-aircraft)
4 M G.

Armour:
4″ Bulkheads, F. & A.
8″ Barbettes ....
13″-4¼″ Gunhouses ....
4″ Box Citadel (over magazines) ......
6″ C.T. ....
1″ Fo'xle & Upper D'ks
4″ Main Deck (Slopes)
2″ Main Deck........
1½″-¾″ Lower Deck ..
Anti-torpedo Pro. Bulges

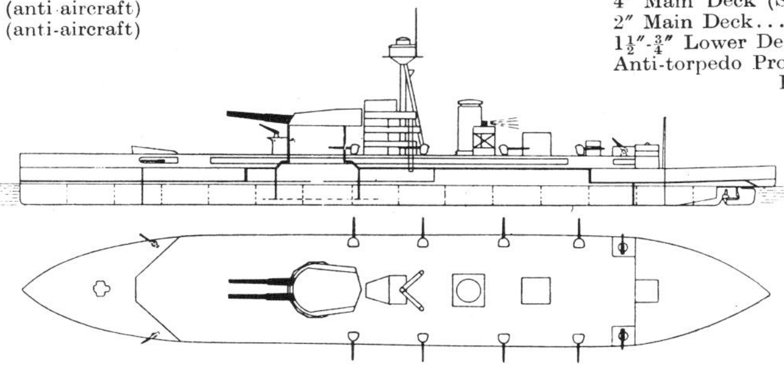

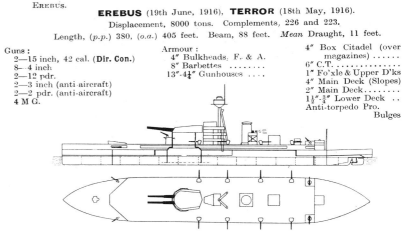

Machinery: Triple expansion. 2 screws. Boilers: Babcock. Designed H.P. 6000 = 12 kts. Fuel: 650 tons *normal*, 750 tons, *maximum*, oil only.

Gunnery Notes.—15 inch are high angle and can range up to 40,000 yards. Smoke screen apparatus fitted. *Erebus* has 15 inch removed from *M. Ney*.

Special Protection.—Bulges about 15 feet deep, sub-divided into 50 w.t.c. *Erebus* hit full amidships by distance-controlled boat, carrying heavy charge. Was repaired in a fortnight and rails were fitted to "blisters" of both ships to prevent distance-controlled boats riding up blisters. *Terror* hit by three torpedoes in succession—2 right forward beyond bulge protection inflicted heavy damage. The third torpedo hit the bulge and did no harm at all.

Name	*Builder and Machinery*	*Begun*	*Completed*	*Trials*
Erebus *Terror*	Harland & Wolff (Govan) Harland & Wolff (Belfast)	Oct., 1915 Oct., 1915	Sept., 1916 Aug., 1916	7244 H.P. = 14·1 kts. 6235 H.P. = 13·1 kts.

General Notes.—Both Emergency War Programme. Designed as an improved "Abercrombie" type to outrange the 15 and 11 inch guns mounted by Germans on Belgian Coast. Their speed, considering their great beam, is remarkable. Were the "crack" monitors of the famous Dover Patrol.

Cancelled 1918.—Large monitor (unnamed) by Messrs. Wm. Hamilton.

BRITISH NAVY—MONITORS.

M. NEY.

Guns: Has only 6—6 inch, 2—3 inch AA., 2—3 pdr. AA.

See Addenda pages

M. SOULT.

Guns: 2—15 inch (DIR. CON., H. A. elevation), 8—4 inch, 2—12 pdr., 2—3 inch AA., 2—2 pdr. AA.

MARSHAL NEY (24th August, 1915), **MARSHAL SOULT** (17th June, 1915).

Displacement, 6670 tons. Complements, *M. Ney* 186, *M. Soult*, 228.

Length, 340 (*p.p.*), 355⅔ (*o.a.*) feet. Beam, 90½ feet. Draught, 10½ feet.

Armour: in *Soult* only, 8″ Barbette, 13″—4½″ Gunhouse: in both, 4″ Bulkheads fore and aft, 6″ C.T., 4″—1″ Box Citadel over Magazine, 1″ Fo'xle Deck, 2″—1½″ Upper Deck, Lower Deck 3″ at bow, 1½″ at stern, 1″ Navig. Position. Deep Bulge Protection.

Machinery: 2 sets Diesel. 2 screws. Designed H.P 1500 = 6·7 kts. Fuel: 235 tons, *maximum* oil only.

Name	*Builder*	*Machinery*	*Begun*	*Completed*	*Trials*
M. Ney *M. Soult*	Palmer Palmer	White Vickers	Jan., 1915 Jan., 1915	Aug., 1915 Nov., 1915	2309 H.P. = 6·3 kts. 1898 H.P. = 6·6 kts.

General Notes.—Emergency War Programme. *M. Ney* practically a failure, on account of her engines being highly unreliable. 15 inch guns and barbette removed from her about 1917, and she was moored as Guard-Ship in the Downs.

ABERCROMBIE, HAVELOCK, RAGLAN, ROBERTS.

Raglan sunk off Imbros 20 Jan. 1918.

SIR JOHN MOORE.

GENERAL CRAUFURD (8th July, 1915), **SIR JOHN MOORE** (31st May, 1915).

Displacement, 5900 tons. Complements, 237.

Length, 320 (*p.p.*), 335½ (*o.a.*) feet. Beam, 87¼ feet. Draught, 10½ feet.

Guns:
2—12 inch, M. VIII, 25 cal.
4 to 2—6 inch
2—12 pdr.
2—3 inch AA.
2—2 pdr. anti-aircraft.
4 M.G.

Armour (Krupp):
6″ Bulkheads F. & A..
8″—2″ Barbettes ......
10½″—2″ Gunhouse...
6″ Conning tower ...
1″ Foxle deck ....
6″ Upper deck (slopes)
2″ Upper deck ....
1½″ Main deck ....
Anti-torpedo protection: Deep bulges.

Machinery: Triple expansion. 2 screws. Boilers: Babcock & Wilcox. Designed H.P. 2310 (?) = 6·7 kts. 2 screws. Coal: 350 tons, *maximum*.

General Notes.—Emergency War Programme. Armed with 12 inch from old *Majestics*. These Monitors are extremely slow and unwieldy—in fact against a strong head wind and sea, they can only make 1 or 2 kts. But most remarkably steady gun platforms, on account of their huge beam and bulges.

Name	*Builder and Machinery*	*Begun*	*Completed*	*Trials*
Gen. Craufurd *Sir Jno. Moore*	Harland & Wolff (Belfast) Scotts S.B. Co.	Jan., 1915 Jan., 1915	Aug., 1915 July, 1915	2523 H.P. = 7·4 kts. 2500 H.P. = 7·75 kts.

Special Note.—All other Monitors of *Abercrombie* (14 inch) type and *Earl of Peterborough* (12 inch) type on Disposal List, 1919—not required for War Fleet and will be broken up soon.

BRITISH NAVY—MONITORS & ARMOURED GUNBOAT.

Monitors.

M 29, M 31 (Workman Clark), **M 32, M 33** (Harland & Wolff, Belfast). All launched and completed during 1915. 535 tons. Complement, 75. Dimensions : 170 × 31 × 6¾ feet. Guns : 2—6 inch (1—3 inch AA. in *M 31, M 33*), 1—6 pdr. AA., 4 or 2 M.G. Designed H.P. 400 = 10 kts. Machinery : Triple expansion. 2 screws. Boilers : Yarrow. Oil fuel : 45 tons. *M 30* lost during the War.

Notes.—All Emergency War Programme.

M 23 (with 7·5 inch gun).

For description, v. next column.

Monitors—*continued.*

For photo, see Addenda pages.

M 19, M 20, M 22, M 23, M 24, M 25, M 26, M 27. All built by Sir Raylton Dixon & Co. Launched May-September, 1915. Completed May-October, 1915. 540 tons. Complement, 67-82. Dimensions : 170 × 31 × 6 feet. Guns : *M 19—20* as *M 16—18* below, *M 22* also as those below, but 1—12 pdr. and 1—3 pdr. extra. *M 23—26*, 1—7·5 inch, 1 or 2—3 inch AA., 1—12 pdr. and (in some) 1—6 pdr. or 2—2 pdr. AA., or pom-pom, 2 M.G. *M 27*, 1—4·7 inch, 2—3 inch AA., 2—2 pdr. pom-pom, 2 M.G. Machinery : *M 19—20, 23—27.* Bolinders oil engines, 640 B.H.P. *M 22*, triple expansion engines and White-Forster boilers. I.H.P. 650. 4 screws in *M 24, 26, 27,* 2 in others. Speed : 12 kts. in all. Oil : 25-28 tons. *M 15, 21, 25, 27* and *M 28* of this class lost during the War.

For photo, see Addenda pages.

M 16, M 17, M 18. Built by Messrs. Gray & Co. Launched April-May, 1915, completed June-July, 1915. Guns : 1—9·2 inch, 1—3 inch AA., 2 M.G. I.H.P. 800 = 12 kts. Triple expansion engines. 2 screws. Boilers : Loco. Oil : 32 tons. All other details as *M 19—27* above, from which they differ in appearance. *M 15* lost during the War.

General Notes.—All Emergency War Programme.

Armoured Gunboat.

Photo, Abrahams, Devonport.

HUMBER (ex *Jarary*, Vickers, 1913). 1260 tons. Dimensions : 261 (*p.p.*), 266¾ (*o.a.*) × 49 × 5¾ feet. Guns : 3—6 inch, 2—4·7 inch howitzers, 4—3 pdr., 1—3 pdr. AA. Armour : 2″ sides, ″ Barbette, ″ C.T. Upper deck is protective. H.P. 1450 = 12 kts. Boilers : Yarrow. Coal : 187 tons + 90 tons oil fuel.

General Notes.—Brazilian River Monitor *Jarary.* Purchased 1914. 1—6 inch gun (salved from old wrecked *Montagu*) was added, mounted on quarter deck. Purchased for British Navy on outbreak of war. Designed for service on the Amazon, S. America, but has actually taken part in several coastal bombardments and other operations entailing long sea voyages. Sister ships, *Mersey* (ex *Madera*), *Severn* (ex *Solimoes*), on Sale List, 1919.

Large China Gunboats.

BRITISH NAVY.

LADYBIRD. (INSECT CLASS—12 BOATS.)

APHIS (1915), **BEE** (1916), **CICALA** (December, 1915), **COCKCHAFER** (December, 1915), **CRICKET** (December, 1915), **GLOWWORM** (February, 1916). All by Barclay Curle.

GNAT (1915), **LADYBIRD** (1915). Both by Messrs. Lobnitz.

MANTIS (1915), **MOTH** (1915). Both by Sunderland S.B. Co.

SCARAB (1915), **TARANTULA** (1915). Both by Wood, Skinner & Co.

645 tons. Complement, 53. Dimensions : 230 (*p.p.*), 237½ (*o.a.*) × 36 × 4 feet. Guns : 2—6 inch, 2—12 pdr., 6 M.G.; also 2—3 inch AA. in a few. Machinery : Triple expansion. Twin screws in tunnels fitted with Messrs. Yarrow's patent balanced flap. Boilers : Yarrow. Designed H.P. 2000 = 14 kts. Fuel (coal or oil) : 35 tons coal + 65 tons oil.

Notes.—Emergency War Programme. Ordered February, 1915. Completed November, 1915-April, 1916. Built to Yarrow design under Messrs. Yarrow's supervision. Originally intended that these boats should proceed to Salonika, be dismantled, transported in sections overland and be re-erected and re-floated on a tributary of the Danube, to fight the Austro-Hungarian Danube Flotilla. To conceal their objective, they were ordered as River Gunboats for the Chinese Rivers—hence their name of "China Gunboats." These were towed out to Malta, but the great "drive" by the enemy armies through Serbia stopped these plans. These ships then proceeded to the Tigris and Euphrates. *Glowworm* badly injured by explosion, 1919, on Dvina River.

Small China Gunboats.

SEDGEFLY. (FLY CLASS—16 BOATS.)

BLACKFLY, BUTTERFLY, CADDISFLY, CRANEFLY, DRAGONFLY, FIREFLY, GADFLY, GRAYFLY, GREENFLY, HOVERFLY, MAYFLY, SAWFLY, SEDGEFLY, SNAKEFLY, STONEFLY, WATERFLY. Built by Messrs. Yarrow, Ltd., in sections, shipped out to Mesopotamia and erected at Abadan, 1915-6—See *Notes* below. 98 tons. Complement, 22. Dimensions : 120 (*p.p.*), 126 (*o.a.*) × 20 × 2 feet. Guns : 1—4 inch, 1—12 pdr., 1—6 pdr. (not in all), 1—3 pdr. AA., 1—2 pdr. pom-pom, 5 or 4 M.G. Machinery : 1 set triple expansion engines. Single screw in tunnel fitted with Messrs. Yarrow's patent balanced flap. Boilers : 1 Yarrow, burning coal or oil. Designed H.P. 175 = 9·5 kts. Fuel : 5 tons coal + 10 tons oil.

Notes.—Twelve of these craft are said to have been ordered by the Admiralty in February, 1915, from Messrs. Yarrow, Ltd. They were intended to police the Tigris against Arab guerillas. After capture of *Firefly* by Turks, the number was increased to 16. *Firefly* was re-captured in the British advance from Kut-el-Amara to Bagdad. They were built in sections and shipped out, the port and starboard sections being numbered and painted red and green, to facilitate erection by native labour at Abadan. *Firefly* began to be erected August, 1915, and entered service in November of the same year. The last of the original twelve were shipped out in August, 1915, and were in service by March, 1916, the extra four (*Blackfly, Caddisfly, Hoverfly, Sedgefly*) following them later. All Emergency War Programme. Eight of these transferred to War Office.

	Begun.	Sent out.		Begun.	Sent out.
Blackfly		4/16	Greenfly	2/15	9/15
Butterfly	2/15	7/15	Hoverfly	11/15	4/16
Caddisfly		12/15	Mayfly	2/15	8/15
Cranefly	7/15		Sawfly	2/15	8/15
Dragonfly		7/15	Sedgefly	11/15	9/16
Firefly	2/15	7/15	Snakefly		
Gadfly		8/15	Stonefly	2/15	
Grayfly		8/15	Waterfly		9/15

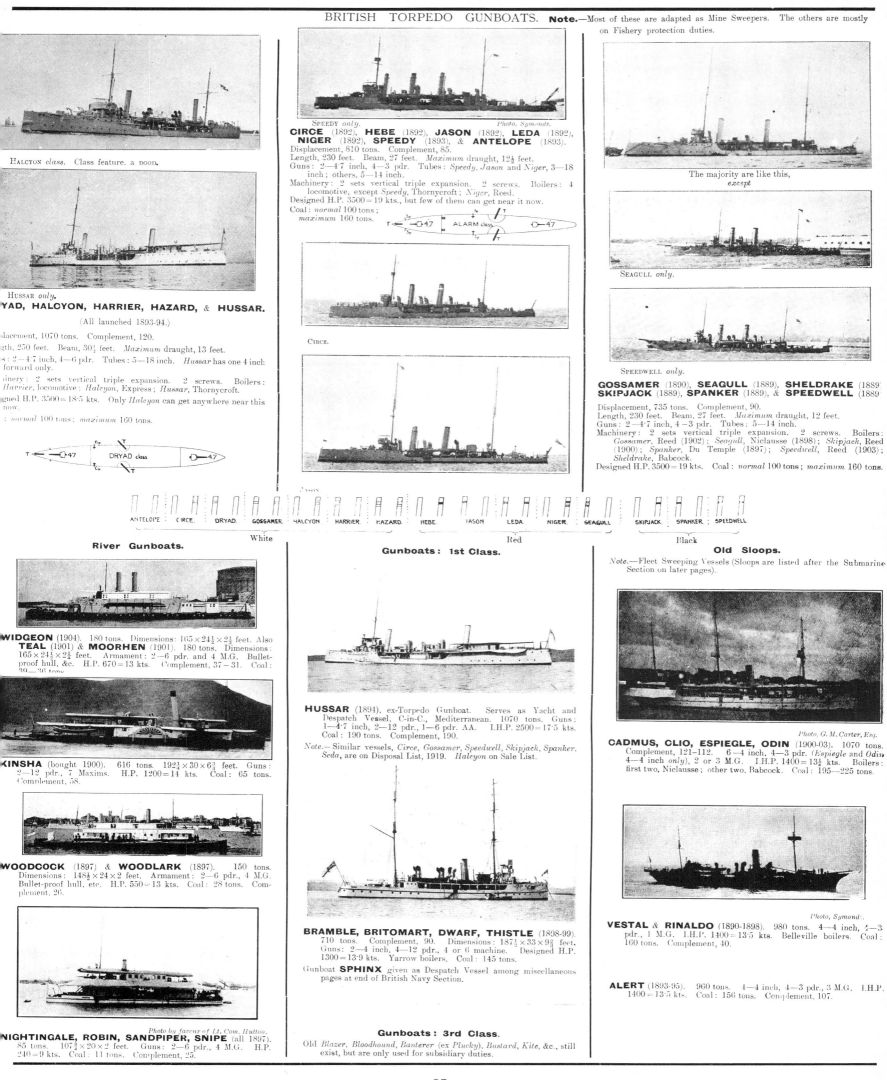

BRITISH TORPEDO GUNBOATS. **Note.**—Most of these are adapted as Mine Sweepers. The others are mostly on Fishery protection duties.

SPEEDY *only.* *Photo, Symonds.*

CIRCE (1892), **HEBE** (1892), **JASON** (1892), **LEDA** (1892), **NIGER** (1892), **SPEEDY** (1893), & **ANTELOPE** (1893).
Displacement, 810 tons. Complement, 85.
Length, 230 feet. Beam, 27 feet. *Maximum* draught, 12½ feet.
Guns: 2—4·7 inch, 4—3 pdr. Tubes: *Speedy, Jason* and *Niger*, 3—18 inch; others, 5—14 inch.
Machinery: 2 sets vertical triple expansion. 2 screws. Boilers: 4 locomotive, except *Speedy,* Thornycroft; *Niger,* Reed.
Designed H.P. 3500 = 19 kts., but few of them can get near it now.
Coal: *normal* 100 tons; *maximum* 160 tons.

ALARM class

CIRCE.

JASON.

The majority are like this, *except*

SEAGULL *only.*

SPEEDWELL *only.*

GOSSAMER (1890), **SEAGULL** (1889), **SHELDRAKE** (1889), **SKIPJACK** (1889), **SPANKER** (1889), & **SPEEDWELL** (1889).
Displacement, 735 tons. Complement, 90.
Length, 230 feet. Beam, 27 feet. *Maximum* draught, 12 feet.
Guns: 2—4·7 inch, 4—3 pdr. Tubes: 5—14 inch.
Machinery: 2 sets vertical triple expansion. 2 screws. Boilers: *Gossamer,* Reed (1902); *Seagull,* Niclausse (1898); *Skipjack,* Reed (1900); *Spanker,* Du Temple (1897); *Speedwell,* Reed (1903); *Sheldrake,* Babcock.
Designed H.P. 3500 = 19 kts. Coal: *normal* 100 tons; *maximum* 160 tons.

HALCYON *class.* Class feature, a poop.

HUSSAR *only.*

DRYAD, HALCYON, HARRIER, HAZARD, & HUSSAR.
(All launched 1893-94.)
Displacement, 1070 tons. Complement, 120.
Length, 250 feet. Beam, 30½ feet. *Maximum* draught, 13 feet.
Guns: 2—4·7 inch, 4—6 pdr. Tubes: 5—18 inch. *Hussar* has one 4 inch forward only.
Machinery: 2 sets vertical triple expansion. 2 screws. Boilers: *Harrier,* locomotive; *Halcyon,* Express; *Hussar,* Thornycroft.
Designed H.P. 3500 = 18·5 kts. Only *Halcyon* can get anywhere near this now.
Coal: *normal* 100 tons; *maximum* 160 tons.

DRYAD class

ANTELOPE. CIRCE. DRYAD. GOSSAMER. HALCYON. HARRIER. HAZARD. HEBE. JASON. LEDA. NIGER. SEAGULL. SKIPJACK. SPANKER. SPEEDWELL.

White   Red   Black

River Gunboats.

WIDGEON (1904). 180 tons. Dimensions: 165 × 24½ × 2½ feet. Also
TEAL (1901) & **MOORHEN** (1901). 180 tons. Dimensions: 165 × 24½ × 2¼ feet. Armament: 2—6 pdr. and 4 M.G. Bullet-proof hull, &c. H.P. 670 = 13 kts. Complement, 37—31. Coal: 30—36 tons.

KINSHA (bought 1900). 616 tons. 192½ × 30 × 6¾ feet. Guns: 2—12 pdr., 7 Maxims. H.P. 1200 = 14 kts. Coal: 65 tons. Complement, 58.

WOODCOCK (1897) & **WOODLARK** (1897). 150 tons. Dimensions: 148½ × 24 × 2 feet. Armament: 2—6 pdr., 4 M.G. Bullet-proof hull, etc. H.P. 550 = 13 kts. Coal: 28 tons. Complement, 26.

Photo by favour of Lt. Com. Hutton.
NIGHTINGALE, ROBIN, SANDPIPER, SNIPE (all 1897). 85 tons. 107¾ × 20 × 2 feet. Guns: 2—6 pdr., 4 M.G. H.P. 240 = 9 kts. Coal: 11 tons. Complement, 25.

Gunboats: 1st Class.

HUSSAR (1894), ex-Torpedo Gunboat. Serves as Yacht and Despatch Vessel, C-in-C., Mediterranean. 1070 tons. Guns: 1—4·7 inch, 2—12 pdr., 1—6 pdr. AA. I.H.P. 2500 = 17·5 kts. Coal: 190 tons. Complement, 190.
Note.— Similar vessels, *Circe, Gossamer, Speedwell, Skipjack, Spanker, Seda,* are on Disposal List, 1919. *Halcyon* on Sale List.

BRAMBLE, BRITOMART, DWARF, THISTLE (1898-99). 710 tons. Complement, 90. Dimensions: 187½ × 33 × 9¾ feet. Guns: 2—4 inch, 4—12 pdr., 4 or 6 machine. Designed H.P. 1300 = 13·9 kts. Yarrow boilers. Coal: 145 tons.
Gunboat **SPHINX** given as Despatch Vessel among miscellaneous pages at end of British Navy Section.

Gunboats: 3rd Class.

Old *Blazer, Bloodhound, Banterer* (ex *Plucky*), *Bustard, Kite,* &c., still exist, but are only used for subsidiary duties.

Old Sloops.

Note.—Fleet Sweeping Vessels (Sloops are listed after the Submarine Section on later pages).

Photo, G. M. Carter, Esq.
CADMUS, CLIO, ESPIEGLE, ODIN (1900-03). 1070 tons. Complement, 121—112. 6—4 inch, 4—3 pdr. (*Espiegle* and *Odin* 4—4 inch *only*), 2 or 3 M.G. I.H.P. 1400 = 13¼ kts. Boilers: first two, Niclausse; other two, Babcock. Coal: 195—225 tons.

Photo, Symonds.
VESTAL & RINALDO (1890-1898). 980 tons. 4—4 inch, 4—3 pdr., 1 M.G. I.H.P. 1400 = 13·5 kts. Belleville boilers. Coal: 160 tons. Complement, 40.

ALERT (1893-95). 960 tons. 4—4 inch, 4—3 pdr., 3 M.G. I.H.P. 1400 = 13·5 kts. Coal: 156 tons. Complement, 107.

BRITISH NAVY—PATROL GUNBOATS.

(KIL CLASS—81 BOATS.)

4 *G. Brown & Co.:* **KILBERRY** (July, 1918), **KILBEGGAN** (September, 1918), **KILBIRNIE** (———), **KILBRACHAN.**

21 *Cochrane:* **KILDALKEY** (March, 1918), **KILDARE** (April, 1918), **KILDANGAN** (March, 1918), **KILDONAN** (April, 1918), **KILDRESS** (April, 1918), **KILDWICK** (April, 1918), **KILFINNY** May, (1918), **KILFREE** (———), **KILGOWAN** (———), **KILKEE** (———), **KILKENNY** (———), **KILKENZIE** (———), **KILKERRIN** (———), **KILHAMPTON** (———), **KILLADOON** (———), **KILLIGAN** (———), **KILLALOO** (———), **KILLANE** **KILLARNEY** (———), **KILLARY** (———), **KILLEGAN** (———).

14 *Cook, Welton & Gemmell:* **KILCHATTAN** (April, 1918), **KILCHVAN** (———), **KILCLIEF** (May, 1919), **KILCLOGHER** (———), **KILCOLGAN** (———), **KILCOMMON** (———), **KILCONNELL** (———), **KILCOOLE** (———), **KILCORNEY** (———), **KILCOT** (———), **KILCREGGAN** (———), **KILCULLEN** (———), **KILCURRIG** (———), **KILDALE** (———).

4 *Hall Russell:* **KILBRIDE** (May, 1918), **KILBURN** (May, 1918), **KILBY** (———), **KILCAVAN** (———),

30 *Smith's Dock Co.:* **KILCHRENAN** (January, 1918), **KILCHREEST** (June, 1918), **KILCLARE** (January, 1918), **KILCOCK** (April, 1918), **KILDARY** (November, 1917), **KILDAVIN** (February, 1918), **KILDIMO** (April, 1918), **KILDORRY** (February, 1918), **KILDOROUGH** (November, 1917), **KILDYSART** (May, 1918), **KILFENORA** (December, 1917), **KILFULLERT** (March, 1918), **KILGARVAN** (May, 1918), **KILGOBNET** (December, 1917), **KILHAM** (June, 1918), **KILKEEL** (March, 1918), **KILLERIG** (July, 1918), **KILLINEY** (July, 1918), **KILLOUR** (August, 1918), **KILMALLOCK** (December, 1918), **KILMANAHAN** (December, 1918), **KILMARNOCK** (March, 1919), **KILMARTEN** (March, 1919), **KILMEAD** (May, 1918), **KILMELFORD** (———, 1919), **KILMERSDON** (———, 1919), **KILMINGTON** (———), **KILMORE** (———), **KILMUCKRIDGE** (———, 1919), **KILMUN** (———. 1919).

8 *(Builders unknown):* **KILDPART** (———), **KILLENA** (July, 1918), **KILLOWEN** (September, 1918), **KILLYBEGS** (September, 1918), **KILLYGORDON** (———), **KILMACRENNAN** (November, 1918), **KILMAINE** (November, 1918), **KILMALCOLM** (October, 1918).

KILDWICK.   *Photo by courtesy of Messrs. Cochrane & Co. (Builders).*

890-893 tons. Complements, 39. Dimensions : 170 (*p.p.*), 182 (*o.a.*) × 30-30¼ × 11⅝ feet. Guns : 1—4 inch (1—4·7 inch in a few). Designed H.P. 1400 = 13 kts. Machinery : 1 set inverted triple expansion. 1 screw. Boilers : Cylindrical return tube. Coal : 330 tons.

General Notes.—All Emergency War Programme. Many completed after end of War without armament. Some now serving as Tenders to Training Ships, Schools, &c.; others laid up.

Cancelled boats.—*Kilglass* (Brown), *Kilbrittan, Kilcar, Kilbane Kilbarchan* (all Hall Russell). Others listed above may have been stopped, September, 1918, but no list available.

BRITISH NAVY—FLOTILLA LEADERS.

7 Admiralty Large Design.

DOUGLAS.

5 *Cammell Laird:* **Bruce, Campbell, Douglas, Mackay** (ex *Claverhouse*), **Malcolm.**
2 *Hawthorn Leslie:* **Montrose, Stuart.**

Displacement : 1801 tons. Dimensions : 320 (*p.p.*), 332½ (*o.a.*) × 31⅔ × 10½ feet (*mean*) draught. Guns : 5—4·7 inch (DIR. CON.), 1—3 inch AA. (*Stuart*, also 2—2 pdr. AA). Tubes : 6—21 inch in two triple mountings. Machinery : Parsons (all-geared) turbines. Designed S.H.P. 40,000 = 36·5 kts. Boilers : Yarrow. Oil : *about* 505/480 tons. Complement, 164.

General Notes.—Emergency War programme boats. *War Losses: Scott* (Cammell Laird) 15 Aug. 1918. *Cancelled 1918: Barrington, Hughes* (both Cammell laird).

	Begun.	Launch.	Comp.		Begun.	Launch.	Comp
Bruce ..	12/5/17	26/2/18	30/5/18	Mackay ..	5/3/18	21/12/18	/6/19
Campbell ..	10/11/17	21/9/18	21/12/18	Malcolm ..	27/3/18	29/5/18	20/5/19
Douglas ..	30/6/17	8/6/18	2/9/18	Montrose ..	4/10/17	10/6/18	14/9/18
				Stuart ..	18/10/17	22/8/18	21/12/18

3 + 2? Thornycroft Type.

As *Douglas*, but Thornycroft funnels.

5 or 3 *Thornycroft: Keppel, Rooke* (both building 1919, but may be stopped), **Shakespeare, Spencer, Wallace.** 1740 tons. Dimensions : 318½ (*p.p.*), 329 (*o.a.*) × 31⅔ × 19½ feet (*mean*) draught. Guns : 5—4·7 inch (DIR. CON.),* 1—3 inch AA., 1—2 pdr. pom-pom. Tubes : 6—21 inch in 2 triple deck mountings.

Machinery : Brown-Curtis all-geared turbines. Designed S.H.P. 40,000 = 36 kts. 2 screws. Boilers : Yarrow. Oil : *about* 550/400 tons.

General Notes.—Built under War Emergency Programme. Appearance almost exactly same as *Bruce, Campbell, &c*, but these boats have the usual big, flat-sided Thornycroft funnels with caged caps. Complement, 164. No War Losses. *Cancelled 1918: Saunders, Spragge (Keppel* and *Rooke* may be stopped in Sept., 1919).

*Unofficial and unverified reports credit *Keppel* and *Rooke* with 4—5·5 inch (DIR. CON.), 1—3 inch AA. or 2—2 pdr. AA.

	Begun.	Launch.	Comp.	Trials.
Keppel ..	10/18	....	....	....
Rooke ..	11/18	....	....	....
Shakespeare ..	10/16	7/7/17	10/17	38.74
Spencer ..	10/16	22/9/17	12/17	37.76
Wallace ..	8/17	26/10/18	2/19	37.72

BRITISH NAVY—FLOTILLA LEADERS.

5 "Admiralty V" Leaders.

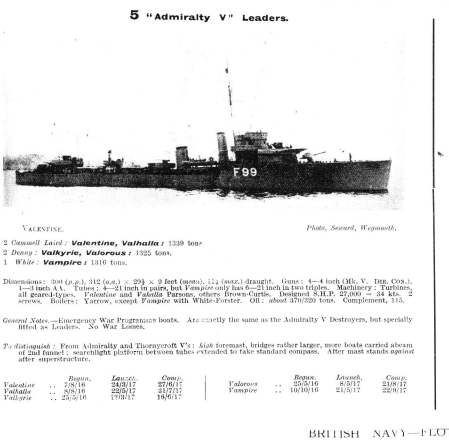

VALENTINE.

Photo, Seward, Weymouth.

2 *Cammell Laird*: **Valentine, Valhalla**: 1339 tons.
2 *Denny*: **Valkyrie, Valorous**: 1325 tons.
1 *White*: **Vampire**: 1316 tons.

Dimensions: 300 (*p.p.*), 312 (*o.a.*) × 29½ × 9 feet (*mean*), 11¼ (*max.*) draught. Guns: 4—4 inch (Mk. V. DIR. CON.), 1—3 inch A.A. Tubes: 4—21 inch in pairs, but *Vampire* only has 6—21 inch in two triples. Machinery: Turbines, all geared-types. *Valentine* and *Valhalla* Parsons, others Brown-Curtis. Designed S.H.P. 27,000 = 34 kts. 2 screws. Boilers: Yarrow, except *Vampire* with White-Forster. Oil: *about* 370/320 tons. Complement, 115.

General Notes.—Emergency War Programme boats. Are exactly the same as the Admiralty V Destroyers, but specially fitted as Leaders. No War Losses.

To distinguish: From Admiralty and Thornycroft V's: *high* foremast, bridges rather larger, more boats carried abeam of 2nd funnel; searchlight platform between tubes extended to take standard compass. After mast stands *against* after superstructure.

	Begun.	Launch.	Comp.			Begun.	Launch.	Comp.
Valentine	7/8/16	24/3/17	27/6/17	Valorous	..	25/5/16	8/5/17	21/8/17
Valhalla	8/8/16	22/5/17	31/7/17	Vampire	..	10/10/16	21/5/17	22/9/17
Valkyrie	.. 25/5/16	13/3/17	16/6/17					

4 Marksman (later) Type.

SEYMOUR.

Photo, C.N.

4 *Cammell-Laird*: **Grenville, Parker** (ex *Frobisher*), **Saumarez, Seymour.** First two 1,666 tons, last two 1673 tons. Dimensions: 315 (*p.p.*), 325 (*o.a.*) × 31½ × 10 feet (*mean*), 12½ (*max.*) draught. Guns: 4—4 inch (DIR. CON.), 2—2 pdr. pom-pom, 1 M.G. Tubes: 4—21 inch in pairs. Machinery: Parsons turbines. 3 screws. Designed S.H.P. 36,000 = 34 kts. Boilers: Yarrow. Oil: *about* 510/420 tons. Complement, 116.

General Notes.—All Emergency War Programme. Same design as *Gabriel*, *Marksman*, &c., but have only three funnels.

War Losses.—Hoste (Cammell Laird). 21 Dec 1916. *Removals.*—Anzac (Denny) presented to Australia, 1919.

	Begun.	Launch.	Comp.			Begun.	Launch.	Comp.
Grenville	.. 19/6/15	17/6/16	11/10/16	Saumarez	..	2/3/16	14/10/16	21/12/16
Parker	.. 19/6/15	16/8/16	13/11/16	Seymour	..	23/11/15	31/8/16	30/11/16

BRITISH NAVY—FLOTILLA LEADERS.

7 Marksman Type.

LIGHTFOOT.

3 *Cammell Laird*: **Gabriel, Ithuriel**, 1655 tons, **Kempenfelt**, 1607 tons.
1 *White*: **Lightfoot**, 1607 tons.
1½ *Hawthorn Leslie*: **Marksman**, 1604 tons.
1 *Denny*: **Nimrod**, 1608 tons.

Dimensions: 325 × 31½ × 11½ feet. Armament: 4—4 inch (DIR. CON.). 2—2 pdr. A.A.* 4—21 inch tubes in pairs. Machinery: Turbines, Brown-Curtis in *Marksman* and *Nimrod*, Parsons in rest. All 3 screws. Boilers: White-Forster in *Nimrod*, Yarrow in others. Designed H.P. 36,000 = 34 kts. Fuel: 510/413 tons oil. Complements, 106-116. *Nimrod 1—3 inch A.A., 1—2 pdr. pom-pom, *Kempenfelt 1—3 inch A.A., 2—2 pdr. pom-poms.

Notes.—*Abdiel*, *Gabriel*, and *Ithuriel*, Emergency War Programme. *Nimrod* and *Kempenfelt*, 1914-15 Programme. *Marksman* and *Lightfoot*, 1913-14 Programme.

	Begun.	Launch.	Comp.			Begun.	Launch.	Comp.
Abdiel	.. 6/5/15	12/10/15	26/3/16	Lightfoot	..	9/6/14	28/5/15	29/5/15
Gabriel	.. 12/1/15	23/12/15	1/7/16	Marksman	..	20/7/14	28/4/15	18/11/15
Ithuriel	.. 14/1/15	18/3/16	2/8/16	Nimrod	..	9/10/14	12/4/15	25/8/15
Kempenfelt	.. 2/10/14	1/5/15	20/8/15					

Cammell Laird: **Abdiel.** 1687 tons. Parsons turbines. Armament: 3—4 inch, 2—2 pdr. Tubes: None. This boat is a Minelayer carrying *about* 60-70 mines behind screens from fourth funnel to stern. Complement, 110. Dimensions, H.P., speed, etc., as *Gabriel*, &c., below.

3 White Boats (ex-Chilean).

FAULKNOR.

3 *White*: **Botha** (ex *Almirante Williams Rebolledo*, 1911), 1742 tons: **Broke** (ex *Almirante Goni*, 1913), 1704 tons: **Faulknor** (ex *Almirante Simpson*, 1913), 1694 tons. Dimensions: 331½ × 32½ × 11 ft. 7 in. Armament: 2—4·7 inch, 2—4 inch, 2—2 pdr. pom-poms. 4—21 inch tubes.* Designed H.P. 30,000 = 31 kts. in *Botha*, = 32 kts. in *Broke* and *Faulknor*. Machinery: Turbines. Boilers: White-Forster. 3 screws. Fuel: (*max.*) 403 coal + 83 oil. Complement, 205.

Note.—Another of the class, *Tipperary*, ex *Almirante Riveros*, sunk in battle of Jutland 1 June 1916. Purchased, August 1914, on outbreak of war, from Chile. re-armed 1918-19.

*Tubes singly mounted in *Botha*, in pairs in *Broke* and *Faulknor*.

1 Special Boat.

1 *Cammell Laird*: **Swift** (1907). 2207 tons. Dimensions: 353 × 34¼ × 13 feet. Oil: 385/280 tons. H.P. 30,000 = 35 kts. Parsons turbines. 4 screws. Yarrow boilers. Armament: 1—6 inch, 2—4 inch, 1—2 pdr. pom-pom. 2—18 inch tubes. Complement, 138. Cost about £280,500.

Notes.—Although 12 years old, still the biggest Leader in British Navy. Extensively rebuilt after action in Dover Straits. 1918.

BRITISH NAVY.—DESTROYERS.

4 + 17 ? "Admiralty V" (with 4·7 inch guns).

WHITSHED.

Photo, Messrs. Swan Hunter (Builders).

	Begun.	Launch.	Comp.		Begun.	Launch.	Comp.
Vansittart ..	1/7/18	17/4/19	....	Whitehall ..	6/18	1919	....
Vimy ..	16/9/18	1919	....	Whitshed ..	6/18	1/19	7/19
Warren* ..			....	Wild Swan ..	7/18	10/5/18	....
Venomous ..	31/5/18	21/12/18	6/19	Werewolf* ..	1918	17/7/19	....
Verity ..	17/5/18	19/3/19	....	Witherington ..	27/9/18	16/1/19	10/19
Veteran ..	30/8/18	26/4/19	....	Wivern ..	19/8/18	15/4/19	....
Volunteer ..	16/4/18	17/4/19	6/19	Wolverine ..	8/10/18	17/7/19	....
Watson* ..			....	Worcester* ..	20/12/18		....
Wanderer ..	1918	1/5/19	1919	Wrangler* ..	3/2/19		....
Whelp* ..		1/18	....	Wren* ..			....
				Wye* ..		1/18	....

*Probably cancelled with some other boats (names unknown) on above List.

Boats cancelled 1918.—*Vashon, Vengeful* (Beardmore), *Vigo, Vigorous, Virulent, Volage, Volcano, Wistful* (Clydebank), *Votary, Wager, Wake, Waldegrave, Walton, Whitaker* (Denny), *Wave, Weazel, White Bear* (Fairfield), *Welcome, Welfare, Wellesley* (Hawthorn Leslie), *Wheler, Whip, Whippet* (Scott), *Whitehead, Willoughby, Winter* (Swan Hunter), *Wishart, Witch* (Thornycroft), *Westphal, Westward Ho!* (White), *Wayfarer, Woodpecker, Yeoman, Zealous, Zebra, Zodiac* (Yarrow).

2 *Beardmore :* **Vansittart, Vimy** (ex *Vantage*).
1 *Chatham D. Y. :* **Warren.***
3 *Clydebank :* **Venomous** (ex *Venom*), **Verity, Veteran.**
1 *Denny :* **Volunteer.**
1 *Devonport D.Y. :* **Watson.***
1 *Fairfield :* **Wanderer.**
1 *Pembroke D.Y. :* **Whelp.***
3 *Swan Hunter :* **Whitehall, Whitshed, Wild Swan.**
6 *White :* **Werewolf,*** **Witherington, Wivern, Wolverine,*** **Worcester,*** **Wrangler.***
2 *Yarrow :* **Wren,*** **Wye.***

*Probably cancelled, Sept., 1919.

Displacement : 1300 tons *average.* Dimensions : 300 (*p.p.*), 312 (*o.a.*) × 29½ × 9 feet (*mean*) draught. Guns : 4—4·7 inch (*Dir. Con.*), 2—2 pdr. pom-poms. Tubes : 6, in two triple mountings. Machinery : Turbines (all-geared type)—all above probably Brown-Curtis, but *Whitehall* (and perhaps one or two others) Parsons. Designed S.H.P. 27,000 = 34 kts. 2 screws. Boilers : Yarrow, except *White* boats with White-Forster. Oil : *about* 350/320 tons. Complement, 127.

General Notes.—Begun under War Emergency Programme, but cost of completion of many may come under post-war Estimates. The position regarding these boats is as follows :—56 were ordered, out of which 35 were stopped in Nov.-Dec., 1918, as list opposite. 21 were proceeding up to Sept., 1919, when further boats (number uncertain) were stopped. Completion of boats launched may be postponed indefinitely. Differ from preceding V's in armament. Sometimes—but unofficially—referred to as " Repeat W Class." No War Losses, none of these boats being finished till 1919.

To distinguish.—Proportions of funnels reversed compared with other V's. These boats have *thick* fore funnel and *thin* after funnel. No 3 inch AA, abaft 2nd funnel. 2 pdr. pom-poms abeam between funnels.

BRITISH NAVY—DESTROYERS.

7 "Yarrow S."

7 *Yarrow :* **Tomahawk, Torch, Tumult, Tryphon,*** **Turquoise, Tuscan, Tyrian.** Displacement, 930 tons. Dimensions : 260½ (*p.p.*) 269½ (*o.a.*) × 25¾ × 9 feet (*mean*) draught. Guns : 3—4 inch (Mk. IV with 30° elevation), 1—2 pdr. pom-pom. Tubes : 4—21 inch in pairs. Machinery : Brown-Curtis (direct drive) turbines. Designed S.H.P. 23,000 = 36 kts. Boilers : Yarrow. Oil : *about* 255/215 tons. Complement, 90.

General Notes.—Emergency War Programme boats. Otherwise as " General Notes " to Admiralty S boats.

To distinguish.—From Admiralty and Yarrow S : shorter fo'xle, sloping Yarrow stern. From other types : as Distinction Notes for Admiralty S boats. No War Losses.

	Begun.	Launch.	Comp.	Trials.		Begun.	Launch.	Comp.	Trials
Tomahawk ..	4/17	16/5/18	7/18	35.15	Turquoise ..	6/17	9/11/18	3/19	39.6
Torch ..	4/17	16/3/18	5/18	39.19	Tuscan ..	6/17	1/3/19	6/19	
Tryphon ..	4/17	22/6/18	9/18	35.37	Tyrian ..	6/17	5/19	1919	39.75
Tumult ..	6/17	17.9.18	12/18	35.70					

Tryphon injured by grounding on Danish Coast. Salved and reported to be re-fitting, 1919.

5 "Thornycroft S."

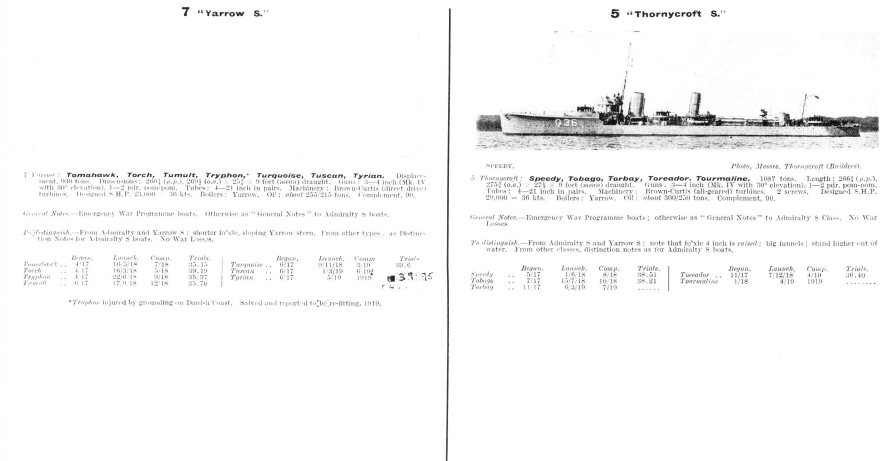

SPEEDY.

Photo, Messrs. Thornycroft (Builders).

5 *Thornycroft :* **Speedy, Tobago, Torbay, Toreador. Tourmaline.** 1087 tons. Length : 266¾ (*p.p.*), 275¾ (*o.a.*) × 27½ × 9 feet (*mean*) draught. Guns : 3—4 inch (Mk. IV with 30° elevation), 1—2 pdr. pom-pom. Tubes : 4—21 inch in pairs. Machinery : Brown-Curtis (all-geared) turbines. 2 screws. Designed S.H.P. 29,000 = 36 kts. Boilers : Yarrow. Oil : *about* 300/250 tons. Complement, 90.

General Notes.—Emergency War Programme boats ; otherwise as " General Notes " to Admiralty S Class. No War Losses.

To distinguish.—From Admiralty S and Yarrow S : note that fo'xle 4 inch is *raised* ; big funnels ; stand higher out of water. From other classes, distinction notes as for Admiralty S boats.

	Begun.	Launch.	Comp.	Trials.		Begun.	Launch.	Comp.	Trials.
Speedy ..	5/17	1/6/18	8/18	38.51	Toreador ..	11/17	7/12/18	4/19	36.40
Tobago ..	7/17	15/7/18	10/18	38.21	Tourmaline ..	1/18	4/19	1919	....
Torbay ..	11/17	6/3/19	7/19	......					

BRITISH NAVY—DESTROYERS.

50 "Admiralty S."

Beardmore : **Tactician, Tara.**

Clydebank : **Scimitar, Scotsman, Scout, Scythe, Seabear, Seafire, Searcher, Seawolf, Simoom.**

Denny : **Senator, Sepoy, Seraph, Serapis, Serene, Sesame.**

Doxford : **Shamrock, Shikari.**

Fairfield : **Sikh, Sirdar, Somme, Spear, Spindrift.**

Hawthorn Leslie : **Tenedos, Thanet, Thracian, Turbulent.**

Palmer : **Steadfast, Sterling, Stonehenge, Stormcloud.**

Scott : **Strenuous, Stronghold, Sturdy, Swallow.**

Stephen : **Sabre, Saladin, Sardonyx.**

Swan Hunter : **Shark, Sparrowhawk, Splendid, Sportive, Tilbury, Tintagel.**

White : **Tribune, Trinidad, Trojan, Truant, Trusty.**

TILBURY.   Photo, Messrs. Swan Hunter (Builders).

975 tons. Dimensions : 265 (*p.p.*), 275-277 (*o.a.*) × 26¾ × 9 feet (*mean*) draught. Guns : 3—4 inch (Mk. IV with 30° elevation), 1—2 pdr. pom-pom. Tubes : 4—21 inch in pairs. Machinery : Turbines (all-geared type). Brown Curtis (A.G.) in all except following :—Palmer boats, Parsons (A.G.); *Tilbury, Tintagel,* Parsons (A.G.). Designed S.H.P. 27,000 = 36 kts. 2 screws. Yarrow boilers in all, except White boats with White-Forster. Oil : *about* 300/250 tons. Complement, 90.

General Notes.—Emergency War Programme boats, but cost of completion of about 40 boats may come under post-war Estimates. Design derived from " Admiralty Modified R " boats. Came into service with a single 14 inch tube on each beam (mounted on turntables or racks) at break of fo'xle, making six tubes in all. These 14 inch have now been removed. Reported to be not quite so successful as the Admiralty M's and R's. No War Losses. *Saturn, Sycamore* (both Stephen) cancelled. *Stalwart, Success, Swordsman, Tattoo, Tasmania,* presented to Royal Australian Navy, 1918.

To distinguish.—Long fo'xle. sheered and slightly turtle-backed. Funnels about equal in size, the extra height of fore funnel not being very prominent. Wedge-shaped bridges built off fo'xle, and open underneath. Features in these boats which also appear in the R and Modified R types are :—Mounting of searchlight on after pair of tubes ; pom-pom on platform just before mainmast ; after 4 inch in bandstand ; boats abeam of 2nd funnel.

		Begun.	Launch.	Comp.			Begun.	Launch.	Comp.
2 B'more	*Tactician* ..	21/11/17	7/8/18	23/10/18	4 H.L.	*Tenedos* ..	6/12/17	21/10/18	6/19
	Tara ..	21/11/17	12/10/18	9/12/18		*Thanet* ..	13/12/17	5/11/18	1919
						Thracian ..	17/1/18	......	......
	Scimitar ..	30/5/17	27/2/18	4/18		*Turbulent* ..	14/11/17	1919	......
9 Clydebank	*Scotsman* ..	10/12/17	30/3/18	6/18	4 Palmer	*Steadfast* ..		8/8/18	3/19
	Scout ..	25/10/17	27/4/18	6/18		*Sterling* ..		8/10/18	3/19
	Scythe ..	14/1/18	25/5/18	7/18		*Stonehenge* ..		1919	9/19
	Seabear ..	13/12/17	6/7/18	9/18		*Stormcloud* ..		30/5/19	
	Seafire ..	27/2/18	10/8/18	11/18					
	Searcher ..	30/3/18	11/9/18	11/18	4 Scott	*Strenuous* ..		9/11/18	1/19
	Seawolf ..	30/4/18	2/11/18	1/19		*Stronghold* ..		5/18	1919
	Simoom ..	30/5/17	26/1/18	3/18		*Sturdy* ..		......	......
						Swallow ..		1/8/18	9/18
6 Denny	*Senator* ..	10/7/17	2/4/18	7/6/18					
	Sepoy ..	6/8/17	22/5/18	6/8/18	3 Stephen	*Sabre* ..	10/9/17	23/9/18	9/11/18
	Seraph ..	4/10/17	8/7/18	25/12/18		*Saladin* ..	10/9/17	17/2/19	11/4/19
	Serapis ..	4/12/17	17/9/18	21/3/19		*Sardonyx* ..	25/3/18	27/5/19	1919
	Serene ..	2/2/18	30/11/18	30/4/19					
	Sesame ..	13/3/18	30/12/18	28/3/19		*Shark* ..		9/4/18	7/18
2 Doxf'd	*Shamrock* ..	......	8/18	1919	6 S.H.	*Sparrowhawk* ..		14/5/18	9/18
	Shikari ..	......	14/7/19	1919		*Splendid* ..		10/7/18	10/18
						Sportive ..		19/9/18	12/18
5 Fairf'ld	*Sikh* ..	......	7/5/18	29/6/18		*Tilbury* ..		13/6/18	9/18
	Sirdar ..	......	6/7/18	6/9/18		*Tintagel* ..		9/8/18	12/18
	Somme ..	......	10/9/18	4/11/18					
	Spear ..	......	9/11/18	17/12/18	5 White	*Tribune* ..	21/8/17	28/3/18	16/7/18
	Spindrift ..	......	30/12/18	2/4/19		*Trinidad* ..	15/9/17	8/5/18	9/9/18
						Trojan ..	3/1/18	20/7/18	6/12/18
						Truant ..	14/2/18	18/9/18	17/3/19
						Trusty ..	11/4/18	6/11/18	9/5/19

BRITISH NAVY—DESTROYERS.

2 Thornycroft "V" (Later Six-tube Boats).

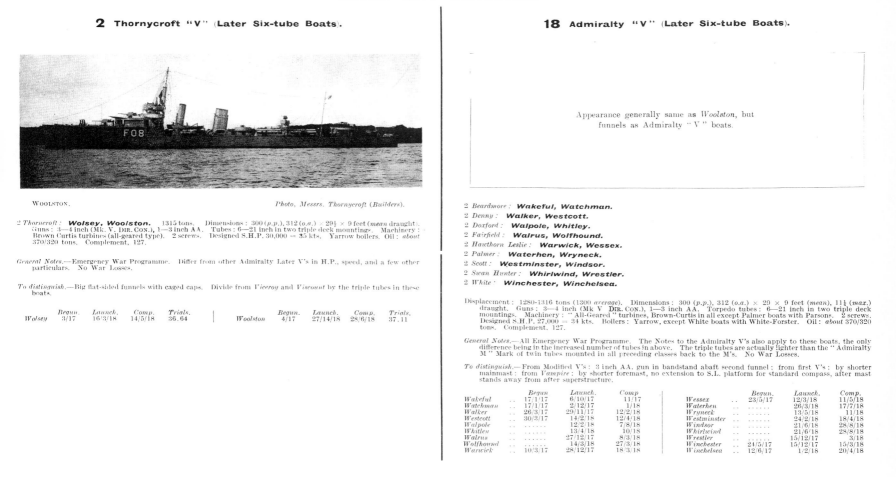

WOOLSTON.   Photo, Messrs. Thornycroft (Builders).

2 *Thornycroft :* **Wolsey, Woolston.** 1315 tons. Dimensions : 300 (*p.p.*), 312 (*o.a.*) × 29½ × 9 feet (*mean draught*). Guns : 3—4 inch (Mk. V. DIR. CON.), 1—3 inch AA. Tubes : 6—21 inch in two triple deck mountings. Machinery : Brown Curtis turbines (all-geared type). 2 screws. Designed S.H.P. 30,000 = 35 kts. Yarrow boilers. Oil : *about* 370/320 tons. Complement, 127.

General Notes.—Emergency War Programme. Differ from other Admiralty Later V's in H.P., speed, and a few other particulars. No War Losses.

To distinguish.—Big flat-sided funnels with caged caps. Divide from *Viceroy* and *Viscount* by the triple tubes in these boats.

	Begun.	Launch.	Comp.	Trials.			Begun.	Launch.	Comp.	Trials.
Wolsey	3/17	16/3/18	14/5/18	36.64		*Woolston*	4/17	27/14/18	28/6/18	37.11

18 Admiralty "V" (Later Six-tube Boats).

Appearance generally same as *Woolston,* but funnels as Admiralty " V " boats.

2 *Beardmore :* **Wakeful, Watchman.**

2 *Denny :* **Walker, Westcott.**

2 *Doxford :* **Walpole, Whitley.**

2 *Fairfield :* **Walrus, Wolfhound.**

2 *Hawthorn Leslie :* **Warwick, Wessex.**

2 *Palmer :* **Waterhen, Wryneck.**

2 *Scott :* **Westminster, Windsor.**

2 *Swan Hunter :* **Whirlwind, Wrestler.**

2 *White :* **Winchester, Winchelsea.**

Displacement : 1280-1316 tons (1300 *average*). Dimensions : 300 (*p.p.*), 312 (*o.a.*) × 20 × 9 feet (*mean*), 11¼ (*max.*) draught. Guns : 3—4 inch (Mk V DIR. CON.), 1—3 inch AA. Torpedo tubes : 6—21 inch in two triple deck mountings. Machinery : " All-Geared " turbines, Brown-Curtis in all except Palmer boats with Parsons. 2 screws. Designed S.H.P. 27,000 = 34 kts. Boilers : Yarrow, except White boats with White-Forster. Oil : *about* 370/320 tons. Complement, 127.

General Notes.—All Emergency War Programme. The Notes to the Admiralty V's also apply to these boats, the only difference being in the increased number of tubes in above. The triple tubes are actually lighter than the " Admiralty M " Mark of twin tubes mounted in all preceding classes back to the M's. No War Losses.

To distinguish.—From Modified V's : 3 inch AA gun in bandstand abaft second funnel ; from first V's : by shorter mainmast : from *Vampire* : by shorter foremast, no extension to S.L. platform for standard compass, after mast stands away from after superstructure.

	Begun.	Launch.	Comp			Begun.	Launch.	Comp.
Wakeful ..	17/1/17	6/10/17	11/17	*Wessex*	23/5/17	12/3/18	11/5/18
Watchman ..	17/1/17	2/12/17	1/18	*Waterhen*		26/3/18	17/7/18
Walker ..	26/3/17	29/11/17	12/2/18	*Wryneck*		13/5/18	11/18
Westcott ..	30/3/17	14/2/18	12/4/18	*Westminster*		24/2/18	18/4/18
Walpole ..	......	12/2/18	7/8/18	*Windsor*		21/6/18	28/8/18
Whitley ..	......	13/4/18	10/18	*Whirlwind*		21/6/18	28/8/18
Walrus ..	......	27/12/17	8/3/18	*Wrestler*		15/12/17	3/18
Wolfhound ..	......	14/3/18	27/3/18	*Winchester*	24/5/17	15/12/17	15/3/18
Warwick ..	10/3/17	28/12/17	18/3/18	*Winchelsea*	12/6/17	1/2/18	20/4/18

BRITISH NAVY—DESTROYERS.

2 "Thornycroft V."

VICEROY.   *Photo. Messrs. Thornycroft (Builders).*

2 *Thornycroft:* **Viceroy, Viscount.** 1325 tons. Dimensions: 300 (*p.p.*), 312 (*o.a.*) × 30′ 7″ × 9½ feet (*mean*) 11¾ feet (*max.*) draught. Guns: 3—4 inch (Mk. V Dir. Con.), 1—3 inch AA. Tubes: 4—21 inch in pairs. **Machinery:** Brown Curtis (all-geared) turbines. 2 screws. Designed S.H.P. 30,000 = 35 kts. Boilers: Yarrow. Oil fuel: *about* 375/320 tons. Complement, 110.

General Notes.—Emergency War Programme boats. Differ from Admiralty V design in dimensions, H.P. and speed. No War Losses.

To distinguish.—Have big, flat-sided funnels with caged caps. The fore funnel not being so prominently raised as in other " V " boats. Other distinctive features as Admiralty V's.

	Begun.	Launch.	Comp.	Trials.
Viscount	12/16	29/12/17	3/18	37.69
Viceroy	12/16	17/11/17	1/18	36.5

21 "Admiralty V."

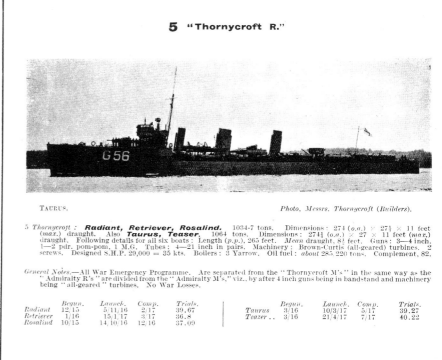

————— as Minelayer.

3 *Beardmore:* **Vancouver, Vanessa, Vanity.**
2 *Clydebank:* **Vanoc,* Vanquisher.***
1 *Denny:* **Venturous.***
2 *Doxford:* **Vega, Velox.**
2 *Fairfield:* **Vendetta, Venetia.**
2 *Hawthorn Leslie:* **Verdun, Versatile.**
3 *Stephen:* **Vesper, Vidette, Voyager.**
2 *Swan Hunter:* **Violent, Vimiera.**
2 *White:* **Vectis, Vortigern.**
2 *Yarrow:* **Vivacious, Vivien.**

                  * Minelayers.

Displacements: 1272-1339 tons (1300 *average*). Dimensions: 300 (*p.p.*), 312 (*o.a.*) × 29½ × 9 feet (*mean*), 11¾ (*max.*) draught. Guns: 4—4 inch (Mk. V Dir. Con.), 1—3 inch AA. Torpedo tubes: 4—21 inch in pairs. Machinery: "All-Geared" turbines: Brown-Curtis in all, except Doxford and Swan Hunter boats with Parsons. 2 screws. Designed S.H.P. 27,000 = 34 kts. Boilers: Yarrow in all, except White-Forster. Oil: *about* 370/320 tons. Complement, 110. Trials: *Viracious* 33·01, *Vivien* 36.79.

General Notes.—All Emergency War Programme. These boats are of remarkable size and power for Destroyers; in fact, five of them, with slight modifications, have been converted to Flotilla Leaders.

To distinguish.—From " W " type, *no triple tubes*; mainmast *short.* From " V Leaders," foremast shorter, forebridges different, no extension to S.L. platform for standard compass, mainmast *away* from after superstructure, fewer boats.

	Begun.	Launch.	Comp.		Begun.	Launch.	Comp.
Vancouver	15/3/17	28/12/17	9/3/18	Vendetta	....	3/9/17	17/10/17
Vanessa	16/5/17	16/3/18	27/4/18	Venetia	....	29/10/17	19/12/17
Vanity	28/7/17	3/5/18	21/6/18	Verdun	13/1/17	21/8/17	3/11/17
Vanoc	20/9/16	14/6/17	8/17	Versatile	31/1/17	31/10/17	11/2/18
Vanquisher	27/9/16	18/8/17	9/17	Vesper	27/12/16	15/12/17	20/2/18
Venturous	9/10/16	21/9/17	29/11/17	Vidette	1/2/17	28/2/18	27/4/18
Vega	....	1/9/17	12/17	Voyager	17/5/17	24/6/18	24/6/18
Velox	....	17/11/17	1/4/18	Violent	11/16	1/9/17	11/17
				Vimiera	10/16	22/6/17	9/17
				Vectis	7/12/17	4/9/17	5/12/17
				Vortigern	17/1/16	15/10/17	25/1/18
				Viracious	7/16	3/11/17	12/17
				Vivien	7/16	16/2/18	28/5/18

War Losses.—*Vehement* (Denny) 2 August 1918, *Verulam* (Hawthorn Leslie) and *Vittoria* (Swan Hunter) lost 1919 in Baltic operations.

BRITISH NAVY—DESTROYERS.

4 Yarrow "Later M."

As illustration of *Mounsey* on page 72 but with sloping stern.

4 *Yarrow:* **Sabrina, Sybille, Truculent, Tyrant.** Displacements: 897-923 tons. Dimensions: 269½ (*p.p.*), 274½ (*o.a.*) × 25¾ × 8½ feet (*mean*), 10½ (*max.*) draught. Guns: 3—4 inch, 1—2 pdr. pom-pom, 1 M.G. Torpedo tubes: 4—21 inch in pairs. Machinery: Brown-Curtis turbines. 2 screws. Designed S.H.P. 23,000 = 36 kts. Boilers: 3 Yarrow. Oil fuel: 256-213/215-200 tons. Complement, 82.

General Notes.—All Emergency War Programme. Generally same as the first group of " Yarrow M's " (*Miranda, Mounsey, Nerissa, Rival, &c.*), but the above boats have the Yarrow form of strongly sloping stern. Note that these have *no* geared turbines, nor is the after 4 inch in a bandstand. Accordingly, there is *no* Yarrow " R " design.

War Losses.—*Strongbow* 17 Oct. 1917, *Surprise* 22 Dec. 1917, *Ulleswater* 15 Aug. 1918 (all Yarrow).

	Begun.	Launch.	Comp.	Trials.		Begun.	Launch.	Comp.	Trials.
Sabrina	8/15	24/7/16	9/16	36.96	Truculent	3/16	24/3/17	5/17	38.27
Sybille	8/15	5/2/17	2/17	39.11	Tyrant	3/16	19/5/17	7/17	37.37

5 "Thornycroft R."

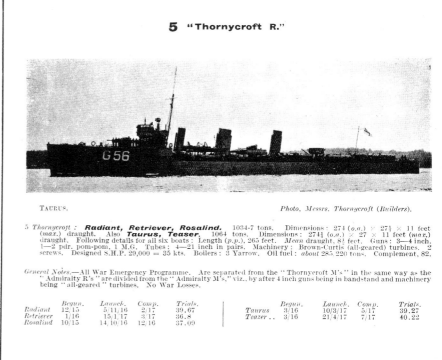

TAURUS.   *Photo. Messrs. Thornycroft (Builders).*

5 *Thornycroft:* **Radiant, Retriever, Rosalind.** 1034-7 tons. Dimensions: 274 (*o.a.*) × 27½ × 11 feet (*max.*) draught. Also **Taurus, Teaser.** 1064 tons. Dimensions: 274¼ (*o.a.*) × 27 × 11 feet (*max.*) draught. Following details for all six boats: Length (*p.p.*), 265 feet. *Mean* draught, 8½ feet. Guns: 3—4 inch, 1—2 pdr. pom-pom, 1 M.G. Tubes: 4—21 inch in pairs. Machinery: Brown-Curtis (all-geared) turbines. 2 screws. Designed S.H.P. 29,000 = 35 kts. Boilers: 3 Yarrow. Oil fuel: *about* 285-220 tons. Complement, 82.

General Notes.—All War Emergency Programme. Are separated from the " Thornycroft M's " in the same way as the " Admiralty R's " are divided from the " Admiralty M's," viz., by after 4 inch guns being in bandstand and machinery being " all-geared " turbines. No War Losses.

	Begun.	Launch.	Comp.	Trials.		Begun.	Launch.	Comp.	Trials.
Radiant	12/15	5/11/16	2/17	39.67	Taurus	3/16	10/3/17	5/17	39.27
Retriever	1/16	15/1/17	3/17	36.8	Teazer	3/16	21/4/17	7/17	40.22
Rosalind	10/15	14/10/16	12/16	37.09					

BRITISH NAVY—DESTROYERS.

10 "Admiralty Modified R."

1 *Beardmore* : **Ulster.** 1086 tons. Brown-Curtis A.G. turbines.
1 *Doxford* : **Umpire.** 1091 tons. Brown-Curtis A.G. turbines.
1 *Fairfield* : **Undine.** 1090 tons. Brown-Curtis A.G. turbines.
2 *Palmer* : **Urchin, Ursa.** 1085 tons. Parsons A.G. turbines.
2 *Scott* : **Tirade, Ursula.** 1076 tons. Brown-Curtis A.G. turbines.
1 *Swan Hunter* : **Tower.** 1087 tons. Brown-Curtis A.G. turbines.
2 *White* : **Trenchant, Tristram.** 1085 tons. Brown-Curtis A.G. turbines.

Dimensions : 265 (*p.p.*), 275½-276 (*o.a.*) × about 26¾ × 10½ feet (*mean*), 11¾ (*max.*) draught. Guns : 3—4 inch (Mk. IV with 30° elevation in *Ulster* and *Ursa*), 1—2 pdr. pom-pom. Tubes : 4—21 inch in pairs. Machinery : "All-Geared" (A.G.) turbines as noted above. 2 screws. Designed S.H.P. 27,000 = 36 kts. Boilers : 3 Yarrow in all except *Trenchant* and *Tristram* by White with 3 White-Forster. Oil : *about* 300/250 tons. Complement, 82.

General Notes.—All Emergency War Programme. These boats are said to be an attempt by the Admiralty to combine the "Admiralty R" design with that of the Yarrow "Later M's." They are said to be not quite so satisfactory as the Admiralty M's and R's, but good sea-boats.

To distinguish.—Very long and high fo'xle, which is *not* sheered or turtle-backed as in "S" boats. Charthouse built on fo'xle. Fore funnel *seen close* to foremast. Funnels nearly equal in size with boats in davits abeam of after funnel. Quarter-deck abaft of mainmast is shorter than in "Yarrow M" boats, and has 4 inch in bandstand.

War Losses.—*Ulysses* (Doxford) 29 Oct 1918.

	Begun.	Launch.	Comp.			Begun.	Launch.	Comp.
Ulster	19/9/16	10/10/17	21/11/17	Tirade		21/4/17		6/17
Umpire		9/6/17	8/17	Ursula			8/17	9/17
Undine		22/3/17	26/5/17	Tower		9/16	5/4/17	8/17
Urchin		7/6/17	8/17	Trenchant ..		17/7/16	23/12/16	30/4/17
Ursa		23/7/17	10/17	Tristram ..		23/9/16	24/2/17	30/6/17

TOWER. *Photo by courtesy of Messrs. Swan Hunter (Builders).*

URCHIN. Some boats have platform on after pair of tubes, as above. *Photo, Topical.*

BRITISH NAVY—DESTROYERS.

34 "Admiralty R."

THISBE. *Photo by courtesy of Messrs. Hawthorn Leslie (Builders).*

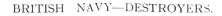

3 *Beardmore* : **Satyr, Sharpshooter,** Parsons A.G. turbines, **Tancred,** Brown-Curtis A.G. turbines.
7 *Clydebank* : **Restless, Rigorous, Romola, Rowena, Skate Tarpon,* Telemachus.***
3 *Denny* : **Rob Roy, Rocket, Redgauntlet.**
1 *Doxford* : **Redoubt.**
1 *Fairfield* : **Tempest.**
6 *Harland & Wolff* (Goran) : **Salmon, Skilful, Springbok, Sylph, Tenacious, Tetrarch.**
5 *Hawthorn Leslie* : **Sarpedon, Stork, Starfish, Thisbe, Thruster.**
3 *Stephen* : **Sceptre, Sturgeon, Tormentor.**
4 *Swan Hunter* : **Radstock, Raider, Sorceress, Torrid.**
1 *White* : **Sable.**

**Tarpon, Telemachus*, Minelayers.

Displacements vary from 1096 to 1036 tons (1065 *average*). Length, (*p.p.*) 265 feet (*o.a.* varies from 274 to 276 feet). Beam, 26¾ feet. *Mean* draught, 9 feet. *Max.* draughts, 11½ to 12 feet. Guns : 3—4 inch, 1—2 pdr. pom-pom (1 M.G., but not in all). Torpedo tubes : 4—21 inch in pairs. Machinery : Turbines—"all-geared" types. Clydebank, Denny, Fairfield, Harland & Wolff, Stephen, Swan Hunter and White boats, Brown-Curtis A.G. turbines ; Doxford and Hawthorn Leslie boats, Parsons A.G. turbines ; Beardmore boats as separately noted. Designed S.H.P. 27,000 = 36 kts. 2 screws in all. Boilers : 3 Yarrow or Modified Yarrow, except *Sable* by White, with White-Forster boilers. Oil fuel : 295-285/250-243 tons. Complement, 82.

		Begun.	Launch.	Comp.			Begun.	Launch.	Comp.
3 B'd-more	Satyr ..	15/4/16	27/12/16	2/2/17	6 H. & W.	Salmon ..	27/8/15	7/10/16	20/12/16
	Sharpshooter ..	23/5/16	27/2/17	2/4/17		Skilful ..	20/1/16	3/2/17	26/3/17
	Tancred ..	6/7/16	30/6/17	9/17		Springbok ..	27/1/16	9/3/17	30/4/17
	Restless ..	22/9/15	12/8/16	10/16		Sylph ..	30/8/16	15/11/16	10/2/17
	Rigorous ..	22/9/15	30/9/16	11/16		Tenacious ..	25/7/16	21/5/17	12/8/17
	Romola ..	25/8/15	14/5/16	8/16		Tetrarch ..	26/7/16	20/4/17	2/6/17
7 Clydebank	Rowena ..	25/8/15	1/7/16	2/16	6 H. L.	Sarpedon ..	27/9/15	1/6/16	2/9/16
	Skate ..	11/1/17	11/1/17	2/17		Stork ..	10/4/16	25/11/16	1/2/17
	Tarpon ..	12/4/16	10/3/17	4/17		Starfish ..	26/1/16	27/9/16	16/12/16
	Telemachus ..	12/4/16	21/1/17	6/17		Thisbe ..	13/6/16	8/3/17	6/6/17
3 D'y	Rob Roy ..	15/10/15	29/8/16	15/12/16		Thruster ..	2/6/16	10/1/17	30/3/17
	Rocket ..	28/9/15	2/7/16	7/10/16	3 Stn.	Sceptre ..	10/11/15	18/4/17	26/5/17
	Redgauntlet ..	30/9/15	23/11/16	7/2/17		Sturgeon ..	10/11/15	11/1/17	26/2/17
(Doxf'd) Redoubt ..			28/10/16	3/17		Tormentor ..	1/5/16	22/5/17	22/8/17
(F'field) Tempest ..			26/1/17	20/3/17	4 S.H.	Radstock ..	9/15	3/6/16	9/16
						Raider ..	9/15	17/7/16	10/16
						Sorceress ..	11/15	29/8/16	12/16
						Torrid ..	7/16	10/2/17	5/17
					(White) Sable ..	20/12/15	18/6/16	30/11/16

TELEMACHUS as Minelayer. After-pair of tubes and 4 inch gun are dummies painted on screens. *Photo, Lt. C. de Brock, R.N.*

STARFISH. *Note.*—*Satyr, Skate, Sharpshooter, Starfish, Stork* only, have mainmast as above illustration.

General Notes.—All Emergency War Programme boats. General design is as the "Admiralty M's" but these boats have geared turbines and 2 screws, and are rather faster than the "Admiralty M's."

To distinguish.—Note that the after 4 inch is mounted in a bandstand.

War Losses.—*Simoon* (Clydebank) 23 Jan 1917, *Recruit* (Doxford) 9 Aug 1917, *Tornado* (Stephen) 22 Dec 1917, *Torrent* (Swan Hunter) 22 Dec 1917, *Setter* (White) 17 may 1917.

BRITISH NAVY—DESTROYERS.

74 "Admiralty M."

(23 "Repeat M" + 45 "M" + 6 "Pre-War M.")

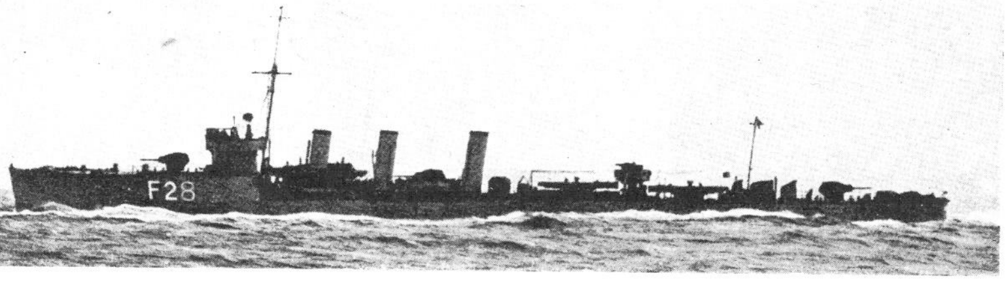

PYLADES ("Repeat M").

2 *Beardmore* : * **Pelican, Pellew.** (Repeat M.)

10 *Clydebank* : **Napier, Penn, Peregrine.** (Repeat M.) **Ossory, Mameluke, Marne, Mons**—also **Milne, Morris, Moorsom.** (Pre-War.)

7 *Denny* : **Petard, Peyton.** (Repeat M.) **Maenad, Marvel, Mystic, Narwhal, Nicator.**

9 *Doxford* : **Norseman, Oberon.** (Repeat M.) **Octavia, Ophelia, Opportune, Oracle, Orestes, Orford, Orpheus.**

11 *Fairfield* : **Observer. Offa, Phœbe.** (Repeat M.) **Mandate, Manners, Mindful, Mischief, Onslaught, Onslow, Orcadia, Oriana.**

3 *Hawthorn Leslie* : **Pigeon, Plover.** (Repeat M.)

8 *Palmer* : **Oriole, Osiris.** (Repeat M.) **Nonsuch, Norman, Northesk, Nugent**—also **Murray, Myngs.** (Pre-War).

6 *Scott* : **Plucky, Portia.** (Repeat M.) **Obdurate, Obedient, Paladin, Parthian.**

5 *Stephen* : **Prince, Pylades.*** (Repeat M.) **Nizam,* Noble** (ex *Nisus*), **Nonpariel.**

4 *Swan Hunter* : **Pasley.** (Repeat M.) Brown-Curtis turbines. **Martial,** Parsons turbines, **Menace,** Brown-Curtis turbines—also **Matchless.** (Pre-War) Parsons turbines.

6 *Thornycroft* : **Michael, Milbrook, Minion, Munster, Nepean, Nereus.**

4 *White* : **Medina** (ex-*Redmill*). **Medway** (ex*Redwing*), (both Repeat M). **Magic, Moresby.**

**Nizam* and *Pylades* were launched by Messrs. Stephen and completed by Messrs. Beardmore.

Displacements vary from 994 to 1042 tons (1025 *average*). Length : 265 feet (*p.p.*) (*o.a.* varies from $271\frac{1}{2}$ to $276\frac{1}{4}$ feet). Beam : $26\frac{5}{8}$ to $26\frac{3}{4}$ feet. *Mean* draught : $8\frac{5}{8}$ feet. *Max.* draught : *about* $10\frac{1}{4}$ feet. Guns : 3—4 inch, 1—2 pdr. pom-pom., 1 M.G. Tubes : 4—21 inch in pairs. Machinery : Clydebank, Fairfield and Stephen boats, Brown-Curtis turbines ; Beardmore, Denny, Doxford, Hawthorn Leslie, Palmer, Scott, Thornycroft, White boats, all Parsons turbines ; Swan Hunter boats as specially noted above. Designed S.H.P. 25,000 = 34 kts. 3 screws in all. Boilers : 3 Yarrow in all, except White boats with White-Forster. Oil fuel : 298-237/243-202 tons. Complement, 80.

General Notes.—Boats with "N," "O" and "P" names, all Emergency War Programme : the War boats with "M" names, Emergency War Programme, but part of their cost was met by the provision in 1914-15 Navy Estimates for ten destroyers. The Pre-War M's, 1913-14 Programme. Proved a remarkably successful type of Destroyer, although not so fast as the Thornycroft and Yarrow "M's."

To distinguish.—Easily distinguished by their three, small round funnels, with 4 inch mounted between second and third funnels. Can be separated from the Admiralty R's by the after 4 inch *not* being mounted in "bandstand." The Repeat M's have *raking* stems ; the Pre-War M's have rather shorter funnels.

War Losses.—Repeat M's : *Pheasant* (Fairfield), *Partridge* (Swan Hunter). War M's : *Narborough* (Clydebank), *Opal* (Doxford), *Mary Rose, Negro, North Star* (all Palmer), *Nomad* (Stephen), *Marmion, Nessus, Nestor* (all Swan Hunter). Pre-War M's : No losses.

		Begun.	Launch.	Comp.
2 B'dmore.	*Pelican* ..	25/6/15	18/3/16	1/5/16
	Pellew ..	28/6/15	18/5/16	30/6/16
10 Clydebank.	*Napier* ..	24/3/15	27/11/16	1/16
	Penn ..	9/6/15	8/4/16	5/16
	Peregine ..	9/6/15	29/5/16	7/16
	Ossory ..	23/12/14	9/10/16	11/15
	Mameluke ..	23/12/14	14/8/15	10/15
	Marne ..	30/9/14	29/5/15	8/15
	Mons ..	30/9/14	1/5/15	7/15
	Milne ..	1914	5/10/14	12/14
	Morris ..	1914	19/11/14	12/14
	Moorsom ..	1914	21/12/14	2/15
7 Denny.	*Petard* ..	5/7/15	24/3/16	23/5/16
	Peyton ..	12/7/15	2/5/16	29/6/16
	Maenad ..	10/11/14	10/8/15	12/11/15
	Marvel ..	11/1/15	7/10/15	28/12/15
	Mystic ..	27/10/14	26/6/16	11/11/15
	Narwhal ..	21/4/15	3/12/15	3/3/16
	Nicator ..	21/4/15	3/2/16	15/4/16
9 Doxford.	*Norseman* ..	....	15/8/16	11/16
	Oberon ..	....	29/9/16	12/16
	Octavia ..	....	21/6/16	11/16
	Ophelia ..	....	13/10/15	5/16
	Opportune ..	....	20/11/16	6/16
	Oracle ..	....	23/12/15	8/16
	Orestes ..	....	21/3/16	6/16
	Orford ..	....	19/4/16	12/16
	Orpheus ..	....	17/6/16	9/16
11 Fairfield.	*Observer* ..	....	1/5/16	15/6/16
	Offa ..	....	7/6/16	31/7/16
	Phoebe ..	....	20/11/16	28/12/16
	Mandate ..	....	27/4/15	13/8/15
	Manners ..	....	15/6/15	21/9/15
	Mindful ..	....	24/8/15	10/11/15
	Mischief ..	....	12/10/15	16/12/15
	Onslaught ..	....	4/12/15	3/3/16
	Onslow ..	....	15/2/16	15/4/16
	Orcadia ..	....	26/7/16	29/9/16
	Oriana ..	....	23/9/16	4/11/16

		Begun.	Launch.	Comp.
2 H. Leslie	*Pigeon* ..	14/7/15	3/3/16	2/6/16
	Plover ..	30/7/15	3/3/16	30/6/16
8 Palmer.	*Oriole* ..	....	31/7/16	11/16
	Osiris ..	....	26/9/16	12/16
	Nonsuch ..	....	8/12/15	2/16
	Norman ..	....	20/3/16	8/16
	Northesk ..	....	5/7/16	10/16
	Nugent ..	....	23/1/17	4/17
	Murray ..	....	6/8/14	12/14
	Myngs ..	....	24/9/14	2/15
6 Scott.	*Plucky* ..	....	21/4/16	7/16
	Portia ..	....	10/8/16	10/16
	Obdurate ..	....	21/1/16	3/16
	Obedient ..	....	16/11/16	2/16
	Paladin ..	....	27/3/16	5/16
	Parthian ..	....	3/7/16	9/16
5 Stephen.	*Prince* ..	27/7/15	26/7/16	21/9/16
	*Pylades** ..	27/7/15	28/9/16	30/12/16*
	*Nizam** ..	11/2/15	6/4/16	29/6/16*
	Noble ..	6/2/15	25/11/15	15/2/16
	Nonpareil ..	24/2/15	16/5/16	28/6/16
4 Swan Hunter.	*Pasley* ..	7/15	15/4/16	7/16
	Martial ..	10/14	1/7/15	10/15
	Menace ..	9/14	9/11/15	4/16
	Matchless ..	11/13	5/10/14	12/14
6 Thorny-croft.	*Michael* ..	10/14	19/5/15	8/15
	Milbrook ..	11/14	12/7/15	10/15
	Minion ..	11/14	11/9/15	11/15
	Munster ..	11/14	24/11/15	1/16
	Nepean ..	2/15	21/1/16	3/16
	Nereus ..	3/15	24/2/16	5/16
4 White.	*Medina* ..	22/9/15	8/3/16	30/6/16
	Medway ..	2/11/15	19/4/16	2/8/16
	Magic ..	1/1/15	10/9/15	8/1/16
	Moresby ..	14/1/15	20/11/15	7/4/16

*Completed by Messrs. Beardmore.

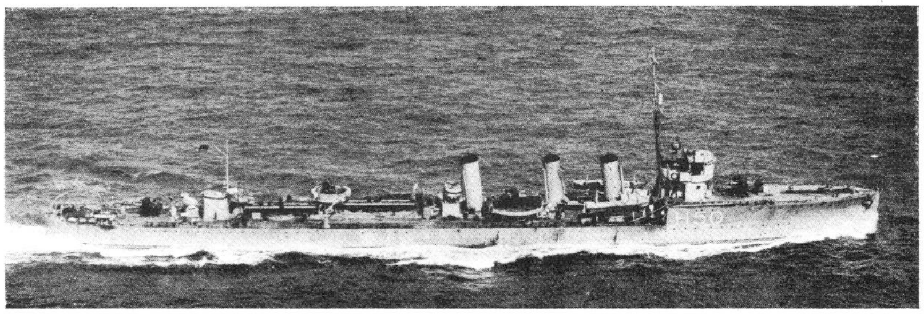

OBDURATE (War M's). *Official R.A.F. Photo.*

BRITISH NAVY—DESTROYERS.

6 "Thornycroft M."

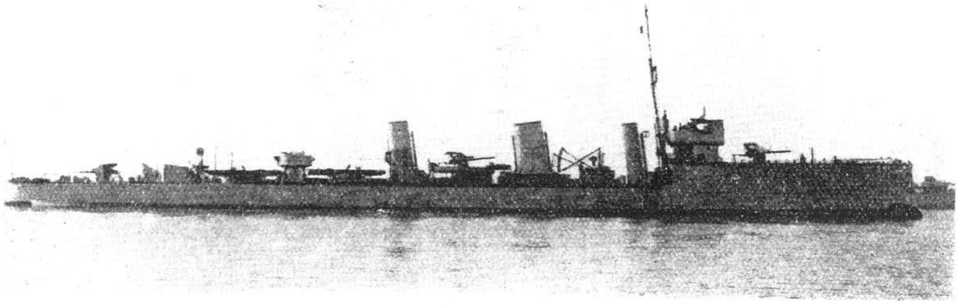

READY. *Photo, Messrs. Thornycroft.*

6 *Thornycroft* : **Rapid, Ready,** 1033 tons. **Patriot, Patrician,** 1004 tons. **Meteor,** 1070 tons. **Mastiff,** 985 tons. Dimensions : 265 (*p.p.*), 271-274 (*o.a.*) × $27\frac{1}{2}$ × $10\frac{1}{2}$-11 feet. Guns : 3—4 inch, 1—2 pdr. pom-pom, 1 M.G. Tubes : 4—21 inch in pairs. Machinery : *Meteor* and *Mastiff*, Parsons turbines, 26,500 S.H.P. = 35 kts. ; other Brown-Curtis turbines, 27,500 S.H.P. = 35 kts. 3 Yarrow boilers. Oil : *about* 285-250/220-200 tons. Complement, 82.

Note.—*Meteor* and *Mastiff* 1913-14 Programme ; rest Emergency War Programme. Proved very successful boats.

6 THORNYCROFT.

	Begun.	Launch.	Comp.	Trials.
Rapid ..	8/15	7/16	8/16	35.45
Ready ..	9/15	8/16	10/16	34.36
Patriot ..	7/15	4/16	6/16	37.34
Patrician ..	6/15	6/16	7/16	35.6
Meteor ..	5/13	7/14	9/14	34.85
Mastiff ..	7/13	10/14	11/14	37.52

10 YARROW.

	Begun.	Launch.	Comp.	Trials.
Relentless	....	4/16	5/16	37.69
Rival ..	5/15	6/16	9/16	36.83
Nerissa ..	11/14	2/16	3/16	36.74
Moon ..	9/14	4/15	6/15	37.86
Morning Star	9/14	6/15	8/15	36.92
Mounsey	9/14	9/15	11/15	39.02
Musketeer	9/14	11/15	12/15	35.6
Miranda	10/12	5/14	8/14	33.53
Minos ..	10/12	8/14	10/14	36.73
Manley ..	10/12	10/14	11/14	33.88

10 "Yarrow M."

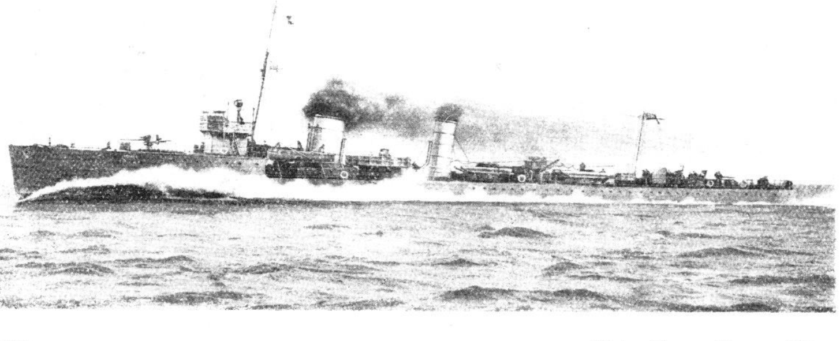

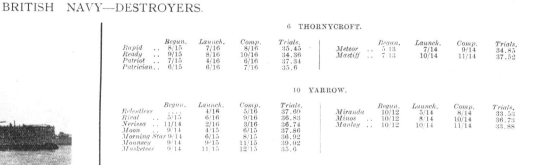

MOUNSEY. *Photo, Messrs. Yarrow, Ltd.*

10 *Yarrow* : **Relentless, Rival, Nerissa, Moon, Morning Star, Mounsey, Musketeer, Miranda, Minos, Manley.** Displace 879-898 tons. Dimensions : $260\frac{1}{4}$ (*p.p.*), $269\frac{1}{2}$-$271\frac{1}{2}$ (*o.a.*) × $25\frac{2}{3}$ - 27 × $10\frac{1}{3}$ feet. Guns : 3—4 inch, 1—2 pdr. pom-pom. Torpedo tubes : 4—21 inch in pairs. Brown-Curtis turbines. 3 Yarrow boilers. Designed S.H.P. 23,000 = 35-36 kts. Oil fuel : 228/202 tons. Complement, 79.

Notes.—*Miranda, Minos, Manley*, 1913-14 Programme ; *Morning Star, Mounsey, Musketeer*, part Emergency War Programme, plus sum voted for ten boats in 1914-15 Estimates ; *Relentless, Rival, Nerissa*, Emergency War Programme. Very successful boats. Design by Messrs. Yarrow, Ltd. These boats have *straight* sterns.

2 "Hawthorn M."

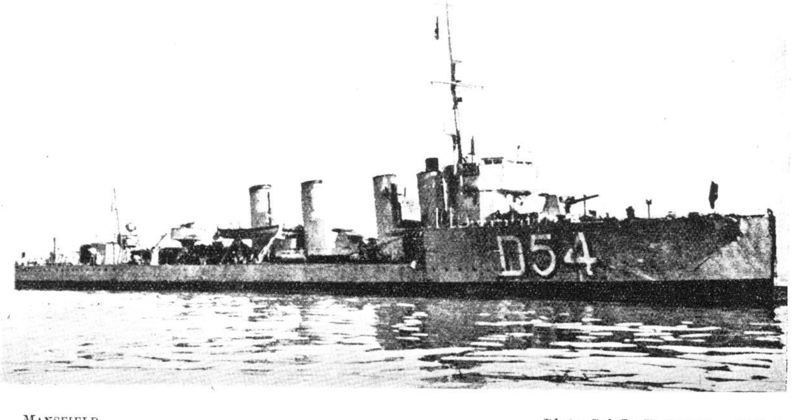

MANSFIELD. *Photo, Sub-Lt. H. Lawrence, R.N.R.*

2 *Hawthorn* : **Mansfield, Mentor.** Launched 1914. 1057 and 1053 tons. Dimensions : 265 (*p.p.*), 271 (*o.a.*) × 27 × $10\frac{3}{4}$ feet. Guns : 3—4 inch, 1—2 pdr. AA., 1 M.G. Tubes : 4—21 inch in pairs. Parsons turbines. 3 screws. Yarrow boilers. Designed S.H.P. 27 000 = 35 kts. Oil : 290/220 tons. Complement, 76.

Notes.—1913-14 Programme boats.

3 ex-Turkish.

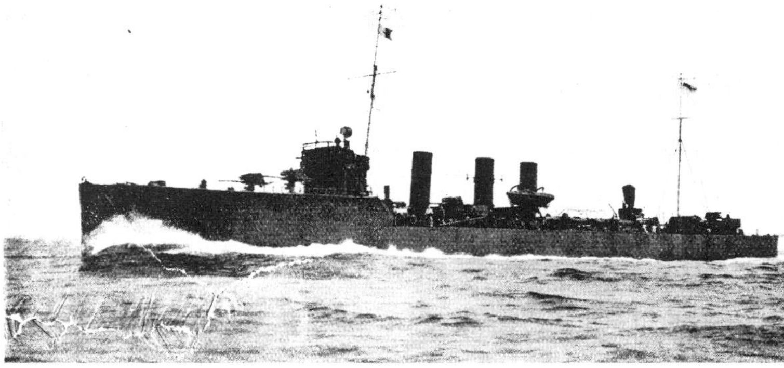

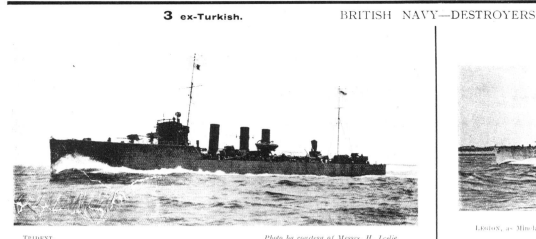

TRIDENT. *Photo by courtesy of Messrs. H. Leslie.*

3 *Hawthorn Leslie*: **Talisman, Termagant, Trident.** 1098 tons. Complement, 102. Dimensions: 309 ft. × 28 ft. 7 in. × 9 ft. 6 in. Guns: 5—4 inch. Torpedo tubes: 4—21 inch in pairs (very light type). Carry D.C. Machinery: Parsons turbines and Yarrow boilers. 3 screws. Designed H.P. 25,000 = 32 kts. Fuel: 237 tons oil. *Turbulent* lost during War. All begun for Turkish Navy, but taken over by Admiralty. Proved so successful, their design formed basis for the later Admiralty V's and W's.

	Begun.	*Launch.*	*Comp.*		*Begun.*	*Launch.*	*Comp.*
Talisman ..	7/12/14	15/7/15	19/1/16	*Trident*	7/1/15	20/11/15	24/3/16
Termagant ..	17/12/14	26/8/15	18/3/16				

3 ex-Greek.

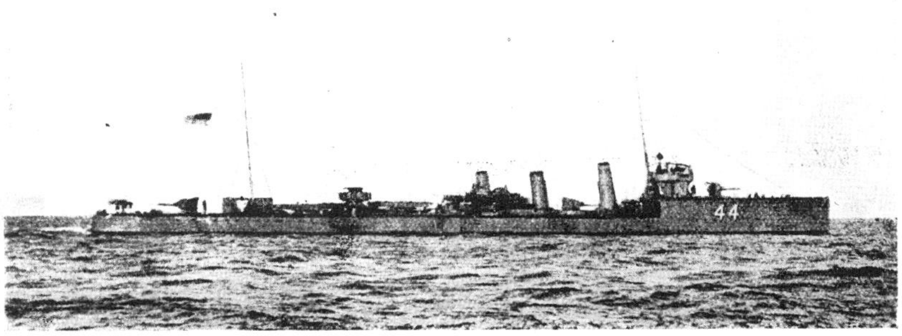

MEDEA.

1 *Clydebank*: **Medea** (ex *Kriti*). 1007 tons.

2 *Fairfield*: **Melpomene** (ex *Samos*), **Melampus** (ex *Chios*). 1040 tons. Complement, 80.

Dimensions: 273⅓ × 26⅜ × 10¼ feet. Guns: 3—4 inch, 1—2 pdr. pom-pom, 1 M.G. Torpedo tubes: 4—21 inch in twin deck mountings. Also usual D.C. Machinery: Brown-Curtis turbines and Yarrow boilers. 3 screws. Designed H.P. 25,000 = 32 kts. Fuel: 276/225 tons.

Notes—Ordered for Greek Navy, and taken over for British Navy, 1914. *Medusa* (ex Greek *Lesvos*), built by Clydebank, lost 25 March 1916.

	Begun.	*Launch.*	*Comp.*		*Begun.*	*Launch.*	*Comp.*
Medea	8/4/14	30/1/15	5/15	*Melampus* ..	....	16/12/14	29/6/15
Melpomene ..	....	1/2/15	16/8/15				

17 L Class (16 Pre-War + 1 War.)

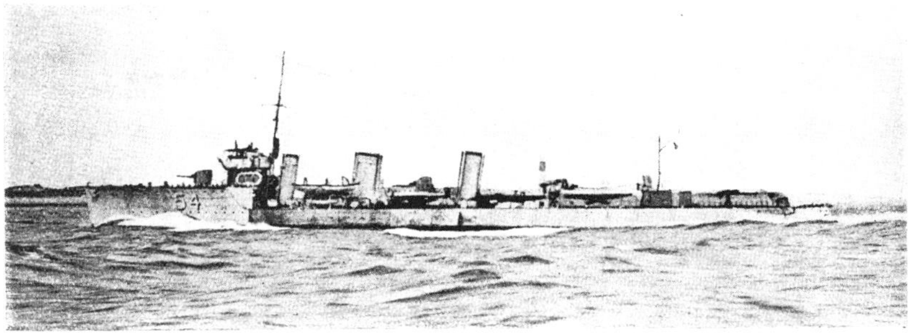

LEGION, as Minelayer. After 4 inch and tubes are dummies painted on screens.

(ALL 3 FUNNELS.)

1 *Beardmore*: **Lochinvar** (Oct., 1915). 1010 tons. Brown-Curtis turbines.

2 *Beardmore*: **Llewellyn** (1913), **Lennox** (1914). 996 tons. Parsons turbines.

2 *Fairfield*: **Lawford** (1913), **Lydiard** (1914). 1003 tons. *Trials*: *Laforey* 29·9 kts.

2 *Parsons (Hawthorn)*: **Leonidas** (1913), **Lucifer** (1913). 987 tons.

2 *Swan, Hunter & W. Richardson*: **Laertes** (1913). 982 tons. **Lysander** (1913). 976 tons. *Trials*: *Laertes* 31·2, *Lysander* 29·9.

2 *Thornycroft*: **Lance** (1914). 997 tons. **Lookout** (1914). 1002 tons.

2 *Denny*: **Loyal** (1913). 995 tons, **Legion** (1914), 1072 tons.

War Losses in above: *Laforey, Louis, Lassoo.*

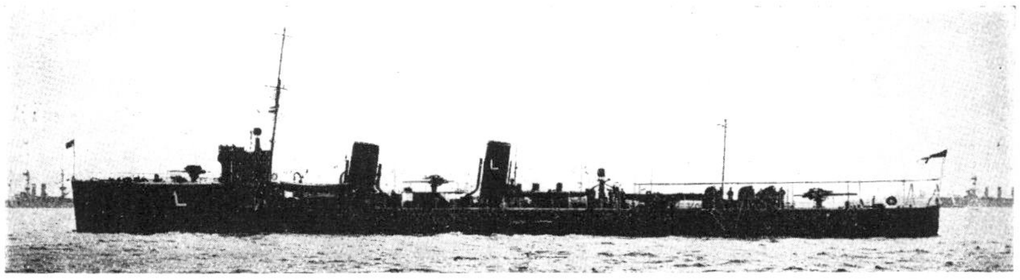

LAUREL. *Photo, Symonds.*

(ALL 2 FUNNELS.)

2 *White*: **Laurel** (1913), **Liberty** (1913). 965-975 tons.

4 *Yarrow*: **Lark** (1913), 968 tons. **Landrail** (1914), 983 tons. **Laverock** (1914), 994 tons. **Linnet** (1913), 970 tons. All Brown-Curtis turbines.

All to Admiralty design. Armament: 3—4 inch, 1—2 pdr. pom-pom, 1 M.G. 4—21 inch tubes in pairs. Machinery: Parsons turbines in all, except where otherwise noted. Designed H.P. 24,500 = 29 kts.; *Leonidas* and *Lucifer* only, 22,500 = 29 kts. Dimensions: 269 × 27½ × 10½ feet. Fuel: 290-270/230-200 tons oil. Complement, 77.

Lochinvar (and lost *Lassoo*), Emergency War Programme; rest 1912-13 Programme.

1911 BRITISH DESTROYERS. 1911

13 K Class.

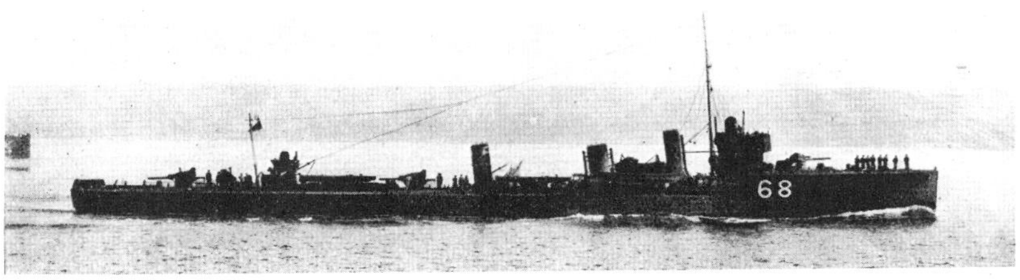

"K CLASS" SPECIAL BOATS. Amidships 4 inch *abaft* funnel and *before* after tube. After S.L. or AA. gun platform *before* mainmast. *Garland* has cut-away stern.

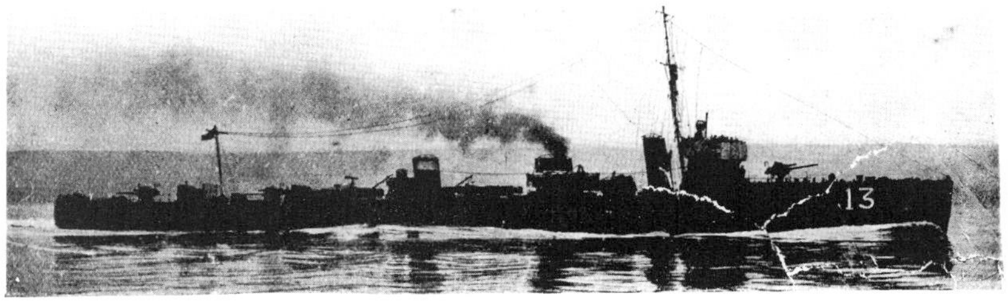

"K CLASS" ADMIRALTY BOATS. S.L. or AA. gun platform *abaft* 3rd funnel, amidships 4 inch *between* after tubes and mainmast. Forefunnel close to foremast.

Special Boats.

3 *Thornycroft*: **Porpoise,** 934 tons, **Unity, Victor,** 954 tons (1913). Designed H.P. 22,500 = 31 kts. All made about 30.3 on trials.

1 *Thornycroft*: **Hardy** (1912). 898 tons. H.P. 21,000 = 32 kts.

1 *Parsons* (hull sub-contracted to Cammell Laird): **Garland** (1913). 984 tons. Dimensions as Admiralty boats. Designed H.P. 24,500 = 30 kts. *Trials*, 31 kts.

Notes to above.—Dimensions (except *Garland*): 265¾ × 26½ × 9¾-10¾ feet. All Parsons turbines. 2 screws. Yarrow boilers. Oil: 250-260/200-220 tons. *Hardy* said to have Diesel engine for cruising speeds; she was so designed, but it is uncertain if this Diesel engine was ever installed or not.

War Losses.—Paragon, Fortune.

Admiralty Design Boats.

3 *Clydebank*: **Acasta,** 996 tons, **Achates,** 982 tons (1912), **Ambuscade,** 935 tons (1913). *Trials*: *Acasta* 29 kts. *Achates* 32·3 kts. *Ambuscade* 30·4 kts. *Acasta* practically destroyed at Jutland and rebuilt. Brown-Curtis turbines in these boats.

2 *Hawthorn Leslie*: **Christopher,** 938 tons, **Cockatrice,** 951 tons (1912). *Trials*: *Christopher* 30.9 kts. *Cockatrice* 29·7 kts.

2 *London and Glasgow*: **Midge, Owl,** 936 tons. (1913); *Trials*: *Midge* 32·9 kts. *Owl* 32·7 kts.

1 *Swan Hunter*: **Spitfire** (1913). 935 tons. *Trials*: 30·3 kts.

Notes to above boats.—Dimensions: 267½ × 27 × 10½ feet. Designed H.P. 24,500 = 29 kts. All Parsons turbines, except Clydebank boats. 2 screws. Yarrow boilers. Oil: 260/200 tons.

War Losses.—Ardent, Contest, Lynx, Sparrowhead, Shark.

General Notes.—All 1911-12 Programme. Guns: 3—4 inch (1—4 inch on AA. mounting in some boats), 1—2 pdr. pom-pom in nearly all, 1 M.G. Tubes: 2—21 inch single. The single tube between 2nd and 3rd funnels is a distinctive feature of this class. Complement, 75-77.

23 I Class (3 this page, 18 next page).

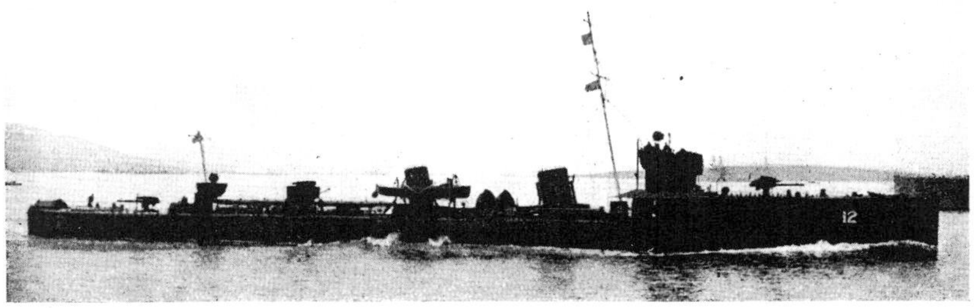

OAK. (LURCHER and FIREDRAKE high mainmasts.)

Special Boats.

3 *Yarrow*: **Lurcher, Firedrake, Oak** (all 1912). 765 tons. *Firedrake* 767 tons. Dimensions: 262 × 25⅔ × 9½ feet. Guns: 2—4 inch, 2—12 pdr., 1—3 pdr. AA., 1 M.G. Tubes: 2—21 inch. Designed H.P. 20,000 = 32 kts. On trials *Firedrake* made 33·1, *Lurcher* 35·34 *mean* of 8 hrs. *Oak*: 32·4. Turbines: Parsons. 2 screws. Boilers: special Yarrow oil burning; oil, *about* 170/155 tons. Built to replace three boats of this class, transferred to Royal Australian Navy, and now H.M.A.S. *Parramatta*, *Yarra* and *Warrego*. Complement, 70.

("I" Class continued on next page).

1911 BRITISH NAVY—DESTROYERS. 1910

23 I Class (18 this page, 3 preceding page).

General Notes to all below.

Built under 1910-11 Programme. Armament of all: 2—4 inch, 2—12 pdr., 1—3 pdr. AA., 1 M G., 2—21 inch tubes. Complement, 70.

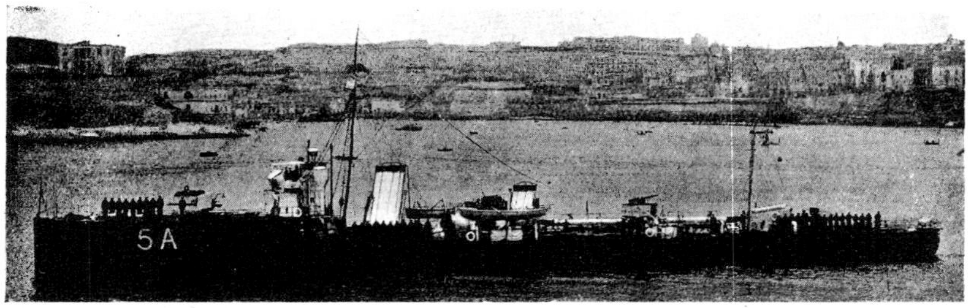

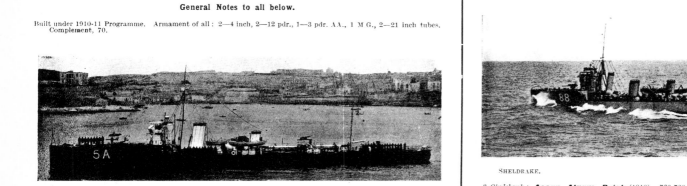

JACKAL. *Photo, Ellis, Malta.*

To Builders' Designs.

2 *Parsons:* **Badger** (1911), 799 tons, **Beaver** (1911), 810 tons. Designed H.P. 16,500 = 30 kts. Hull, etc., contracted for by Hawthorn. *Trials: Badger* 30.7. Parsons turbines.

1 *Thornycroft:* **Acheron** (1911) 773 tons. Designed H.P. 15,500 = 29 kts. On trial, 29.4. Parsons turbines.

1 *Yarrow:* **Archer** (1911). 775 tons. Designed H.P. 16,000 = 28 kts. Brown-Curtis turbines. *Trials: Archer* 30.9.

Notes.—Dimensions: *Acheron*, $252\frac{1}{4} \times 26\frac{1}{3} \times 9\frac{1}{4}$ feet; others about $246 \times 25\frac{3}{4} \times 9\frac{1}{3}$ feet. 2 screws in all. Oil fuel: 182-170/158-150 tons. All Yarrow boilers.

War Losses.—Ariel (Minelayer), *Attack*

Admiralty Design Boats.

1 *Beardmore:* **Goshawk** (1911). 760 tons. Parsons turbines.

3 *Clydebank:* **Hind, Hornet** 1911), **Hydra** (1912). 770-5 tons. *Trials: Hind* 28.1, *Hornet* 28.7, *Hydra* 28.1. Brown-Curtis turbines.

2 *Denny:* **Defender, Druid** (1911). 762-770 tons. *Trials: Defender* 28.3, *Druid* 28.2. Parsons turbines.

2 *Hawthorn:* **Jackal, Tigress** (1911). 745 tons. *Trials: Jackal* 26.9, *Tigress* 28.1. Parsons turbines.

2 *Laird:* **Lapwing, Lizard** (1911). 745 tons. *Trials: Lapwing* 27.2 *Lizard* 27.5. Parsons turbines.

1 *Swan Hunter:* **Sandfly** (1911). 750 tons. *Trials:* 27.7. Parsons turbines.

2 *White:* **Ferret, Forester** (1911). 750 and 760 tons. *Trials: Ferret* 30.2, *Forester* 29.8. Parsons turbines.

Notes.—Dimensions: $246\frac{3}{4} \times 25\frac{7}{8} \times 8\frac{3}{4}$-9 feet. All 3 screws, except the Clydebank boats with Brown-Curtis turbines, which have 2 screws. All Yarrow boilers, except White boats with White-Forster. Oil: *about* 180/148 tons.

War Losses: Phœnix.

20 H Class.

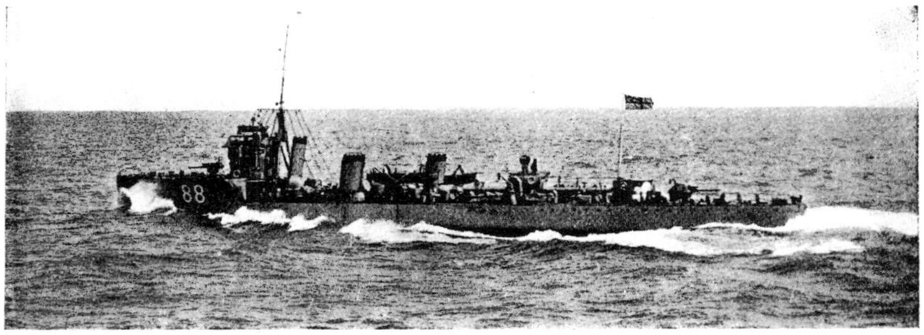

SHELDRAKE.

3 *Clydebank:* **Acorn, Alarm, Brisk** (1910). 760-780 tons. *Acorn* and *Alarm*, Parsons turbines; *Brisk*, Curtis turbines. *Trials: Acorn* 27.2, *Alarm* 27.2, *Brisk* 27.6.

1 *Denny:* **Sheldrake** (1911). 748 tons. Parsons turbines. *Trials: Sheldrake* 28.3.

1 *Fairfield:* **Cameleon** (1910). 747 tons. Parsons turbines. *Trials: Cameleon* 28.03.

3 *Hawthorn:* **Nemesis,* Nereide** (1910), **Nymphe** (1911). All 740 tons. Parsons turbines. *Trials: Nemesis* 27, *Nereide* 27 8, *Nymphe* 27.5.

1 *Inglis:* **Fury** (1911). 760 tons. Parsons turbines. *Trials:* 27.3.

1 *Swan Hunter:* **Hope** (1910). 745 tons. Parsons turbine. *Trials:* 27.1.

4 *Thornycroft:* **Larne, Lyra, Martin** (all 1910), **Minstrel*** (1911). All 730 tons. Parsons turbine. *Trials: Larne* 27.9, *Lyra* 28.7, *Martin* 28.9, *Minstrel* 28.9.

3 *White:* **Redpole, Rifleman, Ruby** (1910). All 720 tons. Parsons turbine. White-Forster boilers. *Trials: Redpole* 29.8, *Rifleman* 28.6, *Ruby* 29.3.

**Minstrel* and *Nemesis* loaned to Japanese Navy, 1917-18, and commissioned as Japanese *Sendan* (*Minstrel*) and *Kanran* (*Nemesis*). Returned to British Navy, 1919.

Notes.—Formerly *Acorn* class. Belong to 1909-10 Programme, laid down end of 1909. About 800 tons. Dimensions: *about* 246½ x 24⅓ x 8⅔ feet. Armament: 2—4 inch, 2—12 pdr., 1—3 pdr. A.A.*. 1 M.G., 2—21 inch tubes. Designed H.P. 13,500 = 27 kts. 3 screws. Yarrow boilers in all, except *Redpole, Rifleman* and *Ruby*, with White-Forster. Fuel: *about* 170/140 tons oil. Complement, 72.

*In a few boats only.

To distinguish.—High bridges, thick middle funnel, no gun or tubes between 2nd and 3rd funnels. 12 pdrs. at break of fo'xle. Big ventilators between funnels.

War Losses.— Comet, Goldfinch, Staunch.

BRITISH NAVY—DESTROYERS AND P. C. BOATS.

16 G Class.

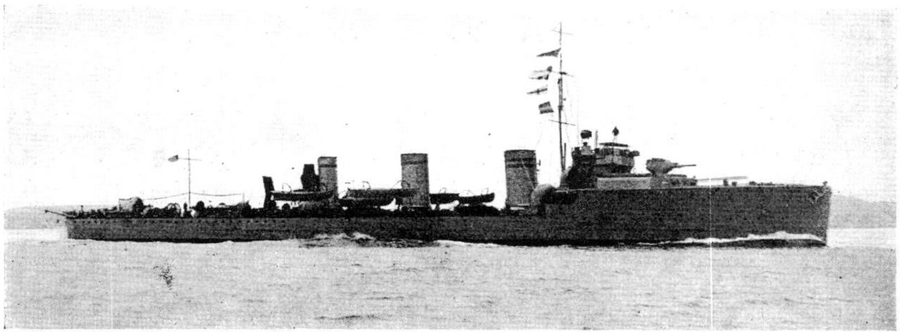

SCOURGE. *Photo, Lieut.-Com. Holberton, R.N.*

3 *Clydebank:* **Beagle, Bulldog, Foxhound** (1909). 950, 952, 995 tons. Parsons turbine. H.P. 12,500.

3 *Fairfield:* **Grasshopper** (1909), **Mosquito** (1910), **Scorpion** (1910). 923, 983, 987 tons. Parsons turbines. H.P. 12,000.

1 *Hawthorn:* **Scourge** (1910). 922 tons. Parsons turbine. H.P. 12,500.

1 *Cammell Laird:* **Renard** (1909). 918 tons. Parsons turbine. H.P. 12,500.

1 *London & Glasgow:* **Rattlesnake** (1910). 946 tons. Parsons turbine. H.P. 12,000.

1 *Thames Ironworks:* **Grampus** (ex *Nautilus*), (1910). 975 tons. Parsons turbine. H.P. 12,000.

1 *Thornycroft:* **Savage** (1910). 897 tons. Parsons turbine. H.P. 12,500.

2 *White:* **Basilisk** (1910). **Harpy** (1909). 972, 976 tons. Parsons turbine. White-Forster boilers. H.P. 12,600.

General Notes.—These boats belong to the 1909-18 Programme, and were formerly known as the *Basilisk* class, or "The Mediterranean *Beagles.*" *Displace 860 to 995 tons. Dimensions: average* 274⅛ x 28 x 10 feet. Armament: 1—4 inch, 3—12 pdr.,* 1—3 pdr. AA.,† 1 M.G., 2—22 inch tubes. *Average* H.P. 12,500 = 27 kts. 3 screws. Boilers: Yarrow in all, except *Basilisk* and *Harpy*, with White-Forster. Coal: 200-241 tons. Complements for all, 96. All made 27 or a little over on *trials*, except *Grampus* 28.1, *Basilisk* 27.9, *Harpy* and *Foxhound* 27.7. Are the only coal-burning Destroyers now in British Navy, and will probably be scrapped within the next two years.

War Losses.—Pincher, Racoon, Wolverine.

**Scorpion* 2—12 pdr.

†3 pdr. AA. not in *Basilisk, Grasshopper, Savage, Scourge.*

19 PC Boats (Converted Patrol Boats).

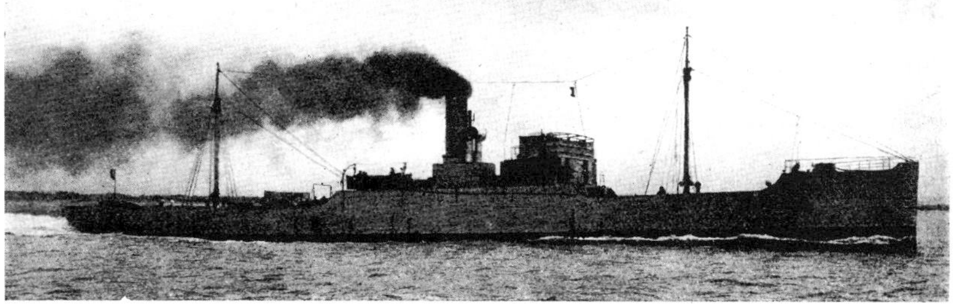

PC 68. *Photo, Messrs. J. S. White & Sons (Builders).*

Note.—Above illustration is typical only: these vessels have varying mercantile disguises as small coasting steamers, tugs, &c. Some have only one mast forward.

2 *Barclay Curle:* **PC 55, PC 56** (both 1917). 682 tons.
2 *Caird:* **PC 42, PC 43** (both 1917). 682 tons.
1 *Connell:* **PC 63** (1917). 682 tons.
2 *Eltringham:* **PC 44.** (682 tons. **PC 65** (both 1917). 694 tons.
1 *Harland & Wolff (Govan):* **PC 62** (1917). 682 tons.
1 *Harkness:* **PC 66** (1918). 694 tons.
1 *Tyne Iron Co.:* **PC 51** (1917). 682 tons.
6 *White:* **PC 67, PC 68** (both 1917). **PC 71–PC 74** (1918). All 694 tons.
2 *Workman Clark:* **PC 60, PC 61** (both 1917). 682 tons. **PC 69, PC 70** (both 1918). 694 tons.

Dimensions: 682 ton boats: 233 (*p.p.*), 247 (*o.a.*) × 25½ × 8-8½ feet. 694 ton boats: 233 (*p.p.*). 247 (*o.a*) × 26¾ × 8 feet. 682 and 694 ton boats reported to have shallow bulge protection. Guns: 1—4 inch. 2—12 pdr. Torpedo tubes: removed. Carry 24-30 D.C. Machinery: Parsons or Brown-Curtis turbines. Yarrow boilers. 2 screws. Designed S.H.P. 3,500 = 20 kts. Oil: 134 tons in 682 ton boats; 164 tons in 694 ton boats: all *max.* These two types carry extra fuel in bulges. Complement, *about* 50-55.

General Notes.—All built under Emergency War Programme. Design as P-boats, but these craft were converted or modified while building, to act as Submarine Decoy Vessels or "Q-boats." The after 4 inch gun was hidden behind various forms of dummy deck loads, *e.g.*, bales or packing cases of merchandise, trusses of hay: in a few boats it was located within a collapsible pantechnicon furniture van, or under a dummy boat built in folding sections. It was expected that, on account of shallow draught, torpedoes fired by U-boats would under-run these *PC*-boats, while, if hit by torpedo, bulge protection and special fillings would keep them afloat long enough to destroy the U-boat.

1909 BRITISH DESTROYERS **1908** and earlier.

12 F Class.

These boats belong (first five) to the 1907-08 programme, the two next to the 1906-07 programme, the remaining five to the 1905-06 programme. They were formerly known as "Ocean-going Destroyers," also as the "Tribal class."

As no two are alike, details are given separately under each boat.

All destroyers from this class to the "A" class had been deleted by mid-1919.

Photo, Cribb.

1 *White :*—**Crusader.** 945 tons. Armament : 2—4 inch (25 pdr.), 2—18 inch tubes. Parsons turbine. White-Foster boilers. Oil fuel. (Fore funnel heightened, 1912).

1 *Denny :* —**Maori** (1909). 980 tons. Armament : 2—4 inch (25 pdr.), 2—18 inch tubes. Parsons turbine. Yarrow boilers. (Fore funnel now heightened, 1912).
Mined off Zeebrugge 7 May 1915.

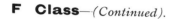

F Class—*(Continued)*.

BRITISH DESTROYERS.

Photo, Oscar Parkes, Esq.

1 *Thornycroft :*—**Nubian.** 990 tons. Armament : 2—4 inch (25 pdr.), 2—18 inch tubes. Parsons turbine. Thornycroft boilers. Oil fuel.
Torpedoed off Folkstone 27 October 1916 (see Zula).

F Class—*(Continued)*.   (2 of 1906-07 programme).

1 *Thornycroft :*—**Amazon** (1908). 966 tons. Dimensions : 280×26½×8½ feet. H.P. 15,500. Parsons turbine. Thornycroft boilers. Oil : 86 tons *normal* ; *maximum*, 185 tons. Armament, 2—4 inch (25 pdrs.), 2—18 inch tubes.

1 *Palmer :*—**Viking** (1909). 1000 tons. Armament : 2—4 inch (25 pdr.), 2—18 inch tubes. Parsons turbine. Yarrow boilers.

Photo, Oscar Parkes, Esq.

1 *White :*—**Saracen.** 970 tons. Dimensions : 272×26×8½ feet. H.P. 15,500. Parsons turbine. White-Foster boilers. Oil : 81 tons *normal* ; *maximum* 185 tons. Armament, 2—4 inch (25 pdrs.) 2—18 inch tubes. (Fore funnel heightened 1911.)

Photo, Oscar Parkes, Esq

1 *Hawthorn :*—**Zulu** (1909). 1000 tons. Armament : 2—4 inch (25 pdr.), 2—18 inch tubes. Parsons turbine. Yarrow boilers. (Fore funnel heightened 1911.)
Mined off Dover 27 October 1916. The undamaged portions of *Zula* and *Nubian* were united to form one destroyer, known as *Zubian.*

BRITISH DESTROYERS (ordered 1906). **1907**
Parsons turbine, and oil fuel in all. *Maximum* radius, 1500—1700 miles.

Unclassed boat of equal date.

1 *Cammell-Laird:*—**Swift** (1907). 1825 tons. Dimensions: 345×34½×10½ feet. Oil: 180 tons. H.P. 30,000 = 36 kts. Yarrow boilers. Armament: 4—4 inch (25 pdr.), 2—18 inch tubes. Cost about £280,500.
(This boat has reached 39 knots).

F Class—*(Continued)*.

1 *Elswick:*—**Afridi** (1907). 836 tons. Dimensions: 250×25×7½ feet. H.P. 14,250 = 32·75. Oil: 92½ tons. Armament: 5—12 pdr., 2—18 inch tubes. Yarrow boilers.

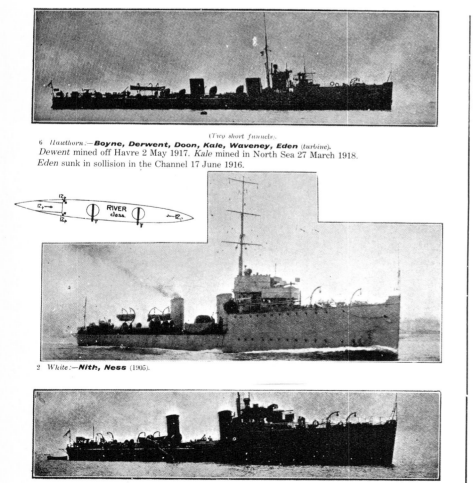

1 *Cammell-Laird:*—**Cossack** (1907). 885 tons. Dimensions: 270×26×8 feet. H.P. 14,000. Oil: 76 tons; *maximum* 185 tons. Armament: 5—12 pdr., 2—18 inch tubes. Yarrow boilers. Cossack has proved to be a remarkably good sea boat.
(Now carries a small mast aft).

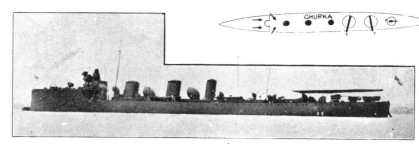

1 *Hawthorn:*—**Ghurka.** 870 tons. Dimensions: 255×25½×8 feet. H.P. 14,250. Oil: 95 tons; *maximum*, 185 tons. Armament: 5—12 pdr., 2—18 inch tubes. Yarrow boilers. Mined off Dungeness 8 February 1917.

Photo, Symonds.
1 *White:*—**Mohawk** (1907). 865 tons. Dimensions: 270×25×8 feet. H.P. 14,500. Oil: 95 tons; *maximum*, 185 tons. Armament: 5—12 pdr., 2—18 inch tubes. White-Foster boilers.

1 *Thornycroft:*—**Tartar** (1907). 870 tons. Dimensions: 270×26×8 feet. H.P. 14,500. Oil: 74 tons; *maximum*, 185 tons. Trial: *maximum*, 37·4 kts.; *mean*, 35·36. Armament: 5—12 pdr., 2—18 inch tubes. Thornycroft boilers.

34 BRITISH **"E Class"** DESTROYERS (1903-05). **1904-06** (ex *River* Class).

(Two short funnels).
6 *Hawthorn:*—**Boyne, Derwent, Doon, Kale, Waveney, Eden** (turbine).
Derwent mined off Havre 2 May 1917. *Kale* mined in North Sea 27 March 1918.
Eden sunk in collision in the Channel 17 June 1916.

(Two high funnels).
4 *Thornycroft:*—**Chelmer, Colne, Jed, Kennet.**

(Four funnels closely paired).
9 *Palmer:* **Cherwell, Dee, Erne, Ettrick, Exe, Swale, Ure, Wear** (1901), **Rother** 1905).

2 *White:*—**Nith, Ness** (1905).

(Four funnels openly paired, and no raised piece in the eyes).
5 *Yarrow:*—**Ribble, Teviot, Usk, Welland** (1904), **Garry** (1905).

(Two medium funnels).
8 *Cammell-Laird:*—**Arun, Foyle, Itchen, Liffey, Moy, Ouse;** also replace boats **Stour, Test.**

Foyle mined off Dover 15 March 1917. *Itchen* torpedoed by U-boat in North Sea 6 July 1917. *Erne* wrecked off Aberdeen 6 February 1915.

Note.—Average displacement, 550 tons. Average dimensions, 225×23½×12 feet (*maximum* draught). Armament: 1—12 pdr., 12 cwt., 3—12 pdr., 8 cwt., 2—18 inch tubes.
Average H.P. 7000 = 25½ kts. Machinery: Reciprocating. Boilers: *Hawthorn* boats, Yarrow; *Palmer*, Reed; others, makers' types. Coal: about 130 tons. Complements: 70.

All these are good sea-boats, and are good for a steady 24 kts. Their endurance at full power is about 12—15 hours. At low speeds they are extremely economical, and their actual radius something like 2000 miles.

BRITISH DESTROYERS. *about* **1897**

8 Class D.

Average 335 tons.   Armament of all, 1—12 pdr. *(forward)*. 5—6 pdr., 2—18 inch tubes.   Designed H.P., *average* 5,700 = 30 kts.   Boilers : Thornycroft in all.   Coal, 80 tons.   Complement, 60.

Special feature : *all boats of D class have only 2 funnels.*

(Cut-away bow, big round stern, both tubes abaft funnels).

8 Thornycroft :— **Angler, Desperate, Fame.** Trials : *Angler,* 30·4 ; *Desperate,* 30·3 ; *Fame.* 30·1.

(Cut-away bow, rudder showing (instead of Thornycroft stern), tubes both aft).

Thornycroft :— **Cygnet, Cynthia, Coquette, Mallard, Stag.**   Trials : *Cygnet,* 30·3 ; *Cynthia,* 30·2 ; *Coquette,* 30·3 ; *Mallard,* 30·1 ; *Stag.* 30·5.

Coquette mined off E. Coast UK, 7 March 1916.

BRITISH DESTROYERS.

35 Class C.

Average 335 tons.   Armament of all, 1—12 pdr. *(forward)*, 5—6 pdr., 2—18 inch tubes.   Designed H.P., *average* 5,700 = 30 kts.   Boilers : Thornycroft in all.   Coal : 80 tons.   Complement : 60.

Special feature : *all boats of C class have 3 funnels.*   Turtleback bow, big bridge.

5 Clydebank :— **Brazen, Electra, Kestrel, Recruit, Vulture.**

Recruit torpedoed by U-boat off the Galloper LV 1 May 1915.

6 Fairfield : **Falcon, Fairy, Gipsy, Leven, Ostrich, Osprey** *(tube between 2 and 3 funnels and abaft).*
Falcon lost in collision 1 April 1918. *Fairy* sunk after ramming UC75 31 May 1918.

(Three equal funnels).

1 Thornycroft :— **Albatross** *(both tubes abaft).*

(High funnels.)

5 Hawthorn :— **Cheerful, Mermaid, Racehorse, Roebuck, Greyhound.**   5 Vickers :— **Avon, Bittern, Leopard, Otter, Vixen.**   2 Earle :— **Dove, Bullfinch.**
Cheerful mined off Shetlands 30 June 1917. *Bittern* sunk in collision 4 April 1918.

5 Palmer :— **Bat, Crane, Star, Fawn, Flying Fish,** *and (with different funnel tops and searchlight on platform abaft bridge)* **Flirt.**   2 Clydebank :— **Vigilant, Thorn.**   2 Doxford :— **Sylvia, Violet.**

Flirt torpedoed off Dover 27 October 1916.

1 Hawthorn :— **Velox** *(tubes as Albatross, s.l. platform abaft bridge, after funnel much smaller than other two).*
Mined off Nab, 25 October 1915.

BRITISH DESTROYERS 1901—1895.

21 Class B.

General details as below. Armament of all except first two is 1—12 pdr. (forward), 5—6 pdrs., 2—18 inch tubes. Were originally classed as 30-knot destroyers.

Special feature of these is the big fore-bridge, and turtleback bow. *All boats of B class have four funnels.*

1 *Clydebank :—* **Arab** (1901). 470 tons. Dimensions: 218×20×5 *(mean).* H.P. 8,600=31 kts. Coal, 90 tons. Comp., 60.

1 *Laird :—* **Wolf** *(details as per Earnest, etc.)*

2 *Palmer :—* **Albacore** & **Bonetta** (1909). 440 tons. Armament: 3—12 pdr., 2—18 inch tubes. Parsons turbine. Coal fuel. *(Replace boats.)*

10 *Laird :—* **Earnest, Griffon, Locust, Quail, Thrasher, Panther, Seal, Orwell, Lively, Sprightly.** *(Funnels very wide apart).* Vary from 395 –355 tons. H.P. in all, 6,300=30 kts. Coal, 80 tons. Complement, 60.

(Middle funnels extremely close together).

5 *Palmer :—* **Kangaroo, Myrmidon, Peterel, Spiteful, Syren.** 1 *Doxford :—* **Success** *(middle funnels still closer together and without the bands which the Palmer boats have).* These average 380 tons. Coal, 85 tons. Complement, 62.

Success wrecked off Fife Ness 27 December 1914, *Myrmidon* lost in collision 26 March 1917.

1 *Laird :—* **Express** *(stern somewhat depressed aft)* (1897). 465 tons. Dimensions: 235×22×9 feet. H.P. 9,250=30·1 kts. *(first trials).* Coal, 80 tons. Complement, 60.

BRITISH DESTROYERS. 1895-93

12 Class A

Old boats dating from 1893-95. Average displacement : 290 tons. Average dimensions : 200×19 × *about* 9 feet *(max.)* Armament in all : 1—12 pdr. (forward), 5—6 pdr., 2—18 inch tubes. Original H.P. *about* 4000 = 27 kts.

Special feature of these, originally classed as 27 kt. t.b.d., is turtleback bow and *small* fore bridge.

2 *Palmer :—* **Lightning, Porcupine.** 1 *Clydebank :—* **Surly.**
Lightning sunk by mine 30 June 1915.

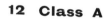

(Ram bow, round Thornycroft stern, small bridge, tubes both aft).

2 *Thornycroft :—* **Boxer, Bruiser.**

Boxer sunk in collision in English Channel 8 February 1918.

(Irregular funnels).

2 *White :—* **Conflict, Wizard** *(very low in water, and with cut-away sterns).*

3 *Hawthorn :—* **Ranger, Opossum, Sunfish.**

2 *Hanna-Donald :—* **Fervent, Zephyr.**

BRITISH NAVY—P-BOATS & TORPEDO BOATS.

43 P-Boats (Patrol Boats.)

P 21. *Photo, Robertson, Gourock, N.B.*

Note.—*P 11, P 21, P 24, P 29*, now have mainmast. *P 17* has mainmast and funnel 4 feet higher. Remainder as above photo.

3 *Barclay Curle:* **P34** (1916), **P53, P54** (1917).
2 *Bartram:* **P23, P41** (both 1916).
2 *Caird:* **P22, P35** (both 1916).
1 *Connell:* **P14** (1916).
2 *Eltringham:* **P27** (1915), **P36** (1916).
4 *Gray:* **P29, P30, P37** (all 1916), **P45** (1917).
4 *Hamilton:* **P75** (ex *P13*, 1916), **P38, P57, P58** (all 1917).
2 *Harland & Wolff (Govan):* **P24** (1915), **P25** (1916).
2 *Harkess:* **P32** (1916), **P46** (1917).
3 *Inglis:* **P18** (1916), **P39, P64** (both 1917).
1 *Napier & Miller:* **P33** (1916).
2 *Northumberland S.B. Co.:* **P19, P20** (both 1916).
3 *Readhead:* **P31** (1916), **P47, P48** (1917).
1 *Russell:* **P21** (1916).
1 *Tyne Iron Co.:* **P50** (1916).
2 *R. Thompson:* **P28** (1916), **P49** (1917).
4 *White (Cowes):* **P11** (1915), **P40, P52** (both 1916), **P59** (1917).
3 *Workman Clerk:* **P15, P16** (both 1916), **P17** (1915).

Displacement: 613 tons. Dimensions: 230 (*p.p.*), $244\frac{1}{2}$ (*o.a.*) × $23\frac{3}{4}$ × 7 feet 7 inch. Guns: Designed to mount 2—4 inch but only *P 52* has this armament: others, 1—4 inch and (in all) 1—2 pdr. pom-pom. Tubes: 2 single 14 inch, removed from old Torpedo Boats. Two depth charge throwers and D.C. Machinery: Brown-Curtis or Parsons turbines. 2 screws. Yarrow boilers. Designed S.H.P. 3500 = 20 kts. Oil fuel: *normal* 50 tons, *max.* 93 tons. Complement, 50-54.

General Notes.—All built under Emergency War Programme. Were designed to relieve destroyers of patrol and escort work and submarine hunting. Outline scheme for these boats stipulated; minimum size consistent with sea-keeping qualities, simplicity of construction, and adequate speed to run down submarines: also shallow draught; low upperworks to reduce visibility; and economy of fuel. Built of mild steel, but with hard steel stem for ramming submarines. Large rudder area and hull strongly cut up aft to give rapid turning. Proved very useful boats and an excellent anti-submarine type in all weathers. Those converted to Decoy Ships or "Q-boats" listed as *PC* boats on the preceding page.

War Losses.—*P 12, P 26.*

P-boat (aircraft view). *Official R.A.F. photo.*

No. 30. *Photo, Ellis, Malta.*

4 *Denny* boats: **30, 29,** also **18, 17.** 272 tons. Dimensions: 183 × 18 × 6 feet. Armament: 2—12 pdr., 3—18 inch tubes. H.P. 4000 = 26 kts. Oil: 51/43 tons.

Note.—All "oily wad" T.B. *1—36* now have pole mainmast and openings under fore bridge screened in, as above illustration.

7 *White* boats: **28, 27, 26, 25** (1908), 283 tons: also **16, 15, 14** (1907), 270 tons. Dimensions: $185\frac{1}{4}$ × 18 × $6\frac{3}{4}$ feet. Armament: 2—12 pdr., 3—18 inch tubes. H.P. 4000 = 26 kts. Parsons turbine. 3 screws. Oil: 50-53/42-45 tons. No. 13 lost during War.

Yarrow boat: **23** (1907). 282 tons. Dimensions: 181 × 18 × *mean* $6\frac{1}{4}$ feet. Armament: 2—12 pdr., 3—18 inch tubes. H.P. 4000 = 26 kts. Parsons turbine. 3 screws. Oil: *normal* 49/41 tons.

To distinguish all above.—*One* tube *before* first funnel. Funnels fairly close together. Eyes set back from stern.

32 Torpedo Boats.

At the outbreak of war there were 106 Torpedo Boats in service.
Of these eleven were sunk (046, 064, 9, 10, 11, 12, 13, 24, 90, 96 and 117).
Of the remainder a large proportion was paid off at the end of the war and those listed below were in service in 1919.

No.	Builders.	Numbers.	Launched.	Displacement.	H.P.	Max. speed.	Tubes.	Coal or oil.	Complement.
				tons. *average.*		kts.		tons	
12	*Various*	36—25 ('07—8 Ests.)	1908—9	290	4000	26	3	53–41*	39
10	*Various*	23—14 ('06—7 Ests.)	1907—8	290	4000	26	3	51–40*	39
9	*Various*	8—1 ('05—6 Ests.)	1906	250	3750—3600	26	3	43–36*	35
1	White	116	1903	197	2900	25	0	44†	38

* Oil only. † Coal.

2 *Palmer* boats: **36, 35** (1909). 313-5 tons. Dimensions: $181\frac{3}{4}$ × $17\frac{3}{4}$ × $7\frac{1}{4}$ feet. Armament: 2—12 pdr., 3—18 inch tubes. H.P. 4000 = 26 kts. Parsons turbine. Oil: 46/41 tons *No. 24* lost during War.

4 *Hawthorn* boats: **34, 33** (1909); also **22; 21.** (1907-8). 325-8 tons. Dimensions: $189\frac{1}{4}$ × $18\frac{1}{2}$ × 7 feet. Armament: 2—12 pdr., 3—18 inch tubes. H.P. 4000 = 26 kts. 3 screws. Parsons turbine. Oil fuel: 48/41 tons.

4 *Thornycroft* boats: **32, 31** (1908), 278 tons; also **20** (1908), 291 tons. **19** (1907), 312 tons. Dimensions: $183\frac{1}{4}$ × $18\frac{1}{4}$-$18\frac{3}{4}$ × $6\frac{1}{2}$ feet. Armament: 2—12 pdr., 3—18 inch tubes. H.P. 4000 = 26 kts. 3 screws. Parsons turbine. Oil: 48/41 tons.

To distinguish all above.—One tube *before* funnel, *big* ventilators between funnels. Eyes set back from stem. Funnels fairly wide apart.

3 *Thornycroft:* **8, 7, 6** (1906). 244-7 tons. Dimensions: $171\frac{1}{2}$ × $17\frac{1}{2}$ × $6\frac{3}{4}$ feet. Armament: 2—12 pdr., 3—18 inch tubes. H.P. 3750 = 26 kts. Parsons turbine. 3 screws. Oil: 42/35 tons. Were originally named in order given: *Gnat, Glow-worm*, and *Gadfly*. *No.* 9 (ex *Grasshopper*), *No.* 10 (ex *Greenfly*), *No.* 11 (ex *Moth*), *No.* 12 (ex *Mayfly*), have been lost during the War.

To distinguish.—One tube *between* funnels: funnels wide apart.

5 *White* boats: **5, 4, 3, 2, 1** (1906). 261 tons. Dimensions: 178 × $17\frac{1}{2}$ × $6\frac{1}{2}$ feet. Armament: 2—12 pdr., 3—18 inch tubes. H.P. 3600 = 26 kts. Parsons turbine. Oil fuel: 44/37 tons. Were originally named in order given: *Spider, Sandfly, Firefly, Dragonfly, Cricket.*

To distinguish.—Tubes *before and abaft* first funnel. *No* tube before after 12 pdr. position. Funnels wide apart.

1 *White* boat: **116** (1903). 197 tons. Dimensions: 165 × $17\frac{1}{2}$ × 7 feet. Armament: *Nil.* H.P. 2900 = 25 kts. 44 tons.

BRITISH NAVY—M. L., C. M. B., AND D. C. B.

M. L. (Motor Launches).

M.L. 381. Some boats have mainmast right at stern for spreading W/T. aerials.

Third type: 30 originally built: ***M.L. 551–580.*** Built 1918. No details known, but similar to first and second types below.

Second type: 500 originally built: ***M.L. 51—550.*** Built 1915. 37 tons. Dimensions: 80-88 × 12$\frac{1}{8}$ feet × 3′ 10″. Guns: 1—3 inch AA. or lesser calibre of AA. and other types. B.H.P. 440-450 = 19 kts. Machinery: 2 sets of Standard petrol motors. Petrol: *about* 1850 gallons. Complement, 9.

First type: 50 originally built: ***M.L. 1—50.*** Built 1915. 34 tons. Dimensions: 75 × 12 × 3$\frac{3}{4}$ feet. Guns: 1—3 pdr. or 2 pdr. AA. and/or 1 or 2 M.G. or Lewis guns. B.H.P. 440-450 = 19 kts. Petrol: *about* 1650 gallons. Complement, 8

General Notes.—Present boats in service can be ascertained by reference to current Navy List. Others now scrapped, being worn out. Mostly built in U.S. and Canadian Yards and shipped across the Atlantic. During War, fitted with D.C., smoke boxes, hydrophones, &c., but special gear now removed from nearly all. Petrol consumption heavy.

War Losses: Twenty-nine boats, detailed in War Losses Section. *M.L. 229,* one of the eleven British M.L. on the Rhine, was almost destroyed by a petrol explosion and fire during 1919. May not be repaired.

C. M. B. (Coastal Motor Boats.

Third Type: (from p 117 bottom left)

Second type: 55-ft. Series numbers, ***a, b, bd, c*** and ***e,*** from about ***13a*** up to ***87 b*** or above. 10 tons. Dimensions: 55 × 11 × 3 feet. Armament: Some had 2 Lewis guns on a paired mounting, others 4 Lewis guns in pairs, with 2—18 inch torpedoes in troughs at stern. Some modified to take 4 Lewis guns in pairs, with only 1—18 inch torpedo and 4 D.C. Other boats, when used for low speed work could carry 4 torpedoes in dropping gears over beams. 1 Thornycroft 375 H.P. "Y" type motor = 35 kts., but have done 41 kts. and over in service. Also Green, F.I.A.T. and Sunbeam motors. W/T. fitted in these. Complement, 3.

C, M. B. 27 = 40-FT. TYPE. *Photo, Cribb, Southsea.*

First type: 40-ft. Original boats ***3—12,*** and later boats numbered up to ***61*** or above. Dimensions: 40 × 8$\frac{1}{2}$ × 3 feet. 350 H.P. Thornycroft motor = over 30 kts. 1 torpedo carried in central trough over stern. Harwich Light Cruisers used to each take a pair of these boats to sea, slung from davits, while, in the Mediterranean, light cruiser *Diamond* served as a special C.M.B. Carrier.

General Notes.—Above types designed by Messrs. Thornycrofts Ltd. Full descriptions have appeared in technical press. It need only be remarked that they discharge their torpedoes tail first from troughs over stern, then swerve on their course and allow torpedoes to run past to target. All stepped hydroplane type hulls with chine to damp down bow wave. Considering their small size, they have exeellent nautical qualities. First boats were secretly built in 1916, and ran trials by night. 13 lost during War and 4 or more in Baltic operations. Boats now in commission can be ascertained from current Navy List. It is little use stating totals and numbers here, as these craft can be laid up and placed out of commission at very short notice. For full description *v.* "Engineer," April 18th, 1919, and Messrs. Thornycroft's own descriptive brochure.

D. C. B.

Are modified C.M.B. No details for publication. A few were finished about August, 1918, and good results were expected from them. The War ended before they could be put into operation.

BRITISH NAVY—SUBMARINES.

127 Submarines (100 Completed, *27 Building*).

No.	Type	First begun.	Last completed.	Displacement (tons)	H.P.	*Max.* speed (kts.)	Fuel (tons)	Complement	T. Tubes	*Max.* draug't (ft.)
12	*R 1—12.*	1917	1918	420/500	250/1000	10/15	...	20	4-6	12
1	*M 1—4.*	1917	'20 ?	1600/1950	...	15/9	...	60	...	10
37	*L 1—71.*	1917	20	890/1070	2400/1600	17·3/10·5	76	36	4-6	13$\frac{1}{2}$
13	*K 2—16, K 22.*	1916	1918	1880/2650	10000/1400	24/9·5	200	55	6	16
32	*H 21—52.*	1917	1919	440/500	180/320	13/10·5	16	22	4	11$\frac{1}{4}$
7	*G 3—13.*	1915	1916	700/975	1600/810	14/10	44	30	5	13$\frac{1}{4}$
(3)	*F 1—3.*	1915	1917	353/525	900/100	14·5/8·8	17$\frac{1}{2}$	20	3	10$\frac{3}{4}$
22	*E 21 – E 55.*	1915	1917	662/807	1600/840	15/10	45	30	3-5	12$\frac{1}{2}$

Notes to above Table.

Excepting *H 21-52* of "Holland" type, all above types are to Admiralty design. Above Table and description by classes on later pages, arranged alphabetically by Class Letters. Rough division by types and building dates is thus:—

61 *Ocean-going* boats: *L 1—71, M 1—4* (Monitors), *K 2—16* and *K 22, G 3—13.*
54 *Sea-going* boats: *H 21—52, E 21—55.*
12 *Coastal* boats: *R 1—12* (*F 1—3* not included).
— *Minelayers:* Various units of *L, H* and *E* types; exact total not known.

As regards the totals given over Table for boats finished and building: These are approximate only, some of the 27 boats given as building may not be finished. Six "Later K" boats not mentioned in Table or included in total, as they seem to be stopped. Coastal *F 1—3* not included in total of completed boats, as they will be sold very soon. The *E* and *G* Classes will probably be sold off within the next eighteen months.

With reference to missing Class Letters in alphabetical order, the following brief notes may be of service. All *A, B, C* and *D* boats sold off or for sale. *J* Class presented to Australia. *N 1* (late *Nautilus*) for sale 1919, having proved more or less a failure. *S 1* (late *Swordfish*) converted into surface patrol boat. *V 1—4* for sale 1919. *W 1—4* presented to Italy during the War. No I, O, P, Q, T, U, X, Y, Z Classes.

Various surrendered German Submarines are in service under the White Ensign, but only for experiments. By agreement with all the Allies, such ex-German boats will not be added to the British Navy, but must be broken up when trials are finished.

12 R Class.

R—. *Photo, Cribb, Southsea.*

R 1—4 by Chatham D.Y., ***R 5, R 6*** by Pembroke D.Y., ***R 7, R 8*** by Vickers, ***R 9, R 10*** by Armstrong Whitworth, ***R 11, R 12*** by Cammell Laird. All launched and finished 1918.

Single hull type to Admiralty designs. Approximate dimensions: 160 × 15-16 × 12 feet. Guns: 1—3 inch or 4 inch in some. Tubes: Unofficially reported to have 4 or 6—18 inch bow. Machinery: No exact details, but said to have 1 set of hot-bulb or heavy oil motors. Oil capacity small, but have an abnormal submerged endurance. Other details as Table.

Notes.—Built under Emergency War Programme. These boats (sometimes called the "Little Arthurs") were produced as a "submarine destroyer of submarines." Their outstanding feature is that—unlike nearly all other submarines in the world—they are faster below water than on the surface. They are short in length, have large rudder and hydroplane areas and small reserve of buoyancy for quick diving and rapid handling. It was intended that they should submerge and chase U-boats, and use their four bow tubes by salvo, specially big torpedo-compensating tanks with rapid flooding gear being placed in bows. Also said to have hydrophones for tracking hostile submarines.

BRITISH NAVY—SUBMARINES.

M Class Submarine Monitors = { **1** Completed. | **3** Completing ? } = 4?

M 1.

Photo, M. Davidson, Esq.

M 1 ex *K 18* (1918). **M 2** ex *K 19* (——), both by Vickers. **M 3** ex *K 20* (——), **M 4** ex *K 21* (——), both by Armstrong Whitworth. Launching dates of *M 2—4* not reported : these three boats may not be finished.

Few details available. Designed by Admiralty ; reported to be double-hulled type. Dimensions : about 200 — 20 × 10 feet. Guns : 1—12 inch, 35 cal., 1—3 inch A.A. Machinery : Type not known, but reported to be Diesel engines. Oil fuel : — tons. Other details as Table.

Gunnery Notes.—12 inch believed to be one of those removed from old *Majestic* Class of Battleships, firing a 520 lb. projectile. No turntable, but high-angle elevation. Reported that gun is loaded and laid to high angle elevation : then boat is dived to about 12-20 feet, leaving muzzle of 12 inch gun above water, and periscopes. There is a bead sight on gun-muzzle, so that gun can be sighted by periscope and fired when running at shallow submersion. To re-load, it is necessary to return to surface.

General Notes.—Begun under War Emergency Programme. These " Submarine Monitors " are a unique design, but reports are not available of *M 1's* performance during War, so that their practical worth is a matter of conjecture.

13 K Class (+ *6 Building ?*)

K 10.   *K 12 & K 16* have gun on high fairwater *before* C.T.

Photo, Cribb, Southsea.

K 15 (higher funnels).

Photo, Topical.

K2, K5 (both by Portsmouth D.Y., 1916), **K6** (Devonport D.Y., 1916), **K3, K8, K9, K10** (all by Vickers, 1916), **K11, K12** (both by Armstrong Whitworth, 1916-17), **K14, K22,** ex *K 13* (both by Fairfield, 1916). **K15** (Scott, 1917), **K16** (Beardmore, 1917).

(**K 23—K 28** : See *General Notes.*)

All double-hulled type, designed by Admiralty for service as " Fleet Submarines " with Grand Fleet. Dimensions : 334 (*p.p.*), 337 (*o.a.*) × 26½ × 16 feet. Guns : 1—4 inch, 1—3 inch A.A., and (in some) 1 D.C. thrower. Torpedo tubes : 8—18 inch, viz., 4 bow, 4 beam. Machinery ; see Notes below. Oil fuel : 170 tons. Other details as Table.

Engineering Notes.—These are *not* the first steam-driven boats in British Navy, having been preceded by *Swordfish* (*S 1*), now scrapped. Surface machinery consists of combined steam turbines and Diesel engine. 2 sets of single reduction turbines, one H.P. and one L.P. in each set, with double helical gearing. 2 screws. 2 Yarrow small-tube type boilers with forced draught, boilers, turbines, funnels being lagged with incombustible non-conducting materials. Small electric motors are fitted for lowering funnels and closing w.t. hatches over funnel wells. Boiler room air vents closed by hydraulic power. To assist in diving quickly, or getting away after breaking surface (while steam motors are being started up), an 800 B.H.P. 8-cylinder Diesel motor is fitted, which can also be used for surface cruising. Drive from Diesel engine is through electric motors, so that these boats have three systems of transmission, (*a*) geared turbines for steam drive, (*b*) Diesel and electric transmission, (*c*) electric battery drive when submerged. 2 high-power compressors to charge 2500 lbs. air bottles : 2 low-power compressors to blow main ballast tanks after breaking surface. 2 electric-power bilge pumps. Hydraulic rams for raising periscopes and telescopic masts. Hydro-electric controlling gear to hydroplanes, forward hydroplanes being of housing type.

Gunnery and Torpedo Notes.—Were first completed with 2 guns before and below C.T. and 1 abaft C.T. on superstructure deck, but these were removed. For a time, these boats had only 1—4 inch, but *K 17* at time of her loss mounted 1—5.5 inch. There were also 2—18 inch tubes in superstructure, above water when in surface trim, making eight tubes in all. The original three guns and superstructure tubes were removed to D.A.M.S. and S.D. Vessels (Q-boats).

General Notes.—All built under Emergency War Programme. Were first completed with flush level bows, but showed a tendency to trim by the head and dive " on their own." To remedy this, bows were raised, as shown in above illustrations. Accommodation for officers and men is remarkably spacious for submarines. Are said to be rather hot on account of steam system of propulsion, but in the North Sea this proved rather an advantage than otherwise. Considering that these boats were of a highly experimental type, they have turned out most remarkably well. Further boats, *K 23—28* reported ordered in 1918, which were to have 6—21 inch bow tubes. Nothing further has been heard of these later boats ; they may be cancelled.

War Losses.—K 1, 4, 17. *K 13* also foundered, but was salved and re-numbered *K 22.*

Removals.—K 7 on Sale List, 1919.

L Classes. (Totals and Description next page).

L 55.

L 20.

Photo, Cribb.

L Classes { About **23*** Completed ? | About **14*** Building ? } = 37*?

19* *Vickers :* **L 1** ex *E 57,* **L 2** ex *E 58,* **L 3** (all 1917), **L 4. L 11. L 12. L 14. L 17—20** (all 1918). **L 21—L 23** (1919), **L 24—27. L 32** (completing 1919 ?).

2* *Swan Hunter :* **L 5** (1918), **L 33** (1919).

2* *Beardmore :* **L 6** (1918), **L 69** (1918).

2* *Cammell Laird :* **L 7. L 8** (both 1917).

2* *Denny :* **L 9** (1918), **L 54** (1919).

5* *Fairfield :* **L 15** (1917), **L 16** (1918), **L 36. L 55. L 56** (all 1919).

2* *Pembroke D.Y. :* **L 34. L 66** (1919-20 ?).

2* *Armstrong Whitworth :* **L 52. L 53** (both 1919).

1 *Scotts :* **L 71** (1919).

*All totals liable to revision. Some of the boats launched 1919 may be abandoned.

Following boats reported stopped 1918 :—

21† boats stopped : *L 28—31* (Vickers), *L 35* (Pembroke D.Y.), *L 50, 51, 63, 64, 65* (Cammell Laird), *L 67, 68* (Armstrong), *L 57—62* (Fairfield), *L 70* (Beardmore), *L 72* (Scotts), *L 73* (Denny).

14 boats never ordered : *L 13, L 37—49.*

†Liable to revision. Some may be completed.

Design and type of hull not known ; reported to be a wing-tank type designed by Admiralty. Dimensions : 222 (*p.p.*), 231 (*o.a.*) × 23½ × 13¾ feet. Guns : 1—3 inch A.A. or 4 inch, but minelayers may have no guns. Torpedo tubes : in earlier boats (*about* L 9), 6, viz., four bow, two beam, all 21 inch ; boats above *L 9,* 6—21 inch, all in bows. Mine-laying boats numbered under *L 9* have no beam tubes—only four bow—21 inch. Machinery : 2 sets 12-cylinder solid injection Vickers type, but others may have Cammellaird-Fullager, Armstrong, and other types. Oil : 76 tons. Other details as Table.

Notes.—The " L Class " is in a highly complex state, owing to the variations in build, giving ten or more types by appearance. Further uncertainty is introduced by inadequate information regarding boats whose construction has been stopped. All built under Emergency War Programme, but funds for completion of some boats will fall within post-war Navy Estimates. In dimensions, H.P., speed, &c., these boats have a marked resemblance to the 1914-18 German ocean-going Submarines. Minelaying boats not known exactly, but unverified reports say *L 2, 14, 17* are equipped for sowing mines.

War Losses.—L 10.

J Class.)

All presented in 1919 to Royal Australian Navy, *q. v.* for details. *War Loss.—J 6.*

H Class { about **20** delivered | about **8** building } = 32.*

*Some adapted for Minelaying.

12 *Vickers :* **H 21—H 32** (launched 1917-18).

8 *Cammell Laird :* **H 33—H 40** (launched 1918-19).

6 *Armstrong Whitworth :* **H 41—H 46** (launched 1918-19).

4 *Beardmore :* **H 47—H 50** (launched 1918-19).

2 *Pembroke D.Y. :* **H 51** (1918), **H 52** (1919).

Single-hull " Holland " (Electric Boat Co.) type modified by Admiralty. Dimensions : 164½ (*p.p.*), 171 (*o.a.*) × 15¼ feet. Guns : Majority have 1—3 inch A.A. Tubes : 4—21 inch bow, but minelaying boats may have only two or none. Machinery : 2 sets of Diesel engines of various types. Oil : 16 tons. Other details as Table.

Notes.—Not known how many of these boats are Minelayers. All built under War Emergency Programme. Not yet certain that all of these will be finished : some may be cancelled. During the War, *H 1—10* type were assembled by the Canadian Vickers Co., Montreal, and crossed Atlantic under their own power. On war service, these boats proved very successful, and were about the most popular type with the British Submarine Service. *H 11—20* were assembled by the Bethlehem Steel Co. and Fore River Co., U.S.A., but were interned by the U.S. Government. On the entry of the U.S. into the War, the boats were released, but were not taken over by British Navy. Six boats (*H 15,* H 16—20) were presented to Chile, *H 14, H 15* presented to Canada, *H 11, H 12* put on Sale List. 1919. *H 21—52* were designed as an improvement on the original *H 1—10* boats, having 21 inch tubes instead of 18 inch.

War Losses.—None in above *H 21—52* Class. Of the *H 1—10* Class, *H 3, 5, 6,* 10 lost during War.

Removals.—H 1, 2, 4, 7, 8, 9, (*H 1—10* Class), H 11, H 12 (*H 11—20* Class), all on Sale List, 1919.

BRITISH NAVY—SUBMARINES.

7 G Class.

Photo, Dr. J. A. Prendergast.

G3, G4, G5 (all Chatham D.Y., 1916). **G6** (Armstrongs, 1916), **G10, G13** (Vickers, 1916). Admiralty double-hull type. Dimensions: 185 (*p.p.*), 187 (*o.a.*) × 22½ × 13¼ feet. Guns: 1—3 inch AA. Torpedo tubes: 5, viz., 2—18 inch bow, 2—18 inch beam, 1—21 inch stern. Diesel engines: Vickers, Armstrong (2 sets). Oil: 44 tons. Other details as Table.

Notes.—All Emergency War Programme. Built as "Bight and North Sea Patrols," being the first genuine ocean-going boats in British Navy. Had their bows raised during War. The above boats will probably be brought home from Mediterranean during the next twelve months and placed on Sale List, except G 3 which is in home waters and may already be for sale. G 1, 2, 12, 14, on Sale List, 1914.

War Losses.—G 7, 8, 9, 11.

3 F Class.

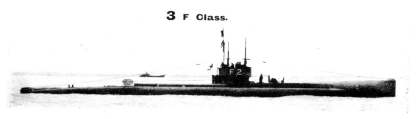

F 2 (and F 3. F 1 slightly different). *Photo, Messrs J. S. White & Sons.*

F 1 (Chatham D.Y., 1915). **F 2** (White, 1917). **F 3** (Thornycroft, 1916). Admiralty double-hull type. F 1, 1913-14 Programme, F 2, F 3, 1914-15 Programme. Dimensions: 150 (*p.p.*), 151 (*o.a.*) × 16 × 10¾ feet. Guns: *Nil*, but were designed to mount a 2 pdr. pom-pom. Tubes: 3—18 inch, 2 bow or beam, 1 stern. Diesel engines, 2 sets. Oil: 17½ tons. Other details as Table.

Note.—Will probably be put on Sale List at an early date.

D 8—2. Diesel motors. Radius: 4000 miles. Armament: 2-12 pdr., 3 tubes. *Photo, Symonds & Co.*

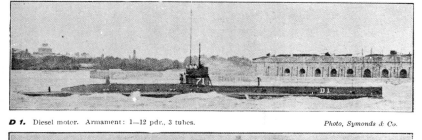

D 1. Diesel motor. Armament: 1—12 pdr., 3 tubes. *Photo, Symonds & Co.*

C 38—C 19. 12 cylinder petrol motors. Radius: $\frac{2000}{150}$ *Photo, Symonds & Co.*

C 18—C 1. Dimensions: 135 × 13½ × 11½ feet. 1 screw. Surface radius, 1500 miles. Engine: 16 cyl. horizontal opposed.

B 11—B 1. Dimensions: 135 × 13½ × 11½ feet. 1 screw. Surface radius, 1500 miles. Engine: 16 cyl. horizontal opposed.

22 E Class.—18 boats + 4 Minelayers.

Now have steel bridge screen.

E 7—20 & LATER CLASS:— 22 boats.

E 21, E 23 (Vickers, 1915), **E 25** (Beardmore, 1915), **E 27** (Yarrow, 1917), **E 31** (Scott, 1915), **E 32** (White, 1916), **E 33** (Thornycroft, 1916), **E 35** (J. Brown, 1916), **E 38** (Fairfield, 1916), **E 39, E 40** (launched by Palmers, 1916-17 and completed by Armstrongs), **E 41,* E 42** (Cammell Laird, 1915), **E 44** (Swan Hunter, 1916), **E 45,* E 46*** (Cammell Laird, 1916), **E 48** (launched by Fairfield 1916, completed by Beardmores), **E 51 *** (Scotts, 1916), **E 52** (Denny, 1916), **E 53, E 54** (Beardmore, 1915-16), **E 55** (Denny, 1916).

*These are Minelayers.

All Admiralty wing-tank type. Built under Emergency War Programme. First British type of submarine with internal sub-division by w.t. bulkheads and with beam tubes. Dimensions: 180 (*p.p.*), 181 (*o.a.*) × 22½ × 12½ feet. Tubes: 3 to 5—18 inch, viz., 2 bow, 0, 1, or 2 beam, 1 stern. Minelayers marked * have no beam tubes, and carry about 20 mines. Diesel engines: 2 sets of Vickers, Sulzer, Carels, M.A.N., or other types. Oil: 45 tons. Other details as Table.

Notes.—Performed splendid work during War, and proved most satisfactory. Heavy losses sustained by this class are an index to the arduous work they performed, 1915-18. E 2, 4 (of E 1—6 type), 11, 12, 20, 45, 56 (all E 7—20 and later type), put on Sale List, 1919 ; the others detailed above will be sold off as new L boats come into service.

War Losses.—E 1,* 3, 5, 6 (E 1—6 type), E 7, 8,* 9,* 10, 13, 14, 15, 16, 17, 18, 19,* 20, 22, 24, 26, 28, 30, 34, 36, 37, 47, 49, 50 (all E 7—20 and later type).

AE1 and AE2, see Australian section. *Scuttled in Baltic.

A 14—A 5. Dimensions: 100 × 12½ × 11½ feet. 1 screw. Surface radius, 1000 miles. Engine: 16 cyl. horizontal.

No.	Type	Date	Displacement	H.P.	Max. speed	Fuel	Complement	T. Tubes	Max. draug't
1	"S" *Fiat* S.G. type	1913	$\frac{300}{345}$	...	$\frac{13}{8\cdot5}$	...	...	2	...
11	E 11—1	1912	$\frac{725}{810}$	$\frac{1750}{600}$	$\frac{16}{00}$	...	...	4	...
7	D 8—D 3	1911 ⎫	$\frac{550}{600}$	$\frac{1750}{550}$	$\frac{16}{10}$	...	...	3	...
1	D 2	1910 ⎭							
8	C 38—C 31	1909 ⎫	$\frac{280}{313}$	$\frac{600}{200}$	$\frac{14}{10}$	15	16	2	12
12	C 30—C 19	1908 ⎭							
1	D 1	1907	$\frac{550}{600}$	$\frac{1200}{550}$	$\frac{16}{9}$	...	...	3	...
7	C 18—C 12	1907 ⎫	$\frac{280}{313}$	$\frac{600}{200}$	$\frac{13}{8}$	15	16	2	12
10	C 10—C 1	1906 ⎭							
10	B 11—B 1	1905	$\frac{280}{313}$	$\frac{600}{200}$	$\frac{13}{8}$	15	16	2	12
8	A 13—A 5	1904	$\frac{180}{207}$	$\frac{550}{150}$	$\frac{11\cdot5}{7}$	7	11	2	11½

C 11, B 4, A 7 and A 3 have been lost.

Note—By 1919 all A, B, C and D classes with the exception of C4 on trials had been paid off.

War losses:
"D" Class — D2, 3, 5 and 6
"C" Class — C3, 16, 26, 27, 29, 31, 32, 33, 34, 35
"B" Class — B10

BRITISH NAVY—AIRCRAFT CARRIERS.

VINDICTIVE (17th Jan., 1918.)   Late Light Cruiser *Cavendish*.

Displacement, 9750 tons.   Complement { R.N. } = –
                                       { R.A.F. }

Length 565 feet (p.p.). 605 feet (o.a.).   Beam, 65 feet.   Draught { Mean 17¼ feet.
                                                                      { Max. 20⅔ feet.

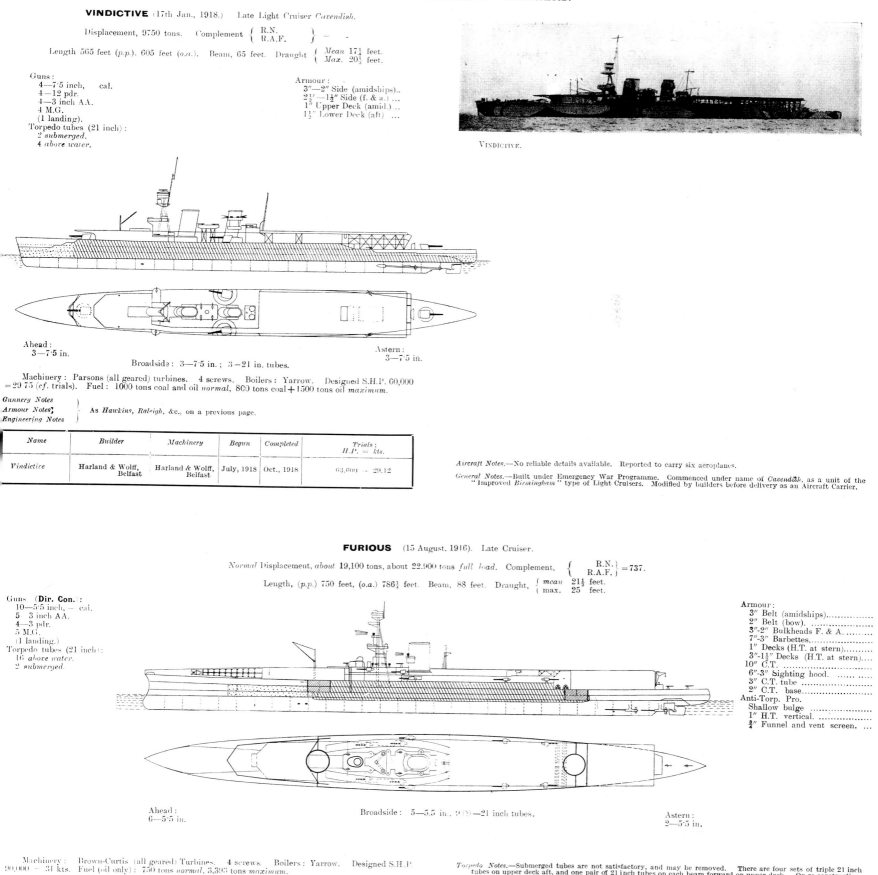

VINDICTIVE.

Guns :
  4—7·5 inch, cal.
  4—12 pdr.
  4—3 inch A.A.
  4 M.G.
  (1 landing).
Torpedo tubes (21 inch) :
  2 *submerged*.
  4 *above water*.

Armour :
  3"—2" Side (amidships)..
  2½"—1½" Side (f. & a.) ...
  1" Upper Deck (amid.) ...
  1½" Lower Deck (aft) ...

Ahead :
3—7·5 in.

Broadside: 3—7·5 in. ; 3—21 in. tubes.

Astern :
3—7·5 in.

Machinery : Parsons (all geared) turbines. 4 screws. Boilers : Yarrow. Designed S.H.P. 60,000 = 29·75 (*cf.* trials). Fuel : 1000 tons coal and oil *normal*, 800 tons coal + 1500 tons oil *maximum*.

Gunnery Notes }
Armour Notes, } As *Hawkins*, *Raleigh*, &c., on a previous page.
Engineering Notes }

Name	Builder	Machinery	Begun	Completed	Trials : H.P. = kts.
Vindictive	Harland & Wolff, Belfast	Harland & Wolff, Belfast	July, 1918	Oct., 1918	63,600 = 29·12

Aircraft Notes.—No reliable details available. Reported to carry six aeroplanes.

General Notes.—Built under Emergency War Programme. Commenced under name of *Cavendish*, as a unit of the "Improved *Birmingham*" type of Light Cruisers. Modified by builders before delivery as an Aircraft Carrier.

FURIOUS (15 August, 1916). Late Cruiser.

Normal Displacement, *about* 19,100 tons, about 22,900 tons *full load*. Complement, { R.N. } = 737.
                                                                                        { R.A.F. }

Length, (p.p.) 750 feet, (o.a.) 786¼ feet. Beam, 88 feet. Draught, { mean 21½ feet.
                                                                       { max. 25 feet.

Guns (**Dir. Con.**) :
  10—5·5 inch, — cal.
  5 3 inch A.A.
  4—3 pdr.
  5 M.G.
  (1 landing.)
Torpedo tubes (21 inch) :
  16 *above water*.
  2 *submerged*.

Armour :
  3" Belt (amidships)................
  2" Belt (bow). ....
  3"—2" Bulkheads F. & A. ...
  7"—3" Barbettes................
  1" Decks (H.T. at stern)........
  3"—1½" Decks (H.T. at stern)....
  10" C.T. ....
  6"—3" Sighting hood. ....
  3" C.T. tube. ....
  2" C.T. base.............
Anti-Torp. Pro.
  Shallow bulge ....
  1" H.T. vertical. ....
  ¾" Funnel and vent screen. ...

Ahead :
6—5·5 in.

Broadside : 5—5·5 in., 9 (?)—21 inch tubes.

Astern :
2—5·5 in.

Machinery : Brown-Curtis (all geared) Turbines. 4 screws. Boilers : Yarrow. Designed S.H.P. 90,000 = 31 kts. Fuel (oil only) : 750 tons *normal*, 3,393 tons *maximum*.

Armour Notes.—3" Belt consists of 2" plating over 1" shell plating, as in Light Cruisers. Belt forward is set inboard, as plans. Barbettes are still in, though no large guns are mounted in them. Fo'xle, Upper Decks, 1" H.T. Main Deck, 1¼"—1". Lower deck at stern, 1½"—1" flat, 2" slopes, 3" over rudder head—all H.T.

Internal Protection.—Bulge deeper than that of *Glorious* and *Courageous*, but *not* filled with oil fuel. There is a complete internal citadel of 1" vertical plating from barbette to barbette, well inboard and covering magazines, shell and boiler rooms. Outside and below this citadel and on each beam, are 1" screens, 250-300 ft. long, covering boiler and engine rooms. From within the citadel rise the 3" screens protecting funnel and boiler room vents.

Gunnery Notes.—Originally designed to mount 2—18 inch and 11—5·5 inch guns, provision being made to mount 4—15 inch if the 18 inch guns proved unsatisfactory. The fore 18 inch gun was never mounted, being replaced by flying-off deck and hangar. When in service in 1917-18, she fired the after 18 inch a few times, and it is said "it shook her up considerably." In 1918, the after 18 inch was also taken out, flying-on deck and after hangar added. At the same time, 1—5·5 inch was removed and other 10—5·5 inch re-distributed. The after tripod mast, with gunnery controls was also removed.

Torpedo Notes.—Submerged tubes are not satisfactory, and may be removed. There are four sets of triple 21 inch tubes on upper deck aft, and one pair of 21 inch tubes on each beam forward on upper deck. On re-construction, the 3" (after) Torpedo Control Tower was removed and controls re-located.

Name	Builder	Machinery	Begun	Completed	Trials H.P. = kts.
Furious	Armstrong Whitworth	Wallsend Co.	June, 1915	July, 1917	90,820 =

General Notes.—Built under Emergency War Programme. Designed as a modified *Courageous*, but altered to Aircraft Carrier (see Gunnery and Aircraft Notes). Since conversion, she is said to be rather light, and is good now for 32-33 kts. Including cost of alterations, this ship is said to have absorbed nearly six million pounds. Flagship, Vice-Admiral Commanding Aircraft.

Aircraft Notes and Illustrations on opposite page.

BRITISH NAVY: AIRCRAFT CARRIERS. FURIOUS—*Continued.*

FURIOUS. **(For details, v. oppposite page.)**

Aircraft Notes.—When first completed, she carried about four Short seaplanes and six Sopwith "Pups." These were easily flown off bows, but there was difficulty in getting seaplanes shipped inboard by derricks. Experiments were made to use the forward flying-off deck for landing also, but it was found too dangerous. Later, the big after flying-on deck was added, and proved satisfactory. Forward flying-off deck is about 160 feet long, tapers to bows, has collapsible wind-breaking pallisades. There is also a power-operated lift before C. T. to hoist seaplanes from forward hangar to flying-off deck. The after flying-on deck is about 300 feet long by 100 feet wide, with stopping net just abaft funnel. There is another lift aft for raising seaplanes from after hangar. Narrow decks on each side of the funnel connect the flying-off deck with flying-on deck, small trolleys on rails being used to move seaplanes forward or aft. No seaplanes are now carried, but only aeroplanes of "Cuckoo" (torpedo dropping) and other types.

FURIOUS. Aircraft View.   *Official R.A.F. Photo.*

ARGUS (2nd Dec., 1917). Late Liner.

Normal displacement, 15,775 tons. Complement $\left\{ \begin{matrix} \text{R.N.} \\ \text{R.A.F.} \end{matrix} \right\}$ = 495.

Length (p.p.), 535 feet (w.l.) 560 feet (o.a.) 565 feet. Beam, 68 feet. Draught, 22¾ feet, *mean.*

Guns :
  2—4 inch, 50 cal.
  2—4 inch AA.
Torpedo tubes :
  Nil.

Armour :
  Nil.

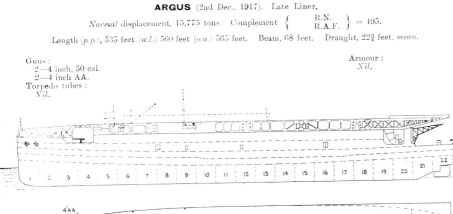

ARGUS (port view).

Machinery : Parsons turbines. 4 screws. Designed S.H.P. 22,000 = 20·5 kts. Can make 20·75 kts. for short periods, but 20 kts. is usually best speed under ordinary conditions. Boilers : 12 cylindrical (6 D.E. and 6 S.E.), with Howdens forced draught. Fuel : 2000 tons oil.

Capacity, &c.—Hangar is 350 ft. long by 68 ft. wide (*over all*) and 48 ft. clear width, 20 ft. clear height. It is divided into four sections by fire-proof screens, and can accommodate 20 seaplanes.

Stores, &c.—Torpedoes are carried for Sopwith "Cuckoo" type torpedo-dropping aeroplanes ; aero-bombs, spare parts, wings, propellers, &c. Full equipment is carried for maintenance and repair of aircraft. There are large carpenters' and engineers' workshops, for executing rapid repairs.

Handling Gear.—Two electrically controlled lifts for raising aircraft from hangar to flying deck. Forward lift, 30 ft. × 36 ft. After lift, 60 ft. × 18 ft. When forward lift is at flying deck level, two roller platforms slide to the sides and uncover well opening. When lift descends, the platforms are closed together and give a 20-ft. platform for flying off. When a deck load of aeroplanes is carried, wind-breaking pallisades can be raised simultaneously to 14 ft. above flying deck. Two derricks with electric winches amidships on flying deck, and two electric cranes at stern on hangar deck level ; all to pick up aeroplanes from the water.

Flying-off.—Flying deck is 68 ft. wide and 550 ft. long. Chart-house is on hydraulic lift ; masts, jackstaff, &c., all fold down to give perfectly level flying-off space.

Landing.—Wind safety mattress (or landing net) fitted. Steam jet indicators fitted for day use and special illumination for night landings. There is a wide safety net all round flying deck.

Engineering Notes.—At the time designs were got out, a ¼-inch scale model was prepared for testing in the air tunnel at the National Physical Laboratory, Teddington, to solve various structural problems and to test eddy-making effects of hull. It was found that the emission of hot furnace gases from the usual type of funnels created such serious air disturbances, safe landings would be very difficult. Accordingly, horizontal smoke-ducts with big expelling fans were fitted, to deliver all furnace gases and smoke out over stern. Designed for 18 kts., but modifications during conversion raised speed by 2 kts.

For all details in these notes, we are indebted to "Engineering," which published a full description of H.M.S. Argus, in its issue of March 28th, 1919.

ARGUS (starboard view.)   *Photo, C. N.*

Note to Illustrations.—Two views are given, as *Argus* exemplifies dazzle-painting excellently. Note the reversed direction of diagonal striping on one beam, compared with the other.

Name	Builder	Machinery	Begun	Completed	Trials ; H.P. = kts.
Argus	Beardmore	Beardmore	1914	Sept., 1918	

General Notes.—Begun 1914, for Italian Lloyd Sabaudo Line, as S.S. *Conte Rosso.* All work on her ceased in 1914. was purchased in 1916 and converted to Aircraft Carrier. In appearance, she is quite unique, and she is sometimes called "The Floating Island." As a mobile hangar and floating aerodrome, she has proved very successful.

BRITISH NAVY: AIRCRAFT CARRIERS.

PEGASUS (ex G. E. Railway Co. s.s. *Stockholm*, built by J. Brown & Co., ——, purchased 1917). 3300 tons. Dimensions: 330 (*p.p.*), 332 (*o.a.*) × 43 × 15 (*mean*), 15⅔ (*max.*) feet. Guns: 2—12 pdr. and 2—12 pdr. AA. S.H.P. 9500 = 20.25 kts. (20.8 trials). Machinery: Brown-Curtis turbines (all-geared). 2 screws. Boilers: Cylindrical. Oil fuel: 360 tons. Complement, 258 R.N. and R.A.F.

ARK ROYAL (Blyth S.B. Co., 1914, purchased 1914). 7450 tons. Dimensions: 352½ (*p.p.*), 366 (*o.a.*) × 50⅚ × 18 feet (*mean*). Guns: 4—12 pdr., 2 M.G. I.H.P. 3000 = 11 kts. Machinery: Vertical triple expansion. 1 screw. Boilers: Cylindrical. Oil: 500 tons. Complement, 180 R.N. and R.A.F.

May be re-conditioned for mercantile service. Photo, Topical.

NARIANA (Denny Bros., ——, chartered 1917). 3070 tons. Dimensions: 315 (*p.p.*), 352 (*o.a*), including projection of stern gantry) × 45½ × 13⅙ feet (*mean*), 13⅚ (*max.*). Guns 2—12 pdr. and 2—12 pdr. AA. S.H.P. 6700 = 19 kts. (20.32 trials). Machinery: Parsons turbines (all-geared). Boilers: Babcock & Wilcox. 2 screws. Coal: 448 tons. Complement, 278 R.N. and R.A.F.

Photo, Messrs. Lobnitz.

SLINGER (——). Experimental Aeroplane Catapult Ship, built by Messrs. Lobnitz. I H P. 1030 = 10 kts. No other details received.

BRITISH NAVY—MINELAYERS.

PRINCESS MARGARET (built 1913-14, chartered and converted during War, purchased 1919). 5440 tons. Complement, 215. Dimensions: 395½ (*o.a.*) × 54 × 16⅚ feet (*max.* draught). Guns: 2—4.7 inch, 2—12 pdr., 2—6 pdr. AA., 1—2 pdr. pom-pom. S.H.P. 15,000 = 22.5 kts. (23.15 on *trials*). Oil fuel: 585 tons.

LONDON (Sept., 1899). Old Battleship of 15,000 tons, converted 1918. Complement, 481. Dimensions: 431¾ (*o.a.*) × 75 × 27⅔ feet (*max.* draught). Guns: 3—6 inch, 1—4 inch AA., 2 M.G., 1 landing. Torpedo tubes (18 inch): 4 *submerged*. Armour: 9″, 6″ and 2″ belt, 6″ casemates, 3″ deck. Old 10″—8″ turrets also left in, though 12 inch guns, shields, etc., are removed. I.H.P. 15,000 = 18 kts. Machinery: 2 sets 3-cylinder vertical triple expansion. 2 screws. Boilers: 20 Belleville. Coal: 2000 tons *max.*

AMPHITRITE (1898). Ex-Cruiser, converted 1917. 11,000 tons. Complement, 409. Dimensions: 466 (*o.a.*) × 69 × 27 feet (*max.* draught). Guns: 4—6 inch, 1—12 pdr. Armour: 4″ deck, 6″ casemates. Machinery: 2 sets 4-cylinder vertical inverted triple expansion. Boilers: 30 Belleville. I.H.P. 18,000 = 21 kts. 2 screws. Coal: 1730 tons.

7 Mine Layers.

IPHIGENIA, THETIS, APOLLO, ANDROMACHE, INTREPID, LATONA, NAIAD (all about 1891) of the *Apollo* class 3400 to 3600 tons. Armament: 6—6 pdrs. *Note*—See Apollo class under Light Cruisers.

EURYALUS (1901). Old Cruiser of 12,000 tons, partially converted to a Minelayer at Hong Kong D.Y., 1918-19, but now laid up in Reserve. Dimensions: 472 (*o.a.*) × 69½ × 27¾ feet *max.* draught. Guns: 2—9·2 inch (probably removed), 2—6 inch, 2—6 pdr. AA., 2—3 pdr. Machinery: 2 sets vertical triple expansion. 2 screws. Boilers: Belleville. I.H.P. 21,000 = 21 kts. Coal: 1600 tons *max.*

Note.

The 20th Destroyer Flotilla (Minelayers) consists of *Abdiel*, *Gabriel* (Leaders), *Vanoc*, *Vanquisher*, *Venturous* (Admiralty "V" type), *Tarpon*, *Telemachus* (Admiralty "R" Class), *Meteor* ("M" Class), used for experiments. Other "V" and "W" Destroyers were fitted as Minelayers during the War.

Submarine Minelayers are units of "L" Classes (numbers not known), *E 41*, *E 45*, *E 46*, *E 51*, carrying about 20 mines.

C.M.B. also used as Minelayers during War. If necessity arises, Warships of nearly all types can be quickly fitted out as Minelayers.

BRITISH NAVY—FLEET SWEEPING VESSELS (SLOOPS).

SIR BEVIS.

ARD PATRICK
DONOVAN
FLYING FOX   } As above view.
MINORU   Mast *before* funnel
ROCK SAND
(and others)

ORMONDE   *Photo by courtesy of Blyth S.B. Co.*

IROQUOIS
SEFTON
SILVIO   } As above illustration.
SIR BEVIS   Mast *abaft* funnel.
(and others)

Photo, by courtesy of Messrs. Osbourne Graham.

("24 CLASS"—21 SHIPS.)

ARD PATRICK (June, 1918), **CICERO** (July, 1918), **FLYING FOX** (March, 1918), **MINORU** (———, 1919), **ORBY** (October, 1918), **ROCK SAND** (July, 1918), **SPEARMINT** (September, 1918), **SUNSTAR** (building ?), all eight by Swan Hunter. **BEND OR** (September, 1918), **HARVESTER** (November, 1918), **IROQUOIS** (August, 1918), **SEFTON** (July, 1918), **SILVIO** (April, 1918), **SIR BEVIS** (May, 1918), all six by Barclay, Curle. **DONOVAN** (April, 1918), **ISINGLASS** (———, 1919), **SANFOIN** (June, 1918), **SIR HUGO** (September, 1918), all by Greenock & Grangemouth Co. **GALITEE MORE** (———, 1919), **LADAS** (September, 1918), **PERSIMMON** (March, 1918), **SIR VISTO** (Dec., 1918), all by Osbourne, Graham. **ORMONDE** (June, 1918), **MERRY HAMPTON** (December, 1918), both by Blyth S.B. Co.

All 1320 tons. First delivered April, 1918, three or four not finished by September, 1919. *Sunstar* not launched and may be stopped. Dimensions : 267½ (*p.p.*). 276½ (*o.a.*) × 34⅝ × 12 feet. Guns : 2—4 inch, as designed ; those completed in 1919 may have only 3 pdr. guns or none at all. Machinery : Inverted 4-cylinder triple expansion. Boilers : Cylindrical return smoke tube. 1 screw. Designed H.P. 2500 = 17 kts. Coal : 260 tons. Complement, 82.

General Notes.—All officially rated as "Fleet Sweeping Vessels (Sloops)" and built under Emergency War Programme Although not built as Submarine Decoy Vessels (or "Q-boats"), they have a resemblance to the Standard Cargo Ships. It is extremely difficult to distinguish bows from stern when these ships are dazzle-painted, or to separat the *Silvio* group (mast *abaft* funnel) from the *Flying Fox* group (mast *before* funnel). The *Silvio* group have rathe higher bridges, mast is close to and *abaft* funnel and ventilators between bridges are rather higher. *Flying Fo* group have mast further away from and *before* funnel. *Minoru* and others completed in the summer of 1919, ha after bridge cut down, the higher fore bridge indicating position of bows. Are said to be indifferent sea-boats and roll a lot : not so successful as the "Flowers." None lost during War. Officially classified as the "24 Class, and not as "Racehorse Class," as this might lead to confusion with the Paddle Minesweepers named afte racecourses. The whole 24 ships may not be completed finally.

BRITISH NAVY—FLEET SWEEPING VESSELS (CONVOY SLOOPS)

"Q" Boat—Flower Type—30 Ships.

POLYANTHUS.

Photo, Messrs. Lobnitz & Co. (Builders).

COREOPSIS.

(ANCHUSA TYPE—26 SHIPS.)

CONVOLVULUS (May, 1917), **COREOPSIS** (Sept., 1917), **DIANTHUS** (Nov., 1917), **EGLANTINE** (June, 1917), **GARDENIA** (Dec., 1917), **GILIA** (Feb., 1918), **HAREBELL** May, 1918), all by Barclay, Curle. **AURICULA** (Oct., 1917), **BRYONY** (Oct., 1917), **CEANOTHUS** June, 1917), **CHRYSANTHEMUM** (Nov., 1917), all by Armstrong, Whitworth. **HIBISCUS** (Nov., 1917), **MARJORAM** (Dec., 1917), **MISTLETOE** (Nov., 1917), all by Greenock & Grangemouth Co. **LYCHNIS** (Aug., 1917), **PELARGONIUM** (March, 1918), both by Hamilton. **POLYANTHUS** (Sept., 1917), **SAXIFRAGE** (Jan., 1918), both by Lobnitz. **SILENE** (March, 1918), **SPIRAEA** (Nov., 1917), both by Simons. **SWEETBRIAR** (Oct., 1917), **TUBEROSE** (Nov., 1917), both by Swan Hunter. **SYRINGA** (Sept., 1917), **WINDFLOWER** (April, 1918), both by Workman, Clark. **IVY** (Blyth S.B. Co., Oct., 1917), **MONTBRETIA** (Irvine S.B. Co., Sept., 1917).

All 1290 tons. Completed Aug., 1917-June, 1918. Dimensions : 250 (*p.p.*), 262½ (*o.a.*) × 35 × 11½-12 (*mean*), 12½-13¾ (*max.*) feet draught. Designed to mount 2—12 pdr., 1—7.5 howitzer or 1—200 lb. stick-bomb howitzer, 4 Depth Charge Throwers, but actually armed with 2—4 inch, 1 or 2—12 pdr. and D.C. Throwers. Machinery : 4-cylinder triple expansion. Boilers : 2 cylindrical. 1 screw. Designed H.P. 2500 = 17 kts., but some only about 16 kts. on this power ; about 2800 = 17 kts. actually. Coal : 260 tons. Complement, 93. Also see *General Notes.*

(AUBRIETIA TYPE—4 SHIPS.)

AUBRIETIA (Blyth S.B. Co., June, 1916), **HEATHER** (Greenock & Grangemouth Co., June, 1916), **TAMARISK** (Lobintz, June, 1916), **VIOLA** (Ropner, July, 1916).

All 1250 tons. Completed Aug.-Oct., 1916. Dimensions : 255¼ (*p.p.*), 267¾ (*o.a.*) × 33½ × 11½ (*mean*), 12¾ (*max.*) feet draught. Designed to mount 3—12 pdr., 2—3 pdr. AA., but have 2—4 inch, 1—3 pdr. AA. and D.C. throwers. Machinery, boilers, as "Anchusa Class," opposite. 1 screw. Designed H.P. 2500 = 17.5 kts., but actually can only make 15-16½ kts. with this power, and require 3000 I.H.P. for 17½ kts. Coal : 255 tons. Complement, 80.

General Notes to Anchusa and Aubrietia types.—All are Fleet Sweeping Vessels (Sloops) of the "Flower Classes," modified in external build for service as Convoy Sloops. Disguised as mercantile vessels, these ships accompanied Convoys, and acted as Submarine Decoy Vessels, or "Q-boats"—hence their popular name of the "Q-boat Flowers." Each builder was allowed to adopt a form of mercantile disguise, with the result that, by appearance, these ships are divided into 15-20 types. All were built under Emergency War Programme.

War Losses.—Owing to the nature of the service these ships were engaged on, war losses were heavy. *Anchusa, Arbutus, Bergamot, Candytuft* (all by Armstrong Whitworth), *Cowslip* (Barclay Curle), *Gaillardia* (Blyth S.B. Co.), *Rhododendron, Salvia* (both by Irvine S.B. Co.), *Tulip* (Richardson, Duck), were all lost during the War. In all, 39 vessels of *Anchusa* and *Aubrietia* types were built. Although nominally rated as "Fleet Sweeping Vessels," they have no gallows at stern, and it is doubtful if they carry sweeping gear, unless of "otter" types.

BRITISH NAVY: FLEET-SWEEPING VESSELS (SLOOPS).
"Flower" Classes—56 Ships.

VALERIAN.

Appearance Notes for all Types.—Majority as *Valerian*, but *Azalea, Buttercup, Campanula, Celandine, Cornflower, Godetia, Hydrangea,* completed with topmasts 40 feet higher; *Lily* completed with topmasts about 20 feet higher. Illustration for *Primrose* shows alterations to ships employed for duty on Mediterranean Convoys, Patrols, &c., mainmast, after gun and gallows, being removed to permit towing of Kite Balloons.

(ARABIS TYPE—26 SHIPS.)

BUTTERCUP (Nov., 1915), **CAMPANULA** (Dec., 1915), **CELANDINE** (Feb., 1916), **CORNFLOWER** (Mar., 1916), all four by Barclay, Curle. **GLADIOLUS** (Oct., 1915). **GODETIA** (Jan., 1916), **HYDRANGEA** (Mar., 1916), all three by Connell. **NIGELLA** (Dec., 1915), **PANSY** (Feb., 1916), both by Hamilton. **ASPHODEL** (Dec., 1915), **BERBERIS** (Feb., 1916), both by Henderson. **WALLFLOWER** (Nov., 1915), **WISTARIA** Dec., 1915), both by Irvine S.B. Co. **CROCUS** (Dec., 1915), **CYCLAMEN** (Feb., 1916), both by Lobnitz. **LOBELIA** (Mar., 1916), **LUPIN** (May, 1916), both by Simons. **MYOSOTIS** (Bow, McLachlan, April, 1916), **VERBENA** (Blyth S.B. Co., Nov., 1915), **AMARYLLIS** (Earle S.B. Co., Dec., 1915), **DELPHINIUM** (Napier & Miller, Dec., 1915), **VALERIAN** (C. Rennoldson, Feb., 1916), **ROSEMARY** (Richardson, Duck, Nov., 1915), **SNAPDRAGON** (Ropner, Dec., 1915), **POPPY** (Swan, Hunter, Nov.,1915), **PENTSTEMON** (Workman, Clark, Feb., 1916).

All 1250 tons. Completed, Dec., 1915-June, 1916. Dimensions : 255¼ (*p.p.*) 267¾ (*o.a.*) × 33½ × 11 (*mean*), 11¼-11¾ *feet* (*max.* draught). *Designed* armament : 2—4.7 inch or 4 inch, 2—3 pdr. AA., but some have only 1—4.7 or 4 inch, with or without the 2—3 pdr. AA. A few are only armed with 2—3 pdr. AA. Designed I.H.P. 1400 = 17 kts., but for this speed they really have to develop about 2400 I.H.P. Machinery : 1 set 4-cylinder triple expansion. Boilers : 2 cylindrical. 1 screw. Coal : 130 tons *normal*, 260 tons *max.* = *about* 2000 miles at 15 kts. Complement, 79. Also see *General Notes.*

General Notes to "Arabis," "Azalea," and "Acacia" Types.—Single-screw Fleet Sweeping Vessels (Sloops), all built under Emergency War Programme. Popularly known as the "Flower Class," but are also referred to as the "Cabbage Class," or "Herbaceous Borders." Have triple hulls at bows to give extra protection against loss when working up mines. Very successful ships, but can only make designed speed with difficulty. Good sea-boats. Copies of this class were built in British yards for the French Navy. The last series of "Flowers" converted to Convoy Sloops (*q.v.*). Several mined during War and extensively re-built.

War Losses, Removals, &c.—*Alyssum, Aster* (both Earle S.B. Co.), *Arabis* (Henderson), *Begonia* (Barclay, Curle), *Genista* (Napier & Miller), *Mignonette* (Dunlop & Bremner), *Lavender, Nasturtium* (both McMillan), *Primula* (Swan Hunter), all lost during War. *Gentian* (Greenock & Grangemouth Co.) and *Myrtle* (Lobnitz), sunk in Baltic, 1919, during anti-Bolshevist operations. *Geranium, Marguerite, Mallow,* presented to Australian Navy. *Peony* (McMillan), sold out. *Petunia* (Workman, Clark), has also gone ; not certain if she has been lost or sold out. In all, 72 of these ships were built.

PRIMROSE.

(AZALEA TYPE—9 SHIPS.)

CARNATION (Sept., 1915), **CLEMATIS** (July, 1915), both by Greenock & Grangemouth Co. **JESSAMINE** (Sept., 1915), **ZINNIA** (Aug., 1915), both by Swan Hunter. **AZALEA** (Barclay, Curle, Sept., 1915). **CAMELLIA** (Bow, McLachlan, Sept., 1915). **HELIOTROPE** (Lobnitz, Sept., 1915). **SNOWDROP** (McMillan, Oct., 1915). **NARCISSUS** (Napier & Miller, Sept., 1915).

All details as "Acacia Type" below, but these ships were designed to mount 2—4.7 inch or 4 inch and 2—3 pdr. AA. Nearly all so armed, but one or two have no 3 pdrs. Complement, 79. Also see *General Notes.*

(ACACIA TYPE—21 SHIPS.)

DAHLIA (April, 1915), **DAPHNE** (May, 1915), **FOXGLOVE** (Mar., 1915), **HOLLYHOCK** (May, 1915), **LILY** (June, 1915), all five by Barclay, Curle. **BLUEBELL** (July, 1915), **DAFFODIL** (Aug., 1915), **DAISY** (June, 1915), all three by Scotts S. B. Co. **MARIGOLD** (May, 1915), **MIMOSA** (July, 1915), both by Bow, McLachlan, **JONQUIL** (May, 1915), **LABURNUM** (June, 1915), both by Connell & Co. **HONEYSUCKLE** (April, 1915), **IRIS** (June, 1915), both by Lobnitz. **ACACIA** (April, 1915), **ANEMONE** (May, 1915), both by Swan Hunter. **VERONICA** (Dunlop, Bremner, May, 1915), **LILAC** (Greenock & Grangemouth Co., April, 1915), **SUNFLOWER** (Henderson, May, 1915), **LARKSPUR** (Napier & Miller, 1915), **PRIMROSE** (Simons, June, 1915).

All 1200 tons. Completed, May-Sept., 1915. Dimensions : 250 (*p.p.*), 262½ (*o.a.*) × 33 × 11 (*mean*), 11¼-12 feet (*max.* draught). Designed to mount 2—12 pdr. and 2—3 pdr. AA. Some still armed in this way ; others have (*a*) 2—4 inch, (*b*) 1—4 inch, (*c*) 1—4 inch and 1—12 pdr., (*d*) 2—12 pdr., with or without the 2—3 pdr. One or two armed *only* with 1 or 2—3 pdr. Designed H.P. 1400 or 1800 = 17 kts., but actually require about 2200 I.H.P. for this speed. Machinery : 1 set 4-cylinder triple expansion. Boilers : 2 cylindrical. 1 screw. Coal : 130 tons *normal*, 250 tons *max.* = *about* 2000 miles at 15 kts. Complement, 77. Also see *General Notes.*

BRITISH NAVY—TUNNEL MINE-SWEEPERS.

(DANCE CLASS—12 BOATS.)

QUADRILLE.

Photo, McClure, Macdonald.

MORRIS DANCE (——), **STEP DANCE** (——), builders not known, **GAVOTTE** (Mar., 1918), and **SARABANDE** (April, 1918), both by Goole Co., **TARANTELLA** (Hamilton, Oct., 1917), **PIROUETTE** (Rennie Forrest, Sept., 1917). These displace 265 tons. I.H.P. 512 = 10.4 kts., *except Gavotte* and *Tarantella*, I.H.P. 450 = 10.4 kts. **COTILLION** (——) and **MINUET** (——), both by Day, Summers, **COVERLEY** (——), and **QUADRILLE** (——), both by Ferguson Bros., **HORNPIPE** (——) and **MAZURKA** (——), both by Murdoch & Murray. All displace 290 tons. I.H.P. 450 = 9½-10 kts. Twin screw (shallow-draught) Minesweepers with screws working in tunnels. Dimensions : 130 (*o.a.*) × 26-27 × 3½ feet. Guns : *Gavotte*, 1—12 pdr., 1—6 pdr. ; *Step Dance*, 1—6 pdr. AA. ; rest, 1—3 pdr. Machinery : Vertical compound. Boilers : Cylindrical. Fuel : 37-41½ tons oil. Complement, 22-26. Completed Nov., 1917-Sept., 1918.

Notes.—All built Emergency War programme. *Sword Dance* and *Fandango,* sunk by Bolshevist mines in River Dvina. Further units of this Class may be completing and others cancelled, but no details are now available of these extra boats.

BRITISH NAVY—TWIN-SCREW MINESWEEPERS.

CRAIGIE.   *Photo, Robertson, Gourock, N.B.*

(TWIN SCREW "HUNT" CLASS—LATER TYPE—87 SHIPS.)

ABERDARE (April, 1918), **ABINGDON** (June, 1918), **ALBURY** (Nov., 1918), **ALRESFORD** (Jan., 1919), **APPLEDORE** (1919), **LEAMINGTON** (ex *Aldeburgh*, Aug., 1918), all six by Ailsa S.B. Co., **BADMINTON** (Mar., 1918), **BAGSHOT** (May, 1918), **BARNSTAPLE** (Mar., 1919), **SWINDON** (ex *Bantry*, 1919), all four by Ardrossan Co., **BANCHORY** (May, 1918), **BLOXHAM** (ex *Brixham*, 1919), **BRADFIELD** (May, 1919), **BURSLEM** (ex *Blakeney*, Mar., 1918), **GOOLE** (ex *Bridlington*, 1919), all five by Ayrshire Co., **BLACKBURN** (ex *Burnham*, Aug., 1918), **BOOTLE** (ex *Buckie*, June, 1919), **CAERLEON** (Dec., 1918), **CAMBERLEY** (Dec., 1918), **CARSTAIRS** (ex *Cawsand*, 1919), **CATERHAM** (Mar., 1919), all six by Bow, McLachlan, **CRAIGIE** (May, 1918), **DERBY** (ex *Dawlish*, Aug., 1918), **FAIRFIELD** (1919), *****FORRES** (ex *Fowey*, Nov., 1918), **DORKING** (Sept., 1918), **DUNDALK** (Jan., 1919), **DUNOON** (Mar., 1919), all seven by Clyde S.B. Co., **BATTLE** (1919), **FERMOY** (1919), **FORFAR** (Nov., 1918), all three by Dundee S.B. Co., **FAREHAM** (June, 1918), **FEVERSHAM** (July, 1918), **FORD** (ex *Fleetwood*, Oct., 1918), **RUGBY** (ex *Filey*, Sept., 1918), all four by Dunlop & Bremner, **BURY** (May, 1919), **CHEAM** (July, 1918), **GADDESDEN** (Nov., 1917), **GAINS-BOROUGH** (ex *Gorleston*, Feb., 1918), **GRETNA** (April, 1919), **HARROW** July, 1918), **HAVANT** Nov., 1918), **HUNTLEY** (ex *Helmsdale*, Jan., 1919), **INSTOW** (ex *Ilfracombe*, April, 1919), **NORTHOLT** (June, 1918), all ten by Jos. R. Eltringham, **IRVINE** (Dec., 1917), **KENDAL** (Feb., 1919), **LYDD** (ex *Lydney*, Dec., 1918), all four by Fairfield Co., **MALLAIG** (Oct., 1918), **MALVERN** (Feb., 1919), **MARAZION** (1919), **MUNLOCHY** (ex *Macduff*, June, 1918), all four by Fleming & Ferguson, **LONGFORD** (ex *Minehead*, Mar., 1919), **MARLOW** (Aug., 1918), **MISTLEY** (ex *Maryport*, Oct., 1918), **MONAGHAN** (ex *Mullion*, May, 1919), all four by W. Harkness, **NAILSEA** (ex *Newquay*, Aug., 1918), **NEWARK** (ex *Newlyn*, June, 1918), **REPTON** (ex *Wicklow*, 1919), **WEYBOURNE** (Feb., 1919), all four by A. & J. Inglis, **PANGBOURNE** (ex *Padstow*, Mar., 1918), **PETERSFIELD** (ex *Portmadoc*, Mar., 1919), **PONTYPOOL** (ex *Polperro*, June, 1918), **PRESTATYN** (ex *Porlock*, Nov., 1918), **ROSS** (ex *Ramsey*, 1919), all five by Messrs. Lobnitz, **SUTTON** (ex *Salcombe*, May, 1918), by Messrs. McMillan, **SALFORD** (ex *Shoreham*, April, 1919), **SALTASH** (July, 1918), **SALTBURN** (Oct., 1918), **SELKIRK** (Dec., 1918), all four by Messrs. Murdoch & Murray, **SHREWSBURY** (Feb., 1919), **SLIGO** (Mar., 1918), **WIDNES** (ex *Withernsea*, June, 1918), **YEOVIL** (Aug., 1918), all four by Messrs. Napier & Miller, **STAFFORD** (ex *Staithes*, Sept., 1918), **STOKE** (ex *Southwold*, July, 1918), both by Chas. Rennoldson, **CLONMEL** (ex *Stranraer*, May, 1918), **ELGIN** (ex *Troon*, Mar., 1919), **SHERBORNE** (ex *Tarbert*, June, 1918), **TIVERTON** (Sept., 1918), **TONBRIDGE** (Nov., 1918), **TRALEE** (Dec., 1918), **TRING** (ex *Teignmouth*, Aug., 1919), **TRURO** (April, 1919), **WEM** (ex *Walmer*, 1919), **WEXFORD** (1919), all ten by Messrs. Simons.

* *Forres* contracted for by Messrs. Dunlop Bremner, but contract and materials transferred to Clyde S.B. Co.

CAMBERLEY (Tender, Navigation School).   *Photo, Robertson, Gourock, N.B.*

All Emergency War Programme. First ship delivered Feb., 1918; all deliveries not completed by Oct., 1919. Displacement, 800 tons. Dimensions: 220 (p.p.), 231 (o.a.) × 28 ft. 6⅝ in. ×7½ (mean), — feet (max. draught). Guns: A few have 1—4 inch and 1—12 pdr. AA. or 2—3 pdr., but majority have only 1—6 or 3 pdr. Several not armed now. Machinery: Vertical triple expansion. 2 screws. Designed I.H.P. 2200 = 16 kts. Boilers: Yarrow. Coal: 185 tons. Complement, 74.

General Notes.—Much the same as original Ailsa Co. design of Twin-Screw Sweepers (*Belvoir, Bicester, &c.*), but slight modifications introduced in these ships by Admiralty. In 1919, several had been assigned to Special Service, *e.g., Marazion, &c.* (Tenders to Submarine Depot Ships), *Salford, Camberley, Caterham* (Tenders to Navigation School), *Petersfield* (Admiral's Yacht and for service on South American Rivers), and so on. Six have been re-named and completed as Surveying Ships (*q.v.*). But on the demobilisation of the Mine Clearance Force, the majority of these ships will be laid up. Those originally named after coastal towns, watering places, fishing ports, &c., were all re-named after inland towns and villages, to obviate misunderstanding of signals and orders.
To distinguish from original "Hunt Class."—Look rather bigger and heavier. Thicker funnel, foremast higher and stepped *through* Chart House. Searchlight on forward extension of bridge. Superstructure runs well towards mainmast and has 4 ventilators arranged in a square. Hull level, *not* broken between mainmast and gallows.

Losses (after-Armistice).—Cupar (ex *Rosslare*, built by McMillan), Kinross (Fairfield), Penarth (Lobnitz). No War Losses.

Cancelled Ships.—Alton (ex *Arbroath*), Ashburton, both by Ailsa S.B. Co.; Bideford, Bolton (ex *Beaumaris*), both by Ardrossan D.D. & S.B. Co.; Atheleney, Bathgate, both by Clyde S.B. Co.; Beccles, Blickling, both by Dundee S.B. Co.; Northrepps, by Messrs. Lobnitz; Tain, Wembdon, Yealmpton, all three by Messrs. Simons. Also the following ships (contractors not known):—Clifton, Crediton (ex *Colyen*), Curragh, Frome, Kew, Kingussie, Knowle, Okehampton, Oundle, Radnor, Reading, Retford, Ringwood, Runcorn, Shifnal. Also Fairburn, Clorelly, either cancelled or re-named; if latter, present names wanted.

BRITISH NAVY—P. W. & T. S. MINESWEEPERS.

(PADDLE SWEEPERS—7 OF LATER GROUP.)

HEXHAM.   *Photo, Robertson, Gourock, N.B.*

BANBURY (Dec., 1917) and **HARPENDEN** (Feb., 1918), both by Ailsa S.B. Co. **HEXHAM** (Clyde S.B. Co., Dec., 1917). **LANARK** (Dec., 1917) and **LEWES** (Mar., 1918), both by Fleming & Ferguson. **SHINCLIFFE** (Dunlop, Bremner, Jan., 1918), **WETHERBY** (Murdoch & Murray, Mar., 1918).

Paddle minesweepers, design by Admiralty, adapted from Ailsa Co. design for *Atherstone, &c.* (v. next page). Completed Jan.-June, 1918. Displacement, 820 tons. Complement. 50-52. Dimensions: 235 (p.p.), 249¾ (o.a.) × 29 ft. 0¼ in. (58 feet outside paddle boxes) × 6¾-7 feet. Guns: 1—12 pdr. (12 cwt.), 1—3 inch AA. Designed I.H.P. 1400 = 15 kts. (actually 1500 = about 14½ kts.). Machinery: Diagonal compound. Boilers: Cylindrical return tube. Coal: 156 tons.

Notes.—All built under Emergency War Programme. Suffer from same defects as *Atherstone, &c.* (next page). To distinguish, note that foremast is stepped *through* chart house; two *high* ventilators abaft fore funnel; *no* derricks abeam of second funnel. Commonly known as the "Improved Racecourse" type.

War Losses.—Nil. *Shirley* (Dunlop, Bremner) sold out for commercial service as a ferry boat, 1919.

(TWIN SCREW "HUNT CLASS"—19 OF EARLIER GROUP.)

CATTISTOCK.   *Photo, Robertson, Gourock, N.B.*

BELVOIR (Mar., 1917) and **BICESTER** (June, 1917), both by Ailsa S.B. Co. **CATTISTOCK** (Clyde S.B. Co., Feb., 1917), **COTSWOLD** (Nov., 1916) and **COTTESMORE** (Feb., 1917), both by Bow, McLachlan. **CROOME** (Clyde S.B. Co., May, 1917), **DARTMOOR** (Mar., 1917) and **GARTH** (May, 1917), both by Dunlop, Bremner. **HAMBLEDON** (Mar., 1917), and **HEYTHROP** (June, 1917), both by Fleming & Ferguson. **HOLDERNESS** (Nov., 1916) and **MEYNELL** (Feb., 1917), both by D. & W. Henderson. **MUSKERRY** (Nov., 1916) and **OAKLEY** (Jan., 1917), both by Lobnitz. **PYTCHLEY** (Mar., 1917), and **QUORN** (June, 1917), both by Napier & Miller. **SOUTHDOWN** (1917) and **TEDWORTH** (June, 1917), both by Simons. **ZETLAND** (Murdoch & Murray, 1917).

Twin Screw Minesweepers, built to design by Ailsa Co. Completed Mar.-Oct., 1917. Displacement, 750 tons. Complement. 71. Dimensions: 220 (p.p.), 231 (o.a.) × 28 × 7 feet (mean draught.) Guns: 2—12 pdr. and 2—2 pdr., but some have temporary armament of 1—12 pdr. and 1—6 pdr. Designed I.H.P. 1800 = 16 kts. Machinery: 3-cylinder triple expansion. Boilers: Yarrow. Coal: 140 tons.

Notes.—All built under Emergency War Programme, and proved very successful. To distinguish from *Aberdare, Abingdon, &c.*, note that searchlight is on tower separated from fore bridges; foremast is stepped *abaft* chart house; superstructure round funnel runs out to beam and does not extend far towards stern; hull at stern breaks level between mainmast and gallows. Generally known as the "Hunt" Class.

War Losses.—Blackmorevale (Ardrossan D.D. Co.).

BRITISH NAVY—PADDLE MINE SWEEPERS.

(PADDLE SWEEPERS—19 OF EARLIER GROUP.)

ERIDGE.   Photo, Robertson, Gourock, N.B.

QUEEN VICTORIA.

* **QUEEN VICTORIA.** Purchased 1915. Used as Net Layer and later as Paddle Mine Sweeper. No details known.

* **PRINCE EDWARD** (ex *Prince of Wales*). Purchased 1915. No details known.

* **DUCHESS OF BUCCLEUCH.** Purchased 1916. No details known.

* *Note.*—Although these three ships were purchased outright for H.M. Navy, it is very likely they will be re-conditioned and sold out for mercantile use in the near future.

ATHERSTONE (Jan., 1916) and **CHELMSFORD** (April, 1916), [both by Ailsa S.B. Co., **CHELTENHAM** (Ardrossan Co., June, 1916), **CHEPSTOW** (April, 1916), **CROXTON** (April, 1916), **DONCASTER** (June, 1916) and **EGLINTON** (Sept., 1916), all by Ayrshire D.Y. Co., **EPSOM** (G. Brown, May, 1916), **ERIDGE** (Clyde S.B. Co., Feb., 1916), **GATWICK** (April, 1916) and **GOODWOOD** (June, 1916), both by Dundee S.B. Co., **HALDON** (Mar., 1916), **HURST** (May, 1916) and **SANDOWN** (July, 1916), all by Dunlop, Bremner (Fleming & Ferguson, April, 1916), **MELTON** (Hamilton, Mar., 1916), **NEWBURY** (A. & J. Inglis, July, 1916), **PONTEFRACT** (Murdoch & Murray, June, 1916), **TOTNES** (McMillan, May, 1916).

Paddle Mine Sweepers, built to designs by Ailsa Co. Completed, April-Oct., 1916. Displacement, 810 tons. Complement, 50. Dimensions : 235 (p.p.), 245¾ (o.a.) × 29 (58 feet over paddles) × 6¾ feet (*mean* draught). Guns : 2—12 pdr. Designed H.P. 1400 = 15 kts. Machinery : Inclined compound. Boilers : Cylindrical return tube. Coal : 156 tons.

Notes.—All built under Emergency War Programme. Fairly good sea-boats, but lose speed badly in a seaway, through paddle boxes getting choked with water. *Eridge* and *Melton* were originally fitted to carry seaplanes. To differentiate from *Banbury*, *Hexham*, &c., note that foremast is stepped *before* fore bridges : also these boats have derricks abeam of second funnel. Unofficially known as the "Racecourse" Class.

War Losses.—*Ascot* (Ailsa Co.), *Redcar* (Ayrshire D.Y. Co.), *Kempton* (Ferguson Bros.), *Ludlow* (Goole Co.) *Plumpton* (McMillan).

Patrol Gunboats *Kildonan, Kilmallock, Kilmanahan, Kilmarnock, Kilmarten, Kilmead, Kilmelford,* all described on an earlier page—are fitted as Mine Sweepers.

In addition to those listed above the following appear in "British Vessels Lost at Sea 1914-18" HMSO. Screw sweepers: *Roedean, Newmarket, Clacton.* Paddle sweepers. *St. Seiriol, Ericks Isle, Queen of the North, Brighton Queen, Duchess of Hamilton, Hythe, Lady Ismay, Fair Maid, Nepaulin, Duchess of Montrose, Marsa, Princess Mary II* lost in Aegean August 1919.

BRITISH NAVY—DEPOT SHIPS.

Depot Ships.

Note—The following old warships have been allocated for service as Depot Ships, but will serve only as Accommodation Ships, Hulks for overflow purposes, &c. Since they will not be required for War Fleet and have no fighting value, details and illustrations are not given for them.

Battleships :—		
Implacable	Cæsar	Mars
Venerable	Hannibal	Victorious
Glory		

Cruisers and Light Cruisers :—

Crescent	Imperieuse	Naiad

The following vessels have been assigned to duty as Depot Ships. They will not serve in a sea-going capacity any longer, but only as Depot Ships to Local Defence Flotillas and Destroyers, Submarines, &c., in Reserve. No illustrations or details given of these ships.

For T.B.D. :—*Prince George, Essex, Europa, Dido, Apollo,*

For Patrol Gunboats :—*Hermione.*

For Anti-Submarine Service :—*Gibraltar.*

For Submarines :—*Rosario, Pactolus, Onyx, Dolphin.*

Destroyer Depot Ships.

Photo wanted.

SANDHURST (ex s.s. *Manipur*, Harland & Wolff, purchased 1915 and converted by Workman, Clerk). 11,500 tons. Dimensions : 470 (p.p.) × 58 × 20 feet (*max.* draught). Guns : 4—4 inch, 2—6 pdr. A.A. I.H.P. 4000 = 10.5 kts. Coal : 1475 tons. Complement, 269. Cyl. boilers.

Tenders : 2 Drifters.

Destroyer Depot Ships—(*Continued*).

Photo. Dr. J. A. Prendergast.

GREENWICH (Dobson & Co., completed by Swan Hunter. Purchased 1915). 8600 tons. Dimensions : 390 (p.p.) × 52 × 19¾ feet (*max.* draught). Guns : 4—4 inch, 2—6 pdr. AA. I.H.P. 2500 = 11 kts. Coal : 960 tons. Complement, 261. Cyl. boilers.

Tenders : 2 Drifters.

WOOLWICH (Scotts. S. & E. Co., 1912). 3380 tons. Dimensions: 320 × 40 × 14¼ feet. Guns : 2—4 inch. H.P. 2600 = 13.5 kts. Coal : 370 tons. Complement, 263.

Tenders : 2 Drifters.

Destroyer Depot Ships—(*Continued*).

DILIGENCE (ex *Tabaristan*, 1907. Purchased 1913). 7400 tons. Dimensions : 390 (p.p.) × 46 × — feet. Guns : 4—4 inch. H.P. 5000 = 14.2 kts. Coal : 780 tons. Complement, 258.

Tenders : 2 Drifters.

BLENHEIM.

BLAKE (1889) & **BLENHEIM** (1890.) Both converted 1907. 9000 tons. Dimensions : 375 (p.p.) × 65 × 25¾ feet (*max.* draught). Guns : 4—old 6 inch, and 2—4 inch in *Blake*; 1—4 inch and 7—12 pdr. in *Blenheim.* Designed H.P. 20,000 = 21.1 kts. Coal : *normal*, 624 tons ; also 650 tons carried in small bags (1 cwt. each) for destroyers.

Tenders : 2 Drifters *each.*

Destroyer Depot Ships—(Continued).

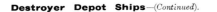

LEANDER (1882). 4380 tons. Dimensions: 300 (p.p.) × 46 × 21¼ feet. (max. draught). Guns: 2—12 pdr., 2—6 pdr., 1 M.G. Armour: 1½″ deck amidships. H.P. 5000 = 16.5 kts. Coal: 813 tons.
Tender: 1 Drifter.

TYNE (purchased 1878). 3590 tons. Dimensions: 320 (p.p.) × 34 × 20 feet (mean draught). Guns: 1—12 pdr., 2—6 pdr. Designed H.P. 1200 = 11.7 kts. Coal: 510 tons. Complement, 172.

HECLA (purchased 1878). 5600 tons. Dimensions: 391½ (p.p.) × 38¾ × 21⅔ feet (mean draught). Guns: 4—4 inch. 1 M.G. Designed H.P. 2400 = 13.4 kts. Coal: 572 tons. Complement, 266.
Tenders: 2 Drifters.

Torpedo Sub-Depot Ships (R.F.A.)

* **SOBO** 4163 tons. Speed: 9 kts. Coal: 413 tons.

* **SOKOTO** 3870 tons. Speed: 9 kts. Coal: 380 tons.

*Purchased 1914. As it is very probable that these ships will be sold out of H.M. Navy in the near future, they are not illustrated

Submarine Depot Ships.

Note.—Light Cruiser, **FEARLESS** and Flotilla Leader **ITHURIEL**, are attached to 1st and 2nd Submarine Flotillas

Photo, Abrahams, Devonport.

AMBROSE (Clyde S.B. Co., 1915. Purchased 1915). 6480 tons. Dimensions: 387¾ (o.a.) × 47½ × 20¼ feet. Guns: 2—12 pdr. I.H.P. 6350 = 14½ kts. Complement, 240.
Tenders: *Marazion* and 1 Drifter. (Also serve for *Pandora*.)

TITANIA (Clyde S.B. Co., 1915, purchased 1915). 5200 tons. Dimensions: 335 (p.p.) × 46¼ × 18¼ feet. I.H.P. 3200 = 14.5 kts. Torpedo tubes: 2. Coal: 498 tons. Complement, 245. Cyl. boilers.
Tenders: *Adamant*, 1 Drifter.

Photo, Dr. J. A. Prendergast.

LUCIA (Furness Withy Co., ex German Prize, *Spreewald*, converted by Clyde S.B. Co., 1916). 6005 tons. Dimensions: 366 (o.a.) × 45¼ × 19¾ feet. Guns: 2—3 pdr. AA. I.H.P. 2700 × kts. Coal: 700 tons. Cyl. boilers. Complement, 245.
Tenders: *Repton*, 1 Trawler.

Submarine Depot Ships—Continued.

PANDORA (ex *Seti*, purchased from Russia, 1914). 4350 tons. Dimensions: 330 × 43 × 16 feet. Guns: *Nil.* H.P. 2200 = 11 kts. Coal: 580 tons. Complement, 70.
Tenders: *Marazion* and 1 Drifter (also serve for *Ambrose*).

Photo, Cribb.

MAIDSTONE (Scott's S. & E. Co., 1912). 3600 tons. Dimensions: 355 × 45 × 17¾ feet. Guns: *Nil.* H.P. 2800 = 14·3 kts. Coal: 465 tons. Complement, 159.
Tenders: *Salford*, 1 Drifter.

ADAMANT and **ALECTO** (both Laird, 1911). 935 tons. Dimensions: 190 × 32½ × 11 feet (mean draught). Guns: *Adamant*, 1—4 inch. Designed H.P. 1400 = 14 kts. Coal: 180 tons. Complement, 63.

No photo available.
Similar to St. George below.

ROYAL ARTHUR (ex *Centaur*) (1891). 7700 tons. Dimensions: 360 (p.p.) × 60¾ × 26¾ feet. Guns: *Nil.* I.H.P. 12,000 = 20 kts., but 7000 = 15-16 kts. may be present *maximum.* Coal: 1230 tons. Complement, —.
Tenders to *Royal Arthur*: 2 Drifters.

Submarine Depot Ships—Continued.

ST. GEORGE (1890). Cruiser of *Edgar* type; converted 1911. 7700 tons. Dimensions: 360 (p.p.) × 60¾ × 23¾ feet (mean draught). Guns: 2—6 inch, 2—12 pdr. AA., 2—3 pdr. AA. Designed H.P. 12,000 = 19.5 kts. (present maximum H.P. 7000 for about 15-16 kts.). Coal: *normal*, 850 tons; *maximum*, 1120 tons. Complement, 301.
Tenders to *St. George*: 2 Drifters.

Submarine Depot Ships—Continued.

VULCAN (1889). Rebuilt 1908. 6620 tons. Dimensions: 350 × 58 × 23¼ feet (max. draught). Guns: 2—8.7 inch. Armour: 5″ deck (amidships), 6″ conning tower, 5″ engine hatches. Designed H.P. 12,000 = 20 kts. Can do now about 16 kts. Coal: *maximum* 1347 tons. Dürr boilers (1909). Complement, 255.
Tenders to *Vulcan*: *Alecto* and 1 Drifter.

THAMES (1885) & **FORTH** (1886). 4050 tons. Dimensions: 300 (p.p.) × 46 × 19¾ feet (max. draught). No guns. Designed H.P. 5700 = 17.2 kts. originally. Coal: 740 tons *maximum*. Fitted as Floating Workshops. Complement, 187.

Tenders to *Thames*: *Fermoy*, 1 Drifter.
Tenders to *Forth*: *Elgin*, *Forres*, 4 Trawlers.

ARROGANT (1896). 5750 tons. Designed H.P. 10,000 = 19 kts. Belleville boilers. Coal: *normal*, 500 tons; *maximum* 1175 tons. (Converted 1911-12.)

BONAVENTURE (1892), of the *Astræa* class. 4360 tons. Armament: 2—6 inch, 8—6 pdrs. Deck 2 on slope. Designed H.P. 9000 = 19.5 kts. Cylindrical boilers. Coal: *normal*, 400 tons; *maximum*, 1000 tons.

BRITISH NAVY—REPAIR & SALVAGE SHIPS.

Repair Ships—(R.F.A.).

SCOTSTOUN Begun, February, 1916. Launched, Completed, July, 1916. Built by Yarrows, as Repair Ship for "Insect," and "Fly" Classes of Gunboats. 300 tons. Dimensions : 132 (*p.p.*), 150 (*o.a.*) × 31 × 2½ feet draught. I.H.P. 200 = 7.7 kts. Compound surface condensing engines. Loco. boiler. Oil : 20/36 tons.

BACCHUS (Hamilton & Co., 1915, purchased 1915). About 3500 tons. Dimensions : 295 × 44 × 12½ feet. Guns : Not known. I.H.P. = kts. Coal : 873 tons.

RELIANCE (ex *Knight-Companion*, 1910, bought 1913). 3250 tons. Dimensions : 470 × 57¾ × — feet. H.P. 3250 = 11 kts. Coal : 1700 tons.

CYCLOPS (ex *Indrabarah*, 1905). 11,300 tons. Dimensions : 460 (*p.p.*) × 55 × 21 feet. Guns : 6—4 inch. Machinery : Triple expansion. Designed H.P. 3500 = 11.75 kts. Coal capacity : 1595 tons. Fitted as Floating Workshop and Distilling Ship. Complement, 294.

Repair Ships—(*Continued*).

ASSISTANCE (1901). 9600 tons. Dimensions : 436 (*p.p.*) × 53 × 20 feet. Guns : 10—3 pdr. Machinery : Triple expansion. Boilers : Cylindrical. Fitted with Howden's forced draught. Designed H.P. (*f.d.*) 4000 = 12 kts. Coal : 2180 tons. Fitted as Floating Workshop and Distilling Ship. Complement, 283.

AQUARIUS (ex *Hampstead*) (1902). 2800 tons. Length (*p.p.*), 268 feet. Beam, 37¾ feet. Draught, 16 feet. Speed, 10·5 kts.

Salvage Vessels.

REINDEER (1884). 970 tons. Re-engined by Fairfield Co., 1918. I.H.P. 1200 = kts.

RACER (1884, rebuilt 1916-17). 970 tons. I.H.P. 1100 = 11 kts. Re-engined with starboard machinery of old T.B. 8 submersible electric, steam centrifugal and compressed air pumps throwing 3000 tons per hour. 2—17 ton derricks.

MELITA (ex *Ringdove*, 1889). Ex-gunboat. 820 tons. H.P. 750 = 11 kts. Coal : 80 tons. Complement, 74.

MARINER (1883). Ex-Sloop and Boom Defence Vessel. 970 tons.

Also *Moonfleet, Hippopotamus* and *Rhinoceros*, built 1917. Are probably only chartered vessels which may no longer be in H.M. Navy.

BRITISH NAVY—OIL TANKERS (R.F.A.).

Oil Tankers (R.F.A.).

Oil Tankers *Birchleaf, Appleleaf* (ex *Texol*), *Plumleaf* (ex *Trinol*), *Erivan*, &c., are understood to have been disposed of, or returned to owners. It is possible that some of the "Ol" Tankers detailed hereafter may have taken up commercial service.

1 funnel with 1 mast just before, both raking and aft of amidships.

PETROBUS, PETRELLA, PETRONEL (Dunlop, Bremner, 1918). 1024 tons. Dimensions : 164 × 28 × 11½ feet. I.H.P. 500 = 9-10 kts. Own oil : 50 tons. Cylindrical boilers. Complement, 16.

Appearance unknown.

DREDGOL (Simons, 1918). About 7000 tons. Dimensions : 326 × 54½ × 18¾ feet. I.H.P. 2400 = 11 kts. Own oil : 360 tons. Cylindrical boilers.

1 funnel with 1 mast before, close together, as in Standard Cargo Ships.

FRANCOL (Earle S.B. Co.), **MONTENOL** (W. Gray), **SERBOL** (Caledon S.B. Co.). All details as *Belgol* below, but of different appearance. All launched 1917.

Oil Tankers (R.F.A.).—*Continued*.

2 masts fore and aft : 1 funnel between. *Rapidol* a little different to other ships.

BELGOL (Irvine D.D. Co.), **CELEROL** (Short Bros.), **FORTOL** (McMillan), **PRESTOL** (Napier & Miller), **RAPIDOL** (W. Gray), **SLAVOL, VITOL** (Greenock and Grangemouth Co.). All launched 1917. 4900 tons. Dimensions : 335 × 41½ × 20½ feet. I.H.P. 3375 = 14 kts. Own oil : 300 tons. Cylindrical boilers. Complement, 39.

1 mast forward. 1 funnel aft.

BIRCHOL, BOXOL (Barclay, Curle), **EBONOL** (Clyde S.B. Co.), **ELDEROL, ELMOL** (Swan Hunter), **LARCHOL, LIMOL,** (Lobnitz). All launched 1917. As *Sprucol, Teakol,* below, but these have triple expansion engines and cylindrical boilers. I.H.P. 700 = 12 kts.

1 mast forward. 1 funnel aft.

SPRUCOL, TEAKOL (Short Bros.), **OAKOL, PALMOL** (W. Gray & Co.). All launched 1917. 1925 tons. Dimensions : 220 × 34 × 12 feet. Bolinders oil engines. B.H.P. 640 = 8-10 kts. Own oil : 40 tons. Complement, 19.

Oil Tankers (R.F.A.).—*Continued*.

1 mast forward. 1 funnel aft.

CREOSOL (Short Bros.), **DISTOL, PHILOL, SCOTOL** (Tyne Iron S.B. Co.), **KIMMEROL, VISCOL** (Craig, Taylor). All launched 1916. 1920 tons. Dimensions : 220 × 34⅔ × 12½ feet. I.H.P. 700 = 9 kts. Own oil : 40 tons. Cylindrical boilers. Complement, 19.

2 masts, 1 funnel at stern.

MIXOL (Greenock & Grangemouth Co., 1916), **THERMOL** (Caledonian S.B. Co., 1916). 4145 tons. Dimensions : 270 × 38½ × 20¼ feet. I.H.P. 1200 = 11 kts. Oil : 150 tons.

TREFOIL (Pembroke, 1913). 4060 tons. Dimensions : 280 × 39 × 18¼ feet. 2 sets 6-cylinder 2-cycle Diesel engines. H.P. 1500 = 12 kts. Deadweight capacity : 2000 tons. Own oil : 200 tons.

"*Ferol,*" "*Servitor,*" "*Attendant,*" *Carol*" one mast forward, one funnel aft.

FEROL (Devonport, 1914). **SERVITOR** (Chatham, 1914). 2007 tons. Dimensions : 200 × 34 × 13 feet. 2 sets 4-cylinder 2-cycle Diesel engines. B.H.P. 450 = 8 kts. Deadweight capacity : 1000 tons. Own oil fuel : 29 tons.

ATTENDANT (Chatham, 1913), **CAROL** (Devonport, 1913). 1935 tons. Dimensions : 200 × 34 × 13 feet. I.H.P. 450 = 8 kts. Coal : 60 tons.

(*Continued on next page.*)

BRITISH MISCELLANEOUS.

Special Service.

Photo, Abrahams & Sons.

FORTITUDE (*ex Neptune*) (1896). 400 tons. H.P. 1200.

MAGNET (1883). 430 tons. Guns: 4—3 pdr. H.P. 650 = 12 kts.

Photo, Abrahams & Sons.

TRAVELLER (1883). 700 tons. Guns: 4—3 pdr. H.P. 1100 = 12 kts.

1 funnel, 2 masts.

IMOGENE (1882). 460 tons. H.P. 390 = 11 kts.

SPHINX (1882). 1130 tons. Guns: 1—old 6 in., 6—old 4 in. H.P. 1100—12·5 kts.

SEAHORSE (1880). 670 tons. Guns: 1—12 pdr. howitzer. H.P. 1100—12·5 kts.

Photo, Abrahams & Sons.

UNDINE (*ex Wildfire, ex Hiawatha*) (1880). 453 tons. Speed 9 kts.

VESUVIUS (1874). 245 tons. 2 torpedo tubes.

Miscellaneous Special Service.

RAVEN (1882). (*ex gunboat*). 465 tons. *Diving School.*

Special Petrol or Oil Ships.

PETROLEUM, KHAKI, ISLA (1903). 4521 tons. Length 370 feet. Beam, 49 feet. *Depth*, 39 feet. Also **BURMA**. 39— tons.

Also *TREFOIL & TURMOIL building.*

Special Collier.

MERCEDES (1902). 9900 tons. Dimensions: 351′ × 50 × 28 feet. H.P. 2350 = kts.

Oil Tankers (R.F.A.)

BURMA (Greenock, 1911). 3945 tons. H.P. 1200 = 11 kts. Cargo capacity: 2500 tons oil fuel. Own fuel: 210 tons.

PETROLEUM (Wallsend, 1901). 9900 tons. Dimensions: 370 × 48¾ × 24 feet. H.P. 2000 = 13 kts. Oil: 426 tons.

KHARKI (1899, bought 1900). 1430 tons. H.P. 775 = 13 kts. Fuel: 90 tons.

ISLA (1903, purchased 1907). 1010 tons. Dimensions: 170 × 26 × 12 feet. H.P. 650 = 10 kts. Petrol-carrying vessel for submarines. Fuel: 75 tons.

INDUSTRY (1901). 1460 tons. H.P. 750 = 10 kts. Fuel: 180 tons.

Collier (R.F.A.)

MERCEDES (1901, purchased 1908). 9930 tons. Dimensions: 350 × 50¼ × 28 feet. H.P. 2350 = 9 kts. Coal: 750/1603 tons.

Hospital Ships.

"*Soudan Type.*"—One ship assigned for duty with Atlantic Fleet, and another for duty with Mediterranean Fleet. Names not known, but one believed to be **ST. MARGARET OF SCOTLAND** of which no photographs or details are available.

Ice Breakers (R.F.A.)

"Ermiak type."
2 funnels, 2 masts

SVIATOGOR (ex-Russian *Sviatogor*, Clyde, 1915-16). No details available.

ALEXANDER (ex-Russian *Aleksandr Nevski*). Built by Armstrongs. Begun June, 1916 (for Russian Government), launched December, 1916, completed December, 1917. 3 screws (2 aft, 1 forward). Cylindrical boilers. No other details known.

Tugs.

ST. ANNE,	ST. COLUMB,	ST. FINBARR,
ST. ARVANS,	ST. CYRUS,	ST. ISSEY,
ST. BLAZEY,	ST. FERGUS,	ST. SAMPSON.

No details available. For Target Work and General Fleet or Squadron duties.
Also many other Tugs, Tanks, &c., but as these are not attached to Fleets or Squadrons, they are not listed.

Despatch Vessels.

WATERWITCH Begun, May 6th, 1914. Launched, October 17th, 1914. Completed, June 7th, 1915. Late Turkish *Rechid Pasha*, purchased 1915. Built by Fairfield. 40— tons. Dimensions: 165 × 26 × 6½ feet (*mean* draught). Designed H.P. 625 = kts. *Trials:* 615 = 13.1. Triple expansion engines and cylindrical boilers. 2 screws. Coal 34 tons. Complement, 14.

SPHINX (1882). 1130 tons. Guns: 4—4 inch, 2 M.G. H.P. 1100 = 12.5 kts. Coal: 220 tons.

Royal Yachts.

ALEXANDRA (1907). 2050 tons. Dimensions: 275 (p.) × 40 × 12½ feet (*mean* draught). Guns: 2—7 pdr. (bronze). Parsons turbines. H.P. 4500 = 18.25 kts. (19.1 on full trials). Yarrow boilers. Coal: 270 tons. Complement, 1— (*Continued on next page.*)

Royal Yachts—*Continued.*

VICTORIA AND ALBERT (1899). 4700 tons. Dimensions : 380 (*p.p.*) × 40 × 18 feet (*mean draught*). Guns : 2—6 pdr. (bronze). H.P. 11,800 = 20 kts. Belleville boilers. Coal : *normal*, 350 tons ; *maximum*, 2000 tons. Comp. 336.

Admiralty Yacht.

ENCHANTRESS (1903). 3470 tons. Dimensions : 320 × 40 × 15 feet. Guns : 4—3 pdr. H.P. 6400 = 18 kts. Yarrow boilers. Coal : 350 tons.

Yachts.

TRIAD Yacht, S. N. O. Persian Gulf. (Caledonian S.B. Co., 1909, purchased 1915). 2354 tons. Dimensions : 264 × 35 × 15¾ feet. Guns : Not known. I.H.P. 2235 = 14 kts. Coal : 480 tons.

BRITISH NAVY—MISCELLANEOUS.

Yachts—*Continued.*

ALACRITY (ex Russian *Mlada*, taken over 1919). No details known. Yacht and Despatch Vessel, C.-in-C., China.

Note.—Gunboat *Hussar* is Despatch Vessel, C.-in-C., Mediterranean. Convoy Sloop *Bryony* has served as Yacht, Rear-Admiral, Ægean. Hunt Class T. S. Minesweeper *Petersfield* may also serve as Yacht on South American Station.

ROSITA (Leith, 1900). 93 tons *gross*. Dimensions : 100 × 16 × feet. I.H.P. 250.

DOTTER. No details known.

Admiralty Whalers.

ZEDWHALE. *Photo, Parry & Sons.*

ARCTIC WHALE,	CACHALOT,	PILOTWHALE,
BALAENA,	COWWHALE,	RIGHTWHALE,
BELUGA,	FINWHALE,	RORQUAL,
BOWHEAD,	HUMPBACK,	ZEDWHALE,
BULLWHALE,	ICEWHALE,	(ex *Meg.*)

Emergency War Programme. Built 1915, by Smiths Dock Co. 336 tons. Dimensions : 139⅞ × 25 × 6½ feet. Guns : 1—12 pdr., but *Zedwhale* has also 1—6 pdr. AA. and 1—3 pdr. H.P. 1000 = 12-13 kts. Coal : 60 tons. Complement, 26.

Admiralty Trawlers.

JAMES CATON. *Builders' Photo, Messrs Lobnitz & Co.*

Nine assigned to Fleet Target Service, Atlantic and Mediterranean Fleets ; about 40 to Training and Experimental Establishments, as detailed on a later page. Disposal of rest not known.

Belong to "Castle," "Mersey," and "Strath" types. Usually as follows :—(*a*) 665 tons, 11 kts. speed, 204 tons coal ; (*b*) 547 tons, 10½ kts., 164 tons coal ; (*c*) 429 tons, 10 kts., 95 tons coal. Guns : Usually 1—12 pdr., but a few have 1—4 inch. Above illustrations typical of appearance.

Admiralty Drifters.

In addition to those detailed on next page as Tenders to Training Establishments, about 60 other Drifters are assigned as Tenders to the Atlantic, Home and Mediterranean Fleets. Displace 199 tons. Speed : 9 kts. Gun : Usually 1—6 pdr. Coal : 34-39 tons.

Surveying Service.

BEAUFORT (ex *Ambleside*, 1919), **COLLINSON** (ex *Amersham*, 1919), by Ailsa S.B. Co. **FITZROY** (ex *Pinner*, ex *Portreath*, 1919), **FLINDERS** (ex *Radley*, 1919), by Lobnitz & Co. **KELLET** (ex *Uppingham*, 1919), **CROZIER** (ex *Verwood*, ex *Ventnor*, 1919), by Simons & Co. Converted Twin Screw Minesweepers of "Hunt Class." 800 tons. Dimensions : 231 (*o.a.*) × 28½ × 7½ feet. Guns : 1—3 pdr. I.H.P. 2200 = 16 kts. Machinery : Vertical triple expansion. 2 screws. Boilers : Babcock or Yarrow. Coal : 185 tons.

ENDEAVOUR.

ENDEAVOUR (Fairfield, 1912). 1280 tons. Dimensions : 200 × 34 × 10 feet. Guns : 1—3 pdr., 2 Maxims. H.P. 1100 = 13 kts. Coal :] 221 tons. Complement, 44. Specially built for survey.

RESEARCH (1888). 520 tons. Guns : 1—old 7 pdr. M.L. Speed about 9½ kts.

SEALARK (1878). 900 tons. Speed about 9-10 kts.

TRITON (1882). 410 tons. Guns : 1—old 7 pdr. M.L. Speed, 9 kts.

Surveying Service—*Continued.*

DAISY (1911) & **ESTHER** (1912) 600 tons. (On surveying service at present.)

MERLIN (1901). 1070 tons. **MUTINE** (1900). 980 tons. Guns : 2—3 pdr., 2 M.G. All about 13½ kts. Belleville boilers. Coal : *about* 160-203 tons.

HEARTY (1885). 1300 tons. Guns : 4—3 pdr. H.P. 2100 = 14 kts.

For Sloop *Fantome*, on Surveying Service, see Australian Navy Section.

Fishery Protection Vessels.

Kilbeggan	*Kilclogher*
Kilfree	*Kilmalcolm*
Kilclief	

Above Patrol Gunboats for Fisheries Protection Service. All are described on an earlier page.

Coastguard Cruisers.

SAFEGUARD (Day, Summers, 1914). 875 tons. Dimensions : 160 × 29 × 10⅜ feet. H.P. 1350 = 15 kts. Guns : 2—3 pdr. Coal : 170 tons. Complement, 39.

Builders' photo, Messrs. Hall Russell & Co.

WATCHFUL (Hall, Russell, 1912). 612 tons. Dimensions : 154 × 25 × 11¾ feet. H.P. 800 = 11.5 kts. Guns : 2—3 pdr. Coal : 150 tons. Complement, 32.

ARGON.

ARGON (ex *Argus*, 1905). 380 tons. H.P. 650 = 12.25 kts. Guns : 2—6 pdr. Coal : 55 tons.

SQUIRREL (1905). 230 tons. H.P. 300 = 10 kts. Guns : 2—3 pdr. Coal : 44 tons.

JULIA (ex *Maretanza*, 1897). 310 tons. H.P. 650. Guns : 2 old 7 pdr. M.L. Coal : 53 tons.

ROYAL INDIAN MARINE.

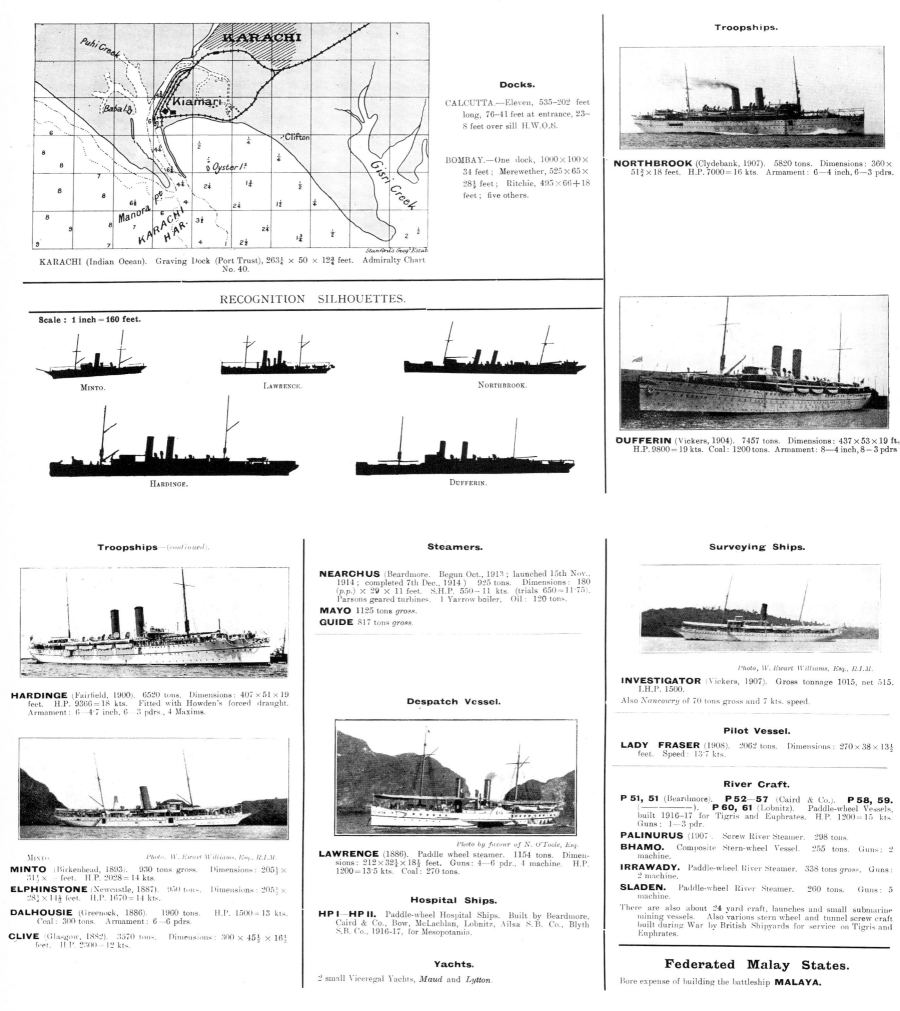

KARACHI (Indian Ocean). Graving Dock (Port Trust), $263\frac{1}{4} \times 50 \times 12\frac{3}{4}$ feet. Admiralty Chart No. 40.

Docks.

CALCUTTA.—Eleven, 535–202 feet long, 76–41 feet at entrance, 23–8 feet over sill H.W.O.S.

BOMBAY.—One dock, $1000 \times 100 \times 34$ feet; Merewether, $525 \times 65 \times 28\frac{1}{2}$ feet; Ritchie, $495 \times 66 + 18$ feet; five others.

Troopships.

NORTHBROOK (Clydebank, 1907). 5820 tons. Dimensions: $360 \times 51\frac{3}{4} \times 18$ feet. H.P. 7000 = 16 kts. Armament: 6—4 inch, 6—3 pdrs.

RECOGNITION SILHOUETTES.

Scale : 1 inch = 160 feet.

MINTO.

LAWRENCE.

NORTHBROOK.

HARDINGE.

DUFFERIN.

DUFFERIN (Vickers, 1904). 7457 tons. Dimensions: $437 \times 53 \times 19$ ft. H.P. 9800 = 19 kts. Coal: 1200 tons. Armament: 8—4 inch, 8—3 pdrs.

Troopships—(continued).

HARDINGE (Fairfield, 1900). 6520 tons. Dimensions: $407 \times 51 \times 19$ feet. H.P. 9366 = 18 kts. Fitted with Howden's forced draught. Armament: 6—4.7 inch, 6—3 pdrs., 4 Maxims.

Minto

Photo, W. Ewart Williams, Esq., R.I.M.

MINTO (Birkenhead, 1893). 930 tons gross. Dimensions: $205\frac{1}{2} \times 31\frac{1}{4} \times$ feet. H.P. 2028 = 14 kts.

ELPHINSTONE (Newcastle, 1887). 950 tons. Dimensions: $205\frac{1}{4} \times 28\frac{1}{4} \times 14\frac{1}{2}$ feet. H.P. 1670 = 14 kts.

DALHOUSIE (Greenock, 1886). 1960 tons. H.P. 1500 = 13 kts. Coal: 300 tons. Armament: 6—6 pdrs.

CLIVE (Glasgow, 1882). 3570 tons. Dimensions: $300 \times 45\frac{1}{2} \times 16\frac{1}{4}$ feet. H.P. 2300 = 12 kts.

Steamers.

NEARCHUS (Beardmore. Begun Oct., 1913; launched 15th Nov., 1914; completed 7th Dec., 1914.) 925 tons. Dimensions: 180 (p.p.) $\times$ 29 $\times$ 11 feet. S.H.P. 550 = 11 kts. (trials 650 = 11.75). Parsons geared turbines. 1 Yarrow boiler. Oil: 120 tons.

MAYO 1125 tons gross.

GUIDE 817 tons gross.

Despatch Vessel.

Photo by favour of N. O'Toole, Esq.

LAWRENCE (1886). Paddle wheel steamer. 1154 tons. Dimensions: $212 \times 32\frac{1}{4} \times 18\frac{1}{4}$ feet. Guns: 4—6 pdr., 4 machine. H.P. 1200 = 13.5 kts. Coal: 270 tons.

Hospital Ships.

HP I—HP II. Paddle-wheel Hospital Ships. Built by Beardmore, Caird & Co., Bow, McLachlan, Lobnitz, Ailsa S.B. Co., Blyth S.B. Co., 1916-17, for Mesopotamia.

Yachts.

2 small Viceregal Yachts, *Maud* and *Lytton*.

Surveying Ships.

Photo, W. Ewart Williams, Esq., R.I.M.

INVESTIGATOR (Vickers, 1907). Gross tonnage 1015, net 515. I.H.P. 1500.

Also *Nancowry* of 70 tons gross and 7 kts. speed.

Pilot Vessel.

LADY FRASER (1908). 2062 tons. Dimensions: $270 \times 38 \times 13\frac{1}{2}$ feet. Speed: 13.7 kts.

River Craft.

P 51, 51 (Beardmore). P 52—57 (Caird & Co.). P 58, 59. (————). P 60, 61 (Lobnitz). Paddle-wheel Vessels, built 1916-17 for Tigris and Euphrates. H.P. 1200 = 15 kts. Guns : 1—3 pdr.

PALINURUS (1907). Screw River Steamer. 298 tons.

BHAMO. Composite Stern-wheel Vessel. 255 tons. Guns : 2 machine.

IRRAWADY. Paddle-wheel River Steamer. 338 tons gross. Guns : 2 machine.

SLADEN. Paddle-wheel River Steamer. 260 tons. Guns : 5 machine.

There are also about 24 yard craft, launches and small submarine mining vessels. Also various stern wheel and tunnel screw craft built during War by British Shipyards for service on Tigris and Euphrates.

Federated Malay States.

Bore expense of building the battleship MALAYA.

COMMONWEALTH OF AUSTRALIA.

ROYAL AUSTRALIAN NAVY.

Personnel :   *Minister of the Navy.*—The Rt. Hon. Sir Joseph Cook, P.C.

Navy Yards.

COCKATOO ISLAND (SYDNEY), with one completed slip, for building Light Cruisers and another large slip building. Employees about 1500–2000. May be closed down owing to labour troubles.

GARDEN ISLAND. Repairs only.

Also a Government yard at Walsh Island, N.S.W., devoted to mercantile construction.

Private Docks, &c.

ADELAIDE (S. AUSTRALIA). Commercial harbour, 7 miles from the town.

BRISBANE (QUEENSLAND, AUSTRALIA). 25 miles up river. Navigable for ships drawing 20 feet. Coaling station. Dry dock : 431½ × 55 × 19 feet.

FREMANTLE (W. AUSTRALIA). Dry dock, originally designed as 594 feet long, but enlarged to 694 feet and may now be 910 × 100 × 34 feet (L.W.O.S.), divisible into two sections (*Dreadnought*).

HOBART (TASMANIA). Coaling station. Anchorage average, 10 fathoms.

KING GEORGE SOUND (W. AUSTRALIA). Coaling station. Fortified.

SYDNEY (N.S.W., AUSTRALIA). Fortified coaling station and base for R.A.N. Harbour excellent. Bar 27 feet at low water. Dry docks : (Sutherland) 638 × 84 × 32 feet (*Dreadnought*), (Fitzroy) 477 × 59 × 21½ feet. Woolwich dock (private) 675 × 83 × 28 feet (*Dreadnought*), and four smaller.

MELBOURNE. Commercial harbour. One dry dock : 470 × 80 × 27 feet, and three smaller. Port Phillip has an area of 800 square miles.

NEWCASTLE (N.S.W., AUSTRALIA). Government floating dock, 426 × 64 × 25 feet. (9500 tons).

T.B.D. & SUBMARINE SILHOUETTES (E. L. KING).

Scale : 125 feet to 1 inch.

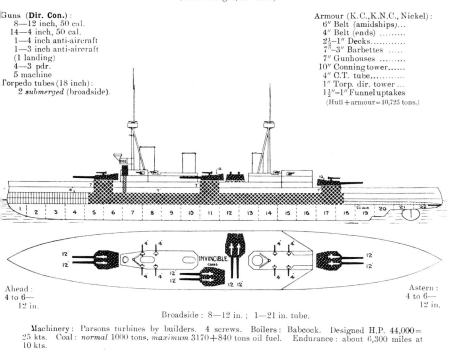

Anzac (*Leader*).

Parramatta *class* t.b.d.

J 1—J 5 (*Submarines*).

J 7 (*Submarine*).

RECOGNITION SILHOUETTES.

RECOGNITION SILHOUETTES.

Scale : 1 inch = 160 feet.

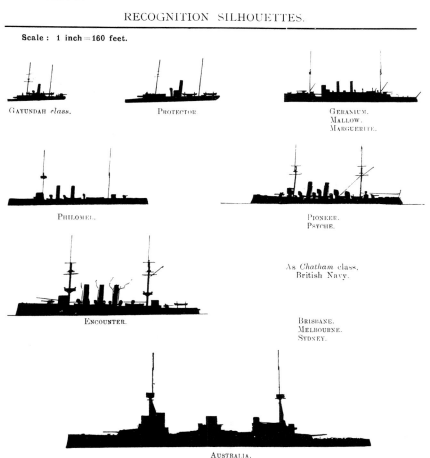

GAYUNDAH *class.*

PROTECTOR

GERANIUM.
MALLOW.
MARGUERITE.

PHILOMEL.

PIONEER.
PSYCHE.

ENCOUNTER.

As *Chatham* class,
British Navy.

BRISBANE.
MELBOURNE.
SYDNEY.

AUSTRALIA.

1910 BATTLE-CRUISER (25 kts.)

(INDEFATIGABLE TYPE—1 SHIP.)

AUSTRALIA (Oct. 25th, 1911).

Normal displacement, 18,800 tons (about 21,300 *full load.*) Complement, 820. (Flagship.)

Length (*waterline*). feet. Beam, 80 feet. { Mean draught, 26½ feet. } Length, (*p.p.*) 555 feet, (*over all*), 590 feet.
{ Max. draught, 30 feet. }

Guns (Dir. Con.) :
8—12 inch, 50 cal.
14—4 inch, 50 cal.
1—4 inch anti-aircraft
1—3 inch anti-aircraft
(1 landing)
4—3 pdr.
5 machine
Torpedo tubes (18 inch) :
2 *submerged* (broadside).

Armour (K.C., K.N.C., Nickel) :
6″ Belt (amidships)...
4″ Belt (ends) ....
2½–1″ Decks............
7″–3″ Barbettes .....
7″ Gunhouses ....
10″ Conning tower......
4″ C.T. tube...........
1″ Torp. dir. tower ...
1½″–1″ Funnel uptakes
(Hull + armour = 10,725 tons.)

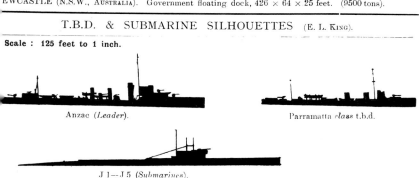

AUSTRALIA. (Topmasts and topgallant masts as Silhouette).

Ahead :
4 to 6—
12 in.

Astern :
4 to 6—
12 in.

Broadside : 8—12 in. ; 1—21 in. tube.

Machinery : Parsons turbines by builders. 4 screws. Boilers : Babcock. Designed H.P. 44,000 = 25 kts. Coal : *normal* 1000 tons, *maximum* 3170 + 840 tons oil fuel. Endurance : about 6,300 miles at 10 kts.

Armour Notes.—Main belt 12 feet deep, closed by 4″ bulkheads and with 1″ deck above. Lower deck 1″ amidships, 2½″ at ends outside belt. For more detailed particulars, r. *New Zealand*, British Navy Section.

Internal Protection.

Name	Builder	Machinery	Laid down	Completed	Trials (mean): 30 hrs. at ⅔ 8 hrs. full power		Boilers	Best recent speed
Australia	J. Brown, Clydebank	J. Brown, Clydebank	June '10	June '13	30,800 = 23·5	48,422 = 26·89	Babcock	

General Notes.—An improved *Indefatigable*, and a sister-ship to *New Zealand*, described on a previous page.

AUSTRALIAN LIGHT CRUISERS.

(CHATHAM CLASS—4 SHIPS.)

MELBOURNE (May, 1912), **SYDNEY** (Aug., 1912), **BRISBANE** (Sept., 1915), and **ADELAIDE** (July, 1918).

Displacement, 5400 tons. Complement, 390–392.

Length (p.p.), 430 feet. Beam, 49⅝ feet. { Mean draught, 15¾ feet. / Max. „ 17¾–18½ feet. } Length (over all), 457 feet.

Guns (**Dir. Con.**) :
8—6 inch, 50 cal.
1—3 inch anti-aircraft
4 —3 pdr.
4 machine
Torpedo tubes (21 inch) :
2 broadside (submerged)

Armour (Hadfield :
2″ Deck (on slopes)

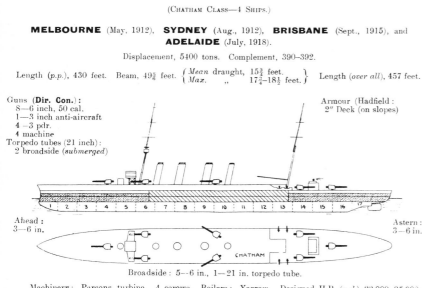

Ahead :
3—6 in.

Astern :
3—6 in.

Broadside : 5—6 in., 1—21 in. torpedo tube.

Machinery : Parsons turbine. 4 screws. Boilers : Yarrow. Designed H.P. (n.d.) 22,000, 25,000 f.d.=25 kts. Coal : normal 750 tons, maximum about 1240 tons+about 260 tons oil fuel. Brisbane, 1196 coal+260 oil.

Gunnery Notes.—Electric ammunition hoists.

Torpedo Notes.—7 torpedoes carried. 4 or more searchlights.

Armour Notes.—Internal protection by longitudinal and transverse bulkheads. Double bottom extends over magazine and machinery spaces. Conning Tower in Sydney (and others) replaced by revolving platform carrying a small aeroplane or seaplane.

Engineering Notes.—500 r.p.m.=full power. Boilers : 3 drum small tube type. Uniflux condensers.

Name	Builder	Machinery	Laid down	Completed	Trials : 30 hrs. at ¾	8 hrs. full power	Boilers	Best recent speed
Melbourne	Cammell-Laird	Cammell-Laird	Apl. '11	Jan. '13		25,800=25·7	Yarrow	
Sydney	L. & Glasgow	L. & Glasgow	Feb. '11	Jun. '13	22,400=	25,572=25·7	„	
Brisbane	Sydney	Vickers	Jan. '13	…			„	
Adelaide	Sydney		1915	…				

General Notes.—Practically same design as British Chatham class. Served during War in North Sea.

MELBOURNE. Can be distinguished from Sydney by director tower placed over control top on foremast.

ENCOUNTER (1902, transferred 1912). 5880 tons. Complement, 457. Dimensions : 376 (o.a.) × 56 × 20⅔ feet (max draught). Armament : 11—6 inch, 4—12 pdr., 4—3 pdr., 3 M.G., 1 landing. 2—18 inch tubes, sub. Designed H.P. 12,500=21 kts. 12 Dürr boilers. Coal : 1300 tons max.

AUSTRALIAN NAVY.

Obsolete Light Cruisers.

Photo, Symonds & Co.

PSYCHE (1897), 2135 tons and **PIONEER** (1899), 2200 tons. Complement, 234. Armament : Psyche, 8—4 inch, 3 M.G. Pioneer has only 4—3 pdr. Tubes : 2—14 inch above water. Designed H.P. 7000 (f.d.)=20 kts. (not over 16 kts. at present). Coal : 520–540 tons.

PHILOMEL (Jan., 1890). 2575 tons. Complement, 222. Dimensions (o.a.) : 278 × 41 × 16⅜ (max.) feet. Armament : 1—3 pdr. Torpedo Tubes : 3—14 inch above water. Armour : 2½″ Deck. Designed H.P. 7500=19 kts. (f.d.) Coal : 450 tons.

12 Destroyers.

No.	Type	Date	Displacement	H.P.	Speed	Oil	Complement	Tubes	Max. draug't
1	Anzac	'16-'17	tons 1666	36,000 t	kts. 34	tons 416/515	116	4	12
5	Admiralty "S"	'17-'19	1075	27,000 t	36	254/301	90	4	12?
3	Swan	'15-'16	700	11,300 t	26	173 189/157	69	3	8½–9
3	Parramatta	'09-'12		10,600 t					

Flotilla Leader.

1 Marksman (later) Type.

1 Denny : **Anzac.** 1,666 tons. Dimensions : 315 ft. (p.p.), 325 ft. (o.a.) × 31 ft. 10 in. × 12 ft. 11½ in. (max. draught aft). Guns : 4—4 inch, 2—2 pdr. pom-poms, 1 M.G. Torpedo tubes : 4—21 inch in 2 rev. deck mountings. Machinery : Brown-Curtis turbines. 3 screws. Boilers : Yarrow small tube. Designed S.H.P. 36,000 = 34 kts. Trials : Oil, 416/515 tons = about 2500 miles at 15 kts. Complement, 116. Begun January 31st, 1916. Launched January 11th, 1917. Completed April 24th, 1917. Begun under Emergency War Programme and presented to Australia, 1919. Sister to Parker, Seymour, &c., of British Navy, but fo'xle of Anzac is 2½ feet higher, and she has a few other small differences.

AUSTRALIAN NAVY.—DESTROYERS & TORPEDO BOATS.

Destroyers—*Continued.*

5 "Admiralty S" type.

2 *Beardmore*: **Tasmania, Tattoo.**

1 *Doxford*: **Success.**

1 *Scott*: **Swordsman.**

1 *Swan Hunter*: **Stalwart.**

1075 tons. Dimensions: 265 (*p.p.*), 276 (*o.a., Success* 277) × 26¾ × 9 feet (*mean*) draught. Armament: 3—4 inch (Mk. IV with 30° elevation), 1—2 pdr. pom-pom, 4—21 inch tubes in two twin deck mountings, 1—24 inch searchlight controlled in unison with guns. May have D.C. Thrower and High Speed type of P.Vs. Machinery: Brown-Curtis all-geared turbines. 2 screws. Boilers: 3 Yarrow small tube. Designed S.H.P. 27000, = 36 kts. Fuel (oil only): 254/301 tons = *about* 2000 miles at 15 kts. Complement, 90.

	Begun.	*Launch.*	*Comp.*
Tasmania ..	18/12/17	22/11/18	29/1/19
Tattoo	21/12/17	28/12/18	7/4/19
Success	....	29/6/18	4/19
Swordsman ..	....	28/12/18	3/19
Stalwart	4/18	23/10/18	4/19

Notes.—Built under Emergency War Programme and presented to Australian Navy, 1919. For any further notes, refer to description of "S Class" in British Navy Section.

Destroyers—*Continued.*

WARREGO.

Parramatta, Yarra (1910, ***Warrego*** (1911), ***Huon*** (ex *Derwent*, 1914), ***Swan*** (Dec., 1915), ***Torrens*** (Aug., (1915). Dimensions: Length (*o.a.*) 250¾ *Houn, Swan, Torrens*, 245¾ *Yarra*, 246 *Parramatta, Warrego* × 24¼ × 8 feet. Armaments: 1—4 inch, 3—12 pdrs., 3—18 inch tubes. Parsons turbines. Yarrow boilers. Radius: 2500 kts. Oil fuel. *Yarra* by Denny, Dumbarton: *Parramatta* and *Warrego* by London & Glasgow Engineering Co., *Warrego* being re-erected at Cockatoo N.Y., Sydney. *Swan, Huon* and *Torrens* built at Cockatoo N.Y., Sydney. Are modified British "I" Class boats.

AUSTRALIAN NAVY—SUBMARINES.

6 Submarines.

Note: *AE1* and *AE2* were transferred to RAN at beginning of the war. Both of British "E" class and both lost – *AE1* off Bismarck Achipelago in September 1914 and *AE2* in Sea of Marmara April 1915.

No.	Class	Begun	Comp.	Displacement	B.H.P. / E H.P.	Speed	Endurance	Tubes	Comp't.
				Tons.		kts.			
6	*J 7*	1916	1917	1200/1760	3600/1400	19/9·5	4,000 miles at 12 kts.	6	44
	J 1—5	1915	1916	1260/1820					

"J Class"—6 Boats.

6 *Admiralty* type: ***J 7*** (Feb., 1917), ***J5*** (Sept., 1915), both by Devonport D.Y. ***J4*** (Feb., 1916), ***J3*** (Dec., 1915), both by Pembroke D.Y. ***J 2*** (Nov., 1915), ***J 1*** (Nov., 1915), both by Portsmouth D.Y. *J 1—5*, completed April-Aug., 1916; *J 7*, Nov., 1917. Dimensions: 270 (*p.p.*), 274¾ (*o.a.*) × 23½ × 14 feet. Armament: 1—4 inch gun and 6—18 inch tubes (4 bow, 2 beam). Surface machinery: 3 sets of Vickers 12 cylinder solid injection, direct reversing 4 cycle 1200 B.H.P. Diesel engines (14½ in. bore × 15 in. stroke, 380 r.p.m.). Oil: 80/91 tons. Built under Emergency Programme as "Bight Patrols." *J 6* lost during War. Presented to Australia, 1918. Other details as Table.

Fleet Sweeping Vessels (Sloops).

See illustration of *Valerian* and *Primrose*—British Navy Section.

GERANIUM (Greenock & Grangemouth Co. Begun Aug., 1915; launched 8th Nov., 1915; completed March, 1916). **MARGUERITE** (Dunlop Bremner. Begua July, 1915; launched 23rd Nov., 1915; completed Jan., 1916). Fleet Sweeping Vessels (Sloops) of *Arabis* type. 1250 tons. Dimensions: 255¼ (*p.p.*), 267¾ (*o.a.*) × 33½ × 10½ feet (*mean*), 11¾ (*max.* draught). Guns: 1—4·7 inch, 2—3 pdr. (AA. in *Geranium*). Designed I.H.P. 2000=17 kts. Trials: *Geranium*, 2312=17: *Marguerite*, 2309=16·1. Machinery: boilers, screws, as *Mallow*, opposite. Coal: 260 tons=2050 miles at 15 kts. Complement, 79. Built under Emergency War Programme; presented to Australian Navy, 1919.

Fleet Sweeping Vessel (Sloop).

See illustration for *Valerian*—British Navy Section.

MALLOW (Barclay Curle. Launched 13th July, 1915; completed Sept., 1916.) Fleet Sweeping Vessel (Sloop) of *Acacia* type. 1200 tons. Dimensions: 250 (*p.p.*), 262½ (*o.a.*) × 33 × 10¼ feet (*mean*), 11¼ (*max.* load). Guns: 1—12 pdr. (12 cwt.), 2—3 pdr. AA. I.H.P. 1800=17 kts. Trials: 2328=16·3 kts. Machinery: 1 set triple expansion inverted and 2 cylindrical boilers. Coal: 250 tons=2000 miles at 15 kts. Complement, 77. Built under Emergency War Programme; presented to the Australian Navy, 1919.

Sloop (Surveying Ship).

UNA (ex-German Surveying Ship *Komet*, built about 1911, captured 1914). 1438 tons. Dimensions: 210½ × 31 × 15¾ feet. Guns: 3—4 inch, 2—12 pdr. H.P. 1300 = 16 kts. Coal; 270 tons. Complement, 114.

FANTOME (1901, lent from Royal Navy, 1915). 1070 tons. Guns: 2—4 inch, 1—3 pdr., 2 M.G. Speed, 13½ kts. Coal: 195 tons. For Surveying Service. Complement, 135.

AUSTRALIAN NAVY.—*Continued*.

Obsolete Gunboats.

PROTECTOR (Elswick, 1884). 920 tons. Guns: 3—4 inch. 2—12 pdr., 4—3 pdr. H.P. 1600 = 14 kts. originally. Re-boilered 1910-11. Tender to Williamstown Gunnery School. (*South Australia*).

GAYUNDAH (Elswick, 1884, reported to have been re-built at Cockatoo N.Y., Sydney, 1914). **PALUMA** (Elswick 1884) 360 tons. Guns: 1—4.7, 2—12 pdr. Speed originally: 10.5 kts.

Also *Cerberus*, now Naval Depot at Williamstown, with Cruiser *Psyche* and 1st Class T.B. *Countess of Hopetoun* and *Coogee, Gannet, Gayundah, Protector* as tenders.

Submarine Depot Ship.

PLATYPUS (J. Brown, Clydebank. Begun Sept. 2nd, 1914; launched Oct. 28th, 1916; completed Mar., 1917.) 2,460 tons. Dimensions: 310 (*w.l*), 325 (*o.a*) × 44 × 15⅔ feet (*max*. draught). Guns: *nil*? I.H.P. 3600 = 15½ kts. Reciprocating engines and cylindrical boilers. 2 screws. Coal: 450 tons. Complement, 357.

Fuel Ships (R.F.A.)

BILOELA. Fleet Collier, built at Cockatoo Island D.Y. Completed 1919. No details known.

KURUMBA (Swan Hunter. Begun Sept., 1915; launched Sept., 1916; completed Jan., 1917; machinery by Wallsend.) Oil Tanker. 8359 tons. Dimensions: 365 (*p.p*), 377¼¼ (*o.a*) × 45½ × 23¼ feet *max*. load draught. Guns: 3 (calibre not known). I.H.P. 2000 = 10 kts. Triple expansion engines and S.E. cylindrical boilers. 2 screws. Fuel: *max*., 688 tons coal + 257 tons oil, exclusive of cargo. Complement, 65–100.

Armed Patrol Vessels.

COOGEE (————). 762 tons *gross*. H.P. = 16 kts. Guns 1—4·7 inch, 2—3 pdr. Coal: 210 tons.

GANNET (ex *Penguin*, ————). 208 tons *gross*. H.P. 420 = kts. Guns: 1—12 pdr. Coal: 87 tons.

MOORILYAN (————). 1349 tons *gross*. H.P. 2330 = 14·4 kts. Guns 1—4·7 inch Q.F., 2—3 pdr. Hotchkiss. Coal: 280 tons.

SLEUTH (ex *Ena*). 108 tons. H.P. 160 = kts. Guns: 1—3 pdr.

Miscellaneous.

NUSA. 64 tons. Ex-German ship seized at Kawieng, 1914.
SUMATRA. No details known.
FRANKLIN (ex-*Adele*). 288 tons. Training Ship for Cadets. Tender to R.A.N. College, Jervis Bay.
TINGIRA. Training Ship.

DOMINION OF NEW ZEALAND.

Battle Cruiser **NEW ZEALAND** was built at the expense of the Dominion. The annual subvention of £100,000 paid by the Dominion is to be devoted to the maintenance of the Light Cruiser **CANTERBURY** and a Training Ship of 3000 tons.

Docks.

AUCKLAND. Coaling station. Excellent harbour; average 40 feet deep. Dry dock (Calliope): 521 × 66 × 33 feet. Also one smaller, able to take torpedo craft.
PORT CHALMERS (S. ISLAND). Otago dry dock, 500 × 70 × 21 feet, *and another smaller*.

Sloop.

FIREBRAND (ex *Torch*, 1894). Transferred from British Navy, 1917. 960 tons. Armament: 4—4 inch, 4—3 pdr., 2 M.G. Speed, 13·4 kts. Coal, 130 tons.

Gunboat.

(*Training Service.*)

AMOKURA (Greenock, 1889). 805 tons. Guns: 6—4 inch, 3—3 pdr. H.P. 1200 = 13 kts. Coal: 105 tons.

Miscellaneous.

A yacht, **HINEMOA,** and two small mining vessels. Also cable ship, **TUTANEKAI.**

DOMINION OF CANADA.

Minister of Marine: Hon. Col. C. C. Ballantyne.
Personnel: *Uniforms*: As British Navy.

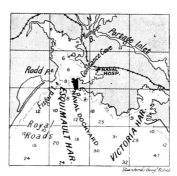

Pacific:—

ESQUIMAULT.—Naval Dockyard. Admiralty Chart No 576. (For Docks, see below.)

Atlantic:—

HALIFAX (NOVA SCOTIA).—Formerly Dockyard. Coaling Station. Anchorage averages 13 fathoms. Examination Base during War. (For Docks, see below.)

Private Shipyards.

CANADIAN VICKERS CO. (MONTREAL).—Affiliated to Messrs. Vickers, Ltd., Barrow-in-Furness. No details available of this establishment. "H" class Submarines built here during the War. For large Floating Dock, see Docks below.
MESSRS. YARROW, LTD. (LANG'S COVE, ESQUIMAULT).—Branch of Messrs. Yarrow, Ltd., Scotstoun, N.B. Can build ships up to 2000 tons. Slipway 315 × 30 feet (3000 tons capacity). Fitting-out Wharf 500 feet long. Repair shops; one 60-ton sheer legs; one 10-ton floating derrick. Yard covers eight acres, with Government Dock adjoining.

Docks.

COLLINGWOOD. Collingwood Dry Dock Co. 524 × 60 × 15½ feet.
ESQUIMAULT. Government Dock 450–480 × 65 × 26¼ feet. Also 2400 tons patent slip.
ST. JOHNS (NEW BRUNSWICK). At Courtenay Bay, new dock *projected*, 1150 × 125 × 40 feet (*over sills*).
HALIFAX (NOVA SCOTIA). Dry dock: Halifax Graving Dock Co., 572 × 89 × 29 feet (*Dreadnought*).
KINGSTON (ONTARIO). Government dock, 290 × 55 × 18 feet.
MONTREAL. Duke of Connaught floating dock (Proprietors, Canadian Vickers Co.), 600 × 100 × 28½ feet. (*Dreadnought*.) Two other private docks, 400 × 45 × 10 feet.
PORT ARTHUR. Dry dock. 700 × 74¼ × 15½ feet.
PORT DALHOUSIE. Muir Bros'. dock, 260 × 16 × 10 feet.
OWEN SOUND. Dock, 300 × 60 × 12 feet.
QUEBEC: Canadian Government dry dock, 1150 × 120 × 30 feet, divisible into two docks, 650 and 500 feet long respectively. (*Dreadnought*.) Levis dock, 600 × 62 × 20½ feet. Three floating docks, 1600, 2200, and 2500 tons lift.

A: ROYAL CANADIAN NAVY.

RECOGNITION SILHOUETTES.

Scale : 1 inch = 160 feet.

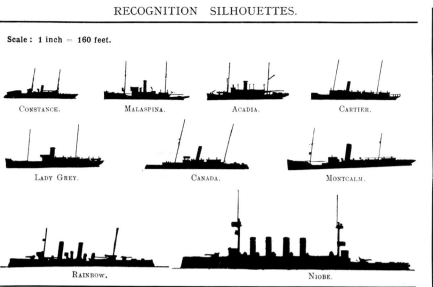

CONSTANCE. MALASPINA. ACADIA. CARTIER.

LADY GREY. CANADA. MONTCALM.

RAINBOW. NIOBE.

Scale : 1 inch = 80 feet.

SUBMARINES.

H 14, H 15, CC 1, CC 2

TORPEDO BOATS AND SUBMARINES.

Grilse (1913). 225 tons. Dimensions : 207 × 18½ × 6 feet. Guns : 2—12 pdr. 1 torpedo tube. Designed H.P. 6000 = 30 kts. Oil : 53 tons.

Tuna (1902). 150 tons. Dimensions : 153 × 15 × 5 feet. Guns : 1—3 pdr. Torpedo tubes : 2. Designed H.P. 2000 = 24 kts. Coal : 27 tons.

4 Submarines.

2 *Holland* type : **H14, H15** (1918). Displacements : 364 tons *surface*, 435 tons *submerged*. Dimensions : 150 × 15¼ × 12¾ feet. Torpedo tubes : 4—18 inch (bow). B.H.P. 480 = 13 kts. *on surface*: H.P. 320 11 kts. *submerged* (for about one hour continuous running). Complement 20—22. Built under Emergency War Programme and presented to Canadian Navy, 1919.

1 *Holland* type : **CC 2** (Seattle Con. & D.D. Co, 1914). Displacements : 310 tons *on surface*, 373 tons *submerged*. Dimensions : 157 ft. 6½ in. × 14 ft. 11½ in. × feet. Torpedo tubes : 3—18 inch. H.P. 600 *on surface* = 13 kts.; 260 *submerged* = 10½ kts.

1 *Holland* type : **CC 1** (Seattle Con. & D.D. Co., 1911). Displacements : 313 tons *on surface*, 373 tons *submerged*. Dimensions : 144 ft. 3½ in. × 14 ft. × 11 ft. 6 in. Torpedo tubes : 5—18 inch. H.P. 600 *on surface* = 13 kts.; 260 *submerged* = 10½ kts.

Note.—Above two boats were begun for Chilean Navy as *Antofagasta* and *Iquique*. They were purchased by Canada just before outbreak of war.

Submarine Depot Ship.

SHEARWATER (1900). Sloop. 980 tons. Guns : 4—4 inch, 4—3 pdr., 2 machine. H.P. 1400 (*f.d.*) = 13¼ kts. Coal : 160 tons. Lent from Royal Navy, 1914.

Sloop.

ALGERINE (1895). 1050 tons. Guns : 4—3 pdr., 3 M.G. H.P. 1400 = 13½ kts. Boilers : cylindrical. Coal 160 tons. Lent from Royal Navy.

Armed Patrol Vessels.

Belongs to the Department of Naval Service.

CANADA (1904). 780 tons. Guns : 2—12 pdr., 2—3 pdr. H.P. 1600 = 14 kts. Coal : 110 tons. (F.)

FLORENCE (———). Guns : 1—3 pdr. Q.F. Speed, 12 kts.

Cruiser.

(Depot Ship—is dismantled.)

NIOBE (1897, transferred 1913). 11,000 tons. Complement —. Guns and torpedo tubes : *Is disarmed.* Armour : Deck, 4″; Casemates, 6″. Designed H.P. 16,500 = 20·25 kts. Present speed : somewhere about 18 kts. or less, owing to damage received by stranding in 1914. Coal : 2000 tons.

Light Cruiser.

(Training Ship for Pacific Coast.)

RAINBOW (1891, bought 1909). 3600 tons. Complement —. Guns and torpedo tubes : *Is disarmed.* Deck : 2″. Designed H.P. 9000 = 19·75 kts. Present speed : about 12 kts. Coal : 560 tons.

HOCHELAGA (———). Guns : 1—12 pdr. Speed, 12 kts.

Belongs to Department of Customs.

MARGARET (1913). 950 tons. Guns : 2—6 pdr. Designed H.P. 2000 = 15½ kts, *max.* speed. Coal : 200 tons.

PREMIER (———). 374 tons *gross*. Guns : 1—6 pdr. Speed, 13 kts.

SEAGULL. Patrol Depot Ship. No details known.

STADACONA (———). Guns : 1—4 inch Q.F. Speed, 12 kts.

STARLING (———). Guns : 1—3 pdr. Speed, 12 kts.

Trawlers and Drifters.

Twenty-seven of these were loaned to U.S. Navy for war duties ; others served with H.M. Navy during the war. No other details available.

B: CANADIAN GOVERNMENT VESSELS.

(From Official List. Arranged *alphabetically*. All speeds are *maximum*.)

Department of the Naval Service.

Note.

Vessels marked (H) were engaged in 1915 on Hydrographic Survey duty, and those marked (F) on Fishery Protection.

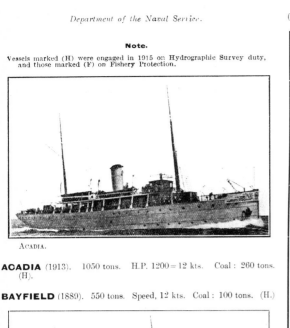

ACADIA.

ACADIA (1913). 1050 tons. H.P. 1200 = 12 kts. Coal : 260 tons. (H.)

BAYFIELD (1889). 550 tons. Speed, 12 kts. Coal : 100 tons. (H.)

CARTIER (1910). 850 tons. H.P. 830 = 12 kts. Coal : 150 tons. (H.)

Department of Marine and Fisheries (continued):—

EARL GREY (ex-Russian *Kanada*, ex-Canadian *Earl Grey*). (Vickers, 1909). 3400 tons. 250 × 47½ × 17¾ feet. H.P. 6000 = 17 kts. (did 18 on trial). Boilers : cylindrical Is specially built for ice-breaking.

LADY GREY.

LADY GREY (1906). 1080 tons. H.P. 2300 = 14 kts. Coal : 200 tons.
LADY LAURIER (1902). 1970 tons. H.P. 1800 = 13 kts. Coal : 175 tons.
LAMBTON (1906). 510 tons. Speed, 11 kts. Coal : 92 tons.

Photo, Lieut. Com. Saul, R.C.N.

MINTO (1899). 2070 tons. H.P. 2900 = 15½ kts. Coal : 290 tons.

Department of the Naval Service—Continued.

CONSTANCE.

CONSTANCE (1891). **CURLEW** (1892). 400 tons. Speed 10 kts. Coal : 46 tons. (F).

GAUSS (1901).

GULNARE (1893). 500 tons. Speed, 10 kts. Coal : 65 tons. (F.)
LILLOOET (1908). 760 tons. Speed, 11¾ kts. Coal : 140 tons. (H.)

Department of Marine and Fisheries (continued):—

MONTCALM (1904) & **CHAMPLAIN** (1904). 1432 tons. 243 × 40 × 18 feet. H.P. 3600 = 14 kts.

NEWINGTON (1889). 475 tons. Speed, 10 kts. Coal : 85 tons.
PRINCESS (1896). 850 tons. Speed, 11 kts. Coal : 124 tons.
QUADRA (1891). 1260 tons. Speed, 11 kts. Coal : 200 tons.
SIMCOE (1909). 1630 tons. Speed, 12½ kts. Coal : 100 tons.
STANLEY (1888). 1890 tons. Speed, 15½ kts. Coal : 250 tons.

Photo, "Syren and Shipping."

VIGILANT (Polson I.W., 1918). No details available.

Also 4 other ships, 1 steel-built and 3 wooden-built. *Wilfrid* (ex S.S. Wilfrid C., 1897), 90 tons *gross*, purchased 1918.

Department of the Naval Service—Continued.

MALASPINA.

MALASPINA (1913). 850 tons. Guns : 1—6 pdr. H.P. 1350 = 14½ kts. Coal : 200 tons. (F.)
PETREL (1902). 400 tons. Speed, 11 kts. Coal : 65 tons. (F.)
Also 4 other vessels under 500 tons, 1 iron-built, 1 composite-built, and 2 wooden-built.

Department of Marine and Fisheries.

ABERDEEN (1894). 1330 tons. H.P. 1510 = 13 kts. Coal : 125 tons.
ARANMORE (1890). 500 tons (net registered). Speed, 13 kts. Coal : 200 tons.
BELLECHASSE (1912). 576 tons. H.P. 900 = 11¼ kts. Coal : 24 tons.
CHAMPLAIN (1904). 800 tons. Speed, 11 kts. Coal : 60 tons.
DOLLARD (1913). 323 tons (net registered). Speed. . Oil fuel.
DRUID (1902). 1000 tons. Speed, 13 kts. Coal : 100 tons.
ESTEVAN (1912). 2100 tons. H.P. 1500 = 12½ kts. Coal : 350 tons.
GRENVILLE (1914). tons. H.P. 900 = kts. Coal : 100 tons.
J. D. HAZEN (1916). Ice breaker. 4900 tons. Dimensions : 275 × 57½ × 19 feet (*max* draught). Designed H.P. 8000 = kts. Coal : 1300 tons. Was transferred to Russia, 1915 or 1916, but is reported to have returned to Canada from the White Sea in 1918

(*Continued on next page.*)

Department of Militia and Defence :—

Three small vessels *Alfreda* (1904), 270 tons : *Armstrong* (1903), 230 tons ; and *Beryl* (1903), 45 tons. All 9½—8 kts. speed.

Department of Public Works.

TYRIAN (1869). 1300 tons. Speed, 10 kts. Coal : 340 tons.

Also *Speedy* (1896). 420 tons. 12 kts. speed.

Department of Railways and Canals :—

DURLEY CHINE (1913). 5173 tons. Speed, 10½ kts. Coal : 457 tons.
MULGRAVE (1892). 925 tons. Speed, 14 kts. Coal : 40 tons.
SCOTIA (1901). 2550 tons. Speed, 12 kts. Coal : 120 tons.
SHEEBA (1912). 5668 tons. Speed, 10½ kts. Coal : 340 tons.

(Also 13 other smaller vessels.)

Department of the Post Office :—

LADY EVELYN (1901). 680 tons. Speed, 14 kts.

Department of Agriculture :—

ALICE (1907). 550 tons. Speed, 11½ kts.

And 4 smaller vessels.

NEWFOUNDLAND.

PETREL. Armed Patrol Vessel. Speed about 10 kts. Guns : 1—3 pdr. Q.F.

Also old *Briton* (ex-*Calypso*) as Training Ship.

EGYPT.

| ENSIGN & JACK. | SULTAN'S STANDARD. |

Red ▨ White ☐

River Gunboats.

MELIK, SHEIK, SULTAN (1897). 140 tons. Speed, 11 kts. 2 screws in tunnels. Guns: 1—12 pdr. + 1—24 pdr. howitzer, 3 machine.

FATEH, NASIR, ZAFIR (1896). 128 tons. Stern-wheel Steamers. Speed, 12 kts. Guns: 1—12 pdr. + 1—24 pdr. howitzer, 4 machine.

ABU KLEA, HAFIR, METEMMEH, TAMAI. Stern-wheel Steamers. Guns: 1—22 pdr. in first; 1—9 pdr. in others.

Also 24 other River Steamers, built 1908-1885.

Transport, &c.

HARBIEH. 3700 tons. Also another steamer, **MUKBIR**, of 420 tons.

There are also 5 Paddle-wheel Steamers and about 15 Tugs.

Yacht.

MAHROUSSA (1865, rebuilt 1906). 3417 tons. Parsons turbine. H.P. 5500 = 17·5 kts.

Also 2 other small Yachts, and 3 Despatch Vessels.

MINOR AFRICAN NAVIES.

Customs Cruisers.

ABDUL MONEIM (Clydebank, 1902). 598 tons. Guns: 1—3 pdr. H.P. 1000 = 13 kts.

ABBAS (1891). 298 tons. Guns: 1—3 pdr. H.P. 650 = 13 kts.

NOUR-EL-BAHR (1884). 450 tons. Guns: 1—3 pdr. H.P. 870 = 13·5 kts.

RESHID. About 650 tons. Guns: 2—6 pdr.

Ports and Lights Administration.

AIDA. 723 tons. 1 gun. H.P. 130 = ?

Also about 25 launches and miscellaneous craft.

NYASALAND.

Gunboat.

GWENDOLEN (1897). 350 tons. Guns: 4—6 pdr., 4 machine. Speed 11½ kts.

Adventure, Pioneer. (1892). 30 tons. Speed, 12 kts.

Dove, Paddle Gunboat of 20 tons. Speed, 8 kts. Armed with 1 M.G.

NORTHERN RHODESIA.

Two Thornycroft motor patrol boats, **Mimi** & **Tou-tou,** originally intended to act as tenders to Greek seaplanes. They were requisitioned and shipped out to Lake Tanganyika in 1915, where they sank the German gunboat *Hedwig von Wissmann* and captured the *Kingani,* now British **Fi-fi.**

BRITISH EAST AFRICA.

Rose (1901). Speed, 8 kts.

M'Vita, Patrol Boat.

NATAL.

Before the war, only possessed a Tug, **Sir John** (1897), and a Surveying Ship, **Churchill.**

NIGERIA.

Empire, Kapelli, Kampala, Sarota, Valiant. Stern-wheel Gunboats, built about 1902. Speed, 10 kts.

Sultan (1907), *Etobe, Egori.* (1909). Stern-wheel Steamers. Speed, 8-10 kts.

Raven (1904). Stern-wheel Steamer. 260 tons. Speed, about 9 kts.

Corona (——). 320 tons. Speed, 9 kts. Governor's Yacht.

Ivy (1896). Yacht.

Also a Stern-wheel Tug of 428 tons. There are also about 18 other small launches and miscellaneous craft.

GERMAN FLEET.

INCLUDING SHIPS SALVED AT SCAPA FLOW AND THOSE TO BE SURRENDERED UNDER PEACE TREATY.

WILHELMSHAVEN to	miles.	KIEL to	miles.
Cherbourg	510	Copenhagen	160
Dover	330	Danzig	280
Gibraltar	1565	Libau	360
Havre	450	Memel	330
Heligoland	48	Kronstadt	670
Hull	330	Skaw	240
Kiao-chau	11100		
Malta	2555	Libau	120
New York	3570	Memel	113
Port Said	3530	Kiel	280
Portsmouth	440		
Rio de Janeiro	5470		
Rosyth	450		
Sheerness	280		

Wilhelmshaven to Kiel, 80 miles (by canal much of the way).
" " 530 " (via Great Belt).

MAP OF GERMAN COAST, SHOWING NAVAL AND PRIVATE YARDS, &c.

Fortifications to be Dismantled.

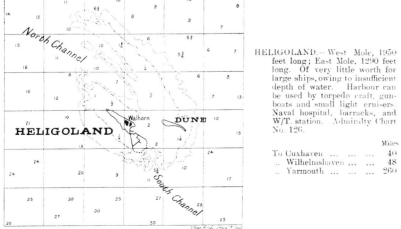

HELIGOLAND.—West Mole, 1950 feet long; East Mole, 1290 feet long. Of very little worth for large ships, owing to insufficient depth of water. Harbour can be used by torpedo craft, gunboats and small light cruisers. Naval hospital, barracks, and W/T. station. Admiralty Chart No. 126.

	Miles
To Cuxhaven	40
" Wilhelmshaven	48
" Yarmouth	260

Flags.

Reported new National Ensign has black, gold and red horizontal and equal stripes. Naval flags not known.

Mercantile Marine.

June, 1919, 3,427,000 tons *gross* but a large amount must be handed over to the Allies and United States.

Coinage.

Mark (100 pfennige *nominal* value = 11¾d. British, 24 cents U.S.A., but rate of exchange has depreciated.

Colour of Ships.

Big ships: light grey all over.
Torpedo craft: varies from black to dull brown.

Active Naval *Personnel.*

Floating Docks.

Note :—Several of these have been sold, though such sales are reported to be contrary to the Treaty of Peace.

GERMAN **SPECIAL SERVICE SHIPS**—RECOGNITION SILHOUETTES.

Scale : 1 inch = 160 eet

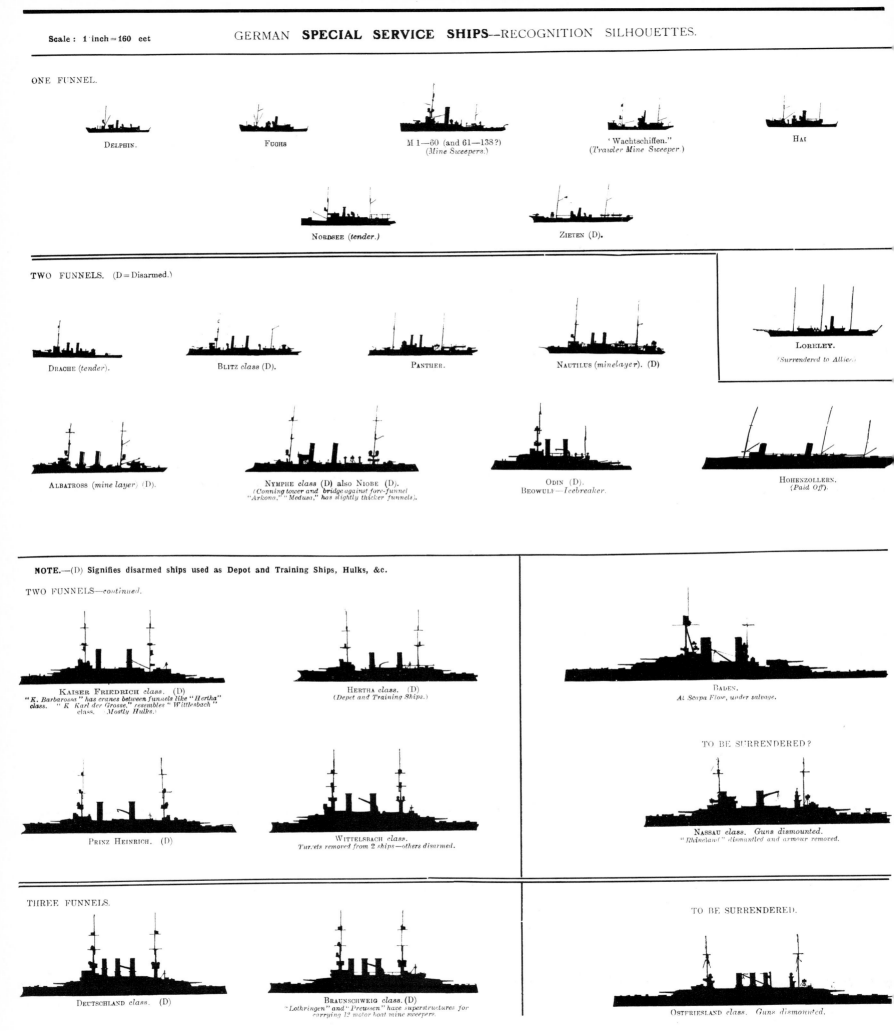

ONE FUNNEL.

DELPHIN.

FUCHS

M 1—60 (and 61—138?)
(Mine Sweepers.)

'Wachtschiffen.'
(Trawler Mine Sweeper.)

HAI

NORDSEE (tender.)

ZIETEN (D).

TWO FUNNELS. (D = Disarmed.)

DRACHE (tender).

BLITZ class (D).

PANTHER.

NAUTILUS (minelayer). (D)

LORELEY.
(Surrendered to Allies.)

ALBATROSS (mine layer) (D).

NYMPHE class (D) also NIOBE (D).
(Conning tower and bridge against fore-funnel
"Arkona," "Medusa," has slightly thicker funnels).

ODIN (D).
BEOWULF—Icebreaker.

HOHENZOLLERN.
(Paid Off).

NOTE.—(D) Signifies disarmed ships used as Depot and Training Ships, Hulks, &c.

TWO FUNNELS—continued.

KAISER FRIEDRICH class. (D)
"K. Barbarossa" has cranes between funnels like "Hertha"
class. "K Karl der Grosse." resembles "Wittlesbach"
class. (Mostly Hulks.)

HERTHA class. (D)
(Depot and Training Ships.)

BADEN.
At Scapa Flow, under salvage.

TO BE SURRENDERED?

PRINZ HEINRICH. (D)

WITTELSBACH class.
Turrets removed from 2 ships—others disarmed.

NASSAU class. Guns dismounted.
"Rhineland" dismantled and armour removed.

THREE FUNNELS.

TO BE SURRENDERED.

DEUTSCHLAND class. (D)

BRAUNSCHWEIG class. (D)
"Lothringen" and "Preussen" have superstructures for
carrying 12 motor boat mine sweepers.

OSTFRIESLAND class. Guns dismounted.

Scale : 1 inch = 160 feet.　　GERMAN **CRUISERS** & **LIGHT CRUISERS** : RECOGNITION SILHOUETTES.

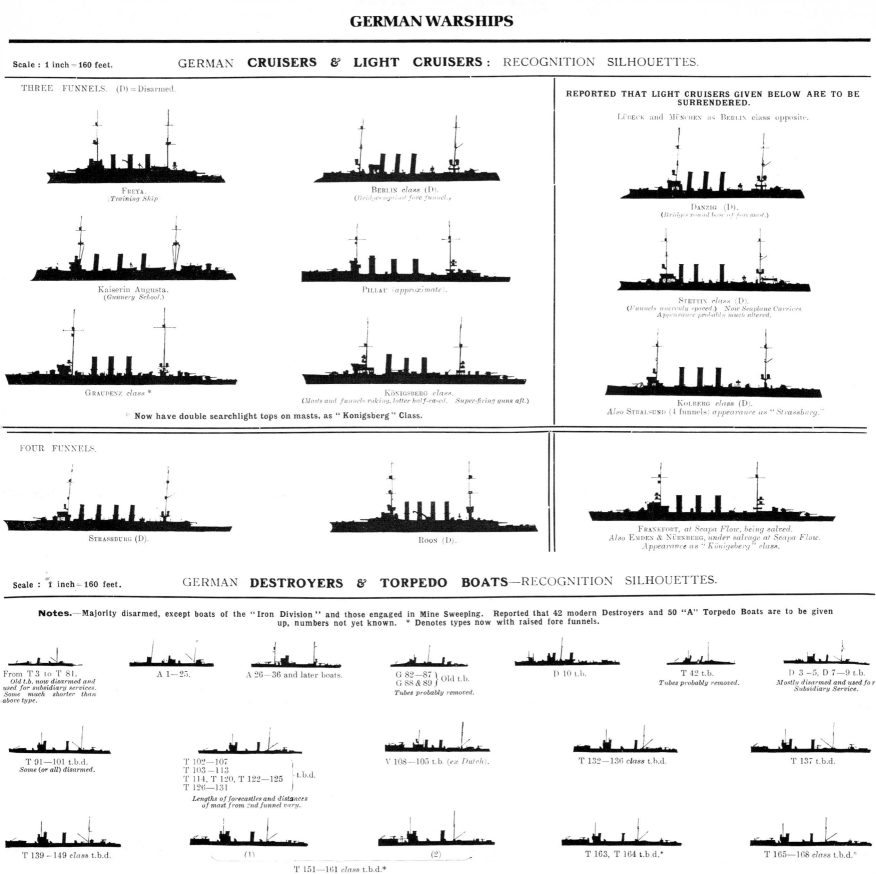

THREE FUNNELS. (D) = Disarmed.

FREYA.
(Training Ship

KAISERIN AUGUSTA.
(Gunnery School.)

GRAUDENZ class *
○ Now have double searchlight tops on masts, as " Konigsberg " Class.

BERLIN class (D).
(Bridges against fore funnel.)

PILLAU (approximate).

KÖNIGSBERG class.
(Masts and funnels raking, latter half-cased. Super-firing guns aft.)

REPORTED THAT LIGHT CRUISERS GIVEN BELOW ARE TO BE SURRENDERED.

LÜBECK and MÜNCHEN as BERLIN class opposite.

DANZIG (D).
(Bridges round base of foremast.)

STETTIN class (D).
(Funnels unevenly spaced.) Now Seaplane Carriers.
Appearance probably much altered.

KOLBERG class (D).
Also STRALSUND (4 funnels) appearance as " Strassburg."

FOUR FUNNELS.

STRASSBURG (D).

ROON (D).

FRANKFORT, at Scapa Flow, being salved.
Also EMDEN & NÜRNBERG, under salvage at Scapa Flow.
Appearance as " Königsberg " class.

Scale : 1 inch = 160 feet.　　GERMAN **DESTROYERS** & **TORPEDO BOATS**—RECOGNITION SILHOUETTES.

Notes.—Majority disarmed, except boats of the " Iron Division " and those engaged in Mine Sweeping. Reported that 42 modern Destroyers and 50 "A" Torpedo Boats are to be given up, numbers not yet known. * Denotes types now with raised fore funnels.

From T 3 to T 81.
Old t.b. now disarmed and used for subsidiary services. Some much shorter than above type.

A 1—25.

A 26—36 and later boats.

G 82—87
G 88 & 89 } Old t.b.
Tubes probably removed.

D 10 t.b.

T 42 t.b.
Tubes probably removed.

D 3—5, D 7—9 t.b.
Mostly disarmed and used for Subsidiary Service.

T 91—101 t.b.d.
Some (or all) disarmed.

T 102—107
T 103—113
T 114, T 120, T 122—125 } t.b.d.
T 126—131
Lengths of forecastles and distances of mast from 2nd funnel vary.

V 108—105 t.b. (ex Dutch).

T 132—136 class t.b.d.

T 137 t.b.d.

T 139—149 class t.b.d.

(1)
T 151—161 class t.b.d.*
(2)

T 163, T 164 t.b.d.*

T 165—168 class t.b.d.*

T 174, T 175*
S 176—179 } t.b.d.

T 180—185 class t.b.d.

T 186, T 189, T 191 t.b.d.*

G 192—197 class t.b.d.*
G 169—173 class t.b.d.*
(Practically identical with each other).

V 1—6*
G 7—11* } classes t.b.d.

" War V & S " t.b.d. :—
V 26—V 130, S 51—S 139
Some boats have short mainmasts. H types said to be same as V & S types. 17 or 19 of these boats salved at Scapa Flow.

G 95 t.b.d.*

G 102 * (ex-Argentine boat). †
(Now has raised forefunnel, with derrick just abaft same and compass platform between third funnel and mainmast.)
† Salved at Scapa Flow.

B 97, B 98, †
(Compass platform actually between after tubes.)
† Seized at Scapa Flow.

V 100.
(Same appearance, but derrick between first and second funnels, with boom slung forward ; big ventilator between second and third funnels.)

GERMAN UNIFORMS, GUNS AND TORPEDOES.

INSIGNIA OF RANK ON SLEEVES FOR EXECUTIVES.

Gross-Admiral (= Admiral of the Fleet) as Admiral but 4 upper stripes.

Crowns may have been removed.

Admiral. Vize-Admiral. Kontre-Admiral. Kommodore. Kapitän zu See. Korvetten- Kapitän- Oberleut z. See. Leutenant z. See
(Vice-Ad.) (Rear-Ad.) (Commodore) (Captain) Kapitän. Leutnant. (Lieut.) (Sub-Lieut.)
  Fregatten-Kapitän & (Commander) (Lieut.-Comm.)
Flaggoffiziere. Stabsoffiziere. Subalternoffiziere.

Note.—Torpedo officers are without the crown on sleeve, as also are all civilian branches. Engineer officers given same official status as Executive, July, 1908.
Torpedo officers have between the gold stripes, *brown*; Engineers, *black*; Doctors, *blue*; Paymasters, *light blue*; Constructors, *black*.

(The colour of the branch is also worn on the epaulettes, full dress, and worked into the shoulder straps).
Paymasters, constructors and legal officers have silver buttons, badges, &c., as well as epaulette fringes, instead of gold, and cloth instead of velvet between the stripes. They are *officials* and not officers.

Torpedoes (1919).

Note : The following details are understood to be based on very sound information.

Size.	Name or Mark.	Air Pressure.	Charge. (lbs.)	Max. Range. (yds.)	at kts.	Type of Heater.
23·6	H 8	2485	616	{ 16350 5450	at 28 at 35 }	Steam
19·7	G VII.⊙☆* (23 feet)	2275	430	{ 11700 5500	at 28 at 35 }	Steam
19·7	G VI. AV ⊙⊙	2275	411	{ 5500 2200	at 27 at 40 }	Dry
17·7	G/125	2133	308	{ 6560 2200	at 24 at 36 }	Dry

Mines (Notes unofficial).

No exact details available. Spherical horned type said to have charge of 220-240 lbs. T.N.T. Pear-shaped "Carbonit" mines said to have charge of 166 lbs. wet guncotton. Marks I and II, soluble safety plugs. Later marks have safety pin attached by rod to sinker. Horns said to be glass tubes (containing battery acid) and covered with lead or soft metal. Bending of horn breaks glass tube and acid runs to battery, which at once becomes active and fires detonator.

Naval Guns (Details unofficial).

Notation.	Calibre.	Usual Naval Designation.	Length in cals.	Date of Model.	Weight of Gun.	Weight of A.P. shot.	Initial Velocity.	Maximum penetration direct impact against K.C. at 9000 yds.	6000 yds.	3000 yds.	Danger space against average ships at 10,000 yards.	5000 yards.	3000 yards.	Approximate
	inch.	c/m.			tons.	lbs.	foot-secs.	in.	in.	in.	yards.	yards.	yards.	foot
A 9*	15	38·1	45	'13	82¼	1675½	2920	16	18½	21	...	...	...	99,0
A 4*	11	28	45	'04	36·3	} 661·4	2920	7	12	15	170	580	950	39,1
A 3*	11	28	40	'01	32·2		2756	6	10	14	150	450	740	31,0
A 2*	9·4	24	40	'99	20·3	} 418·9	2756	4	8	12	130	400	700	22,0
A*	9·4	24	40	'98	20·3		2625	3½	7	10	110	350	620	22,0
A*	8·2	21	40	'01	13·4	275·6	2756	3	6	9	...	...	...	14,7
B*	6·7	17	40	'01	7·5	154·5	2756	...	3	5	80	240	460	8,2
C*	5·9	15	50	...	5·5	} 101·4	3084	...	...	...	...	...	...	6,6
C*	5·9	15	45	'09	5		2920	...	...	5	...	200	420	5,9
E*	5·9	15	40	'01	4·9		2756	...	...	3½	...	140	350	5,3
E*	5·9	15	35	...	4·4		2231	...	...	...	...	...	...	
F*	4·1	10·5	40	...	1·7	35·2	2756	...	...	...	...	...	...	1,8
F*	4·1	10·5	35	...	1·2	38·2	2000	...	...	...	...	...	...	1,6

* Brass cartridge cases to all guns.

Lesser guns : 3.4 inch (88 m/m) firing 22 lb. projectiles in modern and 15 lb. in old models ; also 2 inch (4 pdr.) of 55 and shorter calibres. Also anti-aircraft models, about which no reliable details are available.

Projectiles : Guns of 11 inch and over fire A.P., Ersatz A.P., H.E., and common shell.

The 1899 and later models have the recoil utilized to return the gun to firing position for pieces over 5.9 inch. In 5.9 in. springs are employed. German guns have a lower muzzle pressure than normally obtains, but mountings are arranged to give large degree of elevation.

12 inch, 50 cal. *Helgoland* class.
11 inch, 45 cal. in *Nassau*.
11 inch, 40 cal., M. '01 in *Deutschland* and *Braunschweig* classes (removed from some).

1914 (GERMAN) DREADNOUGHT

(BAYERN CLASS – 2 SHIPS)

BAYERN (1915) BADEN (30th Oct., 1915).

Displacement, *about* 28,000 tons. Complement, over 1100.
Length, 623⅓ (*o.a.*) feet. Beam, 99¾ feet. *Mean draught*, 28½ feet.

Guns :
  8—15 inch, 45 cal.
  16—5·9 inch, 45 cal.
  4—22 pdr. (anti-aircraft).
Torpedo tubes (23·6 inch).
  4 *submerged* (broadside) ?
  1 *submerged* (bow) ?

Armour (Krupp) :⊙
  15″ Belt (amidships) ....
  8″—6″ Belt (ends) ....
  ″ Deck ....
  10″ Side above Belt............
  ″ Turrets ....
  8″ Battery ....
  17½″ Conning Tower . ...
  ⊙Details very approximate.

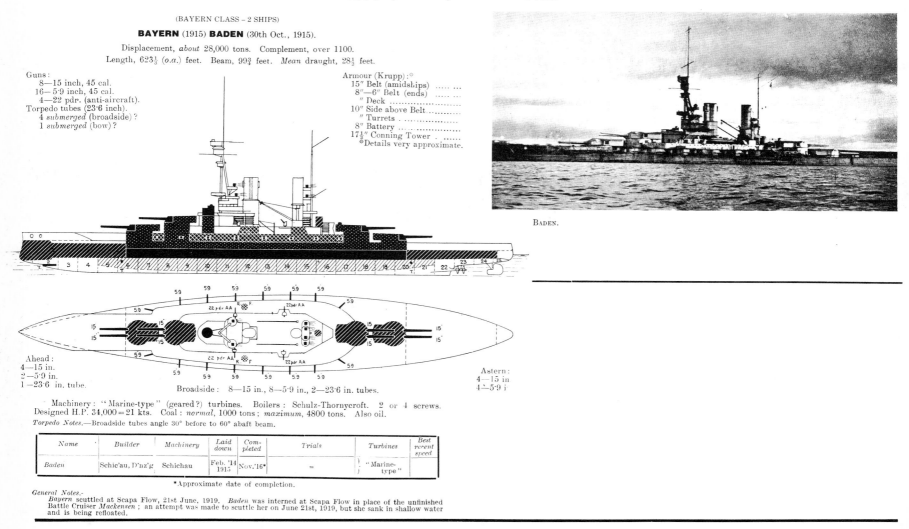

BADEN.

Ahead :
4—15 in.
2—5·9 in.
1—23·6 in. tube.

Broadside : 8—15 in., 8—5·9 in., 2—23·6 in. tubes.

Astern :
4—15 in
4—5·9 in.

Machinery : "Marine-type" (geared ?) turbines. Boilers : Schulz-Thornycroft. 2 or 4 screws. Designed H.P. 34,000 = 21 kts. Coal : *normal*, 1000 tons ; *maximum*, 4800 tons. Also oil.
Torpedo Notes.—Broadside tubes angle 30° before to 60° abaft beam.

Name	Builder	Machinery	Laid down	Completed	Trials	Turbines	Best recent speed
Baden	Schic'au, D'nz'g	Schichau	Feb. '14 1915	Nov.'16*	—	"Marine-type"	

*Approximate date of completion.

General Notes.—
Bayern scuttled at Scapa Flow, 21st June, 1919. *Baden* was interned at Scapa Flow in place of the unfinished Battle Cruiser *Mackensen* ; an attempt was made to scuttle her on June 21st, 1919, but she sank in shallow water and is being refloated.

1911 GERMAN DREADNOUGHTS. Nos. 18, 19, 20 & 22.

KRON PRINZ (1913), **GROSSER KURFÜRST** (May, 1913), & **KÖNIG** (March, 1913),
MARKGRAF (June, 1913).

Displacement, *about* 25,500 tons. Complement, *about* 1100.

Length, *about* 580 feet *over all*. Beam, *about* 96 feet. *Mean draught, about* 27½ feet.

Guns :
10 —12 inch, 45 cal.
14 —6 inch.
12 —24 pdr.
4 —14 pdr. anti-aerial
Torpedo tubes (20 inch) :
4 (broadside) *submerged*.
1 (stern) *submerged*.

Armour (Krupp) :
14″ Belt (amidships)...*aaaaa*
″ Belt (bow) ....
″ Belt (stern) ....
Protection to vitals (*see notes*) :
12″ Turrets ....
8″ Battery ....

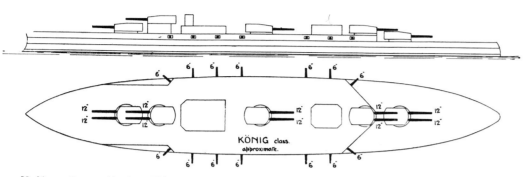

KÖNIG class.
approximate.

Machinery : 3 sets turbine (see table). Boilers : Schulz-Thornycroft. Designed H.P. 34,000＝21·5 kts. Coal : *normal*, 1000 tons ; *maximum*, 4400 tons. Also 700 tons oil. 3 screws.

Gunnery Notes.—There are 2 conning towers, 4 special armoured fire control towers, one torpedo control tower.

Armour Notes.—Funnels, 6 inch armour to height of 20 feet above upper deck. Special under water 3 inch plating for length of 350 feet amidships. Internal protection as for *Kaiser* class.

Name	Builder	Machinery	Laid down	Completed	Trials	Turbines	Best recent speed
Markgraf	Weser, Bremen	Weser	Oct. '11	Oct.'14	=	Bergmann	...
G. Kurfürst	Vulkan, H'b'g	Vulkan	May '11	Oct.'14	=	A.E.G.(Curtis)	...
Koenig	W't'mshav'n Y.	...	Sept. '11	Oct.'14	=	Parsons (mod.)	...
'RINZ *K. Weissenburg*	Krupp	Krupp	Ap'l '12	July'15			...

First three belong to the 1911 programme, *Markgraf* to the 1912.

General Notes.—It was originally intended to fit Diesel motors to the centre engine ; but this was subsequently abandoned.

1909-10 GERMAN DREADNOUGHTS. Nos. 11, 12, *also* 14, 15, 16

(KAISER CLASS—5 SHIPS.)

KAISER (March, 1911), **FRIEDRICH DER GROSSE** (June, 1911), **KAISERIN** (Nov., 1911),
PRINZ REGENT LUITPOLD (Feb., 1913) & **KONIG ALBERT** (April, 1912).

Displacement, 24,700 tons. Complement, 1088.

Length (*waterline*), 564 feet. Beam, 95¾ feet. *Maximum* draught, 27¼ feet.

Guns :
10 —12 inch, 50 cal. (A⁶)
14 —6 inch
12 —24 pdr.
4 —14 pdr. anti-aerial
Torpedo tubes (20 inch) :
4 *submerged* (broadside)
1 *submerged* (stern)

Armour (Krupp) :
14″ Belt (amidships) ...... *aaaa*
6″ Belt (bow) .... *b*
5″ Belt (aft) ....
Protection to vitals ...... =
12″ Turrets .... *aaaa*
7″ Battery .... *a*
(Total weight : 6000 tons).

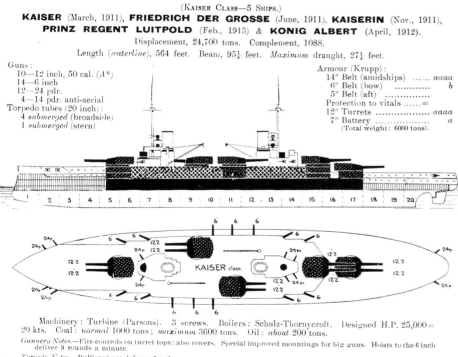

KAISER class.

Machinery : Turbine (Parsons). 3 screws. Boilers : Schulz-Thornycroft. Designed H.P. 25,000＝ 20 kts. Coal : *normal* 1000 tons ; *maximum* 3600 tons. Oil : *about* 200 tons.

Gunnery Notes.—Fire controls on turret tops ; also towers. Special improved mountings for big guns. Hoists to the 6 inch deliver 9 rounds a minute.

Torpedo Notes.—Bullivant net defence fitted.

Armour Notes.—Under water protection consists of double longitudinal bulkheads ; the outer one 2½ inch, the inner 1½ inch. The outer bulkhead is 9 feet away from ship's side ; all bulkheads solid. Minute sub-division : the upper deck is possibly armoured against attacks from aircraft, but no details are available.

Name.	Builder	Machinery	Laid down	Completed	Trials 6 hrs. mean 1 hr.		Boilers	Best recent speed
Kaiser	Kiel Yard		Oct. '09	Oct. '12	31,516＝22·3	35,100＝23·46		23·6
Friedrich der G.	Vulcan, H'b'g	Vulcan Co.	Oct. '09	Oct. '12	31,721＝21·4	42,113＝23·8	Schulz-T.	
Kaiserin	Howalt	Howalt	July '10	Aug. '13			in	
K. Albert	Schichau	Schichau	July '10	Aug. '13			all.	
P. R. Luitpold	Krupp	Krupp	Apl. '10	Aug. '13				

General Notes.—First two, 1909 programme ; the others, 1910 programme. They have *four* bilge keels. The *Kaiser's* 23·6 was for one hour. Average cost, £2,400,000 per ship.

Note.—This class consists of five ships instead of the usual four. Usual anti-rolling tanks.

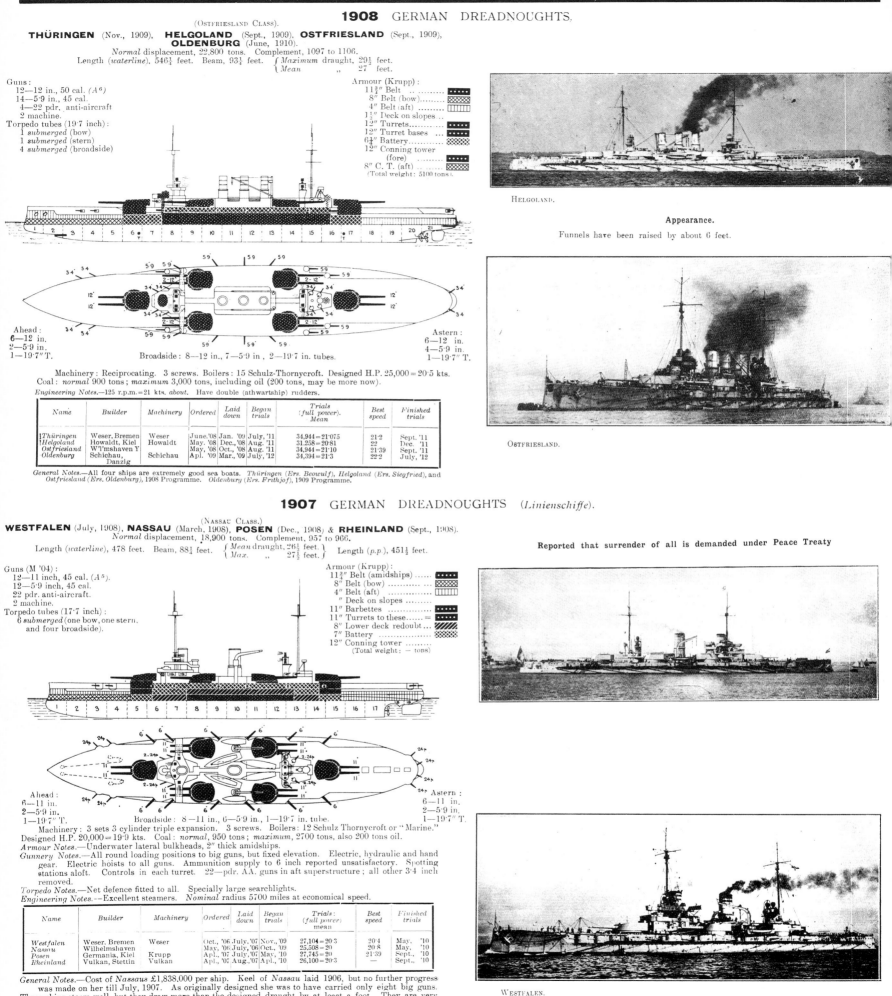

1908 GERMAN DREADNOUGHTS.

(OSTFRIESLAND CLASS).

THÜRINGEN (Nov., 1909), **HELGOLAND** (Sept., 1909), **OSTFRIESLAND** (Sept., 1909), **OLDENBURG** (June, 1910).

Normal displacement, 22,800 tons. Complement, 1097 to 1106.
Length *(waterline)*, 546¼ feet. Beam, 93¼ feet. { Maximum draught, 29½ feet. { Mean „ 27 feet.

Guns:
12—12 in., 50 cal. (A⁶)
14—5·9 in., 45 cal.
4—22 pdr. anti-aircraft
2 machine.
Torpedo tubes (19·7 inch):
1 *submerged* (bow)
1 *submerged* (stern)
4 *submerged* (broadside)

Armour (Krupp):
11¾″ Belt ....
8″ Belt (bow)........
4″ Belt (aft) ....
1½″ Deck on slopes ..
12″ Turrets ....
12″ Turret bases ....
6½″ Battery ....
12″ Conning tower
(fore) ......
8″ C. T. (aft) ......
(Total weight: 5100 tons.)

Ahead:
6—12 in.
2—5·9 in.
1—19·7″ T.

Broadside: 8—12 in., 7—5·9 in., 2—19·7 in. tubes.

Astern:
6—12 in.
4—5·9 in.
1—19·7″ T.

Machinery: Reciprocating. 3 screws. Boilers: 15 Schulz-Thornycroft. Designed H.P. 25,000 = 20·5 kts. Coal: *normal* 900 tons; *maximum* 3,000 tons, including oil (200 tons, may be more now).
Engineering Notes.—125 r.p.m. = 21 kts. about. Have double (athwartship) rudders.

Name	Builder	Machinery	Ordered	Laid down	Began trials	Trials (full power) Mean	Best speed	Finished trials
Thüringen	Weser, Bremen	Weser	June.'08	Jan. '09	July, '11	34,944 = 21·075	21·2	Sept. '11
Helgoland	Howaldt, Kiel	Howaldt	May, '08	Dec., '08	Aug. '11	31,258 = 20·81	22	Dec. '11
Ostfriesland	W'l'mshaven Y		May, '08	Oct., '09	Aug. '11	34,944 = 21·10	21·39	Sept. '11
Oldenburg	Schichau, Danzig	Schichau	Apl. '09	Mar., '09	July, '12	34,394 = 21·3	22·2	July, '12

General Notes.—All four ships are extremely good sea boats. *Thüringen (Ers. Beowulf), Helgoland (Ers. Siegfried),* and *Ostfriesland (Ers. Oldenburg),* 1908 Programme. *Oldenburg (Ers. Frithjof),* 1909 Programme.

HELGOLAND.

Appearance.

Funnels have been raised by about 6 feet.

OSTFRIESLAND.

1907 GERMAN DREADNOUGHTS (*Linienschiffe*).

(NASSAU CLASS.)

WESTFALEN (July, 1908), **NASSAU** (March, 1908), **POSEN** (Dec., 1908) & **RHEINLAND** (Sept., 1908).

Normal displacement, 18,900 tons. Complement, 957 to 966.
Length *(waterline)*, 478 feet. Beam, 88¼ feet. { Mean draught, 26¼ feet. } Length *(p.p.)*, 451½ feet. { Max. „ 27½ feet. }

Guns (M '04):
12—11 inch, 45 cal. (A⁵)
12—5·9 inch, 45 cal.
22 pdr. anti-aircraft
2 machine.
Torpedo tubes (17·7 inch):
6 *submerged* (one bow, one stern,
and four broadside).

Armour (Krupp):
11¾″ Belt (amidships) ......
8″ Belt (bow) ....
4″ Belt (aft) ....
″ Deck on slopes ....
11″ Barbettes ....
11″ Turrets to these ......
8″ Lower deck redoubt ...
7″ Battery ....
12″ Conning tower ....
(Total weight: — tons.)

Reported that surrender of all is demanded under Peace Treaty

Ahead:
6—11 in.
2—5·9 in.
1—19·7″ T.

Broadside: 8—11 in., 6—5·9 in., 1—19·7 in. tube.

Astern:
6—11 in.
2—5·9 in.
1—19·7″ T.

Machinery: 3 sets 3 cylinder triple expansion. 3 screws. Boilers: 12 Schulz Thornycroft or "Marine."
Designed H.P. 20,000 = 19·9 kts. Coal: *normal*, 950 tons; *maximum*, 2700 tons, also 200 tons oil.
Armour Notes.—Underwater lateral bulkheads, 2″ thick amidships.
Gunnery Notes.—All round loading positions to big guns, but fixed elevation. Electric, hydraulic and hand gear. Electric hoists to all guns. Ammunition supply to 6 inch reported unsatisfactory. Spotting stations aloft. Controls in each turret. 22—pdr. AA. guns in aft superstructure; all other 3·4 inch removed.
Torpedo Notes.—Net defence fitted to all. Specially large searchlights.
Engineering Notes.—Excellent steamers. *Nominal* radius 5700 miles at economical speed.

Name	Builder	Machinery	Ordered	Laid down	Began trials	Trials: (full power) mean	Best speed	Finished trials
Westfalen	Weser, Bremen	Weser	Oct., '06	July,'07	Nov., '09	27,104 = 20·3	20·4	May, '10
Nassau	Wilhelmshaven		May, '06	July,'06	Oct., '09	25,508 = 20	20·8	May, '10
Posen	Germania, Kiel	Krupp	Apl., '07	July,'07	May, '10	27,745 = 20	21·39	Sept., '10
Rheinland	Vulkan, Stettin	Vulkan	Apl. '07	Aug.'07	May, '10	26,100 = 20·3		Sept., '10

General Notes.—Cost of *Nassaus* £1,838,000 per ship. Keel of *Nassau* laid 1906, but no further progress was made on her till July, 1907. As originally designed she was to have carried only eight big guns. These ships steam well, but they draw more than the designed draught by at least a foot. They are very cramped internally and it is difficult to accommodate the crews. Some cabins have to accommodate 4 officers. Ventilation is very poor. They are only moderately successful, being overgunned for their displacement, but they are extremely steady gun platforms. The shooting from these ships always averages better than from any others. *Nassau (Ers. Bayern)* and *Westfalen (Ers. Sachsen),* 1906 Programme; *Rheinland (Ers. Württemberg)* and *Posen (Ers. Baden),* 1907 Programme.

WESTFALEN.

1912 GERMAN BATTLE-CRUISERS (*Linienschiff Kreuzer*). Nos. **23, 24** (Dreadnoughts).

DERFFLINGER (June, 1913), **LÜTZOW** (Nov., 1913), ~~ERSATZ HERTHA~~ HINDENBURG (1914).

Displacement. 28,000 tons. Complement,

Length, feet. Beam, feet. Draught, feet.

Guns (see *Note*):
  8—12 inch, 50 cal.
  12—6 inch, 45 cal.
  12—24 pdr.
  —— anti-aerial.
Torpedo tubes (22 inch):
  4 *submerged* (broadside)
  1 *submerged* (stern)

Armour:
  About 13″ Belt (amidships) ... *aaa*
  4″ Belt (ends) .... *d*
  4″ Deck (flat) amidships ......
  3″ Deck (slopes) below it.

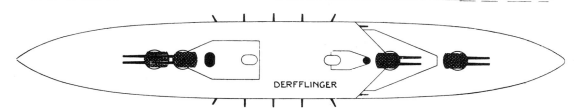

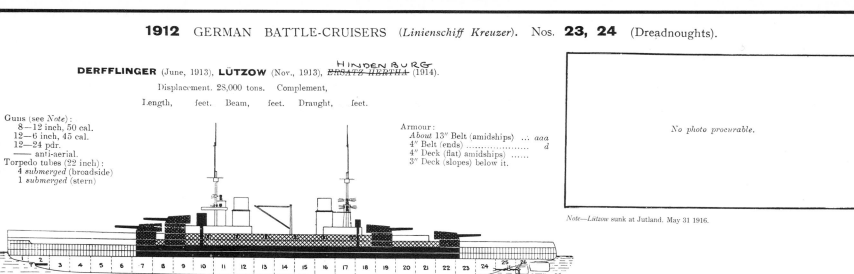

No photo procurable.

Note—Lützow sunk at Jutland. May 31 1916.

Armour Notes.—There is a flat 4″ upper protective deck amidships against aerial attack.

Name	Builder	Machinery	Laid down	Completed	Trials	Turbines	Best recent speed
Derfflinger	Blohm & Voss	Blohm & Voss	Mar. '12	July '14			
Lützow	Schichau, Dan'g	Schichau	Sept. '12	'15			
~~E. Hertha~~	Wilhelmsh'n Y.	...	July '13	'16			

1911 GERMAN BATTLE-CRUISERS. Nos. **17** *and* **21** (Dreadnoughts)

SEYDLITZ (April, 1912).

Displacement, 25,000 tons. Complement,

Length (*over all*), 656 feet (*waterline* 648). Beam, 93⅓ feet. *Maximum* draught, 28 feet *or less* (*mean* 26½).

Guns:
  10—11 inch, 50 cal. (A⁶)
  12—6 inch
  12—24 pdr.
  4—14 pdr. anti-aerial
Torpedo tubes (20 inch):
  1 *submerged* (bow)
  2 *submerged* (broadside)
  1 *submerged* (stern)

Armour (Krupp):
  11″ Belt (amidships)......... *aaa*
  4″ Belt (ends) .... *d*
  3″ Deck (2) (amidships) ..
  8″ Turrets ....
  10½″ Barbettes ....
  6″ Mantlets to funnels ...=*aa*
  4″ Battery .. .. *d*

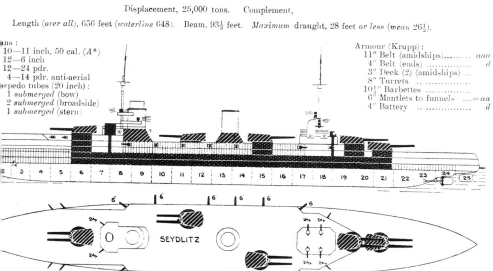

Note raised forecastle.

Machinery : Parsons turbine (2 stage). 3 screws. Boilers : 27 Schulz-Thornycroft. Designed H.P. 63,000 = 26·5 kts.

Armour Notes.—Generally as *Moltke*, but higher forward. The mantlet of fore funnel is 20 feet high, after funnel 12 feet. Main belt is about 400 feet long from turret to turret, of uniform thickness at waterline, reduced at upper and lower edges. Its height is about 15 feet. The double 3″ protective deck is amidships only ; Upper flat, lower curved.
Gunnery Notes.—One of the turrets is electrically and hand manoeuvred ; all the others are hydraulic and hand.
Torpedo Notes.—Net defence fitted. Also special internal protection more or less similar to that of the Argentine *Rividaria*.

Name	Builder	Machinery	Laid down	Completed	Trials	Turbines	Best recent speed
Seydlitz	Blohm & Voss	Blohm & Voss	Feb.'11	May '1?	=	Parsons	29

General Note.—*Seydlitz* 1910 programme. Immensely strong construction is the special feature of this type ; they are specially designed to withstand attack by high explosives. Freeboard forward about 33 feet, aft 18 feet. Except for the high forecastle forward this ship closely resembles the *Moltke* class in appearance.

1909 GERMAN BATTLE-CRUISERS (*Linienschiff Kreuzer*). 9, 13 (Dreadnoughts).

MOLTKE (April, 1910) & **GOEBEN** (March, 1911).

Displacement, 23,000 tons. Complement, 1107.

Length (*waterline*), 590½ feet. Beam, 96¾ feet. *Max.* draught, 28 feet. Length *over all*, 610 feet.

Guns:
10—11 inch, 50 cal. (*A⁶*)
12—6 inch.
12—24 pdr.
Torpedo tubes (20 inch):
2 *submerged* (broadside)
1 ,, (bow)
1 ,, (stern)

Armour (Krupp).
11″ Belt (amidships) .... *aaa*
4″ Belt (ends) .... *d*
3″ Decks (2) (amidships) ...
8″ Turrets .... = *aa*
10½″ Turret bases ....
6″ Mantlets to funnels ...... = *aa*
4″ Battery.................... *d*

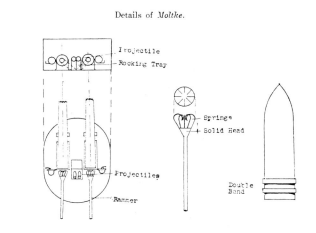

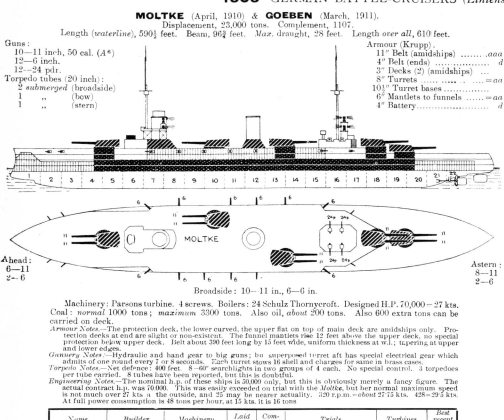

Ahead:
6—11
2—6

Astern:
8—11
2—6

Broadside: 10—11 in., 6—6 in.

Extra Gunnery Notes.—Big guns controlled from two armoured towers amidships. Unprotected spotting po each masthead connected by voice-pipe with the towers. Big guns hand loaded with wooden rammers wh spring coils on head to allow of uniformly seating projectiles. Large holes cut in the back of turret in rea gun to allow the rammers to come out. Turrets are very roomy; no partition between guns. Guns can be at any arc, but at only one fixed elevation. Crew of each turret, including magazine parties, is 70 men. T electric and hand. Loading, hydraulic and hand. Projectiles have 2 copper bands at ends, one for seating rotating. Come up between guns delivered on a rocking tray. Charges come up in brass cylinders, in tw (each 140 lbs.) which are loaded into the guns separately. Breech opens by hand by means of a coarse screw and small fly wheel. At drill using a single dummy charge, loading time has been timed 5 second turret has a range finder and rate instrument, connected with a transmitting station below. The 6 inch g their own control towers. Crew of each 6 inch gun, six men.

Details of *Moltke*.

Machinery: Parsons turbine. 4 screws. Boilers: 24 Schulz Thornycroft. Designed H.P. 70,000 = 27 kts.
Coal: *normal* 1000 tons; *maximum* 3300 tons. Also oil, *about* 200 tons. Also 600 extra tons can be carried on deck.
Armour Notes.—The protection deck, the lower curved, the upper flat on top of main deck are amidships only. Protection decks at end are slight or non-existent. The funnel mantlets rise 12 feet above the upper deck, no special protection below upper deck. Belt about 390 feet long by 15 feet wide, uniform thickness at w.l.; tapering at upper and lower edges.
Gunnery Notes.—Hydraulic and hand gear to big guns; but superposed turret aft has special electrical gear which admits of one round every 7 or 8 seconds. Each turret stows 16 shell and charges same in brass cases.
Torpedo Notes.—Net defence: 400 feet. 8—60″ searchlights in two groups of 4 each. No special control. 3 torpedoes per tube carried. 8 tubes have been reported, but this is doubtful.
Engineering Notes.—The nominal h.p. of these ships is 50,000 only, but this is obviously merely a fancy figure. The actual contract h.p. was 70,000. This was easily exceeded on trial with the *Moltke*, but her normal maximum speed is not much over 27 kts a the outside, and 25 may be nearer actuality. 320 r.p.m. = about 27·75 kts. 428 = 29·5 kts. At full power consumption is 48 tons per hour, at 15 kts. it is 16 tons

Name	Builder	Machinery	Laid down	Completed	Trials		Turbines	Best recent speed
					6 hrs. mean.	runs.		
Moltke	Blohm & Voss	Blohm & Voss	Apr.'09	To be Oct. '11	76,795 = 27·25	85,782 = 28·4	Parsons	28·4
Goeben	Blohm & Voss	Blohm & Voss	July,'09	Oct. '12	71,275 = 27·2	85·661 = 28	Parsons	28

General Notes.—Moltke, 1908 programme; Goeben belongs to the 1909 programme. Designed by Prof. Kretsschner. Meta centric height: 22½ feet. Cost about £2,200,000 per ship. Fitted with Frahm anti-rolling tanks. All cupboards, shelves, etc., are of light sheet iron, the only wood being the tables and chairs. There are no pictures, arm chairs, settees or sofas in the wardroom. There are no ventilators on deck other than the erections around the fore funnel, and mainmast. Freeboard forward 26 feet, aft 18 feet. There are 2 steering engines in separate compartments in tandem. Officers' quarters, aft.

Fire controls of *Moltke* are not amidships as in *Goeben*; but 3 on top of each other at base of each mast.

1907 GERMAN BATTLE-CRUISER (*Linien-Kreuzer*). No. 5.

VON DER TANN (20th March, 1909).

Normal displacement, 19,400; *full load*, 21,000 tons. Complement, 910.

Length (*waterline*), 558 feet. Beam, 85 feet. *Max.* draught, 27½ feet. Length *over all*, 561 feet.

Guns (M. '04) (*see Notes*):
8—11 inch, 45 cal. (*AAAAA*).
10—6 inch.
16—24 pdr.
Torpedo tubes (18 inch):
1 *submerged* (bow)
1 *submerged* (stern)
2 *submerged* (broadside)

Armour (Krupp):
10—7″ Belt (amidships) ...*aaa-a*
4″ Belt (bow) N.C........... *d*
4″ Belt (stern) N.C. .... *d*
″ Deck ....
8″ Turrets .... = *aa*
6″ Turret bases (N.C.) ...... *b*
? 4½″ Battery .... *d*
Protection to vitals .... = *aa*

Torpedo nets now fitted.

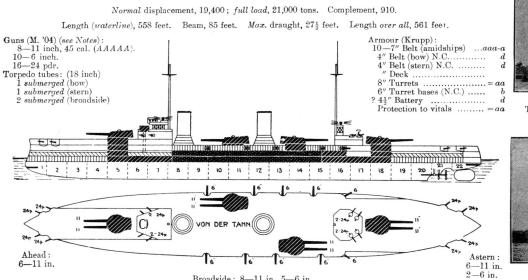

Ahead:
6—11 in.

Astern:
6—11 in.
2—6 in.

Broadside: 8—11 in., 5—6 in.

Machinery: Turbine (Parsons). 4 screws. Boilers: 18 Schulz-Thornycroft. Designed H.P. 50,000 = 25 kts. Coal: *normal* 1000 tons; *maximum* 2800 tons. Also 300 tons oil.
Armour Notes.—Main belt is 14½ feet wide amidships. About 10 feet is above waterline and 4½ below l.w.l. There is a flat armour deck on top of this belt: usual sloping deck from bottom edge. The armour thicknesses given are approximately correct to about an inch. *Exact* thicknesses cannot be ascertained. Belt at ends is about 11½ feet wide, the upper strake being considerably thinner than the lower. Except amidships the belt does not rise to the main deck, though always so represented in plans of German origin.
Gunnery Notes.—
Torpedo Notes.—The stern submerged tube is on the starboard side of the stern post.

Name	Builder	Machinery	Laid down	Completed	Trials	Boilers	Best recent speed.
Von der Tann	Blohm & Voss	Blohm & Voss	Oct.'08	Sept., '10	= 79,802 = 27·4	Schulz-T.	28·1

General Notes.—Cost, £1,833,000. Belongs to 1907 programme, but there was considerable delay in commencing her. The *Von der Tann* is an excellent steamer; but not a particularly good sea-boat. The guns are very well placed, and there is practically no interference at all. All the work in this ship is extremely good, and all details of her internal fittings are most carefully thought out. Frahm tanks. Designed by Prof. Kresschner.

1904 GERMAN BATTLESHIPS (18 knot). PRE-DREADNOUGHTS.

(DEUTSCHLAND CLASS—5 SHIPS).

DEUTSCHLAND (Nov., 1904), **HANNOVER** (Sept., 1905), **POMMERN** (Dec., 1905), **SCHLESWIG-HOLSTEIN** (Dec., 1906), and **SCHLESIEN** (May, 1906).

Displacement, 13,200 tons. Complement, 729.

Length (*waterline*), 410 feet. Beam, 72 feet. *Mean* draught, 25 feet. Length *over all*, 430 feet.

Guns (M. '01):
- 4—11 inch, 40 cal. (*AAA*).
- 14—6·7 inch, 40 cal. (*B*).
- 20—24 pdr.
- 4—1 pdr.
- 4 Machine.

Torpedo tubes (17·7 inch):
- 6 *submerged* (bow, stern, and broadside.

Armour (Krupp) *see Notes*:

9¾″ Belt (amidships) ...	*aaa*
4″ Belt (ends)	*d*
3″ Deck on slopes	
Protection to vitals... =	*aaaa*
11″ Barbettes	*aaa*
11″ Turrets to these	*aaa*
8″ Lower deck (side) ...	*aa*
6¾″ Battery	*a*
6¾″ Casemates (4)	*a*
12″ Conning tower (fore)	*aaa*
5¼″ After C.T.	*b*

(Total weight, 430 tons.)

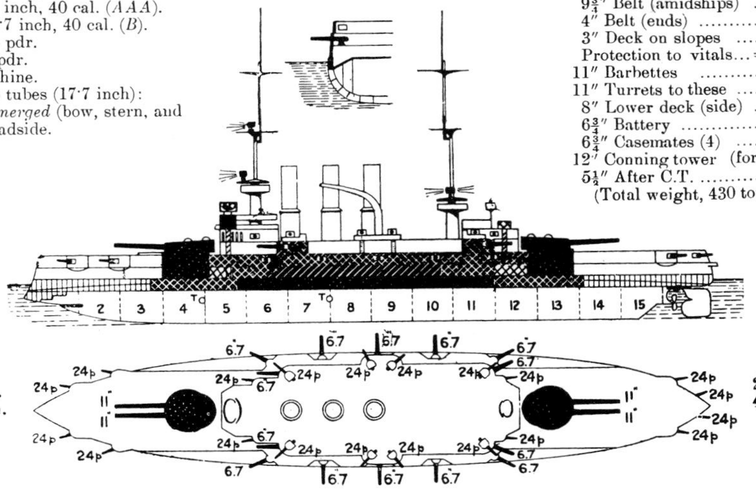

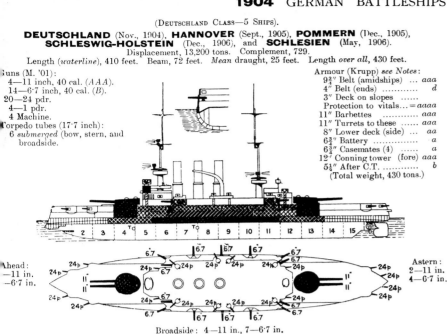

Ahead:
—11 in.
—6·7 in.

Astern:
2—11 in.
4—6·7 in.

Broadside: 4—11 in., 7—6·7 in.

Machinery: 3 sets 3 cylinder vertical triple expansion. 3 screws. Boilers: 12 Schulz Thornycroft. Designed H.P. 16,000 = 18 kts. Coal: *normal* 800 tons; *maximum* 1800 tons. Also 200 tons liquid fuel (in double bottom). *Nominal* radius 5500 kts. at 10 kts.

Armour Notes.—*Deutschland's* belt is only 9 inch, and battery is ½ inch thicker than in the other 4.

Gunnery Notes.—Loading positions, big guns: all round. Hoists: electric, all guns. Big guns manœuvred by electric and hand gear; secondary guns, electric and hand gear.

Arcs of fire: Big guns, 270°; casemates and end battery guns 135° from axial line; other battery guns, 110°.

Engineering Notes.—Coal consumption: *normal* 8½ tons an hour at 17 kts.; about 13 tons at 18 kts. Can steam about 3500 miles at 17 kts. and 2500 at full speed.

Name.	*Builder.*	*Machinery.*	*Laid down.*	*Com pleted*	*Trials: 22 hrs. at ¾.*	*6 hrs. full p.*	*Boilers.*	*Best recent speed.*
Deutschland	Krupp	Krupp	1903	1906	11,377 = 17·1	16,935 = 15·53	Schulz in all.	18·9
Hannover	Wilhelmsh'vn	...	1904	1907	12,153 = 16·9	17,768 = 18·7		19·16
Pommern	Vulkan Co.	Vulkan	1904	1907		17,696 = 18·5		19·21
Schleswig-Holstein	Schichau	Schichau	1905	1908		19,868 = 19		
Schlesien	Krupp	Krupp	1905	1908		19,465 = 18·5		19·03

General Notes.—Cost per ship complete about £1,200,000. These ships of the *Deutschland* class are over-gunned. The secondary guns fire too heavy a projectile for man-handling, and the actual value of the class is well below their paper value. They are very good steamers; but otherwise hardly equal to British, U.S.A., and French ships of equal date.

Note.—In *Deutschland* and *Hannover* the searchlight forward instead of being carried on the fighting top is on a platform just above it.

POMMERN sunk at Jutland 1st June 1916.

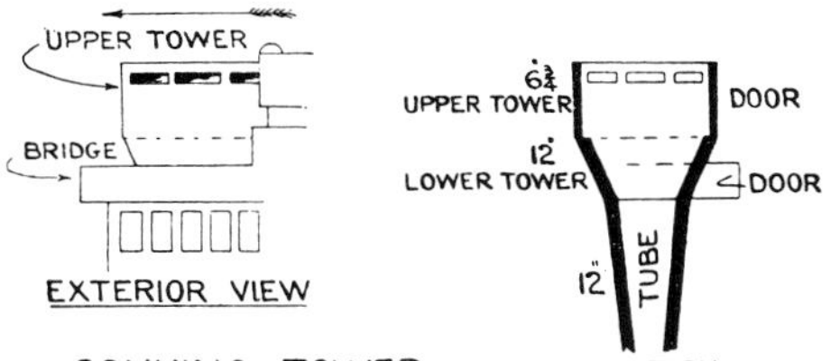

CONNING TOWER

(BRAUNSCHWEIG CLASS—5 SHIPS).

BRAUNSCHWEIG (Dec., 1902), **ELSASS** (May, 1903), **LOTHRINGEN** (May, 1904), **HESSEN** (Sept., 1903), & **PREUSSEN** (Oct., 1903). Displacement, 13,200 tons. Complement, (743 ?). Length (*waterline*), 413⅓ feet. Beam, 72⅘ feet. *Mean* draught, 25¾ feet. Length *over all*, 430 feet. *Guns (M. '01.): 4—11 inch, 40 cal, (A^3), 14—6·7 inch, 40 cal., 18—3·4 inch (22 pdr.) ?, 2 Machine. Torpedo tubes (17·7 inch): 5 *submerged* (bow and broadside), 1 *above water* (stern). Armour (Krupp): 8¾″ Belt (amidships), 4″ Belt (ends), 3″ Deck on slopes, 11″ Barbettes to these, 11″ Turrets (side), 5″ Lower deck, 6″ Battery, 6¾″ Small turrets, 12″ Conning tower, 6″ Conning tower (aft). Machinery: 3 sets 3 cylinder vertical inverted triple expansion. 3 screws. Boilers: 8 Schulz-Thornycroft + 6 cylindrical. Designed H.P. 16,000 = 18 kts. Coal: *normal* 700 tons; *maximum* 1670 tons. Also 200 tons of oil (in double bottom). *Nominal* radius: 5500 miles at 10 kts.

**Note.*—Guns and tubes given, those originally mounted. Present guns and disposal of ships as follows:—

Name	*Guns*	*Service.*
Braunschweig	Disarmed; guns removed.	Accommodation Ship.
Elsass	" "	Accommodation Ship.
Lothringen	" "	Sea-going Parent Ship for Motor Boat Minesweepers.*
Hessen	" "	Accommodation Ship.
Preussen	" "	Sea-going Parent Ship for Motor Boat Minesweepers.*

Name.	*Builder.*	*Machinery.*	*Laid down.*	*Com-pleted.*	*Full power trials: 24 hrs.*	*6 hrs.*	*Boilers.*	*Best recent speed.*
Braunschweig	Germania, Kiel	By Builders	1901	1904	11,382 = 16·3	17,312 = 18·6	8 Schulz-T. and 6 cyl. in all.	18·1
Hessen	Germania, Kiel		1902	1905	11,384 = 16·4	16,900 = 18·23		
Preussen	Vulkan, Stettin		1902	1905	11,304 = 16·2	18,374 = 18·69		
Elsass	Schichau, D'zig		1901	1904	11,554 = 16·7	16,812 = 18·7		18·6
Lothringen	Schichau, D'zig		1902	1906	11,573 = 16·5	16,950 = 18·54		

* Each has superstructures for carrying 12 Motor Boat Minesweepers.

WITTELSBACH (1900), **WETTIN** (1901), **ZÄHRINGEN** (1901), **MECKLENBURG** (1901), **SCHWABEN** (1901). Displacement, 11,800 tons. Complement was 683. Dimensions: 410¾ (*w.l.*), 416½ (*o.a.*) × 68¼ × 28 feet (*maximum* draught). *Guns (M. '99): 4—9.4 inch, 40 cal., 18—5·9 inch, 40 cal., 12—3·4 inch (15 pdr.), 2 M.G. *Torpedo tubes (17·7 inch): 6 *submerged* (bow, stern and broadside). Armour (Krupp): 9″ Belt (ends), 3″ Deck on slopes, 10″ Barbettes, 10″ Turrets to them, 5½″ Lower deck (redoubt), 5½″ Battery, 6″ Casemates (4 bow), 6″ Small turrets, 10″ Conning tower. Machinery: 3 sets vertical triple expansion. 3 screws. Boilers: 6 Schulz-Thornycroft and 6 cylindrical. Designed H.P. 15,000 = 18 kts. Coal: *normal*, 653 tons; *maximum*, 1800 tons. Oil: 200 tons.

*Guns and tubes given, those originally mounted. Present armament and disposal of ships as follows:—

Name	*Guns*	*Service*
Wittelsbach / *Wettin*	Disarmed.	Parent Ships for Minesweepers, Wilhelmshaven.
Zahringen	Turrets removed. 7—5·9 inch.* 4—15 pdr.*	Training Ship, Danzig.
Mecklenburg	Disarmed.	Accommodation Ship, Kiel.
Schwaben	Turrets removed. 6—5·9 inch.* 4—15 pdr.*	Sea-going Parent Ship for Motor Boat Minesweepers, Wilhelmshaven.

*Guns on board, but ships are disarmed.

1890 OLD GERMAN BATTLESHIPS. 1887

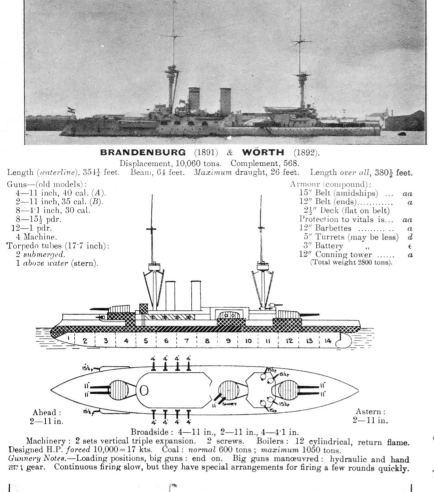

BRANDENBURG (1891) & WÖRTH (1892).

Displacement, 10,060 tons. Complement, 568.

Length (waterline), 354¼ feet. Beam, 64 feet. Maximum draught, 26 feet. Length over all, 380½ feet.

Guns—(old models):
- 4—11 inch, 40 cal. (A).
- 2—11 inch, 35 cal. (B).
- 8—4·1 inch, 30 cal.
- 8—15½ pdr.
- 12—1 pdr.
- 4 Machine.

Torpedo tubes (17·7 inch):
- 2 submerged.
- 1 above water (stern).

Armour (compound):
- 15" Belt (amidships) ... aa
- 12" Belt (ends)........... a
- 2½" Deck (flat on belt)
- Protection to vitals is... aa
- 12" Barbettes .... a
- 5" Turrets (may be less) d
- 3" Battery ,, e
- 12" Conning tower ...... a
- (Total weight 2800 tons).

Ahead:
2—11 in.

Astern:
2—11 in.

Broadside: 4—11 in., 2—11 in., 4—4·1 in.

Machinery: 2 sets vertical triple expansion. 2 screws. Boilers: 12 cylindrical, return flame. Designed H.P. forced 10,000 = 17 kts. Coal: normal 600 tons; maximum 1050 tons.

Gunnery Notes.—Loading positions, big guns: end on. Big guns manœuvred: hydraulic and hand gear. Continuous firing slow, but they have special arrangements for firing a few rounds quickly.

KAISER FRIEDRICH III. (1896), K. WILHELM II. (1897), K. BARBAROSSA (1900), K. WILHELM DER GROSSE (1899), K. KARL DER GROSSE (1899),

Displacement, (reconstructed) 10,790 tons. Complement, 658.

Length (waterline), 384 feet. Beam, 65½ feet. Maximum draught, 27 feet.

Guns—(M. '95):
- 4—9·4 inch, 40 cal. (A).
- 14—6 inch, 40 cal. (K. Karl 18).
- 12—15½ pdr.
- 12—1 pdr.
- 8 Machine.

Torpedo tubes (17·7 inch):
- 5 submerged (bow and broadside).
- 1 above water (stern).

Armour (Krupp):
- 12" Belt (amidships) ... aaa
- 4" Belt (bow) .... d
- 8" Bulkheads (aft) ...... aa
- 3" Deck (flat on belt)
- Protection to vitals is... aaa
- 10" Barbettes .... aa
- 10" Turrets to these ... aa
- 6" on secondary guns ... b
- 10" Conning tower (N.C.) aa
- (Total weight 3,800 tons).

Ahead:
2—9·4 in.
6—6 in.

Astern:
2—9·4 in.
6—6 in.

Machinery: 3 sets vertical 3 cylinder triple expansion. 3 screws. Boilers: 8 cylindrical, 4 Schultz; (in K. Karl der Grosse and K. Barbarossa 6). Designed H.P. 14,000 = 18 knots. Coal: normal 650 tons; maximum 1,050 tons; also 200 tons liquid fuel (double bottom).

Name	Builder	Machinery	Laid down	Completed	Refit	Trials		Boilers	Best recent speed
K. Friedrich III.	Wilhelmsh'vn	...	1895	1898	1908				
K. Wilhelm II.	Wilhelmsh'vn	...	1896	1900	1908				
K. W. der Grosse	Krupp	Krupp	1898	1901	1908				
K. Karl der Grosse	Blohm & Voss	Blohm & Voss	1898	1901					
K. Barbarossa	Schichau	Schichau	1898	1901	1907	7360 = 15·5	13,940 = 18		17·5

ODIN (1894) & ÆGIR (1895), 4150 tons.
and
SIEGFRIED (1889), BEOWULF (1890), FRITHJOF (1891), HEIMDALL (1892), HILDEBRAND (1892), HAGEN (1893). 4100 tons.

Guns (in all): 3—old 9·4 inch, 35 cal. (C); 10—15½ pdr.; 6—1 pdr.; 4 machine. Torpedo tubes: 3—17 inch, submerged. Armour: In first two, nickel, belt (amidships only) 8½"; in others, compound complete belt 9½"—6", barbettes (2 guns forward, 1 aft) 8". Speeds: about 15 kts. (Fuller detail see 1910 and previous editions.)

(Employed on coast defence in the Baltic.)

1906 GERMAN ARMOURED CRUISER (Panzer-Kreuzer).

BLUCHER (April, 1908).

Normal displacement, 15,500 tons. Complement, 847.

Length (waterline), 489 feet. Beam, 80⅓ feet. Maximum draught, 27 feet. Length over all, 493 feet.

Guns (M. '04):
- 12—8·2 inch, 45 cal. (A).
- 8—6 inch, 45 cal.
- 16—24 pdr., 40 cal.

Torpedo tubes:
- 3 submerged.

Armour (Krupp):
- 6" Belt (amidships) ......
- 4" Belt (ends)..............
- " Armour deck ....
- Protection to vitals ......
- 6" Turrets ....

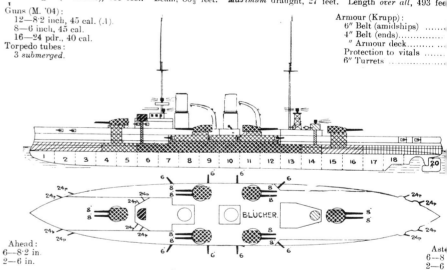

Ahead:
6—8·2 in.
2—6 in.

Astern:
6—8·2 in.
2—6 in.

Broadside: 8—8·2 in., 4—6 in.

Machinery: 3 sets vertical inverted triple expansion. 3 screws. Boilers: 18 Schulz-Thornycroft. Designed H.P. 32,000 = 24·5 kts. Coal: normal 900 tons; maximum 2300; and 200 tons oil.

Gunnery Notes.—Most of big guns replaced, 1912. Fire control in each turret. Masthead spotting stations.

Torpedo Notes.—Nets fitted, 1911.

Name	Builder	Machinery	Laid down	Completed	Trials.	Boilers	Best recent speed.
Blucher	Kiel Yard		Oct'06	Sep'09	mean. 43,886 = 25·86	Schulz Thornycroft	26·4

General Notes.—Total cost, £1,349,000. On her trials this ship touched 26·4 kts. She is a very successful ship in all respects.

Note—Sunk at Battle of Doger Bank 24 February 1915.

BLUECHER, 1914, new rig.

1904 GERMAN ARMOURED CRUISERS (*Panzer-Kreuzer*) (22½ knot).

(SCHARNHORST CLASS—2 Ships).
SCHARNHORST (March, 1906) & **GNEISENAU** (June, 1906).
Displacement, 11,600 tons. Complement, 765.
Length (*waterline*), 449¾ feet. Beam, 71 feet. *Mean* draught, 25 feet. Length *over all*, feet.
Note—Both sunk at Battle of the Falkands 8 December 1914.

Guns :
8—8·2 inch, 40 cal. (A).
6—6 inch, 40 cal.
20—24 pdr., 35 cals.
4 Machine.
Torpedo tubes (18 inch) :
4 *submerged* (bow, stern, and broadside).

Armour (Krupp) :
6″ Belt (amidships)	a
4¾″ Belt (bow)	c
4″ Belt (aft)	d
2″ Armour deck	
Protection to vitals ... =	aa
5″ Bulkheads	b
6″ Barbettes	b
6¾″ Turret hoods	a
6″ Lower deck side	a
6″ Battery (N.C.)	b
6″ Upper battery (N.C.)	b
5″ Battery bulkheads (K.C.)	b
8″ Conning tower	a

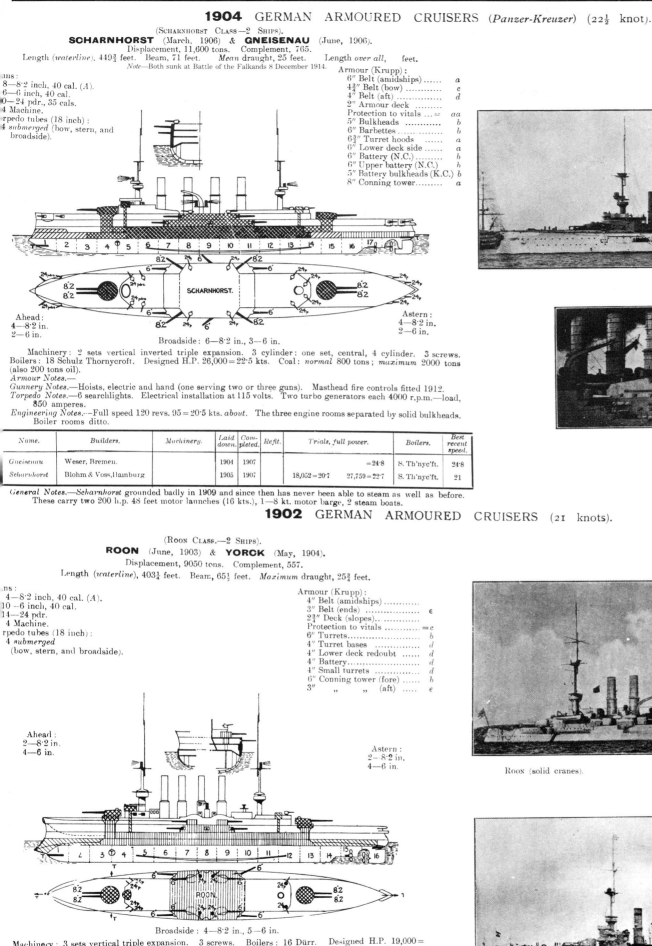

SCHARNHORST.

Ahead :
4—8·2 in.
2—6 in.

Astern :
4—8·2 in.
2—6 in.

Broadside : 6—8·2 in., 3—6 in.

Machinery : 2 sets vertical inverted triple expansion. 3 cylinder : one set, central, 4 cylinder. 3 screws.
Boilers : 18 Schulz Thornycroft. Designed H.P. 26,000 = 22·5 kts. Coal : *normal* 800 tons ; *maximum* 2000 tons (also 200 tons oil).
Armour Notes.—
Gunnery Notes.—Hoists, electric and hand (one serving two or three guns). Masthead fire controls fitted 1912.
Torpedo Notes.—6 searchlights. Electrical installation at 115 volts. Two turbo generators each 4000 r.p.m.—load, 850 amperes.
Engineering Notes.—Full speed 120 revs. 95 = 20·5 kts. *about.* The three engine rooms separated by solid bulkheads. Boiler rooms ditto.

Name.	Builders.	Machinery.	Laid down.	Com- pleted.	Refit.	Trials, full power.		Boilers.	Best recent speed.
Gneisenau	Weser, Bremen.		1904	1907			=24·8	S. Th'nyc'ft.	24·8
Scharnhorst	Blohm & Voss, Hamburg		1905	1907		18,052 = 20·7	27,759 = 22·7	S. Th'nyc'ft.	21

General Notes.—Scharnhorst grounded badly in 1909 and since then has never been able to steam as well as before. These carry two 200 h.p. 48 feet motor launches (16 kts.), 1—8 kt. motor barge, 2 steam boats.

1902 GERMAN ARMOURED CRUISERS (21 knots).

(ROON CLASS.—2 SHIPS).
ROON (June, 1903) & **YORCK** (May, 1904).
Displacement, 9050 tons. Complement, 557.
Length (*waterline*), 403¼ feet. Beam, 65½ feet. *Maximum* draught, 25¾ feet.

Guns :
4—8·2 inch, 40 cal. (A).
10—6 inch, 40 cal.
14—24 pdr.
4 Machine.
Torpedo tubes (18 inch) :
4 *submerged*
(bow, stern, and broadside).

Armour (Krupp) :
4″ Belt (amidships)	
3″ Belt (ends)	ϵ
2¾″ Deck (slopes)..	
Protection to vitals .... =	c
6″ Turrets	b
4″ Turret bases	d
4″ Lower deck redoubt	d
4″ Battery..................	d
4″ Small turrets	d
6″ Conning tower (fore)	b
3″ „ „ (aft)	ϵ

Roon (solid cranes).

Ahead :
2—8·2 in.
4—6 in.

Astern :
2—8·2 in.
4—6 in.

ROON.

Broadside : 4—8·2 in., 5—6 in.

Machinery : 3 sets vertical triple expansion. 3 screws. Boilers : 16 Dürr. Designed H.P. 19,000 = kts. Coal : *normal* 750 tons ; *maximum* 1600 tons ; also 200 tons of oil. 118 revs. = full speed.
General Notes.—Except for some minor details and slightly increased H.P., these ships are identical with the P. Adalbert class (*q.v.*).

Name.	Built at	Laid down.	Completed.	24 hours.	Trials.		Boilers.
Yorck	Blohm & Voss	April, '03	May, '06	13,711 = 19 kts.	20,295 = 21·4 kts.		Dürr
Roon	Kiel Dockyard	Aug., '02	Oct., '05		20,625 = 21·17 kts.		Dürr

YORCK (pierced cranes).

1900 GERMAN ARMOURED CRUISERS. 1899

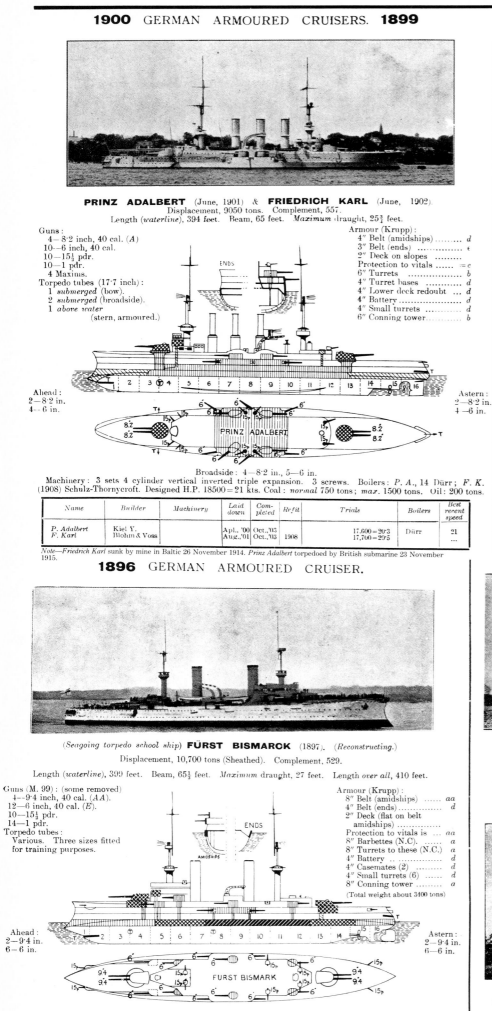

PRINZ ADALBERT (June, 1901) & **FRIEDRICH KARL** (June, 1902).
Displacement, 9050 tons. Complement, 557.
Length (waterline), 394 feet. Beam, 65 feet. Maximum draught, 25¾ feet.

Guns :
  4—8·2 inch, 40 cal. (A)
  10—6 inch, 40 cal.
  10—15½ pdr.
  10—1 pdr.
  4 Maxims.
Torpedo tubes (17·7 inch) :
  1 submerged (bow).
  2 submerged (broadside).
  1 above water
    (stern, armoured.)

Armour (Krupp) :
  4″ Belt (amidships) .... d
  3″ Belt (ends) .... e
  2″ Deck on slopes ....
  Protection to vitals ...... =c
  6″ Turrets .... b
  4″ Turret bases .... d
  4″ Lower deck redoubt .. d
  4″ Battery .... d
  4″ Small turrets .... d
  6″ Conning tower......... b

Ahead :
2—8·2 in.
4—6 in.

Astern :
2—8·2 in.
4—6 in.

Broadside : 4—8·2 in., 5—6 in.

Machinery : 3 sets 4 cylinder vertical inverted triple expansion. 3 screws. Boilers : P. A., 14 Dürr; F. K. (1908) Schulz-Thornycroft. Designed H.P. 18500 = 21 kts. Coal : normal 750 tons; max. 1500 tons. Oil : 200 tons.

Name	Builder	Machinery	Laid down	Completed	Refit	Trials	Boilers	Best recent speed
P. Adalbert	Kiel Y.		Apl., '00	Oct.,'03		17.600=20·3	Dürr	21
F. Karl	Blohm & Voss		Aug.,'01	Oct.,'03	1908	17,700=20·5		...

Note—Friedrich Karl sunk by mine in Baltic 26 November 1914. Prinz Adalbert torpedoed by British submarine 23 November 1915.

1896 GERMAN ARMOURED CRUISER.

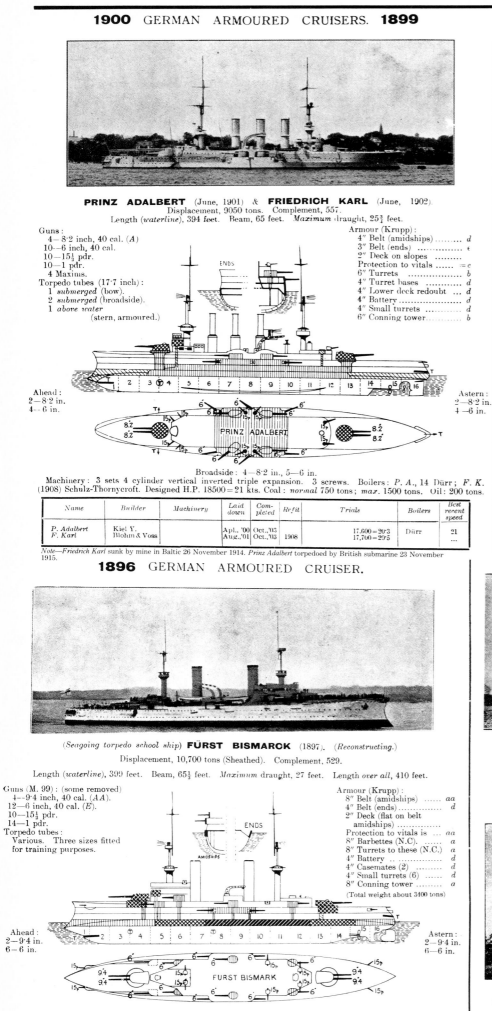

(Seagoing torpedo school ship) **FÜRST BISMARCK** (1897). (Reconstructing.)
Displacement, 10,700 tons (Sheathed). Complement, 529.

Length (waterline), 399 feet. Beam, 65½ feet. Maximum draught, 27 feet. Length over all, 410 feet.

Guns (M. 99) : (some removed)
  4—9·4 inch, 40 cal. (AA).
  12—6 inch, 40 cal. (E).
  10—15½ pdr.
  14—1 pdr.
Torpedo tubes :
  Various. Three sizes fitted
  for training purposes.

Armour (Krupp) :
  8″ Belt (amidships) ...... aa
  4″ Belt (ends)............. d
  2″ Deck (flat on belt
    amidships) ....
  Protection to vitals is ... aa
  8″ Barbettes (N.C.) ...... a
  8″ Turrets to these (N.C.) a
  4″ Battery ....
  4″ Casemates (2) ....
  4″ Small turrets (6) ...... d
  8″ Conning tower .... a
  (Total weight about 3400 tons)

Ahead :
2—9·4 in.
6—6 in.

Astern :
2—9·4 in.
6—6 in.

Machinery : 3 sets vertical triple expansion. 3 screws. Boilers : 8 Schulz Thornycroft and 8 cylindrical. Designed H.P. 13,600 = 19 kts. Coal : normal 1000 tons; maximum 1200 tons.

GERMAN BIG PROTECTED CRUISERS. 1895

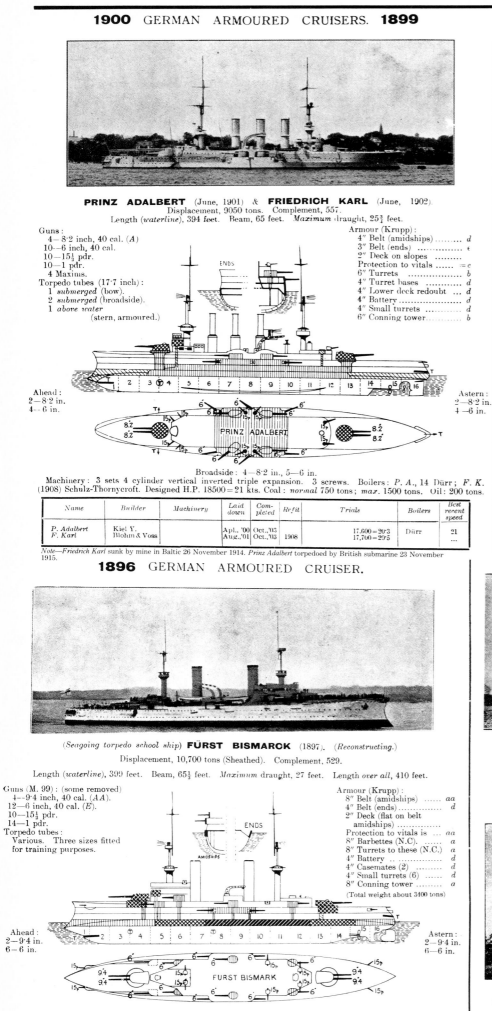

(Training service) **FREYA** (1897), **HERTHA** (1897), **VICTORIA LUISE** (1897), **HANSA** ( )
and **VINETA** (1897).
Displacement, 5660, but last two 5885 tons. Complement, 465.
Length, 344½ feet. Beam, 57 feet. Maximum draught, 23 feet.

Guns :
  2—8·2 inch, 40 cal. (B).
  6—6 inch, 40 cal.
  12—15½ pdr.
  10—1 pdr.
  4 Machine.
Torpedo tubes (17·7 inch) :
  3 submerged (1 in bow).

Armour (Krupp) :
  4″ Deck ....
  Cork belt amidships ...
  Protection to vitals ...
  4″ Turrets and casemates
  5″ Glacis to funnels ...
  3½″ Hoists ....
  8″ Fore C.T. ....

Ahead :
1—8·2 in.
4—6 in.

Astern :
1—8·2 in.
2—6 in.

Broadside : 2—8·2 in., 3—6 in.

Machinery : 3 sets 4 cylinder triple expansion. 3 screws. Designed H.P. 10,500 = 19 kts. normal 900 tons; maximum 1,000 tons.

Name.	Builder	Machinery	Laid down	Completed	Recon-structed		Boilers
Freya	Danzig Y.	Krupp	Oct. '95	1898	1908		8 Schulz Thornycroft except Freya 12 Niclausse
Hertha	Vulk. Stettin	Vulkan Co.	Sep. '95	1898	1907		
V. Luise	Weser, Bremen	Weser, Bremen	Sep. '95	1898	1907		
Hansa	Vulkan Co.	Vulkan Co.	Mar. '96	1898	1907		
Vineta	Vulkan Co.	Vulkan Co.	Jun. '96	1898	1910		

(Stokers' Training Ship.)
PRINZ HEINRICH (March, 1900). Displacement, 8900 tons. Complement (was 567). Dimensions : 409¾ × 64½ × 25½ feet (maximum draught). Guns : None. Torpedo tubes 18 inch) : 1 submerged (bow), 2 submerged (broadside), 1 above water (stern), all probably removed. Armour (Krupp) : 4″ Belt (amidships), 3″ Belt (ends), 2″ Deck, 6″ Turrets, 4″ Turret bases, 4″ Lower deck side, 4″ Battery. Machinery : 3 sets triple expansion 4-cylinder, 3 screws. Boilers : 14 Dürr. Designed H.P. 15,000 = 20·5 kts. Coal : normal, 750 tons; maximum, 1500 tons. Also 200 tons liquid fuel.
Note : Fürst Bismarck sold 1919.

(Gunnery School Ship.)
KAISERIN AUGUSTA (1892). Displacement, 6060 tons. Complement (was 439). Dimensions : 401 × 51 × 25½ feet. Guns : 1—5·9 inch, 4—4·1 inch, 10—3·4 inch (22 and 15 pdr.). Torpedo tubes (13·8 inch) : 1 submerged (bow), 2 above water (broadside). Armour : 3½″ Deck (amidships), 1½″ at ends. Machinery : 3 sets vertical triple expansion. 3 screws. Boilers : 8 two-ended cylindrical. Designed H.P. forced draught 12,000 = 21·5 kts. (much less now). Coal : 810 tons.

GERMAN LIGHT CRUISERS.

(All are officially rated as "Kleine Geschützte Kreuzer" or "Small Protected Cruisers.")

KÖNIGSBERG CLASS.

EMDEN (February, 1916). **NÜRNBERG** (January, 1916).

KÖNIGSBERG (December, 1915).

Displacement, about 4,200 tons.　　Complement, —.

Length, 450 feet.　　Beam, 43½ feet.　　Draught, 16 feet.

Guns :
—5·9 inch, 50 cal. (semi-auto.)
or 3—22 pdr. anti-aircraft
Torpedo tubes (19·7 inch) :
above water
submerged.

Armour :
" Belt (amidships) ....
" Belt (ends) ....
" Deck (amidships) ....
" Gun Shields ....
" Conning Tower (fore)
" Conning Tower (aft)

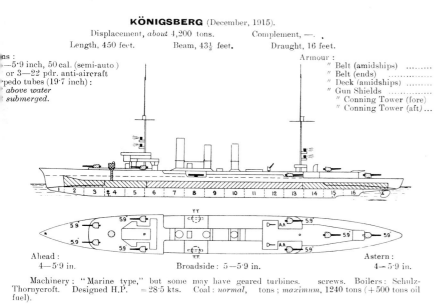

Photo by courtesy of Dr. J. A. Prendergast.

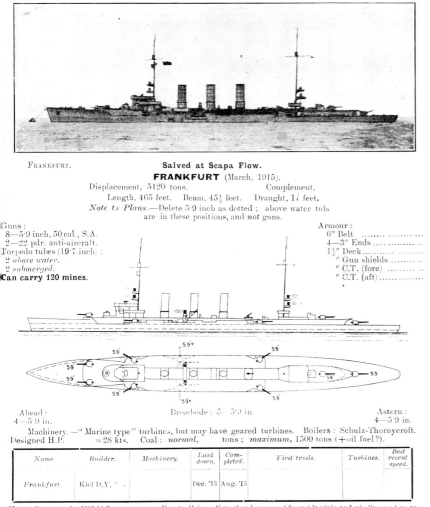

Ahead :
4—5·9 in.　　Broadside : 5—5·9 in.　　Astern :
4—5·9 in.

Machinery : "Marine type," but some may have geared turbines.　screws.　Boilers : Schulz-Thornycroft.　Designed H.P. = 28·5 kts.　Coal : normal, tons ; maximum, 1240 tons (+500 tons oil fuel).

Gunnery Notes.—In Karlsruhe class, the 5·9 inch guns under fore bridges are a deck higher than in *Frankfurt* ; that is, on same level as the forecastle 5·9's.

Name	Builder	Machinery	Laid down	Completed	Trials	Turbines
Emden	Weser, Bremen	Weser, Bremen	1915	Aug.'15		
Nürnberg	Howaldt, Kiel	Howaldt	1915	Nov.'16		
Königsberg	Weser Co., Bremen	Weser Co.	1914	Aug.'16		

General Notes.—Emden begun as *Ersatz Nymphe*, Nurnberg as *Ersatz Thetis*, both under 1915-16 Programme. *Königsberg* begun as *Ersatz Gazelle*, 1914-15 Programme.
Scuttled at Scapa Flow, June 21st, 1919.—*Dresden* (*Ersatz Amazone*, of 1916-17 Programme), launched by Howaldt, Kiel, November, 1916, and delivered 1918 ; *Koln* (*Ersatz Ariadne*, of 1916-17 Programme), launched by Blohm & Voss, Hamburg, October, 1916, and finished 1917 ; *Karlsruhe* (*Ersatz Niobe*, of 1914-15 Programme), launched at Kiel D.Y., February, 1916, and completed November, 1916. Two Minelaying Cruisers, Bremse and Brummer (not of *Königsberg* class), also scuttled at Scapa Flow.

1913 GERMAN LIGHT CRUISERS.

FRANKFURT.

Salved at Scapa Flow.
FRANKFURT (March, 1915).

Displacement, 5120 tons.　　Complement.

Length, 465 feet.　　Beam, 45¼ feet.　　Draught, 17 feet.

Note to Plans.—Delete 5·9 inch as dotted ; above water tubes are in these positions, and *not* guns.

Guns :
8—5·9 inch, 50 cal., S.A.
2—22 pdr. anti-aircraft.
Torpedo tubes (19·7 inch) :
2 above water.
2 submerged.
Can carry 120 mines.

Armour :
6" Belt ....
4—3" Ends ....
1½" Deck ....
" Gun shields..........
" C.T. (fore) ....
" C.T. (aft) ....

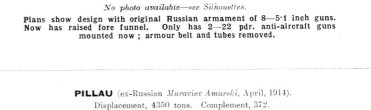

Ahead :
4—5·9 in.　　Broadside : 5—5·9 in.　　Astern :
4—5·9 in.

Machinery.—"Marine type" turbines, but may have geared turbines.　Boilers : Schulz-Thornycroft.
Designed H.P. = 28 kts.　Coal : normal, tons ; maximum, 1500 tons (+oil fuel?).

Name	Builder	Machinery	Laid down	Completed	First trials	Turbines	Best recent speed.
Frankfurt	Kiel D.Y.		Dec. '13	Aug. '15			

Notes.—Begun under 1913-14 Programme as *Ersatz Hela*. Note that her second funnel is plain and wholly cased up to top, instead of being half-cased like first and third funnels. The half-casing to second funnel in above view is not correct.

No photo available—see Silhouettes.

**Plans show design with original Russian armament of 8—5·1 inch guns.
Now has raised fore funnel.　Only has 2—22 pdr. anti-aircraft guns
mounted now ; armour belt and tubes removed.**

PILLAU (ex-Russian *Muraviev Amurski*, April, 1914).

Displacement, 4350 tons.　　Complement, 372.

Length (p.p.), 403 feet.　Beam, 46 feet.　{ Mean draught, 16 feet. { Length (o.a.), 441 feet.
{ Max.　" 19 feet. {

Guns :
8—5·9 inch, 50 cal., S.A.
2—22 pdr. anti-aircraft
Torpedo tubes (19·7 inch) :
2 above water.

Armour :
1½" Deck (on slopes)......
¾" Deck (bow) ....
3" Deck (over rudder) ..
3" Conning tower ......

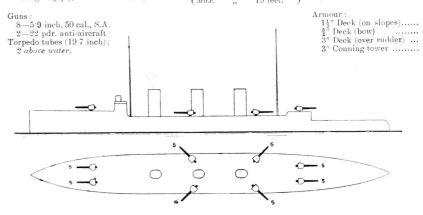

Machinery : Schichau (Melms & Pfenninger) turbines.　3 screws.　Designed H.P. 27,400 = 27½ kts.
Boilers : Yarrow (may be altered to Schulz Thornycroft).　Coal : normal 500 tons ; maximum 1000 tons, and 250 tons oil fuel.

Name	Builder	Machinery	Laid down	Completed	Trials :		Boilers	Best recent speed
					F.P.			
Pillau	Schichau, Danzig	Schichau	Apl., '13	Dec. '15				

General Notes.—Design is based on *Kolberg* class. A sister ship, *Elbing*, sunk in the Battle of Jutland. Both vessels were seized by Germany on outbreak of war with Russia, for whom they were originally laid down.

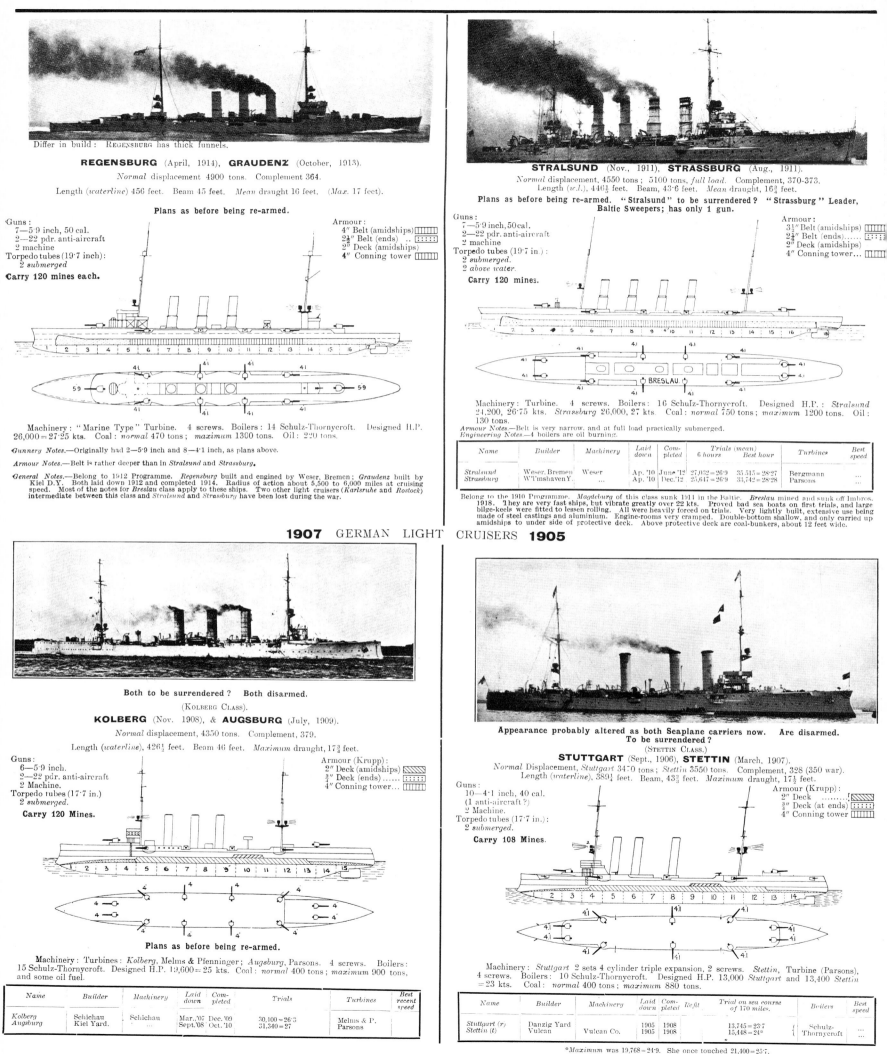

Differ in build : REGENSBURG has thick funnels.

REGENSBURG (April, 1914), GRAUDENZ (October, 1913).

Normal displacement 4900 tons. Complement 364.

Length (*waterline*) 456 feet. Beam 45 feet. *Mean* draught 16 feet. (*Max.* 17 feet).

Plans as before being re-armed.

Guns :
7—5·9 inch, 50 cal.
2—22 pdr. anti-aircraft
2 machine
Torpedo tubes (19·7 inch):
2 *submerged*

Carry 120 mines each.

Armour :
4″ Belt (amidships)
2½″ Belt (ends) ..
2″ Deck (amidships)
4″ Conning tower

Machinery : "Marine Type" Turbine. 4 screws. Boilers : 14 Schulz-Thornycroft. Designed H.P. 26,000 = 27·25 kts. Coal : *normal* 470 tons ; *maximum* 1300 tons. Oil : 220 tons.

Gunnery Notes.—Originally had 2—5·9 inch and 8—4·1 inch, as plans above.

Armour Notes.—Belt is rather deeper than in *Stralsund* and *Strassburg.*

General Notes.—Belong to 1912 Programme. *Regensburg* built and engined by Weser, Bremen ; *Graudenz* built by Kiel D.Y. Both laid down 1912 and completed 1914. Radius of action about 5,500 to 6,000 miles at cruising speed. Most of the notes for *Breslau* class apply to these ships. Two other light cruisers (*Karlsruhe* and *Rostock*) intermediate between this class and *Stralsund* and *Strassburg* have been lost during the war.

STRALSUND (Nov., 1911), STRASSBURG (Aug., 1911).

Normal displacement, 4550 tons ; 5100 tons, *full load.* Complement, 370-373.
Length (*w.l.*), 446½ feet. Beam, 43·6 feet. *Mean* draught, 16¾ feet.

Plans as before being re-armed. "Stralsund" to be surrendered ? "Strassburg" Leader, Baltic Sweepers ; has only 1 gun.

Guns :
7—5·9 inch, 50 cal.
2—22 pdr. anti-aircraft
2 machine
Torpedo tubes (19·7 in.) :
2 *submerged*
2 *above water.*

Carry 120 mines.

Armour :
3½″ Belt (amidships)
2¼″ Belt (ends)......
2″ Deck (amidships)
4″ Conning tower...

Machinery : Turbine. 4 screws. Boilers : 16 Schulz-Thornycroft. Designed H.P. : *Stralsund* 24,200, 26·75 kts. *Strassburg* 26,000, 27 kts. Coal : *normal* 750 tons ; *maximum* 1200 tons. Oil : 130 tons.

Armour Notes.—Belt is very narrow, and at full load practically submerged.
Engineering Notes.—4 boilers are oil burning.

Name	Builder	Machinery	Laid down	Com- pleted	Trials (mean)		Turbines	Best speed
					6 hours	Best hour		
Stralsund	Weser, Bremen	Weser	Ap. '10	June '12	27,032 = 26·9	35,515 = 28·27	Bergmann	...
Strassburg	W'lm'shaven Y.	...	Ap. '10	Dec. '12	25,647 = 26·9	33,742 = 28·28	Parsons	...

Belong to the 1910 Programme. *Magdeburg* of this class sunk 1911 in the Baltic. *Breslau* mined and sunk off Imbros, 1918. They are very fast ships, but vibrate greatly over 22 kts. Proved bad sea boats on first trials. Very heavy bilge-keels were fitted to lessen rolling. All were heavily forced on trials. Very lightly built, extensive use being made of steel castings and aluminium. Engine-rooms very cramped. Double-bottom shallow, and only carried up amidships to under side of protective deck. Above protective deck are coal-bunkers, about 12 feet wide.

1907 GERMAN LIGHT CRUISERS **1905**

Both to be surrendered ? Both disarmed.

(KOLBERG CLASS).

KOLBERG (Nov. 1908), & AUGSBURG (July, 1909).

Normal displacement, 4350 tons. Complement, 379.

Length (*waterline*), 426¼ feet. Beam 46 feet. *Maximum* draught, 17¾ feet.

Guns :
6—5·9 inch.
2—22 pdr. anti-aircraft
2 Machine.
Torpedo tubes (17·7 in.)
2 *submerged*

Carry 120 Mines.

Armour (Krupp) :
2″ Deck (amidships)
¾″ Deck (ends) ......
4″ Conning tower...

Plans as before being re-armed.

Machinery : Turbines : *Kolberg*, Melms & Pfenninger ; *Augsburg*, Parsons. 4 screws. Boilers : 15 Schulz-Thornycroft. Designed H.P. 19,600 = 25 kts. Coal : *normal* 400 tons ; *maximum* 900 tons, and some oil fuel.

Name	Builder	Machinery	Laid down	Com- pleted	Trials	Turbines	Best recent speed
Kolberg	Schichau	Schichau	Mar., '07	Dec. '09	30,100 = 26·3	Melms & P.	...
Augsburg	Kiel Yard.	...	Sept. '08	Oct. '10	31,340 = 27	Parsons	...

Appearance probably altered as both Seaplane carriers now. Are disarmed.
To be surrendered ?

(STETTIN CLASS.)

STUTTGART (Sept., 1906), STETTIN (March, 1907).

Normal Displacement, *Stuttgart* 3470 tons ; *Stettin* 3550 tons. Complement, 328 (350 war).
Length (*waterline*) 389¼ feet. Beam, 43⅔ feet. *Maximum* draught, 17½ feet.

Guns :
10—4·1 inch, 40 cal.
(1 anti-aircraft ?)
2 Machine.
Torpedo tubes (17·7 in.) :
2 *submerged*

Carry 108 Mines.

Armour (Krupp) :
2″ Deck ....
¾″ Deck (at ends)
4″ Conning tower

Machinery : *Stuttgart* 2 sets 4 cylinder triple expansion, 2 screws. *Stettin*, Turbine (Parsons), 4 screws. Boilers : 10 Schulz-Thornycroft. Designed H.P. 13,000 *Stuttgart* and 13,400 *Stettin* = 23 kts. Coal : *normal* 400 tons ; *maximum* 880 tons.

Name	Builder	Machinery	Laid down	Com- pleted	Refit	Trial on sea course of 170 miles	Boilers	Best speed
Stuttgart (r)	Danzig Yard	Vulcan Co.	1905	1908		13,745 = 23·7	Schulz- Thornycroft	...
Stettin (t)	Vulcan	...	1905	1908		15,448 = 24*		...

*Maximum was 19,768 = 24·9. She once touched 21,400 = 25·7.

OLD GERMAN LIGHT CRUISERS.

DANZIG. Has bridges round foremast.

HAMBURG, &c., as above.

DANZIG (September, 1905), **HAMBURG** (July, 1903), **BERLIN** (September, 1903), **LÜBECK** (March, 1904), and **MÜNCHEN** (April, 1904). *Normal* displacement, 3250 tons. Complement, 303. Dimensions : 362.9 × 43.3 × 17½ feet (*maximum* draught). Guns : As noted below. Torpedo tubes (17.7 inch) : 2 *submerged.* Armour (Krupp) : 2″ Deck, ¾″ Deck (at ends), 4″ C.T. Machinery : 2 sets 4-cylinder triple expansion. 2 screws. *Lübeck*, turbine (Parsons), 8 screws on 4 shafts. Boilers : 10 Shulz-Thornycroft. Designed H.P. 10,000 (*Lübeck* 11,200 S.H.P.) = 22 kts. Coal : *normal*, 400 tons ; *maximum*, 860 tons. *Nominal* radius, 5900 at 10 kts. *Danzig* begun 1904, completed 1907 ; others begun 1902-3, completed 1904-5.

Notes.

Reported that DANZIG, MÜNCHEN and LÜBECK are named for surrender in Peace Treaty.

Name	Armament	Mines	Present Service	Station
Danzig ..	10—4.1 inch, 2 M.G.	108	Paid off.	Danzig.
Hamburg ..	,, ,,	,,	,,	Wilhelmshaven
Berlin ..	,, ,,	,,	Headquarters S.N.O. Baltic.	Kiel.
München ..	,, ,,	,,	Paid off.	Kiel.
Lübeck ..	2—5.9 inch, 6—4.1 inch, 2 M.G.	,,	,,	Kiel.

OBSOLETE GERMAN LIGHT CRUISERS.

ARKONA (April, 1902). Displacement, 2700 tons (sheathed). Complement, 281. Dimensions : 342·4 × 40·3 × 17¼ feet (*maximum* draught). Guns : 10—4·1 inch, 2 M.G. Torpedo tubes (17·7 inch) : 2 *submerged.* Can carry 400 mines. Armour (Krupp) : 2″ Deck, 4″ C.T. Machinery : 2 sets 4-cylinder triple expansion. 2 screws. Designed H.P. 8000 = 21·5 kts. Coal : *normal*, 450 tons ; *maximum*, 710 tons. Boilers : 9 Schulz-Thornycroft.

Condition of all Ships named on this page.

Arkona :—Guns on board. Sea-going Parent Ship for Motor Boat Minesweepers (*UZ* boats), North Sea.

Nymphe :—Disarmed. Depot Ship.

Thetis :—Disarmed.

Amazone :—Disarmed.

Medusa :—Guns on board. Sea-going Parent Ship for North Sea Motor Boat Minesweepers (*UZ* boats).

Niobe :—Disarmed and paid off.

(*Gazelle :*—Only Mine Hulk. Is deleted.)

(*Gefion :*—Hulk. Is deleted.)

MEDUSA.   *Photo, Abrahams, Devonport.*

NYMPHE (1899), **THETIS** (1900), **AMAZONE** (1900), & **MEDUSA** (1900). *Normal* displacement, 2650 tons. (Sheathed and Muntz metalled.) Complement, 275. Dimensions : 324·4 × 38·7 × 17¼ feet (*maximum* draught). Guns : 6—4·1 inch, 2 M.G. Torpedo tubes (17.7 inch) : 2 *submerged.* Armour (Krupp) : 2″ Deck (amidships), ¾″ Deck (at ends), 3½″ Glacis to engine room hatches, 3″ C.T. Cofferdam and cellulose amidships. Machinery : 2 sets 4-cylinder triple expansion. 2 screws. Boilers : 9 Schulz-Thornycroft. Designed H.P. 8000 = 21 kts. Coal : *normal*, 380 tons ; *maximum*, 580 tons.

As *Medusa.*

NIOBE (1899). *Normal* displacement, 2600 tons. (Sheathed and Muntz metalled.) Complement, 268. Dimensions : 342·5 × 38·7 × 17¼ feet (*maximum* draught). Guns : 10—4·1 inch, 40 cal., 2 M.G. Torpedo tubes (17·7 inch) : 2 *submerged.* Armour (Krupp) : 2″ Deck (amidships), ¾″ Deck (at ends), 3½″ Glacis to hatches, &c., 3″ C.T., Cofferdam and cellulose amidships. Machinery : 2 sets 4-cylinder triple expansion. 2 screws. Boilers : 5 Thornycroft in *Niobe.* Designed H.P. 8000 = 21·5 kts. Coal : *normal*, 300 tons ; *maximum*, 600 tons.

GERMAN DESTROYERS (*Grosse Torpedoboote*).

90 (a) Modern } Destroyers = 178.
88 (b) Older }

(a) *About 45 of these unfinished.*   (b) *About 12—15 of these quite useless.*

Totals.	Class.	Begun.	Completed.	Displacement.	Nominal H.P.	Nominal Speed.	T. Tubes.	Coal/Oil.†	Complement.
				tons		kts.		tons	
35	G 148—H 190	1917	..	..	..	..	..	..	..
10	S 115—B 124	1916	1919 ?	1400	..	35—38	4	..	..
13	V 125—H 147	1916	1918 }	750—800	..	34—35	4 or 6	..	..
9	S 53—G 95	1915	1916 }						
1	V 100 }	1915	1916	1300	..	34	6	..	..
2	B 97, 98 }								
4	V 43—S 51	1914	1915	700—750	23,000t	34	6	300	..
1	G 102	1913	1915	1250	24,000t	32	6	345	9½
2	V 26, V 28	1913	1915	650	20,000t	32·5	6	290	..
4	S 18—24	1912	1914	570	15,000t	32·5	4	135/55	..
9	{ G 11—7 V 6—1 }	1911	1912	564	15,000t	32·5	4	140/60	73
8	{ T 197—192 T 191—186 }	1910	1911	648—656	16,000t	32·5	4*	165/55	83—93
11	{ T 185—180 T 179—176 T 175—174 }	1909	1910	636—654	16,000t	31·5—32.5	4*	170/45	83
7	{ T 173—169 T 168—165 T 164—163 }	1908	1909	613—636	14,000t	30—32	3*	160/40	83
11	T 161—151	1907	1908	554	10,250	30	3*	160	83
11	T 149—139	1906	1907	530	10,000	30	3*	190	72
1	T 137	1905	1907	572	10,800t	32	3*	170	80
6	T 136—132	1905	1907	487	6500	27	3*	135	60
10	{ T 131—125 T 122—120 T 114	1904 1903 1902	1906 1905 1904	485 470 420	6500 6500 6200	27 27 26	} 3*	116	60—56
6	T 113—108	1901	1903	400	5600	27	}		
6	T 107—102	1900	1902	400	5400	26	3*	92-116	56
11	T 101—91	1899	1900	400	5400	26			

*Tubes removed from nearly all these boats.
†An additional deck load of coal can be carried as follows :—+ 10 tons up to T 114, + 15 tons from T 120 up to T 149, about 20 tons up to V 28, about 25 tons in later boats.

1915-16.

From the "Illustrirte Zeitung."

6 Schichau: **S49, S50, S52, S53,* S60,* S63** } Launched 1915-16.
6 Vulkan: **V69, V71, V73, V79, V80,* V81*** }

*Salved at Scapa Flow.

(Raised fore funnel now).   *Photo, Newspaper Illustrations Co.*
1 Krupp-Germania: **G 95** (1916).

Displacement *about* 750 tons. **Approximate** dimensions : 270 to 272 × 27 × feet. S.H.P. 23,000 Designed speed: 34 kts. Armament: 3—4·1 inch, 2 machine, may also have a small automatic (or semi-auto.) anti-aircraft gun. Torpedo tubes: 6—19·7 inch, in 2 single and 2 twin deck mountings. Complement, 96 to 100. Oil only 330 tons.

V 84-67. S 66-58. S 57-49.

G 96-86.

1917-19 (majority unfinished).

2 Krupp-Germania : G 148, G 149.
6 Howaldt : H 166—H 169, H 188—H 190.
15 Schichau : S 152—S 157, S 179 S 187.
12 Vulkan : V 158—V 165, V 140—V 144.

Launched 1918-19, but all work now stopped. No details available, but said to be about 750 to 800 tons. Believed that G150 and 151 were never begun, and boats numbered 170 to 178 were never contracted for.

1917-19 (majority unfinished).

3 Blohm & Voss : B 122—B 124.
1 Krupp-Germania : G 119.
3 Schichau : S 113—S 115.
3 Vulkan : V 116—118.

Launched 1917-18, but only a few finished. G 120, G 121 abandoned. About 1400 tons. Armed with 4—5.9 inch and 4—23.6 inch tubes. Speed : 35-38 kts. No other details known.

1917-18.

2 Howaldt : H 146, H 147.
6 Schichau : S 132—S 135, S 137, S 139.
5 Vulkan : V 125—V 128, V 130.

Launched 1917-18. About 750-800 tons. Dimensions : about 270 × 27 × 10½ feet. Armament : 3—4.1 inch, 2 M.G., 4 or 6 tubes (size unknown). Speed : about 35 kts.
Notes.—All above H, S and V boats believed to be same in build as boats numbered S 51 to G 95.
Scuttled at Scapa Flow.—H 145, S 131, S 132 (salved), S 136, S 137 (salved), S 138, V 125—127 (all salved).
War Losses.—None.

Notes.

Under the Peace Treaty, Germany may not keep more than 12 Destroyers in commission, and, excepting accidental losses, no boat may be replaced until 15 years old. Any future Destroyers built by Germany must not exceed 800 metric tons in displacement.

Reported that Germany has still to surrender 42 modern Destroyers. Not yet known which boats Germany will retain and which she will hand over.

With the exception of boats engaged in Minesweeping, Germany has only the "Iron Flotilla" in effective condition now. The "Iron Flotilla" consists of H 147, H 146, S 139, S 135, S 134, S 133, V 130, S 116, S 113, B 97

Majority of boats with "T" index letter have had armament removed and are fitted for Minesweeping.

General Notes to Table.

B boats built by Blohm & Voss (Hamburg), G boats at Krupp's Germania Yard, H boats by Howaldt (Kiel), S boats by Schichau, V boats by Vulkan (Stettin). All are officially rated as "Grosse Torpedoboote," or "Big Torpedo Boats," and *not* as Destroyers ("Torpedoboote-Zerstörer"). Unless otherwise noted, all boats have Schulz-Thornycroft (or "Marine Type") boilers. The details tabulated are generally simplified to the average design of each group.

Note to boats in preceding column :—
War Losses.— S 57, S 58, S 59, S 61, S 62, S 64, S 66, V 67, V 72, V 74, V 75, V 76, V 77, V 81, S 84, G 85, G 87, G 88, G 90, G 93, G 94, G 96.
Scuttled at Scapa Flow (not salved).—S 55, S 56, S 65, V 70, V 78, V 82, V 83, G 86, G 89, G 91, G 92.

1915.

Appearance as B 98 below, but derrick is before *second* funnel with boom slung *forward*. Very big ventilator between 2nd and 3rd funnels. Searchlight on aft bridge is not raised on tower.

Under salvage at Scapa Flow.

1 Vulkan : **V 100** (probably built 1915-16). Displacement : *About* 1300 tons. Dimensions : *about* 328 × 32 × 10 feet (*mean* draught). Designed speed : 34 kts. A.E.G.-Curtis or "Marine type" turbines. Armament : about 3—4.1 inch, 2 M.G. May also have an automatic (or semi-auto.) AA. gun. May carry some mines. Torpedo tubes : 6—19.7 inch. Complement, about 140-160. Oil fuel only. V 99 lost during War.

1915.

2 Blohm & Voss : **B 98** and **B 97.** Launched, 1915.

Displacement about 1300 tons. Approximate dimensions 325×32×10 feet (*mean* draught). Designed speed : 31 kts. Turbine engines. Armament : 4—4·1 inch, 2 machine—may also have a small automatic or semi-auto. anti-aircraft gun and carry mines. Complement, about 140-160. Torpedo tubes : 6—19·7 inch. Oil fuel only.
Note.—B 98 arrived at Scapa Flow with German Fleet mails just after German Fleet (and B 109—112) had been scuttled. She was seized at once. Probably boats begun in 1914 for Chinese Navy.

GERMAN DESTROYERS.

1915.

As illustration of *S* & *V* types on preceding page.

1 *Schichau:* **S 51***
3 *Vulkan:* **V 43,* V 44,* V 46***, Launched 1915.

About 700-750 tons. Dimensions : 262-270 × 26-27 × 10-11 feet. Guns : 3—3·4 inch (22 pdr.), 2 M.G. Torpedo tubes : 6—19·7 inch (2 twin, 2 single mountings). Designed S.H.P. *about* 23,000 = 34 kts. Oil fuel only : *about* 300 tons. *V 46* last of pre-war (1914-15) Programme boats.

*Salved at Scapa Flow. *S 50, S 52, V 45* not salved.

V 47, V 48 (special type), both War Losses.

G 37, G 41, G 42 War Loss. *G 38, G 39, G 40*, not salved at Scapa Flow. *G 37—40* class therefore extinct.

1914 *(ex-Argentine)*.

1 ex-*Argentine* boat : **G 102** (Krupp-Germania, 1914). Displacement : *normal*, 1250 tons ; *full load*, 1460 tons. Dimensions : 312¾ × 30 × 8⅝ feet (*mean* draught). *Max.* draught, 9½ feet. Armament : 4—4·1 inch guns, 2 M.G. ; may also have a small automatic (or semi-auto.) AA. gun. Torpedo tubes : 6—19·7 inch. Machinery : Turbines and 5 double-ended boilers. Designed H.P. 24,000 = 32 kts. Fuel : (oil only) 345 tons.

Note.—*G 102* salved at Scapa Flow. *G 101, G 103, G 104*, not salved. These were originally the destroyers *San Luis, Santa Fé, Santiago*, and *Tucuman*, laid down for the Argentine in 1913-14 and appropriated for German Navy after outbreak of war.

1913—14.

S 31—36 class has been totally destroyed, viz.:—*S 31, 33, 35*, War Losses ; *S 32, 36*, scuttled at Scapa Flow and not salved.

2 *Vulkan :* **V 26, V 28.** Launched 1914. *About* 650 tons. Armament : 3—3·4 inch (22 pdr.), 2 M.G. Torpedo tubes : 6—19·7 inch. S.H.P. 20,000 = 32·5 kts. Oil only : *about* 290 tons. Complement, 90.

War Losses.—*V 25, V 27, V 29. V 30* sunk November 20th, 1918.

1912—13.

4 *Schichau :* **S 18, S 19, S 23, S 24.** Launched 1913. *About* 570 tons. Dimensions : 234⅔ × 24½ × 10 feet. Armament : 2—4·1 inch, 1—3·4 inch (22 pdr.). Torpedo tubes : 4—19·7 inch. Designed S.H.P. 15,000 = 32·5 kts. Melms-Pfenninger turbines. Fuel : 135 tons coal + 55 tons oil. Complement, 75.

War Losses.—*S 13, S 14, S 15, S 16, S 17, S 20, S 21, S 22.*

1911-1912 (and 2 1913 Replace Boats).

G 7, 9, 8, 10.   *Photo by courtesy of S. Anderson, Esq.*

Note.—All have raised fore funnels now.

G 9.

4 *Krupp-Germania :* **G 7, G 8, G 9, G 10, G 11** (launched 1911-12).

5 *Vulkan :* **V 1—V 3** (1911), **V 5, V 6** (1913).

Displacement 564 to 570 tons *normal* ; 700 tons *full load* ? Dimensions : 233 × 25 × 9⅝ feet (*mean* draught). Armament : 2—3·4 inch (22 pdr.) 30 cal.,2 machine. Torpedo tubes : 4—19·7 inch. Machinery : turbines, Parsons in Germania boats, A.E.G.-Curtis in Vulkan boats. Designed H.P. 15,000=32·5 kts. *S 23* made 37 kts. on trials, other boats all exceeded designed speeds. Fuel : 110 tons coal, 60 tons oil. 4 Schulz-Thornycroft boilers (1 oil burning). Complement, 75.

Appearance Notes.—Raking stem. Rise of turtle-back strongly marked. Gun on forecastle, large ventilator between bow tubes. W/T. cabin immediately abaft fore-funnel. Mainmast well aft of 2nd funnel.

Notes.—*V 5* and *V 6* built to replace original *V 5* and *V 6* sold to Greece, and now Greek *Keravnos* and *Neagenea. V 4, G 12*, lost during war. *V 2, V 3, V 5*, non-effective.

S—   S 22.
    S 21.   S 20.
                   S 19.

From the " Illustrirte Zeitung."

For description of above T.B.D. see previous page.

GERMAN DESTROYERS

Notes.

Nearly all the Destroyers listed on this and succeeding pages have had their tubes removed and fitted for minesweeping.

About a dozen of them have been mined or otherwise injured during the War and not repaired; they are entirely non-effective for fighting purposes. Boilers and engines of many are in a very poor condition, and the *maximum* speeds given must be taken with reserve.

All these boats were built with the usual *G, S* and *V* builders' index letters, but were given letter *T* to avoid duplication of numbers, with the later boats numbered from *V 1* up to *H 190*, described on preceding pages. In description of *T* boats, *G* refers to Krupp-Germania boats, *S* to Schichau boats, and *V* to Vulkan boats.

1910.

V Boats (V 186). Ventilator between bow tubes *low*.

V186–191
G192–197
650 TONS

Note:— All have raised fore funnel now.

G Boats (G 196). Ventilator between bow tubes *high*.
5 *Krupp Germania*, **T 192, T 193, T 195—T 197.** } launched 1910-11.
3 *Vulkan*, **T 190, T 189** and **T 186.**

Displacements: *G* boats 648 tons, *V* boats 656 tons *normal* (750 tons *full load*?). Dimensions : 213 × 26 × 10½ feet. Armament : 2—3·4 inch (22 pdr.) 30 cal., 2 machine guns. Torpedo tubes : 4—19·7 inch. Machinery : Parsons turbines in *G* boats, A. E. G.—Curtis in *V* boats. Designed H.P. 16,000=32·5 kts. Fuel : 160-170 tons coal, 55 tons oil. 4 Schulz-Thornycroft boilers (1 oil burning). Complement 83 (93 War Complement).

Appearance Notes.—Break between forecastle and bridges small, the space for working bow (beam) tubes being extremely cramped. Heights of bow ventilators vary, see note to illustrations above. Gun on forecastle, W/T. cabin immediately abaft forefunnel. Mainmast well aft of funnels in *G* boats, but not so far in *V* boats.

War Losses : *V 187, V 188, V 191, G 194.* At present *T 190* and *T 196* are quite useless.

1909-10.

G174-175
S176-179
V180-185
640-670 TONS

Now have tall foremasts.
6 *Vulkan*, **T 185—180**
3 *Schichau*, **T 179, T 178,*** **T 176** } launched 1909-10.
2 *Krupp-Germania*, **G 175** and **G 174**

Displacements : *V* boats 637 tons, *S* boats 636 tons, *G* boats 654 tons *normal* (760 tons *full load*?). Dimensions *about* 213 × 26 × 10 feet. Armament : 2—3·4 inch (22 pdr.) 30 cal., 4 or 2 machine guns. Torpedo tubes : 4—19·7 inch. Machinery : A. E. G-Curtis turbines in *V* boats, Schichau (Melms and Pfenninger) in *S* boats. Parsons in *G* boats. Designed H.P. 16,000=31·5 to 32·5 kts. Fuel : *S* and *V* boats, 150 tons coal and 10 tons oil ; *G* boats, 190 tons coal and 50 tons oil. Complement 83.

Appearance Notes.—Break between forecastle and bridges very small. In *G* and *S* boats forecastle is *short*, with big, tall ventilator just abaft. In *V* boats forecastle is *long*, and *small* ventilator (or *none*?) abaft of same. *G* and *S* boats *very big and tall* funnels, standard compass is *on* after bridge and derrick *abaft* of mast. Note that beam torpedo tubes are *not* between forecastle and bridges but *abaft* of bridges and forefunnel. In this type, ventilators between funnels are near to second funnel. Gun mounted on forecastle. *G* boats have big ventilator close to and abeam of mainmast on *port* side only. Boat in davits on port beam and abeam of after funnel may also be a distinguishing feature.

S 178 sunk by *Yorck* in 1913. She was salved. *S 177* War Loss. *T 174, T 185,* both useless.

1908-9.

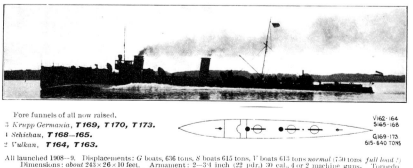

Fore funnels of all now raised.
3 *Krupp Germania*, **T 169, T 170, T 173.**
4 *Schichau*, **T 168—165.**
2 *Vulkan*, **T 164, T 163.**

V162–164
S165–168
G169–173
615-640 TONS

All launched 1908—9. Displacements : *G* boats, 636 tons, *S* boats 615 tons, *V* boats 613 tons *normal* (750 tons *full load*?). Dimensions : *about* 243 × 26 × 10 feet. Armament : 2—3·4 inch (22 pdr.) 30 cal., 4 or 2 machine guns. Torpedo tubes, 4—19·7 inch. Machinery : Turbines : Parsons in *G* boats (*G 173* Zoelly turbines), Schichau (Melms & Pfenninger) in *S* boats and A. E. G.-Curtis in *V* boats. Designed H.P. 11,000=30 to 32 kts. Fuel : 160 tons coal, 40 tons oil. Complement 83.

Appearance Notes.— *G 169—173* almost same as *G 192—197* Class. *V* and *S* boats have slightly longer forecastles, higher funnels and derrick *abaft* mast. Ventilators differently arranged (see Silhouettes). *G 171* lost by collision in 1912. *V 162, T 172,* War Losses. *T 168-170,* quite useless. Original *S 165-168* sold to Turkey. War loss *T 138.*

1907-08.

554 TONS

T 156- T 161 as above photo, and plan.

T 151 T 155.

Two tubes between funnels, with ventilator between same. Ventilator in space between 2nd funnel and mainmast, closer to funnel than to mainmast.

11 *Vulkan*, **T 161 151,** launched 1907-8. Displacement : 554 tons, *normal* (670 tons *full load*?). Dimensions : 236½ × 25¾ × 10 feet *mean draught*. Guns : 2—3·4 inch (15 pdr.) 35 cal., 2 machine. Torpedo tubes : 3—17·7 inch. Machinery : *T 161* has A.E.G.-Curtis turbines, the remainder reciprocating engines. Designed H.P. 10,250=30 kts. Coal : 160 tons ; *T 161*, 170 tons. Complement, 83.

Appearance Notes. Very big funnels ; short and high forecastle, with gun mounted on same. Standard compass not on after bridge, but just before it.

War Losses.- V 150.

GERMAN DESTROYERS (*Grosse Torpedoboote*).

1906.

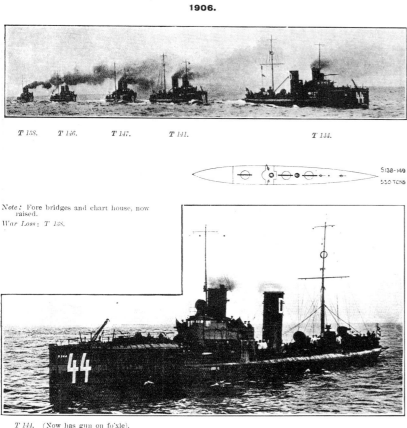

T 138.   T 146.   T 147.   T 141.   T 144.

S138-149
530 TONS

Note: Fore bridges and chart house, now raised.

War Loss: T 138.

T 144.   (Now has gun on fo'xle).

1 *Schichau:* **T 149—139,** launched 1906-7. Displacement: 530 tons. Dimensions: 231 × 25½ × 8⅝ feet (*mean draught.*) Armament: 1—3·4 inch (15 pdr.), 35 cal., 3—4 pdr., 55 cal., 2 machine. Torpedo tubes: 3—17·7 inch. Machinery, reciprocating. Designed H.P. 10,000=30 kts. Coal: 190 tons. Complement, 80.

Appearance Notes.—Break between forecastle and bridges fairly long. Bridges run well aft of forefunnel. Funnels large and *tall*. Mainmast well aft of second funnel with single large ventilator centrally in space between second funnel and mainmast. 4 pdr. gun between mainmast and this ventilator. Compass on raised platform immediately abaft mainmast.

1904-2.

T 130.   Note rudder under forefoot, which is fitted to all German Destroyers.

T 121 OFF THE MOUTH OF THE EMS.   *1917 War Photo.*

9 *Schichau:* (**T 131, T 130,** * **T 128—125** (launched 1901-5). 185 tons.) Plans as given in next column with 1901-1898 boats.
(**T 121—120** (launched 1901). 470 tons.
(**T 114** * (launched 1902). 420 tons.

Armament: 3—4 pdr., 10 cal., 2 machine, 3—17·7 inch tubes. Designed H.P. 6500=27 kts. (T 111, 6200=26 kts.) Coal: 116 tons. Complement, 60.

Appearance Notes.—Low in water. Long forecastle without any gun, long space between forecastle and bridges. Tall funnels, with raised steam pipe to fore funnel.

* T 129, T 121, T 123, T 122, 119, 118, 117, 116 and 115 have been sunk. T 125 useless.

1905-6.

G 137
570 TONS

1 *Krupp-Germania* special boat: **T 137** (launched 1907). Displacement: 565 tons. Dimensions: 231½ × 25 × 9⅝ feet. Armament: 1—3·4 inch (15 pdr.), 35 cal., 3—4 pdr., 55 cal., 2 machine. Torpedo tubes: 3—17·7 inch. Machinery: Parsons turbine. Designed H.P. 10,000=32 kts., made 33·9 on trials. Coal: 170 tons. Complement, 80.

Appearance Notes.—Raised forecastle short. Raised steam pipe to fore funnel. Ventilators between funnels close to fore funnel and mast well aft of second funnel—compare these details with boats below. Distinctive features are the guns on raised platforms, between second funnel and aft as shown in above photo. Steam-pipe to fore funnel *raised*, as boats below.

G 132-136
490 TONS

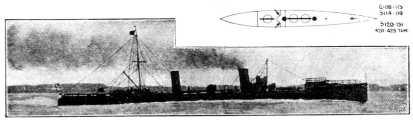

6 *Krupp-Germania:* **T 136—132** (launched 1905-06).

Displacement: 487 tons. Dimensions: 207 × 23 × 7½ feet. Armament: 4—4 pdr., 55 cal., 2 machine. But T 135 (illustrated above) has special armament of 1—3·4 inch (15 pdr.), 35 cal., 2—4 pdr., 55 cal., 2 machine. Torpedo tubes: 3—17·7 inch. Machinery, reciprocating. Designed H.P. 6500=27 kts. Coal: 135 tons. Complement, 68.

Appearance Notes.—Raised forecastle very short, no gun mounted on same. Space between forecastle and bridges long. Steam-pipe raised above forefunnel. Funnels spaced wide apart. Mainmast close to second funnel, with derrick on after side. *Two guns abaft mainmast.*

1901-1898.

G 108-113
S 114-119
S 120-131
420-475 tons

6 *Krupp-Germania:* **T 113—108** (1901-2). 400 tons. Armament: 3—4 pdr., 2 machine. 3—17·7 inch tubes. H.P. 6000= 26 kts. Coal: about 110 tons. Complement, 56.

Appearance Notes.—Much the same as T 131—114 class, but shorter forecastle, no raised steam pipe to forefunnel, mainmast rather more aft.

Plan as given above for T 113—108 boats, but only **one tube midway between** funnels, the third tube being *abaft mainmast.*

6 *Schichau:* **T 107—102** (1900-01). As T 113—108 above, but coal 95 tons and H.P. 5100=26 kts. T 107 useless.

Appearance Notes.—Long fo'xle, funnels and mainmast set well towards stern. Big after funnel.

No Photo available.

See Silhouettes: Also Appearance Notes below.

8 *Schichau:* **T 98—91** * (1899-1900). 400 tons. Armament: 3—4 pdr., 2 M.G. 3—17.7 inch tubes (probably removed from majority). H.P. 5400 = 26 kts. Coal: 95 tons.

2 *Schichau:* **T 101, T 99.** As above boats, but tubes removed and perhaps guns. Both were Submarine Tenders before war.

Appearance Notes.—Much as T 131—111 boats on this page, but have *large and tall* funnels. Single and fairly large ventilator midway between funnels; a similar ventilator before and at foot of mainmast. *High* sterns.

* T 97 bears name **Sleipner.**

War losses: T 100, T 90 and Taku of separate Single class.

GERMAN TORPEDO BOATS (*Torpedoboote*).

74* Modern }
60† Old } Torpedo Boats = 134§

*11 of these interned. †Majority are useless.

§Peace Treaty limits Germany to 12 Torpedo Boats. Not to be replaced unless 15 years old or lost by accident. New boats not to be over 200 tons.

Totals.	Name or Number.	Date.	Displacement.	I.H.P.	Max. Speed.	*Torpedo Tubes.	Coal.	Complement.
3	V 105—108	1914—15	tons. 320	5300t	kts. 32	4	tons. ..	..
1	D 10	1897—99	355	5500	28	2	80	60
1	D 9	1893—94	380	4040	24½		105	59
2	D 8, D 7	1890—92	350	4000	23	3	75	49
2	D 6, D 5	1888—90	320	3600	23		90	49
2	D 4, D 3	1887—89	300	2500	21		65	49
30	A 59—95	1916—17	200	..	24	1	35	..
27	A 26—55	1915—16		..	24	1	35	..
14	A 1—25	1915	80	..	15	2	29	..
2	T 88 & 89	1898	160	1800	25	2	36	24
6	T 87—82							
7	T 81—74	1889— 1897	180—150	1500	25—22	3	30	24—16
5	T 73—69							
6	T 63—55							
2	T 53, T 49	1889— 1897	150	1500	25—22	3	30	16
2	T 45, T 42			1350				
22	T 40—T 3	1885-7	85	1000	20	3	30	16

*Note.—Many have been converted into Mine Sweepers and have no tubes now.

1914 Appropriated Boats.

No Photo available : for appearance as originally designed, v. Silhouettes.

3 *ex*-Dutch boats : **V 108, V 106, V 105** (Vulkan, 1913-14). 320 tons. Dimensions : 201 × 20½ × 6 feet (**mean draught**). Armed with 2—13 pdr. guns and 4—17·7 inch tubes. Designed H.P. 5,300=27 kts. Turbines.

Note.—The above were originally the Dutch *Z 1—Z 4*, and were appropriated for German Navy after the outbreak of war. *War Loss.—V 107.*

"Divisional Boats."

1 *Thornycroft :* **D 10** (1895). 355 tons. Armament : 5—4 pdr., 2—17·7 inch tubes. Speed (originally) 28 kts. Boilers Yarrow.

D 7, with guns and tubes removed, used for Subsidiary Service. *Photo, Seward, Weymouth.*

7 *Schichau.* **D 9** (1891), **D 8, D 7** (1891), **D 6, D 5** (1888-89), **D 4, D 3** (1887). For details, see Destroyer Tables on a preceding page. Armament : 3—4 pdrs., 3—17·7 inch tubes, one *submerged* in bow. Tubes probably removed from all now. Reconstructed and given two funnels 1907-09.

Note.—D 5 had tubes removed and was used for Fisheries Protection before war, being armed with 4—4 pdr. guns. D 5 also had tubes removed and was Tender to Submarine Depot Ships. *D 1* and *D 2* still exist, but are quite useless.

GERMAN FIRST-CLASS TORPEDO BOATS.

1915-17

A 26—36 (later boats similar, but longer fo'xle). *From the "Illustrirte Zeitung."*

30 boats, by various yards : **A 59, A 61—A 66, A 68—A 70, A 74—A 76, A 78, A 80—A 95.** Built about 1916-17.

27* boats, by various yards : **A26 — A 31,* A 33 — A 36, A 37 — A 44, A 46 — A 49,* A 52 — A 55.** Built about 1915-16.

*A 30, A 40, A 42, A 47, interned in Holland on German evacuation of Belgium. Present disposal not known. If deducted, total is 22 boats.

General Notes.—Displace about 200-250 tons. Dimensions : *about* 170 × 16¾ × 5-7 feet. Guns : 2—3.4 inch (22 pdr.). 1 M.G. Torpedo tubes (17.7 inch) : 1 (removed from sweeping boats). Speed : 24 kts. Fuel : Oil only. Complement, 35.

War losses.— A 32, A 50, A 56, A 57, A 58, A 60, A 71, A 72, A 73, A 77, A 79. A 67 does not seem to exist now, but is not reported as War Loss. A 45 destroyed on German evacuation of Flanders.

1915

A 1—25 TYPE. *Photo, L. N. A.*

14* boats, by various yards (several sent in sections to Antwerp and assembled there) : **A 1, A 5,* A 8,* A 9,* A 11,* A 16,* A 17, A 18, A 20,* A 21—25.** Built about 1915.

*Interned in Holland after German evacuation of Belgium. Present disposal not known. If deducted, total is 12 boats.

About 80 tons. Dimensions : 140 × 19½ × 8¼ feet. Guns : 1—4 pdr., 1 M.G. Torpedo tubes (17.7 inch) : 1 or 2 (removed from sweepers). Speed : 15 kts. Coal : *about* 30 tons. Complement, 29.

*War Losses.—A 2, A 3, A 6, A 7, A 10, A 13, A 15, A 19. A 1, A 12, A 14, abandoned in Flanders and now units of Belgian Navy.

OLD GERMAN TORPEDO BOATS (*Kleine Torpedoboote*).
Above-water tubes probably removed.   Now used as Minesweepers, Tenders, &c.

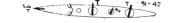

2 *Krupp-Germania,* **T 89** and **T 88** (1897-8).   1—4 pdr., 2—17·7 inch tubes.

6 *Schichau:* **T 87—T 82** (1898).   1—4 pdr., 3—17·7 inch tubes (1 bow *submerged*, 2 deck).

5 *Schichau:* **T 81—74** (1893-4).⁕ Armed as *T 87—T 82* above.
⁕ Less *T 78* War Loss.

Motor Launches.

49 boats: **F ...—F...**   (built 1917-18).   23 tons.   About 55 feet long.

Total Number uncertain: **UZ 1—50**   (built 1916-17).   About 60 tons.   Length, 85 feet.   Speed, 15 kts.
Note.—UZ = *Unterseeboote-Zerstörer* (Submarine Destroyer).   All UZ and F boats fitted as Anti-Submarine craft and Minesweepers.

"Controlled Torpedoes."

These craft were used off the Belgian Coast, and are simply a modern development of the old Brennan and Lay torpedoes.   The "controlled torpedo" is a small boat with twin petrol motors, partly covered in. The crew leave after it has been started.   About 30-50 miles of single-core insulated electric cable connect the boat's steering and control gears with the shore directing station.   A seaplane, escorted by a strong escort of fighting 'planes, "spots" for the "controlled torpedo," sending instructions by W/T. on course, speed, etc., to the shore controlling station.   About 300-500 lbs. of high-explosive are contained in the bows of the "torpedo," being exploded on impact with the target.

Mine Layers (are disarmed).

T 42 (1887).   Appearance after being re-boilered and re-engined.
16 *Schichau:*   **T 73—69, T 63—59, T 55, T 53, T 49, T 45, T 42** (1889-1897).   1—4 pdr., 3—13·8 inch tub
(1 bow *submerged*, 2 deck).
War Losses:—T 43, 46, 47, 50, 51, 52, 54, 56, 58, 58, 61, 65, 66, 68.

2nd & 3rd CLASS.

Like *T 81—74* but shorter and with big funnel.

22 *old boats:*   **T 40—33, T 31—27, T 25, T 24, T 21—20, T 16, T 15—13, T 11, T 3** (1885-1889).   85 tons.
Speed: 17 kts. (probably much less now).   Armament: 1—4 pdr., 3 torpedo tubes (2 deck and 1 *submerged* bow).
Guns and tubes may have been removed from some.   Complement, 16.
Appearance: Similar to *T 81—74* opposite, but much shorter in length.
Notes.—T 36, 35, 31—27 and 25 converted to Mine sweepers, tubes being removed ; some (or all) of the other boats may also have been altered for this service.   T 25 War Loss.

ALBATROSS after naval action of 1/7/15 ; foremast partly shot away.
(Was Mining School Ship before the war.)
ALBATROSS (October, 1907).   2200 tons.   Complement, 197.   Length, 295 feet.   Beam, 42⅔ feet. *Maximum* draught, *about* 13 feet.   Armament : 8—3·4 inch (15 pdr.), 35 cal.   Boilers : Schulz-Thornycroft.   Designed H.P. 6000=20 kts.   Coal, 450 tons.   **Carries 600 mines.**
Note.—Was disabled and driven ashore near Ostergarm Lighthouse, Gothland Island (Baltic), by Russian Cruisers on July 1st, 1915.   Above illustration shows her being towed to internment at Viborg.   Released from internment by Sweden in 1918.

S.M.S. "*Nautilus*," *Minenleger.*

NAUTILUS (1906).   1950 tons.   Complement, 198.   Length, 305 feet.   Beam, 42⅔ feet.   Draught, 13¼ feet.   Armament : 8—3·4 inch, 15 pdr.   Boilers : Schulz-Thornycroft.   Machinery : reciprocating.   Designed H.P. 6000=20 kts.   Coal, 115 tons.   **Carries 200 mines.**

SMALL GERMAN MINE LAYERS AND SWEEPERS.

F.M. 1—36 (Built 1917-18.) 175 tons. *About* 139½ × 19⅔ × 4½ feet. Guns : 1—3·4 inch 22 pdr. I.H.P. 600 = 13·5 kts. Coal, 33 tons. Fitted to carry mines.

Notes.—Shallow draught sweepers. Proved of little worth owing to inadequate fuel supply and dangerous instability.

M 19, M 20, M 21, M 25. (Built 1915.) *About* 400 tons. *About* 164 × 20 × 9 feet. Guns: below. I.H.P. 1500 = 16 kts. Complement, 40. Can carry 30 mines.

War Losses : M 22, M 23, M 24, M 26, M 27.

M 28—30, M 32—35, M 37, M 38, M 42—46, M 48, M 50—54, M 57—62, M 65, M 66, M 68—82, M 84—90, M 93—94, M 96—122, M 125, M 129, M 137, M 138. (Built 1915-18.) *About* 480 tons. *About* 192 × 24 × 8½ feet. Guns : see next column. I.H.P. 1600 = 17 kts. 2 screws. Coal : 150 tons and 12 tons oil. Complement 40. Can carry 30 mines.

War Losses : M 31, M 36, M 39, M 40, M 41 M 47, M 49, M 55, M 56, M 63, M 64. M 67, M 83, M 91, M 92, M 95.

Not finished ?—M 123, M 124, 126—128, 130—136.

M 1—5, M 7, M 8, M 10, M 13, M 17, M 18. (Built 1915.) *About* 350 tons. *About* 106 × 23 × 9 feet. Guns : see below. I.H.P. 1500 = 16 kts. Complement, 40. Carry 30 mines.

War Losses : M 6, M 9, M 11, M 12, M 14, M 15, M 16.

Armaments for all "M" Types.

(a) 3—4·1 inch, or (b) 2—4·1 inch, or (c) 1—4·1 inch, or (d) 2—3·4 inch, 22 pdr. Also 2 machine.

GERMAN GUNBOATS (*Kanonenboote*).

Perhaps never begun.

METEOR ? (Danzig Yard, 1914 or 1915 ?). 1150 tons. Dimensions : 219½ × 33½ × 10½ feet. Guns : 4—4·1 inch, 2—1 pdr., 2 machine. Machinery : 2 sets triple expansion. 2 screws. Boilers : 4 Schulz-Thornycroft. Designed H.P. 1550 = 14 kts. Coal : tons. Was intended for "surveying service" on East African Coast.

DELPHIN (Meyer, Papenburg, 1906). 450 tons. Complement 41. Armament : 4—3·4 inch (22 pdr.), 2—4 pdr., 4 M.G. Speed : 9·5 kts. Coal : 55 tons.

PANTHER (April, 1901). Displacement, 1000 tons. Dimensions 210·3 × 31·8 × 10·2 feet Complement, 130. Guns : 2—4·1 inc 40 cal., 6—1 pdr., 2 Machine. Machinery : Triple expansio 2 screws. Boilers : 4 Schulz-Thornycroft. Designed H.P. 130 = 14 kts. Coal : 275 tons.

DRACHE (Germania, 1908). 790 tons. Complement 64. Guns : 4—3·4 inch (22 pdr.), 4—4 pdr. Speed : 15 kts. Coal : 150 tons.

FUCHS (Meyer, Papenburg, 1905). 640 tons. Complement 51. Armament : 2—4·1 inch, 2—3·4 inch (15 pdr.). Speed : 12·5 kts. Coal : 75 tons.

Photo, S. Anderson, E

BLITZ & PFEIL (1882). 1388 tons. Dimensions : 246 × 34½ 13¼ feet. Complement, 134. Guns : 6—3·4 inch (15 pdr 4 machine. Tubes : 2 *above water* (probably removed), 1 su *merged.* Designed H.P. 2700 = 15 kts. Coal : 250 tons.

HAI (Geestemünde, 1907). 640 tons. Complement 51. Armament : 8—4 pdr. Speed : 12·5 kts. Coal : 75 tons.

(Continued on next pag

GERMAN MISCELLANEOUS.

Gunboats—(continued).

ZIETEN (1876). 1006 tons. Complement, 108. Guns : 6—4 pdr. Tubes (13·8 inch) : 2 *submerged* (bow and stern). Speed : under 13 kts. Coal : 140 tons.

GREIF. No details known.

PRIMULA. Sea-going Parent Ship, 5th Minesweeping Flotilla.

SPERBER. No details known.

Also :

Grille (1857). 350 tons. Speed : 13 kts. Guns : 2—3·4 inch.

Condor (Mine Hulk), *Schwalbe* (Target Hulk).

Admiralty Trawlers.

("Wachtschiffen.")

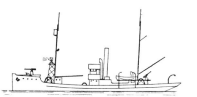

About 250 tons *gross*. H.P. 450 = 10 kts. Guns : 1 or 2 small.

These are Trawler Mine-Sweepers, of which a large number were built by the smaller German Shipyards during the War. The majority have been sold to private owners for fisheries purposes, but a few may still remain for Mine Clearance duties. About 100 were built during the War and 30 were sunk.

Fleet Auxiliaries.

Various Oilers, Colliers, &c., including a few ships used as Auxiliary Mine Layers. Believed that all have reverted to mercantile service, including German Mercantile and Fishing Vessels used as Submarine Decoy Ships (" Q-boats ").

River Gunboats.

(All on Vistula.)

MÖWE. Ex Shallow Draught River Steamer, armed with 1— 1 pdr. and 1 M.G.

LIEBE. Ex Shallow Draught Tug. Guns : 1—3·4 inch (22 pdr.) 1—1 pdr.

GARDENGO. Ex Shallow Draught Tug. Guns : 1—3·4 inch (22 pdr.), 1 M.G.

Submarine Depot and Salvage Ship.

(Surrendered.)

CYCLOP (Danzig, 1914). Dock and Salvage Ship for Submarines, designed for raising 1200 tons deadweight. 2800 tons. Dimensions : 295 × 64 × 13 feet. Guns : None. Machinery : Reported to be Diesel engines. Speed : 9 kts.

Fleet Tender.

NORDSEE (Atlas Werfte, Bremen, 1914). 790 tons. Dimensions : 175¾ × 30¾ × feet. Armed with 2—3·4 inch (22 pdr.) guns. H.P. 1700 = kts. Serves as Leader of North Sea Patrols.

Surveying Ships (*Vermessungsfahrzuge*).

HYÄNE (1878). 493 tons. Complement, 85. Guns : 1—3.4 inch (15 pdr.), 1—4 pdr., 3—1 pdr. H.P. 340 = 8 kts. Coal : 110 tons.

TRITON. No details known. May be the ex-Russian Surveying Ship, launched at and during German occupation of Reval, 1918. If so, her details are :—270 tons. Dimensions : 127¾ × 20 × 10 feet.

Surveying.

PLANET (1905) & **MÖWE** (1906). 600 tons. Speed : 10 kts.

Yachts (*Jachten*).

Not finished.

—— (ex *Ersatz Hohenzollern*, Vulkan, Stettin, 1915). 7300 tons. Complement, 455. Dimensions : 528¼ × 62½ × 20 feet. (Guns : Not known, but is capable of mounting about 12—5·9 inch. Machinery : Turbines. 3 screws. Boilers : 10 Schulz-Thornycroft (2 oil burning). Designed H.P. 25,000 = 24 kts. Coal : 1000 tons + 500 tons oil.

Royal Yacht.

HOHENZOLLERN. (Vulkan, Stettin, 1892 ; re-constructed 1907). 4200 tons. Complement, 348. Dimensions : 380½ × 46 × 19⅓ feet. Armament : 2—4 pdr. Boilers (1907) : Schulz-Thornycroft. Designed H.P. 9500 = 21·5 kts. Coal : 510 tons.

(Surrendered.)

LORELEY (ex *Mohican*, Henderson, Glasgow, 1885). 925 tons. Dimensions : 207·4 × 27·1 × 13½ feet. Guns : 2—4 pdr. Speed : Made 13.4 kts. on trials ; now about 12 kts. Coal : 165 tons. Complement, 60.

Training Ships.

For Gunnery :—

KAISERIN AUGUSTA. Old Cruiser, previously described on an earlier page.

Sea-going Torpedo School Ship :—

WÜRTTEMBERG, (*old*) (1878). 7300 tons. I.H.P. 6000 = 15 kts. Guns : 2—3·4 inch (22 pdr.), 8—1 pdr., 4 M.G. Torpedo tubes : 2—19·7 inch, *submerged* ; 2—13·7 inch, *submerged* ; 1—13.7 inch, *above water*. Coal : 650 tons. Is serving temporarily as Sea-going Tender to Minesweepers.

2 M

(Submarines).

Under the Peace Treaty, Germany is absolutely prohibited from building (or maintaining in service) any Submarines, whether of Naval or Mercantile types.

All unfinished German Submarines—of which there were a considerable number at the end of 1918—have been dismantled, broken up, scuttled outside German ports or otherwise disposed of.

German Submarines, divided among the Allied Navies for investigation and trials noted in each Allied (and U.S.) Navy Section.

Type: Coastal Submarines (1+1+2+4)
Class: "U1","U2", "U3", "U5"
Displacement, tons: U1, 238/283; U2 341/430; U3-4 421/510; U5-8 506/636
Dimensions, feet: Varying from U1 139 x 12.3 x 10.5 to U5 188 x 18.3 x 11.3
Torpedo armament: U1 1 x 18in (bow). Remainder 4 x 18in (2 bow, 2 stern)
Guns: 1 x 37mm in U3 and U5 classes. (1 x 4pdr added in U6 and U8 in 1915)
Main machinery: 2 heavy oil engines of (U1) 400bhp, (U2 and U3) 600bhp, (U5) 900bhp; 2 main motors, (U1) 400bhp, (U2) 630bhp, (U3 and U5-8) 1,040bhp; 2 shafts
Speed: knots: Surfaced U1 – 10.8, U2 13.2; U3 11.8; U5-8 13.4; Dived 9-10 knots
Complement: 22 (29 in U5 class)

Dates: 1906-1911

Notes: Germaniawerft Kiel: U1, U5-8; Danzig DY: U2, U3,4
Although three "Karp" class were ordered in Germany by Russia in 1904, U1 completed in December 1906, was the first U boat built for the German navy. From the start double hulls and twin screws were incorporated. The Germans very sensibly abjured the petrol engine and used Körting heavy oil engines. These, although they emitted clouds of exhaust and sparks through an upper deck exhaust, were much safer than the contemporary engines in British submarines. By 1908 suitable diesels had been evolved, to be used from the U19 class onwards.
The incorporation of stern torpedo tubes in these early submarines gave the Commanding Officers an advantage not achieved in the RN until the "D" class of 1910.

Note: torpedo tube diameters listed as 18in and 20in in earlier classes. Technically these were 17.7in and 19.7in respectively.

U1 (Drüppel)

Type: Patrol Submarines (4+4+4+11+8+6)
Class: "U19", "U23", "U27", "U31", "U43", "U51"
Displacement, tons: U19 650/837; U23 669/864; U27 675/867; U31 685/878; U43 725/940; U51 712/902
Dimensions, feet: U19 210.5 (U23 & U27 & U31 212.5; U43 213.3; U51 214) x 20.5 x 11.7
Torpedo armament: 4 x 20in (2 bow, 2 stern)
Mines: U43 and U44 acted as minelayers from 1916
Guns: 1 x 3.4in in U19, U23, U31, U43 and 2 x 3.4in in U27 and U51. (Some boats also mounted 4.1in guns during the war)
Main machinery: 2 diesel engines of 1,700bhp (U19) – 2,400bhp (U51); 2 main motors of 1,200bhp; 2 shafts
Speed, knots: 15 surfaced (U19 & U43); 17 (remainder) 9-10 dived
Complement: 35
Dates: 1912-1916

Notes: Danzig DY: U19-22, U27-30, U43-50
Germaniawerft Kiel: U23-26, U31-41, U51-56 (U42 unallocated)
These were the first classes to be engined with diesels. With the aim of attacking merchant ships the calibre of the guns was increased to allow the saving of torpedoes by surface action. A number of these guns were designed to fold sideways thus disappearing into the casing.
From U19 onwards net-cutters were provided as well as jumping-wires.

"U 19-51"

Type: Patrol Submarines (3+3+3+5)
Class: "U57", "U60", "U63", "U66"
Displacement, tons: U57 786/954; U60 768/956; U63 810/927; U66 791/933
Dimensions, feet: U57 & U60 219.7 (U63 224.3; U66 228) x 20.6 x 12.5
Torpedo armament: 4 x 20in (2 bow, 2 stern). 5 x 18in 4 bow, 1 stern in U66
Guns: 1 (or 2) x 3.4in or 4.1in)
Main machinery: 2 diesels of 1,800bhp (U57 & U60) 2,200bhp (U63) and 2,300 (U66) and 2 main motors 1,200bhp
Speed, knots: Surfaced 14.7 (U57 & U60); 16.5 (U63 & U66); dived 8.4 (U57 & U60); 9-10 (U63 & U66)
Complement: 39
Dates: 1915-1916

Notes: A.G. Weser, Bremen: U57-59, U60-62
Germaniawerft, Kiel: U63-65, U66-70
The U66 class, completed in 1915, was built for the Austro-Hungarian Navy as U8-U12 but taken over by the Germans.

Type: Patrol Submarines (4+3+1+2)
Class: "U9", "U13", "U16", "U17"
Displacement, tons: U9 493/611; U13 516/644; U16 489/627; U17 564/691
Dimensions, feet: U9 188 (U13 190, U16 200, U17 204.5) x 19.7 x 11.5
Torpedo armament: 4 x 18in (2 bow, 2 stern)
Guns: 1 x 37mm in U9 and U17; 1 x 4pdr in U13 and U16
Main machinery: 2 heavy oil engines of (U9) 1,000bhp; (U13 and U16) 1,200bhp; (U17) 1,400bhp; 2 main motors of 1,150bhp; 2 shafts
Speed, knots: 14/15 surfaced; 8/10.7 dived
Complement: 29
Dates: 1910-1912

Notes: Danzig DY.: U9-15, U17 & 18; Germaniawerft Kiel: U16
These were the last classes with heavy oil engines. U9 sank the British cruisers *Hogue, Cressy* and *Aboukir* on 22nd September 1914 resulting in an appreciation by many hitherto unconvinced people of the capabilities of submarines.

U13 (Drüppel)

Type: Submarine Minelayers (2+2+5)
Class: "U71" (UE-1), "U73" & "U75"
Displacement, tons: U71 755/830, U73 745/829, U75 755/832
Dimensions, feet: 186.3 x 19.3 x 15.7
Torpedo armament: 2 x 20in (external)
Mines: 32 in 2 tubes
Guns: 1 x 3.4in or 4.1in
Main machinery: 2 diesels of 8-900hp; 2 main motors of 8-900hp; 2 shafts
Speed, knots: 10.5 surfaced; 8 dived
Complement: 32-39
Dates: 1915-1916

Notes: AG Vulkan, Stettin: U71-72, U75-80
Danzig DY: U73-74
These were two classes of long-range submarine minelayers to complement the large class of smaller UC boats. It is rumoured that HMS *Hampshire* with Lord Kitchener aboard was lost on a mine laid by U75. The second group, the UE-II, comprised U117-126.

U71

Type: Patrol Submarines (6)
Class: "U81"
Displacement, tons: 808 surfaced; 946 dived
Dimensions, feet: 230 x 20.6 x 13
Torpedo armament: 4 x 20in (2 bow, 2 stern)
Guns: 1 x 4.1in (U81-83), 2 x 3 4in (U84-86)
Main machinery: 2 diesels of 2,400hp; 2 main motors of 1,200hp; 2 shafts
Speed, knots: 17 surfaced; 9 dived
Complement: 38
Dates: 1916

Notes: U81-86 built by Germaniawerft, Kiel. No reason can be found for the reduction of the bow salvo to two but, apart from the "U99" class and the "U151", (Merchant) class this was the end of a plan which must have been both disconcerting for the CO and inefficient in its results.

Type: Patrol Submarines (6)
Class: "U87"
Displacement, tons: 757 surfaced; 998 dived
Dimensions, feet: 215.7 x 20.5 x 12.7
Torpedo armament: 6 x 20in (4 bow, 2 stern)
Guns: 1 x 4in (plus 1 x 3.4in in U87-89)
Main machinery: 2 diesels of 2,400hp; 2 main motors of 1,200hp; 2 shafts
Speed, knots: 15.6 surfaced; 8.6 dived
Complement: 38
Dates: 1917

Notes: U87-92 all built by Danzig DY.

U81 (Drüppel)

Type: Patrol Submarines (6)
Class: "U93" and "U96"
Displacement, tons: 838 surfaced; 1,000 dived
Dimensions, feet: 235.5 x 20.6 x 12.7
Torpedo armament: 6 x 20in (4 bow, 2 stern)
Guns: 1 x 3.4in ("U93" class), 1 x 4.1in ("U96" class)
Main machinery: 2 diesels of 2,400hp, 2 main motors of 1,200hp; 2 shafts
Speed, knots: 16.8 surfaced; 8.6 dived·
Complement: 38
Dates: 1917

Notes: U93-98 all built by Germaniawerft, Kiel.

U93

Type: Patrol Submarines (6)
Class: "U99"
Displacement, tons: 750 surfaced; 952 dived
Dimensions, feet: 221.7 x 20.7 x 11.7
Torpedo armament: 4 x 20in (2 bow, 2 stern)
Guns: 2 x 3.4in (U100 1 x 4.1in)
Main machinery: 2 diesels of 2,400hp; 2 main motors of 1,200hp; 2 shafts
Speed, knots: 16.5 surfaced; 8.5 dived
Complement: 39
Dates: 1917

Notes: U99-104, all built by A.G. Weser (Bremen). Except for "U151" (Merchant) class, the last of the U-boats with only two bow tubes. Otherwise a handy and popular class.

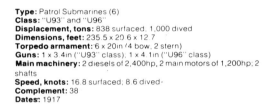

U99 (Drüppel)

Type: Patrol Submarines (6 + 4)
Class: "U105" and "U111"
Displacement, tons: 798 surfaced; 1,000 dived
Dimensions, feet: 235.5 x 20.7 x 12.7
Torpedo armament: 6 x 20in (4 bow, 2 stern)
Guns: 1 x 4.1in; 1 x 3.4in
Main machinery: 2 diesels of 2,400/2,300hp; 2 main motors of 1,200hp; 2 shafts
Speed, knots: 16.4 surfaced; 8.4 dived
Complement: 36
Dates: 1917-1918

Notes: U105-110 and U111-114 all built by Germaniawerft Kiel, although the hulls of U111-114 were built by Bremer-Vulkan (Vegesack)
U115-116 were cancelled whilst building by Schichau, Danzig. These were to have been boats of 1,250 tons dived displacement.

U105 as French submarine (Drüppel)

Type: Minelaying Submarines (5 + 5)
Class: "U117" and "U122" (UE-II)
Displacement, tons: 1,164 surface; 1,612 dived (U122 1,470)
Dimensions, feet: 267.5 x 24.5 x 13.7
Torpedo armament: 4 x 20in. (bow)
Mines: 2 tubes for 42 mines
Guns: 1 x 5.9in (2 guns in some)
Main machinery: 2 diesels of 2,400hp; 2 main motors of 1,200hp; 2 screws
Speed, knots: 14.7 surface; 7 dived
Complement: 40
Dates: 1918

Notes: U117-121 built by A.G. Vulkan, Hamburg and U122-126 by Blohm and Voss, Hamburg. This was the second group of long-range minelayers, designed for operations off the US Atlantic coast and the first to carry the very large 5.9in gun.

U117 (Drüppel)

Type: Coastal Submarines (17 + 30 + 88)
Class: "UB"
Displacement, tons: UBI 127/142; UBII 263/292; UBIII 520/650 (508/639)
Dimensions, feet: UBI 92.3 x 9.7 x 10; UBII 118.5 x 14.3 x 12; UBIII 182 x 19 x 12
Torpedo armament: 2 x 18in (bow) UBI; 2 x 20in (bow) UBII; 5 x 20in (4 bow, 1 stern) UBIII
Guns: 1 x 2in or 3.4in (UBII); 1 x 3.4in or 4.1in (UBIII)
Main machinery: UBI: 1 heavy oil engine of 60hp; 1 main motor 120hp; 1 shaft. UBII: 2 diesels of 284hp; 1 main motor of 280hp; 2 shafts. UBIII: 2 diesels of 1,100hp; 2 main motors of 788hp; 2 shafts
Speed, knots: UBI 6.5/5.5; UBII 9/5.7; UBIII 13.5/8
Complement: 14-23-34
Dates: 1915-1919
Notes: UBI Series "UBI" Class (UB1-8) Germaniawerft, Kiel; "UB9" class (UB9-17) A.G. Weser. (10, 12, 16 and 17 converted for minelaying with 8 mines in 4 chutes length 105ft).
UBII Series: "UB18" Class (UB18-23) Blohm and Voss; "UB24" Class (UB24-29) A.G. Weser; "UB30" Class (UB30-41) Blohm and Voss. (121ft, 274/305 tons); "UB42" Class (UB42-47) A.G. Weser (as "UB30" class).
UBIII Series: "UB48" Class (UB48-132) 48-53 Blohm & Voss, 54-59 A.G. Weser, 60-65 A.G. Vulkan, 66-71 Germaniawerft, 72-74 A.G. Vulkan, 75-79 Blohm & Voss, 80-87 A.G. Weser, 88-102 A.G. Vulkan, 103-117 Blohm & Voss, 118-132 A.G. Weser; "UB133" Class (133-141) surrendered or scrapped before completion; "UB142" Class UB142, 143, 148, 149 A.G. Weser; UB144, 145, 146, 147, 150-153, 155, 170, 178; 196 surrendered or scrapped before completion.
A busy and useful series of boats much employed in the Mediterranean and patrolling as far as the Irish Sea. The UBI Series and "UCI" Class were the only single screw submarines Germany built.

Type: Patrol Submarines (3 + 1)
Class: "U139", "U142"
Displacement, tons: 1,930 surfaced; 2,483 dived
Dimensions, feet: 311 x 29.7 x 17.3
Torpedo armament: 6 x 20in (4 bow, 2 stern)
Guns: 2 x 5.9in
Main machinery: 2 diesels of 3,500hp and 1 auxiliary charging unit of 450hp; 2 main motors of 1,780hp; 2 shafts
Speed, knots: 16 surface; 8 dived
Complement: 62
Dates: 1918
Notes: U139-141 built by Germaniawerft, Kiel. These were very large boats with a formidable gun armament and long range. They were also the first to bear names (U139 *Schwiger* and U140 *Weddigen* (of U9 fame)). U139 was retained in commission by the French Navy to whom she surrendered in November 1918, until 1935 being renamed *Halbronn*.
The subsequent class, "U142", was composed of U142-150 of which only U142 herself was completed one day before the Armistice. In many ways this class was similar to the "U139" although of 300 tons more dived displacement.

U139 (Drüppel)

Type: Patrol Submarines (8)
Class: "U160"
Displacement, tons: 821 surface; 1,002 dived
Dimensions, feet: 235.5 x 20.5 x 13.5
Torpedo armament: 6 x 20in (4 bow, 2 stern)
Guns: 1 or 2 x 4.1in
Main machinery: 2 diesels of 2,400hp; 2 main motors of 1,200hp; 2 shafts
Speed, knots: 16.2 surface; 8.2 dived
Complement: 38
Dates: 1918-1919
Notes: All (U160-167) built by Bremer-Vulkan (Vegesack), being the last class of U boats completed at the war's end. Two (U162 as *Pierre Marrast* and U166 as *Jean Roulier*) were transferred to the French Navy, remaining in commission until 1935. U168-172 were broken up before completion. These boats are interesting because they show a return to the smaller type of submarine with a more reasonable gun-armament. The twelve boats of the "U201" class (U201-212) were similar to the "U160", whilst the "U229" class (U229-246), the "U247" class (U247-262) and the "U263" class (U263-276) were slightly smaller. None of these was completed. The "U173" class (U173-176) and the "U177" class (U177-200) of 2,790 tons dived displacement showed a return to the big boat idea, mounting 2 x 5.9in guns, whilst the "U213" class (U213-218) and "U219" class (U219-228) were of an intermediate size – 1,900 tons dived displacement – mounting four bow and four stern tubes in the "U219" with a single 5.9in gun. Again none of these were completed.

Type: Patrol Submarines (2)
Class: "U135"
Displacement, tons: 1,175 surface; 1,534 dived
Dimensions, feet: 274 x 24.7 x 13.7
Torpedo armament: 6 x 20in (4 bow, 2 stern)
Guns: 1 x 5.9in
Main machinery: 2 diesels of 3,500hp; 2 main motors of 1,690hp; 2 shafts
Speed, knots: 17.5 surface; 8.1 dived
Complement: 46
Dates: 1918
Notes: U135 and U136 built by Danzig DY. U137-138 of same class and the same builders were broken up in 1919 before completion.

U135 (Drüppel)

Type: Ex-Merchant Cruisers (7)
Class: "U151"
Displacement, tons: 1,512 surface; 1,875 dived
Dimensions, feet: 213.3 x 29.3 x 18.5
Torpedo armament: 2 x 20in (bow)
Guns: 2 x 5.9in or 4.1in
Main machinery: 2 diesel engines of 800hp; 2 main motors of 800hp; 2 shafts
Speed, knots: 12.4 surfaced; 5.2 dived
Complement: 56
Dates: 1916-1918
Notes: Built (U151-157) by Germaniawerft, Kiel with hulls built at Flensburg, Hamburg and Bremen. The original design was to provide cargo-carrying submarines to penetrate the British blockade – in fact *Deutschland* (later U155) made two such trips to the USA. *Oldenburg* (later U151) was converted for naval operations. *Bremen* was damaged on her first voyage and converted into a surface ship, whilst U152, 153, 154, 156 and 157 were completed for naval service, two being sunk. Despite the need for maximum numbers for "unrestricted warfare" these must have been brutal boats to take on patrol with their slow speed and minimal torpedo armament.

Type: Coastal Minelaying Submarines (104)
Class: "UC"
Displacement, tons: UCI 168/183; UCII 400/434 to 480/511; UCIII 491/571
Dimensions, feet: UCI 111.5 x 10.3 x 10; UCII 162-173 x 17 x 12; UCIII 185.3 x 18.3 x 12.5
Torpedo armament: UCI nil; UCII 3 x 20in (2 bow external, 1 stern); UCIII 3 x 20in (2 beam external, 1 stern)
Mines: UCI: 12 in 6 vertical tubes; UCII: 18 in 6 vertical tubes; UCIII: 14 in 6 vertical tubes
Guns: UCI: 1 MG; UCII: 1 x 3.4in; UCIII: 1 x 4.1in
Main machinery: UCI: 1 heavy oil engine of 90hp; 1 main motor of 175hp; 1 shaft; UCII: 2 diesels of 500/600hp; 2 main motors of 460/620hp; 2 shafts (UCIII same, 600/770hp)
Complement: 15-28-32
Dates: 1915-1919

Notes: UCI Series: UC1-8 A.G. Vulkan; UC9-15 A.G. Weser.
UCII series: UC16-24 Blohm and Voss; UC25-33 A.G. Vulkan; UC34-39 Blohm and Voss; UC40-45 A.G. Vulkan; UC46-48 A.G. Weser; UC49-43 Germaniawerft; UC53-60 Danzig DY; UC61-64 A.G. Weser; UC65-73 Blohm & Voss; UC74-79 A.G. Vulkan.
UCIII series: UC90-114 Blohm & Voss. (UC106-114 surrendered incomplete, 115-118 scrapped before completion)
In addition to these minelaying submarines UA (building for Norway) was taken over by Germany August 1914. The "UDI" class of large boats and UF series of small submarines were both cancelled.

U151 (Drüppel)

UC1

Note: **For U-boat losses see pages 327-329.**

UNITED STATES FLEET.

Revised from 1918-19 Edition of official handbook, "Ships' Data, U.S. Naval Vessels."

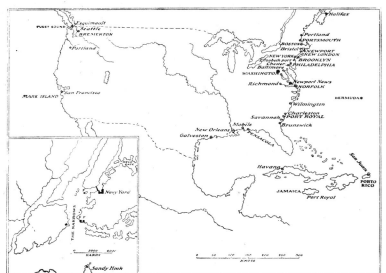

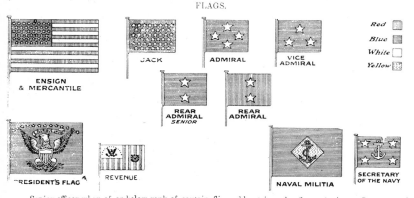

NEW YORK.

to	miles
Bermuda	680
Boston (Mass.)	315
Brest	2954
Cherbourg...	3066
Colon	1985
Galveston	1910
Gibraltar	3670
Havana	1320
Havre	3125
Jamaica	1495
Key West	1180
La Guayra	1840
Liverpool	3062
New Orleans	1710
Norfolk Navy Yard... ...	300
Pernambuco	3690
Philadelphia (Pa.) ...	240
Portsmouth Navy Yard ...	330
Portsmouth (England)	3060
Wilhelmshaven	3570

NEW YORK
(via Panama Canal)

to	miles
Callao	3328
Colon	1981
Hong Kong	11,684

	miles
Iquique	3837
Manila	11,585
Puget Sound	6074
San Francisco	5299
Shanghai	10,885
Sydney	9811
Valparaiso	4630
Yokohama...	9835

PORT ROYAL

to	miles
Bermuda	810
Key West	450
New York	650
Pensacola	785

KEY WEST

to	miles
Bermuda	1100
Boston (Mass.)	1387
Galveston	730
Jamaica (Port Royal Harbour)	850
New York	1180
Pensacola	235
Philadelphia	1020
Port Royal Naval Station	450
Portsmouth Navy Yard ...	1400

MARE ISLAND

to	miles
Auckland (N. Zealand) ...	5965
Esquimault	750
Honolulu	2095
Kiao-chau	5600
Manila	7500
Panama	3424
Puget Sound	800
Yokosuka	4500

KAVITE

to	miles
Amoy...	700
Hong Kong	650
Kiao-chau	1325
Nagasaki	1300
Saigon	875
Singapore	1320
Vladivostock	2080
Yokosuka	1720

Secretary of the Navy: Hon. J. Daniels. *Chief Constructor:* Rear-Admiral D. W. Taylor.

FLAGS.

Senior officer when of or below rank of captain flies a blue triangular flag. Assistant-Secretary of Navy has a flag same as Secretary's with colours reversed, *i.e.*, white ground and blue anchor and stars.

Uniforms.

Admiral of the Navy. — Rear-Admiral. — Captain. — Commander. — Lieut-Commander. — Lieutenant. — Ensign.

Note.—Lieutenants, junior grade, have 1½ stripes. Chief Warrant Officers one stripe broken with blue. Line Warrant Officers star without any stripe. Staff Warrant Officers under Chiefs have no sleeve mark. Engineers same as Line Officers (interchangeable). Other branches than executive wear no sleeve star, but have distinctive colours between the sleeve stripes.

Colour of significance (between the sleeve stripes): *Medical,* dark maroon; *Pay,* white; *Constructors,* purple; *Civil Engineers,* light blue: *Professors of Mathematics,* olive green. In 1919 the undress uniform of U.S. Naval officers was altered to a pattern resembling that of the British Navy.

Personnel.—War, 450,000. Post-war establishment not known yet.

Mercantile Marine.—Lloyds Return, 1919, gives 9,773,000 tons sea-going and 2,160,000 on the Great Lakes.

Coinage.—Dollar (100 cents) = approximately 4s. 2d. British at pre-war rate of exchange.

Overseas Possessions.—Panama Canal Zone, Porto Rico, Virgin Islands, Alaska and Aleutian Islands, Guam, Tutuila, Wake and Johnston Islands, Philippine Islands.

U. S. NAVAL ORDNANCE, TORPEDOES, &c.

Principal Guns in the U. S. Fleet.

(Corrected from the official figures, 1913.)

Built at Washington Gun Factory, proved at Indian Head, Ind., and Potomac Range.

Notation.	Nominal Calibre.	Mark or Model.	Length in Calibres.	Weight of Gun.	Weight of A.P. Shot.	Service Initial Velocity.	Maximum penetration firing *capped* A.P. direct impact against K.C. armour.			Approximate Danger Space average ship, at			Muzzle Energy
							9000	6000	3000	10,000	5000	3000	
	inch.			tons.	lbs.	ft. secs.	in.	in.	in.	yards.	yards.	yards.	
A⁸	16	...	45-50	128 ?	2100 ?	...	...	...	...	...	...	...	...
A⁷	14	...	45	63¼	1400	2600	18	...	...	...	...	...	...
A³	13	I. & II	35	61½	1130	2000	8	9¾	12	110	310	550	31,333
A⁶	12	VII	50	56·1	870	2950	11·0	13·9	17·5	...	...	...	52,483
A⁶	12	VI	45	53·6	870	2850	10·6	13·3	16·6	...	...	...	48,984
A⁵	12	V	45	52·9	870	2700	9·8	12·3	15·5	...	...	...	43,964
A⁴	12	III & IV	40	52·1	870	2600	9·3	11·7	14·8	...	...	...	40,768
A³	12	III & IV	40	52·1	870	2400	8·3	10·5	13·3	39†	126	264	34,738
A²	12	I & II	35	45·3	870	2100	7·2	8·8	11·2	100	390	580	26,596
A²	10	III	40	34·6	510	2700	6·9	9·0	11·9	140	460	700	25,772
	10	I & II	30	25·1	510	2000	5·0	6·1	8·0	...	...	...	14,141
A	8	VI	45	18·7	260	2750	4·4	6·1	8·6	15†	...	...	13,630
B	8	V	40	18·1	260	2500	4·0	5·3	7·5	45	...	...	11,264
C	8	III & IV	35	13·1	260	2100	3·6	4·2	6·0	...	...	...	7,948
C	6	...	52	...	...	...	...	...	...	...	...	...	...
C	6	VIII	50	8·6	105	2800	2·3	3·2	5·2	...	...	...	5,707
D	6	VI	50	8·3	105	2600	2·2	2·9	4·7	75	250	470	4,920
D⊛	6	IX	45	7·0	105	2250	2·1	2·5	3·8	...	...	...	3,685
E⊛	6	IV, VII	40	6·0	105	2150	2·1	2·4	3·6	35	150	355	3,365
E⊛	5	VII	51	5·0	50	3150	1·4	1·8	3·4	...	...	...	3,439
	5	VI	50	4·6	50	3000	1·4	1·7	3·2	...	...	...	3,122
	5	V & VI	50	4·6	60	2700	1·6	2·0	3·5	...	...	...	3,032
F⊛	5	II, III, IV	40	3·1	50	2300	1·4	1·7	2·6	...	...	...	1,834
F⊛	4	VIII	50	2·9	33	2800	1·2	1·5	2·6	...	...	...	1,794
F⊛	4	VII	50	2·6	33	2500	1·2	1·4	2·2	...	...	...	1,430
F⊛	4	III,IV,V,VI	40	1·5	33	2000	...	1·2	1·7	...	...	...	915
F	3	V, VI, S-A	50	1·0	13	2700	...	0·8	1·2	...	...	...	658
F⊛	3	II, III	50	0·9	13	2700	...	0·8	1·2	...	...	...	658

⊛ = Brass cartridge case. † = Calculated for a 20 ft. target.
Guns of 1899 and later have Vickers breech, etc. All guns use nitro-cellulose.
Anti-aircraft guns are 3 inch (13 pdr.) and 1 pdr.

16 inch, 50 cal. in *Massachusetts* class (6) and *Constellation* class (6).

16 inch, 45 cal. in *Colorado* class.

14 inch, 50 cal. mounted in *California* (2), and *New Mexico* (3) classes.

14 inch, 45 cal. mounted in *Texas* (2), *Nevada* (2) and *Pennsylvania* (2) classes.

12 inch, 50 cal. mounted in *Arkansas* (2) and *Utah* (2) classes.

12 inch, 45 cal. mounted in *Delaware* (2), *Idaho* (2), *Louisiana* (2), *Kansas* (4), and *S. Carolina* (2) classes.

12 inch, 40 cal. mounted in *Maine* (3), *New Jersey* (5), and *Ozark* (4) classes.

"Director" fire-controls have been installed in all the Dreadnoughts and Battleships back to the *New Jersey* type. Dreadnoughts have enlarged elevation to main guns, and directors for 5 inch guns. *Star shell* for 3, 4 and 5 inch guns. Range : 3-6 land miles. Time fuze ignites lamp and expels parachute and burner through base of shell. Shell usually detonates at 1000 feet, and 800,000 candle-power burner burns for 30 seconds, lighting up sea over ½ mile radius. *Non-ricochet shell* (flat-nosed) for 3, 4, 5 and 6 inch guns. Fired at elevation over 2° and delay action fuze begins on impact with water. *Y-gun* has two barrels set at 90° with powder chamber common to both barrels. Range : about 30 yards. *Davis non-recoil gun* (9 pdr.) consists of 2 guns placed breech to breech. Recoil absorbed by expulsion of powder charge case from after gun ; aimed by tracer bullets from Lewis gun fixed on barrel. 8 inch Trench Mortar Howitzer under test.

Aircraft Bombs.—20 lb. Cooper, 112, 163, 230, 270, 520 lbs. Mark VI is 10 inch diameter and 6 feet long.

Paravanes.

Generally as British Navy types, with minor modifications in inhaul gear.

Depth Charges.

18 inch diameter, 28 inches long. 300 lb. T.N.T. or Amatol charge. Detonation controlled by hydrostatic valve, with safety device to 20 feet depth. Effective up to 100 feet.

Torpedoes.

Built at the Torpedo Station, Newport (Rhode Island), and the Naval Gun Factory, Washington, D.C. No exact details are available. Ranges of torpedoes were improved by experiments in 1914, and a new type of net-cutter, which gave excellent results on trials, has been adopted. A new torpedo model is said to have been adopted recently of a simplified pattern, possessing few Bliss-Leavitt features. New 24 inch non-gyro model said to be under test. Nearly all ships are now equipped with submarine signalling and receiving sets.